REVELATION 1-7

AN EXEGETICAL COMMENTARY

Kenneth Barker, General Editor

Robert L. Thomas

MOODY PRESS

CHICAGO

All Scripture quotations, unless otherwise noted, are the author's
translation.

Library of Congress Cataloging in Publication Data

Thomas, Robert L., 1928–
    Revelation 1-7 / Robert L. Thomas.
      p.   cm.
    Includes bibliographical references and indexes.
    ISBN 0-8024-9265-7
    1. Bible. N.T. Revelation I-VII—Commentaries. I. Title. II. Series.
BS2825.3.T46 1992
228'.07—dc20   91-45740
                                            CIP

7 9 10 8 6

Printed in the United States of America

*Dedicated to
my children,
Barbara
Bob
Jon
Mark
Mike,
five overcomers whose faith in Christ has been a great encouragement*

Written especially for the informed layman, student, and scholar, all exegesis and exposition is based on the original languages of the Bible books. Translations used are those of the author. Textual criticism and word study are included where appropriate.

This in-depth commentary also includes extended excursuses on important topics of theological, historical, and archaeological interest.

The text is interpreted according to a historical, critical, grammatical hermeneutic and propounds a conservative, evangelical theology. But the reader will not get a narrow view of problem passages. This commentary interacts with a range of major views, both evangelical and nonevangelical.

General Editor
Kenneth L. Barker (B.A., Northwestern College; Th.M., Dallas Theological Seminary; Ph.D., Dropsie College for Hebrew and Cognate Learning) is executive director of the NIV Translation Center (a ministry of the International Bible Society) in Lewisville, Texas, and former academic dean and professor of Old Testament literature and exegesis at Capital Bible Seminary, Lanham, Maryland.

Special Editor
Moisés Silva (B.A., Bob Jones University; Ph.D., University of Manchester, England; B.D., Th.M., Westminster Theological Seminary) is chairman of the New Testament department and professor of New Testament at Westminster Theological Seminary, Philadelphia.

REVELATION

Through the centuries since its writing, the book of Revelation has captured the fascination of the Christian church. Earliest Christians were unanimous in understanding its prophecies as descriptions of events surrounding the premillennial second advent of Jesus Christ, but alongside their exclusively futuristic and premillennial view other hermeneutical approaches to the book began to emerge in the third century. These clouded, and added complexity to, the task of explaining the book's meaning. For most of the Christian era, consequently, many readers have viewed this last of the NT writings as though it were hopelessly embedded in an aura of deep mystery. An avalanche of interpretive literature has evidenced remarkable interest in the book's contents, but along with the interest has come widespread bewilderment.

In post-Reformation times detailed commentaries on the Greek text of Revelation from a futurist and premillennial perspective have been scarce and perhaps even nonexistent. This first of two volumes commences the filling of that void with its exegetical analysis of the first seven chapters of the Apocalypse. It reaffirms the basic framework of eschatology espoused by ancient Christianity, but with added help from centuries of maturing thought and doctrinal progress in the Body of Christ.

About the author
Robert L. Thomas (B.M.E., Georgia Institute of Technology; Th.M., Th.D., Dallas Theological Seminary) is professor of New Testament language and literature at The Master's Seminary, Sun Valley, California. He has written *Understanding Spiritual Gifts* and "1, 2 Thessalonians" in the *Expositor's Bible Commentary* and has edited *A Harmony of the Gospels (NASB)* and *The NIV Harmony of the Gospels*. He is also general editor of the *New American Standard Exhaustive Concordance*.

Table of Contents

General Editor's Introduction   xi

Preface   xiii

Abbreviations   xv

Selected Bibliography   xvii

Introduction to the Commentary   1
    Authorship of the Apocalypse   2
       Dionysius of Alexandria   2
          Personal background   2
          Dionysius's case against apostolic authorship   3
          Summary of Dionysius's evidence   8
          Principles derived from examining Dionysius   10
       Additional Evidence for Apostolic Authorship   11
          Vocabulary   11
          Syntax   13
          Style   15
          Concepts   16
       Differences Between the Apocalypse and John's
          Other Writings   17
    Date of the Apocalypse   20
    Prophetic Style of the Apocalypse   23

Hermeneutics for Interpreting the Apocalypse   29
Language of the Apocalypse   39
Other Scripture in the Apocalypse   40
Text of the Apocalypse   42
Structure of the Apocalypse   43

Part 1—The Preparation of the Prophet: His Past Vision
  (1:1-20)   47

1. The Prologue of the Apocalypse   49
   A. Prologue (1:1-8)   49
      1. Preface (1:1-3)   49
      2. Address and doxology (1:4-6)   63
      3. Theme (1:7-8)   76

2. John's Vision of the Glorified Christ   83
   B. John's Commission to Write (1:9-20)   83
      1. The first commission to write (1:9-11)   83
      2. The source of the commission (1:12-16)   96
      3. The commission restated and amplified (1:17-20) 108

Part 2—The Preparation of the People: Their Present
  Condition (2:1–3:22)   123

3. Church of Loveless Orthodoxy   125
   A. The Message to Ephesus (2:1-7)   125

4. Church of Martyrdom   157
   B. The Message to Smyrna (2:8-11)   157

5. Church of Indiscriminate Tolerance   177
   C. The Message to Pergamum (2:12-17)   177

6. Church of Compromise   205
   D. The Message to Thyatira (2:18-29)   205

7. Church of Complacency   239
   E. The Message to Sardis (3:1-6)   239

8. Church of Promised Deliverance   269
   F. The Message to Philadelphia (3:7-13)   269

9. Church of Lukewarmness   295
   G. The Message to Laodicea (3:14-22)   295

Part 3—The Publication of the Prophecy: Its Future
Expectation (4:1–22:5)   329

10. The One Sitting on the Throne   331
    A. The Opening of the Seven-sealed Scroll (4:1–8:1)   331
        1. The source of the scroll (4:1–5:14)   331
           a. The one sitting on the throne (4:1-11)   332

11. The Seven-sealed Scroll of the Lamb   373
           b. The seven-sealed scroll of the Lamb (5:1-14)   373

12. The First Six Seals, "The Beginning of Birth Pains"   413
        2. The opening of the first seal: peaceful conquest
           (6:1-2)   413
        3. The opening of the second seal: warfare and
           bloodshed (6:3-4)   425
        4. The opening of the third seal: widespread famine
           (6:5-6)   429
        5. The opening of the fourth seal: death to a fourth
           of earth's inhabitants (6:7-8)   434
        6. The opening of the fifth seal: prayers for divine
           vengeance (6:9-11)   439
        7. The opening of the sixth seal: cosmic and
           terrestrial disturbances (6:12-17)   450

13. The Slaves of God   461
        8. The slaves of God (7:1-17)   461
           a. Those on earth: the 144,000 (7:1-8)   461
           b. Those in heaven: the innumerable multitude
              (7:9-17)   482

Excursus 1: The Chronological Interpretation of
Revelation 2-3   505

Excursus 2: The Imprecatory Prayers of the Apocalypse   517

Revelation 8-22, the second volume of this commentary, contains four indexes, each of which covers both volumes. These deal with subjects, ancient literature, modern authors, and Scripture.

General Editor's Introduction

While the various areas of biblical criticism receive at least brief treatment in this volume, the principal emphasis of the commentary is exegesis. By exegesis we mean the application of generally accepted hermeneutical principles to the original (Hebrew, Aramaic, and Greek) biblical text with a view to unfolding (lit. "leading out," Gk. *exēgeomai*) its correct, contextual meaning. The method followed is commonly referred to as grammatico-historical exegesis. A more complete designation would be the grammatical-historical-literary-theological method.

This is a commentary on the Greek and Hebrew texts of the Bible, not on an English translation. Consequently Greek and Hebrew words and phrases appear in their original scripts, but with English transliterations and translations provided at their first occurrence. After that, transliterations alone normally suffice. However, only the original scripts are employed in the Additional Notes and footnote discussions, since scholars and specialists would be the ones most interested in that more technical material (e.g., word studies, grammatical or syntactical points, etymologies, textual variants in the original languages, specialized bibliographies, etc.). Unless otherwise indicated, all Scripture translations are those of the authors of the individual volumes.

This commentary stresses the development of the argument of a given book and its central theme(s). An attempt has been made to show how each section of a book fits together with the preceding and following sections. We do not want the reader to become so preoccupied with the trees (analysis) that he fails to see the forest (synthesis).

Most of the abbreviations and transliterations follow the guidelines of the *Journal of Biblical Literature (JBL)*. The only abbreviations listed are those not found in *JBL*.

Asterisks in either the Translation or the Exegesis and Exposition section refer the reader to discussions of text-critical problems in the Additional Notes section, though these are not the only kinds of discussions one will encounter in the Additional Notes sections (see above).

I trust and pray that this commentary will be used by God to advance the cause of a more exegetically-based, and so more accurate, biblical interpretation and biblical theology. Paul's parting words to the Ephesian elders seem apropos here: "Now I commit you to God and to the word of his grace, which can build you up and give you an inheritance among all those who are sanctified" (Acts 20:32, NIV).

KENNETH L. BARKER
General Editor

Preface

This commentary on Revelation results from a pilgrimage of over thirty years. It started with a doctoral dissertation tracing the book's logical development, "The Argument of the Book of Revelation," under the mentorship of S. Lewis Johnson at Dallas Seminary in the late 1950s. It has continued through a continuous ministry of teaching and specialized research ever since. It is satisfying now to be able to make available some of those results.

My appreciation extends to the staff of Moody Press and to General Editor Kenneth L. Barker for allowing me two volumes to try to do justice to this, the climactic and most question-provoking book of the NT. I am indebted to many students whose research on the Apocalypse has facilitated my own. The thorough work of colleague Dennis A. Hutchison on Revelation 2-3 has been especially helpful.

I must express apprehension about publishing separately the first of a two-volume set, being unable to foresee future developments while the second volume is in production. Literature dealing with the Apocalypse and apocalyptic-type issues is multiplying at an almost unbelievable rate. Who knows what will eventuate? Perhaps an "extroduction" at the end of volume 2 will be needed as a counterpart to the introduction in this volume.

Fifteen chapters of Revelation remain to be covered in volume two. This may seem unbalanced with the seven discussed in volume one, but many of the foundational issues are handled in volume one and need not be treated again.

We owe much to teachers of past generations, people whom Christ has given to instruct His church. We dare not break ranks with these Christian soldiers of the past, or we will in large measure impoverish our understanding of the text. At the same time, much is happening on the current scene in the maturing Body of Christ that causes us to sharpen our focus on interpretive issues more closely than ever before. We must hear and evaluate as many voices as possible as they clamor for our attention, recognizing the utter impossibility of citing all the countless works done on the Apocalypse through the centuries.

Limitations in this work are inevitable. Besides the many personal ones, there is the enigmatic nature of biblical prophecy. Not even the biblical prophets themselves understood the full import of their prophecies. Thorough comprehension of predictive Scripture awaits the arrival of the generation of its fulfillment. The best the contemporary student can do is to draw broad parameters within which the consummation will fall.

With these matters in mind, the following is offered with prayer that it will contribute to the further growth of the Body of Christ.

Abbreviations

In addition to those standard abbreviations found in the *Journal of Biblical Literature*, Instructions for Contributors, please note the following:

EBC	*The Expositor's Bible Commentary*
EDT	*Evangelical Dictionary of Theology*
GTJ	*Grace Theological Journal*
NA	Nestle-Aland, *Novum Testamentum Graece,* 26th ed.
GEL	*Greek-English Lexicon,* ed. J. Louw and E. Nida
NIDNTT	*New International Dictionary of New Testament Theology,* ed. Colin Brown
TrinJ	*Trinity Journal*

Selected Bibliography

Bibliographical resources have been limited to those in English. This allows access to documented sources for a wider audience. The works marked by an asterisk (*) are ones cited most frequently. Often in the comments on the text, references to these after their first mention in each chapter will be noted (without page numbers) in parentheses in the body of discussion rather than in footnotes. Whenever this occurs, the comment cited is at the same chapter and verse location as the relevant point under discussion in this commentary.

Books

Abbott, Edwin A. *Johannine Grammar*. London: Adam and Charles Black, 1906.

_____. *Johannine Vocabulary*. London: Adam and Charles Black, 1905.

Abbott-Smith, G. *A Manual Greek Lexicon of the New Testament*. Edinburgh: T. & T. Clark, 1950.

*Alford, Henry. *The Greek Testament*. 4 vols. London: Longmans, Green, 1903.

Archer, Gleason L. "The Case for the Mid-Seventieth-Week Rapture." In *The Rapture: Pre-, Mid-, or Post-Tribulational*. Essays by Reiter, Feinberg, Archer, and Moo. Grand Rapids: Zondervan, 1984.

Arndt, W. F., and F. Gingrich. *A Greek-English Lexicon of the New Testament*. 2d ed. Walter Bauer's 5th ed. revised and augmented by F.

Wilbur Gingrich and Frederick W. Danker. Chicago: U. of Chicago, 1979.

Aune, D. E. *The New Testament in Its Literary Environment.* Philadelphia: Westminster, 1987.

———. *Prophecy in Early Christianity and the Ancient Mediterranean World.* Grand Rapids: Eerdmans, 1983.

Barclay, William. *Letters to the Seven Churches.* New York: Abingdon, 1957.

———. *The Revelation of John.* 2d ed. 2 vols. Philadelphia: Westminster, 1960.

Barnes, Albert. *The Book of Revelation.* New York: Harper, 1851.

*Beasley-Murray, G. R. *The Book of Revelation.* NCB. Grand Rapids: Eerdmans, 1978.

*Beckwith, Isbon T. *The Apocalypse of John.* New York: Macmillan, 1919.

Biederwolf, William E. *The Millennium Bible.* Grand Rapids: Baker, 1967.

Blass, F., and A. Debrunner. *Greek Grammar of the New Testament.* Edited and translated by Robert W. Funk. Chicago: U. of Chicago, 1961.

Bowman, John Wick. *The Drama of the Book of Revelation.* Philadelphia: Westminster, 1955.

Brown, Colin, ed. *The New International Dictionary of New Testament Theology.* 4 vols. Grand Rapids: Zondervan, 1971-85.

Brown, Raymond E. *The Epistles of John.* Vol. 30 of AB. Garden City, N.Y.: Doubleday, 1982.

———. *The Gospel According to John.* 2 vols. Vol. 29 of AB. Garden City, N.Y.: Doubleday, 1966.

Bruce, F. F. *The Canon of Scripture.* Downers Grove, Ill.: InterVarsity, 1988.

Bruce, F. F. "The Revelation to John." In *A New Testament Commentary.* Edited by G. C. D. Howley. London: Pickering & Inglis, 1969.

———. "The Spirit in the Apocalypse." In *Christ and Spirit in the New Testament.* Edited by B. Lindars and S. S. Smalley. Cambridge: Cambridge U., 1974.

Buchanan, George Wesley. "John of Patmos and the Angel of Revelation." In vol. 1 of *Proceedings of the Sixth World Congress of Jewish Studies.* Edited by Avigdor Shinan. Jerusalem: Academic, 1977.

*Bullinger, E. W. *The Apocalypse or "The Day of the Lord."* London: Eyre and Spottiswoode, n.d.

Bultmann, R. *The Johannine Epistles.* Hermeneia. Philadelphia: Fortress, 1973.

*Caird, G. V. *A Commentary on the Revelation of St. John the Divine.* HNTC. New York: Harper & Row, 1966.

Carpenter, W. Boyd. *Revelation.* Vol. 3 of A New Testament Commentary for English Readers. Edited by C. J. Ellicott. New York: Harper & Row, 1966.

Charles, R. H. *The Apocrypha and Pseudepigrapha of the Old Testament.* 2 vols. Oxford: Clarendon, 1913.

*_____. *The Revelation of St. John.* 2 vols. ICC. New York: Scribner's Sons, 1920.

Chilton, David. *The Days of Vengeance.* Fort Worth, Tex.: Dominion, 1987.

Cremer, Hermann. *Biblico-Theological Lexicon of New Testament Greek.* Translated by William Urwick. Edinburgh: T. & T. Clark, 1895.

Dana, H. E., and Julius R. Mantey. *A Manual Grammar of the Greek New Testament.* New York: Macmillan, 1927.

Düsterdieck, Friedrich. *Critical and Exegetical Handbook to the Revelation of John.* In Meyer's Commentary. Translated and edited by Henry E. Jacobs. New York: Funk & Wagnalls, 1887.

Ellis, E. Earle. "The Role of the Christian Prophet in Acts." In *Apostolic History and the Gospel.* Edited by W. Ward Gasque and Ralph P. Martin. Grand Rapids: Eerdmans, 1970.

Epp, Theodore H. *Practical Studies in Revelation.* 2 vols. Lincoln, Neb.: Back to the Bible, 1969.

Eusebius. *The Ecclesiastical History.* 2 vols. Translated by Hugh Jackson Lawlor and John Ernest Leonard Oulton. London: SPCK, 1954.

Fee, Gordon D., and Douglas Stuart. *How to Read the Bible for All Its Worth.* Grand Rapids: Zondervan, 1982.

Feinberg, Charles L. *Millennialism, the Two Major Views.* 3d ed. Chicago: Moody, 1980.

Feinberg, Paul D. "The Case for the Pretribulation Rapture Position." In *The Rapture: Pre-, Mid-, or Post-Tribulational.* Essays by Reiter, Feinberg, Archer, and Moo. Grand Rapids: Zondervan, 1984.

Feine, Paul, Johannes Behm, and Werner Georg Kümmel. *Introduction to the New Testament.* Translated by A. J. Mattill, Jr. Nashville: Abingdon, 1966.

Fiorenza, Elisabeth Schüssler. *The Book of Revelation, Justice and Judgment.* Philadelphia: Fortress, 1985.

*Ford, J. Massyngberde. *Revelation.* Vol. 38 of AB. Garden City, N.Y.: Doubleday, 1975.

Gentry, Kenneth L., Jr. *Before Jerusalem Fell: Dating the Book of Revelation.* Tyler, Tex.: Institute for Christian Economics, 1989.

Glasgow, James. *The Apocalypse.* Edinburgh: T. & T. Clark, 1872.

Glasson, Thomas F. *The Revelation of John.* CBC. Cambridge: Cambridge U., 1965.

*Govett, Robert. *The Apocalypse Expounded by Scripture*. London: Charles J. Thynne, 1920.

Grant, F. W. *The Revelation of Jesus Christ*. New York: Loizeaux, n.d.

Green, Oliver B. *The Revelation*. Greenville, S.C.: Gospel Hour, 1967.

Grudem, Wayne A. *The Gift of Prophecy in the New Testament and Today*. Westchester, Ill.: Crossway, 1988.

Gundry, Robert H. *The Church and the Tribulation*. Grand Rapids: Zondervan, 1973.

Guthrie, Donald. *New Testament Introduction*. 4th ed. Downers Grove, Ill.: InterVarsity, 1990.

_____. *The Relevance of John's Apocalypse*. Grand Rapids: Eerdmans, 1987.

*Hailey, Homer. *Revelation, an Introduction and Commentary*. Grand Rapids: Baker, 1979.

Harrison, Norman B. *The End*. Minneapolis: Harrison Service, 1948.

Hellholm, David. "The Problem of Apocalyptic Genre and the Apocalypse of John." In SBLSP. Edited by Kent Harold Richards. Chico, Calif.: Scholars, 1982.

*Hemer, Colin J. *The Letters to the Seven Churches of Asia in Their Local Setting*. JSNTSup 11. Sheffield: U. of Sheffield, 1986.

Hendriksen, William. *More Than Conquerors*. Grand Rapids: Baker, 1944.

Hengstenberg, E. W. *The Revelation of St. John*. 2 vols. New York: Carter and Brothers, 1852.

Hill, David. *New Testament Prophecy*. Atlanta: Knox, 1979.

*Hort, F. J. A. *The Apocalypse of St. John*. London: Macmillan, 1908.

Houlden, J. L. *The Johannine Epistles*. HNTC. New York: Harper & Row, 1973.

Ironside, H. A. *Lectures on the Book of Revelation*. New York: Loizeaux, n.d.

Jamieson, Robert, A. R. Fausset, and David Brown. *A Commentary Critical, Experimental and Practical on the Old and New Testaments*. 6 vols. Grand Rapids: Eerdmans, 1945.

Jennings, F. C. *Studies in Revelation*. New York: Publication Office, "Our Hope," n.d.

*Johnson, Alan F. "Revelation." In *EBC*. Edited by Frank E. Gaebelein. Grand Rapids: Zondervan, 1981.

Kaiser, Walter C. "Legitimate Hermeneutics." In *Inerrancy*. Edited by Norman L. Geisler. Grand Rapids: Zondervan, 1979.

Kelly, William. *Lectures on the Revelation*. London: G. Morrish, n.d.

_____. *The Revelation*. London: Thomas Weston, 1904.

*Kiddle, Martin. *The Revelation of St. John*. HNTC. New York: Harper, 1940.

Kittel, Gerhard, and Gerhard Friedrich, eds. *Theological Dictionary of the New Testament.* 10 vols. Grand Rapids: Eerdmans, 1964-76.

Koester, Helmut. *Introduction to the New Testament.* 2 vols. Philadelphia: Fortress, 1982.

*Ladd, George E. *A Commentary on the Revelation of John.* Grand Rapids: Eerdmans, 1972.

Lang, G. H. *The Revelation of Jesus Christ.* London: Oliphants, 1945.

Lange, John Peter. *The Revelation of John.* Lange's Commentary. Edited by E. R. Craven. Grand Rapids: Zondervan, 1968.

Larkin, Clarence. *The Book of Revelation.* Philadelphia: Clarence Larkin, 1919.

*Lee, William. "The Revelation of St. John." In *The Holy Bible.* Edited by F. C. Cook. London: John Murray, 1881.

*Lenski, R. C. H. *The Interpretation of St. John's Revelation.* Columbus, Ohio: Lutheran Book Concern, 1935.

Liddell, Henry George, and Robert Scott. *A Greek-English Lexicon.* 9th ed. Oxford: Clarendon, 1940.

Lindblom, J. *Prophecy in Ancient Israel.* Philadelphia: Fortress, 1973.

Loenertz, R. J. *The Apocalypse of Saint John.* London: Sheed and Ward, 1947.

MacArthur, Jack. *Expositional Commentary on Revelation.* Eugene, Ore.: Certain Sound, 1973.

Makrakis, Apostolos. *Interpretation of the Revelation of St. John the Divine.* Chicago: Hellenistic Christian Education Society, 1948.

Metzger, Bruce M. *A Textual Commentary on the Greek New Testament.* New York: United Bible Societies, 1971.

McClain, Alva J. *The Greatness of the Kingdom.* Grand Rapids: Zondervan, 1959.

Mickelsen, A. Berkley. *Daniel and Revelation: Riddles or Realities?* Nashville: Nelson, 1984.

Milligan, William. *The Book of Revelation.* Vol. 25 of The Expositor's Bible. New York: George H. Doran, 1889.

Moo, Douglas J. "The Case for the Posttribulation Rapture Position." In *The Rapture: Pre-, Mid-, or Post-Tribulational.* Essays by Reiter, Feinberg, Archer, and Moo. Grand Rapids: Zondervan, 1984.

*Moffatt, James. "The Revelation of St. John the Divine." In *The Expositor's Greek Testament.* Edited by W. Robertson Nicoll. Grand Rapids: Eerdmans, n.d.

*Morris, Leon. *The Revelation of St. John.* TNTC. Grand Rapids: Eerdmans, 1969.

Moule, C. F. D. *An Idiom Book of New Testament Greek.* Cambridge: Cambridge U., 1960.

_____. "The Judgment Theme in the Sacraments." In *The Background of the New Testament and Its Eschatology.* Edited by W. D. Davies and D. Daube. Cambridge: Cambridge U., 1954.

Moulton, James Hope. *A Grammar of New Testament Greek. Prolegomena.* 3d ed. Edinburgh: T. & T. Clark, 1908.

Moulton, J. H., and G. Milligan. *The Vocabulary of the Greek Testament.* Grand Rapids: Eerdmans, 1974.

*Mounce, Robert H. *The Book of Revelation.* NICNT. Grand Rapids: Eerdmans, 1977.

Mulholland, M. Robert. *Revelation, Holy Living in an Unholy World.* Grand Rapids: Zondervan, 1990.

Mussies, G. *The Morphology of Koine Greek As Used in the Apocalypse of St. John, A Study in Bilingualism.* Leiden: E. J. Brill, 1971.

Newell, William R. *The Book of Revelation.* Chicago: Moody, 1935.

Payne, J. Barton. *The Imminent Appearing of Christ.* Grand Rapids: Eerdmans, 1962.

Pentecost, J. Dwight. *Things to Come: A Study in Biblical Eschatology.* Grand Rapids: Zondervan, 1958.

*Ramsay, W. M. *The Letters to the Seven Churches of Asia.* New York: A. C. Armstrong, 1904.

Randell, T. *Revelation.* The Pulpit Commentary. Chicago: Wicox and Follett, n.d.

Rienecker, Fritz. *A Linguistic Key to the Greek New Testament.* Edited and translated by Cleon L. Rogers, Jr. Grand Rapids: Zondervan, 1980.

Robertson, Archibald Thomas. *A Grammar of the Greek New Testament in the Light of Historical Research.* Nashville: Broadman, 1934.

_____. *Word Pictures in the New Testament.* 6 vols. Nashville: Broadman, 1933.

Rosenthal, Marvin. *The Pre-Wrath Rapture of the Church.* Nashville: Nelson, 1990.

Ryken, Leland. *Words of Life: A Literary Introduction to the New Testament.* Grand Rapids: Baker, 1987.

Ryrie, Charles Caldwell. *Revelation.* Everyman's Bible Commentary. Chicago: Moody, 1968.

*Scott, Walter. *Exposition of the Revelation of Jesus Christ.* Swengel, Pa.: Bible Truth Depot, n.d.

*Seiss, J. A. *The Apocalypse.* 3 vols. New York: Charles C. Cook, 1909.

*Smith, J. B. *A Revelation of Jesus Christ.* Scottdale, Pa.: Herald, 1961.

*Simcox, William Henry. *The Revelation of St. John the Divine.* Cambridge: Cambridge U., 1893.

Sproule, John A. *In Defense of Pretribulationism.* Winona Lake, Ind.: BMH, 1980.

Stonehouse, Ned Bernard. *The Apocalypse in the Ancient Church.* Goes, Holland: Oosterbaan & Le Cointre, 1929.

Stott, John R. W. *What Christ Thinks of the Church.* Grand Rapids: Eerdmans, 1958.

Strauss, Lehmann. *The Book of Revelation.* Neptune, N.J.: Loizeaux, n.d.

Stuart, Moses. *A Commentary on the Apocalypse.* Edinburgh: Maclachlan, Stewart, 1847.

*Sweet, J. P. M. *Revelation.* Philadelphia: Westminster, Pelican, 1979.

*Swete, Henry Barclay. *The Apocalypse of St. John.* London: Macmillan, 1906.

Tatford, Frederick A. *Prophecy's Last Word.* London: Pickering and Inglis, 1947.

*Tenney, Merrill C. *Interpreting Revelation.* Grand Rapids: Eerdmans, 1957.

Thayer, Joseph Henry. *A Greek-English Lexicon of the New Testament.* New York: American Book, 1889.

Thiessen, Henry Clarence. *Introduction to the New Testment.* Grand Rapids: Eerdmans, 1952.

_____. *Will the Church Pass Through the Tribulation?.* New York: Loizeaux, 1941.

Thomas, Robert L. *Understanding Spiritual Gifts.* Chicago: Moody, 1978.

Thompson, Steven. *The Apocalypse and Semitic Syntax.* Cambridge: Cambridge U., 1985.

*Trench, Richard Chenevix. *Commentary on the Epistles to the Seven Churches in Asia.* London: Parker, Son, and Bourn, 1861.

_____. *Synonyms of the New Testament.* Grand Rapids: Eerdmans, 1953.

Turner, Nigel. *Syntax.* Vol. 3 of *A Grammar of New Testament Greek.* Edinburgh: T. & T. Clark, 1963.

Vine, W. E. *An Expository Dictionary of New Testament Words.* Old Tappan, N.J.: Revell, 1966.

*Walvoord, John F. *The Revelation of Jesus Christ.* Chicago: Moody, 1966.

Zahn, Theodor. *Introduction to the New Testament.* 3 vols. Translated by John Moore Trout et al. Grand Rapids: Kregel, 1953.

Journal Articles

Achtemeier, Paul J. "An Apocalyptic Shift in Early Christian Tradition: Reflections on Some Canonical Evidence." *CBQ* 45, no. 2 (April 1983): 231-48.

Aune, David E. "The Apocalypse of John and Graeco-Roman Revelatory Magic." *NTS* 33, no. 4 (October 1987): 481-501.

_____. "The Apocalypse of John and the Problem of Genre." *Semeia* 36 (1986): 65-96.

———. "The Form and Function of the Proclamations to the Seven Churches (Revelation 2-3)." *NTS* 36, no. 2 (April 1990): 182-204.

———. "The Influence of Roman Imperial Court Ceremonial on the Apocalypse of John." *Papers of the Chicago Society of Biblical Research* 28 (1983): 5-26.

Barr, David L. "The Apocalypse of John as Oral Enactment." *Int* 40, no. 3 (July 1986): 243-56.

Bauckham, Richard J. "The Role of the Spirit in the Apocalypse." *EvQ* 52, no. 2 (April-June 1980): 66-83.

———. "Synoptic Parousia Parables and the Apocalypse." *NTS* 23 (1977): 162-76.

Beale, G. K. "A Reconsideration of the Text of Daniel in the Apocalypse." *Bib* 67, no. 4 (1986): 539-43.

Bell, Albert A., Jr. "The Date of John's Apocalypse. The Evidence of Some Roman Historians Reconsidered." *NTS* 25, no. 1 (October 1978): 93-102.

Blevins, James L. "The Genre of Revelation." *RevExp* 77, no. 3 (Summer 1980): 393-408.

Blomberg, Craig L. "New Testament Genre Criticism for the 1990s." *Themelios* 15, no. 2 (January/February 1990): 40-49.

Boring, M. Eugene. "The Theology of Revelation, 'The Lord Our God the Almighty Reigns.'" *Int* 40, no. 3 (July 1986): 257-69.

Boyer, James L. "Are the Seven Letters of Revelation 2-3 Prophetic?" *GTJ* 6, no. 2 (Fall 1985): 267-73.

Brown, Schuyler. "The Hour of Trial, Rev. 3:10." *JBL* 85 (1966): 308-14.

Callan, Terrance. "Prophecy and Ecstasy in Greco-Roman Religion and in 1 Corinthians." *NovT* 17 (1985): 125-40.

Charlesworth, J. H. "The Jewish Roots of Christology: The Discovery of the Hypostatic Voice." *SJT* 39, no. 1 (1986): 19-41.

Collins, Adela Yarbro. "Reading the Book of Revelation in the Twentieth Century." *Int* 40, no. 3 (July 1986): 229-69.

Collins, Adela Yarbro, ed. *Semeia 36, Early Christian Apocalypticism.* Decatur, Ga.: SBL, 1986.

Collins, John J., ed. *Semeia 14, Apocalypse: The Morphology of a Genre.* Missoula, Mont.: SBL, 1979.

Crutchfield, Larry V. "The Apostle John and Asia Minor as a Source of Premillennialism in the Early Church Fathers." *JETS* 31, no. 4 (December 1988): 411-27.

Deer, Donald S. "Whose Faith/Loyalty in Revelation 2.13 and 14.12?" *BT* 38, no. 3 (July 1987): 328-32.

Edgar, Thomas R. "Robert H. Gundry and Revelation 3:10." *GTJ* 3, no. 1 (Spring 1982): 19-49.

Fackre, Gabriel. "Evangelical Hermeneutics." *Int* 43, no. 2 (April 1989): 117-29.

Fiorenza, Elisabeth Schüssler. "Apocalyptic and Gnosis in the Book of Revelation and Paul." *JBL* 92 (1973): 565-81.

_____. "The Quest for the Johannine School: The Apocalypse and the Fourth Gospel." *NTS* 23, no. 4 (July 1977): 402-27.

Geyser, Albert. "The Twelve Tribes in Revelation: Judean and Judeo Christian Apocalypticism." *NTS* 23, no. 3 (July 1982): 388-99.

Gunther, John J. "The Elder John, Author of Revelation." *JSNT* 11 (1981): 3-20.

Hill, David. "Prophecy and Prophets in the Revelation of St. John." *NTS* 18 (1971-72): 401-18.

Hurtado, L. W. "Revelation 4-5 in the Light of Jewish Apocalyptic Analogies." *JSNT* 25 (1985): 105-24.

Kirby, John T. "The Rhetorical Situations of Revelation 1-3." *NTS* 34, no. 2 (April 1988): 197-207.

Kvanig, Helge S. "The Relevance of the Biblical Visions of the End Time." *HBT* 11, no. 1 (June 1989): 35-58.

Ladd, George E. "New Testament Apocalyptic." *RevExp* 78, no. 2 (Spring 1981): 205-9.

_____. "Why Not Prophetic-Apocalyptic?" *JBL* 76 (1957): 192-200.

Longman, Tremper, III. "The Divine Warrior: The New Testament Use of an Old Testament Motif." *WTJ* 44, no. 2 (Fall 1982): 290-307.

Mazzaferri, Fred. "ΜΑΡΤΥΡΙΑ ΙΗΣΟΥ Revisited." *BT* 3 (1988): 114-22.

Mackay, W. M. "Another Look at the Nicolaitans." *EvQ* 45 (1973): 111-15.

Mendham, Peter. "Interpreting the Book of Revelation." *Saint Mark's Review* 122 (June 1985): 23-28.

Mueller, Theodore. "'The Word of My Patience' in Revelation 3:10." *Concordia Theological Quarterly* 46 (April-June 1982): 231-34.

Muse, Robert L. "Revelation 2-3: A Critical Analysis of Seven Prophetic Messages." *JETS* 29, no. 2 (June 1986): 147-61.

Newport, Kenneth G. C. "Semitic Influence in Revelation: Some Further Evidence." *AUSS* 25, no. 3 (Autumn 1987): 249-56.

_____. "Semitic Influence on the Use of Some Prepositions in the Book of Revelation." *BT* 37, no. 3 (July 1986): 328-34.

_____. "The Use of EK in Revelation: Evidence of Semitic Influence." *AUSS* 24, no. 3 (Autumn 1986): 223-30.

Owens, John J. "The Imprecatory Psalms." *BSac* 13 (July 1856): 551-63.

Parker, Harold M., Jr. "The Scripture of the Author of the Revelation of John." *The Iliff Review* 37, no. 1 (Winter 1980): 35-51.

Peterson, David. "Worship in the Revelation to John." *Reformed Theological Review* 47, no. 3 (September-December 1988): 67-77.

Porter, Stanley E. "The Language of the Apocalypse in Recent Discussion." *NTS* 35, no. 4 (October 1989): 582-603.

_____. "Why the Laodiceans Received Lukewarm Water (Revelation 3:15-18)." *TynBul* 38 (1987): 143-49.

Poythress, Vern Sheridan. "Johannine Authorship and the Use of Intersentence Conjunctions in the Book of Revelation." *WTJ* 47, no. 2 (Fall 1985): 329-36.

Rosscup, James E. "The Overcomer in the Apocalypse." *GTJ* 3, no. 2 (Fall 1982): 261-86.

Rowland, Christopher. "The Vision of the Risen Christ in Rev. i. 13 ff.: The Debt of an Early Christology to an Aspect of Jewish Angelology." *JTS* 31, no. 1 (April 1980): 1-11.

Rudwick, M. J. S., and E. M. B. Green. "The Laodicean Lukewarmness." *ET* 69 (1957-58): 176-78.

Russell, Emmett. "A Roman Law Parallel to Rev. V." *BSac* 115 (July 1958): 258-64.

Satre, Lowell J. "Interpreting the Book of Revelation." *WW* 4, no. 1 (Winter 1984): 57-69.

Smalley, Stephen S. "John's Revelation and John's Community." *BJRL* 69 (Spring 1987): 549-71.

Spinks, Leroy C. "A Critical Examination of J. W. Bowman's Proposed Structure of the Revelation." *EvQ* 50, no. 3 (July-September 1978): 211-22.

Staats, Reinhart. "The Eternal Kingdom of Christ, The Apocalyptic Tradition in the 'Creed of Nicaea-Constantinople,'" *Patristic and Byzantine Review* 9, no. 1 (1990): 19-30.

Strand, Kenneth A. "The Eight Basic Visions in the Book of Revelation." *AUSS* 25, no. 1 (Spring 1987): 107-21.

Swanson, Theodore N. "The Apocalyptic Scriptures." *Journal of Dharma* 8 (July 1982): 313-30.

Thomas, Robert L. "The Glorified Christ on Patmos." *BSac* 122 (1965): 241-47.

_____. "John's Apocalyptic Outline." *BSac* 123 (1966): 334-41.

_____. "Tongues . . . Will Cease." *JETS* 17 (1974): 81-89.

Thompson, Leonard. "A Sociological Analysis of Tribulation in the Apocalypse of John." *Semeia* 36 (1986): 146-74.

Townsend, Jeffrey L. "The Rapture in Revelation 3:10." *BSac* 137 (1980): 252-66.

Trudinger, Paul. "The Apocalypse and the Palestinian Targum." *BTB* 16, no. 2 (April 1986): 78-79.

VanderKam, James C. "Recent Studies in 'Apocalyptic.'" *WW* 4 (Winter 1984): 70-77.

van Unnik, W. C. "A Formula Describing Prophecy." *NTS* 9 (1962-63): 86-94.

Vassiliadis, Petros. "The Translation of ΜΑΡΤΥΡΙΑ ΙΗΣΟΥ in Revelation." *BT* 36 (1985): 129-34.

Vos, Johannes G. "The Ethical Problem of the Imprecatory Psalms." *WTJ* 4 (1941): 123-38.

Wilkinson, Richard H. "The ΣΤΥΛΟΣ of Revelation 3:12 and Ancient Coronation Rites." *JBL* 107, no. 3 (September 1988): 498-501.

Winfrey, David G. "The Great Tribulation: Kept 'Out of' or 'Through'?" *GTJ* 3, no. 1 (Spring 1982): 3-18.

Wood, P. "Local Knowledge in the Letters of the Apocalypse." *ExpTim* 73 (1961-62): 263-64.

Introduction to the Commentary

The first-century churches in the Roman province of Asia were distinctive in several ways. They were the only ones outside Jerusalem and the birthplace of Christianity to benefit from the extended personal ministries of two major apostles. Paul spent three years in Ephesus, the major city of the province (Acts 20:31, probably A.D. 52-55). This was the longest span of ministry devoted to any city during his extensive missionary tours. According to reliable tradition,[1] John the apostle arrived in this city at about the time of Paul's martyrdom in Rome and spent the remainder of his life, approximately thirty years, overseeing churches in the same general area. These churches were also the first recipients of a considerable number of NT books. Paul wrote Ephesians, Colossians, and 1 and 2 Timothy to this general region. He also wrote 1 Corinthians while ministering in Ephesus, so the church there presumably had opportunity to know its contents before it was dispatched. John wrote the gospel of John, three epistles, and the Apocalypse primarily for the benefit of churches in this territory. It is not surprising, therefore, that several

---

1. For a summary of the tradition for placing John in Ephesus during the last portion of his life, see Isbon T. Beckwith, *The Apocalypse of John* (New York: Macmillan, 1919), pp. 366-93; Raymond E. Brown, *The Gospel According to John*, 2 vols., vol. 29 of AB (Garden City, N.Y.: Doubleday, 1966), 1:lxxxviii-xcii. Among other things, these treatments show the weaknesses of theories based on the early martyrdom of John the son of Zebedee, which would militate against John's residence in Ephesus.

prominent church leaders of the second century such as Papias, Polycarp, Ignatius, and Irenaeus had ties to this region. It was an important sector of the cradle of Christianity.[2] Valuable traditions have
been preserved from this area regarding the Apocalypse and other
parts of the NT, but a general attitude of skepticism regarding ancient traditions preserved from here and elsewhere pervades NT
scholarship of the last half of the twentieth century.[3]

AUTHORSHIP OF THE APOCALYPSE

Hesitancy by modern scholarship to accept the ancient church's
strong support for apostolic authorship of the Apocalypse is slightly
less startling than for some other books, however, because of an early
minority opinion that questioned the mainline tradition. The primary discussion disputing apostolic authorship is traceable to a certain
Dionysius of Alexandria. The following will sketch some biographical
data about Dionysius, outline his relevant theological leanings, and
investigate more thoroughly his case against the apostolic authorship
of the Apocalypse. We are indebted to Eusebius's *Ecclesiastical History* for what we know of Dionysius in this connection.[4]

DIONYSIUS OF ALEXANDRIA

Personal background. Dionysius was an outstanding Christian
leader of his time, a man of great influence. He served as overseer of
the Alexandrian church from A.D. 247 to 264 (Eusebius 6.35; 7.18),
having been a distinguished pupil of Origen in that same city. He was
devout in his loyalty to Christ as proved by the severe persecutions he
underwent (Eusebius 7.11). He was staunch in his insistence on correct doctrine. This was demonstrated when he spoke out strongly
against the Novatian heresy (Eusebius 7.8). In short, he possessed
outstanding Christian qualities and was highly respected.

His unusual theological preferences included a strong opposition
to the teaching of a thousand-year kingdom on earth (Eusebius 7.24;
7.25). In keeping with this outlook, he actively campaigned against a
literal understanding of the Apocalypse, being self-characterized in

---

2. A recent discussion pinpoints Asia Minor (i.e., the Roman province of Asia)
   as begetting the doctrine of premillennialism (Larry V. Crutchfield, "The
   Apostle John and Asia Minor As a Source of Premillennialism in the Early
   Church Fathers," *JETS* 31, no. 4 [December 1988]: 411-27).
3. E.g., I. Howard Marshall, *The Espistles of John,* NICNT (Grand Rapids:
   Eerdmans, 1978), pp. 42, 46-47; Alan Johnson, "Revelation," in *EBC,* ed.
   Frank E. Gaebelein (Grand Rapids, Zondervan, 1981), 12:405.
4. Eusebius, *The Ecclesiastical History,* trans. by Kirsopp Lake, 2 vols. (Cam-
   bridge, Mass.: Harvard U., 1953).

his approach to the book as an allegorist. He spoke out in opposition to the teachings of a certain Nepos, who before his death had served as overseer of Christians in another part of Egypt. Nepos had written a book entitled *Refutation of the Allegorists* in which he advocated interpreting the Scriptures after "a more Jewish fashion." This work followed the assumption that there would be what Eusebius calls "a kind of millennium on earth devoted to bodily indulgence" (Eusebius 7.24). Dionysius pictures the followers of Nepos as relying greatly on a work of Nepos "as proving indisputably that the kingdom of Christ will be on earth" (Eusebius 7.24).

His approach to these allegedly misguided followers is quite patronizing. He first praises Nepos in the following words: "I approve and love Nepos, for his faith and devotion to work, his diligent study of the Scriptures and his abundant psalmody, by which many of the brethren have till this day been cheered; and I am full of respectful regard for the man, all the more for that he has gone to his rest already" (Eusebius 7.24). He then goes on in the same treatise to recount how over a period of three days he successfully persuaded a group of Nepos's followers to reject his teaching.

Later on in the same treatise, Dionysius tells of those who had rejected the Apocalypse because they held its teaching to be Cerinthian. Dionysius differs with them on this point, saying, "But for my part I should not dare to reject the book" (Eusebius 7.25). After demonstrating that the book cannot be understood in a literal sense, he moves to a discussion of its authorship. He grants that the book was written by a holy and inspired person named John, but he is not ready to agree that this John was the apostle. He furnishes only scant external evidence to support his premise, but is more extensive in discussing internal factors.

Dionysius's case against apostolic authorship. The extent of Dionysius's external support for rejecting apostolic authorship is revealed in the following statement: "But I think that there was a certain other [John] among those that were in Asia, since it is said both that there were two tombs at Ephesus, and that each of the two is said to be John's" (Eusebius 7.25). This statement follows a lengthier discussion of how common the name John was toward the end of the apostolic period. This highly theoretical conclusion was to play a significant role in influencing Eusebius in his later interpretation of a statement of Papias (cf. 3.39). Furthermore, this conclusion could in no way be classified as reliable tradition received by Dionysius; it was only vague hearsay that may or may not have had anything whatever to do with the John who wrote the Apocalypse.

Turning to Dionysius's more detailed discussion of internal evidence, one observes four categories of evidence: (1) the writer's self-identification; (2) the general construction of the Apocalypse as compared with the authentic writings of John the apostle; (3) the character of these writings; and (4) the nature of the language in these writings.

Speaking of the apostle, he writes, "The evangelist nowhere adds his name, nor yet proclaims himself, throughout either the Gospel or the Epistle." (Eusebius, 7.25. This discussion will assume, along with Dionysius, the authorship of the gospel of John and the three epistles of John by John the son of Zebedee.) In contrast, he points to the triple mention of John's name in Revelation 1 and to its fourth mention in chapter 22. Dionysius makes this difference a big part of his proof that John the apostle did not write the Apocalypse.

He does not, however, allow for the obvious difference in character between the two sets of writings. The strategic importance of a reference to some authoritative figure in apocalyptic/prophetic writing is widely illustrated in similar works coming from this era of history. Furthermore, one may question Dionysius's objectivity and his credentials for deciding such an issue in view of his endorsement of Paul as the author of the epistle to the Hebrews (Eusebius 6.41). It apparently never occurred to him that Paul is careful to give his name in thirteen epistles, but fails to do so in Hebrews, about which there was a dispute over authorship long before Dionysius's time. The same principle applied to Hebrews as to the Apocalypse would have led him to deny Pauline authorship of Hebrews, which he was unwilling to do.

In regard to the general construction of the recognized Johannine apostolic writings, Dionysius notes that the gospel and the first epistle of John begin in similar ways: "In the beginning was the Word" and "That which was from the beginning." In their early verses, both books also bear witness to the author's eyewitness vantage point. Dionysius then contrasts the Apocalypse with these two books, saying that it is utterly different from and foreign to them and scarcely has even a syllable in common with them. On the other side, he notes that the epistle and the gospel contain no mention or thought of the Apocalypse.

As we will point out, Dionysius radically overstates the case in order to try to make his point. There is actually an interesting parallel between the structure of the Apocalypse and that of the gospel and first epistle. Commenting on the prominence of μαρτυρία (*martyria*, "testimony") in 1 John 5:6-11, Haupt has written,

> The idea of μαρτυρία [(*martyria*)] . . . is one that has a remarkable prominence throughout the Johannaean writings. This idea appears at the beginning, and recurs at the end of all the three greater documents which we have received from St. John. In the Apocalypse he commences,

ch. 1.2, with the vindication of his trustworthiness: ὃς ἐμαρτύρησεν τὸν λόγον τοῦ θεοῦ καὶ τὴν μαρτυρίαν Ἰησοῦ Χριστοῦ, ὅσα εἶδεν [(*hos emartyrēsen ton logon tou theou kai tēn martyrian Iēsou Christou hosa eiden,* "who testified the Word of God, even the testimony of Jesus Christ, as many things as he saw")].[5]

Haupt observes that it is a mark of the apostle to introduce a guarantee of his veracity by the mention of his eye-witness-ship: "as many things as he saw." So again at the close of the book, in Revelation 22, "its contents are summed up again and again as a μαρτυρία [(*martyria*)] of our Lord," Haupt continues.

As for the gospel of John, after its prologue it continues with the *martyria* of John the Baptist (John 1:19ff.; Haupt, pp. 196-97). In the body of the gospel Jesus appeals repeatedly to the witness of God to His mission (cf. John 5:32; 8:18; 15:26). It ends with the testimony of the evangelist himself in 21:24 (Haupt, p. 197).

The epistle of 1 John begins with the testimony of John the apostle (1 John 1:1-4) and ends with that of God Himself (1 John 5:6-11; Haupt, p. 197).

Without pursuing this investigation further, one is impressed with how similar the Apocalypse is to the other two works by John. The author of all three writes from the perspective of one who was personally involved in and a witness to the things he writes about.

The fondness of the Apocalypse for triplets (e.g., Rev. 2:2, 9; 4:5; 8:5; 11:19; 16:18) and for sevenfold arrangements (e.g., seven messages, seven seals, seven trumpets, seven bowls) is another characteristic that shows authorial inclination similar to that of the gospel of John.[6]

Dionysius's third piece of internal evidence against apostolic authorship of the Apocalypse deals with the character of the authentic writings of John the apostle. Here he apparently has in mind similarities in vocabulary between the gospel and the epistles that are not shared by the Apocalypse. His list includes the following: "the life" (John 1:4 et al.; 1 John 2:25; 3:14 f., etc.), "the light" (John 1-12; 1 John 1:7; 2:9, etc.), "turning from darkness" (John 12:46; 1 John 1:5), "the truth" (John 1:14 et al.; 1 John 1:8; 3:19, etc.), "the grace" (John 1:14, 16, 17; 2 John 3), "the joy" (John 3:29, etc.; 1 John 1:4; 2 John 12; 3 John 4), "the flesh" (John 1:13, 14; 6:53,56, etc.; 1 John 4:2) and "the

---

5. Erich Haupt, *The First Epistle of St. John* (Edinburgh: T. & T. Clark, 1879), p. 296 (transliteration and translation supplied). See also Stephen S. Smalley, "John's Revelation and John's Community," *Bulletin of the John Rylands University Library* 69 (Spring 1987): 564-65.
6. Edwin A. Abbott, *Johannine Grammar* (London: Adam and Charles Black, 1906), pp. 455-65.

blood" (John 6:53-56; 19:34; 1 John 1:7; 5:6,8) of the Lord, "the judgment" (John 3:19, etc.; 1 John 4:17; cf. 2:18, etc.), "the forgiveness of
sins" (cf. John 20:23; 1 John 1:9; 2:12; cf. 3:5), "the love of God toward
us" (John 3:16; 14:23; 17:23; 1 John 3:1; 4:11, etc.), the "commandment" that we should "love one another" (John 13:34; 15:12, 17; 1
John 3:23, etc.), that we should "keep all the commandments" (John
15:10; 1 John 2:3; 3:22 ff., etc.), the "conviction" of "the world" (John
16:8; 1 John 2:16 f.), of "the devil" (1 John 3:8; cf. 2:14, etc.), of "the
Antichrist" (1 John 2:18 f.), the promise of the Holy Spirit (John 14:16,
etc; 1 John 3:24; 4:13; cf. 2:20), the adoption of the sons of God (John
1:12; 11:52; 1 John 3:1,2, etc.), the "faith" (John 1:7, etc.; 1 John 5:4)
that is demanded of us throughout, "the Father" and "the Son" (John
3:36 et al.; 1 John 4:14, etc.). These, he says, are to be found everywhere in John's gospel and epistles, but the Apocalypse has scarcely a
syllable in common with them (Eusebius 7.25).

One cannot help but question the accuracy of Dionysius's research at this point. Of course, he did not have the advantage of
modern NT concordances or of computer technology, but one wonders why he should make such sweeping generalizations when he did
not have facts to base them on.

To give a specific response, twelve of the nineteen terms or expressions with which Dionysius says the Apocalypse has no connection or
affinity (Eusebius 7.25) *are* found in the book, some of them with
great frequency. "Life" (ζωή, zōē) is found fifteen times, including
among others such expressions as "the book of life," "the water of
life," and "the tree of life" (Rev. 2:7, 10; 3:5; 7:17; 13:8; 17:8; 20:12, 15;
21:6, 27; 22:1, 2, 14, 17, 19). The "blood" (αἷμα, haima) of Christ also
has prominence in Revelation, being referred to five times (Rev. 1:5;
5:9; 7:14; 12:11; 19:13). The same is true of judgment (κρίσις, krisis)
which is found four times (Rev. 14:7; 16:7; 18:10; 19:2). Reference to
the devil (διάβολος, diabolos) by that name is made five times (Rev.
2:10; 12:9, 12; 20:2, 10). To complete the list of words introduced by
Dionysius, the "Father" (ὁ πατήρ, ho patēr) is found five times (Rev.
1:6; 2:27; 3:5,21; 14:1), the "Son" (υἱός, huios) four times (Rev. 1:13;
2:18; 12:5; 14:14), "faith" (πίστις, pistis) four times (Rev. 2:13, 19;
13:10; 14:12), the "Spirit" (πνεῦμα, pneuma) seven times (excluding
references to the "Seven Spirits"; Rev. 2:7, 11, 17, 29; 3:6, 13, 22), the
"commandment" (ἐντολή, entolē) twice (Rev. 12:17; 14:12), "love"
(ἀγάπη, agapē, and ἀγαπάω, agapaō) three times (Rev. 1:5; 2:19; 3:9),
"grace" (χάρις, charis) twice (Rev. 1:4; 22:21), and "light" (φῶς, phōs)
three times (Rev. 21:24; 22:5).

Of the other seven terms mentioned by Dionysius, three are not
found in the gospel of John. These are "forgiveness" (ἄφεσις, aphesis),
"antichrist" (ἀντίχριστος, antichristos), and "adoption" (υἱοθεσία,

huiothesia). One additional word is not used in 1 John: "conviction" (ἔλεγχος, *elenchos*).

This leaves three of the nineteen words unaccounted for. One of them, "truth" (ἀλήθεια, *alētheia*), is not in the Apocalypse, but "genuine" (ἀληθινός, *alēthinos*) is. "Darkness" (σκότος, *skotos*) and "joy" (χαρά, *chara*) are the other two not used in Revelation, but the latter of these is used only once apiece in the three epistles of John.

The fourth argument that Dionysius uses against assigning the Apocalypse to the son of Zebedee is drawn from the writing style of the gospel and epistle in contrast with that of the Apocalypse. These are his words:

> The former [John and 1 John] are not only written in faultless Greek, but also show the greatest literary skill in their diction, their reasonings, and the constructions in which they are expressed. There is a complete absence of any barbarous word, or solecism, or any vulgarism whatever. For their author had, as it seems, both kinds of word, by the free gift of the Lord, the word of knowledge and the word of speech. But I will not deny that the other writer had seen revelations and received knowledge and prophecy; nevertheless I observe his style and that his use of the Greek language is not accurate, but that he employs barbarous idioms, in some places committing downright solecisms. (Eusebius 7.25)

Dionysius is certainly not alone in his observations regarding the style of the Apocalypse. The irregularities in grammar have been noticed frequently.[7] As Guthrie summarizes, "He places nominatives in opposition [sic] to other cases, irregularly uses participles, constructs broken sentences, adds unnecessary pronouns, mixes up genders, numbers and cases and introduces several unusual constructions."[8]

Without any question there are unusual grammatical features in the Apocalypse, but what about John's other writings, his first epistle, for example? Are there not extreme grammatical irregularities here, too? They may be somewhat different in kind, but they are still quite difficult to follow. Houlden characterizes the epistolary Prologue of 1 John (1:1-4) as "bordering on incoherence" and sees these verses as a "lapse into grammatical impossibilities."[9] In regard to 1 John 3:19-21, Brown writes the following: "We have already seen that the epistolary author is singularly inept in constructing clear sentences, but in these verses he is at his worst. Most commentators kindly call

---

7. Steven Thompson, *The Apocalypse and Semitic Syntax* (Cambridge: Cambridge U., 1985), p. 1.
8. Donald Guthrie, *New Testament Introduction*, 4th ed. (Downers Grove, Ill.: InterVarsity, 1990), p. 939.
9. J. L. Houlden, *The Johannine Epistles*, HNTC (New York: Harper & Row, 1973), p. 45.

the passage a *crux interpretum*; less charitably Loisy . . . dubs it 'gib-berish.' . . . At the least, it offers the Prologue competition for the prize in grammatical obscurity."[10] In speaking of the ἐν τούτῳ γιν-ώσκειν (*en toutǭ ginōskein*) in 1 John 5:2, Bultmann says the expression is "almost incomprehensible."[11]

Unusual grammatical phenomena are by no means limited to the Apocalypse in the apostle John's canonical writings. If John deviated from the normal usage in 1 John, why could he not have done so in the Apocalypse? No writer can be put into a straitjacket and required to have no deviations or to practice the same kinds of grammatical deviations in everything he writes. It is shallow thinking, therefore, on the basis of this aspect of writing style to exclude the last book of the canon from among those written by the apostle John.

Summary of Dionysius's evidence. Because both the external and the internal evidence adduced by Dionysius is so weak, his case against the apostolic authorship of the Apocalypse is practically non-existent. Stonehouse summarizes the situation well when he writes, "In spite of this apparently pious regard for the Apocalypse and en-deavor to be objective in his criticisms, it is admitted on all sides that Dionysius's entire criticism is motivated by dogmatic considerations and his arguments are one-sided and overstated."[12]

Stonehouse goes on to say, "There can be no doubt that Dionysius was first of all interested in destroying the influence of this work," that is, the Apocalypse (Stonehouse, p. 127). He adopted two tactics to do this. First, he fought the literalist, chiliastic interpretation of the book, the earliest accepted orthodox interpretation (Stonehouse, p. 4). Nepos's *Refutation of the Allegorists* had been an attack on Origen's principles of interpretation. Dionysius had been a pupil of Origen and, hence, felt compelled to defend him in this way.

His second tactic was to raise questions about apostolic author-ship, but in such a way as to avoid bringing the wrath of the rest of the church upon him. He knew the widespread acceptance of the Apoc-alypse as canonical and dared not reject the book outright.

One might anticipate that the personal influence of Dionysius and that of his ecclesiastical position would carry much weight in this matter, but the only direct evidence that remains is in the writ-

---

10. Raymond E. Brown, *The Epistles of John*, vol. 30 of AB (Garden City, N.Y.: Doubleday, 1982), p. 453.
11. R. Bultmann, *The Johannine Epistles*, Hermeneia (Philadelphia: Fortress, 1973), p. 77.
12. Ned Bernard Stonehouse, *The Apocalypse in the Ancient Church* (Goes, Holland: Oosterbaan & Le Cointre, 1929), p. 126; cf. also G. B. Caird, *A Commentary on the Revelation of St. John the Divine*, HNTC (New York: Harper & Row, 1966), pp. 4-5.

ings of Eusebius, himself a Christian leader of great influence.[13] His
Ecclesiastical History shows how deep his regard for Dionysius was.
He devotes one entire book to this Alexandrian leader and quotes
from his writings extensively. Specifically, he championed Dionysius's criticism of the apostolic authorship (Stonehouse, pp. 129,
131-32). However, Eusebius stopped short of an outright denial of
canonicity because he knew he was at odds with the church in this
matter.

Evidence of Dionysius's impact on Eusebius is found in the way
the latter followed the former's theory about two Johns in Ephesus
when he interpreted a certain statement of Papias.[14] Eusebius also
endorsed Dionysius's strong antichiliastic viewpoint. In citing Papias's chiliastic views (i.e., that there would be a millennium after the
resurrection of the dead with a kingdom of Christ set up in material
form on the earth), Eusebius characterizes them as the result of a
perverse reading of the apostolic accounts without proper allowance
for those accounts having been spoken mystically and symbolically.
He even went so far as to call Papias a man of very little intelligence
(Eusebius, 3.39).

In spite of the questions raised by Dionysius and Eusebius, the
broader judgment of the early church prevailed to give the Apocalypse a place in the NT canon. This recognition was assuredly based
on the book's apostolic authorship (Stonehouse, p. 153) and possibly
on the doctrine of the future millennium presented in the book.[15]
Athanasius is generally given credit for "saving" the book. He valued
the historic position of his church above the critical judgments of
Dionysius and Eusebius (Stonehouse, p. 3).

Even though in modern times R. H. Charles has adduced a case
against apostolic authorship that is more sophisticated than that of
Dionysius, Charles still follows the same general lines of evidence as
Dionysius did.[16] The fact remains that the external evidence for au-

---

13. Indirect evidence illustrates Dionysius's influence also. After he raised a
    question about the authorship of Revelation by the apostle John, the
    Eastern Fathers refrained as much as possible from any use of Revelation
    in their writings. Chiliasm was considered suspect, and they unan-
    imously followed Dionysius's example (Reinhart Staats, "The Eternal
    Kingdom of Christ, The Apocalyptic Tradition in the 'Creed of Nicaea-
    Constantinople,'" *Patristic and Byzantine Review* 9, no. 1 [1990]: 26).
14. Eusebius, *Eccles. Hist.*, 3.29. The second John was called an "elder" to
    distinguish him from the apostle. A recent reconstruction of who this
    alleged elder might have been is given by John J. Gunther, "The Elder
    John, Author of Revelation," *JSNT* 11 (1981): 3-20.
15. Stonehouse, p. 151; Helmut Koester, *Introduction to the New Testament*, 2
    vols. (Philadelphia: Fortress, 1982), 2:256.
16. R. H. Charles, *A Critical and Exegetical Commentary on The Revelation of
    St. John*, 2 vols in ICC (Edinburgh: T. & T. Clark, 1963), 1:xxxviii-l.

thorship by John the apostle is earlier, clearer, more definite, and more positive for Revelation than for the traditional authorship of any other NT book.[17] Testimony of the earliest Fathers is unanimous in favor of the apostolic authorship and authority of the book. These include Papias, Justin Martyr, the Muratorian Fragment, Irenaeus, Clement of Alexandria, Tertullian, Hippolytus, Origen, and Methodius.[18]

Principles derived from examining Dionysius. At the conclusion of such a historical survey as this, it seems appropriate to draw several conclusions.

(1) Theological bias can affect one's approach to the Scripture in very radical ways. Dionysius had a theological axe to grind, and this brought him to the point of questioning an almost unanimous tradition that had been handed down to him. This should serve notice to us to exercise every effort toward objectivity in our biblically related investigations.

(2) Though not the case for every NT book, apostolic authorship was a major, if not the major, factor in the recognition of the Apocalypse as canonical. At this point Caird is incorrect when he says, "The little that we know of the Apostle John would add nothing to our ability to interpret Revelation, and its authority would be neither increased if his authorship of it could be proved nor diminished if it were disproved."[19] Caird is at odds with the testimony of the early church on this point. Some contemporary evangelicals seem to have missed this point too. Without apostolic authorship the book loses its claim to canonicity.

(3) There is severe danger in relying solely on internal evidence for conclusions about authorship when there is a strong consensus of ancient tradition covering the same. One's use of internal criteria can and often does become quite subjective, allowing him to prove just about anything he sets out to prove. Sometimes, when there is no such consensus among the ancients, one must rely on internal matters, as is the case with the epistle to the Hebrews. But to use internal evidence to counteract a consistent tradition coming from the earliest period of church history is very ill-advised.

(4) Tradition preserved from the ancient church is on the whole quite reliable. This is not to say that the Fathers individually were inerrant, but that when one did go astray in his writings there was a

---

17. Guthrie, *NT Introduction*, p. 933; Leon Morris, *The Revelation of St. John*, TNTC (Grand Rapids: Eerdmans, 1969), pp. 26-27.
18. Beckwith, *Apocalypse*, pp 348-51; Morris, *Revelation*, p. 26; William Lee, "The Revelation of St. John," in *The Holy Bible*, ed. F. C. Cook (London: John Murray, 1881), 4:405-24, 438-42; Stonehouse, pp. 7-8, 129-30.
19. Caird, *Revelation*, p. 4.

sufficient response to counteract his error. It is highly insulting to those leaders of the past to assume that we moderns can discover the truth and overrule their early testimony because of allegedly insightful discoveries made in observations of internal criteria of this or that book of the NT. The earliest Christians were not ignorant and uninformed. We who have entered the inheritance which they preserved for us should show the highest respect for their collective accuracy and integrity.

ADDITIONAL EVIDENCE FOR APOSTOLIC AUTHORSHIP

In addition to the elements favorable to apostolic authorship already given in response to Dionysius, more internal elements may be cited. For example, only John's gospel and Revelation call Christ "the Word" (John 1:1; Rev. 19:13). The same is true regarding the imagery of "the lamb," "the water of life," "he who overcomes," "keeping the commandments," and use of the adjective ἀληθινός (*alēthinos*). Both books have a striking form of Zechariah 12:10 (John 19:37; Rev. 1:7), an invitation to the one who is thirsty (John 7:37; Rev. 22:17), and white clothing for angels (John 20:12; Rev. 4:4). Both sets of writings have the same sharp contrasts between absolute good and absolute evil, and they both emphasize witness-bearing and keeping the commandments of God.[20] A more detailed look at similarities is revealing.

Vocabulary. First, a number of vocabulary ties between Revelation and other writings of the apostle John exist. The verb σημαίνω (*sēmainō,* "I signify, indicate") used in Rev. 1:1 is found only five other times in the NT, three of them being in the gospel of John (John 12:33; 18:32; 21:19). In Rev. 1:7 the Greek verb ἐκκεντέω (*ekkenteō,* "I pierce") renders the Hebrew רָקַד (*dāqar,* "I pierce") of Zech. 12:10 in agreement with the rendering of the same word in John 19:37. This rendering differs from that of the LXX, making the agreement even more striking. These are the only two occurrences of the verb in the NT. Κοινωνέω (*Koinōneō,* "I share") with its cognates and συγκοινωνέω (*synkoinōneō,* "I have fellowship with") with its cognates are used five times in John's other writings (1 John 1:3 [twice], 6, 7; 2 John 11) in agreement with John's usage of them in Revelation (Rev. 1:9; 18:4; 21:27). John's use of θλίψις (*thlipsis,* "tribulation") in Rev. 1:9 to refer to the general tribulations of the Christian life harmonizes well with the same usage in John 16:33. The Greek noun ὄψις (*opsis*) is used in

---

20. Beckwith, *Apocalypse,* p. 356; Morris, *Revelation,* p. 31; Henry Barclay Swete, *The Apocalypse of St. John, The Greek Text with Introduction, Notes and Indices* (Grand Rapids: Eerdmans, n.d.), pp. cxvi-cxxx; Henry Alford, *The Greek Testament* (Cambridge: Deighton, Bell, 1903), 4:226-29.

the sense of "countenance" in Rev. 1:16. The only other NT occurrences of the word are in John 7:24; 11:44, with 11:44 carrying this same sense. The preposition ἐκ (ek, "out of") is far more frequent in the gospel of John and Revelation than in any other books in the NT.[21]

The verb νικάω (nikaō, "I conquer, overcome") is a dominant one in John's writings. It is found seven times in his other works (John 16:33; 1 John 2:13, 14; 4:4; 5:4 [twice]; 5:5) and fifteen times in Revelation (Rev. 2:7, 11, 17, 26; 3:5, 12, 21; 5:5; 6:2; 11:7; 12:11; 13:7; 15:2; 17:14; 21:7). Only four instances of it in the NT are outside Johannine writings (Luke 11:22; Rom. 3:4; 12:21 [twice]). Seven of the Revelation uses (Rev. 2:7, 11, 17, 26; 3:5, 12, 21) closely parallel in sense the uses in 1 John 5:4, 5. The use in Rev. 5:5 is quite close in meaning to the use in John 16:33.

The Greek verb πλανάω (planaō, "I deceive") occurs with greater frequency in Revelation (Rev. 2:20; 12:9; 13:14; 18:23; 19:20; 20:3, 8, 10) and 1 John (1 John 1:8; 2:26; 3:7) than anywhere else in the NT. This gives evidence of the composition of the two books by the same author, addressed to the same general audience, at roughly the same time. It seems to have been John's role to rebuke erring church leaders of Asia during the last decade of the first century.

John reflects the frequent teaching of Jesus in his use of βάλλω εἰς (ballō eis, "I cast into") to speak of casting people into the place of eternal torment (cf. Matt. 3:10; 5:29; 7:19; 13:42, 50; 18:8, 9; Mark 9:45, 47; Luke 3:9) both in the gospel of John (John 15:6) and in Revelation (Rev. 20:14, 15; cf. Rev. 20:3, 10). Τηρέω (Tēreō, "I keep") is another word of unusual frequency in writings of the apostle John. In reference to keeping someone's word or command, it occurs twelve times in the gospel of John (8:51, 52, 55; 14:15, 21, 23, 24; 15:10 [twice], 20 [twice]; 17:6) and six in 1 John (2:3, 4, 5; 3:22, 24; 5:3). Comparable uses of it occur nine times in Revelation (1:3; 2:26; 3:3, 8, 10; 12:17; 14:12; 22:7, 9).

Another mark of authorship by John is the use of ζάω (zaō, "I live") to denote life that belongs primarily and essentially to God and Christ. The verb is so used in the gospel of John (4:10, 11; 5:25; 6:51 [twice], 57 [three times], 58; 7:38; 11:25, 26; 14:19 [twice]) and 1 John (4:9) as it is in Revelation (1:18; 2:8; 3:1; 4:9, 10; 7:2; 10:6; 13:14; 15:7; 20:4, 5). The substantive ὁ ἅγιος (ho hagios, "the holy one") as a title for Christ is occasionally a title for the Messiah in the NT. John (6:69), 1 John (2:20), and Revelation (3:7) are among the books that utilize this title.

The adjective ἀληθινός (alēthinos, "true, genuine") is a favorite

---

21. Kenneth G. C. Newport, "The Use of EK in Revelation: Evidence of Semitic Influence," *AUSS* 24, no. 3 (Autumn 1986): 223.

word of the apostle, occurring twelve times in the gospel of John and 1 John (John 1:9; 4:23, 37; 6:32; 7:28; 8:16; 15:1; 17:3 19:35; 1 John 2:8; 5:20 [twice]) and ten times in Revelation (3:7, 14; 6:10; 15:3; 16:7; 19:2, 9, 11; 21:5; 22:6). It appears only five times outside the Johannine writings (Luke 16:11; 1 Thess. 1:9; Heb. 8:2; 9:24; 10:22). The thought of Jesus as a μάρτυς (martys, "a witness") is favored by John (John 3:11, 32, 33; 5:31, 32; 8:13, 14; Rev. 1:5; 3:14), but is not found elsewhere in the NT.

The verb συμβουλεύω (symbouleuō) occurs only four times in the NT, twice in the active voice meaning "advise" or "counsel," and twice in the middle voice meaning "consult." One of the active verbs is in John's gospel (18:14) and the other in Revelation (3:18). The use of φανερόω (phaneroō, "I manifest") in Rev. 3:18 to refer to things hidden from men now, but revealed at the last day agrees particularly well with the use of the same verb in 1 John 3:2 (cf. also 1 Cor. 4:5; 2 Cor. 5:11; Eph. 5:13).

In Rev. 3:18 ἐγχρίω (enchriō, "I anoint") refers to a spiritual anointing of the eyes as does its cognate noun χρίσμα (chrisma, "anointing") in 1 John 2:20, 27 (twice). Both words recall the episode involving Christ, the blind man, and the Pharisees in John 9:6, 11. The verb is ἐπιχρίω (epichriō, "I anoint") in vv. 6, 11. The noun λαμπάς (lampas, "lamp") is relatively rare in the NT outside the parable of the ten virgins (Matt. 25:1-8). It is found only three other times, one of which is in the gospel of John (18:3) and two of which are in Revelation (4:5; 8:10).

Ἀρνίον (Arnion, "lamb"), a word used thirty times in Revelation, appears only one other time in the NT, in the gospel of John (21:15). The noun βροντή (brontē, "thunder") is in only two places in the NT outside Revelation. Both relate to the apostle John. One is in Mark 3:17, where he and his brother are called "sons of thunder." The other is in John 12:29. It occurs ten times in Revelation (4:5; 6:1; 8:5; 10:3, 4 [twice]; 11:19; 14:2; 16:18; 19:6).

The apostle is the only NT writer to use the verb σκηνόω (skēnoō, "tabernacle") (John 1:14; Rev. 7:15; 12:12; 13:6; 21:3). He too is the only one to use ὁδηγέω (hodēgeō, "I lead") to speak of divine guidance (John 16:13; Rev. 7:17). The gospel and the Apocalypse are the only two NT books to refer to Christ as ὁ λόγος (ho logos, "the Word") (John 1:1; Rev. 19:13).

The above sampling furnishes an impressive list of similarities in lexical usage in a comparison of Revelation with other Johannine writings.

Syntax. On the grammatical side an illustration of this similarity is seen in the fondness of the author for articular participles. The frequency of articular participles in the Johannine epistles and in

13

the Apocalypse is substantially higher than in any other NT books. The frequency rate per 1,000 words for 1 John is 19.6; for 2 John, 20.4; for 3 John, 18.3; and for the Apocalypse 17.7. This is compared with an average frequency per 1,000 words of 11.4 for the text of the entire NT. Outside these four books the highest rate is found in the epistle to the Hebrews, where the rate is 15.5.[22] These figures provide additional evidence of a common hand in the writing of the four books.

The anarthrous Ἰησοῦς (*Iēsous*, "Jesus") is used nine times in the Apocalypse (1:9 [twice]; 12:17; 14:12; 17:6; 19:10 [twice]; 20:4; 22:16), an unusually high frequency compared to the rest of the NT books. There are only five anarthrous occurrences. Two other Johannine books bear the same characteristic. The gospel of John has ninety-three anarthrous uses and the first epistle of John has five. This is in great contrast with the epistles of Paul (less than ten) and Peter (no occurrences).

The futuristic use of the present tense of ἔρχομαι (*erchomai*, "I come") is another feature that binds the gospel of John and Revelation close together syntactically. It is a way of emphasizing the imminence of Christ's return in both books (e.g., John 14:3; Rev. 1:7; 2:5, 16; 3:11). In Rev. 1:10, the comparative particle ὡς (*hōs*, "as, like") is followed by a noun. Only three other times in the NT is there a construction like this. One of them is in John 1:14 where the adjective μονογενοῦς (*monogenous*, "one of kind") functions as a substantive (cf. 1 Pet. 1:19; 2:12).

Another striking resemblance between the syntax of Revelation and that of the gospel of John is in its special use of parataxis in Rev. 2:5, 16; 3:3, with one independent clause subordinated in sense to another, according to a Semitic model. This construction matches that in John 7:34 and 10:12. In Revelation as in John's other writings, the preposition ἐκ (*ek*, "from") is often used idiomatically in a partitive sense, meaning "[some] of" (e.g., Rev. 2:10; 3:9; 5:5, 9; 6:1; 7:9, 13; 9:13; 11:9; 13:3; 14:10; 15:7; 17:1, 2, 6[twice], 11; 18:3; 20:12; 21:9; cf. John 1:41; 3:1; 6:8, 70, 71; 7:40, 50; 16:17; 2 John 4). Sometimes the writer combines εἷς (*heis*, "one") with *ek* to provide a partitive sense, another Johannine characteristic (Rev. 5:5; 6:1; 7:13; 9:13; 13:3; 15:7; 17:1; 21:9; cf. John 1:41; 6:8, 70, 71; 7:50; 11:49; 12:2; 13:21, 23; 18:26; 20:24). It is substantial support for the apostolic authorship of the Apocalypse that this combination occurs eleven times in the gospel of John and eight in Revelation, and only ten times in the rest of the NT.[23]

---

22. Statistics are derived from PROJECT GRAMCORD, 1984.
23. Charles, *Revelation*, 1:139; Archibald Thomas Robertson, *Word Pictures in the New Testament*, 6 vols. (Nashville: Broadman, 1933), 6:333; Newport, "Use of EK," pp. 228-29. A variant at John 12:4 accounts for the twelfth occurrence in Charles's count in the gospel of John.

Though the passive of ἀποκτείνω (*apokteinō*, "I kill") is frequent in Revelation (2:13; 6:11; 9:18, 20; 11:5, 13; 13:10, 15; 19:21), twice the author substitutes the active of ἀποθνήσκω (*apothnēskō*, "I die") for it (Rev. 8:11; 14:13). This is always the practice in the gospel of John (11:16, 50, 51; 18:14, 32; 19:7). The nominative absolute is another construction common to the apostle's other writings and Revelation (John 6:39; 7:38; 1 John 2:24, 27; Rev. 2:26; 3:12, 21).[24]

Three unusual uses of the adverbial accusative of time in the NT seemingly designate a point in time, contrary to the usual function of the accusative to indicate extent of time. One of the three is in the gospel of John and another is in Revelation (John 4:52; Rev. 3:3; cf. 1 Cor. 15:30).[25] Future tenses following ἵνα (*hina*, "in order that") are relatively rare in the NT, but do occur in Johannine writings, including Revelation (John 7:3; Rev. 3:9; 6:4, 11; 8:3; 9:4, 5, 20; 13:12; 14:13; 22:14).[26]

The verb προσκυνέω (*proskyneō*, "I worship") is more frequent in the gospel of John and Revelation than in any other NT books. In addition, these two books have the distinction of having the verb govern objects in both the dative and accusative cases.[27] Another feature common to the gospel of John and Revelation is the use of κεῖμαι (*keimai*, "I lie") as a passive of τίθημι (*tithēmi*, "I place") (John 2:6; 19:29; 21:9; Rev. 4:2; 21:16).

These grammatical examples lend additional support to the plausibility of the apostolic authorship of the Apocalypse.

Style. Writing style is another area that bolsters the case for apostolic authorship. The writer of the Apocalypse shows an inclination toward *brachylogy* just as the writer of acknowledged apostolic works does (e.g., John 5:36; 6:58; 13:18; 15:11, 25; 1 John 3:11, 12; Rev. 1:16; 13:11). The apostle is also characterized by his use of the pleonastic οὕτως (*houtōs*, "thus") (John 4:6; 13:25; Rev. 2:15; 3:5, 16; 9:17), another stylistic link between his two major works.

In Rev. 3:10, τηρέω (*tēreo*) is repeated as a means of emphasizing reciprocal action. A comparable play on different meanings of the same verb emphasizes similar reciprocity in John 17:6, 11, 12. The reciprocity reflected in μετ' αὐτοῦ καὶ αὐτὸς μετ' ἐμοῦ (*met' autou kai autos met' emou*, "with him and he with Me") (Rev. 3:20) is also remi-

---

24. Lee, "Revelation," 4:529.
25. Archibald Thomas Robertson, *A Grammar of the Greek New Testament in the Light of Historical Research* (Nashville: Broadman, 1934), p. 470.
26. Well-supported variants in John 15:8; 17:2 also have future indicatives following ἵνα.
27. Matthew, Mark, Paul, and the author of Hebrews consistently use the dative as object of a transitive προσκυνέω. Luke uses the accusative in his gospel and the dative in Acts. A possible exception to this distinctiveness is the gospel of Mark where a variant in Mark 5:6 offers the possibility of the dative or the accusative.

niscent of the apostle's writing habits (John 6:56; 10:38; 14:20; 15:4, 5; 17:21, 26).

In Rev. 6:11, the phrase ἔτι χρόνον μικρόν (*eti chronon mikron*, "yet a little time") represents the delay until the blood of the martyrs under the altar is finally avenged. In John 7:33 and 12:35, Jesus uses the identical words to describe the remaining time He was to be with the Jewish people (cf. also John 13:33). This concurrence is another mark of common authorship.

Concepts. A last group of considerations that show the likelihood that the same person wrote the Apocalypse as wrote the gospel and epistles of John are the similar concepts expressed in the books. The idea of drinking water provided by Christ is in both the gospel and Revelation (John 7:37; Rev. 22:17). Both John's first epistle and Revelation are introduced by references to what John saw, designated in expressions built around ὁ λόγος (*ho logos*, "the word") (1 John 1:1-2; Rev. 1:2).

Christ's references to God as "*My* God" and "*My* Father" in Revelation (Rev. 3:2, 5, 12) are unusual enough to remind the reader of His words in John 20:17. "*My* Father" comes from his lips thirty-five times in the NT outside Revelation, mostly in Matthew (13 times) and John (19 times). Quite possibly the title ἐγώ εἰμι (*egō eimi*, "I am") that begins Rev. 1:8 is the self-designation appropriated by Jesus in the gospels, especially in the gospel of John (e.g., John 8:58).

Roman involvement in the crucifixion of Christ is indicated in the gospel of John (John 19:31-32, 37; Rev. 1:7; cf. Zech 12:10). Some of the same anti-Roman spirit is present in the Apocalypse. The Messianic title "Son of Man" applied to Jesus in Rev. 1:13 and 14:14 fits the usage in the gospel of John. As John notes the prerogative of the Son of Man to execute judgment (John 5:22, 27), Jesus does that very thing in Revelation 2-3. Revelation is also consistent with the gospel of John in its assignment of the title "Son of God" to Jesus (John 1:34, 49; 3:18; 10:36; 11:4, 27; 19:7; Rev. 2:18). In a similar vein, resentment toward certain Jews is reflected in both books (John 8:31 ff.; Rev. 2:9; 3:9).

Representation of Christ's omniscience by the repetition of οἶδα (*oida*, "I know") in Revelation (2:2, 9, 13, 19; 3:1, 8, 15) is quite in keeping with John's picture of Him in the gospel. Peter acknowledges this same attribute in practically the same way with his threefold use of *oidas* ("you know") in John 21:15, 16, 17. Of course, the prominence given to love for both God and man in Revelation accords well with the same emphasis in the apostle's other writings (John 13:34-35; 1 John 3:13-14; 2 John 5-6; 3 John 6; Rev. 2:4, 19). Yet faith is not overlooked in either case (1 John 5:1, 4, 5; Rev. 2:13, 19; 13:10; 14:12). Furthermore, love and works are intimately related in both Revelation and 1 John (1 John 5:2-3; Rev. 2:4-5).

It is typical of apostolic style to delineate clearly between those whose relationship to Christ is merely superficial and those who are genuine (John 8:44; 1 John 1:10; 2:4; Rev. 3:9). Christ's self-characterization as "the beginning of the creation of God" (Rev. 3:14) closely relates to John's earlier crediting of Him with the creation of all things (John 1:3).

John's gospel portrays the unity of the Father and the Son and the participation of believers in their future glory (John 10:30; 17:22, 24). Both elements are graphically pictured in the promise to the overcomer in Rev. 3:21. A comparison of Christ's relationship with believers and the Father's relationship with Him suggested by this verse is also characteristic of the literature of the apostle (John 15:9, 10; 17:21, 22; 20:21). Attention to the passover lamb is also a notable component of each book (John 1:29; 19:14, 31-36; Rev. 1:5; 5:6, 9). The shepherd-figure is another point that the gospel of John and Revelation have in common (John 10:1-30; 21:15-17; Rev. 7:17). God is the fountain of life to whom Christ will lead His sheep (John 4:12, 14; 7:38-39; Rev. 7:17; 21:6; 22:1, 17).

This survey suffices to show that conceptually the Apocalypse is similar to NT writings acknowledged to have been written by the apostle John.[28]

DIFFERENCES BETWEEN THE APOCALYPSE AND JOHN'S OTHER WRITINGS

Marked differences between Revelation and the apostle's other writings are to some degree answerable, but it need not be denied that they do exist. These have been developed extensively elsewhere and a simple mention of them is all that is necessary here.[29] Mussies, after a detailed examination of the Apocalypse's morphology, writes, "The linguistic and stylistic divergence of the Apc. on the one hand and the Gospel and the Letters of St. John on the other, proves beyond any reasonable doubt that all these works as we have them before us were not phrased by one and the same man."[30] Mussies's opinion carries some weight because of the extreme detail of his research, but it also suffers from debilitating limitations. For example, he limits his examination, in large degree, to Codex Alexandrinus. Also, he makes no attempt to balance the differences with the similarities such as are enumerated above. An overlap of his observations with the previously

---

28. For further discussion of the similarities between Revelation and John's other writings see Lee, "Revelation," 4:454-60; Smalley, "John's Revelation," pp. 549-71.
29. Charles, *Revelation*, 1:xxix-xxxvii; Beckwith, *Apocalypse*, pp. 354-60; Elisabeth Schüssler Fiorenza, "The Quest for the Johannine School: The Apocalypse and the Fourth Gospel," *NTS* 23, no. 4 (July 1977): 410-27.
30. G. Mussies, *The Morphology of Koine Greek As Used in the Apocalypse of St. John, A Study in Bilingualism* (Leiden: E. J. Brill, 1971), p. 352.

discussed criticisms of Dionysius is conspicuous. The vocabulary of the Apocalypse differs from the rest. Certain characteristic Johannine theological expressions and phrases are not found in it. Its grammar is different. Its eschatology is futuristic as compared with the realized eschatology of the gospel of John. Its theological perspective is different. It uses the OT in a different way.

Many have interpreted these differences as indicating that the two came from different authors. Besides John the Elder proposed by Dionysius and Eusebius, suggestions as to authorship of the Apocalypse have included a Palestinian Jew but not John the Elder, the author of 2 and 3 John,[31] and John the Baptist.[32] If sameness of authorship is assumed, as this investigation advocates, several ways to explain the differences have been proposed: differences in scope and literary form of the gospel and epistles on the one hand and of Revelation on the other, a substantial time-lapse between the two sets of writings, complementary rather than contradictory theological positions between the two, and the use of an amanuensis for one or both.[33]

The second proposal may be dismissed if a traditional dating of the books is adopted, because they all would come within the same decade. (The gospel of John was probably written between A.D. 85 and 90, the epistles of John in the early nineties, and the Apocalypse about A.D. 95 as will be shown below.) If divine inspiration of the books is applied strictly, the fourth suggestion may be dismissed, for God inspired the author, not his secretary, to record what is written. Introduction of excessive deviations through an amanuensis from what an author dictated, as this proposal implies, strains this doctrine. The author would not have recognized his own work after the amanuensis incorporated changes as radical as the differences between the Apocalypse and the other four NT works by John.

The first and third proposals need not be mutually exclusive. Vocabulary, grammar, style, and concepts of a piece of literature are functions of the subject being treated and the state of mind of the author. The natures of the gospel and the epistles on the one hand and of the Apocalypse on the other differ widely. In addition, John's mental state changed from the first set of books to the last one. Though he was inspired to write them all, the divinely chosen method of conveying what he was to write differed markedly. First, the more common means of impressing his inner consciousness with truths that he

---

31. Charles, *Revelation*, 1:xliv.
32. J. Massyngberde Ford, *Revelation*, vol. 38 of AB (Garden City, N.Y.: Doubleday, 1975), pp. 28-30.
33. Fiorenza, "Quest for the Johannine School," pp. 405-6.

transformed into written words for the sake of his constituency was used. Then, in Revelation another method of prophetic inspiration was adopted, that of dramatization through visions, which he in turn described for the sake of his readers. The result of this last process falls into the category of "apocalyptic" literature.

Yet this analysis of Revelation is an oversimplification. The book actually consists of two distinct styles. Aune limits his observation to Revelation 2-3 when noting, "The seven proclamations contrast sharply with the literary matrix in which they are set."[34] Following different criteria, Poythress treats Rev. 1:9–22:17 as visionary narrative with 1:17b–3:22 being an embedded quotation falling into the category of expository discourse. He calls the rest of the book, Rev. 1:1-8 and 22:18-21, expository discourse.[35] His investigation concludes that sections of expository discourse do not differ significantly in their use of intersentence conjunctions from comparable type material in the gospel and the epistles of John. It is in the visionary narrative where distinctive differences of usage are found.[36]

An implication of Poythress's study may furnish support that John's unusual prophetic state while writing the apocalyptic portions accounts for the widespread differences between the Apocalypse and other literature of the apostle John. The unusual condition characterized by him as being ἐν πνεύματι (*en pneumati*, "in spirit") (Rev. 1:10; 4:2; 17:3; 21:10) revised his thinking and manner of expression to the point that he did not write as he did under other circumstances. He became more a product of his prophetic state than while writing his other NT books.

Whether further investigations such as that of Poythress prove fruitful in bearing out this theory or not, the fact remains that the case for the authorship of the Apocalypse by the apostle John rests solidly on the near-unanimous testimony of the early church and a significant body of internal data that liken it to John's other NT books.[37]

---

34. D. E. Aune, "The Form and Function of the Proclamations to the Seven Churches (Revelation 2-3)," *NTS* 36, no. 2 (April 1990): 184.
35. Vern Sheridan Poythress, "Johannine Authorship and the Use of Intersentence Conjunctions in the Book of Revelation," *WTJ* 47, no. 2 (Fall 1985): 329-30, 332-33.
36. Ibid., pp. 331-32.
37. Mounce correctly portrays the status of affairs in his words, "Internal evidence is not entirely unfavorable to apostolic authorship and . . . external evidence is unanimous in its support" (Robert H. Mounce, *The Book of Revelation*, NICNT [Grand Rapids: Eerdmans, 1977], p. 31), though his use of "unanimous" seemingly excludes the weak-minority testimonies such as those of Dionysius and Eusebius.

DATE OF THE APOCALYPSE

A date during the last decade of the first century, about A.D. 95, is the traditional time assigned to the publishing of the Apocalypse. This tradition is substantiated by contemporary majority opinion as well as those who suggest alternatives.[38] A few have opted for an earlier date, before or just after the death of Nero in the late sixties.

Some late-twentieth-century support for an early date has originated in the movement known variously as "dominion theology," "Christian reconstructionism," or "theonomy." This worldview foresees a progressive domination of world government and society by Christianity until God's kingdom on earth becomes a reality. It represents a recent revival in postmillennial eschatology. Reconstructionism's interest in this subject stems from its optimistic outlook regarding Christianity's ability to gain control of secular society. Because Revelation is admittedly pessimistic in this regard, the system's scheme for disposing of this unfavorable evidence is to relegate its fulfillment almost entirely to the past, to a time prior to A.D. 70.[39]

Theonomist Gentry has developed an extensive apologetic for a Neronic (i.e., early) dating of Revelation.[40] He devotes considerable space to raising questions about the traditional evidence for dating the book in the 90s, during Domitian's reign (pp. 41-109). He acknowledges that his case rests either on challenging the usual interpretation of Irenaeus's statement about the dating of the book, an interpretation that prevailed until modern times, or on the assumption that Irenaeus erred regarding the date (p. 334; cf. Chilton, pp. 3-4). Either explanation is at best tenuous. He then downplays the role of such external considerations in favor of those derived from the book itself (Gentry, pp. 113-14, 334).

His internal evidence depends on the questionable assumption of two future comings of Christ foreseen in the NT: a "Cloud-Coming" that occurred at the destruction of Jerusalem in A.D. 70 (cf. Rev. 1:7), and a "Second Coming" at the end of world history (Gentry, p. 123). With this tactic, the "cloud-coming" to which Revelation is devoted turns out to be *no* coming. It is obvious to most that Christ did not come in A.D. 70, so the hermeneutics used to conclude that He did

---

38. E.g., Albert A. Bell, Jr., "The Date of John's Apocalypse. The Evidence of Some Roman Historians Reconsidered," *NTS* 25, no. 1 (October 1978): 93; J. P. M. Sweet, *Revelation* (Philadelphia: Westminster, Pelican, 1979), pp. 21-27.
39. David Chilton, *The Days of Vengeance, an Exposition of the Book of Revelation* (Fort Worth, Tex.: Dominion, 1987), p. 4.
40. Kenneth L. Gentry, Jr., *Before Jerusalem Fell: Dating the Book of Revelation* (Fort Worth, Tex.: Institute for Christian Economics, 1989).

come are suspect. Gentry's other arguments based on internal evidence also rest upon biased interpretive presuppositions that render them unconvincing.

Like Gentry, reconstructionist Chilton, in *Days of Vengeance*, bases his brief case for an early date on the conclusion that the second-century church Father Irenaeus and most other ancient witnesses were wrong in dating the book's writing late in the first century, at the end of the reign of Domitian (A.D. 81-96) (pp. 3-4). He also proposes that the prophecies in Revelation point primarily to the destruction of Jerusalem in A.D. 70 (p. 4). He adds a further reason: the prophecy of Daniel's seventy weeks (Dan. 9:24-27) received its ultimate fulfillment and the canon of NT books was complete by the time of the destruction of Jerusalem in A.D. 70 (pp. 5-6; cf. also Philip Mauro, *The Seventy Weeks and the Great Tribulation*, rev. ed. [Swengel, Pa.: Reiner, n.d.], pp. 102-4).

As will be shown below, Chilton's last two reasons for an early date rest on questionable hermeneutical methodology. His interpretation rests on the questionable assumption that John the author was a priest and that the book is filled with liturgical allusions and references to Temple services (pp. 2-3). He even suggests that John and other ministers wore distinctive uniforms similar to those of the priests of Israel as indicators of their official status (p. 2). This assumption forces the informality of the early church into a completely unnatural, formalistic mold. Pressing the Apocalypse into this liturgical framework commits violence against a grammatical-historical interpretation of its contents.

Chilton's first reason in support of an early date opposes the strong tide of early church evidence and recent NT scholarship. Grounds for questioning the accuracy of Irenaeus and other early witnesses are purely subjective. Chilton cites Athanasius as proof of the canon's completion by A.D. 70 (pp. 5-6). Careful scrutiny of the Athanasius quotation, his comment on Gabriel's words in Dan. 9:24, reflects that Chilton's interpretation of it is quite forced. Athanasius at that point did not address the issue of the NT canon at all. If Irenaeus had been wrong, later witnesses including Clement of Alexandria, Origen, Victorinus, Eusebius, and Jerome would have corrected him. Instead, they confirmed his dating.[41] Most modern scholars concur with this confirmation.

Several details of internal evidence emerge for preferring a Domitianic date in the 90s over a Neronic date in the 60s. One is the difference in the condition of the Asian churches in the 90s compared to the condition portrayed in Paul's epistles of Ephesians, Colossians,

---

41. Swete, pp. xcix-c; Mounce, *Revelation*, p. 32.

and 1 and 2 Timothy, which were addressed to that area during the 60s.[42] By the time of John's book serious spiritual deterioriation and doctrinal apostasy, not present earlier, had set in. Gentry's attempt to respond to this evidence (pp. 327-29) is brief and unpersuasive.

A second reason for preferring the later date is the timing of John's arrival in Asia. According to the best information, he did not come to Asia from Palestine before the late 60s, at the time of the Jewish revolt of A.D. 66-70.[43] This was after Paul's final visit to Asia in A.D. 65. John was part of a migration of Palestinian Christians from Palestine to the province of Asia before the outbreak of the rebellion.[44] A Neronic dating would hardly allow time for him to have settled in Asia, to have replaced Paul as the respected leader of the Asian churches, and then to have been exiled to Patmos before Nero's death in A.D. 68. Gentry does not respond to this chronological difficulty, but his dating of the book in late A.D. 65 or early A.D. 66 (p. 336) renders its apostolic authorship impossible.

Another serious difficulty to the earlier dating is the earthquake that destroyed Laodicea, one of the seven cities addressed in Revelation, in A.D. 60 or 61.[45] Evidence indicates that the earthquake had long-term effects on the area. Laodicea was deeply involved in reconstruction for the rest of Nero's reign and shortly thereafter.[46] The possibility of the existence of a city, much less a relatively degenerate church in that city, during the 60s is highly questionable. Gentry's attempted rebuttal of this argument (pp. 319-22) is again far-fetched. Other internal considerations favoring the Domitianic date have been cited elsewhere,[47] and need not be repeated.

Persecution under Domitian appears to have spread far enough to include the province of Asia where John was.[48] It was the occasion of John's exile to Patmos and his consequent writing of the Apocalypse

---

42. Swete, *Apocalypse*, pp. c-ci; Morris, *Revelation*, pp. 37-38; Mounce, *Revelation*, pp. 34-35.
43. Brooke Foss Westcott, *The Gospel according to John* (1958 reprint, London: James Clarke), p. xxxiv; Merrill C. Tenney, "The Gospel of John," in *EBC*, ed. Frank E. Gaebelein (Grand Rapids: Zondervan, 1981), 8:10; Richard L. Niswonger, *New Testament History* (Grand Rapids: Zondervan, 1988), p. 274.
44. F. F. Bruce, *New Testament History* (Garden City, N.Y.: Doubleday, 1969), pp. 375-76.
45. Morris, *Revelation*, p. 37; Colin J. Hemer, *The Letters to the Seven Churches of Asia in Their Local Setting* (Sheffield: JSNTS, 1986), p. 182.
46. Hemer, *Seven Churches*, pp. 192-94.
47. Cf. Morris, *Revelation*, pp. 34-40; Mounce, *Revelation*, pp. 32-36; H. Wayne House and Thomas D. Ice, *Dominion Theology: Blessing or Curse?* (Portland, Oreg.: Multnomah, 1988), pp. 249-60.
48. Swete, *Apocalypse*, pp. lxxxv-xci.

(1:9-10, 19). Efforts to disprove a state of persecution[49] during this period are weak. The case for the traditional date of about A.D. 95 remains the most probable option.[50]

PROPHETIC STYLE OF THE APOCALYPSE

Analysis of literary genre has emerged as a relatively new tool for NT study at the end of the twentieth century.[51] This methodology divides the NT books into groups based on comparisons with extrabiblical literature from the periods immediately before, during, and after the composition of the NT. Literary features such as structure, style, content, and function are included in these comparisons.[52] Blomberg identifies the categories of general style to which the Apocalypse has been compared as *prophecy, apocalyptic,* and *epistle.*[53] To these may be added *edict,* to which Aune has recently likened the messages of Revelation 2-3,[54] and *drama,* for which Blevins has argued.[55]

No consensus exists as to a precise definition of genre,[56] so discussions attempting to classify portions of the NT, including Revelation, are at best vague. However, a few general observations regarding genre are in order. The epistolary element is clearly present at certain points of the Apocalypse, such as in Rev. 1:4-5*a*, which has a customary epistolary salutation, and in Rev. 22:21 with its normal epistolary benediction.[57] Yet so much of the book is clearly of another character that this hardly suffices as an overall category. Aune's case for likening chapters 2-3 to a royal or imperial edict has merit too, but he nowhere claims that this applies to the whole book. Blevins's argument for seeing Revelation as a form of Greek tragic drama pro-

---

49. E.g., Bell, "Date," pp. 94-97.
50. Caird, *Revelation,* p. 6; G. R. Beasley-Murray, *The Book of Revelation,* NCB (Grand Rapids: Eerdmans, 1978), pp. 37-38; Sweet, *Revelation,* p. 27; Mounce, *Revelation,* p. 36; Koester, *Introduction,* 2:250-51.
51. Craig L. Blomberg, "New Testament Genre Criticism for the 1990s," *Themelios* 15, no. 2 (January/February 1990): 40.
52. D. E. Aune, *The New Testament in Its Literary Environment* (Philadelphia: Westminster, 1987), p. 13.
53. Blomberg, "Genre," p. 45.
54. D. E. Aune, "Form and Function," p. 183.
55. James L. Blevins, "The Genre of Revelation," *RevExp* 77, no. 3 (Summer 1980): 393-408.
56. D. E. Aune, "The Apocalypse of John and the Problem of Genre," *Semeia* 36 (1986): 66.
57. Paul Feine, Johannes Behm, and Werner Georg Kümmel, *Introduction to the New Testament,* trans., A. J. Mattill, Jr. (Nashville: Abingdon, 1966), p. 321; Poythress, pp. 329-30.

vides interesting historical background derived from the Greek theater at Ephesus, but hardly qualifies as an overall literary type.

A recent trend among some scholars has been to view Revelation as primarily apocalyptic. This complicates the problem of definition even further because in addition to disagreement about what constitutes genre, uncertainty also prevails regarding a definition of apocalyptic.[58] As for terminology, a distinction between "apocalypses" (as literature), "apocalyptic eschatology" (as a worldview), and "apocalypticism" (as a socio-religious movement) appears to have wide acceptance among specialists in this area of study,[59] though acceptance is by no means universal.[60] The purpose of this study is not to advance proposed distinctions in definition, but to comment on the literary result. The socio-religious movement that produced the Apocalypse is the one begun by Jesus and continued by the apostles, not the apocalyptic spirit that developed among the Jews following the abuses of Antiochus Epiphanes (contra Swanson, pp. 321-27). Within this framework apocalyptic eschatology cannot be distinguished from prophetic eschatology as, for example, being more pessimistic (contra Swanson, pp. 314-17). The outlook of the two is no different. The brief evaluation here elaborates on the literary factors of Revelation as compared to other "apocalypses."

Aune launches an effort to solve the problem of definition by formulating a proposed definition from the book itself.[61] This is appropriate because the term *apocalyptic* arose from the first word of the Greek text of Revelation, ἀποκάλυψις (*apokalypsis*, "revelation").[62] Yet such an effort prejudices the case in favor of categorizing Revelation in a certain way by assuming an answer to the question under investigation and not allowing for the book's uniqueness. Revelation certainly has features in common with the *Shepherd of Hermas* and other works of this type, including its extensive use of symbolism, vision as the major means of revelation, focus on the end of the current age and the inauguration of the age to come, a dualism with God and Satan as leaders, a spiritual order determining the course of

---

58. Aune, "The Apocalypse," pp. 67-91.
59. Theodore N. Swanson, "The Apocalyptic Scriptures," *Journal of Dharma* 8 (July 1982): 314; James C. VanderKam, "Recent Studies in 'Apocalyptic,'" *WW* 4 (Winter 1984): 71-72; Aune, "The Apocalypse," p. 67.
60. VanderKam, "Recent Studies," p. 73; Adela Yarbro Collins, "Reading the Book of Revelation in the Twentieth Century," *Int* 40, no. 3 (July 1986): 235-38.
61. Aune, "The Apocalypse," pp. 86-91.
62. D. E. Aune, *Prophecy in Early Christianity and the Ancient Mediterranean World* (Grand Rapids: Eerdmans, 1983), p. 108; Aune, *The New Testament*, pp. 226-27.

history, and pessimism about man's ability to change the progress of events.[63]

But it also differs distinctly from everything else in this class. Other apocalypses are generally pseudonymous, but Revelation is not. The epistolary framework of Revelation also sets it apart from the works that are similar in other respects. Other writings lack the repeated admonitions for moral compliance that Revelation has (2:5, 16, 21, 22; 3:3, 19). Revelation is not as pessimistic about the present as other works in this category. In others the coming of Messiah is exclusively future, but in Revelation He has already come and laid the groundwork for His future victory through His redemptive death.[64]

Most distinctive of all, however, is that this book calls itself a prophecy (1:3; 22:7, 10, 18, 19). Its contents fully justify this self-claim.[65] Of the thirty-one characteristics that have been cited in attempts to define apocalyptic,[66] all when properly understood could apply to prophecy as well, with the possible exception of pseudonymity (which does not apply to Revelation). Alleged differences between the Apocalypse and generally accepted works of prophecy often rest upon inadequate interpretations of the Apocalypse.

The Apocalypse is the product of the NT gift of prophecy, administered by the Holy Spirit, referred to frequently in the NT as a gift (e.g., Rom. 12:6), as a product of the gift (e.g., 1 Tim. 1:18), as a person possessing the gift (e.g., 1 Cor. 12:28, 29; Eph. 4:11), or as an exercise of the gift (e.g., 1 Cor. 14:31). Fully understood, this gift was marked by the following characteristics.

(1) It involved immediate divine inspiration of the spokesperson or writer. Lindblom writes, "Common to all representatives of the prophetic type here depicted is the consciousness of having access to information of the world above and experiences originating in the divine world, from which ordinary men are excluded."[67] The same

---

63. Mounce, *Revelation*, pp. 19-23; Paul J. Achtemeier, "An Apocalyptic Shift in Early Christian Tradition: Reflections on Some Canonical Evidence," *CBQ* 45, no. 2 (April 1983): 232. Ladd is too narrow in his statement that "the central element in apocalyptic is the glorious second coming of Jesus Christ, who will raise the dead, judge persons and usher in the glories of the Age to Come" (George E. Ladd, "New Testament Apocalyptic," *RevExp* 78, no. 2 [Spring 1981]: 205).
64. Morris, *Revelation*, pp. 23-25; Mounce, *Revelation*, pp. 23-25; Blevins, "Genre," p. 393; Lowell J. Satre, "Interpreting the Book of Revelation," *WW* 4, no. 1 (Winter 1984): 60-61.
65. Kümmel, *Introduction*, p. 324; Morris, *Revelation*, p. 23.
66. David Hellholm, "The Problem of Apocalyptic Genre and the Apocalypse of John," in SBLSP, ed. Kent Harold Richards (Chico, Calif.: Scholars, 1982), pp. 164-65.
67. J. Lindblom, *Prophecy in Ancient Israel* (Philadelphia: Fortress, 1973), p. 6.

marked prophets in early Christian communities who regarded themselves as spokesmen for an ultimate authority (Aune, *Prophecy*, p. 204). Possession of a direct revelation from God was one thing that distinguished true prophecy from false prophecy.[68] Evidence of this characteristic is readily available in the Apocalypse where prophets are a group whose special task is to mediate divine revelation to the churches (Rev. 22:6, 9; cf. 1:1) (Aune, *Prophecy*, p. 206). (2) The gift provided exhortation and encouragement (1 Cor. 14:3).[69] (3) It also shared elements in common with the gift of teaching.[70] (4) It incorporated prediction of the future into its function.[71] (5) The gift of proph-

---

68. Wayne A. Grudem, *The Gift of Prophecy in the New Testament and Today* (Westchester, Ill.: Crossway, 1988), pp. 142-43.
69. This characteristic accords with the "forth-teller" etymology of the word προφήτης (Helmut Krämer, "προφήτης κ. τ. λ.," *TDNT* 6:783-84). This part of the present/future structure of the gift is easily illustrated in the teachings of Jesus (Aune, *Prophecy*, p. 188). The prophet gives God's call to repentance which torments some (e.g., Rev. 11:3, 10) but convicts others to turn to God (e.g., 1 Cor. 14:24, 25) (G. Friedrich, "προφήτης κ. τ. λ.," *TDNT* 6:828). He is essentially a proclaimer of God's Word. His παράκλησις results in the οἰκοδομή of the Christian community (David Hill, *New Testament Prophecy* [Atlanta: Knox, 1979], pp. 8-9). In particular, the Apocalypse is a series of messages to bring consolation and exhortations (Colin Brown, "Prophet," *NIDNTT* 2:88).
70. The prophet instructed the church regarding the meaning of Scripture and through revelations of the future (David Hill, "Prophecy and Prophets in the Revelation of St. John," *NTS* 18 [1971-72]: 406). The prophetic gift should not be confused with the gift of a teacher, however. The ministry of prophets was more spontaneous, being based on direct divine revelations. Teachers, on the other hand, preserved and interpreted Christian tradition, including relevant OT passages, the sayings of Jesus, and traditional beliefs of earlier Christian teaching (Aune, *Prophecy*, p. 202). In regard to the OT, the "charismatic exegesis" of traditional materials by NT prophets resembled the practice of the Qumran community in its *pesharim* (ibid., p. 252). The practice consisted of finding hidden or symbolic meanings that could be revealed only through an interpreter possessing divine insight (Hill, *NT Prophecy*, p. 91; Aune, *Prophecy*, p. 133). Paul illustrates this in his handling of Isa. 59:20-21 and 27:9 in Rom. 11:25-27 (Aune, *Prophecy*, p. 252). Aune feels this practice could have been followed by one with the gift of teaching also (*Prophecy*, pp. 345-46), but this is doubtful.
71. This was the "foretelling" part suggested by the προ- prefix, but that was a later development in the evolution of the word's meaning (Krämer, "προφήτης," pp. 783-84; Friedrich, "προφήτης," pp. 832-33). This is the chief sense of the word in the Apocalypse, but Paul also predicted the future (e.g., Acts 20:22-23, 29; 27:22 ff.; Rom. 11:25 ff.; 1 Cor. 15:51-52; 1 Thess. 4:14-17) (Friedrich, "προφήτης," p. 840). Friedrich notes that in Paul, exhortation is dominant in prophecy, but in the Apocalypse prediction is the main focus (ibid., pp. 828-29; cf. Aune, *Prophecy*, p. 5). This, he says, puts John more into the category of OT prophecy than in company with early Christian prophets. Aune disagrees with this appraisal, however (Aune, *Prophecy*, p. 6). The predictive element is one of several features that Colin Brown uses to relate Luke's understanding of the gift to OT prophets, too (Brown, "Prophecy," p. 87). Hill observes that prediction is clearly not the main function of prophets in Acts (Hill, *NT Prophecy*, p.

ecy entailed a degree of authority, which was less than that of the OT prophets and the NT apostles, but some kind of authority was implied.[72] (6) A further characteristic of the NT prophet was his ability to discern the validity of other prophecies.[73] (7) Gifted prophets also had an ability to perceive the thoughts and motives of other persons (cf. Luke 7:39; John 4:19; Acts 5:3-4; 8:21 ff.).[74] (8) The use of prophecy was sometimes accompanied by symbolic acts.[75] (9) Most often prophets were residents of a single locality, but some were also itinerant.[76] (10) Most NT prophecy was oral, but some was written.[77] (11)

---

108). The degree of prediction as compared to exhortation is probably not sufficient ground to remove any NT writer's idea of the gift from the realm of NT prophecy, however. Though he could predict the future, the NT prophet should not be confused with the μάντις. This latter figure belonged strictly to a secular setting and discharged nothing of the hortatory function of a prophet.

72. Because they were spokesmen for God, they claimed no personal part in the communication they gave (Aune, *Prophecy*, p. 204), so it is inevitable that they possessed authority (Hill, *NT Prophecy*, p. 87). The limited nature of this authority is quite obvious, however. Utterances of NT prophets were in many cases challengeable in ways that those of an OT prophet would never have been (1 Cor. 14:30) (ibid., p. 135). This limitation may be missed if one takes the prophecies of Paul (1 Cor. 7:10; 14:37-38) and John (Rev. 22:18-19) as typical. Paul's absolute authority is clear throughout his writings (ibid., p. 114), and in the Apocalypse John seemingly places himself in the category of the OT prophets through such things as his inaugural vision (1:9-20), his use of symbolic acts (10:10), and his use of oracular formulas (chaps. 2-3) (Rolf Rentdorf, "προφήτης κ. τ. λ.," *TDNT* 6:812; Friedrich, "προφήτης," p. 849; Hill, *NT Prophecy*, pp. 87-88). The distinguishing feature was that Paul and John were apostles also, which enabled them to write with a higher degree of authority. This was not possible for the non-apostolic NT prophet (Hill, *NT Prophecy*, p. 132).

73. In 1 Cor. 14:29, Paul speaks of the need for some to evaluate whenever a prophet was speaking in the local assembly. Although there is some disagreement about the identity of the discerners in the verse, the most probable answer is that "the others" referred to are the other prophets in the congregation (Friedrich, "προφήτης," p. 855; Hill, *NT Prophecy*, p. 133; Aune, *Prophecy*, p. 196).

74. Friedrich, "προφήτης," p. 842; E. Earle Ellis, "The Role of the Christian Prophet in Acts," in *Apostolic History and the Gospel*, ed. W. Ward Gasque and Ralph P. Martin (Grand Rapids: Eerdmans, 1970), p. 55. Such ability was widely regarded as a prophetic phenomenon by Jesus' contemporaries (cf. Mark 2:5, 8 and pars.; Mark 9:33 ff.; 10:21 and pars.; 12:15 and pars.; Luke 6:8; 9:47; 11:17; 19:5; Matt. 12:25 and pars.; John 2:24-25; 4:17 ff.; Hill, *NT Prophecy*, p. 60). This ability was a distinctive part of the effectiveness of the gift for Paul (1 Cor. 14:24-25) (Friedrich, "προφήτης," p. 842).

75. Here is another trait it has in common with OT prophecy. Agabus signified Paul's coming imprisonment this way (Acts 21:10-11). John swallows a small book (Rev. 10:8-11) and measures the Temple with a reed (Rev. 11:1) (Friedrich, "προφήτης," p. 849).

76. Hill, *NT Prophecy*, p. 90.

77. Revelation received was fruitless until communicated to others. Without communication, ἀποκάλυψις could not be called prophecy (Grudem, *Gift*

Prophetic language was marked by a variety of literary forms.[78] (12) Exercise of the gift entailed the prophet's being in a special state of mind, sometimes referred to as "ecstasy."[79] (13) The gift of prophecy was in some sense temporary.[80]

In light of Revelation's self-claims (e.g., Rev. 1:3; 22:18-19) and how well it fulfills the qualifications of NT prophecy, the best overall characterization of the literary style of the Apocalypse is to call it prophetic.[81] A blending of genres such as prophetic-apocalyptic[82] or prophetic-apocalyptic-epistolary[83] is not the best answer because it does not allow for the preeminence of the book's prophetic character. As noted already in the descriptive characteristics of NT prophecy (cf. [11] in the list above), sufficient variety exists in how prophets communicated to account for apocalyptic, epistolary, imperial-edict, and dramatic elements, which are doubtless present in the book but are not representative of its overarching literary character.

At least two other NT literary styles reflect methods of divine communication to prophets different from that given to the prophet of the Apocalypse. According to John 14:26, stimulation of the memories of eyewitnesses was a means used by the Spirit to inspire the writing of gospel-style literature. For the epistolary style, according to indications in 1 Cor. 2:6-13, He somehow impressed upon the deep consciousness of the writers some hitherto undisclosed data, which they in turn transformed into words for communication to an au-

---

of Prophecy, pp. 143-44). In spite of the importance attached to written prophecies such as the Apocalypse, most Christian prophets appear to have delivered their messages orally (Hill, *NT Prophecy*, p. 93).

78. For the most part, the NT prophet did not follow stereotyped oracular formulas. A noteworthy exception here is the use of the τάδε λέγει τὸ πνεῦμα τὸ ἅγιον formula by Agabus and John (Hill, *NT Prophecy*, p. 107). Aside from this kind of rare indicator, Christian prophecy had to be recognized on other grounds (Aune, *Prophecy*, p. 317).

79. This point is debated (Terrance Callan, "Prophecy and Ecstasy in Greco-Roman Religion and in 1 Corinthians," *NovT* 17 [1985]: 139). Also, implications of the term *ecstasy* are not agreed upon. Nevertheless, something different distinguished the prophet's condition as he received divine revelation (Friedrich, "προφήτης," p. 829).

80. Hill, *NT Prophecy*, p. 137. First Corinthians 13:8-13 makes this point, though the extent of the limited time is debated (see Robert L. Thomas, "Tongues . . . Will Cease," *JETS* 17 [1974]: 81-89; Thomas, *Understanding Spiritual Gifts* [Chicago: Moody, 1978]: 42-44, 79-81, 106-8, 199-204).

81. G. R. Beasley-Murray, *Revelation*, pp. 19-29; Elisabeth Schüssler Fiorenza, *The Book of Revelation, Justice and Judgment* (Philadelphia: Fortress, 1985), pp. 133-56. Hill's opinion that Revelation is atypical of NT prophecy in general does not have foundation (Hill, *NT Prophecy*, p. 93; Hill, "Prophecy and Prophets," pp. 401-18).

82. George E. Ladd, "Why Not Prophetic-Apocalyptic?" *JBL* 76 (1957): 192-200.

83. Blomberg, "Genre," p. 46.

dience. For the apocalyptic communication the message was passed on to the prophet in the form of visions. Because observed differences in genre relate more to the manner of revelation than anything else, perhaps a better designation for the book of Revelation would be a "visional-prophetic" genre. Such a term would distinguish it from the gospel and epistolary styles, which in a broader sense are also prophetic.

It is inevitable that elements of literary genres resulting from each mode of communication differ somewhat from one another. Yet all fall into the broad category of prophecy as biblically defined. Boring's objection to defining apocalyptic and prophecy as mutually exclusive categories is valid. He says that it leaves "no room for an apocalyptic document such as Revelation to be considered also as a genuinely prophetic document directly concerned with the realities of political history."[84] Mickelsen, on the other hand, makes strict distinctions between genre-types. He deems it impossible for one person to have written three different genres—gospel, epistles, and apocalypse—as tradition attributed to John the apostle.[85] This alleged impossibility is no problem at all, however, if the genre-type was dependent on the manner in which God inspired His prophet.

It may be concluded, therefore, that the literary genre of inspired writings was not the choice of the human author, but was an inevitable result of the manner in which God chose to reveal his message to the prophet. This, of course, distinguishes them from uninspired but similar works whose writers did, in fact, choose a particular genre.

HERMENEUTICS FOR INTERPRETING THE APOCALYPSE

Proposals for hermeneutical guidelines in interpreting Revelation have correlated at least partially with the literary style assigned to the book. Several general approaches to the book reflect, for the most part, the difference between assuming a predominantly apocalyptic genre and one that is more prophetic: the contemporary-historical or preterist, the tradition-historical, the historicist or continuous-historical, the timeless-symbolic or idealist, and the eschatological or futurist.[86] The preterist approach says the book is a sketch of first-

---

84. M. Eugene Boring, "The Theology of Revelation, 'The Lord Our God the Almighty Reigns,'" *Int* 40, no. 3 (July 1986): 261.
85. A. Berkeley Mickelsen, *Daniel and Revelation: Riddles or Realities?* (Nashville: Nelson, 1984), p. 19.
86. Mounce, *Revelation*, pp. 41-43; Helge S. Kvanig, "The Relevance of the Biblical Visions of the End Time," *HBT* 11, no. 1 (June 1989): 36-37. These categorizations deal principally with the core of the book consisting of Rev. 4:1 to 22:5.

century conditions in the Roman Empire, thereby emphasizing its historical background.[87] Quite assuredly the book must be interpreted in light of its historical setting, but to justify this as the limiting factor, one must assume an apocalyptic genre in which the language only faintly reflects actual events. For example, this extreme degree of spiritualization requires that one see the words about Christ's second coming as fulfilled in the destruction of the Temple in A.D. 70, even though He did not appear on that occasion.[88] This does injustice to the prophetic nature of the work, which requires a second personal appearance of Christ on earth in fulfillment of Rev. 19:11-16.

The tradition-historical approach views Revelation from the perspective of background material in Greek or Oriental myths and Jewish tradition.[89] Most certainly the book draws upon these, especially the OT, but it cannot be divested of its predictive element through suppositions of vagueness connected with its alleged apocalyptic language. It is a prophecy whose scope stretches forward to the return of Christ and beyond. To exclude this from its interpretation denies the prophetic genre that most characterizes the book.

The continuous-historical approach treats the book as a panorama of church history from John's time until the second advent. For proof, the view cites events during the intervening centuries that match the happenings under the seal, trumpet, and bowl series. To produce such a match, however, unwarranted allegorization is necessary. It is not uncommon for interpreters to allegorize prophetic portions of Scripture,[90] so the continuous-historical approach does not necessarily favor an apocalyptic genre. It can resort to this rationale, however, whenever it has difficulty finding events of the Christian era to correspond to the data of Revelation. Efforts to match prophecy with fulfillment in this manner have proved futile. For instance, Elliott's suggested equation of the hail and fire mingled with blood under the first trumpet judgment (8:7) with the wars of Alaric the Goth and Rhadagaisus the Vandal against the western Roman Empire[91] is wholly without exegetical merit. The same may be said of his theory proposing that the fallen star following the fifth trumpet (Rev.

---

87. Henry Clarence Thiessen, *Introduction to the New Testament* (Grand Rapids: Eerdmans, 1952), p. 324. A recent variation of the preterist approach is offered by David Chilton, *The Days of Vengeance, an Exposition of the Book of Revelation.* Chilton dates the book in the 60s (pp. 3-6) and sees the entire prophecy as being fulfilled shortly thereafter (p. 40).
88. E.g., Chilton, *Vengeance*, pp. 63-64.
89. Kvanig, "Relevance," p. 36.
90. Charles L. Feinberg, *Millennialism, the Two Major Views*, 3d ed. (Chicago: Moody, 1980), pp. 43-46; Collins, "Reading," pp. 229-31.
91. E. B. Elliott, *Horae Apocalypticae*, 4 vols. (London: Seeleys, 1851), 2:348, 351-53.

9:1) is Mohammed.[92] Such suggestions as these reduce the language of Scripture to meaninglessness because of their propensity to make the words fit some preconceived notion.

The timeless-symbolic or idealist position has the Apocalypse representing the eternal conflict of good and evil in every age, usually in reference to the particular age in which the interpreter lives.[93] The book does not refer to specific events, but expresses the basic principles according to which God acts throughout history.[94] This interpretation leans heavily on the conclusion that Revelation is basically apocalyptic in style, and continues the allegorical approach to the book so characteristic of the middle ages of the Christian era. It is correct in attributing to God certain principles of action that govern His dealings with the world in every era, but it is blatantly inadequate in denying the prophetic genre of Revelation. Fulfillment of the events predicted in the book, most notably the personal return of Jesus Christ to earth, is not found in a repetitive cycle that marks each generation, but will at some future point be historical in the fullest sense of the word.

The timeless-symbolic approach relates closely to the movement of recent hermeneutical trends toward contextualizing in interpretation. *Contextualization* is a term coined in a 1972 publication of the World Council of Churches.[95] It advocates assigning meaning to the text of Scripture based on cultural and sociopolitical factors in contemporary society rather than on the grammatical-historical method of exegesis. It inevitably leads to substituting one or more of the many possible applications for the one correct interpretation of Scripture. Following the assumptions of this approach, various oppressed peoples use the Apocalypse to support their cause. They advocate translating the first-century "rhetorical situation" into a contemporary one in a way that results in meanings that may be diametrically opposed to the original ones. For instance, it is held that "we have become conscious of androcentric language and its socializing function" so that "we can detect a quite different rhetorical function and impact" of the symbolic language regarding women in Revelation.[96] This transposing of rhetorical situations enables an

---

92. Ibid., pp. 417-18.
93. Merrill C. Tenney, *Interpreting Revelation* (Grand Rapids: Eerdmans, 1957), p. 143.
94. Mounce, *Revelation*, p. 43.
95. *Theological Education Fund, Ministry in Context: The Third Mandate Programme of the Theological Education Fund*, 1970-77 (Bromiley, Kent, United Kingdom: New Life Press, 1972); cf. also Gabriel Fackre, "Evangelical Hermeneutics," *Int* 43, no. 2 (April 1989): 128.
96. Fiorenza, *Revelation*, p. 199.

interpreter to use the book according to personal preferences, even to the extent of supporting positions as divergent as the political left and right.[97]

Yet "meaning" in the original setting and "significance" for the present situation must be kept separate if literature is to have any coherence. To apply Scripture carelessly without regard to its meaning is to abuse it for the sake of self-generated crusades. Without a well-defined interpretation in the historical setting of the author, applicational control vanishes and the significance for any given situation becomes a matter of individual whim.[98]

The futurist approach to the book is the only one that grants sufficient recognition to the prophetic style of the book and a normal hermeneutical pattern of interpretation based on that style. It views the book as focusing on the last period(s) of world history and outlining the various events and their relationships to one another. This is the view that best accords with the principle of literal interpretation.[99] The literal interpretation of Revelation is the one generally associated with the premillennial return of Christ and a view of inspiration that understands God to be the real author of every book of the Bible. Though He used human authors whose individual backgrounds and writing styles are reflected, the divine element in inspiration prevails to the point that the unity of Scripture can be assumed.[100] Blomberg's assessment that an "exclusively prophetic interpretation usually insists on an impossibly literal hermeneutic which is therefore inevitably applied inconsistently" ("Genre," p. 46) reflects a premature and biased judgment about a subject on which the last word has yet to be written.

Attempts to combine two or more of the above approaches into a single interpretation without allowing for the dominance of prophecy have produced hermeneutical confusion. An example of such a combination is a merging of the idealist and the futurist.[101] This proposes that apocalypses spoke of the historical context in which they were written and can be transferred to new situations of later generations time after time, with one final reference to the real end-time tribulation. The signs of the end have been present in every generation, but only God can decide when the real end will come. This kind of analy-

---

97. Ibid., p. 203.
98. Walter C. Kaiser, "Legitimate Hermeneutics," in *Inerrancy*, ed. Norman L. Geisler (Grand Rapids: Zondervan, 1979), p. 122; Geisler, "Does Purpose Determine Meaning?" *WTJ* 51, no. 1 (Spring 1989): 153-55.
99. Tenney, *Interpreting*, p. 139; Collins, "Reading," pp. 231-32.
100. Collins, "Reading," pp. 232-33; cf. also Fackre, "Hermeneutics," pp. 121, 123.
101. Kvanig, "Relevance," pp. 46-48.

sis makes the details of the text almost useless and satisfies itself with general conclusions about the description. These details are alleged to be nonhistorical.[102] With a similar approach, Collins's judgment is that the goal of interpretation is "to discern how the text may fulfill its original purpose, or function socially in a way analogous to its effect upon its original readers, in the situation of the interpreter," that "the symbols [of Revelation] are not primarily informational (predicting future events)," and that "a hermeneutic which takes historical criticism seriously can no longer work with an interventionist notion of God" ("Reading the Book," p. 242).

Mickelsen is an example of the combination approach as reflected in his discussion of "Literary Forms in Daniel and Revelation" (*Daniel and Revelation*, pp. 24-27). Other examples of the combination-approach are presented in Gordon D. Fee & Douglas Stuart, *How to Read the Bible for All Its Worth* (Grand Rapids: Zondervan, 1982), pp. 205-17; Leland Ryken, *Words of Life, A Literary Introduction to the New Testament* (Grand Rapids: Baker, 1987), pp. 135-47; and M. Robert Mulholland, *Revelation, Holy Living in an Unholy World* (Grand Rapids: Zondervan, 1990), pp. 17-25. Both Ryken (*Words of Life*, pp. 143-44) and Mulholland (*Revelation*, p. 18) point out the necessity of what the psychologists call "right-brain" activity (i.e., the ability to think by means of images and intuition) in the interpretation of the book; i.e., the effects of parts of the Apocalypse are to be *felt* without cognitive interaction. The assessment of Bauckham is more acceptable than this emphasis of feelings in opposition to rationality: "Out of his visionary experience John has produced a work which enables the reader not to share the same experience second-hand, but to receive its message transposed into a literary medium" (Richard J. Bauckham, "The Role of the Spirit in the Apocalypse," *EvQ* 52, no. 2 [April-June 1980]: 72).

An example of the combination approach is Beasley-Murray's opinion that the importance of the locust-plague prophecies is not in their detail, and therefore, glaring inconsistencies that are present in them are of no concern to the author.[103] Mounce describes the fifth trumpet as the language of ecstatic experience that eliminates any possibility of a consistent pattern. He calls this "a montage of divine judgments upon a recalcitrant world."[104] Leon Morris speaks of this same section as coming from a "fiery, passionate and poetic spirit" whose details cannot be pressed as though it were "a pedantic piece

---

102. Ibid., pp. 49-50; Donald Guthrie, *The Relevance of John's Apocalypse* (Grand Rapids: Eerdmans, 1987), p. 30.
103. Beasley-Murray, *Revelation*, p. 157.
104. Mounce, *Revelation*, p. 184.

of scientific prose."[105] Writing in broader terms, Ladd describes apocalyptic language and vision as generally surrealistic rather than rational and logically consistent.[106]

Ryken is quite explicit regarding a combination perspective of the book. After naming and describing the preterist, the continuous-historical, the futurist, and the idealist as the four major approaches to the Apocalypse, he writes,

> I think that the book is a combination of all of these. We should begin with the situation of the church to which the book was written. Because of the literary form of the book, which portrays events symbolically, its relevance extends throughout the history of the world. Babylon, for example, may have been the Roman empire for John's first century audience, but in Old Testament times it was literally Babylon, and it has taken many forms throughout history. The literary mode of symbolism means that the events portrayed in Revelation are perpetually relevant and will be ultimately relevant at the end of history.[107]

All the authorities cited above as viewing apocalyptic genre to exclude literal interpretation would insist on interpreting it literally, however, when it speaks of the personal return of Christ to earth in Rev. 19:11-16. They are distinctly idealistic in their understanding of earlier sections of the book. Morris is perhaps typical of the rest when he writes concerning the trumpet-plagues, "This is true throughout the ages and it will be so till the End."[108] Yet in their overall approach to the Apocalypse, this group of interpreters mix the idealistic interpretations with a futurist viewpoint regarding the general thrust of the Apocalypse. They have John in a sort of "dream world" until their personally contrived formula has him revert to a literal mode of predicting the future in more precise terms.

To be sure, the bulk of the Apocalypse resulted from John's prophetic trance(s) (cf. ἐν πνεύματι [*en pneumati*, "in the spirit"], Rev. 1:10; 4:2; 17:3; 21:10). There is, however, no justification for equating such a trance with a dream where logical coherence is nonexistent. Though in some sort of ecstatic state, John's spirit was wide awake and its powers were exercised with unusual alertness and clarity.[109] If anything, his senses were *more* alert for details rather than less alert. It is shortsighted to dismiss the details of the Apocalypse as meaningless or to explain them in some idealistic and timeless sense on the basis of John's prophetic state.

---

105. Morris, *Revelation*, p. 123.
106. Ladd, *Revelation*, p. 124.
107. Ryken, *Words of Life*, pp. 144-45.
108. Morris, *Revelation*, p. 123.
109. R. C. H. Lenski, *The Interpretation of St. John's Revelation* (Columbus, Ohio: Lutheran Book Concern, 1935), p. 58.

The combination approach is deficient on another ground: it leaves to human judgment the determination of where the details of a text end and its general picture begins. Allowing this liberty for subjective opinion cannot qualify as objective interpretation. In other words, it cannot satisfy the criteria of a grammatical-historical system of hermeneutics such as has characterized an evangelical Christian understanding of Scripture. This grammatical-historical method must be applied to Revelation also. If Revelation is a prophecy, it must be treated as other prophecy and its details must be objectively meaningful and historical. Only in this way can the general picture of which the details are a part be historical. No provision can be made for elasticity of interpretation that allows for a change in meaning from generation to generation and from place to place.

The preferred approach to the Apocalypse is to interpret according to normal principles of grammar and facts of history, remembering the peculiar nature of predictive prophecy throughout the Bible.[110] This is usually referred to as literal interpretation. One may wonder how a book of symbols and visions such as Revelation can be interpreted literally.[111] This is not so difficult to understand if one keeps in mind that the symbols and visions were the means of communicating the message to the prophet, but they have a literal meaning unless otherwise indicated in the text. They do not furnish grounds for interpreting the text in a nonliteral fashion. They are to be interpreted as one would interpret the rest of the Bible.

The verb ἐσήμανεν (*esēmanen*, "he signified") in Rev. 1:1 furnishes an advance notice of the symbolic nature of God's communication with John. This has nothing to do with how the resultant communication should be interpreted, however. Ryken makes the same basic mistake as Ironside in taking the Apocalypse to be a book of symbols that cannot be interpreted literally.[112] Both men fail to distinguish between the process of revelation and that of interpretation. Ryken's faulty judgment is in not recognizing that literal interpretation makes ample allowance for figures of speech that are clearly represented as such and in seeking to make a distinction between "literal"

---

110. The original historical setting of the prophecy is of utmost importance, but a peculiar characteristic of predictive prophecy is that at times the prophet himself did not grasp the full import of his own prophecy (1 Pet. 1:10-12). This being the case, the same limitation applies to his readership and to succeeding generations, until the fulfillment of the prophecy finally illuminates fully the divinely intended meaning.
111. Peter Mendham, "Interpreting the Book of Revelation," *Saint Mark's Review* 122 (June 1985): 26.
112. Ryken, *Words of Life*, pp. 143-44; H. A. Ironside, *Lectures on the Book of Revelation* (New York: Loizeaux, n.d.), p. 13.

and "historical."[113] By blurring this characteristic of literal interpretation, he opens the door to treat details of the text quite loosely. Literal interpretation sees a distinction between symbols and symbolic or figurative language. The latter receives full recognition, but the former may have a meaning that is quite literal and historical.

The proper procedure is to assume a literal interpretation of each symbolic representation provided to John unless a particular factor in the text indicates it should be interpreted figuratively. For example, John saw in vision form a dramatization of a multitude of 144,000 (Rev. 7:4) which in future fulfillment will be a literal multitude of 144,000 people because nothing in the text indicates that the number should be understood in some hidden sense. On the other hand, the city where the two witnesses will be slain is called "spiritually" (πνευματικῶς, pneumatikōs) Sodom and Egypt (Rev. 11:8), indicating that a figurative rather than a literal interpretation of the proper names is in order.[114] So a literal interpretation is the assumption unless something in the text indicates otherwise.

Literal interpretation refrains from the tendency to find hidden meanings in the Apocalypse. "Green grass" in the first trumpet of Rev. 8:7 has at times been seen as a hidden symbol, the grass standing for human beings and the green portraying the prosperous conditions of those people.[115] Alford points out the incongruity of such an interpretation, noting that the later trumpet judgments distinguish clearly between grass as a natural object and men who are distinctly so labeled in explicit terminology (Rev. 8:11; 9:4, 15).[116] Analogy requires that in the same series of visions, when one part destroys earth, trees, and grass, and another inflicts no injury on earth, trees, or grass, but does harm men, grass must carry the same meaning, i.e., a literal one, in both cases.

The same principle applies, but even more conspicuously, in conjunction with the sixth seal judgment (Rev. 6:12-17). At times, commentators have understood the cosmic disturbances to picture human arrogance and the overthrow of principalities and powers supporting the authority of earthly kings.[117] The most conspicuous

---

113. Ryken, Words of Life, p. 143.
114. Bauckham criticizes the use of πνευματικῶς as justification for a non-literal interpretation of the two cities and says the adverb refers to Spirit-given perception ("The Role," p. 79). Whether the word refers to the Holy Spirit or not is debatable, but the end result is the same: this is not a reference to the literal city Sodom or the literal country Egypt.
115. Walter Scott, Exposition of the Revelation of Jesus Christ (Grand Rapids: Kregel, n.d.), p. 186.
116. Alford, Greek Testament, p. 635.
117. E.g., William Barclay, The Revelation of John, 2d ed., 2 vols. (Philadelphia: Westminster, 1960), 2:15; Caird, Revelation, p. 80.

deficiency of this kind of interpretation is that the thing allegedly symbolized by the convulsion of the heavens (6:12-14), i.e., a convulsion of the nations, is described immediately after the heavenly phenomenon in literal terms (6:15-17) (the same way as in Hag. 2:21-22).[118]

Another clear distinctive of literal interpretation is its avoidance of assumptions not justified in the text. Theories that "Babylon" in Revelation 14 and 16-18 is a code-word for Rome have been widespread.[119] The fact that the text of Revelation locates the city on the Euphrates River (16:12) has been no deterrent to this symbolic understanding. Neither has the fact that Rome, because of its geographical location, has never been and could never be the great commercial city described in Revelation 18.[120] Babylon did eventually become a code-word for Rome, but not during the period of the NT's composition.[121]

Attempts to assign a symbolic connotation to the thousand years in Rev. 20:2-7 have been multiplied. Lewis is typical of the wide assortment of attempts to explain away the literality of a future millennium on earth when he writes, "The biblical millennium . . . is not the glorious age to come, but this present era for giving the message of salvation to the nations."[122] The trend of this view is to take one thousand as a symbolic number and identify the period with the interval between Christ's first and second advents.[123] All who adopt this tactic, however, are at a loss to explain how two resurrections in Rev. 20:4-5 can be described as separated by one thousand years and yet have that thousand years not be future and literal. The two resurrections are designated by the same verb: ἔζησαν (*ezēsan*, "they lived," "they came to life"). By common agreement, the latter resurrection is clearly a bodily one, so the former one must be too, necessitating that both be future and positing a future thousand-year period between them.[124] The literal approach is fair and consistent.

---

118. E. W. Bullinger, *The Apocalypse* or *"The Day of the Lord"* (London: Eyre and Spottiswoode, n.d.), p. 255.

119. Mounce, *Revelation*, p. 274; Beasley-Murray, *Revelation*, p. 225; Mickelsen, *Revelation*, p. 25; Ryken, *Words of Life* pp. 144-45.

120. Alford, *Greek Testament*, p. 471.

121. "Babylon" in 1 Pet. 5:13 is not an exception to this generalization.

122. Arthur H. Lewis, *The Dark Side of the Millennium* (Grand Rapids: Baker, 1980), p. 65.

123. Chilton, *Vengeance*, p. 507; Mulholland, *Revelation*, pp. 304-9; Philip Edgcumbe Hughes, *The Book of Revelation* (Grand Rapids: Eerdmans, 1990), p. 209.

124. Alford, *Greek Testament*, pp. 732-33; George E. Ladd, *Crucial Questions about the Kingdom* (Grand Rapids: Eerdmans, 1952), pp. 141-50.

To interpret otherwise marks an end of "all definite meaning in plain words."[125]

Kuyper acknowledges that the language of Rev. 20:1-10 found anywhere else would require literal interpretation, but thinks that its surroundings in this book require the terminology to be understood nonliterally.[126] Ladd points out the fallacy of this reasoning. He disagrees with the position that "the spiritual interpretation departs from the proper principles of hermeneutics because this is literature of a different type to which the ordinary rules of hermeneutics cannot apply."[127] He finds no contextual clue in Rev. 20:4-6 to support a spiritualized interpretation.[128]

Because in broad perspective the Apocalypse is prophetic in nature as is the rest of the NT, a different set of hermeneutical principles is not needed to interpret it. A normal grammatical-historical methodology is the natural and necessary interpretive framework. To arrive at this goal, other commentaries and analyses are incorporated as resources from past and present generations. Their insights recorded in various exegetical works are invaluable for the present, to the degree that they observed valid hermeneutical principles.[129] Otherwise, the works are valueless except by way of application. The goal of this commentary is to use judiciously these authorities of the past as facilitators in arriving at the one correct interpretation of each of the myriad difficult passages in Revelation.

Judicious use of resource works entails frequent recourse to basic principles of hermeneutics. Interpreters have not consistently used these basic principles. Two examples of relatively recent departures illustrate this. The first relates to the understanding of Greek verb tenses. Responding to frequent abuses of the aorist tense, Stagg proposed in a 1972 essay that the aorist denotes undefined action and therefore is not to be contrasted with other verb tenses in the same context.[130] He is correct about abuses, but overreacts against them. A balanced understanding of the aorist takes into account the aspect of verbal action derived from each context and the contribution of the root idea of the verb itself. This *does* allow for the kinds of contrasts with other tenses that Stagg condemns in a blanket fashion. The

---

125. Alford, *Greek Testament*, p. 252.
126. Abraham Kuyper, *The Revelation of St. John*, trans. John Hendrik de Vries (Grand Rapids: Eerdmans, 1935), p. 263.
127. Ladd, *Crucial Questions*, p. 147.
128. Ibid., p. 146.
129. Citations of sources in this commentary do not necessarily indicate an endorsement of or opposition to the particular view under discussion by that source. Often writers offer helpful discussions of several viewpoints before settling upon the one of their choice.
130. Frank Stagg, "The Abused Aorist," *JBL* 91 (1972): 222-31.

balanced approach will serve as the guideline in the comments below where documentation will reflect the grammatical authorities who oppose Stagg's stand.

Another recent suggestion says that the aorist imperative implies no urgency, which is contrary to what grammatical opinion has long held. Moule is one who has expressed this.[131] On the other hand, the long-term position that urgency is implicit in the aorist imperative has solid grammatical footing.[132] As comments below will reflect, my judgment will favor the notion of urgency whenever encountering an aorist imperative.

In addition to verb tenses, a second example of departures from traditional hermeneutics pertains to synonyms. It has been more customary to see a distinction between similar words used in the same immediate context.[133] In line with modern linguistic trends, however, some have chosen to question any distinction between two synonyms, such as ἀγαπάω (*agapaō,* "I love") and φιλέω (*phileō,* "I love"), in the same context.[134] The plea is usually made that the writer chose to vary his vocabulary for stylistic effect. Yet the NT writers, for the most part, were not aiming for stylistic excellence as classical Greek writers of earlier generations. They wrote in the language of the man on the street. This would have been particularly true of John, writing while in a prophetic trance. So my commentary follows the longstanding view that the writers intended shades of distinction in synonyms. Moule's advice is wise: "The safest principle is probably to assume a difference until one is driven to accept identity of meaning."[135]

LANGUAGE OF THE APOCALYPSE

The nature of the language used in Revelation has resulted in a good bit of discussion. Three classifications of analyses of the issue have been suggested: (1) the language is essentially Greek, any major deviations from "correct" Greek being explainable; (2) the Greek is a

---

131. C. F. D. Moule, *An Idiom Book of New Testament Greek* (Cambridge: University Press, 1960), pp. 20-21.
132. A. T. Robertson, *Historical Research,* p. 856; A. T. Robertson and W. Hershey Davis, *A New Short Grammar of the Greek New Testament,* 10th ed. (Grand Rapids: Baker, 1958), p. 297; Nigel Turner, *Syntax,* vol. 3 of *A Grammar of New Testament Greek* by James Hope Moulton (Edinburgh: T. & T. Clark, 1963), pp. 74-75.
133. E.g., Merrill C. Tenney, "The Gospel of John," in *EBC* (Grand Rapids: Zondervan, 1981), 9:201-2; *NIV Study Bible,* ed. Kenneth L. Barker (Grand Rapids: Zondervan, 1985), p. 1638 (note on John 21:15-17).
134. D. A. Carson, *Exegetical Fallacies* (Grand Rapids: Baker, 1984), pp. 48-54.
135. Moule, *Idiom Book,* p. 198.

translation from Aramaic; (3) the language is a Jewish-Greek in use in Palestine during the first century.[136] The last of these theories has been most actively supported during this century by such men as R. H. Charles, Matthew Black, and Stephen Thompson.[137] More recently Kenneth G. C. Newport has furnished evidence to this effect.[138]

Porter has advanced a case to counteract the movement toward the last of these three analyses, arguing that Semitic interference in the Greek of Revelation cannot be proved.[139] He proposes that the book's language falls within the limits of vulgar Greek usage of the first century, but allows for isolated Semitic enhancements.[140]

The solution to this issue probably lies somewhere between the two extremes. For one so full of the OT as John was, the Greek of the LXX with its unchallenged Semitisms must have had its influence, but it cannot be assumed too quickly that every proposed case of Hebrew or Aramaic influence is a valid one. Each instance must be decided on its own merit. For example, few would question that εἰς τοὺς αἰῶνας τῶν αἰώνων (*eis tous aiōnas tōn aiōnōn*, "forever and ever") (1:6) is based on a Hebrew idiom. In the case of ἔχων (*echōn*, "having") used as a finite verb in 1:16, one cannot be as dogmatic, however. Still more doubtful is the case for taking δέδωκα (*dedōka*) Hebraistically to mean "I have set" in 3:8, the balance of considerations weighing in favor of a more normal Greek sense of "I have given."

The Greek of the Apocalypse assuredly is marked by a Semitic influence, but the interpreter must be wary of looking too often to this factor in his analysis.

OTHER SCRIPTURE IN THE APOCALYPSE

Of the 404 verses in the Apocalypse, 278 allude to the OT Scriptures. No other NT writer uses the OT more than this.[141] Yet the book is marked by an entire absence of formal quotations from the OT.

---

136. Stanley E. Porter, "The Language of the Apocalypse in Recent Discussion," *NTS* 35, no. 4 (October 1989): 582-84.
137. Ibid., pp. 583-84.
138. Kenneth G. C. Newport, "Semitic Influence on the Use of Some Prepositions in the Book of Revelation," *BT* 37, no. 3 (July 1986): 328-34; Newport, "Use of EK": 223-30; Newport, "Semitic Influence in Revelation: Some Further Evidence," *AUSS* 25, no. 3 (Autumn 1987): 249-56.
139. Porter, "Language," p. 599.
140. Ibid., pp. 599-600, 603.
141. Swete, *Apocalypse*, p. cxl. Beale prefers "dependence" to "allusion" as better describing John's use of the OT. He categorizes the dependencies into three kinds, the clear, the probable, and the possible (G. K. Beale, "A Reconsideration of the Text of Daniel in the Apocalypse," *Bib* 67, no. 4 [1986]: 543).

Probably the nature of the work prevented the author from appealing directly to his source as his authority.[142] His allusions are to books from each of the three divisions of the OT, with Daniel leading in number of citations proportionately followed by Isaiah, Ezekiel, and Psalms.[143]

The author shows familiarity with other books of the NT also. He uses these in much the same way as he does the OT. It is fairly conclusive that he reflects some dependence on Matthew and Luke, and it is probable that he knew 1 Thessalonians, 1 and 2 Corinthians, Colossians, and Ephesians. He possibly knew Galatians, 1 Peter, and James also.[144]

An attempt has been made to elevate extrabiblical material referred to by John to the level of the OT among his sources.[145] Yet no conclusive evidence proves that he used sources, written or oral, outside the OT.[146] He certainly was versed in apocalyptic literature of his period, but it can hardly be demonstrated that he used it in the same way as he did the books of the OT. The influence of the OT on Revelation is overwhelming.[147]

Respected authorities disagree on whether John's main source was the Hebrew (or Aramaic) OT or the LXX. For example, Charles preferred the former explanation and Swete the latter.[148] Such a disagreement may mean that John drew from both sources. An investigation of the allusions in this commentary will bear out the conclusion that John drew from both. With a mind steeped in both the Hebrew and Greek OT, it is not too surprising that John might have done this. Quite possibly he was influenced by his familiarity with the Aramaic expanded paraphrases of the OT called Targums. These were used regularly in the Jewish synagogues.[149]

---

142. Swete, *Apocalypse*, p. cxl.
143. Ibid., p. cliii.
144. Charles, *Revelation*, 1:lxv-lxvi. Contrast Fee and Stuart, *How to Read*, p. 209.
145. Harold M. Parker, Jr., "The Scripture of the Author of the Revelation of John," *The Iliff Review* 37, no. 1 (Winter 1980): 35-51.
146. Swete, *Apocalypse*, p. clviii; Martin Kiddle, *The Revelation of St. John*, MNTC (New York: Harper, 1940), p. xxviii. Though some MSS of the LXX contained books of the Apocrypha that are not generally recognized in the canon of the Protestant OT, none of these books figures significantly in the citations of the Apocalypse. The thirty-nine books of our OT were the ones generally agreed upon as the Jewish Scriptures during the first century, though no formal announcement to that effect existed (F. F. Bruce, *The Canon of Scripture* [Downers Grove, Ill.: Inter-Varsity, 1988], pp. 28-32).
147. Guthrie, *Relevance*, p. 19.
148. Swete, *Apocalypse*, p. clv; Charles, *Revelation*, 1:lxvii-lxviii.
149. Sweet, *Revelation*, p. 40; Paul Trudinger, "The Apocalypse and the Palestinian Targum," *BTB* 16, no. 2 (April 1986): 78-79.

It is apparent that John and his readers recognized the same body of Scripture as is referred to elsewhere in the NT as ἡ γραφή (*hē graphē*, "the Scripture") consisting of the same books as the Protestant OT of the twentieth century. His use of these Scriptures fluctuated between the Hebrew originals and the Greek translation, as his Spirit-directed mind led him to do.

TEXT OF THE APOCALYPSE

Textual resources for recovering the autograph of Revelation are fewer than for any other part of the NT, with the book being represented in approximately 230 Greek MSS.[150] Of the few uncial MSS including it, three are relatively early: Codex Sinaiticus (4th century), Codex Alexandrinus (5th century), and Codex Ephraemi (5th century). The first two have the whole book, and the last has most but not all. Of the four papyrus MSS that have some of the book, three are quite fragmentary. Only p[47], a late third-century MS, has a significant portion. The rest are minuscule MSS dating from the tenth to the sixteenth centuries.[151] Ancient versions of the NT and quotations from the early Fathers supplement these sources as a means of restoring the words that were originally written. Of particular importance is the work of Andreas, an early sixth-century Greek commentator on the Apocalypse, who preserved the Greek text he followed.[152] A serious problem with using Andreas's work, however, is the large number of variants in the MSS of his commentary.[153]

In spite of the relatively small number of sources, an unusually large number of variants are encountered. One estimate is about 1,650 in the approximately 400 verses of the book.[154] The nature of most of the variations is minor, however, and therefore they do not have a substantial impact on the meaning of the text.[155] The editors of the third edition of the United Bible Societies' *The Greek New Testament* (1975), the text followed in this commentary, judged just over ninety of these worthy of inclusion in their text.[156] Most of these are commented upon where they occur, by means of the Additional Notes

---

150. Swete, *Apocalypse,* p. clxxxvi.
151. Beckwith, *Apocalypse,* p. 412.
152. Ibid., p. 414.
153. Swete, *Apocalypse,* p. cxcvi.
154. Ibid., p. 411.
155. Ibid.
156. The textual commentary that is a companion volume to the third edition discusses slightly more, about 115 variants (Bruce M. Metzger, *A Textual Commentary on the Greek New Testament* [New York: United Bible Societies, 1971], pp. 731-69).

sections of this commentary. A few variations not cited in the third edition are also discussed.

Reliance upon the internal evidence of readings in Revelation is more necessary than in any other portion of the NT, because of the sparsity of early textual witnesses. Yet usually external evidence is sufficient to give a general idea about the correct reading.[157]

STRUCTURE OF THE APOCALYPSE

Of the many ideas expressed about the structure of Revelation, mention of two examples must suffice. One theory finds eight basic visions in the book.[158] Another discovers seven major acts of a Christian drama.[159] These and other proposals hold a type of fascination, but do not satisfactorily answer the question of why they grant the same prominence to unnumbered series of visions in the book that they do to the numbered series.[160]

The outline below builds upon structural hints in 1:19 and features the numbered series of the book as the author himself does. A conspicuous sevenfold series (though unnumbered) lying outside the apocalyptic part of the book pictures seven simultaneous situations in representative churches of Asia (Rev. 2-3). The other three series are in the apocalyptic portion and denote chronological progression of some sort. The nature of that progression, called herein the "telescopic" arrangement, has the seventh seal consisting of seven trumpets and the seventh trumpet consisting of seven bowls.[161] In outline form, the structure may be pictured as follows.

---

157. A good summary of guidelines for use of external evidence is given by J. Neville Birdsall, "The Text of the Revelation of Saint John: A Review of Its Materials and Problems with Especial Reference to the Work of Josef Schmid," *EvQ* 33, no. 4 (October-December 1961): 228-37.

158. Kenneth A. Strand, "The Eight Basic Visions in the Book of Revelation," *AUSS* 25, no. 1 (Spring 1987): 107-21.

159. Leroy C. Spinks, "A Critical Examination of J. W. Bowman's Proposed Structure of the Revelation," *EvQ* 50, no. 3 (July-September 1978): 215-22; William Hendriksen, *More Than Conquerors* (Grand Rapids: Baker, 1967), pp. 38-39.

160. Guthrie, *Relevance*, p. 25; Ryken, *Words of Life*, pp. 147-49.

161. Lee, "Revelation," 4:595. Loenertz terms the approach "dove-tailing" by which the seventh scene of each act consists of the seven scenes of the following act (R. J. Loenertz, *The Apocalypse of Saint John* [London: Sheed and Ward, 1947], pp. xiv-xvi). He writes, "The complete septenary is dovetailed into the one preceding it as a final section" (p. xv). The other major alternative for explaining the relationship between the seals, bowls, and trumpets is called the "recapitulation" theory. Recapitulation is described in connection with a defense of the telescopic approach in this commentary at Rev. 8:1 (vol. 2).

I. The Preparation of the Prophet: His Past Vision (1:1-20)
  A. Prologue (1:1-8)
    1. Preface (1:1-3)
    2. Address and Doxology (1:4-6)
    3. Theme (1:7-8)
  B. John's Commission to Write (1:9-20)
    1. The First Commission to Write (1:9-11)
    2. The Source of the Commission (1:12-16)
    3. The Commission Restated and Amplified (1:17-20)

II. The Preparation of the People: Their Present Condition (2:1–3:22)
  A. The Message to Ephesus, Church of Loveless Orthodoxy (2:1-7)
  B. The Message to Smyrna, Church of Martyrdom (2:8-11)
  C. The Message to Pergamum, Church of Indiscriminate Tolerance (2:12-17)
  D. The Message to Thyatira, Church of Compromise (2:18-29)
  E. The Message to Sardis, Church of Complacency (3:1-6)
  F. The Message to Philadelphia, Church of Promised Deliverance (3:7-13)
  G. The Message to Laodicea, Church of Lukewarmness (3:14-22)

III. The Publication of the Prophecy: Its Future Expectation (4:1–22:21)
  A. The Opening of the Seven-Sealed Scroll (4:1–8:1)
    1. The Source of the Scroll (4:1–5:14)
      a. The One Sitting on the Throne (4:1-11)
      b. The Seven-sealed Scroll of the Lamb (5:1-14)
    2. The Opening of the First Seal: Peaceful Conquest (6:1-2)
    3. The Opening of the Second Seal: Warfare and Bloodshed (6:3-4)
    4. The Opening of the Third Seal: Widespread Famine (6:5-6)
    5. The Opening of the Fourth Seal: Death to a Fourth of Earth's Inhabitants (6:7-8)
    6. The Opening of the Fifth Seal: Prayers for Divine Vengeance (6:9-11)
    7. The Opening of the Sixth Seal: Cosmic and Terrestrial Disturbances (6:12-17)
    8. The Slaves of God (7:1-17)
      a. Those on Earth: The 144,000 (7:1-8)

      b. Those in Heaven: The Innumerable Multitude (7:9-17)

      9. The Seventh Seal: The Seven Trumpets Awaited (8:1)

B. The Sounding of the Seven Trumpets (8:2–11:19)

      1. The Setting of the Trumpets: The Prayers of the Saints (8:2-6)

      2. The First Trumpet: Burning of a Third of Vegetation (8:7)

      3. The Second Trumpet: Destruction of a Third of Sea-Life (8:8-9)

      4. The Third Trumpet: Poisoning of a Third of the Fresh Water (8:10-11)

      5. The Fourth Trumpet: Darkening of a Third of the Heavenly Bodies (8:12-13)

      6. The Fifth Trumpet: Demonic Locust Plague (9:1-12)

      7. The Sixth Trumpet: Death to a Third of Earth's Inhabitants (9:13-21)

      8. The Announcement of the End of Delay (10:1-11)

      9. The Measurement of the Temple and Worshipers (11:1-14)

     10. The Seventh Trumpet: The Seven Bowls Awaited (11:15-19)

C. The Pouring Out of the Seven Bowls (12:1-18:24)

      1. The Background of the Bowls (12:1–14:20)

         a. The Woman, the Male-Child, and the Dragon (12:1-18)

         b. The Beast Out of the Sea (13:1-10)

         c. The Beast Out of the Earth (or Land) (13:11-18)

         d. The Victorious Followers of the Lamb (14:1-5)

         e. Four Climactic Announcements (14:6-13)

           (1) The Everlasting Gospel (14:6-7)

           (2) The Fall of Babylon (14:8)

           (3) The Torment of the Beast-Worshipers (14:9-12)

           (4) The Blessedness of Those Dying in the Lord (14:13)

         f. The Harvest and the Vintage (14:14-20)

      2. The Rejoicing Over the Seven Last Plagues (15:1-4)

      3. The Preparation for the Seven Last Plagues (15:5-8)

      4. The First Bowl: Incurable Sores on the Beast-Worshipers (16:1-2)

      5. The Second Bowl: Death to All Sea-Life (16:3)

      6. The Third Bowl: Transforming of All Fresh Water into Blood (16:4-7)

7. The Fourth Bowl: Scorching of All through the Sun's Intensity (16:8-9)
8. The Fifth Bowl: Darkening of the Beast's Kingdom (16:10-11)
9. The Sixth Bowl: Preparation for the Doom of Earth's Kings (16:12-16)
10. The Seventh Bowl: The Destruction of Babylon (16:17– 18:24)
    a. The Bowl Summarized (16:17-21)
    b. Religious Babylon Destroyed (17:1-18)
    c. Commercial Babylon Destroyed (18:1-24)
D. The Closing Visions of John (19:1–22:5)
    1. Rejoicing Over the Fall of Babylon (19:1-10)
    2. The Coming of the King of Kings (19:11-16)
    3. The Great Supper of God (19:17-21)
    4. The Binding of Satan (20:1-3)
    5. The Thousand-Year Kingdom (20:4-10)
    6. The White-Throne Judgment (20:11-15)
    7. The New Heaven and the New Earth (21:1-8)
    8. The Holy City (21:9-22:5)
E. Epilogue (22:6-21)
    1. The Testimony of the Angel (22:6-7)
    2. The Testimony of John (22:8-11)
    3. The Testimony of Jesus and John's Response (22:12-20)
    4. The Benediction (22:21)

PART 1
The Preparation of the Prophet: His Past Vision (1:1-20)

1

The Prologue of the Apocalypse

The first chapter of the Apocalypse describes how God prepared John to receive subsequent portions of the revelation that were to constitute the book. After John introduces the work in its prologue (1:1-8), he describes a vision of Christ especially designed to direct the prophet's thinking into channels appropriate to what follows in subsequent chapters (1:9-20).

A. PROLOGUE (1:1-8)

These eight verses contain a preface with such things as the book's title, the content of the revelation, and other elements (1:1-3), the book's address and a doxology (1:4-6), and a statement of the book's theme (1:7-8).

1. PREFACE (1:1-3)

Translation

¹The Revelation of Jesus Christ, which God gave Him to show His slaves, the things that must happen soon, and He signified [it] by sending through His angel to His slave John, ²who testified the Word of God, even the testimony of Jesus Christ—as many things as he saw. ³Blessed is the one who reads and those who hear the words of the prophecy and keep the things that are written in it, for the time is near.

Exegesis and Exposition

The opening verses of Revelation (1:1-3) fill the all-important role of directing the audience's mind to the topics covered in the book as a whole. The preface (or superscription, as it is sometimes called) of Revelation (1:1-3) effectively fulfills this function by means of an overview of seven broad features. To begin, it states *the title* of the book (v. 1). Then follow words about *the channels* used to communicate the book's contents (v. 1). *The content* is featured next in an expression that shows this to be the climax of a prophetic line of thought rooted in the OT (v. 1). *The time of fulfillment* is said to be near (v. 1). There is some elaboration on *the method of communicating* the message to John (v. 1), who makes a brief allusion to *the prophetic process* (v. 2). A clear statement of the book's *practical purpose* culminates the three-verse preface (v. 3).

1:1 *The title.* The last book of the Bible is a book with its title incorporated into its own text. Ἀποκάλυψις Ἰησοῦ Χριστοῦ (*Apokalypsis Iēsou Christou,* "The Revelation of Jesus Christ"), the first three words of the book, provides as suitable a name as can be found for the twenty-two chapters that follow: "The Apocalypse (or Revelation) of Jesus Christ." These words tell the story of the whole book in a nutshell.

"Revelation," the title most often given in English translations, is a counterpart of a transliterated name often assigned to this work of John, "the Apocalypse." The latter word serves immediate notice that we are dealing with a category of literature that has come to be referred to as "apocalyptic."[1] The "apocalyptic" mold of thought characterized the outlook of many who were contemporaneous with the NT era. This book displays a number of similarities to such thinking, but distances itself in many respects from all nonbiblical apocalyptic literature of the day.

Apokalypsis, with the combination force of taking "away" (ἀπό [*apo*]) "a cover" (κάλυψις [*kalypsis*]), has a literal sense of "an uncovering" or "a laying bare."[2] Referring as it does to "a disclosure of what had been concealed,"[3] the word implies prior hiddenness and is a convenient vehicle to express the further ideas of "a disclosure of divine truth" or "a manifestation from God."[4] This more developed

---

1. See the more extended discussion of "Prophetic Style of the Apocalypse" in the Introduction.
2. G. Abbott-Smith, *A Manual Greek Lexicon of the New Testament* (Edinburgh: T. & T. Clark, 1937), p. 50.
3. Merrill C. Tenney, *Interpreting Revelation* (Grand Rapids: Eerdmans, 1957), p. 28.
4. Abbott-Smith, *Manual Greek Lexicon* p. 50.

reference to matters that are derived from God is characteristic of the NT usage of this noun and the related verb ἀποκαλύπτω (*apokalyptō,* "I reveal"). The word group takes on this more specialized significance in two ways, each of which has a possible application to Rev. 1:1.

One of the ways is the use of "revelation" as a name for the events connected with the revealing of Jesus Christ at the time of His second advent to the earth (e.g., 1 Cor. 1:7; 2 Thess. 1:7). This will be the unveiling of a Person who in His incarnate form has been personally hidden since His first advent. The other way "revelation" is used is in a disclosure of propositional data from God through a human instrument (e.g., Rom. 16:25; 1 Cor. 14:26). This understanding involves the use of persons such as apostles and prophets who were inspired by God to write or speak His message (cf. Eph. 3:5).

Obviously both senses of the noun would be appropriate in this book, but their connotations result in significantly different meanings. The former meaning would have the title focus on the personal appearance of Jesus Christ at His second advent, whereas the latter would focus on Jesus Christ as the inspired agent who reveals future happenings. Both are true, but which is the intended meaning of this book's three-word title *apokalypsis Iēsou Christou?*

Before this question is answered, a further related factor must be brought to bear. This is the meaning of the genitive case of *Iēsou Christou.* Is the genitive objective or subjective? In other words, is Jesus Christ the one revealed, or is He the one doing the revealing? The objective genitive goes with the former meaning of *apokalypsis* cited above, and the subjective genitive goes with the latter.

Favorable to Christ's being pictured as the revealed one is the mention of the angel as the revealer later in v. 1 (cf. διὰ τοῦ ἀγγέλου [*dia tou angelou,* "through the angel"]).[5] Yet this is not decisive because Christ later in the book reveals through angels (cf. 17:1; 21:9).

Some argue against Christ's being pictured as the revealed one in this title because the words "which must happen soon" in 1:1 preclude a reference to His personal appearance. The series of prophecies in Revelation require a prescribed period of time before His appearance in chapter 19.[6] To this objection it may be replied that *apokalypsis* in its technical eschatological sense may refer to the whole series of end-time happenings and not just to that phase when Christ returns personally (cf. 2 Thess. 1:7). There is nothing that must

---

5. J. A. Seiss, *The Apocalypse,* 3 vols. (New York: Charles C. Cook, 1909), 1:17.
6. Isbon T. Beckwith, *The Apocalypse of John* (New York: Macmillan, 1919), p. 418.

intervene before He returns to begin inflicting wrath during the Tribulation.

Further support for Christ's being the revealed one is derived from NT usage of a genitive following *apokalypsis*. In such cases the genitive is said always to be objective (Rom. 2:5; 8:19; 1 Cor. 1:7; 2 Cor. 12:1; Gal. 1:12; 2 Thess. 1:7; 1 Pet. 1:7, 13).[7] This conclusion may be debated, however. A good case can be made for a subjective genitive in at least two of the cases (2 Cor. 12:1; Gal. 1:12).[8]

The evidence favoring Christ as the revealer (i.e., subjective genitive) is more impressive. The strongest single consideration on either side of the issue is the plain fact that Christ functions in the role of revealer throughout the book: He addresses the seven churches in chapters 2-3;[9] He opens the scroll of destiny (5:5, 7) and discloses its contents (6:1, 3, 5, 7, 9, 12; 8:1).[10] His activity in this respect supports viewing Christ as the revealer in Revelation.

When this is coupled with the plain statement of 1:1 that the revelation is given by Jesus Christ to John as God gave it to Him,[11] the case for the subjective genitive is even more convincing. The words "which God gave Him to show His slaves" most naturally convey this meaning.

With the above conclusion we can now determine what John meant by his title to this book: it refers to data that Jesus Christ was inspired by God to reveal to His servants. Part of that revelation, to be sure, will be His own personal advent in chapter 19, but that is only a part. The revelation includes all other happenings prior to and subsequent to His own personal appearance.

Channels of communication for the revelation. After stating the title of his book, John proceeds in 1:1 to clarify some of the features of the revelation contained in the Apocalypse. The relative clause ἣν ἔδωκεν αὐτῷ ὁ θεός (*hēn edōken autō ho theos*, "which God gave Him") identifies the ultimate source of the matters that Christ reveals. God, presumably God the Father, gave them to Christ with the stipulation that He show them to God's servants (δεῖξαι τοῖς δούλοις αὐτοῦ [*deixai tois doulois autou*, "to show His slaves"]) (1:1). The aorist tense of

---

7. E. W. Bullinger, *The Apocalypse* or *"The Day of the Lord"* (London: Eyre and Spottiswoode, n.d.), pp. 31-34.
8. Beckwith, p. 418; Henry Barclay Swete, *The Apocalypse of St. John* (London: Macmillan, 1906), p. 1.
9. William Lee, "The Revelation of St. John," in *The Holy Bible*, ed. F. C. Cook (London: John Murray, 1881), 4:497.
10. Robert H. Mounce, *The Book of Revelation*, NICNT (Grand Rapids: Eerdmans, 1977), p. 64.
11. R. H. Charles, *The Revelation of St. John*, 2 vols., ICC (New York: Charles Scribner's, 1920), 1:6; Swete, *Apocalypse*, p. 1.

deixai views the mission of Christ as one great showing[12] just as the singular number of *apokalypsis* sees the separate revelations as one great revelation. This is the verb chosen by the author when he wants to describe communication of a divine revelation by means of visions (Charles).

Whether *doulois* refers to Christian prophets or to believers in general is problematic. Consulting Amos 3:7 and other uses in the Apocalypse (10:7; 11:18; 22:6), one might conclude for the former group (Charles). But he would look in vain throughout this book to find more than one prophetic recipient besides the one who at the end of v. 1 is referred to as τῷ δούλῳ αὐτοῦ 'Ιωάννῃ (*tō doulō autou Iōannē*, "to His slave John"). It is more feasible, therefore, to identify Christians in general as the ultimate destination of the revelation. Admittedly, this is an unusual name for such a group, but it can be paralleled in the early chapters of Acts (2:18; 4:29). Besides this, the seven churches of chapters 2-3 are composed of Christians, and they are the obvious recipients of these words.[13]

Content of the revelation. The data to be shown the churches, that is, the content of the revelation, are described by the highly significant words ἃ δεῖ γενέσθαι (*ha dei genesthai*, "things that must happen") (1:1). They depict a theme of longstanding interest that has its roots in the OT. These "things that must happen" first come into view in Daniel's description and interpretation of Nebuchadnezzar's dream about the great statue (Dan. 2:28[LXX]; cf. also 2:29, 45). The statue stands for four kingdoms, and a stone cut without hands out of the mountain that destroys the statue stands for an everlasting kingdom that will supersede the other four. The prophet, using the king's dream as a vehicle, clearly predicts the eventual establishment of God's kingdom on earth.

On Tuesday of the week He was crucified, Jesus in His Olivet discourse resumes this theme with the identical wording δεῖ γενέσθαι (*dei genesthai*, "they must happen") (Matt. 24:6; cf. Mark 13:7; Luke 21:9). In the process of teaching His disciples, Jesus points out that these things that "must happen," spoken of by Daniel, had not yet run their course. They were at that point still future. When discussion of the seal judgments is given in connection with Revelation 6, the close parallelism between Jesus' Olivet discourse and the symbolism of the seals will be noted. Jesus in His discourse was clearly anticipat-

---

12. R. C. H. Lenski, *The Interpretation of St. John's Revelation* (Columbus, Ohio: Lutheran Book Concern, 1935), p. 28.
13. William Henry Simcox, *The Revelation of St. John the Divine* (Cambridge: U. Press, 1893), p. 40.

ing what He was to show John in much greater detail more than six decades later here on the island of Patmos.

At this point John picks up the baton of this long-awaited series of happenings and develops them in far more detail than ever before. *Ha dei genesthai* is the basis for the framework of this book. The same clause is used in 4:1 at the beginning of the portion of the book that is specifically apocalyptic in nature. It is found again in 22:6 at the conclusion of the main body of the book. Rev. 4:1–22:5 is thereby marked out as comprising "the things that must happen soon." All that precedes this central section is preliminary, and all that follows it is conclusion.

To these occurrences may be added the closely related ἃ μέλλει γενέσθαι (*ha mellei genesthai*, "the things that are about to happen") of 1:19. This verse, generally acknowledged as furnishing the outline of Revelation, is another way of referring to ἃ δεῖ γενέσθαι ἐν τάχει (*ha dei genesthai en tachei*, "the things that must happen soon"). In 1:19 the expression follows references to two preliminary sections that precede chapter 4.

The revelation contained in this book thus is to bring to a climax an expectation that began at least as early as Daniel 2.[14] This is the ultimate detailed account of events that must (*dei*) transpire in the outworking of God's program regarding the institution of the ever-lasting kingdom that will replace other earthly, temporary kingdoms. That this is the goal toward which this book moves is very obvious from a casual review of subsequent passages such as 11:15 ("The kingdom of the world has become the kingdom of our Lord and of His Christ") and 20:4 ("And they lived and reigned with Christ for a thousand years").

Time of fulfillment of the revelation. The perspective of the Apocalypse regarding the establishment of this future kingdom differs in one important respect from that of both Daniel and Christ. Daniel placed the fulfillment of these things "in the latter days" (Dan. 2:28) and "after this" (2:29, 45). Jesus says that these things must happen "first" (Luke 21:9) and that the end is "not yet" (Matt. 24:6; Mark 13:7) or "not immediately" (Luke 21:9). Writing in the closing decade of the first century A.D., John is able to express a new viewpoint regarding these events of the last days. He writes that these are things that must happen ἐν τάχει (*en tachei*, "soon").

Two meanings have been proposed for this phrase. One makes it descriptive of the speed with which the events will be carried out once they have begun. They will occur in "rapid-fire" sequence or

---

14. G. K. Beale, "The Influence of Daniel upon the Structure and Theology of John's Apocalypse," *JETS* 27, no. 4 (December 1984): 415-16, 420.

"speedily." The meaning of the phrase in other NT passages is cited in support of this meaning of "suddenly" (cf. Luke 18:8; Acts 12:7; 22:18; 25:4; Rom. 16:20),[15] but in at least two of these passages the conclusion is debatable (cf. Luke 18:8; Rom. 16:20). The strongest support for this view is by way of an objection to the other alternative, that the phrase means "soon" and has reference to nearness of fulfillment for the events predicted. The objection is that such an alternative is impossible because a futurist approach to the book would require the events to have taken place close to John's lifetime. As the matter stands, it has been almost nineteen hundred years since the prediction and much of what the book predicts still has not begun to happen.[16]

In spite of the foregoing objection, however, the view that sees *en tachei* meaning "soon" and thereby focuses on the imminence of the predicted events is impressive. A major thrust of Revelation is its emphasis upon the shortness of time before the fulfillment. In the midst of persecution God's people do not have long to wait for relief to come. To say that the relief will come "suddenly" offers no encouragement, but to say that it will come "soon" does.[17] That fulfillment of the divine purpose will come soon is the consistent expectation of prophecy and apocalyptic (cf. 22:6; Deut. 9:3; Ezek. 29:5[LXX]; Luke 18:8; Rom. 16:20). Throughout apocalyptic literature and the NT the Messianic kingdom with its immediate precursors is viewed as near (Charles; Beckwith).

The meaning of nearness assigned to *en tachei* also derives support from ὁ γὰρ καιρὸς ἐγγύς (*ho gar kairos engys*) in 1:3, "for the time is near," and from the parallel statement of 22:6, "behold, I come soon."[18] The response of this view to the seeming difficulty raised by the delay of more than nineteen hundred years is not that John was mistaken[19] but that time in the Apocalypse is computed either relatively to the divine apprehension as here and in 22:10 (cf. also 1:3; 3:11; 22:7, 12, 20) or absolutely in itself as long or short (cf. 8:1; 20:2).

---

15. John F. Walvoord, *The Revelation of Jesus Christ* (Chicago: Moody, 1966), p. 35.

16. Alan F. Johnson, "Revelation," in *EBC*, ed. Frank E. Gaebelein (Grand Rapids: Zondervan, 1981), 12:416; Homer Hailey, *Revelation, an Introduction and Commentary* (Grand Rapids: Baker, 1979), p. 96; Mounce, *Revelation*, pp. 64-65.

17. James Moffatt, "The Revelation of St. John the Divine," in *The Expositor's Greek Testament*, ed. W. Robertson Nicoll (Grand Rapids: Eerdmans, n.d.), 5:335.

18. Henry Alford, *The Greek Testament*, 4 vols. (London: Longmans, Green, 1903), 4:545.

19. Contra G. V. Caird, *A Commentary on the Revelation of St. John the Divine*, HNTC (New York: Harper & Row, 1966), p. 12.

When measuring time, Scripture has a different standard from ours (cf. 1 John 2:18) (Lee). The purpose of *en tachei* is to teach the imminence of the events foretold, not to set a time limit within which they must occur (Johnson). It must be kept in mind that God is not limited by considerations of time in the same way man is (cf. 2 Pet. 3:8).

The presence of *en tachei* in 1:1 shows that for the first time the events predicted by Daniel and foreseen by Christ stood in readiness to be fulfilled. Therefore, John could speak of them as imminent, but earlier prophets could not.

Method of communicating the revelation. The end of v. 1, καὶ ἐσήμανεν ἀποστείλας διὰ τοῦ ἀγγέλου αὐτοῦ τῷ δούλῳ αὐτοῦ Ἰωάννῃ (*kai esēmanen aposteilas dia tou angelou autou tō doulō autou Iōannē*, "and He signified [it] by sending through His angel to His slave John"), tells the means by which the revelation was passed on. The graphic term *esēmanen* deserves special notice because in nonbiblical literature it already had a usage related to symbolic divine communications with men (Tenney). At other times, however, the notion of symbolism in the word seems to have vanished (cf. John 12:33; 18:32; 21:19; Acts 11:28). Nevertheless, the present instance is more in keeping with the symbolic import in light of the many signs and symbols that make up the apocalyptic portion of this book (cf. 4:1 ff.).

This symbolism must be assigned to the process by which John was inspired to write the book. Sometimes it has mistakenly been used as justification for interpreting the book in a nonliteral fashion.[20] It in no way gives license for a departure from the normal grammatical-historical system of hermeneutics. To clarify this point Govett proposes that *esēmanen* be translated "represent."[21] The revelation given to John, symbolic though it be, is to be interpreted just as one would interpret the rest of the Bible.

The angelic part in passing on the revelation is carefully noted by διὰ τοῦ ἀγγέλου αὐτοῦ (*dia tou angelou autou*, "through His angel"). Though Christ dealt directly with John at times (e.g., 6:9-17), He at other times used angels to reveal (e.g., 17:1; 21:9). It is quite possible that the four living beings and the twenty-four elders who are first encountered in chapter 4 are also included as angelic beings used for disclosing aspects of God's plan (cf. 6:1, 3, 5, 7; 7:13-17).[22]

---

20. H. A. Ironside, *Lectures on the Book of Revelation* (New York: Loizeaux, n.d.), p. 13.
21. Robert Govett, *The Apocalypse Expounded by Scripture* (London: Charles J. Thynne, 1920), p. 243.
22. Swete, *Apocalypse*, p. 2; Moffatt, "Revelation," 5:336. Buchanan presents a case for identifying τοῦ ἀγγέλου as a human messenger who brought John a book containing the material incorporated as Rev. 4:1-22:5 (George Wesley Buchanan, "John of Patmos and the Angel of Revelation," *Proceed-*

A further link in this chain of communication is John, the writer of this book. As clarified by the extended discussion in the introduction, this is traditionally held to be John the apostle, one of the Twelve, and nothing substantial has arisen to show this tradition to be in error (see Introduction to the Commentary). This John outlived the rest of the twelve, dying some time around the turn of the first century A.D. He is called a "slave" (*doulō*), which identifies him with the group earlier in the verse who are called "slaves" (cf. 1:9), but in this case there is justification for placing him on the same plane of authority as the OT prophets (cf. Isa. 49:5; Amos 3:7). As is true with all prophecy, it is important that the prophet's name be given so that the reader may know the credentials of the writer. For this reason, no writing of Scripture that is prophetic in a narrower sense is ever anonymous (Lee).

1:2 *The prophetic process.* John offers a further description of his prophetic activity in v. 2, though this conclusion is not without controversy. He speaks of his testimony (ἐμαρτύρησεν [*emartyrēsen*, "he testified"]) in this connection. The aorist tense of *emartyrēsen* has been explained in at least three different ways: as a testimony borne prior to the writing of the Apocalypse, one that had nothing directly to do with this book; as a constative aorist looking back to the writing of Rev. 1:4–22:21, assuming that the superscription (1:1-3) was the last part of the book to be written; and as an epistolary aorist, the past time expressed by the verb being explained by the perspective of the readers (i.e., when they received it, the writing of the whole book would be a thing of the past).

The strongest reason for surmising that this is a reference to a testimony prior to the Apocalypse is a more general sense assigned to τὸν λόγον τοῦ θεοῦ καὶ τὴν μαρτυρίαν 'Ιησοῦ Χριστοῦ (*ton logon tou theou kai tēn martyrian Iēsou Christou*, "the Word of God, even the testimony of Jesus Christ") on the basis of similar expressions found in Rev. 1:9; 6:9; 12:17; and 20:4 (Moffatt). These make the present expression refer more naturally to what John had written earlier in his gospel and epistles. Other points of coincidence between this book and John's other writings include the reference of Rev. 22:17 to John 7:37 (i.e., the idea of drinking the water provided by Christ) and Rev. 1:2 to 1 John 1:1 (i.e., references to the Word of God and to what John saw) (Lee).

The difficulty of having Rev. 1:2 refer to John's other writings is great, however. Εἶδεν (*Eiden*, "he saw"), as a part of the limiting

---

ings of the Sixth World Congress of Jewish Studies [vol. 1, edited by Avigdor Shinan; Jerusalem: Academic Press, 1977]: 36). His evidence is unconvincing.

phrase "as many things as he saw," must in the setting of Revelation refer to apocalyptic visions, not to the kinds of material that are found in the gospel of John and the Johannine epistles (Alford; Swete). Furthermore, if John for some strange reason had wanted to refer to his earlier writings at this point, he most probably would have written "who *also* testified" rather than simply "who testified" (Alford).

The need to take *tēn martyrian Iēsou Christou* in the sense, "the testimony borne by Jesus Christ," as will be pointed out below, makes it compelling to refer *emartyrēsen* to the contents of the book in light of 22:16, 20. These two verses are statements summarizing the contents of the book, and both connect the testimony borne by Jesus with said contents.[23] The question remains, however, as to how the contents are referred to.

One viewpoint is that the aorist tense of *eiden* (1:2) shows that John had already seen the visions and is in the process of prefixing his superscription (or introduction) to a book that is already otherwise complete (Beckwith; Bullinger). In support it is offered that common practice was to write a book's superscription last in those days and that τὰ . . . γεγραμμένα (*ta . . . gegrammena*, "the things written") (1:3) shows that the work was completed when John wrote the superscription (Beckwith). To this position it may be replied that *eiden* could be a constative aorist even if *emartyrēsen* is epistolary. John could have seen the visions and written them down at a later time, the same time he wrote the superscription. There is nothing to interrupt the flow of thought from 1:3 to 1:4 to indicate that there was a break of any kind between the two parts. Generally the "title" of such a work, as this superscription has been characterized, would not be the last thing to be added. How would John have known how much space to reserve at the beginning of his papyrus scroll for these words? The idea is impractical. As for the *ta . . . gegrammena* of 1:3, such an articular participle bears the characteristics of a substantive and does not indicate absolute time in the past.

Bullinger's proposal that all of chapter 1 was written last runs into even greater obstacles (Bullinger). The messages of chapters 2-3 are dependent on the vision of chapter 1 in their characterizations of Christ. John could not have comprehended the messages in their fullness without the background of chapter 1 to precede them.

The best explanation is to understand that John's testimony as contained in this book was written in the past from his initial readers' point of view.[24] The objection that this is not an epistle and conse-

---

23. Beckwith, *Apocalypse*, pp. 421, 780.
24. Swete, *Apocalypse*, p. 3; Charles, *Revelation*, 1:7; Moffatt, "Revelation," 5:336; Simcox, *Revelation*, p. 41; Leon Morris, *The Revelation of St. John*, TNTC (Grand Rapids: Eerdmans, 1969), p. 46.

quently the epistolary aorist should not be identified here is countered by the observation that the Apocalypse is written in epistolary form (Alford).

John's use of the aorist *emartyrēsen*, then, is best explained by his adoption of the perspective of his readers in regard to his composition of this book. When they received it, his testimony as recorded in its pages would be a thing of the past.

With *emartyrēsen* referring to John's writing of this book, *ton logon tou theou* must be a further characterization of the contents of this book. The expression denotes "any declaration, revelation, or truth coming from God" (Beckwith). More specifically, it is the common idiomatic phrase for a direct prophetic communication, exactly what this book purports to be (Bullinger).

"The Word of God" is elaborated upon by "the testimony of Jesus Christ" (v. 2). Because the genitive following *martyria* is probably always subjective, this must refer specifically to "the testimony borne by Jesus Christ."[25] The *kai* that joins *tēn martyrian Iēsou Christou* to *ton logon tou theou* is epexegetical, a frequent use of the conjunction in this book. The fuller description of the book's contents is "the Word of God, that is (or 'even'), the testimony borne by Jesus Christ." The testimony given by Jesus Christ in this case is His communication to John of the contents of this book.

John has even more to add to his elaboration on the contents. Another relative clause, ὅσα εἶδεν (*hosa eiden*, "as many things as he saw"), further defines "the Word of God, even the testimony of Jesus Christ." This clause points forward to the frequent use of εἶδον (*eidon*, "I saw") throughout the apocalyptic portion of the book and indicates that the book's general character is that of prophetic vision (Swete). Descriptions of these visions constitute the subject matter of John's testimony to the slaves of God as found in the Apocalypse.

1:3 *The practical purpose of the revelation.* A feature that distinguishes this prophecy from other apocalyptic writings of the time is the blessing pronounced in 1:3. Μακάριος (*Makarios*, "blessed") offers something by way of incentive, which was not found in other similar literature in circulation in that day (Tenney). The writer draws upon Jesus' earlier practice (cf. Matt. 5:3-12) of promising special blessing to the reader and to the ones hearing and complying with the moral

---

25. Vassiliadis has argued for an objective genitive here, basing his case on a martyrological meaning of μάρτυς and its cognates in Revelation (Petros Vassiliadis, "The Translation of ΜΑΡΤΥΡΙΑ ΙΗΣΟΥ in Revelation," *BT* 36 [1985]: 129-34). The case offered by Mazzaferri for attaching a prophetic rather than a martyrological significance to the word-group is much more convincing, however. This bears out the subjective genitive as correct (Fred Mazzaferri, "ΜΑΡΤΥΡΙΑ ΙΗΣΟΥ Revisited," *BT* 3 [1988]: 114-22).

and ethical standards to be advocated in the following chapters' words. Already the distinctly practical purpose is evident (Beckwith).

The participial expression ὁ ἀναγινώσκων καὶ οἱ ἀκούοντες (*ho anaginōskōn kai hoi akouontes*, "the one who reads and those who hear") reflects the early Christian practice of reading aloud the Scriptures in the services of the church. This, in turn, was a carryover from the procedure followed in the Jewish synagogues where most of the earliest Christians had participated. Because writing materials were expensive and scarce, so were copies of the books that were parts of the biblical canon. As a rule, one copy per Christian assembly was the best that could be hoped for. Public reading was the only means that rank-and-file Christians had for becoming familiar with the contents of these books.

An individual would therefore read aloud for the benefit of the rest of those assembled. It behooved the listeners to pay close attention, a habit in which they had been well-trained. When written resources were unavailable, the memory had to be keen or else the data were lost.[26]

A good memory was vital not only for the sake of retaining information. Obedience also depended on remembering what was commanded. Listening (*akouontes*) was only the first step in obtaining God's blessing (*makarios*). The other requirement was obedience. Two participles in v. 3 are connected by καὶ and governed by one article οἱ: οἱ ἀκούοντες . . . καὶ τηροῦντες (*hoi akouontes . . . kai tērountes*, "those who hear . . . and keep"). This construction depicts one group, not two. There is not one group of listeners and another group of obedient ones. To inherit the promised blessing, every individual in the group had to combine obedience with hearing.

It has been suggested that *tērountes* be taken in the sense of "remember" or "ponder upon," with no notion of compliance with the things heard (Bullinger). In light of common NT usage of the word and this book's frequent exhortations to repentance, faith, endurance, obedience, and the like, it is much preferred to assign it the sense of "give heed to" or "observe."[27] This is a call to be a doer of the word and not a hearer only (cf. James 1:22). Once again, the practical purpose of this book is in the forefront.

The expression τοὺς λόγους τῆς προφητείας (*tous logous tēs proph-*

---

26. Barr, in commenting on the various clues and memory aids incorporated into Revelation, points out that the ancients had better-trained memories than twentieth-century generations and could keep the whole of the book in mind in perhaps one or, at the most, very few public readings (David L. Barr, "The Apocalypse of John as Oral Enactment," *Int* 40, no. 3 [July 1986]: 244).

27. Abbott-Smith, *Lexicon*, p. 445; Alford, *Greek Testament*, 4:548.

ēteias, "the words of the prophecy") is important in determining the nature of the literary genre of the Apocalypse. Whether it is to be classed as "apocalyptic" or not, its self-claim is that it is prophecy (Alford; Swete). John was endowed with the gift of prophecy (cf. Rom. 12:6; 1 Cor. 12:10, 28; Eph. 4:11), which enabled him to communicate inspired messages from God, including words about the future.[28] The Apocalypse begins and ends on this note of authoritative revelation (cf. 22:7, 10, 18, 19).

The reason for the blessing pronounced is introduced by γάρ (*gar,* "for") (1:3). The reason consists of the nearness of the accomplishment of the things predicted in the book. Compliance with the moral and ethical standards is much more urgent because final accountability for personal behavior is imminent.

Καιρός (*kairos,* "time") (1:3) frequently has a technical sense in the NT, referring to the end times when the earthly kingdom of Israel will be instituted (cf. Acts 1:7; 3:20; 1 Thess. 5:1). The events of this book are thus identified with the last of the "critical epoch-making periods foreordained of God."[29] From the perspective of prophetic anticipation this period is declared to be ἐγγύς (*engys,* "near") (1:3) (Beckwith). This declaration echoes and reinforces the ἐν τάχει (*en tachei,* "soon") of v. 1.

Additional Notes

1:1 Book titles in Greek New Testaments (e.g., Ἀποκάλυψις Ἰωάννου) and English Bible translations are separate from the text and have been added subsequent to the initial writing of the books. Though they appeared very early, they are therefore recognized as not having come from the books' original authors. It is rare for a book to include a title *within* its own text.

The suggestion that Ἰησοῦ Χριστοῦ is a possessive genitive (Morris) has little to commend it. It is less precise than the other two possibilities, the objective and subjective genitives. The revelation was His and His alone, either in the sense of His prerogative of being revealed or in the sense of being given to Him so that He might reveal it. In which sense it was His possession needs to be determined.

"Which God gave Him" has been punctuated in two ways. One way is to place a comma after "Him," in effect making the relative clause parenthetical (*The Greek New Testament,* UBS 3d edition, KJV). This punctuation favors the objective genitive by syntactically sepa-

---

28. See the Introduction for a comparison between apocalyptic and prophetic as related to the Apocalypse.
29. Richard Chenevix Trench, *Synonyms of the New Testament* (reprint; Grand Rapids: Eerdmans, 1953), p. 211; Lenski, *Revelation,* p. 33.

rating δεῖξαι from ἔδωκεν. In other words, God did not give the revelation to Christ to show. The other possibility omits punctuation after "Him" (NA, ASV, RSV, NASB, NIV), which has the effect of making δεῖξαι the purpose of ἔδωκεν: God gave it Him to show. Because no adequate reason exists for treating this relative clause as parenthetical, the latter punctuation is preferable.

1:2 The failure of some grammarians, including A. T. Robertson, to identify ἐμαρτύρησεν as an epistolary aorist[30] may be attributed to oversight inasmuch as Robertson calls this occurrence an epistolary aorist in another of his works.[31] A grammarian is mistaken, however, if he limits the NT usage of the epistolary aorist so as to exclude such an instance as this.[32]

1:3 This verse is one of seven "beatitudes" found in Revelation. The other six are in 14:13; 16:15; 19:9; 20:6; 22:7; 22:14. As would be expected, all seven "blessings" are for those who comply with this book's high standards of righteousness. They either declare their blessed estate in an absolute way (1:3; 14:13; 16:15; 22:7) or elaborate on their blessing by way of a rich promise for the future (19:9; 20:6; 22:14).

Public reading is a consideration that made the opening words of a book extremely important. Introductory comments had to be chosen carefully so as to alert the listeners' minds to major themes to be treated in subsequent parts of the book. Earlier comments about the first two verses have shown how well this goal is attained by John in this book.

Another important function of public reading became more evident during the first four centuries of the Christian era. A crucial decision faced by many churches related to which books were to be read in their public services. The reason for this concern was the place accorded such books when read alongside the OT Scriptures. To grant such a recognition was to acknowledge a book's authority as inspired Scripture. The early church faced hard decisions in separating such books from the many other early writings vying for recognition. For this reason, the obvious intention that the Apocalypse was to be read publicly argued strongly from the start that it be included

---

30. E.g., Archibald Thomas Robertson, *A Grammar of the Greek New Testament in the Light of Historical Research* (Nashville: Broadman, 1934), pp. 845-46; BDF, p. 172, par. 334; Nigel Turner, *Syntax*, vol. 3 of *A Grammar of New Testament Greek*, by James Hope Moulton (Edinburgh: T. & T. Clark, 1963), pp. 72-73.
31. Cf. Archibald Thomas Robertson, *Word Pictures in the New Testament*, 6 vols. (Nashville: Broadman, 1933), 6:284.
32. E.g., BDF, p. 172, par. 334.

among those books that eventually would be recognized as part of the NT canon. Only two other NT books contain such direct indications regarding public reading: Colossians and 1 Thessalonians (cf. Col. 4:16; 1 Thess. 5:27). In addition, there is perhaps an indirect indication regarding the public reading of the gospel of Luke, which is found in 1 Tim. 4:13 and 5:18. If 4:13 is talking about the public reading of Scripture and if the second quotation of 5:18 is taken from Luke and is included under the designation of ἡ γραφή in 5:18, the implication is strong that Paul included at least one NT book as something that should be read publicly.

2. ADDRESS AND DOXOLOGY (1:4-6)

Translation

⁴John to the seven churches that are in Asia: Grace to you and peace from the one who is and who was and who is coming and from the seven spirits who are before His throne ⁵and from Jesus Christ, the faithful witness, the first-born from the dead and the ruler of the kings of the earth.

To the one who loves us and loosed us from our sins by His blood—⁶and He made us a kingdom, priests to His God and Father—[let] glory and strength [be] to Him forever and ever. Amen.

Exegesis and Exposition

As is true of NT epistles in general, the address of Revelation contains three elements: the writer, the addressees, and the greeting. The writer is Ἰωάννης (*Iōannēs*, "John"), the addressees are noted in ταῖς ἑπτὰ ἐκκλησίαις ταῖς ἐν τῇ Ἀσίᾳ (*tais hepta ekklēsiais tais en tē Asia*, "to the seven churches that are in Asia"), and the greeting is χάρις ὑμῖν καὶ εἰρήνη (*charis hymin kai eirēnē*, "grace to you and peace").

Appended to the greeting are three prepositional phrases at the end of v. 4 and the beginning of v. 5 that name and describe the source of the greeting extended by the writer. From the middle of v. 5 through v. 6 John, by means of a doxology that ascribes glory and strength to Jesus Christ, focuses on the third member of the triune source of the greeting.

1:4 *The address. Tais hepta ekklēsiais tais en tē Asia* are the recipients of this "epistle." A good bit of discussion has centered on why John chose seven churches and not more. There were certainly churches in more than seven cities in the first-century Roman province of Asia. Though he may have chosen only seven because seven is the number that denotes completeness (Swete), the likelihood is greater that he chose them because they were typical assemblies with

63

regard to their histories and spiritual states.[33] These adequately represented the various spiritual situations of the surrounding churches at the time. Then too they were probably the ones with which John enjoyed the closest relationship. The possibility of their being representative of consecutive future periods of church history is discussed in Excursus 1 at the end of this volume.

It is well attested by writings from the early centuries of the Christian church that John the apostle spent the last years of his life in this province of Asia, which was in the western part of modern-day Turkey. He apparently left Jerusalem in the late sixties of the first century A.D. while the Jewish people were in rebellion against Rome and went to Asia where he became the recognized leader of the Asian churches.[34]

Charis hymin kai eirēnē is an epistolary greeting that came into general use among Christians. It is used by Paul in all his epistles except the pastorals (1 and 2 Timothy replace *hymin kai* with ἔλεος [*eleos*, "mercy"] and Titus uses *charis kai eirēnē*, omitting *hymin*). The identical expression is also used in 1 and 2 Peter.

Charis is a "Christianized" form of the more secular χαίρειν (*chairein*, "greeting") that was used widely in earlier Christian writings and in Greek letters of a non-Christian type (cf. Acts 15:23; 23:26; James 1:1). It was transformed from the infinitive *chairein* into the noun *charis*, perhaps by Paul, to reflect the distinctive spiritual benefit that belongs to Christians. The favor of God has been freely bestowed on them, though they deserve the opposite. The grace of God is a highly developed theme in NT epistolary literature.

Eirēnē was a commonly used greeting among the Jews. Its Hebrew counterpart שָׁלוֹם (*šālôm*, "peace") is a familiar greeting in the OT (e.g., Judg. 6:23; 19:20; Isa. 57:19). It is a wish of well-being to the other party, including all aspects of his person. The NT *eirēnē* goes even deeper, however, because of Christ's death and the fulfillment of the OT anticipations accomplished thereby. A person can experience and know he has peace with God through Jesus Christ (cf. Rom. 5:1), a peace resulting from the grace of God and the ultimate peace that a person can enjoy. Such a completed meaning lies behind the Christian use of the word.

The source of the greeting. At the end of v. 4 and the beginning of v.

---

33. William R. Newell, *The Book of Revelation* (Chicago: Moody, 1935), p. 8.
34. That John would use his own name rather than ascribe his work to a figurehead of antiquity, as was the practice in extrabiblical apocalypses, indicates that he was known to the addressees as a reliable and authoritative figure. In other words, the *ēthos* he had with them even before writing was quite positive (John T. Kirby, "The Rhetorical Situations of Revelation 1-3," *NTS* 34, no. 2 [April 1988]: 199).

5 three prepositional phrases using ἀπό (*apo*, "from") give the three-fold source of the greeting "grace to you and peace." In Pauline practice it was common to name Deity as the origin of the theological concepts denoted by the terms *charis* and *eirēnē* (cf. Rom. 1:5; 1 Cor. 1:3; 2 Cor. 1:2; Gal. 1:3; Eph. 1:2; Phil. 1:2; Col. 1:2; 2 Thess. 1:2; 1 Tim. 1:2; 2 Tim. 1:2; Tit. 1:4; Philem. 3). The assumption must be that such is the source designated here also.

The first part of the threefold source is named by ἀπὸ ὁ ὢν καὶ ὁ ἦν καὶ ὁ ἐρχόμενος (*apo ho ōn kai ho ēn kai ho erchomenos*, "from the one who is and who was and who is coming"). Though one might at first see a reference to Jesus Christ here, such a possibility is excluded by His being named as the third part of the source in 1:5 (Swete). Instead, this refers to God the Father.

This title for the Father is unusual in a number of respects. The nominative case of the article *ho* in the three members of the expression is surprising because the preposition *apo* is usually followed by a genitive inflectional ending. In fact, this has been cited as one of the many examples of alleged grammatical errors in Revelation (Moffatt). As is the case with all such allegations, a satisfactory explanation exists without the need for concluding that the text has errors. *Ho ōn kai ho ēn kai ho erchomenos* is to be regarded as an undeclinable proper name. Proper names were frequently not declined as other nouns were, and so their inflectional endings remained unchanged regardless of their functions in the sentence structure (Swete).

Another rare grammatical phenomenon of this title is the finite verb *ēn* doing duty for a participle (Simcox). It is modified by a definite article and is parallel with participles in the first and third members of the expression. The reason for this peculiarity lies in a limitation of the verb εἰμί (*eimi*, "I am"), which has no participial form to express continuing action in past time. The writer wanted to describe the Father's being by including His eternal and continuing existence prior to the present moment. The imperfect indicative was the only linguistic device for doing so.

With the first member *ho ōn* speaking of the Father's continuing existence in the present and the second *ho ēn* of His continuing existence in the past, ὁ ἐσόμενος (*ho esomenos*, "who will be") could have been expected as the third member of this title. For his own reasons, however, the writer varied from the expected and chose the present participle *ho erchomenos*. Several reasons for this variation may be suggested. For one thing, it corresponds with the keynote of the book in 1:7 (ἔρχεται [*erchetai*, "he is coming"]), the second advent of Christ (Moffatt). Also, the present tense of the participle acquires a future significance through the meaning of the word, i.e., that which is coming is not yet here.[35] Such a means of referring to the future also heightens the focus upon the imminence of His coming: He who is already on His way may arrive at any moment.

This is a title that is used several times in Revelation (cf. 1:8; 4:8; 11:17; 16:5). A notable feature about the last two uses (11:17; 16:5) is the absence of the third member *kai ho erchomenos*. A reasonable explanation for this omission is that by the time these points in the book are reached, the prophetic perspective has reached the time of the second advent and the coming thus can no longer be spoken of as future. A legitimate question is, then, Why is this title not referred to the Son rather than the Father, since it is the Son's advent that is in view in *ho erchomenos*? The answer to the question lies in the close identity of the Son with the Father. Though two separate Persons, they along with the Holy Spirit are nevertheless one God. The Son possesses equal dignity with the Father, and when the Son returns, He will come as the representative of the Father (Lee). So there is a legitimate sense in which it will be the advent of the Father also.

The second part of the threefold source of the greeting "grace to you and peace" is given by the words ἀπὸ τῶν ἑπτὰ πνευμάτων ἃ ἐνώπιον τοῦ θρόνου αὐτοῦ (*apo tōn hepta pneumatōn ha enōpion tou thronou autou*, "from the seven spirits who are before His throne"). The identification of the seven spirits is problematic. The name occurs again in 3:1; 4:5; 5:6, and these other mentions must figure into efforts to identify the meaning. Two main proposals for identification are that they are angels (i.e., supernatural created beings) or the Holy Spirit, the third Person of the Holy Trinity.

To support the identification of the seven spirits as angels, it is sometimes noted that πνεῦμα (*pneuma*, "spirit") is frequently used for angels, both fallen and unfallen, in the NT (Walvoord). It is also observed that the location of the seven spirits before God's throne shows that they are created beings. This, a position of subordination, is quite inappropriate for a divine being, but angels are regularly positioned in this manner.[36] Furthermore, the similarity of the language here to that of Luke 9:26 and 1 Tim. 5:21 (Moffatt) and the prominence of angels in connection with the Tribulation period (cf. Matt. 13:41), which is presumably the period covered by Revelation 6-18 (Smith), are further factors that favor the angelic identification.

Arguing against angels, some have noted that though seven angels are mentioned in 8:2, these angels are never referred to as *pneumata*, and that angels in this book are distinctly called angels and are seen in distinct angelic form whereas the seven spirits are always represented in symbolic form (Alford; Beckwith). Both the singular

---

35. F. J. A. Hort, *The Apocalypse of St. John* (London: Macmillan, 1908), p. 11.

and plural of *pneuma* in this book refer only to the Spirit of God or to demons, with the exception of Rev. 11:11 and 13:5, and neither of these exceptions refers to angels (Lee; Johnson).

The most decisive consideration against a reference to angels is the impossibility that created beings could be seen as a source of an invocation of grace and peace in 1:4-5. This would place them alongside the Father and the Son as equals, and the strict prohibitions against angel worship elsewhere in the book (19:10; 22:9) make it inconceivable that angels would be placed side-by-side with the Father and the Son in such a role (Charles; Beckwith).

It is more satisfying to identify "the seven spirits" as a reference to the Holy Spirit, and thus as an additional *divine* source for the greeting of v. 4. It is improper to associate anyone less than Deity with the Father (1:4) and the Son (1:5) (Swete; Morris; Mounce). Further confirmation is noted in Christ's hold upon the seven spirits (3:1) and in the relationship of the seven spirits to both God and Christ (4:5; 5:6). This is in keeping with NT usage where the procession of the Holy Spirit from both the Father and the Son is taught (e.g., John 15:26). He is both the Spirit of God and the Spirit of Christ (cf. Rom. 8:9) (Beckwith).

Against the Holy Spirit identification it has been contended that this passage does not purpose to portray the Trinity, but to designate the high court of heaven as having jurisdiction on earth, with angels as those who assess the situation (Bullinger). It is further argued that nowhere else is the Holy Spirit associated with the Father and the Son in an epistolary salutation (Bullinger). These objections, however, do not appear to be sufficient to counteract the stronger consideration that a reference to angels would indeed be an intrusion of created beings into the Holy Trinity.

It is better, then, to see in "the seven spirits" of 1:4 a reference to the Holy Spirit. But this raises a further question: Why is He referred to in this way? In thirteen or fourteen places in this book He is referred to in a more conventional fashion as "the Spirit" or something comparable (e.g., 19:10). Suggestions have varied. Is it because the churches in which He operates are seven in number?[37] This proposal is inadequate because the descriptions of 4:5 and 5:6 relate to what is fundamental and universal, not just to the seven churches (Beckwith).

Another idea is to trace the title to Isa. 11:2 where a supposedly

---

36. Bullinger, *Apocalypse*, p. 140; J. B. Smith, *A Revelation of Jesus Christ* (Scottdale, Pa.: Herald, 1961), pp. 38, 82.
37. Swete, *Apocalypse*, p. 6; H. B. Swete, *The Holy Spirit in the New Testament* (London: Macmillan, 1919), p. 274.

sevenfold designation of the Spirit is found (Lenski; Walvoord; Morris; Caird). This notion is inadequate, however, because Isa. 11:2 points out only six, not seven, energies of the Spirit (Alford; Beckwith). The fact that the LXX breaks the poetic parallelism of the three couplets by inserting εὐσέβειας (*eusebeias*, "godliness") to increase the number to seven (Mounce) is not sufficient to carry this view because in the Apocalypse little weight is assigned to the LXX.[38]

Another approach is to see "seven spirits" as a means for expressing the Spirit's perfection and His sevenfold energies.[39] Rationale for this derives from the symbolic use of the number seven to denote completeness (Alford) and from the manifold working of the Spirit indicated in such passages as 1 Cor. 12:10; 14:32; Heb. 2:4; Rev. 22:6.[40] Though it is true that the Spirit operates in a variety of ways (Rom. 12:6; 1 Cor. 12:4) and that seven can express the fullness and perfection of those operations, an emphasis on such fullness is absent in all four contexts where this title is used for the Holy Spirit (Charles; Beckwith). The uses of the title require a reference to a concrete being, not to abstract energies.

The most satisfactory explanation for the title "the seven spirits" traces its origin to Zech. 4:1-10.[41] Zechariah 4:2, 10 speaks of the seven lamps (cf. Rev. 4:5) that are "the eyes of the Lord, which range throughout the whole earth." This has a close similarity to John's "sent out into all the earth" in Rev. 5:6 (Mounce). Because Revelation 4 and 5 carry the same symbolism as Zechariah 4 and the title used in the opening of this book must relate to themes occurring later on, the tracing of the title to this OT passage is an obvious solution (Beckwith). The prominence of the Holy Spirit's activity in the world in Zech. 4:2-10 is established by the words "not by might or power, but by my Spirit, says the Lord of hosts" (Zech. 4:6). John's use of Zechariah 4 furnishes an example of his kaleidoscopic variations on OT imagery (Caird). In deriving the title, John identifies the seven eyes of Zechariah with the seven spirits that belong to the Lord (Zech. 4:10; cf. Rev. 5:6).[42] The seven lamps of Zechariah (Zech. 4:2) are also synonymous with the seven spirits (Rev. 4:5).

---

38. Swete, *The Apocalypse*, p. 6.
39. Seiss, *Apocalypse*, 1:45; John F. Walvoord, *The Holy Spirit* (Wheaton, Ill.: Van Kampen, 1954), p. 10; Morris, *Revelation*, p. 48.
40. Swete, *The Apocalypse*, p. 6; Charles, *Revelation*, 1:11.
41. Beckwith, *Apocalypse*, pp. 426-27; F. F. Bruce, "The Spirit in the Apocalypse," in *Christ and Spirit in the New Testament*, ed. B. Lindars and S. S. Smalley (Cambridge: U. Press, 1974), p. 336; Caird, p. 15.
42. Charles, *Revelation*, 1:141; cf. also Kenneth L. Barker, "Zechariah," in *EBC*, ed. Frank E. Gaebelein (Grand Rapids: Zondervan, 1985), 7:626, 630.

1:5 The third part of the threefold source of greeting is Ἰησοῦ Χριστοῦ (*Iēsou Christou*, "Jesus Christ"). Usually He is named in second position among the persons of the Holy Trinity, but the writer chooses to name Him last in this case to facilitate an elaboration upon several aspects of His Person and work in the remainder of vv. 5 and 6 (Moffatt).

This is the last time in the Apocalypse that this Person is referred to as "Jesus Christ," with the exception of the benediction in 22:21 (see also 11:15; 12:10; 20:4, 6 where "Christ" is used alone). From this point on "Jesus" is the usual name given to Him. By this means the author emphasizes His glorified humanity.[43]

Jesus Christ is next characterized by three descriptive titles in v. 5. The first of these, ὁ μάρτυς ὁ πιστός (*ho martys ho pistos*, "the faithful witness"), is repeated in 3:14. He is also called "faithful" in 19:11. "The faithful witness" is an allusion to Ps. 89:37 where regarding the throne of David it is written, "It shall be established forever like the moon, and the witness in the sky is faithful." Jesus Christ is of the seed of David and will sit on the Davidic throne that will endure forever as the sun (Ps. 89:36). Psalm 89 in its entirety is an inspired commentary on the Davidic covenant of 2 Sam. 7:8-16.

The next title ὁ πρωτότοκος τῶν νεκρῶν (*ho prōtotokos tōn nekrōn*, "the first-born from the dead") also finds its source in Psalm 89. God promises to make David's seed, His "first-born," "the highest of the kings of the earth" (Ps. 89:27). "The first-born from the dead" is almost identical with the title of Christ in Col. 1:18: πρωτότοκος ἐκ τῶν νεκρῶν (*prōtotokos ek tōn nekrōn*, "first-born from the dead"). The two differences in Colossians are the absence of the article before *prōtotokos* and the presence of the preposition *ek* before *tōn nekrōn*. The absence of the article is attributable to the predicate nominative function of the noun in the sentence structure of Col. 1:18. The presence of *ek* reflects the ablatival sense of *tōn nekrōn*: He is the first-born "from among the dead ones" (cf. Acts 4:2). The same function should probably be understood in Rev. 1:5 even though the *ek* is not used (cf. also Acts 26:23; Rom. 1:4). This promised seed who will sit on David's throne is "the first-born from (among) the dead (ones)" (cf. Acts 2:29-32). Others will be raised from the dead, but Jesus Christ is the firstfruits (1 Cor. 15:23).

The third title of v. 5 is ὁ ἄρχων τῶν βασιλέων τῆς γῆς (*ho archōn tōn basileōn tēs gēs*, "the ruler of the kings of the earth"). John is once again drawing from Psalm 89 where the psalmist notes God's promise to make David's seed "the highest of the kings of the earth" (Ps. 89:27).

---

43. Swete, *The Apocalypse*, p. 5.

Here is a clear foreshadowing of Jesus Christ's future role as "King of kings and Lord of lords" (Rev. 19:16). As with the first two titles, this too is by virtue of His Davidic lineage.

The three titles taken together have been variously construed. One defines them as speaking of divine testimony, revelation of the risen Lord, and the forecast of the issues of history.[44] Another sees the past, present, and future works of Christ in the three (Tenney). The most precise explanation sees all three as referring to Jesus Christ's future dominion over the earth (Bullinger). Some secondary reference may be acknowledged to the faithful witness He has borne in the past, to His present ministry as the resurrected Lord, and to His future role as King of kings, but the origination of all three expressions from Psalm 89 reflects a major authorial intent to direct attention to the fulfillment of the promises made to David regarding an eternal kingdom in 2 Samuel 7.

The doxology. Continuing his elaboration upon the work of Jesus Christ, the author in the middle of v. 5 turns his words to ascribe praise to this second Person of the Holy Trinity. The doxology begun by τῷ ἀγαπῶντι ἡμᾶς* (*tō agapōnti hēmas*, "to the one who loves us") culminates at the end of v. 6 with an ascription of glory and strength to Jesus Christ. The durative force of the present participle gains heightened significance in contrast with the aorist participial expression λύσαντι ἡμᾶς* (*lysanti hēmas*, "loosed us"), which follows immediately. Here Christ's love for His own is pictured as continuing in the present. This is the only NT instance where His love is so described. Usually an aorist tense tells of His past love (e.g., Gal. 2:20).

The article *tō* preceding *agapōnti* governs both *agapōnti* and *lysanti*, joining them together to describe one person. The one who "loves" us has also "loosed" us from our sins by means of His blood. The action of Jesus Christ has provided for our release from bondage to sin (ἐκ τῶν ἁμαρτιῶν ἡμῶν [*ek tōn hamartiōn hēmōn*, "from our sins"]). This pictures sins in the role of slave-master in much the same way as Paul sees sin in Rom. 6:12-14. A similar redemption will come to Israel in the future according to Ps. 130:8.

The blood Jesus shed at Calvary was the purchase price to obtain our release. 'Εν in the phrase ἐν τῷ αἵματι αὐτοῦ (*en tō haimati autou*, "by His blood") is instrumental. It was "by means of" His blood that He provided this great benefit for believers.[45]

---

44. Ibid., p. 7.
45. Another suggestion is that ἐν in imitation of the Hebrew בּ has the meaning here and in 5:9 of "at the price of" (e.g., Isa. 7:23) (BDF, par. 219[3]; Kenneth G. C. Newport, "Semitic Influence in Revelation: Some Further Evidence," *AUSS* 25, no. 3 [Autumn 1987]: 251-52).

The total participial expression that begins the doxology therefore carries this sense: praise is ascribed "to the one who has an abiding love for believers which is demonstrated by His completed past work of redemption from sins by means of His blood shed for them."[46]

1:6 As the apostle continues his doxology in v. 6, he varies the construction, changing from a participle in the dative case (*tō agapōnti*, 1:5) to the finite verb ἐποίησεν (*epoiēsen*, "he made"). This verb in the indicative mood marks a sort of parenthetical statement, because the dative construction of 1:5*b* is resumed by the αὐτῷ (*autō*, "to Him") in 1:6*b*.[47] "Parenthetical" is not to be taken to mean "less emphatic," however, because the finite verb form *epoiēsen* carries more emphasis than a participle.

The sense of the aorist indicative of the verb is to mark what has been ideally or potentially accomplished in the purpose of God (Beckwith). The completed work of Christ in making believers a kingdom is offered as another evidence of His on-going love expressed in the previous verse.

Βασιλείαν* (*basileian*, "kingdom") is a collective designation for all believers in Christ. This corporate designation recalls a continuing NT theme traceable to the beginning of Jesus' parabolic teaching regarding the mysteries of the kingdom (Matt. 13:1-52). This theological entity is noticed from time to time by other NT writers (e.g., Col. 1:13). The present kingdom pales into minor significance in the context of Revelation, however. *Basileia* is the word used most often in the LXX, and the NT to speak of the messianic rule and kingdom,[48] an emphasis that most vividly carries over into John's Revelation. It reaches a climax in chapter 20 where the future share of the saints in Christ's earthly rule is expressly stated (20:4; cf. 5:10; 11:15).

Another evidence of Christ's on-going love for believers is His appointment of them as priests (ἱερεῖς [*hiereis*, "priests"]). Corporately they are a "kingdom," but individually they are "priests" (Alford). The priestly office established by the OT law was hereditary, and only members of Aaron's family were eligible. Jesus Christ has provided a new family relationship by which all believers have a priestly ministry to God (Bullinger). Their opportunity for priestly service is a continuing theme in the remainder of the Apocalypse (5:10; 20:6; cf. Ex. 19:6; Isa. 61:6; 1 Pet. 2:5, 9).

The combination *basileian, hiereis* has been identified as a *hen-*

---

46. Swete, *The Apocalypse*, p. 7.
47. Ibid., p. 8.
48. Abbott-Smith, *Lexicon*, p. 77.

diadys, a pair of nouns, one of which functions as a superlative adjective (Bullinger). Believers are either "royal priests of the highest order" (Bullinger) or "a kingdom of subjects with direct priestly access to God." The latter is the more probable sense because of Revelation's emphasis upon the kingdom and ruling as kings (5:10; 20:4, 6).

The priestly service is directed to "His God and Father" (τῷ θεῷ καὶ πατρὶ αὐτοῦ [*tō theō kai patri autou*]) (1:6). This naming is unlike "*our* God and Father" used so often in Paul's writings (e.g., Gal. 1:4, but see elsewhere such as 2 Cor. 1:3), but John 20:17 expresses the common Pauline relationship in addition to the one found here (Bullinger).

With αὐτῷ (*autō*, "to Him") the writer returns to the dative case with which he began the doxology in v. 5. Without doubt the antecedent is "Jesus Christ," the same as the antecedent of *autou* at the end of v. 5. He is the object of ἡ δόξα καὶ τὸ κράτος (*hē doxa kai to kratos*, "glory and strength"). "Glory and strength" are among the tributes to the one who sits upon the throne in the doxology of 5:13. Among John's later apocalyptic visions the earliest addressed to Jesus is in 5:12.

The sense of some verb such as ἔστω (*estō*, "be") is to be understood in this doxology: "*let* glory and strength *be* to Him."

The words εἰς τοὺς αἰῶνας τῶν αἰώνων* (*eis tous aiōnas tōn aiōnōn*, "forever and ever") express the unending duration of the deserved glory and strength that are attributed to Jesus Christ. This strengthened expression for eternity, literally "to the ages of the ages," is the rendering of a Hebrew idiom. It was unknown among classical writers. The Hebrew counterpart is עַד־עוֹלְמֵי עַד (*'ad-'ôlĕmê 'ad*, "for the futurities of perpetuity") (cf. Isa. 45:17) (Bullinger).

The doxology closes with the word ἀμήν (*amēn*), a common practice with doxologies in the NT (Rom. 1:25; 15:33; Gal. 1:5; 1 Tim. 1:17). Among Jews and Christians this was the customary solemn response to show approval of the words of others, probably including a commitment to what is expressed in those words also. The Greek term comes from the Hebrew word אָמֵן (*'āmēn*, "be firm").[49] That it was a regular part of Christian worship is the indication of 1 Cor. 14:16 where "amen" is the response to a prophetic utterance.[50] In the synagogue it was the response to the prayers of the leader of the meeting.[51] In this verse it marks the assent and commitment of

---

49. D. E. Aune, *Prophecy in Early Christianity and the Ancient Mediterranean World* (Grand Rapids: Eerdmans, 1983), p. 165.
50. Ibid., p. 327; Swete, *Apocalypse*, p. 9.
51. J. Massyngberde Ford, *Revelation*, vol. 38 of AB (Garden City, N.Y.: Doubleday, 1975), p. 379.

the writer to the truthfulness of all the affirmations about Jesus Christ, His identity and accomplishments, but especially His worthiness to receive glory and strength, as expressed in the doxology of vv. 5b-6. *Amēn* is used this way six other times in this book (cf. 1:7; 5:14; 7:12 [twice]; 19:4; 22:20).[52]

Additional Notes

1:4 A literary style known as "drama" is common to apocalyptic writings of John's time, but the feature of this work that distinguishes it from all other apocalyptic writings is that it combines the epistolary style of writing with the dramatic.[53] The most distinctly epistolary aspects of this book are confined to 1:4-6 and 22:21, but some elements of epistolary style may be detected in chapters 2-3 also.

The three-member title ἀπὸ ὁ ὢν καὶ ὁ ἦν καὶ ὁ ἐρχόμενος bears a strong resemblance to the OT name of God called the "Tetragrammaton" (יהוה, *YHWH*) (cf. Ex. 3:14).[54] It focuses upon His eternal being as does the Tetragrammaton, but this title sees Him as the eternal being of the past and present who in addition is to come in future judgment (Lee). Such an allusion to this OT name of God is reminiscent of similar references to the name in John's gospel by means of ἐγὼ εἰμί (e.g., John 8:58).

The suggestion that "the seven spirits" are a reference to the attributes (or exercise of them) of Christ falters in all the contexts of the phrase except 3:1 where it has been interpreted to refer to His communicating of the spiritual powers of life, His omniscient and heart-searching knowledge, and His unlimited power to punish and reward.[55] Because of the absence of substantial support for this suggestion, discussion is limited to the possibilities of the spirits being angels or the Holy Spirit.

One effort to support the angelic identity of "the seven spirits" resorts to the seven archangels who were known to Jewish tradition of the time: Uriel, Raphael, Raguel, Michael, Saraquael, Gabriel, and Remiel (1 Enoch 20:1-8; cf. Tobit 12:15; Esd. 4:1; Dan. 10:13) (Mounce). These originally were astral deities who supposedly were

---

52. A seventh possible use of ἀμήν (cf. 22:21) involves a questionable textual variant.
53. John Wick Bowman, *The Drama of the Book of Revelation* (Philadelphia: Westminster, 1955), pp. 2, 11.
54. Alford, *Greek Testament*, 4:548; for a discussion of יהוה see Kenneth L. Barker, "YHWH Sabaoth: 'The LORD Almighty,'" in *The NIV: The Making of a Contemporary Translation*, ed. Kenneth L. Barker (Grand Rapids: Zondervan, 1986), pp. 106-9.
55. E. W. Hengstenberg, *The Revelation of St. John*, 2 vols. (New York: Carter, 1852), 1:162.

degraded into angels to protect the monotheism of Judaism (Charles). This suspicious rationale for the angelic identification represents a strange intrusion of Jewish tradition into Christian thought, however (Mounce).

A further consideration to oppose this view of identifying the seven spirits with the Holy Spirit here is derived from 3:1 where the καί can be given an ascensive sense ("even"). This in turn identifies the seven spirits with the seven stars who are identified as seven angels in 1:20 (Smith). Although the ascensive use of καί is an established characteristic of Revelation, nevertheless there is no contextual basis for understanding it in that sense in 3:1. Just because the seven spirits are grammatically parallel with the seven stars in this verse, it does not necessarily follow that they are placed on the same footing. One expression speaks of a divine Being and the other of created beings.

1:5 The anarthrous Ἰησοῦ is used nine times in the Apocalypse (1:9 [twice]; 12:17; 14:12; 17:6; 19:10 [twice]; 20:4; 22:16), an unusually great frequency compared to the rest of the NT books. There are only five articular occurrences. Two other Johannine books bear the same characteristic. The gospel of John has 93 anarthrous uses and the first epistle of John has five. This is in great contrast with the epistles of Paul (less than 10) and Peter (no occurrences).[56]

The alleged grammatical error of having nominative inflectional endings ὁ μάρτυς, ὁ πρωτότοκος, and ὁ ἄρχων in apposition with the genitive Ἰησοῦ Χριστοῦ is in reality a figure of speech utilized for the sake of rhetorical force. The other alternative of using genitive inflectional forms for these three titles would have resulted in ten consecutive words in the genitive form (sixteen consecutive words if the καί is discounted). Such a phenomenon would have obscured the meaning of a text that is quite clear in the form in which we have it.[57]

Some less reliable manuscripts read the aorist ἀγαπήσαντι instead of the present participle ἀγαπῶντι cited in the discussion above. In addition to enjoying this weaker manuscript support, the aorist participle would have been less difficult for a scribe to copy because Christ's love for believers is most commonly spoken of in the aorist in the rest of the NT. Some scribes could have assumed that the present participle resulted from an earlier scribal error, because Christ's love

56. J. H. Moulton and A. S. Geden, *A Concordance to the Greek Testament* (Edinburgh: T. & T. Clark, 1926), pp. 478-85.

57. Apostolos Makrakis, *Interpretation of the Revelation of St. John the Divine* (Chicago: Hellenistic Christian Education Society, 1948), p. 17.

is not elsewhere depicted by a present tense, and arbitrarily changed it to an aorist. Hence, the present participle is the preferred reading.

An alternative reading for λύσαντι ἡμᾶς is λούσαντι. This latter reading has some impressive manuscript support, but all things considered, the balance of external evidence is more in support of the former. The figure is that of being loosed by means of Christ's blood rather than being washed or cleansed from impurity in His blood. The picture of washing one's robe and making it white in the blood of the Lamb *is* found in 7:14.

1:6 The finite verb ἐποίησεν connected to an earlier articular participle (τῷ ἀγαπῶντι) by καί is a Hebraism. Other instances of this construction are in 2:20 (ἡ λέγουσα . . . καὶ διδάσκει) and 7:14 (οἱ ἐρχόμενοι . . . καὶ ἔπλυναν).[58] The idiom is also found in 1:18; 2:2, 9; 3:9; 14:2-3; 15:3. After using a participle or an infinitive, Hebrew writers often followed with a finite verb.[59] This construction in the Hebrew OT is occasionally reproduced by the LXX (e.g., Gen. 49:17; Ps. 92:8; Jer. 23:32; Amos 5:7) (Charles). Because of John's frequent employment of this participle-finite verb idiom in Revelation, Charles doubts the parenthetical nature of the expression. Although John's fondness for the construction may be acknowledged, it is still infrequent enough to warrant special attention whenever it occurs. Besides this, he returns to the dative construction of the participles with the αὐτῷ in the middle of v. 6, proving the parenthetical nature of the finite verb clause.

Βασιλείαν has much better MS support than βασίλειον or βασιλεὶς καί. Βασίλειον would have focused on the priesthood of believers as the primary emphasis of the clause (cf. 1 Pet. 2:9). Βασιλεὶς καί would have pictured individual believers as kings. The accepted reading βασιλείαν looks at believers corporately and calls them "a kingdom." A few MSS, including one that reads βασίλειον rather than βασιλείαν earlier in v. 6, read ἱεράτευμα (cf. 1 Pet. 2:9) instead of ἱερεῖς. Their witness is so slight, however, that it does not merit serious consideration.

Two strong witnesses (p[18] A) omit τῶν αἰώνων from εἰς τοὺς αἰῶνας τῶν αἰώνων, but the assortment of witnesses favoring its inclusion is sufficient to attest its genuineness. This longer form of the expression is the more common one in Revelation (cf. 1:18; 4:9, 10; 5:13; 7:12; 10:6; 11:15; 14:11; 15:7; 19:3; 20:10; 22:5).

---

58. Robertson, *Word Pictures*, 6:353.
59. S. R. Driver, *A Treatise on the Use of the Tenses in Hebrew* (Oxford: Clarendon, 1892), par. 117.

3. THEME (1:7-8)

Translation

> ⁷**Behold, He comes with the clouds,**
> **and every eye will see Him,**
> **even those who pierced Him,**
> **and all the families of the earth will mourn over Him.**
> **Yes, amen.** ⁸**"I am the Alpha and the Omega, says the Lord God, who**
> **is and who was and who is coming, the Almighty."**

Exegesis and Exposition

1:7 Without warning, following the address and doxology, the writer inserts the first prophetic oracle of the book (1:7-8). It is characteristic of the Apocalypse that ἰδού (*idou*, "behold") indicates a special divine intervention. This usage is no exception. Sayings thus introduced are not always oracles in a technical sense, but this one meets the oracular criteria, with John the speaker in v. 7 and God in v. 8.[60] The only other oracle in the book where God speaks is 21:5-8, a factor that reflects the importance of these two verses in the overall structure of the Apocalypse.[61]

The content of v. 7 confirms its important contribution. It tells the topic of the whole book: the coming of Jesus Christ. To do so, it uses a conflation of two OT passages: Dan. 7:13 and Zech. 12:10. Jesus Himself had earlier used the same combination of passages in His Olivet discourse to speak of His second advent (Matt. 24:30) in a statement John had heard with his own ears about sixty-five years before penning these words (cf. Mark 13:4). John's use of *idou* in the present verse is an added feature, however. Though not an invariable indicator of oracular speech, it is often so used in the OT and NT (e.g., 1 Cor. 15:51; Rev. 2:10, 22; 3:8, 9, 20). This writer uses the word twenty-six times. Five of the other uses are in conjunction with the verb ἔρχομαι (*erchomai*, "I come"). Three of the five call special attention to the personal return of Christ as 1:7 does (cf. 16:15; 22:7, 12). In each case the particle fastens the reader's attention on the importance of the forthcoming announcement.

"The coming one" (ὁ ἐρχόμενος [*ho erchomenos*]) is Christ's "great name in Old Testament prophecy" (cf. Matt. 11:3) (Lenski). It is therefore no surprise that the understood subject of ἔρχεται (*erchetai*, "He comes") in v. 7 is "Jesus Christ" (cf. 1:5) who is the object of praise in the doxology of 1:5b-6. This same verb is used directly or indirectly eleven more times in this book in reference to the return of Christ (cf.

---

60. Aune, *Prophecy*, pp. 280, 433 n. 7.
61. Ibid., p. 280.

1:4, 8; 2:5, 16; 3:11; 4:8; 16:15; 22:7, 12, 20 [twice]), seven coming from the lips of Christ Himself (2:5, 16; 3:11; 16:15; 22:7, 12, 20). The current verse obviously is the theme verse for the whole book (Tenney). Sequentially in the book's development, His personal coming is described in 19:11-16, but the verb also describes preliminary phases of His return for judgment (cf. 2:5, 16).

Though not a precise quotation of Daniel 7:13 in either the Aramaic or its Greek translation in the LXX, the first five words of v. 7 are clearly dependent on it (see also Matt. 24:30; Mark 13:26; Luke 21:27). This OT statement tells of Daniel's vision in which he saw the future coming of the Son of Man to assume rule over a worldwide and unending kingdom (Dan. 7:14, 27). Though details of His coming are not developed at this point, the phrase μετὰ τῶν νεφελῶν (*meta tōn nephelōn*, "with the clouds") indicates that He will come from above. The heavenly origin of His return is made even clearer in 19:11, 14.[62]

The remainder of v. 7 alludes to Zech. 12:10, 12, 14. The context of Zechariah 12 is the future repentance of the tribes of Israel in the day the Lord restores Jerusalem and the nation to a place of supremacy. In adapting the passage to the Apocalypse, John emphasizes a universality of interest in the advent of the Lord. Such widespread attention is implied in Zechariah 12, but the words πᾶς ὀφθαλμός (*pas ophthalmos*, "every eye") in this verse make it quite explicit. It is inevitable that the whole human race witness the return of Christ (Alford).

Clarification of who is intended by "every eye" is offered in the third clause of the verse. The καὶ (*kai*, "even") that introduces καὶ οἵτινες αὐτὸν ἐξεκέντησαν (*kai hoitines auton exekentēsan*, "even those who pierced Him") is one of the frequent ascensive uses of *kai* in this book (cf. 1:2) (Beckwith). Those referred to in this clause are a class within the human race indicated by "every eye" of the previous clause (Beckwith). This prominent class within the larger group is composed of the ones who pierced Him. The smaller group surely includes the Jewish people responsible for the crucifixion of Christ. Zechariah 12:10 indicates their involvement, but so does John 19:37 where John again cites Zech. 12:10 in connection with the crucifixion of Christ. Roman involvement in His execution is also indicated in that gospel context (cf. John 19:31) (Charles). The inclusion of the Romans is likely in the present clause because anti-Romanism is so readily ap-

---

62. Longman finds a continuation of an OT theme of the Divine Warrior as a "Cloud Rider" in this verse because of its use of Dan. 7:13 (Tremper Longman III, "The Divine Warrior: the New Testament Use of an Old Testament Motif," *WTJ* 44, no. 2 [Fall 1982]: 296). The Divine Warrior image is a frequent one in Revelation, especially in 19:11ff. (ibid., pp. 297-300).

parent elsewhere in the Apocalypse (Beckwith). Obviously that earlier generation of Jews and Romans is dead and will not be alive to witness the Lord's return, but a class of people closely akin to them in opposing Christ will be among those future witnesses.

The final clause of v. 7 lends itself to two possible interpretations. The first suggestion is that πᾶσαι αἱ φυλαί (*pasai hai phylai*, "all the tribes") refers to the tribes of Israel, τῆς γῆς (*tēs gēs*, "the land") refers to the land promised to Abraham, and κόψονται (*kopsontai*, "they shall mourn") refers to a mourning of repentance (Hort; Seiss). The merit of this explanation is that it matches the meaning of the OT source passage, Zech. 12:10 ff.[63] When the leading role played by the Jews in the crucifixion of Christ is noted (cf. John 19:37; Acts 2:22, 23; 3:14, 15), the case for this explanation of the words is even stronger (Moffatt; Smith). Another supporting consideration is the consistent use of *hai phylai* in the LXX and NT to refer to the tribes of Israel (Johnson). Then too it is well known that the repentance of Israel and her consequent national blessing are associated with the return of Christ that is so prominent in this book as a whole (Bullinger). This first proposal regarding the mourning of v. 7 has much to commend it.

A second way of explaining the last clause of v. 7 is as follows: (1) *pasai hai phylai* refers to "all the families" of the earth, not just to Jewish tribes; (2) *tēs gēs* refers to "the earth" in the sense of the whole world; and (3) *kopsontai* refers to a mourning of despair by a sinful world over the judgment of Christ at His return.[64] That Jesus uses the same passage to denote a mourning of despair in Matt. 24:30 strongly favors this approach (Lee; Charles). Inasmuch as John's use of these words in Rev. 1:7 agrees more in form with Matt. 24:30 than with Zech. 12:12, the sense of the Olivet Discourse is a more decisive factor (Beckwith; Charles). Probably the strongest evidence favoring this second view is the later context of the book where mourning is generally remorse that accompanies the disclosure of coming divine judgment (cf. 16:9, 11, 21) (Mounce). Here then is an issue where the two diverse explanations both have respectable support.

In weighing the two options, one is impressed that a significant difference between this passage and Matt. 24:30 is the absence of ἐπ' αὐτόν (*ep' auton*, "over Him"), which is found here, but not there. To some this can only be explained by a difference of meaning in the two places, mourning there and repentance here (Beckwith). Yet on the other side, not too much can be made of the limited Jewish scope of

---

63. Lee, "Revelation," 4:502; J. P. M. Sweet, *Revelation* (Philadelphia: Westminster, Pelican, 1979), p. 67; Caird, *Revelation*, p. 18.
64. Richard Chenevix Trench, *Commentary on the Epistles to the Seven Churches in Asia* (London: Parker, Son, and Bourn, 1861), p. 17.

hai phylai in the LXX and the rest of the NT, because the Apocalypse uses the word more broadly to refer to peoples of all nations (cf. 5:9; 7:9; 11:9; 13:7; 14:6).[65] The weightiest consideration of all appears to be the worldwide scope of the book. "Those who dwell on the earth" (3:10; 6:10; 8:13; 11:10 [twice]; 13:8, 12, 14 [twice]; 17:2, 8) are the objects of the wrath that is pictured in its pages, and evidence points to the multi-ethnic nature of this group. The scope of the judgments of the book is also worldwide, not localized (e.g., 14:6; 15:4). Besides this, the people on whom these judgments fall do not respond by repenting as the first view suggested above might imply (cf. 9:20, 21; 16:9, 11). A weighing of all considerations points to the second option as the correct meaning of this clause. This carries the sense, "All the families of the earth will mourn over Him with remorse because of the severity of punishment inflicted upon them in conjunction with His return." Taken in this sense, the statement provides a grim preview of what lies ahead for the world. The return of Christ is anything but a comfort to those who continue in their rebellion against Him.

Verse 7 ends with a double affirmation of the certainty of fulfillment of the prophetic oracle just given. Ναί (*Nai*, "yes") is the usual word of affirmation in the Greek language, and it is followed by the Hebrew word of affirmation *amēn* (cf. 1:6). Combined this way, the two words constitute the figure of speech called *synonymia*, whose function is to strengthen the certainty of what has just been prophesied (Bullinger). They are used in a similar way in 22:20 with the effect of saying, "It is so, amen" (Charles). It is absolutely fixed that the coming of Christ will happen as prophesied and will bring with it the resultant effects noted earlier in the verse.

1:8 As though not satisfied that he has made the prophecy's certain fulfillment plain, in v. 8 the prophet adds the emphatic declaration of God the Father as further verification of this fact. The implied thought is that the prophecy of v. 7 is just as sure to be fulfilled as is the credibility of the speaker who identifies Himself in v. 8 by these very significant titles. The sentence can be paraphrased, "I, the Almighty Lord of hosts, the unchangeable God, will accomplish all My will, fulfill all My word, and execute all My judgments" (Bullinger).

---

65. Johnson, "Revelation," 12:423. The handling of Rev. 1:7 by reconstructionist authors errs badly in limiting the scope of judgment to the land of the Jews, specifically the judgment of A.D. 70 (cf. David Chilton, *The Days of Vengeance: An Exposition of the Book of Revelation* [Fort Worth, Tex: Dominion, 1987], pp. 65-67; Kenneth L. Gentry, Jr., *Before Jerusalem Fell: Dating the Book of Revelation* [Fort Worth, Tex: Institute for Christian Economics, 1989], pp. 123-32). Not only do they miss the worldwide scope of the book's implications, they also fail to furnish a satisfactory explanation of Christ's non-appearance on that earlier occasion.

The specific identity of the speaker of these words is not immediately clear. Is the spokesman God the Father or God the Son? Persuasive evidence has been advanced in favor of the latter identification. Ἐγώ εἰμι (Egō eimi, "I am"), the words with which the verse begins, is a frequent self-designation appropriated by Jesus in the NT, especially in the gospel of John (e.g., John 8:58) (Caird). Τὸ Ἄλφα καὶ τὸ Ὦ (to Alpha kai to Ō, "the Alpha and the Omega") is a self-description by Jesus in Rev. 22:13. It more probably carries the same force in this verse.[66] Jesus Christ has been the central figure in vv. 1-7. A switch to God the Father in v. 8 is improbable because it is so abrupt (Walvoord). The case is further strengthened by a comparison of this verse with Rev. 1:17-18, where similar titles are without question applied to Christ (Smith). Lastly, because erchetai in v. 7 clearly refers to Christ's coming, the same must be the case with ὁ ἐρχόμενος (ho erchomenos, "the coming one") in v. 8. The evidence in favor of seeing Christ as the speaker is impressive.

Yet so is the evidence favoring the Father. Κύριος ὁ θεός (kyrios ho theos, "the Lord God") is a title of God the Father throughout the OT, beginning in Genesis 2 (Bullinger; Alford). Furthermore, ὁ ὢν καὶ ὁ ἦν καὶ ὁ ἐρχόμενος (ho ōn kai ho ēn kai ho erchomenos, "the one who is and who was and who is coming") is a title for the Father in 1:4, as shown there. It is only plausible that it should have that connotation here also (Smith). In the LXX ὁ παντοκράτωρ (ho pantokratōr, "the Almighty") renders the Hebrew expression for "Lord of hosts," except in Amos 4:13 where it renders "God of hosts," and in the book of Job where it is used for the Hebrew "Shaddai" (Bullinger; Alford). Remembering that similar words are spoken by the Father in 21:6 (Mounce), one cannot help being impressed by the strength of the case for seeing God the Father as the speaker in v. 8.

Whichever conclusion is correct, it is clear that a close affinity exists between the Father and the Son in this book. Undoubtedly this results from Christ's being all the fullness of the Godhead (cf. Col. 2:9) and sharing in all the attributes, deity, and totality of the Father (cf. Heb. 1:3) (Hailey). Still, the above issue of identity must be resolved. A weighing of evidence, especially in light of the OT "flavor" of the expressions and a recollection that the Father in the OT refers to Himself as "I am" (i.e., the Tetragrammaton, Ex. 3:14; cf. Isa. 48:12), tips the balance ever so slightly to the side of concluding that God the Father speaks in v. 8. This is His affirmation to confirm the truthfulness of the prophetic oracle of v. 7.

Τὸ Ἄλφα καὶ τὸ Ὦ (to Alpha kai to Ō, "the Alpha and the Omega") is interpreted by ἡ ἀρχὴ καὶ τὸ τέλος (hē archē kai to telos, "the beginning and the end") in 21:6 and by ὁ πρῶτος καὶ ὁ ἔσχατος (ho prōtos kai

---

66. Swete, Apocalypse, p. 11.

ho eschatos, "the first and the last") in 22:13. The primary addressees of the Apocalypse are Greeks, so the first and last letters of the Greek alphabet are used. There is little doubt, however, that a reference is made to the first and last letters of the Hebrew alphabet in Jewish literature to indicate the same truth. The expression stands for totality, a fact about God that is stated in Isa. 41:4; 43:10; 44:6; 48:12. It expresses not only eternity, but also infinitude, "the boundless life which embraces all while it transcends all."[67]

Λέγει κύριος ὁ θεός (*Legei kyrios ho theos,* "Says the Lord God") is frequent in the writing of the OT prophets, particularly Ezekiel (e.g., 6:3, 11; 7:2). By its use here John associates himself with this body of OT spokesmen.[68]

The title "the one who is and who was and who is coming" is fully discussed at v. 4. At this point the eternal Being of the past and present who is to come in judgment adds His affirmation to verify further the certainty of fulfillment of the prophecy of 1:7.

Ὁ παντοκράτωρ (*Ho pantokratōr,* "the Almighty") is used eight other times in the Apocalypse (4:8; 11:17; 15:3; 16:7, 14; 19:6, 15; 21:22). It occurs only once more in the NT and this in an OT quotation (2 Cor. 6:18). In the LXX of Job it translates שַׁדַּי (*šadday,* "Shaddai"), but in the rest of the OT it renders צְבָאוֹת (*ṣĕbā'ôt,* "hosts"). Etymologically, *pantokratōr* is equivalent to ὁ πάντων κρατῶν (*ho pantōn kratōn,* "the one who holds all") or ὁ πάντων ἐξουσιάζων (*ho pantōn exousiazōn,* "the one who has authority over all"). The term focuses on God's sovereignty, and with its emphasis on authority might be rendered "all-ruler" as well as "almighty."[69]

God's declaration in v. 8 thus ends with a note of authority. The omnipotent one will surely implement what His prophet has predicted by way of future judgment.

Additional Notes

1:7 In each place where ἰδού is used, the one who speaks is either God (21:3, 5), Christ (1:18; 2:10, 22; 3:8, 9, 20; 16:15; 22:7, 12), an angel (5:5), or the prophet John speaking in the spirit (4:1, 2; 6:2, 5, 8; 7:9). The identification mark in each such case is the first person singular used by a divine revealer.[70]

---

67. Ibid., pp. 10-11. Aune contends that "the Alpha and the Omega" is a title derived from Greek literature, having closest associations with Hellenistic magical revelation (D. E. Aune, "The Apocalypse of John and Graeco-Roman Revelatory Magic," *NTS* 33, no. 4 [Oct 1987]: 489-91). This can hardly be the case, however. The rest of the titles in the verse have too strong an OT flavor, as does the book as a whole, for this to be true.
68. Swete, p. 11.
69. Ibid.; cf. Barker, "YHWH," pp. 109-10.
70. Aune, *Prophecy,* pp. 279-80.

The verb form ἔρχεται is an example of the futuristic use of the present tense, the future connotation being provided by the word's meaning. The idea is that Christ is already on His way, i.e., He is in the process of coming and hence *will* arrive. This use of the present tense enhances emphasis on the imminence of that coming (cf. ἔρχομαι, John 14:3).

In the LXX the prepositional phrase represented here by μετὰ τῶν νεφελῶν is ἐπὶ τῶν νεφελῶν. Matthew's wording of the phrase is the same as in the LXX. Mark and Luke differ from the others and from each other. Mark has ἐν νεφέλαις, and Luke uses ἐν νεφέλῃ. John too is distinctive in Rev. 1:7 in his use of μετὰ τῶν νεφελῶν ("with the clouds"). No great difference in meaning attaches to the four variations of the expression. They all indicate an upward direction in relation to the earth. The Son of Man will return "upon the clouds *of heaven*" as the text of Dan. 7:13 points out. His return will be from the direction of the sky above.

The choice of ἐκκεντέω to render the Hebrew דָּקָר of Zech. 12:10 in John 19:37 and Rev. 1:7 adds strength to the case that the two books had the same author. Both uses differ from the LXX's obviously erroneous choice of κατορχέω to render the same Hebrew word.

1:8 No conjunction connects v. 8 with v. 7. The impact of this asyndeton heightens further the already emphatic nature of v. 8.

2
John's Vision of the Glorified Christ

B. JOHN'S COMMISSION TO WRITE (1:9-20)

After including God's emphatic declaration (1:8) that confirms the prophetic theme of the book (1:7), John turns his attention to a description of his first revelatory encounter with Christ on the island of his exile. Initially he tells the circumstances of his *first commission to write* (1:9-11). Then he furnishes a detailed description of *the source of the commission* (1:12-16). He closes with words about interaction with the one who gave him the commission and a *restatement of the commission* which expands the initial command with a more detailed statement of what he was to write (1:17-20).

1. THE FIRST COMMISSION TO WRITE (1:9-11)

Translation

⁹I John, your brother and fellow-partaker in the affliction and kingdom and endurance in Jesus, came to be in the island that is called Patmos because of the Word of God, even the testimony of Jesus. ¹⁰I came to be in the spirit on the Lord's day, and I heard behind me a loud sound as [that] of a trumpet, ¹¹saying, "Write what you see in a scroll and send it to the seven churches, to Ephesus and to Smyrna and to Pergamum and to Thyatira and to Sardis and to Philadelphia and to Laodicea."

Exegesis and Exposition

1:9 With the self-designation ἐγὼ Ἰωάννης (*egō Iōannēs*, "I John") the writer names himself for the third time in the short span of nine verses (cf. 1:1, 4). Setting aside the preliminaries of the prologue, he gives an account of his initial vision of Christ and the commission to write that resulted therefrom. In contrast with what might be termed ecstatic words in 1:7-8, he begins addressing the seven churches directly. The form of self-designation represented in *egō Iōannēs* is customary among apocalyptic writers (cf. Dan. 7:28; 8:1; Enoch 12:3; 4 Esdr. 2:33; Rev. 22:8),[1] but it is not limited to apocalyptic style. Elsewhere in the NT usages of this sort carry the connotation of a claim of authority by a writer or speaker, a force quite appropriate in the present context.

John relates himself to his readers in a twofold manner: ὁ ἀδελφὸς ὑμῶν καὶ συγκοινωνός (*ho adelphos hymōn kai synkoinōnos*, "your brother and fellow-partaker"). With the former term *adelphos* he puts himself on the same level as his readers. He could have claimed the official status of an apostle or elder, an authoritative posture that would serve an important function in his conflicts with some elements in the seven churches (e.g., 2:20-22), but he claims no official status. He is satisfied to use a title that the apostles and elders shared with all Christians (cf. Acts 15:23; 2 Pet. 3:12) (Swete).

With the latter term, *synkoinōnos,* he draws upon the thought of fellowship or sharing that was quite common among early Christians. *Koinōneō* with its cognates and *synkoinōneō* with its cognates are used more by Paul than anyone else (thirty times; e.g., Rom. 12:13; Phil. 4:14), but Peter (three occurrences; e.g., 1 Pet. 4:13; 5:1) and John (eight occurrences; e.g., 1 John 1:3; Rev. 18:4) make frequent use of them also.[2]

The joint participation of which John writes is defined by a prepositional phrase with a compound object: ἐν τῇ θλίψει καὶ βασιλείᾳ καὶ ὑπομονῇ (*en tēthlipsei kai basileiᾳ kai hypomonē* "in the affliction and kingdom and endurance"). The combination of *synkoinōnos* and the first of the three objects, *thlipsei,* is quite similar to Phil. 4:14 where Paul commends the Philippian church for its participation with him by way of financial help in his time of need (συγκοινωνήσαντές μου τῇ θλίψει, *synkoinōnēsantes mou tē thlipsei,* "sharing with

---

1. Henry Barclay Swete, *The Apocalypse of St. John* (London: Macmillan, 1906), p. 11.
2. Ibid., pp. 11-12. Luke is also quite fond of this word group, making use of it ten times (e.g., Luke 5:10; Acts 2:42). Mark (seven uses), Matthew (five uses), the writer of Hebrews (five uses), and Jude (one use) round out the list, which includes all writers of NT books except James.

me in my affliction"). Hebrews 10:33 where θλίψεσιν (*thlipsesin,* "through afflictions") and κοινωνοὶ (*koinōnoi,* "sharers") occur together is also similar, but not quite so close lexically and grammatically. Yet the thought of the Hebrews statement is basically the same: sharing in persecution with other Christians.

Afflictions are not the only thing that Christians have in common, of course. The grammatical combination συγκοινωνός ἐν (*synkoinōnos en,* "fellow-partakers in") closely resembles the κοινωνείτω . . . ἐν (*koinōneitō . . . en,* "share . . . in") of Gal. 6:6. There the one who is instructed in the Word is told to "share in" all good things with the one who instructs. This illustrates the broad spectrum of other areas, besides afflictions, that are shared by believers, but fellowship in suffering is one of the most frequent, if not the most frequent, among the stock of primitive Christian ideas.[3] This is an indispensable element of Christian discipleship and following the example of Jesus (1 Thess. 1:6; 1 Pet. 2:21; 4:13; cf. also 2 Cor. 1:7; Phil. 3:10; 1 Pet. 5:1).

Thlipsei in Rev. 1:9 is linked closely with two other words, *basileią* and *hypomonę,* which combine with it in constituting the sphere of fellowship. The grammatical signal pointing to this is the governance of all three nouns by a single article *tę.* Yet the nature of the relationship of these three is not easy to define. Many explain that the three are viewed separately with the unusual sequence of their listing accounted for by the following rationale: the present experience of tribulation is that which is bringing in the kingdom (Acts 14:22), but endurance is mentioned to remind the readers that the kingdom in its fullness is not yet here; there is still a struggle before it will be attained.[4] The appropriateness of this reasoning is obvious. It fits well against a backdrop of a persecuted church awaiting a future kingdom-deliverance. The unusual nonchronological sequence can be accounted for by noting that, added as an afterthought, *hypomonę* is a quality that must be manifest in tribulation as a condition of inheriting the kingdom.[5] This aligns with Paul's exhortation that "through many afflictions we must enter the kingdom of God" (Acts 14:22). A

---

3. Ibid., p. 12. The grammatical combination συγκοινωνός ἐν is nearly duplicated also in Matt. 23:30 where the κοινωνοί ἐν conveys the idea of "participants in." In the Matthew passage Jesus cites the claim of the scribes and Pharisees that they would not have been among those who "share in" or had a part in shedding the blood of the prophets of OT times.
4. Henry Alford, *The Greek Testament,* 4 vols. (London: Longmans, Green, 1903), 4:553; Swete, *Apocalypse,* p. 12; Isbon T. Beckwith, *The Apocalypse of John* (New York: Macmillan, 1919), p. 433.
5. Beckwith, *Apocalypse,* p. 433; James Moffatt, "The Revelation of St. John the Divine," in *The Expositor's Greek Testament,* ed. W. Robertson Nicoll (Grand Rapids: Eerdmans, n.d.), 5:341.

severe drawback to this understanding of the three concepts, however, is a grammatical one. It simply does not account adequately for the unity of the three indicated by the single article governing them.

An alternative understanding is to see that John has used a figure of speech called *hendiatris*, i.e., the use of three words with only one thought intended. The one idea is "affliction" and the other two words characterize that affliction as being not what the world experiences but what is particularly connected with the "kingdom" (Acts 14:22; 2 Tim. 2:12; Rev. 20:6) and one that requires "endurance" or patient waiting (Rev. 2:2, 3, 19; 3:10; 13:10; 14:12).[6] This view's elevation of θλίψει (*thlipsei*, "affliction") to the prominent role gives due recognition to the grammatical construction (Bullinger) and coincides well with the end of 1:9 where John's exile comes into view. Such a focus on persecution sets a more appropriate stage for the vision and commission that came to John in 1:10 ff. What Jesus had to reveal to and through him must be seen in the light of his own sufferings and those of other Christians. This second view regarding the relationship of the three nouns is superior to the first and should be accepted.

Another issue remains regarding *thlipsei*. Is it the specific tribulation of the last time, identified with "the great tribulation" of 7:14 and "the hour of testing that is about to come on all the inhabited earth" of 3:10,[7] or is it the general tribulation that accompanies Christian living during the present age (Swete)? The former alternative has superficial plausibility because it strikes a note that is predominant throughout the book, that of tribulation immediately preceding the return of Christ.[8] On the other hand, this special eschatological sense would probably have been identified more specifically as "the great tribulation" (cf. 2:22; 7:14). Furthermore, Acts 14:22 furnishes an instance where "kingdom" is eschatological and "tribulation" or "affliction" is not specifically end-time.

The latter option is more persuasive. General tribulation of the Christian life, although it may foreshadow that of the end-time, is not identical with it. John was drinking of the cup of suffering that Jesus had predicted according to Matt. 20:22-23. This cup had already brought the death of John's brother James (Acts 12:2) and was evidenced in the lives of many others (cf. Acts 14:22; Rom. 8:17; 2 Tim. 2:12).[9] This more general meaning of the term better parallels other

---

6. E. W. Bullinger, *The Apocalypse* or *"The Day of the Lord"* (London: Eyre and Spottiswoode, n.d.), p. 149.
7. R. H. Charles, *The Revelation of St. John*, 2 vols., ICC (New York: Scribner's, 1920), 1:21.
8. Beckwith, *Apocalypse*, p. 433; G. V. Caird, *A Commentary on the Revelation of St. John the Divine*, HNTC (New York: Harper & Row, 1966), p. 20.
9. William Lee, "The Revelation of St. John," in *The Holy Bible*, ed. F. C. Cook (London: John Murray, 1881), 4:503.

uses of the word (John 16:33; Acts 14:22) and related words in the NT (e.g., 2 Tim. 3:12).[10]

Little difference of opinion exists over the meaning of *basileią* in 1:9. It is the millennial kingdom described more fully in Revelation 20 (Charles). It is the future kingdom spoken of by Christ (e.g., Luke 12:32; 22:29), Paul (e.g., 1 Thess. 2:12; 2 Thess. 1:5) and James (e.g., James 2:5). Anticipation of this kingdom is an integral part of present Christian experience (Swete). This conclusion is confirmed further by the virtue of "endurance," which is next in the series of three. This is a quality that has as its motivation an expectation of coming deliverance (cf. 1 Thess. 1:3).

Hypomonę̄ is a quality that is constantly connected with Christian living (e.g., Rom. 5:3; 8:35-36; Rev. 2:2-3, 19; 3:10) (Swete). It is the "spiritual alchemy" that transforms those such as John who share in tribulation into citizens of the future kingdom (Charles).

Ἐν Ἰησοῦ (*en Iēsou*, "in Jesus") (1:9) clarifies the realm of John's joint participation in the affliction that relates to the kingdom and requires endurance. This phrase marks such experiences as distinctly Christian, and excludes any reference to sufferings for other causes. He will elaborate on this subject more fully later in v. 9 while detailing the reason for his exile to Patmos.

Ἐγενόμην ἐν τῇ νήσῳ τῇ καλουμένῃ Πάτμῳ (*egenomēn en tę̄ nēsǭ tę̄ kaloumenę̄ Patmǭ*, "I came to be in the island that is called Patmos") explains that the prophet John found himself relocated in new surroundings, an island off the coast of Asia Minor in the Icarian Sea. The thirteen-square-mile island (i.e., ten miles long and five miles wide at its extremities) called Patmos was about forty miles west of the coastal city of Miletus (cf. Acts 20:15, 17; 2 Tim. 4:20). The island is one of a group of about fifty islands called the Dodecanese. Patmos is located between two other islands named Icaria and Leros. Patmos, shaped like a crescent with its horns facing eastward, was a safe place for vessels to anchor during storms and was therefore important to navigators. It was the last stopping place when traveling from Rome to Ephesus and the first stopping place on a return trip to Rome. Being a rocky and barren place, it was chosen as a penal settlement by the Romans, as were other islands in the group. Early Christian tradition says John was sent here during Domitian's reign over Rome (A.D. 81-96) and was forced to work in the mines. Another tradition adds that when Domitian died, John was permitted to return to Ephesus.[11]

---

10. Robert H. Mounce, *The Book of Revelation*, NICNT (Grand Rapids: Eerdmans, 1977), p. 75.
11. Swete, *Apocalypse*, p. 12; Charles, *Revelation*, 1:21; John F. Walvoord, *The Revelation of Jesus Christ* (Chicago: Moody, 1966), p. 41.

Assuming a general awareness that Patmos was an island for criminals, John follows immediately with a clarification of why he was there: διὰ τὸν λόγον τοῦ θεοῦ καὶ τὴν μαρτυρίαν Ἰησοῦ (*dia ton logon tou theou kai tēn martyrian Iēsou,* "because of the Word of God, even the testimony of Jesus"). A good bit of discussion has surrounded the meaning of this expression. Does it mean that John was sent to Patmos to receive the revelations that were to compose this Apocalypse (Alford)? This meaning parallels the experience of Paul in going to Arabia to receive his revelation (Bullinger). The strongest support for this interpretation is that it best coincides with the meaning of the almost identical expression in 1:2.[12] The phrase is, in other words, another name for the book of Revelation (Bullinger). The major weakness of this view is an important difference that exists between the phrase in v. 2 and the one in the present verse. In v. 2 the relative clause ὅσα εἶδεν (*hosa eiden,* "as many things as he saw") defines the meaning of the expression, but no such defining clause is present in v. 9 (Moffatt). Furthermore, the use of *dia* in similar phrases of 6:9 and 20:4 makes it impossible that John was a voluntary resident on Patmos "for the purpose of" receiving the Word of God (Lee).

Another approach to the expression is to see it as meaning that John went to the island to carry out Christ's great commission of making disciples of all nations, in accord with the ordinary apostolic calling (Alford). That the expression, or one very close to it, uniformly refers to the preaching of the gospel through the remainder of the book (cf. 6:9; 12:17; 19:10; 20:4) is the chief evidence for this explanation (Beckwith). It is highly doubtful, however, that John would have left the open door of the mainland urban center of Ephesus to go to a remote, sparsely populated island such as this to preach the gospel (Beckwith; Moffatt).

The most probable meaning of the words is that John was exiled here because of the preaching of the gospel that he had done in other places (Alford). The closely related use of *dia* in 6:9 and 20:4 supports the idea of banishment as the cause, because both passages speak of death by persecution. Also, throughout the remainder of the book the expression refers uniformly to the gospel (cf. 6:9; 12:17; 19:10; 20:4) (Beckwith). This is the sense of "the Word of God" elsewhere also (cf. 1 Thess. 2:13; 2 Tim. 2:9; 1 John 2:7) (Swete). This too is in agreement with an early and practically unanimous tradition regarding the reason for John's presence on Patmos.[13] A final confirmation comes from

---

12. Beckwith, *Apocalypse,* p. 434; J. P. M. Sweet, *Revelation* (Philadelphia: Westminster, Pelican, 1979), p. 67.
13. Alford, *Greek Testament,* 4:553; Beckwith, *Apocalypse,* pp. 434-35; J. B. Smith, *A Revelation of Jesus Christ* (Scottdale, Pa.: Herald, 1961), p. 49; Walvoord, *Revelation,* p. 41; Alan F. Johnson, "Revelation," in *EBC* (Grand

noting the emphasis on affliction and persecution earlier in the verse. Only this viewpoint follows through with that line of thinking (Alford). One objection is worth mentioning. The claim is that because John had leisure to receive visitors and to write, he could not have been under the penalty of some kind of banishment (Bullinger). This is countered, however, by noting Paul's situation of house arrest during his earliest imprisonment in Rome. He enjoyed freedom of ministry while a prisoner. There is no reason John could not have been extended the same.

Dia ton logon tou theou is taken, therefore, as supplying the reason John was sent to Patmos as a prisoner, an imprisonment by the Roman emperor because of his preaching of the gospel in Ephesus and the rest of Asia.

Following the pattern of the similar expression in 1:2, καί (*kai*, "even") is once again taken in an ascensive sense. This means that *tēn martyrian Iēsou* supplies a more specific definition of what is meant by "the Word of God." The genitive *Iēsou* is subjective as it was in 1:2, but further clarification is necessary. Is it the testimony that Jesus bore in conveying to John the contents of the Apocalypse or more generally the one He bore through the preaching of John, without reference to the contents of the book? Earlier discussion of *ton logon tou theou* shows the latter sense to be correct. John's ministry of preaching is viewed as an activity of Jesus, with the Lord testifying through His apostle.

1:10 John follows his note about a geographical change of locations (*egenomēn*, 1:9) with a word about another kind of change (ἐγενόμην [*egenomēn*, "I came to be"], 1:10). The precise nature of the latter change depends on the meaning of ἐν πνεύματι (*en pneumati*, "in the spirit") of v. 10. This is one of a number of NT passages where it is difficult to distinguish whether *pneumati* refers to the human spirit of a Christian or to the Holy Spirit who indwells him. In Rom. 8:9 the identical phrase occurs and clearly speaks of being in the Holy Spirit.[14] That context is quite different, however. Explicitly it refers to the Spirit of God (cf. πνεῦμα θεοῦ [*pneuma theou*, "Spirit of God"], Rom.

Rapids: Zondervan, 1981), 12:424. A recent objection questions the validity of Christian tradition regarding persecution under Domitian and the penal banishment of John, attributing the tribulation mentioned in this verse, and alluded to throughout the book, to John's "symbolic" world (Leonard Thompson, "A Sociological Analysis of Tribulation in the Apocalypse of John," *Semeia* 36 [1986]: 147-74). The likelihood of this theory compared to the early and longstanding tradition regarding John's exile is not very high. Whatever the repression under Domitian, it was sufficient in kind and degree to result in hard times for Christians, including John.

14. Richard J. Bauckham, "The Role of the Spirit in the Apocalypse," *EvQ* 52, no. 2 (April-June 1980): 66-67.

8:9c) and His presence in and control of believers in contrast with those who are under the control of the flesh.

In the present context of Revelation, however, the phrase designates the ecstatic condition into which God placed John for the sake of granting him the revelations of this book (Charles). It has been described as a "state in which the ordinary faculties of the flesh are suspended, and the inward senses opened."[15] In this kind of condition the natural senses, mind, and spirit are not operative in relation to and responsive to the natural world. God brings a man's spirit into direct contact with the invisible spiritual world and with the things in God's own mind, yet in ways accommodated to finite human perception. Luke calls it "ecstasy" (ἔκστασις [*ekstasis*, "trance"], Acts 10:10; cf. Acts 11:5; 22:17) because the spirit is taken temporarily from the ordinary range of contact to one that is wholly new and superior. This was not a revelation through a dream because, unlike Peter in Acts 10:10 and Paul in Acts 22:17, John never slept during the process. His spirit was wide awake, and its powers were exercised with exalted clarity.[16]

The time of this spiritual relocation is expressed in another prepositional phrase, ἐν τῇ κυριακῇ ἡμέρᾳ (*en tę̄ kyriakę̄ hēmerą*, "on the Lord's day"). The meaning of *tę̄ kyriakę̄ hēmerą* is problematic with two conflicting possibilities of meaning dominant. (1) It refers to the eschatological day of the Lord referred to by the OT prophets. According to this approach, John in his ecstatic state was "mystically drawn down among the scenes of the last day."[17] (2) It refers to Sunday, the first day of the week, as "the Lord's day." The ecstatic experience that the prophet has just begun describing took place on a Sunday.[18] A third possible meaning that refers the expression to Easter Sunday (Johnson) has little support.

A reference to the eschatological day of the Lord is certainly relevant to the book as a whole (cf. 6:17; 16:14) (Charles). This coupled with the NT practice of referring to the day of Christian worship as "the first day of the week" (Matt. 28:1; Mark 16:2; Luke 24:1; John 20:1, 19; Acts 20:7; 1 Cor. 16:2) rather than "the Lord's day" adds support to the case for this meaning (Bullinger; Walvoord). A weakness of this explanation includes the observation that the genitive of

---

15. F. J. A. Hort, *The Apocalypse of St. John* (London: Macmillan, 1908), p. 15.
16. R. C. H. Lenski, *The Interpretation of St. John's Revelation* (Columbus, Ohio: Lutheran Book Concern, 1935), p. 58.
17. Bullinger, *Apocalypse*, p. 12; cf. J. A. Seiss, *The Apocalypse*, 3 vols. (New York: Charles C. Cook, 1909), 1:20, 22; Walvoord, *Revelation*, p. 42.
18. Alford, *Greek Testament*, 4:554; Charles, *Revelation*, 1:22-23; Walter Scott, *Exposition of the Revelation of Jesus Christ* (Swengel, Pa.: Bible Truth Depot, n.d.), pp. 35-36.

the noun, κυρίου (*kyriou*), and not the adjective *kyriakē* is always used elsewhere to name the eschatological day of the Lord (Bullinger; Mounce). Another weakness observes that though the eschatological day of the Lord is prominent in the book elsewhere, it is out of place in this immediate context that portrays Christ in His current role as present with the church on earth (Swete; Beckwith).

Referring *kyriakē hēmera* to Sunday agrees with the terminology of a number of Christian writings from the same general area of Asia Minor a short time after the writing of the Apocalypse there.[19] "The Lord's day" came to be the customary way of referring to Sunday by the end of the second century because it was the day of the week on which the Lord was raised from the dead (Swete; Lee; Charles). This understanding of the expression finds further confirmation in the similar expression κυριακὸν δεῖπνον (*kyriakon deipnon*, "the Lord's supper") (1 Cor. 11:20), which was customarily observed by the early church on the first day of the week (cf. Acts 20:7).[20]

The position that has a slight edge is the one that takes the meaning as Sunday. Even though John was carried away in an ecstatic state, he was not carried forward to a future time. To be "in spirit" was not the same as being "transported by the Spirit into" the day of the Lord. A parallel usage of the phrase in 4:1 does not permit this (Alford). *Kyriakē hēmera* as a temporal designation, then, means that John received this first vision on the first day of the week. Quite possibly, this is the first use of this name for Sunday in Christian history. If so, it began a habit picked up by other Christian writers shortly after John's time.

The prophet's experience in this ecstatic state began the same way as Ezekiel's experience of Ezek. 3:12 when he heard a sound behind him (ἤκουσα ὀπίσω μου [*ēkousa opisō mou*, "I heard behind me"], 1:10). Whereas Ezekiel heard "a sound of a great earthquake," however, John heard "a loud sound as [that] of a trumpet" (φωνὴν μεγάλην ὡς σάλπιγγος [*phōnēn megalēn hōs salpingos*]). As throughout the Apocalypse, the loud sound or voice clearly indicates the importance and solemnity of what is about to be spoken (cf. 5:2, 12; 6:10; 7:2, 10; 8:13; 10:3; 11:12, 15; 12:10; 14:2, 15, 18; 16:1, 17; 19:1, 17).[21] The question remains whether it also connotes divine inspiration or authority, however. This latter connotation is probably not present in

---

19. Didache 14:1; Evang. Petri, 35; Ignatius, Ad Magn. 9:1; Melito of Sardis, cited by Eusebius, *H.E.*, 14. 26. 2.
20. Charles, *Revelation*, 1:23; Homer Hailey, *Revelation, an Introduction and Commentary* (Grand Rapids: Baker, 1979), p. 107.
21. David E. Aune, *Prophecy in Early Christianity and the Ancient Mediterranean World* (Grand Rapids: Eerdmans, 1983), pp. 282, 434.

the *phōnēn megalēn* alone,[22] but the addition of *hōs salpingos* does give the total expression the concept of authority.[23] The sound (i.e., voice) that John heard behind him was as loud and clear as a trumpet blast, signaling the necessity to submit to whatever it commanded. Such significance contrasts to trumpet blasts later in the book that relate more to the battlefield as signals to action in conflict (e.g., 8:2, 6, 13; 9:14) (Bullinger).

1:11 The substance of what John heard from the loud voice is introduced by the participle λεγούσης (*legousēs*, "saying"). The voice told the prophet to write what he sees (γράψον [*grapson*, "write"]). This is one of twelve times in the book that he receives such a command (cf. also 1:19; 2:1, 8, 12, 18; 3:1, 7, 14; 14:13; 19:9; 21:5). Such an emphasis on his commission to write and the follow-up instructions to circulate what is written aligns with the author's claim of canonical authority for his work. During this period a literary work of this nature required a special guarantee of its authoritative nature such as is latent in this kind of repetition (cf. Tobit 12:20 and 2 Esdr. 12:37) (Mounce).

The substance of the writing John was to produce comes emphatically at the beginning of its clause: Ὁ βλέπεις (*Ho blepeis*, "What you see"). Sometimes the reference of this relative clause is limited to the vision of 1:12-16,[24] because John receives another command to write in 1:19, this time with an aorist tense ἃ εἶδες (*ha eides*, "what you saw") rather than a present tense *blepeis* found in v. 11. Such a proposal limits the scope of the clause too much, however. The fact that the command to write is followed by instructions that the writing is to be sent to the seven churches shows that it must encompass more than just five verses. "What you see" may just as legitimately be rendered "what you are seeing," which could quite easily carry the action to the end to include everything in the book. Such a force characterizes the present tense in this book (cf. "are proceeding," 4:5; "is descending," 16:21) (Bullinger). The relative clause *ho blepeis* must refer to the actions of the entire book that John was to witness. Another characteristic of the prophet's style also supports the broader understanding. Sometimes he uses a brief statement and follows it up later with one that is more specific or full (cf. 1:4 with 1:11; 7:9 with 7:13-17; 10:3a with 10:6; 12:6 with 12:13-17; 13:1-8 with 17:7-17; 14:1 with 14:4-5; 14:8 with 14:18; 15:1 with 15:5-8; 16:19b with 18:1-24;

---

22. Ibid.
23. Charles, *Revelation*, 1:24; Moffatt, "Revelation," 5:342; William R. Newell, *The Book of Revelation* (Chicago: Moody, 1935), p. 25.
24. Richard Chenevix Trench, *Commentary on the Epistles to the Seven Churches in Asia* (London: Parker, Son, and Bourn, 1861), p. 25.

21:1-2 with 21:9-22:5).[25] This is apparently what he does here, stating in a general way the Lord's command to him in v. 11 and repeating it in 1:19, where he gives more detail regarding the outline of the visions that make up the Apocalypse.

John was to put his written data into a βιβλίον (*biblion*, "scroll") (1:11). This term specifies a roll made of papyrus material, the less expensive of the writing materials used in that day. The more expensive material was parchment made from animal skins, whereas papyrus was made from a plant grown in Egypt. Both writing materials are mentioned in 2 Tim. 4:13, τὰ βιβλία, μάλιστα τὰς μεμβράνας (*ta biblia, malista tas membranas*, "the scrolls, especially the parchments"). After completion, the Apocalypse was a μονόβιβλον (*monobiblon*, "single scroll"), the length of which must have been about fifteen feet.[26]

John's instructions continued with a command to send (πέμψον [*pempson*, "send"]) the scroll to the seven churches already referred to in the epistolary greeting of 1:4. Earlier the province of Asia was noted as the general location of the churches, and in v. 11 the seven cities where these churches were located are named. These cities were centers of seven postal districts, which made them well-suited to publicize the message further, once they received it (Charles).

The order of the names of the seven cities indicates the route the messenger(s) would follow in delivering the Apocalypse to its immediate addressees: εἰς Ἔφεσον καὶ εἰς Σμύρναν καὶ εἰς Πέργαμον καὶ εἰς Θυάτειρα καὶ εἰς Σάρδεις καὶ εἰς Φιλαδέλφειαν καὶ εἰς Λαοδίκειαν (*eis Epheson kai eis Smyrnan kai eis Pergamon kai eis Thyateira kai eis Sardeis kai eis Philadelpheian kai eis Laodikeian*, "to Ephesus and to Smyrna and to Pergamum and to Thyatira and to Sardis and to Philadelphia and to Laodicea"). Starting from Ephesus and moving clockwise, the party of messengers would have proceeded northward about forty miles to Smyrna and about forty more miles to Pergamum. From Pergamum they moved in a southeasterly direction about forty-five miles to Thyatira, then about thirty miles south to Sardis, then about thirty miles east-southeast to Philadelphia, and finally about forty miles southeast to Laodicea. A messenger from each city would present the scroll to his own church who would read and probably make a copy of it before the remaining messenger(s) moved on with the original to the next city (Swete; Charles).

The seven cities chosen as recipients of the Apocalypse were situated on a great circular road that tied together the most populous,

---

25. Beckwith, *Apocalypse*, pp. 242, 436.
26. Frederic G. Kenyon, *Handbook to Textual Criticism of the New Testament* (London: Macmillan, 1912), p. 30.

wealthy, and influential part of the Asian province, the west-central part. Pergamum was the center of communication for the north; Thyatira for an inland district on the northeast and east; Sardis for the wide middle valley of the Hermus; Philadelphia for Upper Lydia, to which it was the door (cf. 3:8); Laodicea for the Lycus Valley and for central Phrygia; Ephesus for the Cayster and Lower Maeander Valleys and coasts; Smyrna for the Lower Hermus Valley and the North Ionian coasts.[27] Two of the seven cities were relatively small, Thyatira and Philadelphia, while several well-known cities of Asia were not included as recipients: Colosse, Hierapolis, Troas, and Tralles (Charles). The seven were apparently seen as locations of the churches with the most representative spiritual situations.

Additional Notes

1:9 Although ἐγώ followed by a proper noun is indeed a combination utilized by apocalyptic writers, it is by no means limited to them. In the NT Paul uses it five times: 2 Cor. 10:1; Gal. 5:2; Eph. 3:1; Col. 1:23; Philem. 19. These five occurrences seem to convey a special compulsion with perhaps an implicit idea of apostolic authority connected with the statement or plea in each case. For example, as Lightfoot observes, the usage in Gal. 5:2 is an assertion of authority, parallel to the force of the same words in Eph. 3:1, though it may include also an indirect refutation of calumnies against Paul, as "I Paul" does in 2 Cor. 10:1.[28]

A sixth use of this ἐγώ-proper name combination is in Rom. 16:22 where Tertius, the amanuensis of Romans, identifies himself. To our knowledge, no reason exists to assign special emphasis to this combination.

The other three uses of the combination in the NT are in the Apocalpyse, two by John (1:9; 22:8) and one by Jesus (22:16). Once again, it is natural to see a special compulsion in the usages because of the authoritative office of each speaker. John speaks authoritatively as a prophet of God and Jesus as the member of the Godhead who made the revelations to the prophet.

Because five of the six combinations of ἐγώ followed by a proper noun in Paul's writings carry an implicit reference to the authority of the speaker or writer, John probably intended for his readers to catch this shade of emphasis in his two uses in the present chapter and in chapter 22.

---

27. W. M. Ramsay, *The Letters to the Seven Churches of Asia* (New York: A. C. Armstrong, 1904), pp. 191-92.
28. J. B. Lightfoot, *The Epistle of St. Paul to the Galatians* (1865; reprint, Grand Rapids: Zondervan, 1982), p. 203.

1:10 The genitive case σάλπιγγος following ὡς is understood in the sense of "as [the sound of] a trumpet." Charles finds such a pregnant construction four other times in the Apocalypse (4:1, 7; 13:2; 16:3) (Charles). He apparently fails to notice the same combination ὡς λεόντων in 9:8 and ὡς κιθαρῳδῶν in 14:2. This comparative particle followed by either a noun or an adjective occurs elsewhere in the NT only in John 1:14; 1 Pet. 1:19; 2:12.

1:11 Though λεγούσης agrees with σάλπιγγος in gender, number, and case, σάλπιγγος is not the true antecedent. Φωνήν is what John heard speaking and the accusative singular λέγουσαν would have been expected (Swete). The grammatical practice of a participle agreeing with a dependent genitive rather than the governing noun is called *hypallage* (Swete). It recurs in Rev. 4:1 where λαλούσης rather than λάλουσα is used (Charles). Another instance of hypallage occurs in 6:7 where λέγοντος rather than λέγουσα is used following φωνὴν . . . ζῴου (Charles).

John receives the opposite command not to write in 10:4, right after the utterance of the seven thunders. Something about the timing of writing may possibly be learned from this one instance of such a prohibition, if it is typical of the rest. Possibly this may mean that he wrote immediately after receiving each vision (Smith). He was about to write the content of the thunders' utterance immediately after hearing it, but was prohibited from doing so. In this case, he was stopped, but in other cases when he was not stopped, he would have written while in his ecstatic condition. Another approach sees the utterances of the seven thunders as atypical and his effort to write immediately afterward as limited to that one occasion. It understands that he did not write while in an ecstatic condition, but after he returned to a normal state following his last vision. This stands to reason inasmuch as he could not send the written message, as commanded later in 1:11, until he returned to normalcy (Beckwith). Dogmatism is impossible in a choice between these two reconstructions, but the latter understanding of John's prophetic experience seems more probable. The repetitive nature of the writing necessitated by the former assumption does not fit as well with the constative aorist γράψον of 1:10.

If the interpretation that 1:19 is a more detailed restatement of the commission of 1:11 is followed, the οὖν of 1:19 marks that verse as a continuation of 1:11. If the scope of ὃ βλέπεις in 1:11 is limited to 1:12-16, the οὖν of 1:19 marks v. 19 as a continuation of 1:18.

The author of Revelation does not often use εἰς for ἐν,[29] so the

---

29. Nigel Turner, *Syntax*, vol. 3 of *A Grammar of New Testament Greek* (Edinburgh: T. & T. Clark, 1963), p. 255.

directional meaning of "to" is chosen over the locational meaning of "in." Therefore, the seven prepositional phrases with εἰς are the practical equivalent of the dative case of ταῖς ἑπτὰ ἐκκλησίαις with which they stand in apposition.

2. THE SOURCE OF THE COMMISSION (1:12-16)

After hearing the initial statement of his commission, John turned to look at the one who gave it to him. Verses 12-16 furnish a rather detailed description of the one he saw when he did so.

Translation

¹²And I turned to see the voice that was speaking with me; and having turned, I saw seven golden lampstands, ¹³and in the middle of the lampstands [I saw] one like the Son of Man, clothed down to the feet and girded at the breast with a golden girdle; ¹⁴and His head and His hair were white as white wool, as snow, and His eyes were as a flame of fire, ¹⁵and His feet were like gleaming bronze as when it is aglow in a furnace, and His voice was like the sound of many waters, ¹⁶and [He was] holding in His right hand seven stars, and from His mouth [was] proceeding a sharp two-edged sword, and His appearance was as the sun shines in its strength.

Exegesis and Exposition

1:12 Since John's commission to write came with his back turned to where the commission was spoken (1:10), his natural response was to turn around to see who was behind him. This obvious purpose in his turning around is stated in βλέπειν τὴν φωνήν (*blepein tēn phōnēn*, "to see the voice") (1:12). This conceptual combination is striking because a voice cannot be seen. Two figures of speech may be identified in explanation of this paradox. One is metonymy of the effect, i.e., "the voice" is used to represent the person speaking (Bullinger). The other is called catachresis or incongruity. This incongruity results from the nature of the metonymy and the use of the verb *blepein* with this particular noun. When the use of metonymy and catachresis are allowed for, the sense of these words becomes, "and I turned to see Him who spoke with me."[30]

---

30. Bullinger, *Apocalypse*, p. 155. Charlesworth argues that the statement is to be understood literally and that the "voice" in 1:10, 12 is a heavenly being or hypostatic creature. He depends heavily on Jewish apocalyptic literature to make his point (J. H. Charlesworth, "The Jewish Roots of Christology: The Discovery of the Hypostatic Voice," *SJT* 39, no. 1 [1986]: 19-41). By his own admission, his case is not decisive (p. 39). His questionable assumption is that the Apocalypse lies in the continuum of Jewish apocalypses (p. 40).

After turning around, John's eyes first saw seven golden lamp-stands. As familiar in common usage, λυχνίας (*lychnias*, "lamp-stands") were stands for portable oil lamps.[31] In the Apocalypse, as the speaker will explain shortly (cf. 1:20), they are emblems of churches in separate cities. The reason for such symbolism is par-tially attributable to the standing of each church in divine favor and its capacity for usefulness in God's work (cf. 2:5). Local Christian assemblies are designed to embody and give forth the light of God throughout the earth (Charles).

The heavy dependence of Revelation on the OT in general proba-bly reflects an even deeper symbolism, however. That the lampstands were seven in number (ἑπτά [*hepta*, "seven"]) and made of gold (χρυσᾶς, [*chrysas*, "golden"]) ties them closely to Zechariah's one golden lampstand with seven lamps, each fed by a pipe from a com-mon reservoir (Zech. 4:2), and to the seven-branched golden lamp-stand that stood inside the first and outside the second veil of the tabernacle of Israel (Ex. 25:31-40) (Swete; Charles). These too were symbolic of the witness that God's people were to bear to surround-ing Gentile peoples.

1:13 The next detail that caught John's eye was a human form located in the middle of the row of lampstands (ἐν μέσῳ τῶν λυχνιῶν [*en mesǭ tōn lychniōn*, "in the middle of the lampstands"]), either behind the fourth lampstand or moving freely from one to another.[32]

At this point commences a series of phrases describing the one whom John saw in this first vision. The titles of Jesus Christ found in the introductions to six of the seven messages in chapters 2 and 3 are drawn largely from this vision of 1:12-20 and its descriptive phrases. Only the message to Laodicea (3:14-22) is devoid of one of these. One of the titles is used in two messages (cf. 2:1 and 3:1) (Charles). It is apparent that the appearance of Christ in this vision is designed to emphasize the aspects of His nature that are most relevant to the needs and circumstances of the seven churches who are the primary recipients of this book.

"One like the Son of Man." John first notes the similarity of this figure to a human form with ὅμοιον υἱὸν ἀνθρώπου (*homoion huion*

---

31. William Henry Simcox, *The Revelation of St. John the Divine* (Cambridge: U. Press, 1893), p. 47.
32. Swete, *Apocalypse*, p. 15. Through a comparison of the following descrip-tion of Christ with several OT passages and other Jewish literature, Row-land sees a development in Jewish angelology whereby a human figure is regarded as an embodiment of the divine, eventually leading to elements of the doctrine of Christ in the early church (Christopher Rowland, "The Vision of the Risen Christ in Rev. i. 13 ff.: The Debt of an Early Christology to an Aspect of Jewish Angelology," *JTS* 31, no. 1 [April 1980]: 1-11). The reasoning leading to his conclusions is farfetched.

anthrōpou, "one like the Son of Man") (1:13). The accusative case of *homoion* indicates that the sense of εἶδον (*eidon*, "I saw") (1:12) carries over from the previous clause and governs this word as its direct object. *Huion*, which follows *homoion*, is also accusative, one of only two times in Revelation when this adjective is not followed by a dative case (cf. 1:15; 2:18; 4:3, 6, 7; 9:10, 19; 11:1; 13:2, 4, 11; 18:18; 21:11, 18). The other use of an accusative following *homoion* is this identical expression *homoion huion anthrōpou* in 14:14 (Swete). In this book ὅμοιος (*homoios*, "like") is practically the equivalent of ὡς (*hōs*, "as") in meaning and construction (Charles).

The sight John witnessed undoubtedly called to his mind an OT passage with which he was quite familiar, Dan. 7:13. This is a passage which Jesus had, in John's presence, applied to Himself some sixty-five years earlier (Mark 13:26) (Swete; Charles). There has not been complete agreement regarding the exact force of the expression, however. Some have understood the expression to convey the human-like form of the one whom John saw and nothing more (Swete). Though "Son of Man" is a Messianic title in the gospels and in Acts 7:56, the Messianic connotation is said to be absent here because in the other passages the title is always articular: ὁ υἱὸς τοῦ ἀνθρώπου (*ho huios tou anthrōpou*, "*the* Son of Man"). The use of a simile, i.e., "[to be] *like* a son of man," rather than a direct identification, i.e., "[to be] the Son of Man," may also be taken as demonstrating the non-Messianic import of the words.

This reasoning is unconvincing, however, and the interpretation that takes *huios anthrōpou* as an exact equivalent of *ho huios tou anthrōpou* is preferred in light of its similarity to כְּבַר אֱנָשׁ (*kĕbar 'ĕnāš*, "like a Son of Man") in Dan. 7:13, where the Messianic connotation is undoubtedly present (Charles). That Jesus applied the same passage from Daniel to Himself in Mark 13:26 is further evidence (Bullinger; Charles). In apocalyptic writings such as Ezekiel and 1 Enoch 37-71 (cf. also 83-90) "man" was used to symbolize an angel. It stands to reason that such an idea, that of a supernatural being, is present here too. Yet the figure is not an angel, but *like* an angel (Charles). That Christ, and not an angel, is meant is obvious from the context (cf. Rev. 1:17-18) (Beckwith).

The appropriateness of the Messianic title "Son of Man" to this context lies in a twofold usage of the words. It is a title related to Jesus' capacity as judge (cf. John 5:22, 27; Acts 17:31), a function that He proceeds to carry out in Revelation 2-3. It also was used by the early church as Christ's title whenever the suffering of believers and Christ's suffering and glory were in view, as they are in this book.[33]

---

33. Richard N. Longenecker, *The Christology of Early Jewish Christianity* (Naperville, Ill.: Alec R. Allenson, 1970), p. 92. For general discussions of

"Clothed down to the feet." The next feature of the speaker's appearance in this first vision of John was the manner in which He was clothed: ἐνδεδυμένον ποδήρη (*endedymenon podērē*, "clothed down to the feet"). The significance of this type of dress has been debated. Early church commentators and some modern ones have taken this aspect of Christ's appearance to signify His high priestly function (cf. Ex. 28:4; Zech. 3:4).[34] Another modern approach is to see in the *podērē* an emblem of rank or dignity as it was in the OT prophets (cf. Ezek. 9:2-3, 11; Dan. 10:5).[35]

In favor of the priestly notion is the usage of *podērēs* in the OT. Six of its seven OT occurrences refer to the attire of the high priest (Mounce). It refers to the breastplate (cf. Ex. 25:6[7]; 35:8[9]), the ephod (cf. Ex. 28:27[31]), and the robe of the ephod (cf. Ex. 28:4; 29:5) (Swete). It designates the high priest's robes of state in Zech. 3:4 (Swete). Yet priests were not the only ones in the OT who wore long robes.[36] If *podērēs* is an intended rendering of the Hebrew מְעִיל (*mᵉyl*, "robe") (cf. Ex. 28:4; 29:5), the term was a common one for men of high rank (e.g., 1 Sam. 18:4; 24:5, 12; Ezek. 26:16). The long robe was a mark of dignity among Orientals (Charles).

The weight of evidence favors the more general meaning of dignity when the same two Greek words come together in Ezek. 9:2 (ἐνδεδυκὼς ποδήρη [*endedykōs podērē*, "clothed down to the feet"). The man so clothed in Ezekiel 9 has the responsibility of setting a mark on some of the Jerusalemites before the destruction of the rest. This setting of impending judgment from Ezekiel fits one of the principal thrusts of the visions to follow in the Apocalypse. In such an environment Christ is often seen extending mercy to those exempted from the punishments about to fall, very similar to the way some of Jerusalem's people in Ezekiel were passed by while this man and six others engaged in striking down the sinful inhabitants of the city. Christ acts to administer mercy in the midst of God's wrath in Revelation (cf. especially Rev. 7:2-3; 9:4), but never in a priestly capacity elsewhere in the book.

In light of these factors the connotation of dignity or high rank is

---

the title "Son of Man," see also Carsten Colpe, "ὁ υἱὸς τοῦ ἀνθρώπου," in *TDNT*, ed. Gerhard Friedrich, trans. and ed. Geoffrey W. Bromiley, 10 vols. (Grand Rapids: Eerdmans, 1976), 8 (1972):400-77; Otto Michel, "ὁ υἱὸς τοῦ ἀνθρώπου," in *NIDNTT*, ed. Colin Brown (Grand Rapids: Zondervan, 1978), 3:613-34; R. G. Gruenler, "Son of Man," in *EDT*, ed. Walter A. Elwell (Grand Rapids: Baker, 1984), pp. 1034-36.

34. Swete, *Apocalypse*, pp. 15-16; Charles, *Revelation*, 1:cxiii; Walvoord, *Revelation*, p. 44.

35. Swete, *Apocalypse*, pp. 15-16; Charles, *Revelation*, 1:26-27; Robert L. Thomas, "The Glorified Christ on Patmos," *BSac* 122 (1965): 243-44.

36. Leon Morris, *The Revelation of St. John*, TNTC (Grand Rapids: Eerdmans, 1969), p. 53.

the more probable connotation of this symbol, with the added idea of the wearer's functioning in conjunction with judgment as in Ezekiel 9 (Beckwith).

"Girded at the breast with a golden girdle." There have been three major suggestions as to the symbolic connotation of περιεζωσμένον πρὸς τοῖς μαστοῖς ζώνην χρυσᾶν (*periezōsmenon pros tois mastois zōnēn chrysan*, "girded at the breast with a golden girdle"): (1) The reference is to the dress of the high priest who wore a priestly girdle on the breast a little above the armpits (Ex. 28:4; 29:5; 39:29; Lev. 16:4) (Moffatt; Charles). (2) The reference is to the divine messenger in Dan. 10:5 who is similarly clad (Swete). (3) The reference is to a description of the angels of the seven last plagues of the Apocalypse (Rev. 15:6).[37]

In defense of the first view, the dignity of an important office associated with high girding has been cited along with the observation that the high priestly office was such a high office (Mounce). Yet the absence from this book of any other reference to Christ's priestly office leaves this connection in doubt (Beckwith). The use of similar terminology to describe the apparel of angels in Rev. 15:6 and the allusion in this phrase and the one immediately before to Dan. 10:5, where priestly dress is absent, serve as further evidence against this view (Charles).

This similarity of the words to Dan. 10:5, along with the fact that the girdle in the Daniel passage was made of gold as is the one in this passage (not made with large amounts of gold thread as the high priest's girdle), enhances the strength of the second proposed meaning. It is further strengthened by the allusion of the previous part of the description, *endedymenon podērē*, to Dan. 10:5. Yet this second meaning does not incorporate the important similarity to the dress of the angels of the seven last plagues in Rev. 15:6 (third view). The best conclusion is to combine the last two views: John thought first of the messenger of Dan. 10:5 when he saw this aspect of the speaker's apparel, but eventually came to realize (as succeeding visions unfolded) that this aspect of the Son of Man's appearance foreshadowed the judgment to be inflicted by the angels of the seven last plagues (Rev. 15:6).

1:14 *"His head and His hair were white as white wool."* After descriptions of two aspects of the speaker's apparel John begins to tell about His person. The allusion of the next part, ἡ . . . κεφαλὴ αὐτοῦ καὶ αἱ τρίχες λευκαὶ ὡς ἔριον λευκόν, ὡς χιών (*hē . . . kephalē autou kai hai triches leukai hōs erion leukon, hōs chiōn*, "His head and His hair were white as white wool, as snow"), is obviously to Dan. 7:9. In the

---

37. Thomas, "Glorified Christ," pp. 243-44.

OT passage comparable words describe the Father, but John refers them to Christ. This is in line with his Christological practice of granting to the Second Person of the Trinity attributes and titles previously reserved for the Father (cf. 1:18; 2:8; 5:12; 22:13) (Swete).

The symbolism in this case pictures the eternal pre-existence of Christ. The idea that white hair suggests Christ's unchangeableness in contrast to decay (Swete), sinlessness (Swete), or suffering[38] is to be rejected. In the Daniel passage it is the "Ancient of Days" who is so described. Thus the focus is on Christ's longevity here.

"His eyes were as a flame of fire." The second feature of the speaker's personal appearance is given in the words οἱ ὀφθαλμοὶ αὐτοῦ ὡς φλὸξ πυρός (*hoi ophthalmoi autou hōs phlox pyros*, "His eyes were as a flame of fire"). The OT source of this expression is Dan. 10:6. In this passage the messenger clothed in linen had eyes "as lamps of fire" (LXX) or "as torches of fire" (Hebrew text). This description of Christ is repeated in Rev. 2:18 and 19:12.

The biblical force of this simile is sometimes that of fierceness against adversaries (e.g., Dan. 10:6), a meaning common in classical writers. It can also convey the notion of penetrating vision and the associated idea of supernatural intelligence in regard to what is seen. This penetrating intelligence, which was associated with quick intelligence and, when appropriate, with righteous wrath, is now attributed to the risen and glorified Christ (cf. Mark 3:5, 34; 10:21, 23; 11:11; Luke 22:61) (Swete; Charles; Beckwith).

1:15 *"His feet were like gleaming bronze as aglow in a furnace."* Next the prophet describes the speaker's feet: οἱ πόδες αὐτοῦ ὅμοιοι χαλκολιβάνῳ ὡς ἐν καμίνῳ *πεπυρωμένης (*hoi podes autou homoioi chalkolibanōhōs en kaminōpepyrōmenēs*, "His feet were like gleaming bronze as when it is aglow in a furnace"). In the NT feet sometimes symbolize movement (cf. Luke 1:79; Acts 5:9; Rom. 3:15; 10:15; Heb. 12:13). Such significance is applicable here to picture Christ's movement among the churches.[39]

The meaning of *chalkolibanō* is uncertain. It is also used in Rev. 2:18, but has not been found elsewhere in extant literature. In ancient times it was interpreted as a "mixed metal of great brilliance," a burnished brass or bronze, a brightly gleaming metal or metallic compound. Similar terminology in Dan. 10:6 refers to "gleaming bronze" (LXX) or "polished bronze" (Hebrew text) (cf. Ezek. 1:7). The emphasis of the term seems to be on the purity of the metal, which is evident in its glowing quality (Swete; Beckwith).

---

38. Arthur E. Bloomfield, *All Things New* (Minneapolis: Bethany Fellowship, 1959), p. 45.
39. Thomas, "Glorified Christ," pp. 244-45.

Pepyrōmenēs describes *chalkolibanǭ* even though the nature of their grammatical agreement is not immediately obvious, the participle being feminine and genitive and the noun being usually regarded as neuter and dative. This problem is only apparent, however, in that the noun is actually feminine and the participle part of a genitive absolute construction.

Another issue is, What is it that the participle says about the "gleaming bronze"? One explanation assigns it the meaning of "smelted" or "refined," referring to metal that has been purified and therefore has a greater shine to it (Charles; Beckwith). The defense of this meaning lies in a comparable usage of the word in Rev. 3:18 with this meaning (Beckwith). Also cited in support of this is the word's OT equivalent צרף (*ṣrp*, "refine"), which always has this meaning (cf. Pss. 12:6; 46:10; Dan. 12:10; Zech. 13:9) (Charles). The question is, however, whether the thought of refinement goes far enough in emphasizing the concept of judgment that pervades the present context (Swete).

It is better to go further and attach to the idea of shining purity that of metal that is still aglow (i.e., in its high-temperature molten state) as though it were still in a crucible (Swete). The main support for this meaning comes from a similar picture of glowing metal in Ezek. 1:13, 27 and Dan. 10:6. In these OT instances the brightness pictures the appearance of the glory of God (Johnson). This understanding also provides better for the idea of judgment in the context and for retaining the contextual reference to fire from the *pyros* of 1:14. This explanation does not exclude an emphasis on purity. It rather adds to it the thought of judgmental enforcement.

The total impact of this feature of the description, then, is to bring attention to Christ's movement among the churches to inculcate purity. This inculcation was done by Christ's rendering of judgment in cases of moral shortcoming.

"*His voice was like the sound of many waters.*" As he penned ἡ φωνὴ αὐτοῦ ὡς φωνὴ ὑδάτων πολλῶν (*hē phōnē autou hōs phōnē hydatōn pollōn*, "His voice was like the sound of many waters"), John had before him as a reminder the endless pounding of the shores of Patmos by waves of the Aegean Sea. Biblically, wording of this sort suggests a powerful force (cf. Ps. 93:4; Isa. 17:13). The angelic hymns of Rev. 14:2 and 19:6 also draw on this power symbol. The specific source of the present words is the Hebrew text of Ezek. 43:2, this simile being absent in the LXX. In the OT passage Ezekiel sees and hears the glory of the God of Israel returning to His Temple in Jerusalem. Christ's voice is here described in exactly the same terms as the voice of God. In the Hebrew of Dan. 10:6, which the writer has followed through much of this description, the messenger's voice is compared to the sound of a multitude, suggesting the idea of confused roar. He moves to Ezekiel at this point, however, so he can identify the speaker with God and the power of His utterance as He returns to dwell with His people (Swete; Charles).

This is the same voice that at the beginning of the vision was described as "loud" and "as a trumpet" (1:10). It is not difficult to explain why John should mention the voice at two separate points of his description. As he writes, he is trying to recall details of an experience that is now wholly in the past. The trumpet similitude is appropriate for the voice's introductory function, and the sound of many waters appropriately suggests the divine authority behind the commission to write the whole book (1:19), especially the seven messages (Revelation 2-3), which John is about to receive for transmission purposes (Beckwith).

1:16 *"[He was] holding in His right hand seven stars."* Of the ten features of the description of 1:12-16, ἔχων ἐν τῇ δεξιᾷ χειρὶ αὐτοῦ ἀστέρας ἑπτά (*echōn en tē dexiā cheiri autou asteras hepta*, "[He was] holding in His right hand seven stars") is the only one that does not draw directly upon the OT, though it does follow OT imagery. It relates strictly to the circumstances of John and the impartation of revelation to him on Patmos. Revelation 2:1 and 3:1 also refer to Christ's holding of the seven stars, but the former verse substitutes a stronger word, κρατέω (*krateō*, "I hold fast"), for ἔχω (*echō*, "I hold") which is found here.

Two suggested meanings for this symbolic representation have arisen: (1) The main idea is that of Christ's absolute authority and complete control over the seven stars (Charles). (2) As in John 10:28, holding in Christ's right hand implies the notion of safekeeping (Beckwith). The latter notion of safekeeping finds support in its being an acknowledged Johannine sense of the figure (Beckwith) and in the customary association of the right hand's being the position of favor and protection (Morris). This certainly fits this setting where John and these churches were objects of persecution.

The former idea of authority and control focuses on references to "stars" elsewhere in Revelation and in the OT where they picture angels (Job 38:7; Rev. 9:1) or faithful witnesses (Dan. 12:3). Because messengers are always in view, control is a more appropriate thought than protection. Also, the right hand is expressive of majestic power and strength (Ps. 110:1; Heb. 1:3, 4) (Hailey), such strength as is needed for the commissioning of messengers. In John 10:28 it is not the *right* hand of Christ that is specified. Perhaps most convincing of all is the usage of the titles in Rev. 2:1 and 3:1 where the nature of the problems in the two churches does not call so much for the idea of protection as for authority and control.

103

Though it is hard to exclude completely either of the suggested meanings of this expression, it does seem that the former, that of control, is uppermost in importance in this description of Christ. Christ's control of the stars is another way of stating His control of the messengers from the seven churches, as 1:20, where the identification of the stars with these messengers is explicitly stated, makes clear. The manner in which the messengers represent the churches is relevant. They represent the churches in such a way as to be practically identical with them. Thus this figure stands for Christ's authority and control over the churches as well as their messengers.

"From His mouth [was] proceeding a sharp two-edged sword." John uses equivalents of the next part of the description, ἐκ τοῦ στόματος αὐτοῦ ῥομφαία δίστομος ὀξεῖα ἐκπορευομένη (*ek tou stomatos autou rhomphaia distomos oxeia ekporeuomenē*, "from His mouth [was] proceeding a sharp two-edged sword"), again in 2:12, 16 and 19:15. The OT source of the words is Isa. 11:4: "He shall strike the earth with the rod of His mouth" (cf. also Isa. 49:2) (Charles). Other NT passages are relevant because they either liken the Word of God to a sword (Eph. 6:17; Heb. 4:12) or else predict that the returning Christ will destroy the man of lawlessness "with the breath of His mouth" (2 Thess. 2:8).

The *rhomphaia* (found elsewhere in the NT only in Luke 2:35) was a large-bladed sword of Thracian origin. For the sword to be regarded, like the spoken word, as coming from the mouth is quite understandable, because the short Roman sword was shaped like a human tongue.[40] For a sword to be "double-edged" meant greater sharpness. Ancient Greek poets also used *distomos*, meaning "double-mouthed" or "double-edged," to describe swords (Swete).

The resultant focus of this part of the description is upon the judicial authority of Christ. It combines the force of a warrior defeating his enemies in battle and the pronouncement of his sentence of judgment upon them.[41]

"His appearance was as the sun shines in its strength." The last part of the speaker's description is ἡ ὄψις αὐτοῦ ὡς ὁ ἥλιος φαίνει ἐν τῇ δυνάμει αὐτοῦ (*hē opsis autou hōs ho hēlios phainei en tē dynamei autou*, "His appearance was as the sun shines in its strength"). This is a portion of the song of Deborah and Barak found in Judg. 5:31. In that passage it describes those who love the Lord. The faces of the righteous are also said to shine like the sun in Matt. 13:43 as is the face of an angel in Rev. 10:1 (cf. 2 Enoch 1:5) (Charles). For John the words had the added association of his experience on the Mount

---

40. James Hastings, *Dictionary of the Bible*, 5 vols. (Edinburgh: Scribner's, 1911), 4:634.
41. Trench, *Seven Churches*, p. 41; Charles, *Revelation*, 1:30; Beckwith, *Apocalypse*, p. 440.

of Transfiguration. On that occasion more than sixty-five years ear-lier Christ's face had "shone like the sun" (Matt. 17:2) as John and two other apostles had witnessed an anticipatory glimpse of the glory to be witnessed in full at Christ's second coming to earth. On this occa-sion the aged apostle is distinguished as being the only one to be given a second foreview of that glory.[42] This feature forms the climax of his initial vision with its allusion to the overwhelming nature of the glory of the ascended Christ.

This first vision of John, then, included an indication of Jesus' Messianic office with its associated functions: judgment of the un-righteous and comfort of the suffering righteous, His high rank that fits Him as an agent of imposing divine wrath, His activity in impos-ing that wrath, His preexistence along with God the Father, His penetrating intelligence that enables Him to perform righteous judg-ment, His movement among the churches to enforce standards of moral purity, His identification with the Father in the power of His utterance, His authority over the seven messengers and the churches they represent, His power to overcome His enemies and pronounce judgment upon them, and His return to earth to implement judg-ment upon mankind.

Additional Notes

1:13 Further relationships between Christ's appearance in the vi-sion of 1:12-20 and the seven messages of chapters 2 and 3 may be delineated. One of the carryover descriptions ὁ περιπατῶν ἐν μέσῳ τῶν ἑπτὰ λυχνιῶν τῶν χρυσῶν in 2:1 bears a verbal resemblance to a warn-ing in the same letter, κινήσω τὴν λυχνίαν σου in 2:5. The thought of the clause ὃς ἐγένετο νεκρὸς καὶ ἔζησεν of 2:8 very possibly is taken up in γίνου πιστὸς ἄχρι θανάτου, καὶ δώσω σοι τὸν στέφανον τῆς ζωῆς of 2:10. In the message to Pergamum ὁ ἔχων τὴν ῥομφαίαν τὴν δίστομον τὴν ὀξεῖαν in 2:12 anticipates τῇ ῥομφαίᾳ τοῦ στόματός μου of 2:16. It also is very easy to see ὁ ἔχων τοὺς ὀφθαλμοὺς αὐτοῦ ὡς φλόγα πυρός (2:18) as looking forward to ὁ ἐραυνῶν νεφροὺς καὶ καρδίας (2:23) in the message to Thyatira (Charles).

The passages where ὅμοιος is followed by dative-case nouns are Rev. 1:15; 2:18; 4:3, 6, 7; 9:10, 19; 11:1; 13:2, 4, 11; 18:18; 21:11, 18. Grammatically these should be considered to be instrumentals of association (or associative datives) as commonly used with words of likeness, the substantive following the noun defining the area of like-ness in the comparison.[43] The two accusatives following ὅμοιος in this

---

42. Thomas, "Glorified Christ," p. 246; Swete, *Apocalypse*, p. 19; Charles, *Rev-elation*, 1:19.
43. A. T. Robertson, *A Grammar of the Greek New Testament in the Light of Historical Research* (Nashville: Broadman, 1934), p. 530; BDF, par. 194[1].

verse and in Rev. 14:14 should be construed as adverbial accusatives of reference, likewise defining the area of likeness.[44] The difference in case usage may be traceable to the fact that these two comparisons are the only two that involve persons. The rest are objects or animals. Every comparable use of this adjective outside Revelation is followed by a dative of reference (cf. Matt. 11:16; 13:31, 33, 44, 45, 47, 52; 20:1; 22:39; Luke 6:48, 49; 7:32; 12:36; 13:18, 19, 21; John 8:55; 9:9; Acts 17:29; Gal. 5:21; 1 John 3:2; Jude 7).

The ἐνδεδυκὼς ποδήρη translates the לָבוּשׁ בַּדִּים in Ezek. 9:2. The same Hebrew expression in Daniel 10:5 is represented by ἐνδεδυμένος βύσσινα in the LXX. It is rather clear that John depended on the LXX for his terminology in Rev. 1:13, in which case Charles's words are surprising: "John translated directly the O. T. text. He did not quote from any Greek version though he was often influenced in his rendering by the LXX and another later Greek Version."[45] Swete's evaluation seems more probable: "The Apocalyptist generally availed himself of the Alexandrian version of the Old Testament. . . . On the other hand many of the references depart widely from the LXX, in particular words where the writer has either rendered [the Hebrew] independently, or has used another version."[46]

The best attempt to find Christ related to a priestly ministry in the Apocalypse cites the thirty-eight occurrences of "the Lamb" in the book,[47] but this attempt is futile. A lamb is a sacrificial victim but nowhere is "the Lamb" said to serve as a priest offering the sacrifice.

Besides the three connotations discussed more fully, other suggestions regarding the meaning of περιεζωσμένον πρὸς τοῖς μαστοῖς ζώνην χρυσᾶν have included "majesty," "princely rank," and "kingly office."

1:14 One of John's habits is to state first a general term and then follow it up with a more specific one. His use of "head" followed by "hair" is a good illustration of this.[48] The phrasing of ἡ . . . κεφαλὴ αὐτοῦ καὶ αἱ τρίχες λευκαὶ ὡς ἔριον λευκόν is closer to the LXX than it is to the Masoretic text of Dan. 7:9. The latter gives "the hair of His head like pure (i.e., cleansed) wool," whereas the former has "the hair of His head like pure white wool" (Charles).

The suggestion that the addition of ὡς χιών to emphasize the whiteness of the hair pictures sinlessness (cf. Ps. 51:7 [50:9]; Isa. 1:18; Matt. 28:3) (Swete) is not convincing. When describing garments, as the expression does in Dan. 7:9, it is more likely to refer to sinlessness

---

44. H. E. Dana and Julius R. Mantey, *A Manual Grammar of the Greek New Testament* (New York: Macmillan, 1927), pp. 93-94; BDF, par. 160.
45. Charles, *Revelation*, 1:lxvi.
46. Swete, *Apocalypse*, p. clv.
47. Charles, *Revelation*, 1:cxiii.
48. Beckwith, *Apocalypse*, pp. 241-42, 438.

and its associated quality of righteousness (cf. Rev. 19:8) than it is when describing hair color. This is the marked difference between Rev. 1:14 and Dan. 7:9.

1:15 The words οἱ πόδες αὐτοῦ ὅμοιοι χαλκολιβάνῳ ὡς ἐν καμίνῳ πεπυρωμένης compose the last of several features of this first vision of John that bear a striking resemblance to the figure described in Dan. 10:5-6. Bullinger has summarized thus: "The only other place in the whole Bible where we have anything like it is in Daniel x.5, 6, where in every particular the resemblance is the same. His girdle is of *gold*; his eyes *fire*; his feet as *brass*; his voice as many *waters* (Rev.) and as a *multitude* (Dan.); his countenance as the *sun* (Rev.), and appearance as *lightning* (Dan.)" (Bullinger).

The purposes of the two messengers is apparently quite similar. In Daniel the man came to make Daniel "understand what shall befall your people in the latter days" (Dan. 10:14). In light of the context of Revelation subsequent to the messages to the seven churches, it appears that this book too is designed to reveal what is to befall Daniel's people, the people of Israel, in the latter days. It is not limited to Israel alone, however, but broadens to forecast the future of the whole world.

Some MSS read πεπυρωμένῳ rather than πεπυρωμένης, thereby resolving the problem related to the grammatical agreement of the participle with the noun it modifies, χαλκολιβάνῳ. A few sources give πεπυρωμένοι, a nominative ending, making the participle modify οἱ πόδες rather than χαλκολιβάνῳ. The nominative alternative has weak manuscript support and need not be taken seriously. The dative reading has good external support, even more impressive than the genitive. The unanswered question is, however, if the neuter dative had been the original reading, why would a scribe ever have changed it to a feminine genitive? Therefore, with the choice a difficult one, the decision has generally gone in favor of the feminine genitive because it is the harder reading (Swete).

The lack of agreement between χαλκολιβάνῳ and πεπυρωμένης has been cited as another of the grammatical errors of the Apocalypse, but one should not be too hasty in drawing such a conclusion. The distinct possibility exists that χαλκολιβάνῳ is feminine rather than neuter, with a nominative singular of χαλκολίβανος (i.e., a third-declension noun). Further, the difference between the dative and genitive inflectional endings may be accounted for by considering πεπυρωμένης as part of a genitive absolute construction with an unexpressed τῆς χαλκολιβάνου supplying the other part. The sense of the total expression becomes, "His feet were like gleaming bronze as when it (i.e., the gleaming bronze) is aglow in a furnace" (Swete; Beckwith).

1:16 The participle ἔχων is a Semitic idiom for εἶχε, the imperfect indicative of the same verb, which is rendered "he was holding." Occasionally Koine Greek used a participle as a finite verb, but frequent Semitisms through the Apocalypse argue for the Hebrew influence in this case.

Some have suggested a reference to the constellation of the Bear or some other group of stars in the ἀστέρας ἑπτά (Swete; Charles). The evidence for this is unconvincing.

It is difficult to explain how visual pictures such as the sword proceeding from the mouth of Christ were conveyed to John, since John was in the unusual state described as a prophetic trance (i.e., "in spirit," 1:10). The idea of graphic reproduction of such details has been repugnant to some. They correctly point out the importance of the meaning conveyed, as opposed to any kind of pictorial representation. Yet for John to have received the visual impression, there must have been some correlation to the features of a corresponding physical appearance.

Ὡς ὁ ἥλιος φαίνει is patterned after a corresponding Hebrew construction (e.g., Isa. 61:10; Jer. 23:29). "As the sun shines" is short for "like the sun when it shines." This is an example of *brachylogy*, which is illustrated elsewhere in Johannine writings in John 6:58 and 1 John 3:12 (Swete; Charles; Beckwith).

Ὄψις may mean either "countenance" or "appearance." The former is preferred here because the rest of the traits in this description refer to a single part of the Person and not His whole appearance (Beckwith). This noun is used as an equivalent of πρόσωπον, as is commonly the case in the LXX. The only NT uses of it in this sense are here, in John 11:44, and possibly in John 7:24 (Swete).

Ἐν τῇ δυνάμει αὐτοῦ heightens the picture of the brightness of Christ's face. It indicates that no clouds or mist were present to diminish the intensity of the sun's rays (Beckwith).

3. THE COMMISSION RESTATED AND AMPLIFIED (1:17-20)

Quite obviously John was overcome by the impressiveness of the sight he has just witnessed, and his reactions demonstrate it (1:17*a*). Jesus reassures him, however, and restates the commission for John to write, this time with some amplifications of the details about what he is to write (1:17*b*-20).

Translation

17And when I saw Him, I fell at His feet as a dead one; and He placed His right hand on me, saying, "Stop fearing; I am the first and the last, 18and the living one, and I came to be dead and behold, I am living for ever and ever, and I have the keys of death and Hades.

¹⁹**Write, then, the things which you have seen and the things which are and the things which will happen after these things. ²⁰The mystery of the seven stars that you have seen on My right hand and the seven golden lampstands—the seven stars are messengers of the seven churches, and the seven lampstands are seven churches."**

Exegesis and Exposition

1:17 John responded to his vision of the glorified Christ in a manner similar to Daniel's response to the messenger in Dan. 10:7-9. In fact, the whole passage is fashioned along the same general lines as Daniel 10 (Swete; Charles). The clause ἔπεσα πρὸς τοὺς πόδας αὐτοῦ (*epesa pros tous podas autou*, "I fell at His feet") vividly expresses John's state of mind, which was one of being completely overwhelmed. Prostration to the earth was a frequent reaction of those who received visions and the accompanying supernatural manifestations (cf. Ezek. 1:28; 3:23; 9:8; 11:13; 43:3; 44:4; Dan. 2:46; 8:17; 10:9; Matt. 17:6; Luke 5:8; Acts 26:14) (Beckwith).

The simile ὡς νεκρός (*hōs nekros*, "as a dead one") expresses his motionless and even lifeless appearance in his stupefaction. Outwardly he looked the same as the child from whom Jesus had just cast the unclean spirit, "as a dead one" (Mark 9:26). Of course, John's lifelessness was for an altogether different reason. He and his fellow disciples had responded in a similar way on the earlier occasion of Jesus' transfiguration, with prostration and fear (Matt. 17:6). This time, however, he was overcome even more and compares his experience to death itself.

Jesus followed His usual procedure. He touched John and told him to stop being afraid as He had the three disciples on the Mount of Transfiguration (Matt. 17:7). Ἔθηκεν τὴν δεξιὰν αὐτοῦ ἐπ' ἐμέ (*Ethēken tēn dexian autou ep' eme*, "He placed His right hand on me") might be considered problematic, since Jesus' right hand had previously been holding seven stars (1:16). This is no great problem, nor is it necessary to resort to the explanation that the whole representation is symbol and not art.⁴⁹ In accord with the abrupt changes that are natural in visions, He could have shifted the stars to the other hand or some other position before touching John (Beckwith).

The touch of the hand was designed to bring comfort and assurance. By recalling the transfiguration experience, John should have remembered this as the same one on whose breast he had lain at the Last Supper some sixty-five years earlier (Swete). This method of reassurance continues in the pattern of the messenger's comforting of

---

49. Contra Swete, *Apocalypse*, p. 19.

Daniel in Dan. 10:10, 12, 18 (Charles). Though not explicitly stated, it must be assumed that John responded positively and rose and dismissed his fear.

Accompanying Jesus' touch was His spoken word (λέγων, *legōn*, "saying"), presumably with the loud voice like the sound of a trumpet (1:10) and the sound of many waters (1:15). He told John to stop being afraid (μὴ φοβοῦ [*mē phobou*, "stop fearing"]). In a number of other places a "fear not" accompanies a touch of the hand (e.g., Dan. 10:10, 12, 18), but the words are also used separately several times (e.g., Isa. 44:2; Matt. 14:27; Luke 1:13, 30; Acts 27:24). The function of the words is to bring comfort to the person who is, or thinks himself to be, in a difficult situation (Charles).

After His word of reassurance, the Lord continued with some words of self-identification to reinforce the comfort and secondarily to provide a foundation for the commission to John He was about to reiterate. He began with ἐγώ εἰμι ὁ πρῶτος καὶ ὁ ἔσχατος (*egō eimi ho prōtos kai ho eschatos*, "I am the first and the last"). John must have had some recollection of the first two words, *egō eimi*, from earlier days when Jesus calmed the stormy sea. In fact, he along with Mark and Luke included these very same words in conjunction with Jesus' word of reassurance at that time: ἐγὼ εἰμι, μὴ φοβεῖσθε (*egō eimi, mē phobeisthe*, "I am, stop fearing") (Matt. 14:27; Mark 6:50; John 6:20).

The title "I am" has a rich OT background, being traceable to the origination of the Tetragrammaton יהוה (*YHWH*, "the LORD" or "Yahweh"), the OT personal name of God in Ex. 3:14.[50] An OT link of this title with Ex. 3:14 is Isa. 48:12 where the Hebrew text אֲנִי הוּא (*'ănî hû'*, "I am He") gives the self-identification of God and is represented in the LXX rendering of the verse by *egō eimi*. In that OT passage the full statement closely represents the same statement as here in Rev. 1:17, "I am the first and the last." This is a divine title applied by the Lord to Himself frequently in the gospels, a notable example of which is John 8:58: "Before Abraham came to be, I am (*egō eimi*)." The title undoubtedly struck this familiar note in the ear of the prophet in his awe-stricken state and provided immediate encouragement. He was once again in the presence of the God-man with whom he had spent those precious years some six decades earlier.

A question has arisen over the primary function of this divine title. One suggestion says that its main purpose is to provide a foundation for the commission about to come in v. 19 (Beckwith). Little proof can be adduced for this idea. It is far better to connect the words closely with the command not to fear, which it immediately follows, furnishing a ground for that prohibition as in the gospel

---

50. See additional note on 1:4 in connection with this name.

passages cited (Beckwith). The comparable words in Isa. 48:12 fulfill a similar purpose in reassuring Israel (cf. also Isa. 44:6) (Charles; Hailey).

Ho prōtos kai ho eschatos demonstrates another habit of this writer, that of ascribing an OT title of the God of Israel to the exalted Christ (cf. Isa. 44:6; 48:12; cf. also Isa. 41:4 and 43:10 where the concept, not the wording, is the same). The same title is applied to Christ in Rev. 22:13 with elaboration that leaves no doubt as to its significance (Swete). Used alongside "the alpha and the omega" and "the beginning and the end," it can hardly connote anything else than His eternality (cf. *to Alpha kai to Ō* in 1:8). To John's mind these words must have told him he was in the midst of an encounter with the God of Israel. This is the aspect of Christ's person that is of particular comfort to the persecuted church at Smyrna (cf. 2:8).

1:18 The second in the series of self-claims given by Christ to relieve John of his fear is ὁ ζῶν, καὶ ἐγενόμην νεκρὸς καὶ ἰδοὺ ζῶν εἰμι εἰς τοὺς αἰῶνας τῶν αἰώνων (*ho zōn, kai egenomēn nekros kai idou zōn eimi eis tous aiōnas tōn aiōnōn*, "the living one, and I came to be dead and behold, I am living for ever and ever"). The total expression includes references to the ever-abiding life He possessed independently of the world and to His humiliation even to the point of undergoing physical death (Charles). These two stand in sharp contrast with each other.

"The living one" is a common description of God in both the OT and the NT (Josh. 3:10; Pss. 42:2; 84:2; Hos. 1:10; Matt. 16:16; 26:63; Acts 14:15; Rom. 9:26; 2 Cor. 3:3; 6:16; 1 Thess. 1:9; 1 Tim. 3:15; 4:10; Heb. 3:12; 9:14; 10:31; 1 Pet. 1:23; cf. Deut. 32:40; Isa. 49:18; Jer. 5:2; Dan. 12:7). In essence, it says He has life in His essential nature. This contrasts Him to the dead or inanimate gods of heathenism. Christ has this same essential nature (cf. John 5:26). In Johannine Christology the Son is *ho zōn* through the communication of the Father's life. This title is broader than the following words about resurrection and serves as the basis for that statement (Swete; Beckwith; Seiss).

Egenomēn nekros kai idou zōn eimi involves a twofold contrast, one between the verbs and the other between the adjective and participle. The verb contrast pits a single occurrence in history, "came to be [dead]" (i.e., Christ's death), against a continuous state of existence, "am [living]" (Christ's life). The latter contrast compares the temporary, but real, state of Christ's death, "[came to be] dead," with the endless life that He now lives, "[am] living" (Swete; Simcox; Moffatt). His was not just a semblance of death as John's prostration to the ground just before (cp. *hōs nekros*, 1:17). It was the real thing (Swete). *Idou*, "behold," in v. 18 draws special attention to the state of life found in Christ following His resurrection.

111

Daniel 4:34 and 12:7 describe God the Father as living forever, as do Rev. 4:9, 10 and 10:6. Comparable terminology is here applied to Christ (Charles). The initial *zōn* in v. 18 designates the essential life of the Godhead, but the second occurrence of the same word denotes His restored human life following death. Yet it is not just a reference to the historical fact of His resurrection. It focuses more on the fullness of the life that He now lives (Alford).

The third in Christ's series of self-claims is closely connected to the first two. Because He is the eternal one (1:17*b*) and has life in Himself (1:18*a*), He has power to give life (cf. John 5:26-28) and either consign to death permanently or to release therefrom (Beckwith). He possesses the "keys of death and Hades" (τὰς κλεῖς τοῦ θανάτου καὶ τοῦ ᾅδου [*tas kleis tou thanatou kai tou hạdou*]) (1:18*b*). Christ makes essentially this same claim in John 5:28. These are the keys that lock or unlock the "gates of death" (Pss. 9:13; 107:18) and the gates of "Sheol" (Isa. 38:10) or "Hades" (Matt. 16:18). They control the prison-house of the dead (Beckwith). Keys symbolize authority. Hence, the present expression means that He is in charge of death and Hades, a divine prerogative according to Rabbinic tradition of the time.[51]

Because a quasi-personification of death and Hades occurs in Ps. 49:14 and Hos. 13:14 (cf. 1 Cor. 15:54-55) and because the two are personified in Rev. 6:8, some have explained this verse as a personification of them (Swete). Little merit attaches to this, however, since the reference to keys requires the present instance to have local connotations (Swete; Mounce). As noted above (cf. Pss. 9:13; 107:18; Isa. 38:10; Matt. 16:18), use of the term to designate a locality is common. Early Christians taught that Christ descended into Hades at the time of His death (Charles), and death was commonly viewed as a prison-house of the dead from the time of Homer's writings and continued to be so in the Scriptures (Beckwith). These backgrounds confirm a local reference in the present passage.

As to what distinction exists between *tou thanatou* and *tou hạdou*, a precise line is difficult to draw. Probably the former points more to the state of death and the latter to the place of death. Because of Christ's victory over death no one can be a prisoner in death and Hades except by His own choice. Christ has the keys.

---

51. Swete, *Apocalypse*, pp. 20-21. Aune finds the source of this imagery in the Hellenistic conceptions of Hekate, the patron goddess of magic and sorcery. In Hellenism this goddess was the primary mythological figure associated with having the keys to Hades (David E. Aune, "The Apocalypse of John and Graeco-Roman Revelatory Magic," *NTS* 33, no. 4 [October 1987]: 484-89). It is difficult to see, however, that John as one so deeply imbued with OT revelation could have looked primarily to Hellenistic magic as a source of his terminology.

1:19 After His reassuring words to John, Jesus returns to the task at hand, that of directing the prophet to write. Oὖν (*oun*, "then") provides the transition to the new commission. One alternative is to base the new commission on Christ's self-description of 1:17c-18. This idea is, "Since I am the eternal one and the Lord of life and death, I send to my churches the commands and promises of this book" (Beckwith). The proximity of this thought in the context, i.e., immediately before v. 19, certainly commends the idea, but there seems to be compelling evidence of a more fundamental connection than this. The repetition of γράψον (*grapson*, "write") from v. 11 indicates that the *oun* is resuming the earlier command where it had left off. Such a resumption was no doubt necessary after the paralyzing fear of John in 1:17 (Moffatt). The best solution is to see the resumption of v. 11 as the major thrust of v. 19, with only a secondary connection with vv. 17c-18.

Earlier, after His resurrection, Jesus had appeared to His followers (Matt. 28:16-17), reminded them of His authority (Matt. 28:18), and commissioned them to go and make disciples (Matt. 28:19-20) (Swete; Charles). John's experience on Patmos was similar: an appearance of Christ (Rev. 1:12-16), a reminder of His conquest of death (Rev. 1:17-18), and a commission to write (1:19-20).

The difference between this and the earlier commission (v. 11) is that now the commission is given in a more comprehensive and specific form. In this book the writer frequently follows a general statement with a more detailed account of the same (Beckwith). What John was to write was ἃ εἶδες καὶ ἃ εἰσὶν καὶ ἃ μέλλει γενέσθαι μετὰ ταῦτα (*ha eides kai ha eisin kai ha mellei genesthai meta tauta*, "the things which you have seen and the things which are and the things which will happen after these things"). As widely agreed, these three clauses encompass the entire contents of the Apocalypse (Swete; Charles; Beckwith). Disagreement comes, however, in describing *how* the contents are summarized by the three.

Do they speak of the Apocalypse as one unbroken division covered by *ha eides*, which in turn is amplified by *ha eisin* and *ha mellei genesthai meta tauta*?[52] Or do they summarize it as falling into two parts, *ha eides* and *ha mellei genesthai meta tauta* with *ha eisin* providing a further definition of *ha eides* (Alford)? Another possibility is a three-division designation, the first being *ha eides*, the second *ha eisin*, and the third *ha mellei genesthai meta tauta*.[53]

---

52. Bullinger, *Apocalypse*, pp. 60-63; Moffatt, 5:347; Theodore Zahn, *Introduction to the New Testament*, trans. John Moore Trout et al., 3 vols. (Grand Rapids: Kregel, 1953), 3:404; Beckwith, *Apocalypse*, pp. 442-43.
53. Swete, *Apocalypse*, p. 21; Lee, "Revelation," 4:507; A. T. Robertson, *Word Pictures in the New Testament*, 6 vols. (Nashville: Broadman, 1933), 6:294.

One approach to the single-division viewpoint understands chapter one to have been written after chapters 2-22. In this case the *eides* of 1:19 looks back to what has already been seen and written down before the writing of chapter one. This meaning could be paraphrased, "Write, then, the things which you saw, and what they are . . . even the things which shall happen . . . after these things" (Bullinger). Since this view takes *ha eisin* in the sense of "what they represent" and this is the same sense as *eisin* has twice in 1:20, the view has merit, but the dependence of chapters 2-22 on the contents of chapter one for their meaning makes it impossible for chapter one to have been written after the rest of the book had been completed.[54]

Another option with taking 1:19 to designate the Apocalypse as one unbroken division sees chapter one as having been written first and takes *eides* as a proleptic aorist, i.e., as referring to what John will have seen after the visions have been completed. A rendering that brings out the sense of this is, "Write, then, the things which you will have seen, even those which are and those which will come about after these things."[55] To the credit of this view, it is persuasive to compare "the things which you saw" with 1:11 where "what you see" covers the contents of the entire book, and then to understand the two additional clauses of 1:19 as making the first more specific: "that is, both what now is and what lies yet in the future" (Beckwith; Mounce). It is also correct to observe that the initial *kai* of 1:19 taken ascensively (i.e., "even" or "that is") accords with the writer's habit (Beckwith). The greatest deficiency, and it is a crippling one, of this view is identifying *eides* as a proleptic aorist in a nonapocalyptic context such as chapter one. This is a rarity, if not an impossibility. Couple with this the difficulty of ignoring the grammatical symmetry of the three relative clauses in 1:19, and this option looks even less promising.

To understand 1:19 as dividing the Apocalypse into two divisions is to take *ha eides* as referring to the first, chapters 1-3, and *ha mellei genesthai meta tauta* as referring to the second, chapters 4-22. This presupposes that *ha eisin*, following an ascensive *kai*, further defines *ha eides*. The resultant sense is, "Write, then, the things which you saw, even what they represent, and the things which will happen after these things" (Alford). Assigning *eisin* the meaning "represent" is advantageous because the word has this sense in 1:20 and elsewhere in the book (cf. 4:5; 5:6, 8; 7:14; 17:12, 15) (Alford; Johnson). The view also is impressive in uniting chapters 2-3 with chapter one in recogni-

---

54. Robert L. Thomas, "John's Apocalyptic Outline," *BSac* 123 (1966): 335.
55. Moffatt, "Revelation," 5:347; Zahn, *Introduction*, 3:404; Beckwith, *Apocalypse*, pp. 442-43.

tion of the fact that the three chapters constitute a single vision for John.[56] Yet giving *eisin* the meaning of "represent" in 1:19 is not that convincing, because εἰμί (*eimi*, "I am") is such a common verb and must draw its meaning from its own sentence. In regard to the uniting of chapter one to chapters 2-3, the single-vision argument does not give adequate attention to the abruptness of the transition from the end of chapter one to the beginning of chapter two. From a recording of John's experiences there is a switch to the recording of the words addressed to existing churches. Such a drastic change is sufficient to justify a major break in outline after the first chapter.[57] Perhaps the most damaging observation against the two-division idea is that John had not yet "seen" the contents of these two chapters at the time he received this commission, and chapters 2-3 cannot be regarded merely as interpretations of 1:10-18 as this view would necessitate.[58] These factors are sufficient to render this an improbable interpretation.

The interpretation that understands a three-part division of 1:19 sees the past vision of the glorified Christ (chap. 1, esp. vv. 11-18) pointed out by *ha eides* as the first part, the present condition of the churches (chaps. 2-3) indicated in *ha eisin* as the second part, and as the third part, the future happenings (chaps. 4-22) represented by *ha mellei genesthai meta tauta*. This position is represented in the words, "Write, then, the things which you have seen and the things which are and the things which will happen after these things."[59]

The threefold division is the most natural understanding of the symmetrical grammatical construction of 1:19[60] and fits the contents of the Apocalypse quite well. *Eides*, an aorist tense, is best explained as looking back to the vision of Christ that is now past (contrast *blepeis*, present tense, in 1:11). "The things which are" (*ha eisin*) is accurate as a description of the messages to the seven churches that detail specific conditions in the churches of John's day and throughout the period until the events foretold in 4:1 ff. begin to unfold. The similarity of *ha mellei genesthai meta tauta* to *ha dei genesthai* of 1:1 (see earlier discussion at 1:1) and 22:6 and to *ha dei genesthai meta tauta* of 4:1 is strong evidence that the third relative clause of 1:19 points to chapters 4-22, which constitutes the main body of the book (Swete; Charles; Smith). It is natural that this is the longest of the three sections.

---

56. Zahn, *Introduction*, 3:392.
57. Thomas, "Apocalyptic Outline," p. 338.
58. Moffatt, "Revelation," 5:347; Thomas, "Apocalyptic Outline," p. 338.
59. Swete, *Apocalypse*, p. 21; Charles, *Revelation*, 1:33; Lee, "Revelation," 4:507; Robertson, *Word Pictures*, 6:294.
60. Thomas, "Apocalyptic Outline," pp. 338-39.

The strengths of the three-part view of 1:19 combined with the weaknesses of the other views make it the most desirable choice. John, therefore, was commissioned to write a three-part work, the bases for which were the vision of Christ he had just received, the messages of Christ about to be dictated to the seven churches of Asia, and revelations about the future period after conditions represented in the churches are past.

1:20 To provide a transition from the vision of Christ he had just received to the messages of Christ about to be dictated, v. 20 explains part of the symbolism of the vision. Τὸ μυστήριον (*To mystērion*, "The mystery") denotes "the inner meaning of a symbolical vision," a meaning the noun has elsewhere in Dan. 2:47 [LXX] and Rev. 17:7 (Swete). The word speaks of something secret or hidden and is used here in a derived sense of something that contains a hidden or symbolical meaning and something that can be interpreted (Beckwith). This "something" is beyond the reach of natural human understanding and can only be grasped through special revelation through God's Spirit. *Mystērion* is directly antithetical to ἀποκάλυψις (*apokalypsis*, "revelation") (cf. Rev. 1:1) (Lee).

The part of the vision to be unveiled at this point relates to τῶν ἑπτὰ ἀστέρων οὓς εἶδες ἐπὶ τῆς δεξιᾶς μου (*tōn hepta asterōn hous eides epi tēs dexias mou*, "the seven stars that you have seen on My right hand") and τὰς ἑπτὰ λυχνίας τὰς χρυσᾶς (*tas hepta lychnias tas chrysas*, "the seven golden lampstands"). The stars that in v. 16 were said to be "in" (*en*) Christ's right hand are now observed as resting "upon" (*epi*) the palm of His open right hand (Swete; Beckwith). The seven golden lampstands first seen in v. 12 are the second feature to be explained.

The seven stars are identified as ἄγγελοι τῶν ἑπτὰ ἐκκλησιῶν (*angeloi tōn hepta ekklēsiōn*, "messengers of the seven churches"). A major discussion revolves around who these messengers were. Four major approaches to the issue of their identity have been delineated. Are they unfallen angels who are guardians of the seven churches, personified spirits of the churches, men who are bishops or chief teachers who represent the churches, or men who are representatives of the churches but are without a unique leadership function (Lee; Beckwith)?

To support the theory of their being unfallen angels, the consistent use of ἄγγελος (*angelos*, "angel") with this meaning throughout the Apocalypse is impressive evidence (Alford; Johnson), as is the analogy of guardian angels for individual persons. If people have guardian angels, why should not churches have the same (Alford)? Existence of angels of this type is well attested in Scripture (Alford). The extension of such guardianship from individuals to nations is a key to apocalyptic interpretation (cf. Dan. 10:13, 20, 21; 12:1). Why should there not be an analogous extension to local churches (Alford; Swete)? Because stars symbolize angels elsewhere in the Bible (cf. Job 38:7; Isa. 14:12ff.) (Alford), the case for this identification is quite solid.

The view encounters serious difficulties, however. The complexity of the communication process is one thing that raises problems with it. It presumes that Christ is sending a message to heavenly beings through John, an earthly agent, so that it may reach earthly churches through angelic representatives (Beckwith). An even more decisive consideration against the view of guardian angels lies in the sinful conduct of which these angels are accused. Most of the rebukes of chapters 2-3 are second person singular, messages that look first at the individual messengers and presumably through them to the churches they represent. Unfallen angels do not sin, neither are they in need of repentance as these messengers along with their churches were (e.g., 2:4-5, 14, 20; 3:1, 2, 3, 15, 17, 19) (Lee).

Taking the *angeloi* to be personified spirits of the churches alleviates some of these difficulties. The obvious blending of *angelos* and church in stating the destination of each message (cp. 1:11 with the address and contents of each of the seven messages) finds its best explanation in this interpretation (Beckwith). This is the only view that provides for the obvious intention of Christ that each message go to the church as a whole (Mounce; Hailey). When the frequency of personification in Revelation is added to the case for personified spirits (cf. 7:1; 9:11; 14:18; 16:5), the evidence is still more impressive (Lee; Beckwith).

The obstacles to endorsing the view are strong, however. That the churches represented by the lampstands, the other part of the symbolism explained in 1:20, are objective realities argues strongly for the objective reality of the *angeloi* (Alford). Furthermore, the double symbolism involved in the "personified spirit" meaning renders its validity doubtful. It entails understanding a star to be a symbol for an angel who in turn is a symbol for a church. If this is the case, the stars and the lampstands have identical meanings (Lee). This is too strained to be the correct meaning.

Another approach is to take *angeloi* as referring to human messengers, each of whom was a bishop or main leader in the church in his own city. This is in accord with the scriptural practice of having a star to represent highest dominion (Num. 24:17; Isa. 14:12; Matt. 2:2) and a faithful or a false teacher (Dan. 12:3; Jude 13). Either of these symbolisms would be appropriate to church leadership (Lee). The fact that the messengers of chapters 2 and 3 represent and are responsible for the actions of the churches also points to people in leadership positions (Alford). The selection of these seven by the individual churches to go and minister to John on Patmos would seem to necessitate their holding some type of leadership role (Walvoord).

The drawbacks in identifying these as bishops or main leaders include the fact that the office of bishop had not yet been instituted in the church (Alford; Swete). The plurality of leadership in local churches of the NT era militates against singling out a single leader who could have borne the sole responsibility for the behavior of the whole church. No individual officer could have been directly responsible for so much (Beckwith). Furthermore the unvarying use of *angelos* elsewhere in the Apocalypse is against referring it to a human being (Charles; Beckwith). This latter factor is not as strong a reason as the former, that of the absence of a single leadership style of church at this early date, for rejecting this view. If there had been such a leader, it is certainly unparalleled to refer to him by *angelos* (Beckwith).

The fourth possibility is that *angeloi* refers to human messengers who in some sense are representative of the churches, but who possess no unique leadership functions. Two men named Epaphroditus and Epaphras, representing churches in Philippi and Colosse, went to Rome to offer help to the prisoner Paul while he was under house arrest in Rome (Phil. 2:25; 4:18; Col. 4:12). It is quite probable that churches from seven cities in Asia, where John had served for about thirty years prior to the writing of Revelation, sent representatives to offer comparable assistance to him in his exile. *Angelos* is used frequently enough to refer to human messengers (e.g., Matt. 11:10; Luke 7:24; 9:52; James 2:25) to make this a viable option in this part of the Apocalypse (Lee). Also the reference in 2 Cor. 8:23 to "apostles of the churches" shows that churches had a policy of selecting delegates to perform such tasks as visiting and assisting the apostles in ministry (Swete). As observed earlier, a human being is a much more natural recipient of a message to a church than a heavenly being (Morris).

The objection that these were responsible for moral conditions in the churches and must have had authority as leaders because of this responsibility may be countered by noting that each messenger may have been one of the rulers in his church without being the sole ruler, as was apparently the case with Epaphroditus in Philippi and Epaphras in Colosse. It would not take *full* responsibility for the church's behavior for each to be viewed as an embodiment of the church he represented. He could have been a moral representative without being the sole leader.

The view that takes the *angeloi* as men who are representatives of the churches but are without a unique leadership function appears to be the most probable choice, largely because objections to it are easier to answer than objections to the other three views. If this is

118

correct, Christ's explanation of the stars informed John that they stood for seven visitors to Patmos, either already present or soon to arrive, men who come to help John but will return home with a specific mission to the churches that sent them. They will be bearers of a message to their own city as part of the larger package of the whole contents of the Apocalypse.

As Jesus continued His explanation, He noted that the lampstands stood for the churches in the seven cities. The controller of the messengers to the churches stood symbolically in the middle of the churches and was about to commence dictating a particular message to each church.

Additional Notes

1:17 In the construction μὴ φοβοῦ the supposition is that the prophet was already afraid and Jesus told him to quit being afraid. It is assumed that μή followed by the present imperative of any verb commands the cessation of action already in progress.[61] Only some contextual indication can alter this assumption, and no such indication is present here. On the contrary, John's falling to the ground makes perfectly clear that John was gripped by fear.

In Ex. 3:14 the Hebrew אֶהְיֶה is at one point in the LXX translation of the verse represented by ἐγώ εἰμι. It is evident that Isa. 48:12 looks back and takes its cue from the Exodus passage.

John's rendering ὁ πρῶτος καὶ ὁ ἔσχατος follows the Masoretic text of אֲנִי רִאשׁוֹן וַאֲנִי אַחֲרוֹן (Isa. 44:6) and אֲנִי רִאשׁוֹן אַף אֲנִי אַחֲרוֹן (Isa. 48:12). In both verses the LXX gives free renderings of the text that are not as close to John's rendering.

1:18 The construction of 1:18 reflects Semitic influence once again: a participle is resolved into a finite verb, i.e., ζῶν is elaborated upon by the ἐγενόμην and εἰμί clauses, particularly the latter (Charles). This construction places greater emphasis on Christ's death in comparison with His ever abiding life. The aorist tense of γίνομαι, "I became," often in the NT stands in contrast to the present tense of εἰμί as it does in 1:18 (e.g., John 1:1, 14; 8:58; cf. Phil. 2:5-7). This is one of the clearest ways of comparing a single happening with an ongoing state or action.

Ζῶν εἰμι should be distinguished from both ζῶν ἐγενόμην and ἔζησα (Rom. 14:9), which speak of the historical fact of resurrection. It refers to the life that the Lord still lives so that the risen life of the Lord is henceforth concurrent with His divine life. He lives "forever and ever" (cf. Rom. 6:9) (Swete).

The genitives τοῦ θανάτου and τοῦ ᾅδου would fulfill a possessive

---

61. Turner, *Syntax*, pp. 74-75.

function if death and Hades were intended as personifications (Beckwith). Since they are construed locally, however, the two genitives are objective, i.e., the keys lock or unlock death and Hades (Swete; Charles).

Hades is the intermediate abode of only the wicked in Revelation (cf. 6:8; 20:13) as in Luke 16:23. In the Luke passage Hades is set opposite Paradise. No such connection exists in the Apocalypse, however, nor does one appear in Luke 23:43 and 2 Cor. 12:4. The only NT reference to Hades as containing Paradise is Acts 2:27, 31. No soul can enter Paradise except through death. By submitting to death, Christ won the victory over death, so that neither death nor Hades can resist His power any longer. Through His resurrection He also came away with a victory over Hades, having descended there at the time of His death.[62]

1:19 In the Apocalypse οὖν occurs only here and in 2:15, 16; 3:3, 19. In the gospel of John it is found 195 times (Charles). The predominance of the resumptive use of the conjunction in the gospel[63] adds further to the likelihood that the resumptive use is the correct meaning in this verse.

The view of 1:19 as presenting the Apocalypse in one unbroken division is rendered still more improbable by the use of the relative pronoun ἅ instead of the interrogative pronoun τίνα to introduce the εἰσίν clause. The latter more naturally conveys the sense "and what they are."[64] The assumptions of this view that εἶδες of 1:19 looks back to the εἶδεν of 1:2 and that the aorist indicative of both indicates that John's visions lie completely in the past are not well-founded. Very probably the εἶδεν of 1:2 is an epistolary aorist through which John adopts the perspective of his readers when they will have received the book (see discussion at 1:2) (Charles).

The apocalyptic portion of Revelation begins at chapter 4 and a number of proleptic aorists have been identified in the book subsequent to that point (e.g., ἐτελέσθη, 10:7; ἐγένετο, 11:15). The present passage is straight dialogue between Jesus and John. A correlative problem to taking εἶδες proleptically is with the βλέπεις of 1:11. This present tense must be taken either as proleptic—a grammatical unknown—or as futuristic. There is little or no contextual justification for either.[65]

Other inadequacies of the two-division theory in 1:19 may be

---

62. Charles, *Revelation*, 1:32. For a discussion of Christ's descent in connection with his death and/or resurrection, see D. Edmond Hiebert, *First Peter, an Expositional Commentary* (Chicago: Moody, 1984), pp. 226-31.
63. Dana and Mantey, *Grammar*, p. 253.
64. William Kelly, *The Revelation* (London: Thomas Weston, 1904), p. 37.
65. Thomas, "Apocalyptic Outline," p. 336.

cited. It forces μετὰ ταῦτα to refer back to ἃ εἶδες (Alford), but the plain reference of the ταῦτα is to ἃ εἰσίν instead (Lee). It also ignores the evident contrast between ἃ εἰσίν and ἃ μέλλει γενέσθαι (Beckwith). Further, it is weak in understanding the second relative pronoun ἃ to function as an interrogative pronoun τίνα while treating the first and third occurrences as relative pronouns.[66]

Μέλλει followed by an aorist infinitive as here may mean "be on the point of, be about to" (cf. Rev. 3:2, 16; 12:4) or "be destined, be inevitable" (cf. Gal. 3:23).[67] The former meaning, "be about to," is the usual one in this book, but the latter meaning is to be preferred in 1:19 (Charles). The choice of this meaning does not eliminate the idea of imminence, however, because μέλλω with an infinitive always expresses imminence.[68]

Μετὰ ταῦτα conveys the sense of "hereafter" (cf. 9:12; John 13:7) (Beckwith). In this verse, however, there is advantage in keeping the literal rendering of "after these things" so that the antecedent of ταῦτα may be pointed out more specifically.

The common use of a threefold division in pagan and Christian literature as a device for indicating that a work was prophetic is further evidence that Rev. 1:19 views the totality of the book in three parts.[69] The objection that εἶδες in agreement with βλέπεις of 1:11 must apply to the whole book (Beckwith) fails to take into account a writing characteristic of this author. He often gives a general word and then returns later to the same with a more specialized amplification of what has been given previously.[70] In this case all three parts of 1:19, not just εἶδες, are an amplification of βλέπεις.

1:20 Τὸ μυστήριον functions as an accusative absolute in its sentence, a grammatical usage that is unusual in the NT. It is not the object of γράψον (1:19), nor is it in apposition to ἃ εἶδες (1:19). Rather it is best construed as an accusative in apposition with the nominatives οἱ ἑπτὰ ἀστέρες ἄγγελοι . . . αἱ λυχνίαι αἱ ἑπτὰ ἑπτὰ ἐκκλησίαι later in the same sentence (1:20). Other NT uses of the accusative absolute are Acts 26:3; Rom. 8:3; 12:1; 2 Cor. 6:13; 1 Tim. 2:6 (Charles; Beckwith).

Τὰς ἑπτὰ λυχνίας τὰς χρυσᾶς is accusative where a genitive inflectional ending would have been expected to match τῶν ἑπτὰ ἀστέρων, with which it stands in a coordinate relationship. Both expressions

---

66. Kelly, *Revelation*, p. 37; Thomas, "Apocalyptic Outline," pp. 337-38.
67. W. F. Arndt and F. Gingrich, *A Greek-English Lexicon of the New Testament*, 2d ed. (Cambridge: U. Press, 1979), p. 501.
68. BDF, par. 181.
69. W. C. van Unnik, "A Formula Describing Prophecy," *NTS* 9 (1962-63): 86-94.
70. Beckwith, *Apocalypse*, p. 242.

are clarifications of τὸ μυστήριον. John, however, does the grammatically unusual by using the accusative λυχνίας to bring the noun into agreement with the accusative case of μυστήριον (Charles; Beckwith).

The meaning of each occurrence of εἰσιν in 1:20 is clearly "represent" or "signify." This is always the case with this verb and the figure of speech called metaphor which is used here (Bullinger).

PART 2
The Preparation of the People:
Their Present Condition (2:1–3:22)

3
Church of Loveless Orthodoxy

A. THE MESSAGE TO EPHESUS (2:1-7)

A common practice of NT writers is to present doctrinal teaching first and follow it with instructions about behavioral patterns that are consistent with it. Paul's epistle to the Ephesians is an example. The first three chapters of that epistle furnish substantive teaching about positional features of Christianity, and the last three tell obligations of Christian living that stem from those (cf. also the doctrinal nature of Romans 1-11 and the practical nature of Romans 12-15).

The Apocalypse follows the reverse sequence, however. Chapters 2-3 are devoted to describing practical standards of behavior for the seven churches, and chapters 4-22 follow with substantive teaching about future events, which serves as motivation for compliance with the standards upheld in chapters 2-3. The seven messages emphasize practical patterns heavily[1] and in so doing recall that the Apocalypse was written for a distinctly practical purpose. The beatitude of 1:3 notes the blessing of those who hear *and keep by way of obedience* the things written in the book. Chapters 2-3 are devoted to detailing the desired practical impact of the "unveilings" that compose the book from chapter 4 on.

With a few exceptions, the seven messages have the same general structure. (1) An *address* opens each letter and is followed by (2) the

---

1. J. A. Seiss, *The Apocalypse*, 3 vols. (New York: Charles C. Cook, 1909), 1:152.

citation of certain *attributes of the speaker*. (3) An assertion of complete *knowledge about the people* addressed comes next. (4) A description of the *state of the church* by way of praise, promise, censure, or warning follows. (5) A promise of *the Lord's coming*, (6) a universal *command to hear*, and (7) a *promise to the overcomer* conclude the messages (Seiss). In almost every case part (2) is derived from John's vision of Christ in chapter 1. Part (5) speaks of a coming of Christ which is imminent for six of the seven churches. In part (6) is a universal call to all the churches to hear what has been spoken to each church individually. The seventh part anticipates millennial and eternal blessings described later in the book. The last four messages reverse the order of parts (6) and (7).

The writer has already built his bridge between the vision of chapter one and the seven messages by introducing the seven messengers and the seven churches (1:20). The first message now commences.

Translation

¹To the messenger of the church which is in Ephesus, write:

"These things says the one who holds fast the seven stars in His right hand, who walks in the middle of the golden lampstands: ²I know your works, even your labor and endurance, and that you cannot bear evil ones, and you have tested those who call themselves apostles—and they are not—and you have found them [to be] liars; ³and you have endurance and you have borne up because of My name, and you have not grown weary. ⁴But I have against you that you have left your first love. ⁵Remember, therefore, whence you have fallen, and repent and do the first works. But if not, I will come to you and remove your lampstand from its place, unless you repent. ⁶But you have this, that you hate the works of the Nicolaitans, which I also hate. ⁷The one who has an ear, let him hear what the Spirit says to the churches. To the one who overcomes, I will grant to him to eat from the tree of life, which is in the Paradise of God."

Exegesis and Exposition

2:1 *The address.* The address is composed of the words τῷ ἀγγέλῳ τῆς ἐν Ἐφέσῳ ἐκκλησίας γράψον (*tō angelō tēs en Ephesō ekklēsias grapson*, "to the messenger of the church which is in Ephesus, write"). The comparable formula introduces each of the seven messages in these two chapters.[2] *Tō angelō* is a pure dative, reflecting personal interest with regard to the addressee: "to the messenger." The article *tō* identi-

---

2. Walter Scott, *Exposition of the Revelation of Jesus Christ* (Swengel, Pa.: Bible Truth Depot, n.d.), p. 56.

fies the particular messenger in view, distinguishing him from the messengers to the other six churches as well as messengers elsewhere in the Apocalypse.[3]

The word referred to an envoy sent to carry a message. The cognate verb ἀγγέλλω (angellō, "I announce") and a cognate noun ἀγγελία (angelia, "message") bear out this meaning.[4] Angelos is used of both human envoys (cf. Luke 9:52) and spirit beings (cf. Luke 1:11), of good angels (cf. Heb. 1:13-14) and evil spirits (cf. Jude 6; 2 Pet. 2:4).[5]

The issue of the messengers' identification has been discussed in conjunction with their first mention in 1:20. It was concluded that the seven were men who represented their churches, but not in the sense of being sole leaders of the individual churches. These were moral representatives, so to speak, who as individuals epitomized the conditions of the churches they represented. Hence, each letter is addressed to the church's representative, not directly to the church itself.

A question has arisen regarding this more "distant" kind of communication. In other words, why did Paul write to the Ephesians (and other cities of Asia, if Ephesians is a circular letter) directly, addressing his words to "the saints" (Eph. 1:1), whereas John wrote his words only to the churches' representatives? Why the difference in intimacy? One explanation is that the more distant style of the Apocalypse is traceable to the low moral state to which the churches of Asia had sunk by the time it was written. Thirty-five years after Paul penned Ephesians, conditions were so deplorable that the Lord could address the churches only through their representatives (Scott). This explanation reads too much into the method of communication, however. Communication with churches was possible in various ways. There is also the marked difference that Ephesians was written in a complete epistolary form but these seven paragraphs are included in one common epistle sent to all seven cities.[6]

A further difference lies in the circumstances of the writers. John as a resident of Asia Minor for almost thirty years had much more of a pastoral interest in these churches than Paul who had lived there for only three years and had been away from Ephesus for about five years by the time he wrote his epistle. Another difference lies in the natures

---

3. John F. Walvoord, *The Revelation of Jesus Christ* (Chicago: Moody, 1966), p. 53.
4. W. F. Arndt and F. Gingrich, *A Greek-English Lexicon of the New Testament*, 2nd ed. (Cambridge: U. Press, 1979), p. 7.
5. W. E. Vine, *An Expository Dictionary of New Testament Words* (Old Tappan, N.J.: Revell, 1966), p. 55.
6. Isbon T. Beckwith, *The Apocalypse of John* (New York: Macmillan, 1919), pp. 446-47.

of the epistle and the seven messages. Christ dictated the seven to John, but Paul's letter was his own composition under the inspiration of the Holy Spirit. For these reasons it is best to conclude that no difference in intimacy exists and that these messages were addressed to the messengers because they were the ones who had to take them to the churches.[7]

Ekklēsias is a compound of ἐκ (*ek*, "out of") and καλέω (*kaleō*, "I call"). In general usage, it has lost some of its etymological force of "called out," but a good possibility exists that some of this meaning is retained when it refers to the special group composing the Christian church (Acts 15:14; Rom. 9:24). The church is "called out" from previous relationships so as to constitute a body with special relation to God (cf. 1 Cor. 10:32).[8]

Politically the word referred to a regularly assembled body of people.[9] In the LXX it denotes the gathering or assembling of Israel.[10] In the NT it came to have three meanings. First was its technical sense designating all Christians, a group referred to figuratively as "the body of Christ" (cf. Col. 1:18, 24). Jesus first employed the word in this sense (cf. Matt. 16:18).[11] Its second use was to designate a particular assembly in a given location (cf. Rom. 16:5; 1 Cor. 16:19; Col. 4:15). A third meaning was to speak of all the assemblies in a single city (cf. Rom. 16:1; 1 Cor. 1:2).[12] This final possibility must be the force of the term here, because in a city the size of Ephesus, by this time, there must have been a large number of house-churches meeting separately from one another.

Ephesus was a thriving metropolis by the end of the first century A.D. Commercially, it was the largest city in the Roman province of Asia. Originally it had been a prosperous seaport, but the silt that found its way down from the mountains with the help of the Cayster River was gradually filling the harbor. Through continuing attempts to clean the harbor, certain channels were kept open, but the port was

---

7. Walvoord, *Revelation*, p. 53. The fact is Ephesians and Colossians were conveyed to their destinations through a messenger named Tychicus (cf. Eph. 6:21-22; Col. 4:7-9) as were these messages, but Ephesians was not dictated to Tychicus because he was not a representative, moral or otherwise, of the Ephesian church. It is difficult to view the moral states of the churches as so bad as to have caused this method of transmission, because no fault is attributed to the intermediaries of the churches of Smyrna and Philadelphia.
8. Robert L. Thomas, "1 Thessalonians," in *EBC*, ed. Frank E. Gaebelein (Grand Rapids: Zondervan, 1978), 11:238.
9. Arndt and Gingrich, *Lexicon*, p. 240.
10. Vine, *Dictionary*, pp. 83-84.
11. Ibid.
12. Thomas, "1 Thessalonians," p. 238.

accessible only with difficulty and was slowly losing its importance.[13] The city was also accessible by land. Highways connected it with most of the important cities of the Roman provinces composing Asia Minor. The combination of accessibility from land or sea made the city the prominent commercial center of Asia for a long time.[14]

The city was termed "a free city" in the organizational scheme of the Roman Empire. Such a status was granted because of fidelity and services to the Empire and, within certain limits, this allowed the city to be self-governing. No military was stationed there, but Roman provincial governors visited occasionally and held special court sessions.[15] The chief drawing card in the city was the athletic games held annually. These attracted large crowds of people from throughout the province of Asia.[16]

The religious life of Ephesus revolved about the worship of the Greek goddess Artemis (identified with the Roman goddess Diana) (cf. Acts 19:24, 27, 28, 34, 35), for whom it served as the center of worship. Her 425-foot long by 220-foot wide temple was one of the seven wonders of the ancient world. Each of its 120 columns was donated by a king. The image of Artemis was one of the most sacred objects of worship in the ancient world, but it was not beautiful. It was a grotesque, squat, black, many-breasted figure that was reputed to have fallen from heaven (cf. Acts 19:27, 35). Nevertheless, the citizens were fanatically devoted to worshiping the image.[17] Besides being a religious center, the temple was a gathering place for criminals and the scene of widespread immorality. Criminals came there in droves because it provided them an asylum where they were safe after committing a crime. Prostitution thrived there because the immoral activities were looked upon as sacred, and the prostitutes themselves were viewed as priestesses.[18]

The population of the city was of diverse backgrounds. One group was the original natives who inhabited the area before the arrival of the Greeks. Added to these were the direct descendants of the original colonists from Athens. A third group was composed of three other tribes of Greek lineage. Finally, the city had a substantial Jewish population.[19]

---

13. Merrill C. Tenney, *Interpreting Revelation* (Grand Rapids: Eerdmans, 1957), p. 55.
14. William Hendriksen, *More Than Conquerors* (Grand Rapids: Baker, 1944), p. 76.
15. William Barclay, *The Revelation of John*, 2d ed., 2 vols. (Philadelphia: Westminster, 1960), 1:71.
16. Ibid.
17. Ibid.; Tenney, *Revelation*, p. 56.
18. Barclay, *Revelation*, 1:72.
19. Ibid.

In such unpromising circumstances as these the gospel won some of its greatest triumphs. Paul visited the city while returning from Corinth to Jerusalem at the close of his second missionary journey about A.D. 52 (Acts 18:19-21). He left Priscilla and Aquila there (Acts 18:26). Their stay coincided with the persuasive ministry of Apollos in the city (Acts 18:25). On his third missionary journey Paul returned to the city (Acts 19:1 ff.) and spent three years there (Acts 20:31).[20] At the instigation of the metallurgists' union, the citizenry opposed Paul's preaching and eventually forced him to leave the city, but not before a strong church had been established. This became the center of evangelism in Asia (Acts 19:26). The same inclinations that made the people fanatic worshipers of Artemis also made them enthusiastic Christians. The response of the heathen populace to the missionaries reflected this. Their violent reaction against Christians can be explained only by an overwhelming response of some of their fellow citizens to the gospel (Tenney). The sale of shrines dropped drastically because of the impact of Christianity.

Paul had a close relationship to this church. He spent more time there during his missionary tours than anywhere else. His farewell to the Ephesian elders is most touching (Acts 20:17-38). Later he wrote them a letter while a prisoner in Rome and quite possibly visited them following his release. He apparently left Timothy in charge of the church after this visit (1 Tim. 1:3). A few years later (approximately A.D. 66) John the apostle arrived in the city and began a ministry there.[21] John remained in the area until his exile to Patmos. About forty years passed between the founding of the church and the writing of Revelation to this and the other churches of Asia. The prominence of this church is reflected in its being the possible recipient of as many as eight NT books: the gospel of John, Ephesians, 1 and 2 Timothy, 1, 2, and 3 John, and Revelation. Besides, Paul was ministering in Ephesus at the time he wrote 1 Corinthians.

Today Ephesus is in ruins and because of the silt is six miles from the sea. The coast is "a harborless line of sandy beach, unapproachable by a ship."[22]

The command to John at this point, as well as in the addresses of the other six messages, is to begin writing specifically to the messenger of the church in Ephesus. He has already been commanded to write (cf. 1:11, 19), but now his writing has a particular addressee. (For a discussion of possible predictive-prophetic elements in this

---

20. Hendriksen, *Conquerors*, p. 76.
21. Ibid.
22. Barclay, *Revelation*, 1:73.

and the other six messages, see Excursus 1, "The Chronological Interpretation of Revelation 2-3," at the end of this volume.)

Attributes of the speaker. As is typical of Koine Greek, *tade legei*
("these things says [the one]") is used sparingly in the NT, only eight
times. Seven of these are in Revelation 2-3 and the eighth is in Acts
21:11.[23] In each of its eight uses it introduces a strong, authoritative,
emphatic assertion.[24] In Revelation the statements are from the majestic Christ and in Acts it is from the Holy Spirit through the prophet
Agabus. The nature of the NT uses aligns with secular uses of *tade*.
Persian kings used it to introduce their decrees, and prophets employed it in introductions to their prophetic utterances.[25] The reference of "these things" is, of course, to what follows, not to what has
preceded (Beckwith).

After the introductory prophetic formula Christ identifies Himself, figuratively claiming authority and calling attention to His
movement among the seven churches. Both figures come from John's
vision of Christ in chapter 1 (cf. 1:13, 16) with this difference: in the
vision Christ appears in the middle of the lampstands holding the
stars in His right hand, but now *walks* in the middle of the lampstands and has a *firm hold* on the seven stars. The slight change in
expression brings attention to His majestic activity.[26] This amounts
to His absolute control of the messengers as He constantly moves
about among the churches and keeps a watchful eye upon them
(Beckwith).

The shift to *kratōn* from *echōn* of the earlier part of the vision
(1:16) is not viewed by all as a change in emphasis from "hold" to
"hold fast."[27] The rationale is that if Christ is the Son of Man, the
character of such a being guarantees that *echōn* contains the idea of

---

23. R. H. Charles, *The Revelation of St. John*, ICC, 2 vols. (New York:
    Scribner's, 1920), 1:48; A. T. Robertson, *Word Pictures in the New Testa-
    ment*, 6 vols. (Nashville: Broadman, 1933), 6:297.
24. David E. Aune, *Prophecy in Early Christianity and the Ancient Mediterra-
    nean World* (Grand Rapids: Eerdmans, 1983), p. 328.
25. Arndt and Gingrich, *Lexicon*, p. 553. Muse uses τάδε and other elements of
    the seven messages to conclude that they are dominantly prophetic in
    nature. Five of the messages are warning-of-judgment messages
    (Ephesus, Pergamum, Thyatira, Sardis, and Laodicea) and two are
    promise-of-salvation messages (Smyrna and Philadelphia) (Robert L.
    Muse, "Revelation 2-3: A Critical Analysis of Seven Prophetic Messages,"
    JETS 29, no. 2 [June 1986]: 147-61).
26. R. C. H. Lenski, *The Interpretation of St. John's Revelation* (Columbus,
    Ohio: Lutheran Book Concern, 1935), p. 84.
27. James Moffatt, "The Revelation of St. John the Divine," in *The Expositor's
    Greek Testament*, ed. W. Robertson Nicoll (Grand Rapids: Eerdmans, n.d.),
    5:349.

kratōn. This is no mere man, they say (Charles). Yet it is indisputable that κρατέω (*krateō*, "I hold fast") is a stronger and more forceful word than ἔχω (*echō*, "I have").[28] It is also true that *krateō* is the opposite of ἀφίημι (*aphiēmi*, "I let go"), whereas *echō* is not.[29] *Krateō* is certainly intended to have this stronger sense in Rev. 2:25 and 3:11. Why not here?[30] The addition of *peripatōn* to the second part of Christ's self-description in this verse adds to the case for understanding a distinction between the comparable expressions in chapter 1 and those found here.[31]

The same issue exists here as was discussed in connection with 1:16: Is the authority of Christ over the messengers the primary idea, or is it His watchful care over the churches? The latter notion has its supporters,[32] but for the same reasons reviewed in the earlier discussion the former emphasis is primary. This conclusion finds further confirmation in the present verse through the parallel picture of Christ *walking* in the middle of the lampstands. His constant movement among and watchful eye over the churches have more to do with control than with protection. This involves His knowledge of the circumstances and, in the Ephesian situation, may very well relate to the removal of the church's lampstand from its place (cf. 2:5). His constant vigil of the churches determines whether or not the churches as lampstands are shining as they should (Scott). This activity is reminiscent of the OT priests who tended the lamps of the holy place of the Tabernacle to keep them trimmed, oiled, and burning.

2:2 *Knowledge about the people.* Moving to the next part of His message to the church in Ephesus, Christ states His knowledge about the people, specifically their spiritual achievements. The section consists of three couplets found in 2:2-3: Οἶδα τὰ ἔργα σου καὶ τὸν κόπον καὶ τὴν ὑπομονήν σου, καὶ ὅτι οὐ δύνῃ βαστάσαι κακούς (*Oida ta erga sou kai ton kopon kai tēn hypomonēn sou, kai hoti ou dynē bastasai kakous*, "I know your works, even your labor and endurance, and that you cannot bear evil ones") (v. 2a), καὶ ἐπείρασας τοὺς λέγοντας

---

28. William Lee, "The Revelation of St. John," in *The Holy Bible*, ed. F. C. Cook (London: John Murray, 1881), 4:515; Beckwith, *Apocalypse*, p. 448; Robertson, *Word Pictures*, 6:297.
29. Henry Barclay Swete, *The Apocalypse of St. John* (London: Macmillan, 1906), p. 24.
30. Henry Alford, *The Greek Testament*, 4 vols. (London: Longmans, Green, 1903), 4:562.
31. J. B. Smith, *A Revelation of Jesus Christ* (Scottdale, Pa.: Herald, 1961), p. 63.
32. F. J. A. Hort, *The Apocalypse of St. John* (London: Macmillan, 1908), p. 20; George E. Ladd, *A Commentary on the Revelation of John* (Grand Rapids: Eerdmans, 1972), p. 38; Walvoord, *Revelation*, p. 54.

ἑαυτοὺς ἀποστόλους καὶ οὐκ εἰσίν, καὶ εὗρες αὐτοὺς ψευδεῖς (kai epeirasas tous legontas heautous apostolous kai ouk eisin, kai heures autous pseudeis, "and you have tested those who call themselves apostles—and they are not—and you have found them [to be] liars") (v. 2b), and καὶ ὑπομονὴν ἔχεις, καὶ ἐβάστασας διὰ τὸ ὄνομά μου, καὶ οὐ κεκοπίακες (kai hypomonēn echeis, kai ebastasas dia to onoma mou, kai ou kekopiakes, "and you have endurance and you have borne up because of My name, and you have not grown weary") (v. 3).[33] The theme of the statement is ta erga sou, which is immediately defined as being composed of ton kopon kai tēn hypomonēn at the beginning of v. 2. Each of the subordinate themes is then portrayed in more detail, kopon being developed in the last half of v. 2 and hypomonēn in v. 3.[34]

Oida (v. 2) expresses the Lord's self-claim of knowledge in each of the seven messages (cf. also 2:9, 13, 19; 3:1, 8, 15). In contrast to γινώσκω (ginōskō, "I know"), which speaks of progress of knowledge, oida reflects full or complete knowledge. It depicts absolute clearness of mental vision, which photographs all facts of life as they pass.[35] It, not ginōskō, is always the word used of Christ's knowledge in Revelation (Swete). The concept of Christ's absolute knowledge of the situation in Ephesus recalls v. 1 where He reminds the readers that He walks among the churches and consequently knows all things (cf. John 21:17), the areas deserving of commendation (2:2-3, 6) and condemnation (2:5-6).[36]

The Lord's knowledge of ta erga is restated in four of the other six messages (2:19; 3:1, 8, 15). Even though the noun can refer to good or bad works, it is conspicuous in the context of this message that it refers to good works (Alford). The unusual prominence of the noun in this book is reminiscent of the OT conception of the fear of God, which as a religious principle displays itself effectively in works (Moffatt). These deeds are contrasted to God's rest on the Sabbath after He had ceased His good work of creation (Heb. 4:3-4). The plural

---

33. For clarity's sake it may be helpful to furnish the skeleton of the three couplets: (1) "I know your works . . . and that you cannot bear . . ."; (2) "you have tested . . . and you have found . . ."; (3) "you have endurance . . . and you have not grown weary. . . ."

34. Charles, Revelation, 1:49. Charles also notes two paronomasias in vv. 2-3 that cannot be accidental: τὸν κόπον and οὐ κεκοπίακες, and οὐ δύνῃ βαστάσαι and ἐβάστασας. The chiastic arrangement of these two pairs is striking also.

35. Robertson, Word Pictures, 6:297.

36. Walvoord, Revelation, p. 55; Charles, Revelation, 1:49. In 2:19; 3:1, 8, 15 the genitive of the personal pronoun σου precedes rather than follows τὰ ἔργα, as it does here. The sequence in these other places represents the vernacular or unemphatic possessive (Edwin A. Abbott, Johannine Grammar [London: Adam and Charles Black, 1906], pp. 414, 422, 601-7).

of the noun indicates the general course and moral conduct of life, which are exemplified especially in its active and passive sides as exertion (*kopon*) and endurance (*hypomonēn*).[37]

The Ephesian church was engaged in slavish toil to the point of exhaustion and endured with lasting patience every burden it encountered. These qualities represent two sides of *erga*, an outward activity of labor (*kopon*) and an inward disposition of perseverance (*hypomonēn*). Κόπος (*Kopos*) originally meant "a beating accompanied by wailing and grief."[38] It developed into the connotation of hard work to the point of perspiration. The word is frequently connected closely in Revelation and in the rest of the NT with Christian work, carrying with it the idea of the weariness resulting from hard work (cf. 1 Thess. 1:3; Rev. 14:13) (Charles; Moffatt). *Hypomonē* expresses patience with respect to circumstances, whereas a synonym μακροθυμία (*makrothymia*, "longsuffering") is patience that relates to people.[39] Perseverance triumphs over all opposition, as illustrated in the history of the Maccabean martyrs who are praised for their courage (4 Macc. 1:11) (Moffatt). This Christian quality of endurance in the midst of hard labor has the highest ethical standards. It is the brave patience through which Christians contend against hindrances, persecutions, and temptations that come in their conflict with the world.[40] Doubtless the Christians in this city encountered a wide variety of testings, but the following words indicate a good share of it came from their obligation to try impostors and prove them to be liars.[41]

The second couplet describing Christ's knowledge of the people of

---

37. Moffatt, "Revelation," 5:349; Arndt and Gingrich, *Lexicon*, pp. 307-8. The καί immediately following τὰ ἔργα σου is ascensive and the entire phrase which it introduces, τὸν κόπον καὶ τὴν ὑπομονήν σου, is epexegetical and explains ἔργα (Alford, *Greek Testament*, 4:562). Τὸν κόπον and τὴν ὑπομονήν are tied together by σου.

38. Edward Robinson, *Greek and English Lexicon of the New Testament* (New York: Harper & Brothers, 1850), p. 407.

39. Richard Chenevix Trench, *Synonyms of the New Testament* (Grand Rapids: Eerdmans, 1953), p. 171. Spencer challenges Trench's analysis of these two words, but does so on the basis of questionable assumptions about language (F. Scott Spencer, "Beyond Trench's Study of Synonyms," *ExpTim* 99 [1988]: 140-44). He sides with the viewpoint that two words may be absolutely synonymous (ibid., p. 140), a viewpoint that appears to be unrealistic (see my discussion of Hermeneutics of the Apocalypse in the Introduction to the Commentary). After discarding Trench's proposed distinction between the two words, however, Spencer proceeds to arrive at his own distinction between them in certain cases.

40. Robertson, *Word Pictures*, 6:298; Charles, *Revelation*, 1:49-50.

41. W. M. Ramsay, *The Letters to the Seven Churches of Asia* (New York: A. C. Armstrong, 1904), p. 241; Lenski, *Revelation*, p. 84.

the Ephesian church is in v. 2*b* and is a further development of the earlier *ton kopon*.[42] Their toil includes their incapability of putting up with bad people. Though *dynē* is singular and therefore addressed immediately to the messenger representing the Ephesian church, with the negative particle *ou* it unquestionably describes a church-wide intolerance toward those evil ones. *Bastasai* means "to bear" or "to carry" and conceives of the base ones as a burden to be thrown off. In Gal. 6:2 Christians are commanded to bear the burdens of the weak (βαστάζετε [*bastazete*, "bear"]), but to do so for the evil ones would have been a serious flaw in the Ephesian church (Moffatt). The intolerance had to do with people who were bad as to the quality of their deeds and character. The *kakous* (not πονηρούς [*ponērous*, "viciously wicked"]) are good for nothing in regard to the things in which they ought to excel as good. In other places the word speaks of a cowardly soldier or a lazy student, and so here it refers to a profess-ing Christian who does not live up to proper standards.[43]

An associated question arises as to the possibility of a more spe-cific identification of this group of evil persons. Although it may be impossible to go beyond speaking of them only in general terms as backslidden Christians (Lenski), the fact that a group in the church had to be tested (*epeirasas*, v. 2) and that they were found to be false (*pseudeis*, v. 2) indicates the presence of sham or deception and more than just a backslidden condition. Verse 6 reveals that this church was troubled by Nicolaitans, and the very next clause of v. 2 discloses the presence of false apostles. This stated presence of heretics in the Christian community leads to the conclusion that the next clause, *kai epeirasas tous legontas heautous apostolous*, particularizes the more general statement about the evil persons and gives a further hint as to their identity (Alford; Swete).

At some earlier time[44] this church had by some kind of experien-tial observation[45] evaluated self-claims of apostleship by the evil per-sons (v. 2) and had found them to be false (*heures autous pseudeis*, v. 2), with which finding the author of this message agrees (*kai ouk eisin*, v.

---

42. The ὅτι of v. 2 connects with οἶδα at the beginning of the verse and furnishes a further detailing of the Lord's knowledge.
43. Vine, *Dictionary*, p. 94; Lenski, *Revelation*, p. 85.
44. The aorist tense of ἐπείρασας is constative. It is impossible to know whether it looks back to one past happening or a series of several past "testings" as composing one entity (Robertson, *Word Pictures*, 6:298). One would suppose that a prolonged period of observation would constitute testing of the latter nature.
45. The use of δοκιμάζω would have spoken of putting someone to the test with a view to approval. On the other hand, this use of πειράζω views a trial for the purpose of knowing better or assaying (Alford, *Greek Testa-ment*, 4:562).

2). Several proposals have been advanced regarding the identity of these false apostles and the nature of their claims.

One proposal supposes that these were the apostle Paul and his followers because members of the Pauline group were characterized by freedom from the law, as were the Nicolaitans who apparently bear some relationship to the "evil men" (cf. 2:14-15) (Charles). A further likelihood of this explanation is that a few decades earlier Paul had exerted a great influence on Ephesus and the whole Roman province of Asia (Charles). Yet this suggestion is rather far-fetched because no animosity of John the apostle toward Paul is detected anywhere else. John seems to have enjoyed a wholesome relationship with the churches Paul founded after he arrived in Ephesus in the late sixties. The theory of two hard-line factions (representing John and Paul) within the first-century church is an unproved product of modern scholarship and has no roots in the NT or early Christian tradition.

Another proposal holds the false apostles to be "teachers of the true Gospel" who claimed their message was the truth (Lenski). This view understands "apostle" in the nontechnical and wider sense of "one who is sent." No special authority beyond that of any Christian teacher is involved. Such a nontechnical sense of the word has NT parallels (e.g., 2 Cor. 8:23). The widespread presence of such false teachers is well attested (cf. Matt. 7:15-16; 1 Cor. 14:29; 1 Thess. 5:20-21; 1 John 4:1) (Beckwith). That such people would claim special apostolic authority from Christ is doubtful because by this last decade of the first century almost all the recognized apostles were dead and few would have dared to appropriate the term *apostle* in the technical sense. On the other side of the issue, what would have been the value of claiming apostleship as only another name for the office of teacher? A teacher can be excluded from teaching, but an authoritative apostle of Christ, if he is such, must be heard. These people must have claimed to be more than teachers. They were claiming the same authority as the Twelve before them, and this is what forced the Ephesian church to take its stand against them. These had probably claimed apostolic authority much earlier and had been an influence in the church for a considerable period. The impossibility of their having been eyewitnesses of Christ's resurrection, one of the prerequisites of apostleship, had probably escaped the notice of most. The false teachers simply claimed a direct appointment by Christ.

A third proposal for identifying the self-proclaimed apostles describes them as itinerant Nicolaitan missionaries who posed as equal or superior to the original apostles in authority. Paul had warned the elders of this church about such false leaders years before (Acts

20:29).[46] The proposal that these were identical with Judaizers who are seen elsewhere (cf. 2 Cor. 11:13-14; Rev. 2:9; 3:9) (Hort) is not probable because the Nicolaitans were antinomians rather than legalists.[47] The Nicolaitan identification with a claim of apostolic authority in the highest sense receives its strongest support from the fact that 2:6, where the Nicolaitanism is named, is a resumption of this discussion of 2:2 (Lee; Charles) and from the dominance of "apostle" in the NT to denote authoritative representatives of Christ. Accompanying this is the use of "Jew" in its normal sense in 2:9, which would argue for assigning "apostle" its normal NT sense.[48] One consideration that weakens this view is to observe that a lack of genuineness could have been immediately detected through the inability of these to perform miracles (cf. 2 Cor. 12:12), but Christians are not always alert to a criterion such as this. Apparently these men had some credentials that made their falseness harder to discern (cf. 2 Cor. 11:4-15) (Sweet). Another objection to this higher identification of "apostle" is John's failure to recognize anyone other than the Twelve as apostles, as attested by the twelve foundations of the new Jerusalem (Rev. 21:14). Certainly no one, it is said, would lay claim to being one of the Twelve.[49] This objection is met, however, by noting that a wider group of authoritative apostles existed. James the Just, Barnabas, Paul, Silas, Andronicus, and Junias were also apostles (Acts 14:14; Rom. 16:7; 1 Cor. 15:7; Gal. 1:19; 1 Thess. 2:6) (Caird). There is good ground in the NT for allowing for more than just the Twelve in this select company (cf. 2 Cor. 11:5, 13; 12:11) (Beckwith). A proper reconciliation seems to be that the technical sense of "apostle" referred to a wider authoritative group than just the Twelve, but that the Twelve were a special segment within that group because they had been Christ's original apostles.

Kai ouk eisin is a parenthetical insertion of John into the message of Christ to the church.[50] A question has come about the reason for

---

46. Robertson, *Word Pictures*, 6:298.
47. Robert H. Mounce, *The Book of Revelation*, NICNT (Grand Rapids: Eerdmans, 1977), p. 87.
48. J. P. M. Sweet, *Revelation* (Philadelphia: Westminster, Pelican, 1979), p. 81.
49. G. V. Caird, *A Commentary on the Revelation of St. John the Divine*, HNTC (New York: Harper & Row, 1966), p. 30.
50. Such parentheses are typical throughout the Johannine canon (cf. John 2:9; 3:9; 1 John 3:1; Rev. 2:9). Grammatically speaking, the present participle ὄντας instead of the present indicative εἰσίν would normally be expected to correspond to λέγοντας (Robertson, *Word Pictures*, 6:298). The variation in construction calls attention to the parenthetical nature of the clause.

the present tense of *eisin*. The participle *legontas*, which it parallels, seems to speak of a past claim. Why did John not use an imperfect tense? The answer lies in noting that *legontas* is actually timeless,[51] and a sweeping generalization to parallel it must be in the present tense: "they were not apostles in the past and are not now, nor will they ever be in the future."

In the words "and you found them [to be] liars" the tense connotation of *heures* is the same as that of *epeirasas* earlier in the verse.[52] Both point to some definite and recent crises in which the false apostles were confronted. The aorist tense of both verbs may be contrasted with the present tense of μισεῖς (*miseis*, "you hate") in 2:6 where the ongoing hatred discloses some permanent obstacles that remain in the local situation (Moffatt). The past confrontations resulted in the verdict that these people were self-deceived deceivers.[53]

2:3 After having related the toilsome aspect of the Ephesians' works that the Lord commends (i.e., the painful conflict with evil people of the Nicolaitan school) (v. 2*b*), Christ proceeded with the third couplet of vv. 2-3, which details the second part of their works, *hypomonēn* or "endurance" (cf. 2:2*a*).[54] "You have endurance" acknowledges their continued possession of endurance, and the rest of the verse elaborates on that endurance.

Ebastasas restates the fact of their "bearing" or "bearing up" (see *bastasai kakous*, v. 2), but this time it does not specify what the church has borne. Possibly Christ now means that they bear up under pressures of various kinds, not just those created by the evil men of v. 2 (Alford), but this is not the most natural exegesis in the context. The best sequel to v. 2 is to see a reference to the same problem. Because

---

51. Λέγοντας is articular and adjectival and has no reference to time. It is essentially a substantive. The present indicative εἰσίν is a dramatic or static use of the present tense (H. E. Dana and Julius R. Mantey, *A Manual Grammar of the Greek New Testament* [New York: Macmillan, 1927], p. 186).
52. Robertson, *Word Pictures*, 6:298.
53. Ibid., 6:298. Αὐτοὺς ψευδεῖς is the second double accusative of the verse. Like the earlier ἑαυτοὺς ἀποστόλους, it is composed of a personal object and a predicate object (cf. Dana and Mantey, *Grammar*, p. 94),
54. Lange has suggested that v. 3 is a third area of commendation, noting that βαστάζω and κοπιάω have different senses in v. 3 and that it is too redundant to take this verse as a summary of v. 2 (John Peter Lange, *The Revelation of John*, Lange's Commentary, ed. E. R. Craven [Grand Rapids: Zondervan, 1968], 10:115). His exception furnishes a good opportunity to clarify that v. 3 is not merely a repetition of v. 2, but is a further explanation of ὑπομονήν in v. 2. Wordplays upon βαστάζω and κοπιάω are a typical method of elaboration: "you have *borne* up, though you cannot *bear* evil men, and in spite of your *toil*, you have not *grown weary*" (Sweet, *Revelation*, pp. 80-81).

of Christ's name, they had borne or put up with the labor of resisting the errorists and had endured their taunts.[55]

They had so persevered *dia to onoma mou,* "because of My name," says Christ. Here the name of Christ has in view the gospel revelation through which He makes Himself known (Lenski). The identical phrase occurs in Matt. 10:22 and 24:9 in contexts where Christ's persecuted followers were engaged in spreading the gospel (Hort). Before leaving earth Jesus had predicted the very thing that Ephesian Christendom was now experiencing. They persevered for the sake of the purity of the message they preached.

In spite of toil to the point of weariness (see *kopon,* v. 2) they had not grown weary (*ou kekopiakes*). This is a great paradox. Never did they entertain any thought of giving up (Scott). It was labor to the point of weariness without weariness setting in (Hort). Their loyalty to the Lord preempted weariness.[56]

2:4 *The state of the church.* Verse 4 changes abruptly from the tone of commendation to that of condemnation: ἀλλὰ[57] ἔχω κατὰ σοῦ ὅτι τὴν ἀγάπην σου τὴν πρώτην ἀφῆκες (*alla echō kata sou hoti tēn agapēn sou tēn prōtēn aphēkes,* "but I have against you that you have left your first love"). In one brief statement Christ isolates a critical problem in the church. Though the loss of their "first love" is the only thing the church is censured for, this is not to say their problem was not a serious one (Scott).

The phraseology gives special attention to *tēn prōtēn,* "first": "you have left your love, at least the love of the first days" (Swete). The cure for their problem includes a return to "the first works" in 2:5, which indicates that part of the problem was the absence of certain works that would have resulted from the missing love. The Lord expected a growth in works comparable to the growth for which He later commends the church in Thyatira (2:19). The addressees had works (2:2), but not of a magnitude they would have had if they had retained their "first love."

Johannine literature gives great prominence to love for fellow Christians. In fact, brotherly love was very early regarded as authen-

---

55. Swete, *Apocalypse,* p. 26; Homer Hailey, *Revelation, an Introduction and Commentary* (Grand Rapids: Baker, 1979), p. 121.
56. Moffatt, "Revelation," 5:350. The perfect tense of κεκοπίακες is expressive. Lenski proposes a consummative perfect, "all along in the past to the very present 'you have not wearied'" (Lenski, *Revelation,* p. 87), but Swete's proposal of an intensive perfect to indicate their state following endurance has more merit: "you are not weary" (Swete, *Apocalypse,* p. 26).
57. The strong adversative conjunction is appropriate because the strong reproach about to be delivered is so completely opposite from the positive words just concluded (Lenski, *Revelation,* p. 86).

tic proof of faith in Christ (v. 19; John 13:34-35; 1 John 3:13-14; 2 John 5-6; 3 John 6). At the same time, brotherly love cannot be separated from love for Christ, because it is proof of that love (cf. 1 John 4:20). An example of love that serves also as a definition is given in 1 John 4:10: "In this is love, not that we loved God, but that He loved us and sent His Son [to be] a propitiation for our sins." Love is not a reciprocation. It takes the initiative, is sacrificial in nature, and meets the needs of its object. In addition, love is inseparable from obeying God's commands (1 John 5:2; cf. Rom. 13:8-10). Love and moral purity go together (Moffatt).

Something was missing in the relationships among these Ephesians, but this only reflects a deeper need. Most basically, their love for Christ had grown cold, causing the relational problems, and it is this root problem that is primarily addressed. "The love of first conversion had waxed cold, and given place to a lifeless and formal orthodoxy" (Alford). Some vital element that had characterized their initial relationship to the Savior had now disappeared. A closer look at the implications of "leaving one's first love" will help to understand the spiritual status of the Ephesian addressees.

One opinion is that "leaving one's first love" does not mean the loss of all love, the commendations of 2:2-3, 6 presupposing a continuing love of some kind (Beckwith). On this basis it is concluded that these were real Christians whose love had decreased instead of increasing since their conversion (Lenski). The result for Ephesus was that the church had lost its testimony before the world. Another idea is that "leaving one's first love" means that the love that had characterized the church in earlier times was now entirely missing, leaving no proof in their lives to back up the reality of their profession of faith in Christ. With this situation, the danger was infinitely greater and these readers needed to examine their own profession to ascertain whether or not it was genuine.

The first viewpoint finds support in an earlier word from Paul to this church when he told them to place more emphasis on love for one another, but did not question the genuineness of their conversion experience (Eph. 4:2; 5:2) (Lee). Their coldness and lifeless orthodoxy could easily have derived from their zeal against teachers of error (cf. 2:2, 6) rather than from a lack of real conversion (Beckwith; Caird). Neglect of brotherly love was a cardinal fault in contemporary Gnostic tendencies (cf. 1 Tim. 1:5,6; 1 John 2:9), and could easily have accompanied the church's jealous regard for doctrinal purity and unwavering loyalty in trial (Beckwith; Moffatt). Paul warns against this very tendency in 2 Thess. 3:14-15 and 2 Tim. 2:24-26 (Sweet). "First love" speaks of the first fervent, chaste, and pure love of the newly-wedded bride (cf. Jer. 2:2; 2 Cor. 11:2) (Alford) and can only characterize those whose faith in Christ is real. Furthermore, hatred for the deeds of the Nicolaitans (2:6) would hardly have been commended if the Lord were addressing unbelievers. The problem of these readers was not a lack of faith in Christ or of yieldedness to Him. For some reason the ardor they had once exhibited had simply grown cold (Walvoord).

The second viewpoint regarding the meaning of leaving one's first love, i.e., that a lingering of such a condition is proof that real conversion never took place, emphasizes the test of love for the brethren that John himself had posed in his first epistle not too long before this (1 John 2:9-11; 3:13-14). If a loss of the first love entailed the absence of such love, which surely it must have, it is impossible for the professing Christians in Ephesus to have been in possession of new life in Christ when Jesus spoke these words.[58] Coupled with this is the threat of the removal of the church's lampstand (2:5). It is hardly probable that such strong language would have been spoken to believers who had grown lethargic.

Both viewpoints are persuasive, but both also have weaknesses. The position that holds all the addressees to be born again but lethargic fails to note the time lapse between the founding of the Ephesian church and the writing of the Apocalypse. Though the earliest Christians at Ephesus had been noted for their ardent love (cf. Acts 20:37; Eph. 1:15), a new generation had now taken their place (Swete). The present words are an indictment against the new generation. The other perspective that holds that the profession of the addressees is not genuine cannot use the criteria derived from John's first epistle because that epistle never grants that the secessionists had ever possessed a "first love." Besides, Rev. 2:1-7 gives no indication of the existence of a group who had abandoned the Christian community as in 1 John.

A proper reconstruction of the situation must incorporate valid elements from both views. It is evident from the singling out of the overcomer in 2:7 that some in the second generation of Ephesian Christians had not experienced genuine salvation, and so the word spoken to the church corporately about having possessed a "first love" does not necessarily apply to every individual. It simply observes that what the church had possessed as a body when founded was now missing. More than forty years had passed and the warmth of love that characterized the former generation was absent from the present group. This does not imply that every one of John's current generation was unregenerate any more than it implies that every member of the earlier generation had been regenerate. It simply

---

58. Robertson, *Word Pictures*, 6:299.

notes a greater proportion of unregenerate now than before. The level had reached the point that it affected the corporate body adversely, resulting in the verdict, "You have left your first love." This influential minority was quite orthodox in its doctrinal persuasions, but devoid of spiritual life. Jesus urges such persons to become real in their relationship with Himself. The majority of church members were genuinely converted, as reflected in the present works (cf. 2:2-3, 6). To these Christ's word is to shake off their lethargy and cultivate a warmth of love toward Him and hence toward their fellow Christians also.

2:5 *The Lord's coming.* Based on His negative appraisal of the church's condition in 2:4,[59] the Lord now issues a plea for repentance based on His own return: μνημόνευε οὖν πόθεν πέπτωκας, καὶ μετανόησον καὶ τὰ πρῶτα ἔργα ποίησον· εἰ δὲ μή, ἔρχομαί σοι καὶ κινήσω τὴν λυχνίαν σου ἐκ τοῦ τόπου αὐτῆς, ἐὰν μὴ μετανοήσῃς (*mnēmoneue oun pothen peptōkas, kai metanoēson kai ta prōta erga poiēson; ei de mē, erchomai soi kai kinēsō tēn lychnian sou ek tou topou autēs, ean mē metanoēsēs,* "Remember, therefore, whence you have fallen, and repent and do the first works. But if not, I will come to you and remove your lampstand from its place, unless you repent").

Memory is important in responding to this plea. Christ urges the Ephesian church to "keep on remembering"[60] because they were not ignorant unbelievers without a background in Christianity. They had a generation of Christian tradition behind them and knew about the church's former condition. They had simply lost their bearings, like the prodigal son, and needed to regain them.[61] The church's previous condition is alluded to in *pothen peptōkas* ("whence you have fallen"). Pure love resided on the cliff high above, as it were, and they had fallen deep into the valley below.[62] Their departure from their first love (2:4) is now viewed as a fall from a previous position. The perfect tense of *peptōkas* reflects their existent fallen state.

The purpose of their recollection was repentance and a return to the performance of their first works. *Metanoēson* calls for a decisive change of attitude with its resultant action. It is a reversal of the status quo, a deliberate repudiation of former sins and a complete

---

59. The οὖν of 2:5 is resumptive as in 1:19.
60. Μνημόνευε is a present active imperative and carries the force of "continue mindful," "keep on calling to (or bearing in) mind" (Robertson, *Word Pictures,* 6:299). This present tense does two things: (1) it shows that some remembrance already existed and (2) it urges the readers to "keep on remembering." Constant remembering was and is an impulse toward recovery (Lenski, *Revelation,* p. 87).
61. Barclay, *Revelation,* 1:78.
62. Robertson, *Word Pictures,* 6:299.

return to the standards and will of God.[63] It is an appeal to begin at this moment a complete change. It calls for a quick and effective decision.[64]

The urgency that is to characterize the repentance should also mark the return to the first works, according to *ta prōta ta erga poiēson*: "Start doing those works which characterized your church at its earliest stage of existence, do it at once!"[65] "First" looks back to "first love" of the previous verse. Love and works are intimately related (cf. 1 John 5:2). The first works consist of the love shown when the commandments of God are kept in relationships with other believers (cf. Matt. 24:12). This church had works that were outwardly good (cf. 2:2), but they were different in kind and quality from what Jesus now requires. They were not of the quality that the Lord could commend because they arose from inferior motives, not from love. Further in their favor, they had a disdain for the inferior works, those hated also by Christ (2:6). Yet to hate what Christ hates cannot replace works that are prompted by the love of God that has been poured out in believers' hearts by the Holy Spirit (Rom. 5:5). So in spite of His commendations of this church, Jesus calls members to return to the actions prompted by love that they as a church had formerly known.

Anticipating a negative response to His commands, the speaker tells the consequences of non-repentance. *Ei de mē*, translated "but if not" above, can also mean "otherwise," i.e., "if you choose not to repent and do the first works."[66] Jesus promises to come and remove the church's lampstand from its place if the members fail to respond with repentance. Various ideas of what this threatened action entails have been advanced, some relating it to Christ's second advent and others seeing a reference to a special "coming in judgment" to the Ephesian church alone. The latter is supported as being more natural to the context than a threat of judgment to this local church alone at the coming of Christ.[67] Also such a preliminary judgment is said to be

---

63. Ibid., 6:299; Tenney, *Revelation*, p. 57.
64. Alford, *Greek Testament*, 4:563. The verb is aorist imperative and carries the note of urgency that normally accompanies that form.
65. Robertson, *Word Pictures*, 6:299; Lenski, *Revelation*, p. 87; Tenney, *Revelation*, p. 57. Ποίησον is an aorist imperative as is μετανόησον.
66. Εἰ δὲ μή is an elliptical condition, the verb implied but not expressed being μετανόησον. It is a common idiom (e.g., 2:16) usually appearing without a verb in Classical Greek as it does in the NT (Robertson, *Word Pictures*, 6:299; BDF, par. 376). It introduces a supposition opposed to something just said (H. W. Smyth, *Greek Grammar*, rev. Gordon M. Messing [Cambridge, Mass.: Harvard U., 1956], p. 543).
67. G. R. Beasley-Murray, *The Book of Revelation*, NCB (Grand Rapids: Eerdmans, 1978), p. 75. Lee calls specific attention to the removal of *one*

paralleled in Rev. 2:22 (Beckwith), but in that verse the same debate exists in relation to the message to Thyatira. That the coming is not pictured as a worldwide crisis but a crisis private to the church concerned is another evidence that this is a special coming in judgment because of the condition of the church in Ephesus (Caird).

Preference for understanding this as a reference to Christ's second advent attributes more importance to the broad context of the book. It notes that if this were merely a local and preliminary visitation, it would bear no relationship to the apocalyptic portion of the book (Rev. 4:1–22:5), nor would its connection with the theme of Rev. 1:7 be explicable. Seeing this as a reference to Christ's second coming, however, harmonizes quite well with the use of *erchomai* in this book and elsewhere to refer to His return (cf. 1:7; 2:16; 3:11; 22:7, 12, 20).[68] A special coming or visitation, anything short of a personal coming of Christ, fails to satisfy the technical sense this verb must have in a book such as this. In addition, the metaphor chosen by John is the same as that used for the actual occurrence when the Roman conquerors removed the seven-branched lampstand from the Temple in A.D. 70 (Lee). The NT connects that Roman plundering of the Temple with Christ's second coming in a number of places (e.g., Luke 21:5-28). Another factor that gives weight to identifying this with the *parousia* is to note that abandoning the first love is one of the signs of the end (cf. Matt. 24:12) (Sweet). Reasons for associating this threat with the second advent of Christ are compelling, particularly those that relate to the Apocalypse's broad context and the use of *erchomai*. Though the threat is vague, it is probably eschatological.[69]

---

lampstand, not several or seven, as proving that the judgment is local, not catholic (Lee, 4:517). Mounce notes Christ's walking in the midst of the churches as more compatible with an immediate visitation of preliminary judgment (Mounce, *Revelation*, p. 89).

68. The present tense of ἔρχομαι has a futuristic force. A present form is used frequently to speak of Christ's coming (Robertson, *Word Pictures*, 6:299). It has practically the same meaning as ἐλεύσεσθε throughout the Apocalypse (Charles, *Revelation*, 1:52), except for bringing more attention to the imminence of that coming than the future form would have. This future notion recalls the idea of "the coming one" of 1:7, 8 (Lenski, *Revelation*, p. 89).

69. Moffatt, "Revelation," 5:351. Moule and Sweet note a eucharistic emphasis in connection with this threat. The eucharistic pattern of promise and threat are paralleled with the seven messages of Rev. 2-3 and the epilogue of Revelation. In the eucharist *parousia* and judgment are constantly anticipated (cf. 1 Cor. 11:28-32) (C. F. D. Moule, "The Judgment Theme in the Sacraments," in *The Background of the New Testament and Its Eschatology*, ed. W. D. Davies and D. Daube [Cambridge: Cambridge U., 1954], pp. 464-81; cf. also Sweet, *Revelation*, pp. 35, 41-42). Aune, on the other hand, perceptively treats this and other words about negative aspects of the *parousia* as signaling a threat of imminent eschatological judgment

The apparent necessity of taking this threat to connect with Christ's second advent raises a further issue. Because this coming, like the ones at 2:16 and 3:3, is conditioned upon the failure of the church to repent, how could it refer to the *parousia* (Swete; Sweet)? Some take these conditioned threats to Ephesus, Pergamum, and Sardis to show that an imminent *parousia* was not one of the events John believed were "bound to happen soon" (cf. 1:1) (Caird). They assume it to be inaccurate to make the return of Christ dependent on man's refusal to respond in repentance. One solution to this dilemma is to suppose that Christ's coming will occur at an appointed time, no matter what the church's response is, and that the removal of the lampstand is the only thing conditioned on repentance. It does injustice to Christ's statement to ignore His advent completely, however.

Yet a reference to both the advent and removal of the lampstand can be included through attention to a common grammatical characteristic of biblical Greek. Such a special sense for the words is justified by the unconditioned nature of Christ's coming in Rev. 2:25 and 3:11. The unconditional nature of that coming is possible in 2:5 also, and a legitimate meaning for the words is, "When I come, I will remove your lampstand, if you shall not have repented before that coming, whenever it happens" (Sweet; Beckwith). Emphasis upon the imminence of Christ's coming is an acknowledged characteristic of the Apocalypse. For this first-century generation, as for all generations of Christians since, the coming of Christ has been and is imminent. The threat to the people of this church lay in the possibility that His coming might happen while they were alive and catch them in a state of non-repentance. So this sense of the words to the Ephesian recipients stressed the importance of their immediate response to Christ's command to repent, but it did not condition His coming upon their failure to do so.

A remaining issue in 2:5 is Christ's meaning in the threat to remove the lampstand. Does it mean a removal, by some special act of judgment, of the light that at one time had shone so brightly in Ephesus, or does it mean a removal through allowing an unsaved remnant of the church to pass into the future tribulation to be associated with the return of Christ? The extinguishing of the light through special judgment could happen through destruction of the whole city and a closing of its harbor. Such was eventually the fate of Ephesus,

---

(David E. Aune, "The Form and Function of the Proclamations to the Seven Churches [Revelation 2-3]," *NTS* 36, no. 2 [April 1990]: 192; cf. also Muse, pp. 153-54, and Fred Mazzaferri, "ΜΑΡΤΥΡΙΑ ΙΗΣΟΥ Revisited," *BT* 39, no. 1 [January 1988]: 119).

the site the city once occupied, which now lies desolate and barren (Smith; Walvoord). Its harbor was constantly filling with silt at the mouth of the Cayster River, and the city of necessity had to keep relocating (Ramsay; Sweet; Hailey). One can also see a fulfillment of these words in the gross darkness of Islam, which dominates these seven cities of proconsular Asia, including Ephesus (Scott). The difficulty in affirming this meaning of the words lies in noting that the threat does not pertain to the whole city, but to the church within the city. There is a further point of interest: some early Fathers say the Ephesian church *did* repent and turn back to the Lord in response to these words, thus alleviating the applicability of the words to that generation.[70]

Again, an extinguishing of the light through special judgment could entail, not destruction, but a loss of testimony. Light emanating from a lampstand is symbolic of testimony. Κινέω (*Kineō*, "I remove") is different from ἀφαιρέω (*aphaireō*, "I destroy"). It denotes deliberation and judicial calmness in comparison to the other verb. It is not a sudden uprooting as in anger, but a gradual movement that results in loss of the place the church had once filled (Swete). It is quite possible for a church to remain but have no testimony, just as the Temple of Jerusalem was devoid of God's glory after His judgment fell on it (cf. Ezek. 11:22, 23) (Beasley-Murray). Losing its "lamp" most naturally means that it ceases to be a real church (Caird). Without the "first love" (2:4), which includes brotherly love, a church must become extinct (Beckwith). This view has some cogency, but it is hard to conceive of a loss of testimony as an act of divine removal. Testimony is lost automatically through human neglect. No additional judgmental notion is necessary.

Very conceivably, the added dimension of judgment comes through the tribulation associated with Christ's return, which has been connected above with the removal of the lampstand. The casting of the unsaved remnant of the church into the end-time tribulation inevitably accompanies the deliverance of the saved remnant into Christ's presence. The two occur simultaneously, leaving the church on earth without a single person whose profession of faith in Christ is genuine. In this situation loss of testimony is inevitable for the church. Beyond this, it will mean untold suffering for the remaining church, though this is not expressed here (cf. 2:22; 3:10).

The object removed, *tēn lychnian*, may symbolize the source that gives off light, the church (cf. 1:20) (Swete; Charles), or that which holds the light, but not the source of the light. More probably, the

---

70. Ignatius *Epistle to the Ephesians.*

former is the connotation. As is true of the two witnesses of Rev. 11:4, also referred to as lampstands, a lampstand is the source of light that takes the form of the testimony borne. Without genuine Christians remaining, it is impossible for a church to produce light.

Whether or not the first recipients repented as Christ required is a moot point. Since His second advent has not yet occurred, the challenge has remained for all churches since that day.

2:6 The Lord appends to His announced coming and threat a further word regarding His knowledge of the people in the church. His earlier words on this subject were, on the whole, commendatory (2:2-3). His commendation of the readers continues in 2:6 as a strong contrast[71] to His stern words about their shortcomings and need for repentance in 2:4-5: ἀλλὰ τοῦτο ἔχεις, ὅτι μισεῖς τὰ ἔργα τῶν Νικολαϊτῶν, ἃ κἀγὼ μισῶ (*alla touto echeis, hoti miseis ta erga tōn Nikolaitōn, ha kagō misō*, "but you have this, that you hate the works of the Nicolaitans, which I also hate"). Three features contribute to greater emphasis upon these words: the strong adversative *alla* ("but"), the placement of the verse late in the context of the letter in conjunction with the promise of the Lord's return, and the strength of the Lord's reaction to the problem as reflected in His hatred (*misō*) of the deeds (Beckwith).

This return to the subject of 2:2-3 amounts to a repetition and expansion of what is found there, a writing pattern that characterizes the fourth gospel also. The false teachers of v. 2 are now identified as Nicolaitans, and further emphasis comes to the Lord's despising of their teachings (Beckwith). They still retain their past intolerance of these errorists.[72] Though they had left their first love, they had not left their former hatred for evil.

The substance of their virtue consists of their hatred for the works of the Nicolaitans.[73] The commendation relates to their reaction to evil deeds in contrast with their condemnation that related to their lack of love for people. Perhaps their hatred had transferred from the deeds to the people guilty of committing the deeds. Their attitude toward the deeds was altogether proper. This is no mere disapproval. It is hatred in the absolute sense. It is the diametric opposite of the tolerance of the church in Pergamum toward the teachings and deeds of the Nicolaitans (cf. Rev. 2:14-15). It matches the hatred of the Lord

---

71. The strong adversative ἀλλά is used for the second time in the message (cf. v. 4).
72. Note the present tense of ἔχεις as compared with the aorist tenses of ἐπείρασας and εὗρες in 2:2.
73. Ὅτι introduces an accusative object clause in apposition with τοῦτο (Robertson, *Word Pictures*, 6:300).

Himself toward abomination and impurity (*ha kagō misō*; cf. Isa. 61:8; Jer. 44:4; Amos 5:21; Zech. 8:17) (Alford; Swete). To share His hatred is to manifest affinity of character with Him, which is a sign of grace in churches and individuals.

A mystery surrounds the identity of the Nicolaitans. Three major suggestions have been forthcoming. First, Irenaeus took the sect to be followers of Nicolaus of Antioch, one of the seven original deacons (Acts 6:5), a Jewish proselyte, who is said to have apostatized. It is possible that the Balaamites of v. 15 were a variety of this sect.[74] Second, the sect began through a misinterpretation of a statement by Nicolaus. They lived a life which indulged in the lust of the flesh and were an early sect of Gnostics.[75] Third, the word Nicolaitan comes from the Greek compound νῖχος (*nikos*) and λαός (*laos*) and means "conqueror of the people." Its Hebrew counterpart is "Balaam," "devourer of the people." These were forerunners of the clerical hierarchy.[76]

The explanation that takes the Nicolaitans to be composed of followers of Nicolaus of Antioch has strong support in the early church. Added to Irenaeus are the testimonies of Tertullian, Hippolytus, Dorotheus of Tyre, Jerome, Augustine, Eusebius and others (Lee; Moffatt). They all say this was a sect of licentious antinomian Gnostics who lapsed into their antinomian license because of an overstrained asceticism. Hippolytus adds that Nicolaus was the forerunner of Hymenaeus and Philetus who are condemned in 2 Tim. 2:17 (Lee). Eusebius adds that after the group was censured by John in the Apocalypse, the sect disappeared in a very short time (Lee). On the other side of the issue, some have noted that Clement and others give a favorable view of Nicolaus (Alford; Hort). At best, they say, early church history is uncertain and throws no real light on the identity of the Nicolaitans (Beckwith). All that such sources will venture is that they were "a heretical sect, who retained pagan practices like idolatry and immorality contrary to the thought and the conduct required in Christian churches"[77] and a Christian group within the churches of Asia Minor whose professed insight into the divine allowed them freedom to become part of their syncretistic pagan society.[78] For these sources, to try to go beyond such descriptions to discover the origin of the group is futile (Mounce).

The second approach to identifying the Nicolaitans also notes

---

74. Ibid.
75. Lange, *Revelation*, p. 116; Lenski, *Revelation*, p. 90.
76. Lange, *Revelation*, p. 116; Walvoord, *Revelation*, p. 58.
77. Mounce, *Revelation*, p. 89.
78. E. S. Fiorenza, "Apocalyptic and Gnosis in the Book of Revelation and Paul," *JBL* 92 (1973): 565-81.

their licentious tendencies and possible relationship to Gnosticism, but looks upon Nicolaus not as an apostate, but as a dangerously lax teacher who had one of his tenets exploited immorally by others (Moffatt). The group, says this approach, claimed a lineage from Nicolaus, but identification of Nicolaus as its originator cannot be verified (Swete). The connection of Nicolaitans with licentious habits has been contested,[79] but the contesting evidence is not convincing. The major problem with this view is in explaining why the claim of this sect's connection with Nicolaus went uncontested in the early church. Certainly some voice would have been raised to point out the falsity of the claim and protect his good name if there were nothing to it.

A third way of explaining the Nicolaitans says nothing about Nicolaus, but bases their identification on the etymology of the word. The two components are νῖκος (*nikos*, "victory") and λαός (*laos*, "people"), resulting in the meaning "conqueror of the people." This idea is akin to the meaning of the Hebrew word for "Balaam": "devourer of the people."[80] This view sees the Nicolaitans as forerunners of the clerical hierarchy in the church (Walvoord). The mystical interpretation of "the teaching of Balaam" in 2:14 is said to point to the "teaching of the Nicolaitans" in 2:15, providing support for this identification (Alford; Lee). The tempters of the church in the apostolic age were those who, like Balaam (Num. 31:16), introduced the freedom of the flesh (Acts 15:20; 2 Pet. 2:15; Jude 11). Even apart from the etymology of the name, the licentious Nicolaitans may appropriately have been named with a designation comparable to Balaam (Lee). This also accords with John's custom of using Hebrew and Greek counterparts to name the same object (e.g., "Apollyon" and "Abaddon," Rev. 9:11) (Lee). The practices of the Balaamites (Rev. 2:14) and of the followers of Jezebel (Rev. 2:20) were very much the same as those of the Nicolaitans (Rev. 2:15), so the groups must have been akin to each other.[81]

This third view is weak in its suggestion that this is a veiled reference to a clerical hierarchy, because this like other proper names in the book was probably an actual historical sect (Alford; Beckwith). The alleged identity of the Greek word Νικόλαος (*Nikolaos*, "Nicolaus") with the Hebrew בִּלְעָם (*Bil'ām*, "Bilaam" or "Balaam") is improbable (Swete; Beckwith). A play on the two words without specific declaration of their equivalency is too subtle for this writer (Swete).

---

79. W. M. Mackay, "Another Look at the Nicolaitans," *EvQ* 45 (1973): 111-15.
80. Lange, *Revelation*, p. 116.
81. Leon Morris, *The Revelation of St. John*, TNTC (Grand Rapids: Eerdmans, 1969), p. 62.

Of the three possible explanations for the origin of the Nicolaitan sect, the first is most persuasive. The few ancient voices that defend Nicolaus against charges of apostasy raise some questions, but are not sufficient to negate the strain of tradition that traces this sect back to Nicolaus. The charge is too early and too widespread to be neglected. Besides, it was not in the interest of later tradition for the early church to propagate such demeaning reports about the character of an apostolic Christian. Irenaeus and other early Fathers would not have transmitted such without some basis in fact (Moffatt).

Whatever the origin of the Nicolaitans, this church's members had the right attitude toward their works. Jesus Himself joins them in hatred for such deeds, which unquestionably included works of abomination and impurity. Otherwise, the Lord's language would not have been so strong (cf. Isa. 61:8; Jer. 44:4; Amos 5:21; Zech. 8:17) (Walvoord). The Ephesians are refreshing in this kind of response, especially when compared with those at Pergamum where the deeds of the Nicolaitans were tolerated rather than hated (Rev. 2:14-15).[82]

2:7 *Command to hear.* Approaching the end of His message to Ephesus, the speaker extends a personal invitation to each individual to pay special heed to the recommendations given: ὁ ἔχων οὖς ἀκουσάτω τί τὸ πνεῦμα λέγει ταῖς ἐκκλησίαις (*ho echōn ous akousatō ti to pneuma legei tais ekklēsiais*, "The one who has an ear, let him hear what the Spirit says to the churches"). This recalls the individualizing note of the first "beatitude" of the book (1:3; cf. also 13:9) and is formulated much like some of Jesus' invitations in the synoptic gospels (cf. Matt. 11:15; 13:9, 43; Mark 4:9, 23; Luke 8:8; 14:15).[83] The same exhortation to listen comes in the other six messages (2:11, 17, 28; 3:6, 13, 22). In the first three of the seven it precedes the promise to the overcomer, and in the last four it follows it and constitutes the closing words of the messages.

At first, the suggestion of relating this invitation to the content of this first message only appears to have merit, but more compelling considerations dictate otherwise. The use of the plural *tais ekklēsiais* indicates the universal character of the invitation each time it occurs in these two chapters (cf. Mark 13:37; Rev. 2:23) (Lee; Charles). By means of this call the message to a single congregation is extended to all the churches of Asia and through them, as representatives, to the church throughout the world (Swete; Beasley-Murray). Any effort to limit this invitation to the promise to the overcomer that follows it in 2:7 is also futile because the promise to the overcomer precedes it in four of the messages (2:29; 3:6, 13, 22) (Alford).

---

82. Robertson, *Word Pictures*, 6:300.
83. Ibid.

With this kind of invitation the writer exchanges the visional representation suited to an apocalyptist for the customary one of a prophet, and accordingly substitutes the ordinary title "the Spirit" for the visional symbol of "the seven Spirits" (Beckwith). Similarly, the exalted Son of Man pictured in the vision and speaking in the rest of the message is now conceived as having given His message through the Spirit rather than in oral words spoken directly to the prophet (Hort; Beckwith). This too makes a close connection with the contents of one specific message less necessary. A further factor provides this invitation with a more general force. This is the use of it or its variations in other settings as the usual way to command solemn attention (cf. Matt. 11:15; 13:9, 43; Mark 4:9, 23; Luke 8:8; 14:35; Rev. 13:9) (Lee). It invites the recipients to hear and to respond properly by complying with norms and values of the Christian faith as outlined in the message just before.[84]

So with this "command to hear" comes a broadening focus. It certainly includes the church of Ephesus, being a part of its message, but the call is wider and extends to all the churches. The mention of the "ear" suggests an ability to perceive or understand. The one who possesses this ability is invited to pay special attention to what the Holy Spirit is saying to the churches in this particular message. Because Christ is the speaker (cf. 2:1), the Spirit is functioning particularly as the Spirit of Christ in this instance (cf. Rev. 14:13; 19:10; 22:17) (Charles). He bids every church to heed what is said to each church seven times in these two chapters.

Promise to the overcomer. The incentive to heed the moral lessons of the message is centered in the promise to the overcomer: τῷ νικῶντι δώσω αὐτῷ φαγεῖν ἐκ τοῦ ξύλον τῆς ζωῆς, ὅ ἐστιν ἐν τῷ παραδείσῳ τοῦ θεοῦ (*tǭ nikōnti dōsō autǭ phagein ek tou xylon tēs zōēs, ho estin en tǭ paradeisǭ tou theou*, "To the one who overcomes, I will grant to him to eat from the tree of life, which is in the Paradise of God"). Νικάω (*Nikaō*, "I conquer, overcome") is common in John's writings[85] as πιστεύω (*pisteuō*, "I believe") is dominant in Paul's works.[86] The question that needs resolving involves a proper identification of this overcomer. Does he belong to a special class of Christians composed of those who are spiritual and not carnal? Or is he part of a special group of Christians who are set apart for eventual martyrdom? Or is "overcomer" simply another name for those who are genuinely regenerate believers?

---

84. Anne-Marit Enroth, "The Hearing Formula in the Book of Revelation," *NTS* 36, no. 4 (October 1990): 602-3, 607-8.
85. Cf. John 16:33; 1 John 2:13, 14; 4:4; 5:4, 5; Rev. 2:7, 11, 17; 3:5, 12, 21; 5:5; 12:11; 15:2; 17:14; 21:7.
86. Robertson, *Word Pictures*, 6:300.

To make overcomers a special class of Christians divides regenerate persons in Ephesus and the other cities into two groups, one that obeys the Lord's command to repent and one that does not. It assumes that all in the church are regenerate, but that only part of their number qualifies for the promise made to the overcomer. The difficulty with this approach is that this promise to the overcomer (as well as those in the other six messages) entails participation in eternal blessings that belong to all the saved. For example, eating of the tree of life is synonymous with possessing eternal life (cf. Rev. 22:2, 14). A further weakness of this identification is its failure to note that *nikaō* in John's writings is synonymous with saving faith in Christ (cf. 1 John 5:4-5). This is not a special group of Christians distinguished by their spirituality and power from other genuine Christians who lack these. This is a general designation for what is expected of all true Christians.[87] While the promise to the overcomer in Ephesus is tailored to the special circumstances of that church (and the same with the other churches), it still belongs to all believers. This is what the Spirit says to all the churches (2:7a).[88]

An even more restricted definition of the overcomer limits him to the persecuted Christian whose martyr's death is his victory, just as Christ's cross was His victory (cf. 3:21). This group is a limited number of believers through whom Christ wins again the victory of Calvary through weapons of love (cf. 2:26; 7:14; 12:11; 15:2).[89] Not all Christians will experience martyrdom, and the joys of paradise are not limited to martyrs, according to this approach. The inadequacies of this explanation are rather evident. Limiting the statements of 2:26 and 3:21 to martyrs is to neglect both the immediate and the broad contexts of the verses (Beasley-Murray). At the consummation of the book only two categories of people exist: those inside the eternal city and those outside (cf. 21:7, 8) (Sweet). It is true that all Christian martyrs will be inside, but it is not true that all nonmartyrs will be outside. Among those inside the city, no distinction exists between overcomers and nonovercomers. They are all overcomers.

"Overcomer" is best understood as a general designation applicable to all believers. This promise of eating from the tree of life, along with the promises in 2:11, 28, is the common privilege of all the redeemed, not just a select class of believers or just believers in the

---

87. Walvoord, *Revelation*, p. 59; Charles Caldwell Ryrie, *Revelation*, Everyman's Bible Commentary (Chicago: Moody, 1968), pp. 22-23.
88. Lee, "Revelation," 4:518; Ryrie, *Revelation*, p. 23.
89. Charles, *Revelation*, 1:54; Caird, *Revelation*, p. 33; Martin Kiddle, *The Revelation of St. John*, MNTC (London: Hodder and Stoughton, 1940), pp. 62-63.

Ephesian church (Moffatt). "The tree of life" recalls Gen. 2:9 and 3:22 and anticipates Rev. 22:2, 14. Sin barred man from the tree, and overcoming sin restores his right to eat from the tree and thus live forever (Smith). All the promises to the conquerors (2:7, 10, 17, 26-28; 3:5, 12, 21) are fundamentally symbolic promises to the faithful of the benefits of Christ's redemption and of participation in the kingdom of God described in the closing vision of this book.[90]

The identical form denoting God's gift to the overcomer (*dōsō*, "I will grant") occurs several times in these two chapters, usually denoting a gift of one's own accord and good will (cf. 2:10, 17, 26, 28; 3:21). God's gift here consists of the privilege of eating from the tree of life (cf. Gen. 2:9; 3:22; Rev. 22:2, 14), i.e., immortality or unending life in the new Jerusalem.[91] This promise, like all the overcomer promises, looks forward to the last three chapters dealing with the millennial kingdom (chapter 20) and the new Jerusalem (chapters 21-22).[92] Never is the overcomer called upon to anticipate the dreaded woes of chapters 4-19.

The tree of life stands in "the Paradise of God." *Paradeisọ* is derived from a Persian word describing a pleasure garden and park with wild animals built for Persian monarchs.[93] Two other NT uses of the word (Luke 23:43; 2 Cor. 12:4) with the present verse show it to be a name for the abode of God, a permanent home of the redeemed with Christ. What was originally a garden of delight has taken on the connotation of the new heavens and the new earth.[94]

The beauty and satisfaction of such a future existence furnish ample incentive and more for those in this church to overcome by heeding the words of Him who holds fast the seven messengers and walks in the middle of the seven churches (2:1).

Additional Notes

2:1 The KJV incorrectly translates the preposition ἐν with the English "of" rather than by "in." The church "of Ephesus" could be taken to imply that the words are addressed to the pagan inhabitants of the city rather than a church composed of professing Christians. This is the locative use of the preposition to designate the location of the church, not its constituency (Scott).

---

90. Beasley-Murray, *Revelation*, pp. 77-79. James E. Rosscup furnishes a thorough theological rationale for this identification of an overcomer in "The Overcomer in the Apocalypse," *GTJ* 3, no. 2 (Fall 1982): 261-86.
91. Robertson, *Word Pictures*, 6:301.
92. Richard Chenevix Trench, *Commentary on the Epistles to the Seven Churches in Asia* (London: Parker, Son, and Bourn, 1861), p. 95.
93. Robinson, *Lexicon*, p. 547.
94. Robertson, *Word Pictures*, 6:301.

Τῆς ἐκκλησίας is conceivably a possessive genitive if τῷ ἀγγέλῳ is understood as meaning "angel," i.e., "the angel belonging to the church." If "messenger" is taken as the meaning of the latter noun, however, an objective genitive is more probable, "the messenger to the church." This genitive limits the messenger to a specific body and the article τῆς points out this church in distinction from the other six.

The tense and mood of γράψον are aorist and imperative. This combination commands the listener to start doing something he was not doing prior to receiving the instructions. John was already writing, but not to the messenger of Ephesus in particular.

The nominative singular forms of τάδε are ὅδε, ἥδε, τόδε. This demonstrative pronoun meaning "this" is formed by a combination of δέ with ὁ, ἡ, τό.[95]

2:5 A special nuance for parataxis appears to be justified in the case of ἔρχομαί σοι καὶ κινήσω τὴν λυχνίαν σου because of two references to Christ's coming in these messages that are not conditioned on a human response or nonresponse (2:25; 3:11). This means that what is conditioned is not the coming, but its effect (Sweet). The aorist subjunctive of the final clause ἐὰν μὴ μετανοήσῃς thus takes the force of a future perfect: "if you shall not have repented" (i.e., before the coming) (Beckwith). According to Turner, καί is often used in place of subordination according to a Semitic model that also coincides with popular Greek.[96] Matthew 18:21 carries the sense, "How often, if (or when) my brother sins against me, shall I forgive him?" but the statement consists of two independent clauses connected with καί. Another example of such parataxis with subordination is Luke 14:5: "Which of you having a son or an ox, if (or when) he falls into a pit, will not immediately snatch him up on the day of the Sabbath?" Even more to the point are examples from other Johannine writings. John 7:34 has a comparable paratactic construction and means, "If (or when) you seek me, you shall not find me." Similarly, John 10:12 says, "If (or when) the hired servant . . . beholds the wolf coming, he leaves the sheep and flees." Other examples could be adduced (cf. Matt. 26:53; Rom. 13:3). With this kind of parataxis so prevalent elsewhere, it is quite reasonable to allow for it in the linguistics of the Apocalypse, which is so noted for other kinds of Semitic influence.

2:7 The repetition of νικῶντι by the αὐτῷ, which follows it in the verse, is a type of Hebraism frequent elsewhere in John's writings (cf. John 6:39; 7:38; 10:35-36; 15:2-5; 17:2; 1 John 2:24, 27).[97] The position

---

95. Arndt and Gingrich, *Lexicon*, p. 553; Robinson, *Lexicon*, p. 497.
96. Nigel Turner, *Syntax*, vol. 3 of *A Grammar of New Testament Greek* (Edinburgh: T. & T. Clark, 1963), p. 342.
97. Abbott, *Grammar*, pp. 32-33, 309; Charles, *Revelation*, 1:53.

of the participle at the beginning of the sentence (as well as its repetition in the αὐτῷ) emphasizes the victor, giving it the sense of "him alone" (Lenski). This is the dative of the present participle to indicate a continuous victory.[98] Continuous victory characterizes genuine believers who will receive eschatological rewards.

---

98. Robertson, *Word Pictures*, 6:300.

4
Church of Martyrdom

B. THE MESSAGE TO SMYRNA (2:8-11)

Turning His attention to a new church and a new situation, the speaker adds a second message, this time addressed to the church in the city of Smyrna, about thirty-five to forty miles north of Ephesus. In delivering this message, the party of messengers probably dwindled to six with the messenger to the Ephesian church remaining in Ephesus, which was his home.[1]

Translation

8And to the messenger of the church which is in Smyrna, write:
"These things says the first and the last, who came to be dead and lived: 9I know your affliction, even [your] poverty (but you are rich) and the slander [against you] by those who say that they themselves are Jews—and they are not but are the synagogue of Satan. 10Stop fearing anything which you are about to suffer. Behold, the devil is about to cast [some] of you into prison that you may be tested, and you will have affliction for ten days. Be faithful to death, and I will give you the crown of life. 11The one who has an ear, let him hear what the Spirit says to the churches. The one who overcomes will in no way be hurt by the second death."

---

1. See discussion of this probability in connection with the sequence of city names in 1:11.

Exegesis and Exposition

2:8 *The address.* In the address of this, the shortest of the seven messages, the city name Ἐφέσῳ (*Ephesō*, "Ephesus") is, of course, replaced by Σμύρνῃ (*Smyrnē*, "Smyrna"): Καὶ τῷ ἀγγέλῳ τῆς ἐν Σμύρνῃ ἐκκλησίας γράψον (*Kai tō angelō tēs en Smyrnē ekklēsias grapson*, "And to the messenger of the church which is in Smyrna, write"). The only other difference between this and the address to Ephesus is the addition of *kai* ("and") at the beginning of the address, an addition found in the remaining five messages also.

Σμύρνα (*Smyrna*) means "bitter," certainly an appropriate description for the lot of the Christians who lived there. They experienced severe persecution and all the hardships that accompany it. The Greek term is used in the LXX to translate מֹר (*mōr*) or מוֹר (*môr*) which means "myrrh," a resinous gum used as an unguent and for embalming (e.g., Ex. 30:23; Ps. 45:8 [45:9, MT; 45:8, English]; Cant. 5:5, 13).[2] This "embalming" idea suggested by "Smyrna" increases the name's appropriateness to the church situation in light of the martyrdom for which these saints were apparently destined.

The city lay near the eastern end of a gulf off the eastern shore of the Aegean Sea. The gulf was deep and provided an unusually good harbor with a larger port for a mooring ground and a smaller, inner port with a narrow entrance. The wealthy and beautiful city also lay at the end of a road serving the rich valley of the Hermus River on the interior. All the trade of that valley flowed into the city's markets and found an outlet through its harbor.[3] Smyrna's modern name is İzmir, a city which still has a Christian church.[4]

Smyrna began as a colony of Greece some time before 1000 B.C., first as an Aeolean colony, but later becoming an Ionian colony when the Ionian Greeks to the south captured it. Ionia became a powerful state with territory extending far to the east of the Aegean. As late as the seventh century B.C., it fought against the Lydian kingdom whose capital was Sardis, but was unable to prevail, was captured and destroyed in 627 B.C. by Algattes, king of Lydia. The site remained a barren waste until the time of Alexander the Great, though a loosely knit state called Smyrna, consisting of a conglomerate of scattered villages, remained between 600 and 290 B.C. Alexander intended to reestablish the city, but two of his successors, Lysimachus and Anti-

---

2. G. Abbott-Smith, *A Manual Greek Lexicon of the New Testament* (Edinburgh: T. & T. Clark, 1950), p. 411.
3. William Barclay, *Letters to the Seven Churches* (New York: Abingdon, 1957), p. 29.
4. John F. Walvoord, *The Revelation of Jesus Christ* (Chicago: Moody, 1966), p. 59; *NIV Study Bible*, ed. Kenneth L. Barker et al. (Grand Rapids: Zondervan, 1985), p. 1928.

gonus, did it in 290 B.C. When the new city was founded, it was planted on flat land near the southeastern shore of the gulf, about two miles away from the old site on a steep hill north of the extreme eastern end of the gulf. This provided a better location to maximize the advantages of a good harbor and travel overland to the east. The city's maritime activity brought it into contact with the Romans with whom it entered into an alliance against Mithradites, Carthage, and the Seleucid kingdom to the east. In 195 B.C. a temple honoring Rome was built, marking a longstanding relationship to which Smyrna remained true. Rome reciprocated in A.D. 26 by naming Smyrna over all the other cities of Asia as the place for a new temple to be dedicated by the confederacy of that province to Tiberius.[5] The city was destroyed by an earthquake in A.D. 177, but it was rebuilt by Marcus Aurelius. It has suffered many other earthquakes and conflagrations, but survives to the present as the city of İzmir with a population of several hundred thousand.[6]

The city of Smyrna was remarkable for its beauty. Though rivaled by Ephesus and Pergamum as the chief city of Asia in other respects, it was easily the most beautiful. Its picturesque natural surroundings were enhanced by its attractive and well-paved streets. In outlying areas the streets were lined with groves. The city was surrounded by sturdy walls, and on the Pagos ("the Hill") above the city were stately public buildings that, because of their orderly arrangement, were called "the crown of Smyrna." "The Street of Gold" curved around the sloping hill from east to west and had a temple to Cybele at one end and a temple to Zeus at the other. Because of its length and fine buildings along the way, including temples to Apollo, Asklepios, and Aphrodite, the street was compared to a necklace of jewels around the neck of a statue. To some this was the ideal city on earth (Ramsay).

Smyrna was noted as a center of learning, especially in science and medicine. It claimed to be the birthplace of Homer, who was reportedly born and reared beside the Meles River. Traditionally this river has been identified with the present Caravan Bridge River that flows northward to the vicinity of the Pagos and then around its eastern base before entering the sea to its northeast. More recently, however, the Meles has been related to the stream called Chalka-bounar. Whichever identification is made, it appears that this is where Homer spent his early years.[7]

---

5. James Hastings, *Dictionary of the Bible*, 5 vols. (Edinburgh: Scribner's, 1911), pp. 926-27; W. M. Ramsay, *The Letters to the Seven Churches of Asia* (New York: A. C. Armstrong, 1904), pp. 251-52; R. H. Charles, *The Revelation of St. John*, 2 vols., ICC (New York: Scribner's, 1920), 1:55.

6. Albert Barnes, *The Book of Revelation* (New York: Harper, 1851), p. 156; Merrill F. Unger, *Unger's Bible Dictionary* (Chicago: Moody, 1966), p. 1033.

The protecting deity of the city was a local adaptation of Cybele, known as the Sybeline Mother. The Greeks identified her with Nemesis, the Greek goddess of retributive justice. The towers and battlements of her headdress obviously resembled the appearance of the city. Only here in the Greek world was she worshiped.[8] Another religion very important to the city was worship of the Roman emperor. This was an enthusiastic center for such because of its close ties with Rome. Under Domitian (A.D. 81-96) emperor worship was made compulsory for every Roman citizen. Failure to comply meant death. Each year every citizen had to burn incense on Caesar's altar, after which he was issued a certificate. To be without a certificate, as must have been the case for Christians obedient to Christ, was to risk discovery and the death penalty. About a half-century after John's time Polycarp was burned alive at the age of eighty-six as the "twelfth martyr in Smyrna."[9] Joining hands with the Romans to oppose Christianity was a very large Jewish community in Smyrna. The Jews repeatedly informed against Christians or incited the local governor to attack them.[10]

The founding of the Christian church in the city is a mystery. Perhaps it came during Paul's three-year stay in nearby Ephesus. Whatever its origin, it is safe to say that nowhere was life more dangerous for a Christian. If anyone refused to confess "Caesar is Lord" along with his burning of incense, he was considered disloyal and became the object of persecution by the local and imperial governments. The martyrdom of Polycarp was not an isolated case; mass executions of Christians happened on numbers of occasions.[11] It is no wonder that Jesus' message to this church "drips" with words of encouragement to believers in a very perilous situation.

Attributes of the speaker. Jesus' self-acknowledged attributes in this message, attributes that are still fresh in John's mind from the vision of chapter 1, are contained in the words Τάδε λέγει ὁ πρῶτος καὶ ὁ ἔσχατος, ὃς ἐγένετο νεκρὸς καὶ ἔζησεν (*Tade legei ho prōtos kai ho eschatos, hos egeneto nekros kai ezēsen*, "These things says the first and the last, who came to be dead and lived"). As seen earlier in the discussion of Rev. 1:17, "the first and the last" is a title used by Isaiah

---

7. Hastings, *Dictionary*, pp. 926-27.
8. Ibid.
9. Marvin R. Vincent, *Word Studies in the New Testament* (New York: Scribner's, 1906), 2:443; Barclay, *Seven Churches*, pp. 30-31; Alan F. Johnson, "Revelation," in *EBC*, ed. Frank E. Gaebelein (Grand Rapids: Zondervan, 1981), 12:437.
10. Frederick A. Tatford, *Prophecy's Last Word* (London: Pickering and Inglis, 1947), pp. 50-51; Barclay, *Seven Churches*, p. 31.
11. J. A. Seiss, *The Apocalypse*, 3 vols. (New York: Charles C. Cook, 1909), 1:57; Vincent, *Word Studies*, 2:448; Barclay, *Seven Churches*, pp. 30-31.

for the God of Israel (cf. Isa. 41:4; 44:6; 48:12). Also noted in the earlier discussion is the connotation of the title, Jesus' eternality, in agreement with its placement in Rev. 22:13 alongside another title, "the Alpha and the Omega." In the role of the eternal and infinite one He launches His word of encouragement to a church exposed to fierce persecution. He was already in existence at the beginning of all things, and will be after all comes to an end. He is the eternal and abiding one.[12] Two aspects of eternity are placed side-by-side to describe the Lord as eternal.[13] Neither time nor things within time pose any limitation for Him.

This eternal one became a part of time and history, however, as the words *hos egeneto nekros kai ezēsen* reveal. As the eternal God, He became fully human and underwent the agony of death and the victory of resurrection. Once again, Jesus draws upon His appearance to John in the vision of chapter 1 (1:17-18) for His introduction to one of the churches. *Egeneto nekros* is the same as the expression in 1:18 except for a change from the first person to the third, but ζῶν εἰμι (*zōn eimi*, "I am living") of 1:18 is replaced by *ezēsen* in the present verse. The focus of Christ's self-description in 1:18 is a contrast between a single occurrence in history (death) and a continuous state of existence in life, but here the contrast is between two single occurrences in history, His death and His resurrection. He died and He came back to life.[14]

The two characterizations of Christ in 2:8 bring together what Jesus accomplished on earth and what He is by nature. His death and subsequent life as well as His eternal nature are especially relevant to those to whom He promises life subsequent to their death for His sake.[15] As an eternal and living Savior He is able to perform His promises (2:10c, 11).[16] As He experienced death and rose in triumph over it, so will the martyrs, a fact guaranteed by His eternal nature.[17]

---

12. Tatford, *Last Word*, p. 55.
13. Henry Barclay Swete, *The Apocalypse of St. John* (London: Macmillan, 1906), pp. 30-31; John Peter Lange, *The Revelation of John*, Lange's Commentary, ed. E. R. Craven (Grand Rapids: Zondervan, 1968), 10:117. Since both adjectives have an article and are connected by καί in the expression ὁ πρῶτος καὶ ὁ ἔσχατος, the two aspects are viewed as separate entities.
14. The aorist ἐγένετο is constative, but the aorist ἔζησεν is ingressive and focuses on the beginning of life. Christ "began to live" after death. Ζάω is used to depict restoration of life in Matt. 9:18; John 4:50; 5:25; and Rev. 13:14.
15. William Henry Simcox, *The Revelation of St. John the Divine* (Cambridge: U. Press, 1893), p. 55.
16. Moses Stuart, *A Commentary on the Apocalypse* (Edinburgh: Maclachlan, Stewart, 1847), pp. 470-71.
17. Swete, *Apocalypse*, p. 31; A. T. Robertson, *Word Pictures in the New Testament*, 6 vols. (Nashville: Broadman, 1933), 6:301.

2:9 *Knowledge about the people.* Christ's knowledge about the Smyrnan Christians centers in their persecution and consequent sufferings: Οἶδά σου τὴν θλῖψιν καὶ τὴν πτωχείαν, ἀλλὰ πλούσιος εἶ, καὶ τὴν βλασφημίαν ἐκ τῶν λεγόντων Ἰουδαίους εἶναι ἑαυτούς, καὶ οὐκ εἰσὶν ἀλλὰ συναγωγὴ τοῦ Σατανᾶ (*Oida sou tēn thlipsin kai tēn ptōcheian, alla plousios ei, kai tēn blasphēmian ek tōn legontōn Ioudaious einai heautous, kai ouk eisin alla synagōgē tou Satana,* "I know your affliction, even [your] poverty (but you are rich) and the slander [against you] by those who say that they themselves are Jews, and they are not but are the synagogue of Satan").

One way to understand the three terms *sou tēn thlipsin kai tēn ptōcheian . . . kai tēn blasphēmian* is as affliction and blasphemy with poverty falling between the two because it is the result of persecution. The prominence of persecution in this message (cf. 2:10) and its consequent effect of producing a shortage of material possessions support this understanding.[18] This approach is doubtful, however, because placing poverty in the middle lessens rather than heightens the emphasis on it. Another way of taking the three terms is at face value, expressing three distinct characteristics of the church's situation. Although this may be the normal way to explain the meaning if it were expressed by some other author, the proclivity of this author for an ascensive use of *kai* is established[19] and probably affects this phrase too. The preferred relationship between the three is to assign the first term a general connotation and to make the second and third explanatory of it. This aligns with the force of the comparable triplet in Rev. 2:2 by giving the former *kai* its frequent ascensive meaning: "your affliction, even [your] poverty and the slander [against you]."

That this church suffered great affliction is beyond dispute. *Thlipsin* denotes a restricting pressure that burdens the spirit. In the NT the word speaks of the calamities of war, of want, of the distress of a woman in childbirth, and of persecution from which Christ's followers are not to shrink.[20] The context of the message shows that persecution was causing their affliction. The church is commended for its endurance of this suffering (Swete; Beckwith).

The church's affliction is further defined as poverty. *Ptōcheian* has a wide usage in the NT, but the Greek word for ordinary poverty, πενία (*penia,* "poverty"), is not used at all. A cognate noun, πένης (*penēs,* "a poor man"), occurs in 2 Cor. 9:9 in a quotation from the

---

18. R. C. H. Lenski, *The Interpretation of St. John's Revelation* (Columbus, Ohio: Lutheran Book Concern, 1935), p. 97.

19. Isbon T. Beckwith, *The Apocalypse of John* (New York: Macmillan, 1919), p. 421; cf. BDF, par. 442.

20. W. E. Vine, *An Expository Dictionary of New Testament Words* (Old Tappan, N.J.: Revell, 1966), pp. 398-99.

LXX (cf. Ps 111:9 [LXX]). The poverty denoted by *ptōcheian* is much more abject; as Trench notes, "The *penēs* has nothing superfluous, the *ptōchos* nothing at all."[21] The origin of the poverty in Smyrna bears some relationship to the church's affliction, according to the statement of v. 9. It is unlikely that it can be traced to the converts' belonging to a poorer class of society.[22] Smyrna was too rich a city for this (Swete). Nor is it probable that the Christians' deprived condition came from losing their property when put out of the synagogues at conversion to Christ. In such a Gentile city the church population would have been mostly non-Jewish. Possibly their goods had been pillaged by Jewish or Gentile mobs (Swete), as seems to have been the fate of some (cf. Heb. 10:34).[23] The context suggests that something of this nature was at least a contributing cause of their poverty (cf. 2:9-10).[24] Without excluding this as a factor, the best explanation is that their poverty resulted from demands made of them because of their faith in Christ. The context of the message does not attribute violence to the opponents of Christianity in this city, but it hints that their slander and false accusations (cf. 2:9) brought pressure on the civil authorities to put Christians in prison (cf. 2:10). In such an antagonistic environment, making a living as a Christian would have been quite difficult and poverty would have resulted (Mounce).

Material goods are not of ultimate value, however. Spiritual resources are far more lasting and important. With a contrasting parenthetical remark, the Lord notes the prosperity of His addressees in Smyrna: *alla plousios ei*. While poor in a material sense, they were spiritually rich before God.[25] Though this brief word of encouragement is grammatically parenthetical, through the strong adversative conjunction *alla* this second half of the paradox gains special emphasis.[26] Such brief parentheses are habitual with this writer.[27]

Another factor besides poverty contributed to the affliction of the

---

21. Richard Chenevix Trench, *Synonyms of the New Testament* (1880; reprint, Grand Rapids: Eerdmans, 1958), p. 129.
22. Contra Walter Scott, *Exposition of the Revelation of Jesus Christ* (Swengel, Pa.: Bible Truth Depot, n.d.), p. 67.
23. Robert H. Mounce, *The Book of Revelation,* NICNT (Grand Rapids: Eerdmans, 1977), p. 92.
24. Swete, *Apocalypse,* p. 31; G. R. Beasley-Murray, *The Book of Revelation,* NCB (Grand Rapids: Eerdmans, 1978), p. 81.
25. In Laodicea the opposite was true. Professing Christians there were materially rich but spiritually poor (cf. Rev. 3:17-18). "You are rich" in this verse stands in strong contrast to "I am rich" of 3:17. See also Matt. 6:20; 19:21; Luke 12:21; 2 Cor. 6:10; 1 Tim. 6:17, 18; James 2:5.
26. Richard Chenevix Trench, *Commentary on the Epistles to the Seven Churches in Asia* (London: Parker, Son, and Bourn, 1861), p. 136; Stuart, *Apocalypse,* p. 471; Robertson, *Word Pictures,* 6:301-2.
27. Beckwith, *Apocalypse,* pp. 242-44, 453.

Smyrnans: *tēn blasphēmian ek tōn legontōn Ioudaious einai heautous, kai ouk eisin alla synagōgē tou Satana.* Conceivably, *tēn blasphēmian* could be blasphemy against God directly. Both the word and the broad context of the NT allow this (cf. Acts 13:45). The immediate context requires a direct reference to slander against Christians. However, it was the kind of slander that exposed them to the penalties of the law (Simcox; Beckwith). In a city such as Smyrna with its strong ties to Rome, false charges laid before the magistrates could easily have resulted in imprisonment for those accused (Mounce). Such Jewish agitation against Paul in other cities is well documented: at Antioch in Pisidia, Acts 13:50; at Iconium, Acts 14:2, 5; at Lystra, Acts 14:19; at Thessalonica, Acts 17:5 (Mounce). During the first century six types of slander were leveled against Christians: cannibalism, lust and immorality, breaking up of homes, atheism, political disloyalty, and incendiarism.[28] Probably the one capitalized upon most in Rome-oriented Smyrna was that of political disloyalty.

The source of the slander is identified by the words *ek tōn legontōn Ioudaious einai heautous.*[29] These professing Jews were physical descendants of Abraham or proselytes to Judaism who were obviously not Christians (cf. Phil. 3:3; Rom. 2:28, 29).[30] Widespread animosity by Jews toward Christians is well known from the pages of Acts. Likewise the Jews at Smyrna were numerous and aggressively hostile. They took an active part in the martyrdom of Polycarp about fifty years later (Swete). A circular letter from the church at Smyrna to other churches in the Christian world relates how the Jews joined the heathen in demanding that Polycarp be cast to the lions or burned alive. They led the way in bringing firewood to burn him to death and in attempting to prevent his remains from being given to fellow-Christians for burial.[31] Three sources of antagonism to Christians

---

28. William Barclay, *The Revelation of John*, 2 vols., 2d ed. (Philadelphia: Westminster, 1960), 1:98.
29. Lenski, *Revelation*, pp. 97-98. Ἐκ followed by the ablative is one of several ways of expressing agency in the NT (H. E. Dana and Julius R. Mantey, *A Manual Grammar of the Greek New Testament* [New York: Macmillan, 1927], p. 112). Without the preposition the genitive participle τῶν λεγόντων could have been subjective or objective genitive (Stuart, *Apocalypse*, p. 471), but the preposition specifically marks the professing Jews as the agents of the slander. Ἰουδαίους εἶναι ἑαυτούς is an accusative of general reference (or adverbial accusative of reference) and the infinitive of indirect discourse after λέγω. Constructions very close to this occur in Acts 5:36 and 8:9 (Stuart, *Apocalypse*, p. 471; Robertson, *Word Pictures*, 6:301-2).
30. Henry Alford, *The Greek Testament*, 4 vols. (London: Longmans, Green, 1903), 4:566; William Lee, "The Revelation of St. John," in *The Holy Bible*, ed. F. C. Cook (London: John Murray, 1881), 4:519.
31. Vincent, *Word Studies*, p. 582; Stuart, *Apocalypse*, p. 471.

emerge in these seven messages, Jewish (here), pagan (2:13), and heretical (2:24). It is ironic that the Jews surpassed the heathen in their
hostility (Swete).

Theological bias that refuses to acknowledge an ongoing distinction between the physical lineage called "Jews" and a spiritual lineage called "the church" has produced some strange identifications of
the self-proclaimed Jews of this verse. Some have held that these
were of all racial backgrounds who claimed they were Jews inwardly
and that the Lord says they were not inward Jews. Whether they
descended from Abraham or not is not the point in this book, it is
contended; the Jews are the people of God, the true Israel (Lee). Romans 2:28-29 makes this inward sense the only proper connotation of
the word (Lee). It is claimed that with this writer as with Paul (cf. Gal.
6:16) Christians are "the Israel of God" (Beckwith), that true Jews are
those who have believed in Christ and thereby won a legitimate claim
to the name and spiritual privileges belonging to the Jews (Charles).
Real Jews are those who worship by the Spirit of God and glory in
Christ Jesus (cf. Phil. 3:3).[32]

This method of identifying Jews is hard-pressed to produce any
exegetical support either within the Apocalypse or in the rest of the
NT. Besides this, if they had called themselves Jews in this mystical
sense, why would they be named as the principal source of calumny
against the church (Alford)? If the designation were only spiritual
and applied to a multi-racial group, why the reference to "synagogue"
in the next part of the verse (Beasley-Murray)? It is inexplicable why
a person who was not a physical descendant of Abraham would claim
to be so and then turn to persecuting fellow-Christians without re-
canting his claim. The context demands that the offenders be of the
physical descent of Abraham. Whether or not the title properly applies to Gentile Christians is not an issue in this verse.

On the other hand, the persecution of Christians by Jews of physical descent is well known in the NT (cf. Acts 13:50; 14:2, 5, 19; 17:5;
26:2; 1 Thess. 2:14, 15) (Lee). Never is this identification denied elsewhere. This is the normal meaning of the word in the NT, and to take
it otherwise would render language meaningless.[33] Like the Jews of
John 8:31-47 who claimed to be descendants of Abraham, these were
instead children of the devil (Mounce). The NT often denies the title
to those of the Abrahamic lineage physically but not spiritually (cf.
Matt. 3:9; 2 Cor. 11:22; Phil. 3:4 ff.) (Alford). Some of the Christians in

32. Homer Hailey, *Revelation, an Introduction and Commentary* (Grand
   Rapids: Baker, 1979), p. 126.
33. E. W. Bullinger, *The Apocalypse* or *"The Day of the Lord"* (London: Eyre
   and Spottiswoode, n.d.), p. 175.

Smyrna must have been converted Jews. Otherwise, the antagonism of the rest of the Jewish community would not have been so strong (Ramsay).

A second parenthesis of the verse corrects the false claim of these professing Jews. *Kai ouk eisin* duplicates another refutation of a false claim, this one at Ephesus, found in the parenthesis of 2:2.[34] By birth and religion these may have been Jews, but this was only an outward sense. Inwardly they did not meet the condition of a circumcised heart (cf. Rom. 2:28-29). They could not be classed as Jews in the truest sense.[35]

According to Jesus' own words, they are rather the synagogue of Satan. This is not a synagogue building, of course, but the people who gathered there. They assembled and planned their assault on the church, putting themselves at the disposal of the devil to carry out his will. They may have claimed to be the assembly of the Lord (cf. Num. 16:3, 9; 20:4; 31:16) (Charles), but in heaven's eyes these people were not true Jews, but emissaries of the prime adversary of God and His people, the devil or Satan.[36]

2:10 *State of the church.* In elaborating on the condition of the church Jesus encourages them to stop fearing what they were about to suffer: *μηδὲν φοβοῦ ἃ μέλλεις πάσχειν (mēden phobou ha melleis paschein,* "stop fearing[37] anything which you are about to suffer"). Apparently this church, already involved in tribulation, was expecting worse things still to come, and thus was facing the future with trepidation. Jesus commands them to do this no longer (Moffatt). Even though worse trials were imminent,[38] He does not want His people to be apprehensive about them.

To relieve their apprehensions, the Lord does not promise deliverance. This message has no promise of the Lord's coming as the other six do. Rather He reveals specifically what the nature of this inten-

---

34. In both 2:2 and here καὶ οὐκ εἰσίν is a Hebraism standing for καὶ οὐκ ὄντων (Charles, *Revelation*, 1:57). For a fuller discussion of this writer's fondness of such a construction, see Additional Notes in connection with a comparable one in 1:6.

35. Simcox, *Revelation*, p. 55; James Moffatt, "The Revelation of St. John the Divine," in *The Expositor's Greek Testament*, ed. W. Robertson Nicoll (Grand Rapids: Eerdmans, n.d.), 5:354; Lenski, *Revelation*, pp. 97-98.

36. Tatford, *Last Word*, p. 59; Lenski, *Revelation*, p. 98.

37. The negative μηδέν with the present imperative of φοβέομαι indicates that the Lord was commanding cessation of a fear they already had (Robertson, *Word Pictures*, 6:302).

38. Μέλλεις πάσχειν derives the element of imminence from μέλλεις. The immediate future was undoubtedly in view, but the thought of subsequent persecutions (e.g., Polycarp's martyrdom fifty years later) could also be implied (Simcox, *Revelation*, p. 56).

sified persecution will be: ἰδοὺ μέλλει βάλλειν ὁ διάβολος ἐξ ὑμῶν εἰς φυλακὴν ἵνα πειρασθῆτε, καὶ *ἕξετε θλῖψιν ἡμερῶν δέκα (idou mellei ballein ho diabolos ex hymōn eis phylakēn hina peirasthēte, kai hexete thlipsin hēmerōn deka, "behold, the devil is about to cast [some][39] of you into prison that you may be tested, and you will have a ten-day affliction"). Idou directs special attention to this announcement. This particle signals a declaration that is oracular in nature and is one of five such markers in these messages of Christ (cf. 2:22; 3:8, 9, 20).[40] While holding no prospects of immediate relief from persecution, the announcement divulges the next stage of persecution and is followed by a promise of eternal life for the faithful. Herein lies the element of incentive to endure bad treatment.

The Lord's advance knowledge of further persecution shows His sovereign wisdom in allowing it to happen, but the real author of it was Satan. The devil, working through his servants, the Jews and the Romans, instigated these and other unjustified actions against Christians (Beckwith). The early church was convinced that he was the one prompting persecutors of Christians to carry out their acts of violence.[41]

The devil was about to "keep on casting"[42] some of these Christians into prison. One after another, certain members of the Christian community could expect to be seized by the Roman authorities in Smyrna as a result of accusations brought by the Jewish community in the city (cf. 2:9).[43] Satan's purpose in bringing these hardships was to try the faith of the whole body of believers by casting some of their number into prison (Swete). He hoped to bring them to renounce their faith in Christ by promoting conditions of physical suffering.

39. Ἐξ is often employed as an idiom to mean "some of" (cf. Luke 11:49; Rev. 3:9; 11:9). It implies a τινὰς before the ἐξ (Beckwith, Apocalypse, p. 454; Robertson, Word Pictures, 6:302). This kind of construction, usually with ἐκ, is typical of Johannine writings (cf. John 6:39; 21:10; 2 John 4) (Colin J. Hemer, The Letters to the Seven Churches of Asia in Their Local Setting, JSNTSup 11 [Sheffield: U. of Sheffield, 1986], p. 267 n. 43).
40. David E. Aune, Prophecy in Early Christianity and the Ancient Mediterranean World (Grand Rapids: Eerdmans, 1983), pp. 276, 279, 433 n. 184.
41. Swete, Apocalypse, p. 32; Vincent, Dictionary, 2:444.
42. The durative idea of the present tense of βάλλειν is in keeping with the continuation of imprisonment suggested by the ten-day length of the imprisonment (Beckwith, Apocalypse, p. 454).
43. The plural pronoun ὑμῶν deserves special attention. Rarely in these seven messages does the speaker refer to His addressees in the plural. Normally He views each church corporately (e.g., φοβοῦ, γίνου, and σοι at the beginning and end of 2:10). In the middle of the current verse, however, He views the individuals making up the corporate body with ὑμῶν and two other plural words, πειρασθῆτε and ἕξετε. This is perhaps necessary because some members of the body were to be imprisoned whereas others were not.

Because *peirasthēte* ("you may be tested") is passive and no agent of the testing is stated, a question has arisen regarding the identity of the agent. Because of God's purpose in allowing trials in the Christian life, a strong case to make God the agent exists. James 1:2, 3 and 1 Pet. 1:6, 7 elaborate upon God's use of trials to bring growth in a Christian.[44] Whatever Satan intends to accomplish through persecution, behind him is the divine intention to use suffering to ensure the approved character of those for whom the kingdom is being prepared.[45] Added support for God's part in the trial is *mellei*, which carries overtones of divine destiny each time it is used (Swete). In spite of the obvious truth that nothing adverse enters a Christian's life without God's permission, several factors rule out taking this as the principal teaching of this passage. If this had been the meaning, δοκιμασθῆτε (*dokimasthēte*, "may be approved") rather than *peirasthēte* would have been used (Alford). The former verb carries the connotation of testing with a view to approval, but the latter does not. Even more impressive is the clear statement of the verse that the trial was authored by the devil, and that he was the agent who was to cast them into prison for the purpose of such a prolonged trial (Alford).

God's indirect involvement in such treatment of Christians cannot be denied. He permits it, yet His part is not referred to directly in this context. The prominent thing is the declared role of Satan in soliciting Christians to sin by renouncing their faith.[46] As noted above, *peirasthēte* does not mean a trial for the purpose of proving them, but a trial by way of enticing them to fall away. The same word refers to the demonic attacks destined to befall unbelievers on earth during the future hour of trial (cf. Rev. 3:10), but here its sense is that of testing by persecution (Alford; Charles).

The ten-day affliction that is predicted appears to be an intensification of anything individuals within the church had endured up to this point. So far they had undergone the deprivation of their material possessions, but they had not been imprisoned. No reason exists to take "prison" in any other than a literal sense. Peter, James, and Paul, for example, had been imprisoned (cf. Acts 12:1, 3; 16:23), with James's imprisonment ending in martyrdom (Acts 12:2). Apparently prospects of martyrdom were present for the imprisoned Smyrnans too.

Different interpretations of the ten days of affliction have emerged.

---

44. Trench, *Seven Churches*, pp. 112-13.
45. Beckwith, *Apocalypse*, p. 454; G. V. Caird, *A Commentary on the Revelation of St. John the Divine*, HNTC (New York: Harper & Row, 1966), p. 36; Beasley-Murray, *Revelation*, p. 81.
46. J. B. Smith, *A Revelation of Jesus Christ* (Scottdale, Pa.: Herald, 1961), p. 67.

A widely held view says it refers to ten specific periods of persecution under the Roman emperors during the first three centuries of the Christian era. The ten persecuting emperors that are sometimes listed are Nero (A.D. 54), Domitian (A.D. 81), Trajan (A.D. 98), Hadrian (A.D. 117), Septimus Severus (A.D. 117), Maximin (A.D. 235), Decius (A.D. 249), Valerian (A.D. 254), Aurelian (A.D. 270), and Domitian (A.D. 284).[47] Besides these persecutions being well-known facts of history, this interpretation is weak. It is somewhat fanciful (Alford) in light of the writing date of the Apocalypse. In A.D. 95, if this view were valid, one of the persecutions would have been in the past and the second one almost at its end. This would render the future tense *hexete* ("you will have") inexplicable. That this prediction pertained to the church in Smyrna only, not to the church throughout the Roman Empire, is another negative consideration against this view.

Another way of understanding the ten days is to take "day" symbolically to refer to a year. This then is a prediction of ten years of affliction (Lee). This symbolism is used elsewhere in Scripture (e.g., Ezek. 4:6), and the fact is that the persecution under Diocletian lasted for approximately ten years, from February 23, 303 to June 13, 313.[48] Furthermore, the persecution under Decius and Valerian lasted for ten years, from 249-259, as did that under Domitian, from 81-91 (Lee). The prophecy of Daniel's seventy weeks is best explained on the basis of the year-day theory too (cf. Dan. 9:24-26; cf. Rev. 11:2, 3; 12:6). The problems with this view include the fact that the persecution of 81 to 91 transpired before the writing of the book and could hardly fulfill this prediction. Also the nature of the prediction necessitates its fulfillment to that generation, not to a generation many years later. The year-day symbolism is appropriate to the apocalyptic portion of the book, from chapter 4 on, but not to these seven messages that are epistolary in style. Various schemes have sought to apply this theory, and each has proved inadequate (Lee).

A third explanation of the ten days is also symbolical, making it refer to a long period of time (Lee). In the Bible ten often represents a very large number (cf. Gen. 31:41; Num. 14:22; Job 19:3; cp. Deut. 23:3 with Neh. 13:1). This view is more in keeping with the seriousness of the impending crisis the Lord predicts.[49] The immediate context dooms this attempted solution, however. Whatever else this pre-

---

47. Scott, *Revelation*, p. 72(n.); William R. Newell, *The Book of Revelation* (Chicago: Moody, 1935), p. 46; Smith, *Revelation*, p. 67. The dates cited are the beginnings of reigns, not necessarily the beginning of the persecution under that emperor.
48. Lee, "Revelation," 4:481, 520, 532.
49. Ray Summers, *Worthy is the Lamb* (Nashville: Broadman, 1951), p. 113; Mounce, *Revelation*, p. 94.

diction may do, it is provided as an encouragement for those in Smyrna. To accomplish this, the period of their suffering must be of limited duration rather than being so extended. Were the latter the case, their incentive to be faithful would be quelled rather than strengthened.

A further attempt to find symbolic import in the ten days sees the words referring to an indefinite period of persecution, in a short and limited time (Alford; Swete; Scott; Walvoord). "Ten" is said to be a well-known symbol for a very short period (cf. Gen. 24:55; Num. 11:19; 14:22; 1 Sam. 1:8; 25:38; Job 19:3; Dan. 1:12).[50] It is a round number denoting fullness or completeness quite often in the Bible and in apocalyptic writings. Here it denotes a period that is not long, but long enough to bring severe trial to the sufferers (Lee; Beckwith). Ten days of suffering and suspense might seem an eternity while they lasted, but in retrospect they would be but a moment (cf. 2 Cor. 4:17). The trial might be long, but it had a limit known to God (Swete). This view also accords with the significance of the case of *hēmerōn*. As an adverbial genitive of time it does not denote duration of time, which would have been expressed by an accusative case. It indicates the kind of time period during which this affliction transpires.[51] This view encounters difficulty in two areas, however. First is the observation that numerical symbolism is more characteristic of the apocalyptic portions of the book, which begin at chapter 4. The OT examples cited in support are literal ten-day periods and are not symbolic. A second difficulty is to observe that nothing in the context of this message indicates that the expression is intended to be symbolic (Bullinger).

In light of these difficulties a fifth interpretation of the ten days is preferable. The ten days are literal and refer to an unknown persecution within a definite period of time during the generation to which this message was addressed. Such limited periods of persecution are well known in biblical history (Gen. 7:4; 40:12, 13, 20; Num. 14:33; Esth. 3:13; Ezek. 4:1-8; Matt. 12:40).[52] This is the most natural understanding of the expression in epistolary literature such as this. No reason to take the ten days as symbolic exists. This explanation also allows for a proper understanding of the genitive case of *hēmerōn*, which was cited above in connection with the fourth view. It is a "ten-day" affliction. The view is illustrated by, but not fulfilled by, the

---

50. Alford, *Greek Testament*, 4:567; Trench, *Seven Churches*, pp. 114-15.
51. Swete, *Apocalypse*, p. 32; A. T. Robertson, *A Grammar of the Greek New Testament in the Light of Historical Research* (Nashville: Broadman, 1934), p. 495; BDF, par. 186.
52. Swete, *Apocalypse*, p. 32; Robertson, *Word Pictures*, 6:302.

persecution of Polycarp in this city in the mid-second century.[53] A similar surge of opposition against some Christians in Smyrna apparently came a short time after the publication of the Apocalypse.

The Lord's word of encouragement to this persecuted church is not complete without a final command with its attached promise: γίνου[54] πιστὸς ἄχρι θανάτου, καὶ δώσω σοι τόν στέφανον τῆς ζωῆς (*ginou pistos achri thanatou kai dōsō soi ton stephanon tēs zōēs*, "be faithful to death, and I will give you the crown of life"). A little more faithfulness will gain for this church the crown of life as a reward for its faithfulness.

Ginou, the imperative commanding faithfulness, has occasioned three differing interpretations. Is it equivalent to an imperative of εἰμί (*eimi*, "I am"), with the simple meaning of "keep on being"? Probably the latter word would have been used to convey this meaning. Is it to be given the usual force of γίνομαι (*ginomai*, "I become"): "keep on becoming"? The force of this meaning would imply a need for an increase in degree of faithfulness to meet the higher intensity of trials they were to face (Alford). The possibility that Jesus would convey His desire for a greater degree of faithfulness in this obscure manner is rather remote. The other option is that *ginou* has another of its possible meanings here: "keep on *proving* yourselves faithful." The present tense of the command carries the note of continuance (Alford). Trepidation was to cease (*mēden phobou*), but they were to continue demonstrating their faithfulness.

The extent to which faithfulness should go is given in the words *achri thanatou* ("even to death"). Although *achri* can mean "until," this usage does not deal with the duration of the faithfulness, but with its degree.[55] Christians should not shrink from dying for Christ's sake, even if the death is to be a violent one.[56] This charge to faithfulness does not necessarily mean that everyone in the church would die as a martyr, but it does mean that with each one in the corporate body there should be a willingness to make such a sacrifice (Lenski).

---

53. Eusebius *The Ecclesiastical History*, 2 vols., trans. Hugh Jackson Lawlor and John Ernest Leonard Oulton (London: SPCK, 1954), 4.15; Lee, "Revelation," 4:520.

54. The change from the plural ἕξετε to the singular γίνου recalls that whatever is said to the messenger of a church is intended for the church as a whole (Alford, *Greek Testament*, 4:567).

55. Alford, *Greek Testament*, 4:576; Joseph Henry Thayer, *A Greek-English Lexicon of the New Testament* (New York: American Book, 1889), p. 91; Swete, *Apocalypse*, p. 33; Vincent, *Word Studies*, p. 583; Smith, *Revelation*, p. 68. Other examples of ἄχρι which emphasize degree are Acts 22:4 and Rev. 12:11.

56. Stuart, *Apocalypse*, p. 473.

One's willingness to give his life is the ultimate proof of his loyalty as a Christian disciple.

In return for this caliber of faithfulness the Lord promises the Smyrnan church *ton stephanon tēs zōēs* ("the crown of life"). Two issues related to this reward need clarification, the source of the symbolism of *stephanon* and the symbolic connotation of the same word. The sources of the symbolism that have been suggested include a crown of royalty, an emblem of festivity, an adornment similar to that worn by heavenly beings, and a garland of victory. The suggestion of a crown of royalty derives its main impetus from the "golden crowns" of Rev. 4:4, 10, which appear to be royal crowns, and from the employment of this same word by three of the four evangelists to specify Christ's crown of thorns, apparently a caricature of royalty (Matt. 27:29; Mark 15:17; John 19:2).[57] The weakness of seeing royalty as a source is that διάδημα (*diadēma*, "crown") is the usual word for a crown of royalty (cf. Rev. 12:3; 13:1; 19:12).[58] Besides this, it cannot be affirmed with absolute certainty that the evangelists understood Christ's "crown" as a caricature of royalty. Roman emperors did not wear *kingly* crowns. They wore laurel wreaths, and this was a mock laurel wreath (Lee).

To trace the source of *stephanos* to an emblem of festivity resorts to a Jewish use of the word. For Jews the crown was an emblem of joy (Ecclus. 6:31; 15:6; 3 Macc. 7:16) and festive decorations (1 Macc. 4:57) (cf. στέμματα [*stemmata*, "wreath"], Acts 14:13) (Lee). They used such garlands at feasts (cf. Isa. 28:1, 3; Ezek. 23:42) (Lee). Because John was writing the Apocalypse for predominantly Gentile churches in the province of Asia, however, it is doubtful that he would draw on Jewish symbolism.

The idea that *stephanos* suggests primarily an adornment similar to what is worn by heavenly beings derives from a heathen practice according to which Greek gods were frequently pictured with crowns of light or nimbuses (Charles). Comparable uses of the word are also found in pseudepigraphical books (cf. 2 Enoch 14:2; 3 Bar. 6:1) (Charles). It is doubtful, however, that John would derive his symbolism from apocryphal and heathen religious sources.

The most natural explanation of John's source for *stephanos* is the garland of victory awarded in athletic contests of the day and to the victorious general (Lee). Probably the widest NT use of the word is in conjunction with the Greek games as parallels to the Christian life (cf.

---

57. Trench, *Synonyms*, p. 81.
58. Swete, *Apocalypse*, p. 33; Lee, pp. 521, 532-34.

1 Cor. 9:24, 25; Gal. 2:2; Phil. 3:14; 2 Tim. 2:5; 1 Pet. 5:4).[59] Such would be quite appropriate in a message addressed to Smyrna, a city famous for its games (Mounce). This is the picture that would come to the readers' minds (Swete). The contextual reference to struggle and victory leads naturally to the promise of an eschatological victory over evil, both here and in 3:11 (cf. 2 Tim. 4:8; James 1:12) (Beckwith). A possible weakness in this explanation is the use of the identical expression in the epistle of James, an epistle addressed to a predominantly Jewish audience (cf. Jas. 1:12). Athletic contests were well known among the Jews also, however, so this is not a real problem. Tertullian objected that nowhere in the Apocalypse is there a single image drawn from the range of heathen antiquity, including references to athletic contests.[60] This negative generalization is somewhat offset by the use of τὸ τόξον (*to toxon*, "bow") to denote a rainbow in 4:3 and 10:1 (cf. Gen. 9:13, 14, 16; Ezek. 1:28) and perhaps also by Rev. 2:17 and 13:16 (Lee). Nevertheless, it is probably wise not to push the athletic part of the image here and to dwell mainly on the connotation of victory.

The symbolic connotation of *stephanon* is another issue. Does the crown symbolize eternal life with the understanding that *tēs zōēs* is a genitive of apposition, or does the crown signify some special reward that is over and above the eternal life that all believers will receive? In this latter case *tēs zōēs* is a genitive of possession. The special-reward connotation notes that this is not promised to all believers, and hence must be only for those who are faithful and willing to face martyrdom (Scott). Yet because all believers, not even all in this particular church, were not called upon to face the test of giving their lives, other believers besides martyrs can hardly be excluded from this promise. It is hard to grasp how the full consummation of immortality (Charles) could surpass the eternal life that is the lot of all true Christians. A genitive of apposition, "the crown which is life," renders a more satisfactory sense for the expression.

The same construction has this sense in James 1:12, and a similar one, "the crown of righteousness," in 2 Tim. 4:8 does too (Alford; Swete; Lee). This is a promise practically equivalent to eating from the tree of life (Rev. 2:7), but it is phrased differently (Swete). This does not mean that faithfulness is a means of earning eternal life, but that such perseverance through suffering furnishes tangible assurance that they will receive eternal life through their faith in Christ

---

59. F. J. A. Hort, *The Apocalypse of St. John* (London: Macmillan, 1908), p. 26; Lee, "Revelation," pp. 520-21.
60. Tertullian *Scorp.* 6.

(Walvoord). Unlike the other churches, the promise (or threat) to this church is not linked to the Lord's coming. The only incentive for faithfulness given to Smyrna is life after death, whether that death comes by martyrdom or otherwise. Appropriately the promise comes from the lips of Him who died and came back to life (Rev. 2:8).

2:11 *Command to hear.* The command to hear is identical with the one to the church at Ephesus (cf. 2:7). That earlier discussion should be consulted. It is noteworthy that the Lord's anticipation of possible martyrdom for some of the saints in Smyrna has some applicability to the other churches also (cf. ταῖς ἐκκλησίαις [*tais ekklēsiais*, "the churches"], 2:11), though undoubtedly its special relevance was for the church at Smyrna.

Promise to the overcomer. The promise to the overcomer in the message to Smyrna is protection from the second death: ὁ νικῶν οὐ μὴ ἀδικηθῇ ἐκ τοῦ θανάτου τοῦ δευτέρου (*ho nikōn ou mē adikēthē ek tou thanatou tou deuterou*, "the one who overcomes will in no way be hurt by the second death"). *Adikēthē* ("will be hurt") has two components, the alpha-privative (or alpha-negative) and δική (*dikē*, "justice"). It points to a lack of justice, morally speaking, but in the Apocalypse elsewhere it never refers to mere moral wrong, but focuses on physical harm or injury as well (cf. 6:6; 7:2, 3; 9:4, 10, 19; 11:5 [twice]).[61] The *ou mē* combination negates the possibility of harm coming to the overcomer. It is the strongest negative assertion about the future of which the Greek language is capable.[62]

One means by which[63] harm will come to nonovercomers is the second death, but overcomers are exempt from this. Unbelievers are given over to this destiny at the great white throne judgment. John identifies the second death with the lake of fire in 20:14 and 21:8. This is more than physical death; it is eternal death (Beckwith; Walvoord). The idea behind the second death is implicit in Dan. 12:2 and John 5:29. It was current in Jewish circles as in the Jewish Targum on Deut. 33:6 and in Philo. It is not annihilation, but conscious unending punishment.[64] As is true of the promise in Rev. 2:7, this one also ties in with the early chapters of the Bible (cf. Gen. 2:17; 3:22; cf. also Rev. 20:6) (Smith). The incentive to overcome is an eternal one.

---

61. Robertson, *Word Pictures*, 6: 303; Vine, *Dictionary*, p. 240; Charles, *Revelation*, 1:59.
62. BDF, par. 365.
63. Charles, *Revelation*, 1:59. Following a passive verb ἐκ governs the agent or instrument as its object (cf. Rev. 3:18; 9:2, 18; 18:1).
64. Robertson, *Word Pictures*, 6: 303.

Additional Notes

2:10 The textual variant μή instead of μηδὲν has the respectable MS support of A C 046 and other sources, but μηδὲν is the harder reading. This coupled with its widespread external support makes it the preferable reading.

Some sources have ἔχετε and others have ἔχητε rather than ἕξετε. Manuscript support for both alternatives is limited. The present indicative offers a reading that is extremely difficult to comprehend. The present subjunctive makes the verb part of the ἵνα purpose clause and is an easing of the difficulty raised by the future indicative, i.e., an oracular declaration of future persecution. The future indicative is probably original. Though it is harder than the present subjunctive, it is not impossible.

5

Church of Indiscriminate Toleration

C. THE MESSAGE TO PERGAMUM (2:12-17)

The third church to which Christ addressed a message was at Pergamum (sometimes spelled "Pergamus"), located about fifty-five miles north of Smyrna and twenty miles from the Aegean Sea.[1] The city name occurs in the NT only in the accusative (cf. 1:11) and dative (here), so it is impossible to tell whether the gender is feminine, Πέργαμος (*Pergamos*, "Pergamos" or "Citadel"), or neuter, Πέργαμον (*Pergamon*, "Pergamon" or "Citadel"). It is written both ways in secular writings. This city, whose name means "parchment," was where parchment was first manufactured. It gave this writing material made from animal skins its name (περγαμένη [*pergamenē*, "pergamenized"]).[2] With their number reduced to five by leaving behind the messengers to Ephesus and Smyrna, the messengers arrived at Pergamum with the following message:

---

1. Henry Barclay Swete, *The Apocalypse of St. John* (London: Macmillan, 1906), p. 34; John F. Walvoord, *The Revelation of Jesus Christ* (Chicago: Moody, 1966), p. 65.
2. J. H. Moulton and G. Milligan, *The Vocabulary of the Greek Testament* (Grand Rapids: Eerdmans, 1974), p. 503; G. Abbott-Smith, *A Manual Greek Lexicon of the New Testament*, (Edinburgh: T. & T. Clark, 1950), p. 353; W. F. Arndt and F. Gingrich, *A Greek-English Lexicon of the New Testament*, 2d ed. (Cambridge: U. Press, 1979), p. 649.

Translation

¹²And to the messenger of the church which is in Pergamum, write:
"These things says the one who has the sharp two-edged sword:
¹³I know where you dwell, where the throne of Satan is, and [yet] you
are holding fast My name, and have not denied My faith even in the
days of Antipas, My faithful witness, who was killed among you,
where Satan dwells. ¹⁴But I have a few things against you because
you have there those holding the teaching of Balaam, who taught
Balak to cast a stumbling-block before the children of Israel, to eat
things sacrificed to idols and to commit fornication. ¹⁵Thus you have
also those holding the teaching of the Nicolaitans likewise. ¹⁶Repent
therefore; but if not, I will come to you soon, and will make war
against them with the sword of My mouth. ¹⁷The one who has an ear,
let him hear what the Spirit says to the churches. To the one who
overcomes, I will give to him of the hidden manna,³ and I will give to
him a white stone and upon the stone a new name written which no
one knows except the one who receives it."

Exegesis and Exposition

2:12 *The address.* The standard address this time uses the name
Περγάμῳ (*Pergamō,* "Pergamum"): Καὶ τῷ ἀγγέλῳ τῆς ἐν Περγάμῳ ἐκκλησίας γράψον (*Kai tō angelō tēs en Pergamō ekklēsias grapson,* "And to
the messenger of the church which is in Pergamum, write"). Pergamum was on the site of the modern city Bergama. Its history can
be traced back to the fifth century B.C., but its leadership in Asia
began in 282 B.C., the year that Philetaerus refused continued subjection to King Lysimachus and founded the kingdom of Pergamum. For
the next 151 years the succession of kings was named either Eumenes
or Attalus. During this period the kingdom of which the city was
capital varied in size from as small as only part of the Caicus Valley
to as large as "all the land on this side of the Taurus." In the early
years of the kingdom the Seleucid dynasty supported Philetaerus in
opposition to Lysimachus, but later a rivalry arose between the Seleucid and Pergamanian kings. The kings of Pergamum controlled
until 222 B.C. when Antiochus the Great regained control. He reduced
the territory of Attalus I to the original boundaries of the Pergamanian dynasty. In 190 B.C. the Romans assisted in the expulsion of
Antiochus and again enlarged the boundaries to their previous wide
extent. In 133 B.C. Attalus III turned the whole province over to Rome,

---

3. Τοῦ μάννα is a partitive genitive functioning as the object of the verb δίδωμι.
It is the only example of this in the NT (Isbon T. Beckwith, *The Apocalypse of
John* [New York: Macmillan, 1919], p. 461; A. T. Robertson, *Word Pictures in
the New Testament,* 6 vols. [Nashville: Broadman, 1933], 6:307).

which in turn designated it as the province of Asia. Pergamum was the official capital of the province for two and a half centuries. The city's authority over this large territory had not yet ended by the time of this writing (A.D. 95).[4] Its modern counterpart Bergama has lost much of the city's original greatness and glory, however.[5]

Pergamum used much of its plentiful wealth to build temples devoted to idol worship. Statues, altars, and sacred groves filled the city (Walvoord). A 1,000-foot-high hill, the earliest site of the city, was covered with such temples and altars.[6] The primary local deities to whom temples had been erected were Zeus, Athena, Dionysos, and Asklepios. Zeus, the savior-god, and Athena, the victory-bearing goddess, were testimonials to the Greek spirit and influence. The other two, reflecting more of an Anatolian spirit, were more dominant in the religious life of the city. Dionysos, the god of the royal family, had a mystical name "Bull." Asklepios, like Dionysos more of an animal-god, was associated with serpents. The shrine of Asklepios, who was noted as a "god of healing," attracted people from all over the world. Feeding a living serpent in the temple was the manner of practicing this worship.[7] The sick spent the night in the darkness of the temple where nonpoisonous snakes were allowed to roam. If a person was touched by one of these snakes (i.e., by the god himself), he was cured of his illness.[8]

Despite the city's fascination with idol worship, it was the first in Asia to have a temple devoted to the worship of the Roman emperor. This temple was erected in 29 B.C. in honor of Augustus along with the goddess Roma. From this point on, Pergamum continued as a leader in this form of cult-worship (Beckwith). A second temple for emperor worship was added during the reign of Trajan, earning for the city the title *neokoros*, "temple-sweeper (or warden)." It preceded both Ephesus and Smyrna with this distinctive, which marked the city's greatest privilege of rendering even the most menial service to the god who had taken up residence there. Compared to all the surround-

---

4. W. M. Ramsay, *The Letters to the Seven Churches of Asia* (New York: A. C. Armstrong, 1904), pp. 282-83; Colin J. Hemer, *The Letters to the Seven Churches of Asia in Their Local Setting*, JSNTSup 11 (Sheffield: U. of Sheffield, 1986), p. 78.
5. Clarence Larkin, *The Book of Revelation* (Philadelphia: Clarence Larkin, 1919), p. 22.
6. R. H. Charles, *The Revelation of St. John*, ICC, 2 vols. (New York: Scribner's, 1920), 1:60-61.
7. Marvin R. Vincent, *Word Studies in the New Testament* (New York: Scribner's, 1906), 2:446; Ramsay, *Seven Churches*, pp. 284-85; Leon Morris, *The Revelation of St. John*, TNTC (Grand Rapids: Eerdmans, 1969), p. 95.
8. William Barclay, *Letters to the Seven Churches* (New York: Abingdon, 1957), p. 43.

ing cities, Caesar-worship was the most intense here. In other cities a Christian might be in danger on only one day a year when a pinch of incense had to be burned in worship of the emperor. In Pergamum, however, Christians were in danger every day of the year for the same reason.[9]

The city was noted for two other reasons. It was the birthplace of Galen who was second only to Hippocrates as the most famous physician in ancient times. It also developed a well-known library whose collection rivaled that of the renowned library of Alexandria. At its start the library depended on papyrus material imported from Egypt, the only place the papyrus plant was grown in large quantities, but Ptolemy Epiphanes of Egypt learned of the project and terminated the export of papyrus to Pergamum about 180 B.C. In response, Eumenes of Pergamum developed a new writing material manufactured from animal skins and called "parchment," a name that owes its derivation to the name of the city.[10] Several kings continued the library project, which eventually grew to 200,000 volumes. It was later transported by Cleopatra to Alexandria, where it remained until destroyed by the Saracens in A.D. 642.[11]

Attributes of the speaker. Christ identifies Himself to the church at Pergamum by a single descriptive title: ὁ ἔχων τὴν ῥομφαίαν τὴν δίστομον τὴν ὀξεῖαν (*ho echōn tēn rhomphaian tēn distomon tēn oxeian,* "the one who has the sharp two-edged sword"). This description comes from 1:16 where it was seen to denote the judicial authority of Christ, combining the force of a warrior defeating His enemies in battle and pronouncing judgment upon them. This connotation is continued in Rev. 2:16 and 19:15, 21 where the principal thought is the punishing power of Christ's word and the defeat of His enemies.[12]

A reference back to 1:16 is in line with Christ's words of self-description in the other six messages. The only difference in wording is the use of the article *tēn* with each of the three words of the expression, whereas in 1:16 there is no article. The explanation for this difference lies in the custom of the Greek in using the article to denote reference to the same thing in the previous context. Some have questioned the backward look to 1:16 and its OT roots and the forward

---

9. Barclay, *Seven Churches*, p. 45; Morris, *Revelation*, pp. 65-66.
10. Everett Ferguson, *Backgrounds of Early Christianity* (Grand Rapids: Eerdmans, 1987), p. 92.
11. E. J. Banks, *International Standard Bible Encyclopaedia*, 1952, s.v. "Pergamos."
12. Henry Barclay Swete, *The Apocalypse of St. John* (London: Macmillan, 1906), p. 18; Robert L. Thomas, "The Glorified Christ on Patmos," *BSac* 122 (1965): 245-46.

look to 19:15, 21 because the proconsul in Pergamum (the capital of the province) was granted the "right of the sword," i.e., the power to carry out capital punishment at will.[13] They see the sharp two-edged sword in this message as indicating a higher authority for Christ than that bestowed by the Roman Empire. The connection with the immediate situation in Pergamum need not exclude the OT connotations of the expression, however. Apparently the manner of Christ's appearance to John in the vision of chapter 1 was prompted by the specific situations in which these churches found themselves as well as by the OT expressions that are the source of the figures by which He is described in the vision. The ultimate meaning of the sharp, two-edged sword goes far beyond just Pergamum in its significance. It denotes Christ's ultimate conquest of all the world powers, not just Rome (cf. Rev. 19:15, 21).

2:13 *Knowledge about the people.* Once again, Christ's knowledge about the people in this church and their situation is in three parts (cf. Rev. 2:2, 9). The first aspect of His knowledge of them is ποῦ[14] κατοικεῖς (*pou katoikeis*, "where you dwell"). *Katoikeis* is a word that denotes settled residence. It means to have one's home or permanent residence in a place.[15] It is used frequently in Revelation, most of the time carrying a deeply moral significance. Its most frequent use is to point to a class of people who are not simply on earth, but whose sole interests are in it and are bounded by it (e.g., Rev. 6:10).[16] This is not characteristic of Christians (cf. Phil. 3:20). The word seems to lack this moral connotation in the present instance, however, simply pointing to the permanent residence of the addressees in this city. Both Christians and Satan, as v. 13 later discloses, had made a home here.

The second aspect of Christ's knowledge about this church pertains more directly to Satan than does the first aspect: ὅπου ὁ θρόνος τοῦ Σατανᾶ (*hopou ho thronos tou Satana*, "where the throne of Satan is"). This is a local clause giving a further description of the place where these Christians live. A similar clause at the end of v. 13 identifying the place where Antipas was killed describes Pergamum as the

---

13. Ramsay, *Seven Churches*, pp. 292-93; Robert H. Mounce, *The Book of Revelation*, NICNT (Grand Rapids: Eerdmans, 1977), p. 96.
14. Ποῦ is an interrogative adverb used here to introduce an indirect question as in John 1:40 (R. C. H. Lenski, *The Interpretation of St. John's Revelation* [Columbus, Ohio: Lutheran Book Concern, 1935], p. 304).
15. Swete, *Apocalypse*, p. 35; William Barclay, *The Revelation of John*, 2 vols. (Philadelphia: Westminster, 1960), 1:112.
16. Walter Scott, *Exposition of the Revelation of Jesus Christ* (Swengel, Pa.: Bible Truth Depot, n.d.), p. 74.

place where Satan dwells. *Thronos* refers to a chair of state and implies some special authority or consecration.[17] *Tou Satana* is a subjective genitive: Satan controls and gives power to his throne.

Suggestions as to what special role this clause assigns to Satan have been numerous. One has it that this throne is the seat of worship of Asklepios whose traditional image portrayed the god holding a serpent, an image that would remind Christians of Satan (cf. Rev. 12:9; 20:2).[18] The idolatry at Pergamum was well known. The image of Asklepios rivaled the fame of Diana at Ephesus and of Apollo at Delphi.[19] The popularity of this god in Pergamum caused the city to be viewed as the center for this kind of worship throughout the province of Asia.[20] On every hand, the serpent was visible because of the prominence of this cult. The statement does not exclude the presence of the serpent's throne from other cities, but it associates the visible supremacy of the serpent with the invisible supremacy of the power of the evil one (Hort).

For Christ to tie the worship of this familiar idol directly to Satan would have been most shocking to believers in the city. Because the priesthood of this cult allegedly possessed precious medical secrets that could impart physical health, perhaps of all the institutions of the pagan world it was closest to the Christian priesthood (Moffatt). Further commonality between Christianity and this idol lies in the designation of Asklepios as "Savior" by its worshipers, an evident effort of Satan to imitate Christ's saviorhood (Mounce). As convincing as this suggestion is, it perhaps goes too far in identifying Pergamum as *the* leading place in the fulfillment of later prophecies of the Apocalypse (cf. 12:9: 20:2).[21] Pergamum would hardly have possessed such prominence for this author (Beckwith). Furthermore, Asklepios was not the only god connected with the serpent. The serpent also symbolized Zeus, another god who was also known as "Savior."[22]

A second suggestion of the meaning of "where the throne of Satan

17. F. J. A. Hort, *The Apocalypse of St. John* (London: Macmillan, 1908), p. 27.
18. James Moffatt, "The Revelation of St. John the Divine," in *The Expositor's Greek Testament*, ed. W. Robertson Nicoll (Grand Rapids: Eerdmans, n.d.), 5:355-56; G. V. Caird, *A Commentary on the Revelation of St. John the Divine*, HNTC (New York: Harper & Row, 1966), p. 37. In some places, though not at Pergamum, Asklepios was actually worshiped under the form of a serpent.
19. William Lee, "The Revelation of St. John," in *The Holy Bible*, ed. F. C. Cook (London: John Murray, 1881), 4:523.
20. Charles, *Revelation*, 1:60; G. R. Beasley-Murray, *The Book of Revelation*, NCB (Grand Rapids: Eerdmans, 1978), p. 84.
21. Henry Alford, *The Greek Testament*, 4 vols. (London: Longmans, Green, 1903), 4:568.
22. J. P. M. Sweet, *Revelation* (Philadelphia: Westminster, Pelican, 1979), p. 87.

is" turns to the great altar of Zeus Soter, which had been set up in the city to commemorate a victory over the Gauls by Attalus two centuries earlier. This altar, found on the acropolis of the altar platform of Zeus, was enormous in its dimensions and featured beautiful pieces of sculpture (Moffatt). Such magnificence could easily suggest a special throne, even that of Satan. As a symbol of "rampant paganism," this altar could easily have pictured for John all the idolatry that dominated Pergamum (Swete; Beasley-Murray). Once again, however, Pergamum's prominence over other cities where Zeus was also worshiped is not justified (Beckwith). Neither John nor his fellow Christians saw this as the center of satanic power.

A further proposal is to make Pergamum the throne of Satan because in a special sense it was the home of the satanic spirit of persecution.[23] The martyrdom of Antipas mentioned later in v. 13 evidences a fierceness of Satan's power unseen in the other Asian cities (Alford; Lee). This martyrdom is associated with Satan's dwelling-place at the end of the verse. Persecution occasions an earlier reference to Satan in the message to Smyrna also. Persecution against Christians in that city was especially intense through the early centuries of Christianity.[24] This proposal encounters the same difficulty as the first two, however—that of assigning too much prominence to Pergamum as compared to the other cities (Beckwith). It also ignores, as do the first two views, any reference to Rome in a city where religion and politics were allies. Somehow the repeated reference to Satan must relate to the civil effort to maintain emperor worship in a city where it was so prominent (Beckwith).

A fourth suggested identification of the throne of Satan makes it a figurative reference to the power or influence that works against the church and all who belong to it (Ramsay). This idea is based largely on Paul's use of "Satan" in 1 Thess. 2:18 (Ramsay), but it fails the test of plausibility because in epistolary literature such as this, special grounds for figurative interpretation are required. No such grounds exist here.

A fifth explanation sees this city as the worst of the seven, even though all seven were thoroughly pagan (Lenski). That Satan had his throne here and ruled as king is evidenced by temples to at least four of the most prominent Greek gods that were there: Zeus, Athena, Dionysos, and Asklepios (Beckwith). Not only were they worshiped, but their representations were found on the coins used in the city. In

---

23. William Henry Simcox, *The Revelation of St. John the Divine* (Cambridge: U. Press, 1893), pp. 15-16.
24. Eusebius *The Ecclesiastical History*, trans. Kirsopp Lake, 2 vols. (Cambridge, Mass.: Harvard U., 1953), 4.15.

addition, emperor worship was prominent, and even some professing Christians adhered to the teaching both of Balaam and of the Nicolaitans. The combination of all these made Pergamum the worst and combined to produce a heavy, oppressive satanic atmosphere in the city.[25] Though impressive on the surface, this view lacks persuasiveness for the same reason as the first three views: Why should Pergamum have such prominence among the cities? This explanation also fails to analyze the situation definitively enough to determine which of the anti-God forces was most dominant in the daily life of Christians there.

A sixth way of approaching the issue limits the existence of this church as well as the other six to the future day of the Lord.[26] The throne of Satan connects somehow with Rev. 13:2 and the impartation of power, a throne, and great authority to the beast out of the sea by the dragon of Revelation 12. The throne of the beast mentioned in Rev. 16:10 will be at Pergamum. This is none other than the place where Satan's throne will be set up on earth during that future day (Bullinger). The martyrdom prominent in this message will characterize that future time (cf. Rev. 6:9-10; 13:10; 20:4) (Bullinger). Yet martyrdom has also been characteristic of the past. In itself, this is no reason to find a future reference for the words. Even more difficult for this approach is assigning a future reference to literature that is epistolary in nature. This is unnatural and unjustified.

A last suggestion about the throne of Satan is the most impressive: emperor worship was prominent in Pergamum. The city was a leader in this form of worship, which was relatively new to the province of Asia (Beckwith). This form of heathenism best explains the strong terminology regarding the presence of the evil one here, where the imperial cult had its headquarters (Charles). A temple erected to the divine Augustus and the goddess Roma had stood in the city since 29 B.C. (Moffatt). Later a temple was erected in honor of Trajan, giving the city the title "twice *neokoros* (i.e., temple warden [or sweeper])" (Mounce). A special priesthood was also devoted to this kind of worship. Throughout the Apocalypse the specter of Caesar-adoration is in the background. Emperor worship is constantly viewed as an agency of Satan's power (Moffatt; Beckwith). Probably Antipas, the city's Christian martyr (2:13), was the victim of Rome, because only the imperial cultus had the power of capital punishment. John's personal circumstances probably made him believe that Rome was the most

---

25. Homer Hailey, *Revelation, an Introduction and Commentary* (Grand Rapids: Baker, 1979), p. 130.
26. E. W. Bullinger, *The Apocalypse* or *"The Day of the Lord"* (London: Eyre and Spottiswoode, n.d.), p. 180.

recent and strongest agent of Satan because of its totalitarian demands for absolute allegiance to the state and because in her was embodied the epitome of all paganism and worldliness (Caird). The sword (cf. Rev. 2:12) was emblematic of the almost unlimited imperial power wielded by the senatorial governor of Asia stationed in Pergamum (Caird).

This suggested meaning alone offers a satisfactory explanation of Pergamum's preeminence in being the location of the throne of Satan. Most of the other suggestions can be matched by pagan worship practiced in other cities (Morris). This new Caesar-worship, it appears, was the greatest menace to the existence of the church in this city (Swete). Though Rome is nowhere mentioned in the message to Pergamum, this appears to be the root meaning of the presence of the throne of Satan in Pergamum.

The third item of Christ's knowledge of this people concerns their faithfulness: καὶ κρατεῖς τὸ ὄνομά μου, καὶ οὐκ ἠρνήσω τὴν πίστιν μου *καὶ[27] ἐν ταῖς *ἡμέραις Ἀντιπᾶς ὁ μάρτυς μου ὁ πιστός μου, ὃς ἀπεκτάνθη παρ' ὑμῖν, ὅπου ὁ Σατανᾶς κατοικεῖ (*kai krateis to onoma mou, kai ouk ērnēsō tēn pistin mou kai en tais hēmerais Antipas ho martys mou ho pistos mou, hos apektanthē par' hymin, hopou ho Satanas katoikei*, "and [yet] you are holding fast My name, and have not denied My faith even in the days of Antipas, My faithful witness, who was killed among you, where Satan dwells"). The first *kai* carries an adversative notion by virtue of the context, because this statement contrasts with what has just been said (Lee; Lenski). In spite of having permanent residence in a setting where Satan has his throne, these Christians were continuing faithful. What it means to hold fast Christ's name deserves a closer scrutiny.

Does "my name" speak of the revelation by which Jesus made Himself known (Lenski) or does it refer to personal loyalty to Christ as Lord and Master with a consequent refusal to submit to the worship of Caesar (Beckwith)? In the former case, doctrinal conformity is the meaning. In the latter, it means faithfulness to Christ in spite of adverse pressures. Admittedly doctrinal conformity and personal faithfulness cannot be completely separated, but personal faithfulness is more in keeping with this part of the message, whereas doctrinal conformity fits better with vv. 14-16. *To onoma* can have an objective sense referring to all that Jesus is, i.e., His deity, authority, and lordship over God's entire universe, thereby supporting the doctrinal meaning (Lee; Hailey). Yet because the remainder of the sen-

---

27. Here is another of this book's frequent uses of an ascensive καί. This time it shows the refusal of the church to deny Christ's name came on the same occasion as the death of Antipas, Christ's faithful witness.

tence proceeds to speak of Antipas's faithfulness to Christ under duress, the meaning of faithfulness is more likely. In the trial of Polycarp in this city a few years later, the test of his loyalty was whether or not he would curse Christ (Moffatt; Caird). In later contexts of the Apocalypse, holding fast to Christ's name is manifested in not receiving the mark of the beast (cf. Rev. 11:18; 13:13-17) (Bullinger).

The faithfulness of this congregation is further reflected in its unwillingness to deny faith in Christ.[28] The aorist tense of *ērnēsō* speaks of a specific incident in the past when some of the members had apparently been asked to deny their faith in Him (Beckwith; Caird). This was probably a persecution undergone by the church about which nothing is now known (Charles), one that illustrates their constancy in holding fast to Christ's name.[29] *Pistin* could possibly refer to "*the* faith" or doctrine of Christ (Lenski), inasmuch as personal loyalty to Christ has already been mentioned in the previous part of the statement (Walvoord). However, the noun is never so used in this book. It means personal trust in Christ (e.g., Rev. 14:12) (Lee; Charles). This meaning is natural here and coincides with personal loyalty to Christ's name in the clause just before.

Specific information about this particular persecution through which the church had displayed such loyalty locates it "in the days of Antipas, My faithful witness." Apparently Antipas[30] was part of the resistance to imperial pressure upon Christians to compromise their loyalty to Christ. Nothing certain is known about this man except what this passage tells (Simcox), but tradition suggests that he was burned to death in a bronze bull during the reign of Domitian (Swete). He is never listed among the martyrs of the first two centuries mentioned elsewhere in connection with Pergamum: Carpus, Papylus, and Agathonice. This is possibly explained by his not being a native of the city, having been brought there from a smaller town to suffer (Swete). Proposed identifications of him with Athanasius or Timothy hold little plausibility.[31]

---

28. Mου gives the most natural sense if taken as an objective genitive (Swete, *Apocalypse*, p. 34; Charles, *Revelation*, 1:61; Robertson, *Word Pictures*, 6:304; Donald S. Deer, "Whose Faith/Loyalty in Revelation 2.13 and 14.12?" *BT* 38, no. 3 [July 1987]: 328-30). The objective genitive with the noun πίστις elsewhere is common (cf. Mark 11:22; Rev. 14:12) (Swete, *Apocalypse*, p. 35).
29. Note the present tense of κρατεῖς earlier in v. 13 to indicate the continuing faithfulness of the church.
30. Ἀντιπᾶς means "against all" and could be a commentary on his stand against evil until his death (Walvoord, *Revelation*, p. 67). This point cannot be pressed, however, as he may have had the name before becoming a Christian.
31. Swete, *Apocalypse*, p. 35; J. B. Smith, *A Revelation of Jesus Christ* (Scottdale, Pa.: Herald, 1961), p. 35.

This verse discloses what is important about Antipas, however: he was Christ's faithful witness. *Martys* is the usual NT word for *witness* (cf. Rev. 17:6; Acts 1:8; 22:20).[32] In a very similar expression in Rev. 1:5, it refers to Christ as "the faithful witness" (cf. Ps. 89:37).[33] Quite possibly this exhausts the meaning of the word here, with Jesus giving Antipas his own title because he was true. But the question remains, How does this meaning distinguish Antipas from other faithful believers? By the third century A.D., *martys* had developed the meaning *martyr* because so many witnesses of Christ had given their lives for the Christian cause. The end of the first century may be too early to attach this developed meaning to the word,[34] but this also may be the beginning of a transition in the word's meaning from witness to martyr.[35] The way had been prepared for development of this meaning by Acts 22:20, where Stephen is called a *martys* (Charles). The likelihood is that John captures this technical sense of the noun, though the clear-cut use of it in the sense of martyr was not yet in evidence elsewhere. This passage doubtless expedited the transition to the new meaning.

To be sure that the sense of martyr is attached to *martys*, the Lord clarified that Antipas had been killed, presumably because of his faith. Though persecution of the church had been widespread on this occasion, apparently only one had been put to death among the Christians at Pergamum.[36] That was Antipas. Because pressure was on the whole church and only one was killed, his death may have happened through mob violence. If execution of Christians had become an official policy, there would have been no reason for the government to stop with one (Beasley-Murray). Yet persecution took the form of trial before the proconsular court in Pergamum (Ramsay), making it more probable that Antipas was only the first in a series of martyrs (Sweet).

"Where Satan dwells" locates the martyrdom of Antipas in Per-

---

32. Robertson, *Word Pictures*, 6:305.
33. Barclay, *Seven Churches*, p. 50.
34. Swete, *Apocalypse*, p. 36; Robertson, *Word Pictures*, 6:305.
35. F. F. Bruce, "The Revelation to John," in *A New Testament Commentary* (London: Pickering & Inglis, 1969), p. 638; Beasley-Murray, *Revelation*, p. 85; Sweet, *Revelation*, p. 88. For another suggestion of the influence of this book on later Christian terminology, see the discussion of "the Lord's day" at Rev. 1:10.
36. Albert Barnes, *The Book of Revelation* (New York: Harper, 1851), p. 75. The plural ὑμῖν here and in 2:10 recalls that Christ's words were not solely for the individual church messengers, but pertain to the entire church in each case. The phrase παρ᾽ ὑμῖν replaces the local dative (or locative) without a preposition. The latter has almost disappeared from the NT (Nigel Turner, *Syntax*, vol. 3 of *A Grammar of New Testament Greek* [Edinburgh: T. & T. Clark, 1963], p. 273). The phrase could be translated "at (or by) your side" (Robertson, *Word Pictures*, 6:305).

gamum, because the verse has earlier indicated the presence of Satan's throne in the city. This appended clause implicitly traces the martyrdom and related persecution to Satan as the ultimate source.

2:14 *State of the church.* As in the messages to Ephesus (2:4) and Thyatira (2:20), ἀλλ᾽ (*all'*, "but") introduces a strong complaint, this time against the church at Pergamum: ἀλλ᾽ ἔχω κατὰ σοῦ ὀλίγα (*all' echō kata sou oliga,* "But I have a few things against you"). The complaint comes as a strong contrast to the Lord's commendation of the church's faithfulness in persecution (2:13). Though few numerically, the matters were nonetheless important.

One opinion is that the plural of *oliga* refers generically to only one thing (Charles). The plural is explained as a word of comparison with the far greater number of approved things that remained (Alford). The singular ὀλίγον (*oligon,* "small"), it is said, would not have indicated objective fewness, but rather the subjective unimportance of the grounds of the complaint. At times the plural has such a generic use as this.[37] The one ground of criticism against the church is its indifference to those who held the teaching of Balaam and that of the Nicolaitans, probably an indifference that arose from contempt or fear rather than ignorance (Moffatt). Because the following context proceeds to reduce the "few things" to one by identifying those holding the teaching of Balaam with those embracing that of the Nicolaitans, the basis for the complaint is singular (Beasley-Murray). Yet this is not the whole story. It is true that the root problem may have been indifference, but the speaker does not cite the root problem. He cites the presence of this group and then the presence of that group (Scott). Two groups explain the plural. If the teaching of the Nicolaitans were identical with that of Balaam, this could have been expressed more clearly. Since the church tolerated two classes of heretics, the better course is to take the plural *oliga* in its normal plural sense as referring to more than one ground of complaint.

The Lord next furnishes the reason for His complaint: ὅτι[38] ἔχεις ἐκεῖ κρατοῦντας τὴν διδαχὴν Βαλαάμ, ὃς ἐδίδασκεν τῷ Βαλὰκ βαλεῖν σκάνδαλον ἐνώπιον τῶν υἱῶν Ἰσραήλ, φαγεῖν εἰδωλόθυτα καὶ πορνεῦσαι (*hoti echeis ekei kratountas tēn didachēn Balaam, hos edidasken tō Balak balein skandalon enōpion tōn huiōn Israēl, phagein eidōlothyta kai por-*

---

37. G. B. Winer, *A Grammar of the Idiom of the New Testament* (Andover, Mass.: Warren F. Draper, 1897), par. 27.2.

38. A causal ὅτι is preferred over the epexegetical sense indicating the content of the ὀλίγα because ὅτι does not usually indicate content in such an appositional situation as this. The particle introduces substantive clauses more commonly when direct or indirect discourse is involved. The epexegetic sense might provide for the remainder of v. 14, but it would not account for how v. 15 fits into the picture.

neusai, "because you have there those holding the teaching of Balaam, who taught Balak to cast a stumblingblock before the children of Israel, to eat things sacrificed to idols and to commit fornication"). *Ekei* ("there") designates the same place as *par' hymin* ("among you") and the two *hopou* ("where") clauses of v. 13 (Alford; Charles). Because Pergamum has just been noted as the death-site of Antipas, special attention is drawn to the locality once again. "You have there" shows that the persons whose presence was being tolerated were not teachers from abroad as at Ephesus (2:2), but members of the local congregation of the city (Beckwith). While the congregation as a whole was commended for "holding fast" (*krateis*) to the name of Jesus (2:13), it is condemned for tolerating some of their number who were "holding fast" (*kratountas,* 2:14, 15) to the teaching of Balaam and the Nicolaitans.

The fault of the church as a whole was not adherence to the teaching or doctrine of Balaam, but rather indifference to those within who were in sympathy with it (Moffatt). *Balaam* is derived from two Hebrew words, בָּלַע (*bala',* "he swallows") and עָם (*'ām,* "people"). Interestingly, according to the derivative meanings of the names, the two groups troubling this church were "swallowers of the people" (i.e., the Balaamites) and "conquerors of the people" (i.e., the Nicolaitans; cf. discussion at 2:6).

In Numbers 24 Balaam persistently refused the request of Balak, king of Moab, to curse Israel (Beckwith). In the account of Israel's seduction to worship Baal in Num. 25 no mention is made of Balaam's agency in causing this defection. Nevertheless, according to Num. 31:16, he had apparently advised Balak that Israel would forfeit God's protection if he could induce them to worship idols, which he did. This tragic incident at Baal-Peor made a deep impression on subsequent generations of Israelites (Morris). The doctrine relevant to the downfall resulting from Balaam's counsel advocates that the people of God commit sexual immorality or intermarry with the heathen and compromise in the matter of idolatrous worship (Walvoord). Balaam bears more guilt than even antagonistic King Balak. As an alleged prophet of God, he betrayed his calling and is viewed as the real instigator of the seduction in which 24,000 of God's people fell into idolatrous worship and practices (Scott).

Two other NT passages refer to the negative example of Balaam, 2 Pet. 2:15 and Jude 11. It is possible to view the lesson to be learned as the same in all three cases. Balaam sold his gift for profit, and whenever he is mentioned in the NT, his sin of greed is the primary sin to be avoided (Beckwith). This conclusion derives from the fact that desire for gain was Balaam's ultimate motive in carrying out the will of Balak (Smith). This idea does not do justice to the total expression *tēn didachēn Balaam* ("the teaching of Balaam") as compared with τῇ ὁδῷ τοῦ Βαλαὰμ (*tȩ hodȩ tou Balaam*, "the way of Balaam") in 2 Pet. 2:15 and τῇ πλάνῃ τοῦ Βαλαὰμ (*tȩ planȩ tou Balaam*, "the error of Balaam") in Jude 11. The contexts of the three mentions of Balaam as well as the difference between "teaching," "way," and "error" warrant some distinction in meaning (Walvoord).

The emphasis here is not on selling his prophetic gift for money as in 2 Peter or on assuming erroneously that God would curse Israel as in Jude. It is simply on teaching them to eat things sacrificed to idols and to commit fornication. These Balaamites at Pergamum taught others to relax their principles the way Balaam did (Moffatt). They advocated that it was legitimate for a Christian to buy food in the open market that had already been consecrated to an idol. In Jewish midrash the story of Balaam served two purposes: his acceptance of Balak's bribe exemplified a mercenary spirit (alluded to in 2 Peter and Jude) and his responsibility for the defection at Baal-Peor made him the father of religious syncretism. The latter lesson is the main focus of the present discussion (Caird).

The relative clause that closes v. 14 confirms that this was the nature of the local problem. A comparison of *edidasken* with the *didachēn* a few words before discloses the strict correspondence between the thing held by some in Pergamum and the erroneous teachings of Balaam. The person taught by Balaam was *tȩ Balak*.[39] Numbers 31:16 does not identify the recipient of the counsel,[40] but tradition had accurately said that it was Balak. Balaam taught Balak how to put a stumbling block into the path of Israel. *Skandalon*, along with its cognate verb, occurs only in the LXX and NT. It is a trap or more precisely that part of a trap where the bait is placed which, when touched, triggers the trap to close on its prey. The trap could be small enough to catch a bird or large enough to entangle a man's foot and cause him to stumble.[41] Metaphorically the word referred to anything over which a person might fall or stumble into sin, the occasion of one's sin.[42]

Tōn huiōn Israēl identifies the victims of the trap as the physical descendants of Abraham, the only sense that *Israel* ever carries in the

---

39. Robertson, *Word Pictures*, 6:305.
40. Alford, *Greek Testament*, 4:570. The imperfect tense of ἐδίδασκεν shows that this kind of teaching was Balaam's habitual method. This is what made him "the prototype of all corrupt teachers" (Charles, *Revelation*, 1:63).
41. Richard Chenevix Trench, *Commentary on the Epistles to the Seven Churches in Asia* (London: Parker, Son, and Bourn, 1861), p. 160; Swete, *Apocalypse*, p. 36; Morris, *Revelation*, p. 67.
42. Trench, *Seven Churches*, p. 160; Barnes, *Revelation*, p. 61.

NT.[43] The women of Moab were deliberately thrown in the way of unsuspecting people of Israel for the purpose of causing their downfall (Num. 25:1-2), and the plan worked (Swete). The two infinitives *phagein* ("to eat") and *porneusai* ("to commit fornication") are epexegetic in explanation of *skandalon* (Lenski). The order of Num. 25:1-2 is reversed. There fornication preceded and led to idolatry, the same order as indicated in the related problem at Thyatira (cf. Rev. 2:20). In Pergamum, however, idolatrous practices seem to have come first. It has been proposed that the problem at Pergamum resembled that introduced by Balaam in a general way and that the idolatry and fornication of this church amounted only to taking a laxer attitude than John did toward pagan society and religion. This is defended by noting that the sin of Jezebel, mentioned in Rev. 2:20, was never that of literal harlotry (Caird). Since a metaphorical sense is necessary in connection with Thyatira, the similarity must not be pushed to a literal sense in connection with Pergamum (Beasley-Murray). Idolatry is often referred to as spiritual "fornication" in the OT (cf. Isa. 1:21; Ezek. 23:37).[44]

To limit the meaning to a general similarity by saying that literal idolatry and fornication happened only to ancient Israel does injustice to the natural sense of v. 14, however. The sins of participation in idolatrous feasts and sexual immorality were so characteristic of the pagan surroundings in Asia Minor that a literal sense is preferable (Moffatt; Johnson). Civic and religious life in this community were so intertwined that intermarriage with the heathen and spiritual compromise were inevitably real issues for the church (Walvoord). Further, grammatically speaking, the function of the relative clause introduced by *hos* (v. 14) in giving the reason the teaching of Balaam was so objectionable is to give the content of the doctrine being propagated among the readers. The practices of eating meat sacrificed to idols and immorality are the same two that Paul, under slightly different circumstances, decried in 1 Cor. 10:19-28 and 1 Cor. 6:15-18 (Scott).

The term *eidōlothyta* names things offered to idols as viewed by Christians and Jews. This was sacrificial meat, part of which was burned on the altar, part of which was eaten at a solemn meal, and part of which was sold at the market for home use. From the Jewish viewpoint, it was unclean and therefore forbidden, no matter which

---

43. It is abusive of the exegetical process to say this expression marks the church as the true Israel (cf. Hort, *Apocalypse*, p. 28). The church is never so identified in the NT. See discussion of the 144,000 sons of Israel at 7:4.
44. Alan F. Johnson, "Revelation," in *EBC*, ed. Frank E. Gaebelein (Grand Rapids: Zondervan, 1981), 12:441.

use it had.[45] The practice in view in Pergamum was only partially similar to the one that Paul addresses at Corinth, that of eating things purchased at the meat markets after being consecrated to an idol and personal sharing in the heathen feasts (cf. 1 Cor. 8:7-13; 10:20-30) (Charles). The cities were separated too far in time and distance to assume complete identity. In Pergamum, personal involvement in idolatrous feasts was the major issue. It had come to be viewed as morally indifferent by the Balaamite advocates.

To this, Christ objects. In this environment the searching test for converts from idolatrous religions was whether or not they made a clean break with this aspect of pagan worship. It was extremely difficult to do so because such feasts were an integral part of social life in the city (cf. 1 Cor. 10:21-22).[46] Yet to participate in the feast was tantamount to the actual offering of sacrifices to these idols as the children of Israel had done under Balaam's influence (cf. Num. 25:1-2) (Alford). It was the mixed company at these feasts that led to the other sin of fornication (Swete). Feasting on sacrificial meat and licentious conduct are the usual accompaniments of idol worship in both the OT and the NT (Morris). Yet some in Pergamum who professed to be Christians had yielded to cultural pressure, and the church had not pronounced against them.

The other practice tolerated was that of fornication. Only a weak case can be made for referring the term to religious infidelity. The usage of πορνεύω (*porneuō*, "I commit fornication") and its cognate noun in Revelation is mostly metaphorical, conveying the sense of religious infidelity to the true God (Moffatt). It is commonly used this way in both Testaments (Caird; Beasley-Murray). Because the intercourse of Israelite men with Moabite women was religious infidelity as well as sexual license, John could be speaking of either one in v. 14. Yet to theorize a metaphorical meaning here is to ignore that spiritual fornication has already been covered in the phrase *phagein eidōlothyta*. The literal sin of fornication was closely associated with this city's pagan feasts and was an inescapable consequence of them (Mounce; Sweet). The compromisers had given their approval to this practice also. It is no wonder that Christ voices this strong complaint against the church for not raising its voice in protest.

2:15 Christ's complaint against the church's condition continues in v. 15: οὕτως ἔχεις καὶ σὺ κρατοῦντας τὴν διδαχὴν Νικολαϊτῶν ὁμοίως (*houtōs echeis kai sy kratountas tēn didachēn Nikolaitōn homoiōs*, "Thus you have also those holding the teaching of the Nicolaitans

---

45. Trench, *Seven Churches*, pp. 161-62; Arndt and Gingrich, *Lexicon*, p. 221.
46. Trench, *Seven Churches*, pp. 161-62; Swete, *Apocalypse*, p. 37; Vincent, *Word Studies*, p. 448; Lee, "Revelation," p. 524.

likewise"). A major issue here concerns whether the adverbs *houtōs* ("thus") and *homoiōs* ("likewise") serve to identify the Nicolaitans of v. 15 with the Balaamites of v. 14. One proposal says that "thus" relates the Nicolaitans with the Balaamites and "likewise" relates them to the Nicolaitan influence in Ephesus (cf. 2:6) (Charles). This makes the sense of the verse, "you too (as well as the Ephesian church) in like manner (with the Ephesian church)." As ingenious as it is, this suggestion cannot justify an adverbial comparison with something as remote as the message to Ephesus. The remaining possibilities are that the two groups are the same and that they are similar. In favor of the former option is the observation that "the teaching of Balaam" is merely John's opprobrious name for "the teaching of the Nicolaitans." Whether or not they claimed to follow Nicolaus, they certainly did not profess to be followers of Balaam (Caird). An alternative way of identifying the two is to allow that v. 14 shows their affinity with corrupt teachers of the past, and v. 15 with teachers of the present (Charles).

A major obstacle to making the two groups the same, however, is that it would destroy the historical illustration by which the present sect is described (Alford). Another problem with it is that John could have made it much plainer that they are the same if this were true. That the teaching of the two groups is identical (Charles; Beckwith) does not demand that the two groups be the same. Support for the sameness of the two groups notes that both verses speak of an antinomian group accepting the religious and social requirement of that pagan society, one church being too small for two groups of the exact same kind (Mounce). Yet the view of a single group is questionable, because it must view the *homoiōs* at the end of the verse as merely emphasizing the *houtōs* that begins the verse (Swete). *Echeis* ("you have") would take up the thread of v. 14, and *houtōs echeis kai* would compare the situation with Israel of old. The above-stated objections to the view are stronger than its supports.

A better case exists for distinguishing the two groups. *Houtōs* reflects that they were like, but not identical with, those who held the Balaamite doctrine. The introduction of the Nicolaitans with *kai* ("also") and *homoiōs* ("thus" or "in like manner") also argues for two separate groups.[47] The best conclusion is that there were two different but similar groups in this church, both of which had disobeyed the decision of the Jerusalem council in regard to idolatrous practices and fornication (cf. Acts 15:20, 29).[48]

---

47. Hailey, *Revelation*, p. 132. The οὕτως may be understood as pleonastic as at 3:5, 16; 9:17 (Lee, p. 524).
48. Robertson, *Word Pictures*, 6:306.

A related question to be answered centers in the *kai* ("also") of v. 15. Does it compare the situation at Pergamum with that of Israel of old, with that at neighboring Ephesus, or with something else within the church at Pergamum? A comparison with Israel of old may be ruled out on the basis of the form of the text and the context (Charles). One or both of the adverbs account for this comparison. A comparison with Ephesus would emphasize the position of *kai* just before *sy* ("you"): "in addition to others *you* have these false teachers." This sense requires that the *houtōs* also reinforces the *sy*. The main difficulty with this sense, as already stated, is the remoteness of the message to Ephesus. Two adverbs could hardly draw such a comparison.

The comparison indicated by *kai* must be within the local church itself. The second occurrence of *echeis* (v. 15; cf. v. 14) addressed to the same messenger necessitates that "also" points to a second deficiency in that same church. The second deficiency is another group holding a false doctrine similar to the first group. The following rendering accounts for the three adverbs *houtōs*, *kai*, and *homoiōs*, assuming that John uses *houtōs* pleonastically as he does on other occasions (3:5, 16; 9:17; cf. John 4:6; 13:25): "You have also [in addition to those who hold the teaching of Balaam] those who hold in like manner [to the way the Balaamites hold their teaching] the teaching of the Nicolaitans."

An earlier discussion has investigated the origin and nature of the Nicolaitan party (cf. 2:6), but a word of clarification about the doctrine being tolerated at Pergamum is desirable. Though 1 John indicates the widespread influence of incipient Gnosticism in Asia by this time, these were not Gnostics,[49] but followers of Nicolaus. It is true that the two groups arrived at the same goal, that of eating meat sacrificed to idols and fornication, but they followed different paths to get there.[50] The teachings of this group were an attempt to reach a compromise between the Christian life and the cultural customs of the Graeco-Roman society, with special attention to including as much as possible from the latter category (Ramsay). The connection of the Nicolaitans with the end of v. 14 shows this (Alford; Swete). Because they represent an excessively liberal or even antinomian outlook with regard to Jewish Christianity, the Nicolaitans have sometimes been connected with the teaching of Paul (Sweet). The connection is unfounded, however. Paul argued against eating things sacrificed to idols because it offended weaker brethren (1 Cor. 8:4, 9, 10) and because of the connection between idol worship and demons

---

49. Contra Beasley-Murray, *Revelation*, p. 86; J. Massyngberde Ford, *Revelation*, vol. 38 of AB (Garden City, N.Y.: Doubleday, 1975), p. 387.
50. Edward Hayes Plumptre, *A Popular Exposition of the Epistles to the Seven Churches of Asia* (London: Hodder, 1879), p. 121.

(1 Cor. 10:20). The Nicolaitan syncretism was rather a perversion of the liberty that Paul advocated.

2:16 *The Lord's coming.* In light of Christ's complaint He enjoins the church to repent: μετανόησον οὖν[51] (*metanoēson oun*, "repent therefore"). *Oun* shows repentance to be the logical outcome of the Lord's hatred of the grave evils in their midst (Scott; Morris). The church allowed some to continue in its fellowship who held to the teaching of Balaam and that of the Nicolaitans. They had not purged themselves of such as had the church in Ephesus (cf. 2:6) (Alford; Swete). They were guilty of unjustified tolerance. So the Lord issues an urgent command for them to repent.[52]

To strengthen his plea for immediate action, He appends a threat of punishment if the church fails to purge itself: εἰ δὲ μή, ἔρχομαί[53] σοι ταχύ, καὶ πολεμήσω μετ᾽ αὐτῶν ἐν τῇ ῥομφαίᾳ τοῦ στόματός μου (*ei de mē, erchomai soi tachy, kai polemēsō met᾽ autōn en tȩ̄ rhomphaiȩ̄ tou stomatos mou*, "but if not, I will come to you soon, and will make war against them with the sword of My mouth").

Ei de mē is an abbreviation for εἰ δὲ μή μετανοήσεις (*ei de mē metanoēseis*, "but if you will not repent"). It is always elliptical in this book (Charles). The same elliptical expression is used in the message to Ephesus to introduce the consequences of failure to repent (cf. 2:5). Such failure will mean for this church what it meant for the one at Ephesus: punishment when Christ comes. The same issue exists here as in the first of the seven messages. Does *erchomai* refer to a special coming in judgment to this church only, or does it refer to His second advent for the whole church? A special coming in the form of some pestilence or physical calamity could have taken place a short time later in punishment of this church (Moffatt). Ethnic conscience in general and early Christianity shared the belief that punishment inflicted by a divine being could take this form. This was the way Balaam met his punishment (Num. 22:23, 31; 25:5; 31:8) (Alford; Moffatt). Such a judgment has come against the Balaamites and the Nicolaitans who are gone and have left behind no records or institutions (Hailey). The inclusion of the pronoun *soi* ("you") can serve also to support that this was a special coming to this church only.

---

51. Οὖν is an important indicator of Johannine style (Lee, p. 524).
52. The verb always signifies to change one's mind or purpose with respect to sin (W. E. Vine, *An Expository Dictionary of New Testament Words* [Old Tappan, N.J.: Revell, 1966], p. 280). As customary, the aorist imperative stresses urgency (Robertson, *Word Pictures*, 6:306). The singular number addresses the messenger who stands as representative of the whole church (Lenski, *Revelation*, p. 108).
53. Ἔρχομαι is once again the futuristic use of the present tense, the time of occurrence coinciding with the time of the future tense of πολεμήσω. See additional note on ἔρχεται at 1:7.

Yet the coming of Christ as the theme of the Apocalypse is clearly a reference to His second advent, as the earlier discussion of *erchomai* in 2:5 has shown. This conclusion is strengthened in the present verse by the addition of *tachy*. Every other combination of *erchomai tachy* in this book refers to Christ's second advent (cf. 3:11; 22:7, 12, 20).[54] The adverb is equivalent to the ἐν τάχει (*en tachei*, "soon") of 1:1 and 22:6.[55] Both teach the imminence of Christ's return. *Polemēsō met' autōn en tę̄ rhomphaią tou stomatos mou* is further confirmation of a reference to Christ's eschatological return rather than a special coming to this church. This is the language of 19:11-15, especially v. 15, which is the full prophecy of Christ's triumphant return. It shows that at the final moment of truth this church will be on the wrong side unless it repents (Charles; Sweet). That faithful believers will have access to the tree of life (2:7) and receive the crown of life (2:10) is no argument for making this a historical judgment rather than the second coming.[56] Unwillingness to repent shows that a person is not a faithful believer. Little doubt can be entertained that from the perspective of the first century, *erchomai* referred to the second or final coming of Christ (Mounce).

The apparent problem of making the second coming of Christ conditioned upon the nonrepentance of the Pergamene church has been discussed in connection with the similar issue regarding Ephesus (cf. 2:5, Exegesis and Exposition and Additional Notes). Applied to the present verse, the proposed grammatical analysis produces the following meaning: "When I come quickly, I will make war against them with the sword of My mouth, if you shall not have repented before that coming, whenever it happens."

The issue of whether *tachy* denotes imminence or swiftness of action has been discussed at 1:1 in connection with *en tachei*. The conclusion must be the same here, that the coming is imminent. The latter idea of rapidity of movement makes little sense here as the coming must be explained in conjunction with victory in battle. Swiftness of action is meaningful only where a series of events is in view. Since only one event is here, the point must be imminence.

The threatened action connected with Christ's coming is *polemēsō met' autōn* ("I will make war[57] against[58] them"). The identity of those

---

54. Lee, "Revelation," 4:524-25; Robertson, *Word Pictures*, 6:306.
55. Robertson, *Word Pictures*, 6:306.
56. George E. Ladd, *A Commentary on the Revelation of John* (Grand Rapids: Eerdmans, 1972), p. 49.
57. The words for "war" or "make war" occur more often in the Apocalypse than in any other NT book.
58. Μετά with the genitive provides the idea of "in conflict with" (C. F. D. Moule, *An Idiom Book of New Testament Greek* [Cambridge: Cambridge U.,

against whom Christ threatens to battle, *autōn*, must be resolved. The change of pronouns from *soi* to *autōn* provides a reason for saying the threat applies only to those who hold heretical teaching. Κρατοῦντας τὴν διδαχὴν Νικολαϊτῶν (*kratountas tēn didachēn Nikolaitōn*, "those holding the teaching of the Nicolaitans," 2:15) provides a natural antecedent for the plural pronoun. It is true that the church had tolerated the Nicolaitans and some of her members had listened to their teaching, but she had not as a whole identified herself with the party (Swete). So goes the argument to limit the threat to the error-ists. Yet the plain truth is that the church is called on to repent of its leniency earlier in v. 16. Being tolerant of the Nicolaitans makes the church as guilty as those who hold false doctrine. Failure to repent of this uncleanness in her midst must evoke the punishing sword of Christ upon the whole church (Beckwith). The change from a singular to a plural pronoun and from second to third person is a Hebraism that is common in the LXX.[59] The two pronouns refer to the same group.

Christ's instrument of warfare is *tē̦ rhomphaia̦ tou stomatos mou*. The threat clarifies why Christ's self-description in 2:12 was ὁ ἔχων τὴν ῥομφαίαν τὴν δίστομον τὴν ὀξεῖαν (*ho echōn tēn rhomphaian tēn distomon tēn oxeian*, "the one who has the sharp two-edged sword"). This prepared the way for the threat associated with His return. "The sword of My mouth" is not just a forensic condemnation.[60] Making war with it suggests conquest by force as in Rev. 19:11-21. The vic-torious warrior depicted in this later description of Christ's advent overcomes through means similar to what are pictured here.

In essence, this is a call to the church at Pergamum to demon-strate its genuineness by repenting of its lenience toward the errorists who had become part of that local fellowship. Failure to do so would mean dreadful consequences for them.

2:17 *Command to hear.* The command to hear, ὁ ἔχων οὖς ἀκουσάτω τί τὸ πνεῦμα λέγει ταῖς ἐκκλησίαις (*ho echōn ous akousatō ti to pneuma legei tais ekklēsiais*, "the one who has an ear, let him hear what the Spirit says to the churches"), is the same as the comparable com-mands to Ephesus (2:7) and Smyrna (2:11). A mode of address often

---

1960], p. 61). This preposition rather than κατά commonly has this sense in the LXX (e.g., 1 Kings 17:33; 4 Kings 19:9), but this sense is found in the NT only here and in Rev. 11:7; 12:7, 17; 13:4, 7; 17:14; 19:19. It is another indication of Semitic influence on the Greek used by John (Robertson, *Word Pictures*, 6:306; Kenneth G. C. Newport, "Semitic Influ-ence in Revelation: Some Further Evidence," *AUSS* 25, no. 3 [Autumn 1987]: 249-50).

59. Charles, *Revelation*, 1:65.
60. Contra Charles, *Revelation*, 1:65.

employed by the Lord, this is designed to arrest the attention of the listeners and to denote that what has been said is of special importance.[61]

Promise to the overcomer. The incentive to heed the moral lesson of the message closes this message as it has the first two (2:7, 11). The form of this promise to the overcomer resembles more closely the one to Ephesus: τῷ νικῶντι δώσω αὐτῷ[62] τοῦ μάννα[63] τοῦ κεκρυμμένου, καὶ δώσω αὐτῷ ψῆφον λευκὴν καὶ ἐπὶ τὴν ψῆφον ὄνομα καινὸν γεγραμμένον ὃ οὐδεὶς οἶδεν εἰ μὴ ὁ λαμβάνων (*tō nikōnti dōsō autō tou manna tou kekrymmenou, kai dōsō autō psēphon leukēn kai epi tēn psēphon onoma kainon gegrammenon ho oudeis oiden ei mē ho lambanōn,* "to the one who overcomes, I will give to him of the hidden manna, and I will give to him a white stone and upon the stone a new name written which no one knows except the one who receives it"). None of the seven participles of νικάω (*nikaō,* "I conquer") in these messages has an object, but victory over hostile forces is implied. Their thought is not that of victory finally achieved at the end of life, which would have been an aorist participle. It is rather the picture of a believer who from the beginning of his faith in Christ to the end of life stands victorious because he keeps on overcoming whatever the enemy has to offer (Lenski).

In this message the promise to the overcomer does not anticipate the end of the Apocalypse as it did in the first two messages. It must pertain to the future as they do, however (Charles). As with the others, the conqueror is promised full and final enjoyment of something of which he already has a foretaste (Sweet). Yet both promises are enigmatic. Suggested meanings for "the hidden manna" include future reward when the struggle is over (Scott), Christ as the bread from heaven,[64] the present spiritual food of the saints (Walvoord), and the pot of manna in the Ark of the Covenant within the Tabernacle (Charles). The last of these is most convincing, but the other three have elements of truth in them.

According to the fourth view, tradition taught that Jeremiah hid the ark before the destruction of Jerusalem, and it will not be re-

---

61. Barnes, *Revelation,* p. 68.
62. The twofold occurrence of δώσω αὐτῷ strengthens the emphasis on the promised blessings to the Pergamene church. The future tense of δώσω recalls that the reward will be bestowed in the future when the struggle is over (Scott, *Revelation,* pp. 78-79). The dative pronoun stresses "the victor" in the sense of "to him alone" (Lenski, *Revelation,* p. 94).
63. Τοῦ μάννα is a partitive genitive functioning as the object of the verb δίδωμι. It is the only such example of this in the NT (Beckwith, *Apocalypse,* p. 461; Robertson, *Word Pictures,* 6:307).
64. Vincent, *Word Studies,* p. 450.

covered until Israel is restored in the future (cf. 2 Macc. 2:5 ff.; Apoc. Bar. 7:7-9; 19:8).[65] Revelation 11:19 notes the heavenly location of the true ark of which the earthly ark is a picture (cf. Heb. 8:5; 9:24). The manna within that ark is the proper and heavenly food of God's people in contrast to the unhallowed food offered to idols (Alford). As with promises to the other churches, there is special appropriateness in connection with a current activity from which the church is to abstain (Trench). As the first two promises were reminiscences of the OT, the promise to Ephesus recalling Genesis 2 and that to Smyrna Genesis 3, so this promise looks back to the manna of Ex. 16:32-34 (Hort; Bullinger). This was the manna the children of Israel were eating when they encountered Balaam, who has been discussed earlier in this message (cf. v. 14) (Beasley-Murray). The other three suggestions may be incorporated with this identification. The symbolism of future reward, an allusion to Christ as the true manna, and present satisfaction of believers with this spiritual bread as a foretaste of future fullness are all in the background of "the hidden manna."

The "white stone" is even more difficulty to identify. Is the white stone symbolic of the victor himself, seen as white because he has overcome in the final strife (Charles)? This proposal finds support in 3:12 where God's name *is* inscribed on the victor. The new name inscribed on the stone may be a parallel idea.[66] The problem with this suggestion is that v. 17 says the victor is *given* the stone. He himself is not the stone.

Does the white stone allude to the practice in the Greek surroundings of the Asiatic churches where such stones were used as counters in calculations (cf. Rev. 13:18) (Swete)? If so, they may mean that if a man is faithful, he will be counted among the people of God. This idea has little merit, however, because of its failure to explain the whiteness of the stone and the presence of an inscription on it. Furthermore, it does not do justice to the solemnity of the victory that is described.

Could the stone symbolize a happy day, a day of victory (Charles)? The Roman writer Pliny speaks of a day "marked with the whitest of stones." Once again, however, stones of this sort had no inscription on them. It is also doubtful that the Lord would look to a pagan source for His symbolism in the same message where he has warned so strongly against worldly relations (Smith).

The same argument holds against the suggestion that the white

---

65. Moffatt, "Revelation," 5:358; Beckwith, *Apocalypse*, pp. 460-61; Robertson, *Word Pictures*, 6:307.
66. Charles, *Revelation*, 1:67; Robertson, *Word Pictures*, 6:307.

stone is an amulet that keeps a person safe.[67] These were often made of white or precious stones and were considered doubly effective if none but the wearer knew what was written on it (Swete; Beckwith; Moffatt). The amulet proposal goes along with the contextual idea of the victor's having a charmed life and fits in with the superstitious mood of the day regarding the invincibility of the possessor of an amulet (cf. Acts 19:19). But why would the author of this message condone non-Christian and even anti-Christian practices to teach about victory in the future messianic kingdom? The answer is that he would not (Smith).

Another view tries to explain the white stones by resorting to rabbinic speculations that when manna fell from heaven, it was accompanied by precious stones. This tradition rests on weak evidence, however, and even if it were true, such stones had no inscriptions (Charles).

Could the white stone be an allusion to the stones in the breastplate of the high priest, each of which had the name of a tribe written on it (cf. Ex. 28:36-37; 39:8-13) (Lee; Bullinger)? This would furnish an analogy whose source was contemporaneous with the giving of the manna alluded to in the first half of this promise to the overcomer (Alford). It would also appropriately represent the priestly dignity of the victorious Christian (Alford). This explanation is unsatisfactory, however, because the stones in the high priest's breastplate were not white (Charles). Neither is there any hint of an allusion to priestly dignity in the context.

Another way of identifying the white stone is to say it is the Urim that was hidden beneath the twelve stones of the high priest's breastplate of judgment (cf. Exod. 28:30) (Trench). This white stone, or diamond, was the most precious stone of all, and no one knew what was written on it. The problem with this identification is that Exodus 28 does not list this stone among those having names engraved on them (Lee). It is also problematic that λίθος (*lithos*, "stone"), not ψῆφος (*psēphos*, "pebble"), is the NT word to designate a precious stone such as the Urim (e.g., Luke 21:5; 1 Cor. 3:12; Rev. 4:3; 17:4) (Lee).

Stones were inscribed with writing for various purposes in that day. One approach says the imagery belongs to the occasion itself (Alford). The occasion here is said to dictate that white signifies victory with the inscription of the recipients being the thing that gives the stones value (Alford). But how could a recipient's name impart value to the stone? This view also fails to suggest a picture that would

---

67. Barclay, *Seven Churches*, p. 54.

have been imparted to the initial readers by the figurative representation.

A view that has NT support is the one that sees the white stone in light of the ancient practice of juries reaching judicial decisions by casting stones into an urn.[68] A white stone was for acquittal, and a black one for condemnation. The noun *psēphos* is used with this connotation in Acts 26:10, where Paul tells about "casting his pebble" against Christians before becoming one himself. The debilitating deficiency of this view is its inability to explain the inscription mentioned in v. 17 (Charles). "Voting pebbles" had nothing written on them. It is also difficult to see how the verdict of acquittal is an appropriate reward for one who has fought and overcome in the strength of an acquittal obtained by Christ long before he entered the battle (Alford).

The most satisfactory understanding of the white stone derives significance from the free doles of bread and free admission to entertainments that people of the Roman Empire received from time to time.[69] These were in exchange for "tickets," which often took the form of white stones (Alford). Such a white stone with one's name on it was the basis for admission to special events. It was also a well-established custom to reward victors at the games with such a token enabling them to gain admission to a special feast. This practice coincides with the victor's participation in the feast of Rev. 3:20 (cf. also 19:9) (Lee). The "hidden manna," the other part of the reward in v. 17, suggests a reference to the Messianic feast. The white stone is, then, a personalized *tessara*, which would serve as his token of admission to this great future feast (Mounce). This furnishes sufficient incentive for faithfulness to Christ in the meantime. Admittedly, limited information about ancient customs makes identification of the white stone difficult, but repeated contextual reminders about the future Messianic feast make this the most probable of the proposals made to date.

The "new name" inscribed on the white stone is one that is qualitatively new, not one that is recent. *Kainon* does not mean new in contrast to what is old, but something that is different in nature. *Onoma* is perhaps an allusion to Jesus' name to which this church has held fast, according to 2:13. In return, they will get another name that is of superior quality.

One suggestion is that the new name is that of Christ or God (Charles). The parallel with 3:12 supports this, as does the unknown

---

68. Robertson, *Word Pictures*, 6:307.
69. Ibid.

name of Christ in 19:12.[70] Popular superstition attributed the mysterious power of such stones to the name of a supernatural being that
was inscribed on them, demonstrating that this must have been God's
name (Charles; Beasley-Murray). Yet this assumes a derivation of the
stone symbolism from pagan sources, an unlikely possibility. Also a
parallel with 3:12 is not probable because three names, not one, are
promised there. Nor can it be exactly parallel with 19:12 because
Christ alone knows that name (Beckwith). This verse attributes such
knowledge to the one receiving the name. The secretive nature of the
name is against its belonging to Christ or God (Alford; Morris).

Clearly the new name is the recipient's own name, a new one,
reflecting his status as belonging to Christ.[71] This is verified in its
being a secret name given to the man himself. Somehow it reflects
those personal marks and signs of God's peculiar adoption of him
with which no one else is acquainted (Alford). Various other religious
traditions reflect this same kind of unique privilege (Moffatt). The
new name denotes the victor's new state in the time of the consummation. The practical identity of the name and the personality in
biblical thought leads to the familiar representation of the bestowal
of a new name upon entrance into that new state (cf. Gen. 32:28; Isa.
62:2; 65:15) (Lee; Beckwith; Morris). A secret name suggested invul-
nerability (Sweet). Its value depended upon others not knowing it and
appropriating it for themselves (Beckwith).

The antecedent of the neuter relative pronoun *ho* ("which") in
2:17 is *onoma* ("name"), but its sense also includes a reference to
psēphon ("stone"). The knowledge pertains to the new name, but the
reception of it (i.e., *ho lambanōn* ["who receives"]) includes both
the stone and the name. Possession and knowledge of the stone with
the new name inscribed on it are the peculiar privilege of the recipient. This indicates the security of his most treasured possession.

Additional Notes

2:13 Some MSS omit the καὶ immediately after πίστιν μου. Docu-
mentary support for its inclusion is sufficient, however, and its inclusion is the harder of the two readings because such an ascensive use of
the conjunction is rare elsewhere in the NT. Its inclusion is therefore
the preferable reading.

Other sources read either ἡμέραις αἷς or ἡμέραις ἐν αἷς in order to
make the nominative case of Ἀντιπᾶς fit into the sentence's syntax
(Alford). Still other sources change the proper name to a genitive for

---

70. Ibid.; Smith, *Revelation*, p. 74.
71. Alford, *Greek Testament*, 4:572; William R. Newell, *The Book of Revelation*
(Chicago: Moody, 1935), p. 52.

the same reason (Beckwith). The nominative has occasioned a good number of variations in different MSS. The nominative reading is preferable, the author viewing the proper name as an indeclinable noun. It functions as a genitive, showing possession.

Outside the Apocalypse the passive form of ἀποκτείνω occurs only three times, each time in connection with the events at Caesarea-Philippi when Jesus predicted His coming death (cf. Matt. 16:21; Mark 8:31; Luke 9:22). In Revelation the passive is frequent, being found in 2:13; 6:11; 9:18, 20; 11:5, 13; 13:10, 15; 19:21. Twice ἀπο-θνήσκω is substituted for the passive of ἀποκτείνω (Rev. 8:11; 14:13), as it always is in the fourth gospel (cf. John 11:16, 50, 51; 18:14, 32; 19:7) (Charles).

The nominative case of μάρτυς requires explanation. Because it is in apposition with the indeclinable ᾿Αντιπᾶς, which is genitive, a genitive of this noun would have been expected. One proposal explains the nominative as caused by attraction to the case of the relative pronoun ὅς, which follows it (Lenski). In another NT writer this might be possible, but hardly so in Revelation. Another explanation regards ᾿Αντιπᾶς as nominative rather than genitive (Alford), but this is incorrect. The best answer to the grammatical dilemma comes from the acknowledgement that such solecisms are common in this book.[72] Μάρτυς is in characteristic irregular apposition with an indeclinable noun (Alford; Moffatt). This kind of solecism is actually a Hebraism, since the Hebrew noun is not inflected (cf. 1:5; 2:20; 3:12; 7:4; 8:9; 9:14; 14:12, 14; 20:2).[73]

2:14 The dative inflectional ending of τῷ Βαλὰκ is puzzling. One suggestion is that it is a dative of advantage rather than a direct object, noting that the action resulted from Balak's original request (Alford). Balaam's action could hardly have been for the benefit of Balak, however, because 2 Pet. 2:15 says he acted because of personal greed. Another explanation calls the construction a Hebraism, which simply names the person taught as the direct object of the verb (Alford; Lee). Though Num. 31:16 does not specify Balak as the recipient of the counsel (Alford; Swete), he was the one in power and the one most likely to implement the scheme (Alford). Josephus confirms that after his departure, Balaam went to the Euphrates, summoned Balak and other rulers, and gave them this advice. If this is to be construed as a Hebraism, it follows the pattern of לְמַד לְ in Job 21:22. Calling this a Hebraism is not justified, however, because it is exceptional in the OT for ירה or למד to govern such a construction as its object (Charles). The best course is to see this dative as a colloquialism with the verb

---

72. Robertson, *Word Pictures*, 6:305.
73. Charles, *Apocalypse*, 1:13, 62.

διδάσκω. This verb governs a dative twice in Plutarch's writings as well as in writings of later writers (Hort; Swete; Charles). Sometimes it governs a double accusative, with both the person taught and the lesson taught in the accusative case. It is not unnatural, however, to conceive of the teaching being to or for a person, necessitating a dative case of indirect object for the person.

6
Church of Compromise

D. THE MESSAGE TO THYATIRA (2:18-29)

Next on the itinerary of the remaining messengers to the last four cities was Thyatira, the smallest of the seven cities but one that receives the longest of the seven messages. It was about forty miles southeast of Pergamum, situated in a long north-south valley connecting the Hermus and Caicus valleys. It was a rich agricultural area but lacked natural fortifications to protect it from invasion. On either side were gently sloping hills of moderate elevation.[1]

Translation

[18]And to the messenger of the church which is in Thyatira, write:
"These things says the Son of God, the one who has eyes as a flame of fire, and His feet are like gleaming bronze. [19]I know your works, even your love and faith, that is, [your] service and endurance, and [that] your last works are greater than the first. [20]But I have against you that you tolerate the woman Jezebel, who says that she herself is a prophetess, and she teaches and deceives My slaves to commit fornication and to eat things sacrificed to idols. [21]And I gave

---

1. W. M. Ramsay, *The Letters to the Seven Churches of Asia* (New York: A. C. Armstrong, 1904), pp. 316-17; R. H. Charles, *The Revelation of St. John*, 2 vols., ICC (New York: Scribner's, 1920), 1:68; John F. Walvoord, *The Revelation of Jesus Christ* (Chicago: Moody, 1966), p. 71; William Hendriksen, *More Than Conquerors* (Grand Rapids: Baker, 1944), p. 87.

her time that she might repent, and she does not desire to repent of her fornication. ²²Behold, I am casting her into a bed, and those who commit adultery with her into great tribulation, if they do not repent of her works. ²³And I will kill her children with pestilence, and all the churches will know that I am the one who searches the reins and hearts, and I will give to each one of you according to your works. ²⁴But I say to the rest who are in Thyatira, as many as do not have this teaching, who have not known the deep things of Satan, as they say, I do not cast on you another burden, ²⁵other than [this]: hold fast what you have until I come. ²⁶And the one who overcomes and keeps My works until the end,

> I will give to him authority over the nations
> ²⁷And he will destroy them with a rod of iron,
> As vessels of a potter are dashed to pieces,

as I also received from My Father, ²⁸and I will give him the morning star. ²⁹The one who has an ear, let him hear what the Spirit says to the churches."

Exegesis and Exposition

2:18 *The address.* The conventional address uses the city name Θυατίροις (*Thyatirois,* "Thyatira"): Καὶ τῷ ἀγγέλῳ τῆς ἐν Θυατίροις ἐκκλησίας γράψον (*Kai tō angelō tēs en Thyatirois ekklēsias grapson,* "And to the messenger of the church which is in Thyatira, write"). Seleucus I, founder of the Seleucid dynasty, whose realm extended from the Hermus Valley to the Himalayas, founded this city by importing large numbers of people to settle there after he gained control of the military garrison that was already there. He was not responsible for the origination of the military garrison, however. The northwestern boundary of the Seleucid domain was limited only by the strength of the neighboring ruler Lysimachus, whose territory included parts of Thrace, Mysia, and the coastlands as far south as Ephesus. Seleucus apparently controlled the Hermus Valley, and Lysimachus the Caicus Valley. Between 300 and 282 B.C. Lysimachus established a colony of Macedonian soldiers at Thyatira between the two valleys to protect Pergamum and the Caicus Valley from Seleucid conquest. In 282 Philetaerus revolted against Lysimachus and founded the Pergamenian kingdom. At first Seleucus encouraged Philetaerus in order to weaken Lysimachus's hand in dealing with the revolt, but soon the common bond of enmity was dissolved with the death of the enemy. Thyatira then became a useful garrison to discourage attacks by the Pergamenians on the north, and later served the same purpose against attacks by the Seleucid kings from the south. In this sense, the two cities of Thyatira and Pergamum became very close. If Pergamum controlled the city, it was safe from the Seleucids. If not, its strength was severely weakened. The status of Thyatira was the best measure of the power of Pergamum (Ramsay).

About 190 B.C. control of Thyatira was assumed by Rome, which made it a part of the province of Asia. Roman peace did not bring immediate prosperity to the city, but eventually, after greed for the wealth of the province had brought oppression and extortion, prosperity in the area resulted in a favorable situation for trade in the city. An important road ran from Pergamum to Thyatira, then to Sardis and through Philadelphia to Laodicea. This location produced a healthy commerce and a multiplication of related craftsmen's guilds for which the city was famous (Ramsay; Charles).

Since the first century A.D., the city has been destroyed and rebuilt a number of times as a result of centuries of fighting between Muslims and Christians. The nature of its situation exposed it to necessary destruction by every conqueror, and required complete restoration after every siege. It was right in the way of an invasion and had to be captured before the invader could move on. It guarded a rich region and had to be defended to the last, causing the conqueror to accomplish a complete devastation. Yet because of natural conditions it could never be a very strong fortress, so successful resistance was nearly impossible. After conquest, however, the new power had to refortify the city if he wanted to hold his ground. Such has been the history of Thyatira.[2]

The period of Thyatiran prosperity had just begun in the last decade of the first century A.D. Vivid memories of her military origin remained even though fortifications had disintegrated or been dismantled. As a communications center, the city had become a commercial city with multiplied trade guilds outnumbering those in every other city. Guilds for wool workers, linen workers, manufacturers of outer garments, dyers, leather workers, tanners, potters, bakers, slave dealers, and bronze smiths were known. Membership in a guild was compulsory if one wanted to hold a position. Dyeing and manufacturing of woolen goods appears to have been a foremost industry of the city. Lydia, "a seller of purple" (Acts 16:14), appears to have been an agent of a Thyatiran establishment who lived in Philippi.[3]

The population of the city was predominantly Gentile, a fact re-

---

2. Ramsay, *Seven Churches*, p. 323; Hendriksen, *Conquerors*, p. 87.
3. Ramsay, *Seven Churches*, pp. 322-26; Isbon T. Beckwith, *The Apocalypse of John* (New York: Macmillan, 1919), pp. 463-64; Hendriksen, *Conquerors*, p. 88.

flected in the absence of any reference to a Jewish element in the message.[4] Most were of Macedonian descent, but a great deal of mixture of nationalities had resulted from the varied military and commercial history (Beckwith). Apollo was the chief deity here, and emperor worship was not a major factor.[5] Pagan worship was associated with trade guilds in that each guild had its guardian god. Guild members were expected to attend the guild festivals and to eat food, part of which had been offered to the tutelary deity and which was acknowledged as being on the table as a gift from the god. At the end of the feast grossly immoral activities would commence. To exit at the time of such activity would lay a person open to ridicule and other kinds of persecution, a situation well reflected in the message to the church in this city.[6] The moral issue of whether Christians were justified in participation in such common meals with their associated activities was a major one for this church (Charles). Besides this pagan influence, Thyatira also had its temples to Apollo, Artemis, and Tyrimnaios, and a shrine to Sambathe, an oriental Sibyl connected with the area (Charles).

The defects of the local church were related to those at Pergamum, but were far worse. Not only did the Christians lack zeal for godly discipline and correct doctrine; they also obliged those who erred in these ways and condoned their errors. Falsehood and idolatry permeated almost the whole church. The NT has no record of how Thyatira was evangelized. Perhaps it was through Lydia (Walvoord), but more likely the church was planted by Paul or some of his fellow missionaries during his long stay in Asia (Acts 19:10) (Beckwith). According to tradition, the church here ceased to exist at the end of the second century, having become a center of Montanism before dying (Charles). No record of a great achievement by this church has been preserved.[7]

Attributes of the speaker. Three expressions, two of which are taken from the introductory vision of chapter one, compose Christ's self-identification in this message. The first is not taken from the earlier vision: ὁ υἱὸς τοῦ θεοῦ (*ho huios tou theou*, "the Son of God") (2:18). Revelation is at one with the gospel of John in assigning this name to

---

4. Lydia, a "god-fearer" from this city, had come under the influence of a Jewish synagogue somewhere. It may have been in Thyatira, but this is not certain (Ramsay, *Seven Churches*, pp. 322-23).
5. A. T. Robertson, *Word Pictures in the New Testament*, 6 vols. (Nashville: Broadman, 1933), 6:308.
6. Beckwith, *Apocalypse*, p. 464; Hendriksen, *Conquerors*, p. 88.
7. Henry Barclay Swete, *The Apocalypse of St. John* (London: Macmillan, 1906), p. 41; J. A. Seiss, *The Apocalypse*, 3 vols. (New York: Charles C. Cook, 1909), 1:160; Leon Morris, *The Revelation of St. John*, TNTC (Grand Rapids: Eerdmans, 1969), pp. 69-70.

Christ (cf. John 1:34, 49; 3:18; 5:25; 10:36; 11:4, 27; 20:31).[8] The title is used only here in this book, but is implied in 1:6; 2:27; 3:5, 21; 14:1. It is practically the equivalent of "Messiah" (cf. Luke 4:41). It refers to the superhuman personality of Jesus as divinely commissioned to implement God's purpose for His people (cf. John 10:36).[9] In the vision of chapter one Christ is identified as "the Son of Man," but in keeping with the character of judgment pronounced on this church, He is "the Son of God." A reiteration of His deity is necessitated by the seriousness of this church's diversion from the true worship of Jesus Christ, the Son of God (Walvoord). This is the first instance in these messages when the self-identification of the speaker takes the form of a title rather than a descriptive attribute.[10]

Some have found both a pagan and Jewish coloring in the title "Son of God" (Moffatt). Because the imperial cultus used similar terminology and because Domitian imposed claims of worship, an apologetic purpose may have been behind its use here. Apollo, also called Tyrimnos, was the divine guardian of the city, and his worship was combined with that of the emperor. He was along with the emperor acclaimed a son of Zeus.[11] The pagan coloring is open to serious question, however, because pressure from Rome to impose emperor worship in Thyatira was negligible compared to that imposed in neighboring Pergamum. Jewish coloring is present without question. Allusion to Psalm 2 and the reference to God's Son there (Ps. 2:12) is quite clear in light of the use of Ps. 2:8-9 later in this message (Rev. 2:26-27).[12] Without connection with the imperial cultus, Jesus claimed this relationship to the Father during His earthly ministry (cf. Matt. 11:27; 26:63-64; Luke 10:22; John 11:4).[13] Peter called Him by this title in His great confession (Matt. 16:16), and the claim to be God's Son was the ground for His indictment before the Sanhedrin (Matt. 26:63; John 19:7) (Charles). No pagan background for the title

---

8. J. P. M. Sweet, *Revelation* (Philadelphia: Westminster, Pelican, 1979), p. 93.

9. James Moffatt, "The Revelation of St. John the Divine," in *The Expositor's Greek Testament*, ed. W. Robertson Nicoll (Grand Rapids: Eerdmans, n.d.), 5:359-60; cf. also Richard N. Longenecker, "The One and Only Son," in *The NIV: The Making of a Contemporary Translation*, ed. Kenneth L. Barker (Grand Rapids: Zondervan, 1986), pp. 119-26.

10. E. W. Bullinger, *The Apocalypse* or *"The Day of the Lord"* (London: Eyre and Spottiswoode, n.d.), p. 186.

11. G. V. Caird, *A Commentary on the Revelation of St. John the Divine*, HNTC (New York: Harper & Row, 1966), p. 43; Robert H. Mounce, *The Book of Revelation*, NICNT (Grand Rapids: Eerdmans, 1977), pp. 101-2.

12. Henry Alford, *The Greek Testament*, 4 vols. (London: Longmans, Green, 1903), 4:573; William Lee, "The Revelation of St. John," in *The Holy Bible*, ed. F. C. Cook (London: John Murray, 1881), 4:527; Beckwith, *Apocalypse*, p. 465.

13. Robertson, *Word Pictures*, 6:308.

is present in any of these. Rather, it suggests the joint rule of the overcomer with Christ in the future kingdom foreseen in Psalm 2, as the message will develop later (cf. 2:26-27).

The second description through which Christ makes Himself known to the Thyatirans is ὁ ἔχων τοὺς ὀφθαλμοὺς αὐτοῦ ὡς φλόγα πυρός (*ho echōn tous ophthalmous autou hōs phloga pyros*, "the one who has eyes as a flame of fire"). This description is applied to Christ in His initial appearance to John (1:14) and in His climactic return as a victorious warrior (19:12).[14] As noted in the discussion of 1:14, the notion of fierceness against adversaries is present in the OT use of the expression (e.g., Dan. 10:6) as well as in classical writers. Yet a related meaning of surpassing intelligence[15] is more appropriate in a message where Christ will claim ability to search the reins and the hearts (cf. 2:23). He exercises a prerogative of God (i.e., "the Son of God") in such a probing of the inner man and can do so only on the basis of His omniscience (i.e., "the one who has eyes as a flame of fire"). These first two expressions lay the groundwork for the severe warnings that follow to the Thyatirans.

The third expression, also derived from the earlier vision to John (cf. 1:15), is οἱ πόδες αὐτοῦ ὅμοιοι χαλκολιβάνῳ (*hoi podes autou homoioi chalkolibanō*, "his feet are like gleaming bronze"). The earlier discussion of *chalkolibanō* saw an emphasis on the purity of the metal reflected in its great brilliance.[16] The emblematic meaning of the feet was seen to be movement among the churches.[17] The theme of moral purity circulating among the churches goes along with the purging out of all impurity suggested in the trampling into small fragments later in the message (cf. v. 27) (Alford; Lee; Charles).

2:19 *Knowledge about the people.* The first part of Christ's knowledge about this church is composed of five nouns connected by καί (*kai*, "and" or "even"): σου τὰ ἔργα καὶ τὴν ἀγάπην καὶ τὴν πίστιν καὶ τὴν διακονίαν καὶ τὴν ὑπομονήν σου (*sou ta erga kai tēn agapēn kai tēn pistin kai tēn diakonian kai tēn hypomonēn sou*, "your works, even your love and faith, that is, [your] service and endurance"). Each noun has its article, and the genitive of the personal pronoun *sou* precedes the first and follows the last. This arrangement raises several questions regarding the relations of these words to one another.

As was the case in 2:2, it appears that the first *kai* introduces an elaboration or explanation of *sou ta erga* ("your works").[18] A gram-

---

14. Ibid.
15. Robert L. Thomas, "The Glorified Christ on Patmos," *BSac* 122 (1965): 244.
16. See discussion of χαλκολιβάνῳ at 1:15.
17. See discussion of πόδες at 1:15.
18. Charles, *Revelation*, 1:69; Robertson, *Word Pictures*, 6:308. This is the epexegetic use as in John 1:16 (Alford, *Greek Testament*, 4:573).

matical feature that confirms this is the use of *sou* with *erga*, but not with each of the other characteristics, the last four in the list being covered by one *sou* (Alford). This being the case, the expression "your works" is more specifically declared to be "your love and faith and service and endurance."

Erga is a neutral word. Whether the works are good or bad must be determined from each context where it is used. In these messages the Lord constantly views works as a mirror of the character of the churches (cf. 2:2, 5, 22, 26; 3:1, 8, 15) (Swete). Four items that constitute the works furnish the grounds for His praise of this church. This is a longer list than at Ephesus (cf. 2:2), the other church where an extensive list of worthwhile qualities is found. To Ephesus and Thyatira more praise is given when considerable cause for blame follows than to Smyrna and Philadelphia where no fault is found.[19]

In usual Johannine fashion love comes first in the list, even before faith. Yet faith is not overlooked (cf. 2:13; 13:10; 14:12). The frequent Pauline order of faith followed by love is reversed (cf. 1 Thess. 3:6; 5:8; 1 Tim. 1:14; 2:15; 2 Tim. 1:13; 2:22; Tit. 2:2) (Swete; Moffatt). One opinion is that there are four classes of works indicated in the last four nouns: "love, faith (or faithfulness), service, endurance" (Walvoord). Two classes of works are more probable, however. Love and faith are abstract qualities or motive forces for Christian activity, and service and endurance are outward fruit or the results that flow from these motive forces (Charles; Mounce). This arrangement, in agreement with the frequent ascensive use of *kai* in this book, takes the last two words to be in apposition with the first two (Beckwith). In other words, love is demonstrated in service to others and faith is shown through endurance of hardship imposed through persecution.[20] It is true that in some contexts service is a natural proof of faith as it is of love (Alford), but the symmetry of the present statement requires faith to be seen as the cause of endurance.

As elsewhere, this love is doubtless directed toward God and man.[21] Neither of the three previous churches is commended for love as Thyatira is (Walvoord). Unlike Ephesus (cf. 2:4), Thyatira still has love.[22] Thyatira is distinguished among all seven churches as being the only one commended for both love and service.[23] This church

---

19. Robertson, *Word Pictures*, 6:308.
20. John Peter Lange, *The Revelation of John, Lange's Commentary*, ed. E. R. Craven (Grand Rapids: Zondervan, 1968), 10:121.
21. Alford, *Greek Testament*, 4:573. See discussion of love at 2:4.
22. R. C. H. Lenski, *The Interpretation of St. John's Revelation* (Columbus, Ohio: Lutheran Book Concern, 1935), p. 114.
23. Walter Scott, *Exposition of the Revelation of Jesus Christ* (Swengel, Pa.: Bible Truth Depot, n.d.), p. 83.

deserves credit for its standards in maintaining this emblem of discipleship called love (cf. John 13:35).

The *pistis* for which this church is commended may signify faith or faithfulness. Faith is a firm persuasion, a conviction based upon hearing, always in the NT having as its object God or Christ or spiritual things.[24] Faithfulness connotes an unwavering devotion in following Christ.[25] A case for the latter meaning claims this is the usual meaning of the noun in Revelation (cf. also Gal. 5:22) (Sweet). This is possibly true in 13:10, but in 2:13 and 14:12 the meaning faith is more probable. The case for faithfulness also notices that faithfulness is the quality necessary to withstand the pressure being brought against the faithful remnant of the church (cf. 2:25) and to produce a steadfast endurance under trial mentioned later in v. 19 (Beckwith). Yet the meaning faithfulness is so close to the meaning endurance, one wonders whether both would have found a place in the same list. It is preferable, therefore, to adopt faith as the meaning of *pistin* in this verse. Alongside *agapēn*, a general quality is more probable (Alford).

Diakonia ("service") is a ministry to the needs of others (cf. Acts 11:29; 1 Cor. 16:15). This is *voluntary* service as compared with that rendered by the δοῦλος (*doulos*, "slave"), whose obligation was to render service to his master (Alford; Swete; Lenski). A number of NT instances of such voluntary service involved the supplying of food to the needy. Such acts in Thyatira appear to have been of the kind indicated in Rom. 15:25, 31; 1 Cor. 16:15; 2 Cor. 8:4; 9:1; Heb. 6:10. Here such manifestations of love were on the increase, as compared to Ephesus where they were declining (cf. 2:4-5) (Swete).

The endurance of this church resulting from the strong faith of its members also receives commendation. This quality, which implies hardships imposed through persecution, was one of the commendable features of the Ephesian church too.[26] To withstand such pressure without wavering is expected of all followers of Christ (cf. Matt. 16:24-26).

The last part of Christ's knowledge of this church comes at the end of v. 19: καὶ τὰ ἔργα σου τὰ ἔσχατα πλείονα τῶν πρώτων (*kai ta erga sou ta eschata pleiona tōn prōtōn*, "and [that][27] your last works are greater than the first"). The later deeds of this church were in some sense more in number or in quality, perhaps both, than their earlier

---

24. W. E. Vine, *An Expository Dictionary of New Testament Words* (Old Tappan, N.J.: Revell, 1966), p. 71; Morris, *Revelation*, p. 70.

25. Robertson, *Word Pictures*, 6:308.

26. See the discussion of ὑπομονήν at 2:2.

27. Only καὶ is found in the text, but the sense of ὅτι also is without question to be understood with it (Robertson, *Word Pictures*, 6:308).

ones. As time progressed, their works had grown. This highly commendable state of affairs was the opposite of what had happened in Ephesus (cf. 2:5; cf. Matt. 12:45; 2 Pet. 2:20) (Alford; Moffatt; Lenski). Whatever else may be yet to come in this message, in the ground already covered this was an exemplary church.

2:20 *The state of the church.* Sad to say, the high praise of v. 19 yields to censure in v. 20 (Beckwith). To the defects that offset the earlier virtues the speaker now turns (Morris): ἀλλὰ ἔχω κατὰ σοῦ ὅτι ἀφεῖς τὴν *γυναῖκα Ἰεζάβελ, ἡ λέγουσα ἑαυτὴν προφῆτιν (*alla echō kata sou hoti apheis tēn gynaika Iezabel, hē legousa heautēn prophḗtin,* "but I have against you that you tolerate the woman Jezebel, who says that she herself is a prophetess"). *Alla* ("but") is a strong adversative marking the distinct contrast with what has preceded.

Apheis ("you tolerate") is quite revealing. It shows that the dangers to this church were not external but internal, not a pagan deity but a false prophetess (Charles). Their guilt was greater than that of their neighbors in Pergamum because *apheis* implies a tolerance of evil that is not suggested by the ἔχεις (*echeis,* "you have") of 2:14. Even more conspicuous is the disparity between their attitude toward the Nicolaitans and that in Ephesus. The Ephesians hated the deeds of the Nicolaitans, yet the Thyatirans not only had the problem among them, but also *permitted* it to remain (Swete).

Jezebel was the name of the Phoenician wife of Ahab (1 Kings 16:31) who sought to carry the Northern Kingdom of Israel into the worship of Baal and Astarte (2 Kgs. 9:22) and to engage in associated immoralities and magical practices (Swete). To whom or what the name applies here is problematic. One idea is that she was the wife of the messenger representing that church on Patmos (Beckwith). This view usually accompanies a preference for the reading that includes the genitive of the second person pronoun following *gynaika,* yielding the translation "your wife" (Alford). This reading is probably not correct, however.[28]

Another meaning attached to Jezebel is that she is a personification of heresy. This notion is supported in connection with the view that the *angelos* ("messenger") of the church is a personification of the church.[29] Since the allusion here is to 1 Kings 21:25, the thought is suggested that this Jezebel was to the church in Thyatira what the other Jezebel was to Ahab (Alford). Thyatira allowed the Nicolaitans the position of being a teaching sect with the power to persecute, just as Ahab allowed Jezebel to teach and persecute (Lee). This understanding also lends itself to the inclusion of the pronoun *sou* and

---

28. See Additional Notes at the end of this chapter.
29. See discussion of the second view of the meaning of ἄγγελοι in 1:20.

213

observes that the choice of the name Jezebel and its coupling with *tēn gynaika sou* proves that an actual woman cannot have been meant. Therefore the statement moves from fact to symbolism (Alford). Yet, besides the weakness of the reading *sou* already observed, this interpretation lacks persuasiveness because in vv. 22-23 Jezebel is distinguished from her followers (Beckwith). For a woman to be so used figuratively is unparalleled. Furthermore, the context of the message furnishes no hint of such symbolic language.

Other explanations hold either that she was a woman named Jezebel or that she represented a Jewish synagogue in the city.[30] The former is inadequate to explain her analogy with Jezebel of the OT, and the latter ignores the definiteness of her personality, the fact of her situation within a Christian church that had jurisdiction over her, and her associations with the practices of the Nicolaitans who were members of the church (Moffatt; Beckwith; Morris; Mounce). The trade guilds, not the Jewish synagogue, were the problem for Christians in Thyatira (Moffatt). This last fact also militates against another view that takes Jezebel as a reference to a Sibylline prophetess at Thyatira (Lee). That the presence in Thyatira of a Sibyl Sambetha could mean a Jewess lending her aid to a syncretism of different religions (Lee) is not strong enough proof to sustain such a view.

The approach that has the least objection to it is to take Jezebel as a symbolical name for some prominent woman in the church of Thyatira. She was like the infamous wife of Ahab and claimed to be a prophetess, seeking to mislead the people.[31] The claim to be a prophetess (*hē legousa heautēn prophētin*, v. 20) can hardly refer to anything else than an individual (Alford). A cult would hardly claim to have the gift of prophecy. Ahab's queen was notorious for her support of idolatry in Israel (1 Kings 18:4, 19) and adultery, as 2 Kings 9:22 is interpreted here (Beckwith). The same is true of the Thyatiran leader. As her OT prototype, she was an influential woman.[32] She may have attained her dominance in the church partially through the example of another woman, Lydia (cf. Acts 16:14), who may have been the first one to bring the gospel to this city (Walvoord). The two women shared the same characteristics of leadership, hard work, and spiritual activity, but they were totally different in character from one another (Hailey). More is revealed about this woman called by the symbolical name of Jezebel as the message continues.

Hē legousa is an articular participle of λέγω (*legō*, "I say") used to

---

30. Lange, *Revelation*, 10:122.
31. Robertson, *Word Pictures*, 6:309.
32. Homer Hailey, *Revelation, an Introduction and Commentary* (Grand Rapids: Baker, 1979), pp. 136-37.

indicate Jezebel's claim of being a prophetess. Similar constructions with the same verb are used elsewhere in these messages to indicate self-proclaimed titles that are inaccurate just as this one is.[33] The feminine noun προφῆτις (prophētis, "prophetess") is only here and in Luke 2:36 in the NT. It names Anna, whose prophetic gift enabled her to recognize Jesus when His parents presented Him in the Temple shortly after His birth. Yet females possessing the legitimate gift of prophecy were not limited to her in the NT, because the daughters of Philip engaged in prophesying (Acts 21:9). In the first-century church a prophet was an inspired messenger of God who ranked high, just behind the apostles, in the capability of edifying the church (cf. 1 Cor. 12:28). But the early church also had false prophets.[34] In her own eyes, Jezebel's alleged special revelations from God qualified her as an authoritative teacher in the church. Some others agreed and she became a recognized leader, the critical problem being that she was leading people astray.[35]

The Lord delineates the specifics of the problem: καὶ διδάσκει καὶ πλανᾷ τοὺς ἐμοὺς δούλους πορνεῦσαι καὶ φαγεῖν εἰδωλόθυτα (kai didaskei kai planą tous emous doulous porneusai kai phagein eidōlothyta, "and she teaches and deceives My slaves to commit fornication and to eat things sacrificed to idols"). Didaskei ("she teaches") particularizes Jezebel's leadership function of teaching, an ecclesiastical role much earlier denied to women by Paul (cf. 1 Tim. 2:12), and planą ("she deceives") states the consequences of her teaching.[36] Πλανάω (Planaō, "I deceive") occurs with greater frequency in the Apocalypse than in any other book of the NT. Its relative frequency is also high in another of John's writings from the same decade, the epistle of 1 John. In the Apocalypse it always speaks of a fundamental departure from the truth (cf. 13:14; 18:23) (Lee; Sweet). Its participial form is a title for

---

33. The nominative case of ἡ λέγουσα is in apposition to the accusative noun γυναῖκα. This construction is similar to the apposition of the nominative ὁ μάρτυς with the genitive ᾿Αντιπᾶς in 2:13. It is an irregular absolute construction, the participle functioning very similarly to a relative pronoun. It should be considered a Hebraism as in Mark 12:38-40 where οἱ κατεσθίοντες is in apposition to γραμματέων (cf. also οἱ . . . φρονοῦντες in apposition to τοὺς ἐχθρούς in Phil. 3:16-19) (Moffatt, "Revelation," 5:361; Charles, Revelation, 1:70).
34. Robertson, Word Pictures, 6:309.
35. Swete, Apocalypse, p. 43; Beckwith, Apocalypse, p. 466; George E. Ladd, A Commentary on the Revelation of John (Grand Rapids: Eerdmans, 1972), p. 51.
36. The two finite verbs, διδάσκει and πλανᾷ, are participles resolved into finite verbs (Robertson, Word Pictures, 6:309). This is on the order of the construction occurring a number of times in this book, the first time being 1:5-6. For further discussion of the force of this Hebraism, see Exegesis and Exposition and Additional Notes on 1:6.

the devil in 12:9.[37] As hard as it is to understand, this woman through some devious means had led God's servants astray in this church, and was continuing to do so current to the writing of this book. The present tense of the two verbs shows this (Swete). Jesus had given her an opportunity to repent, yet she chose to continue her destructive activity (cf. 2:21). Jesus calls the ones deceived *tous emous doulous*, "My *own*[38] slaves." That these are His slaves implies their obligation to obey the voice of God and flee the evil deception of this woman (Lenski), an obligation made explicit in v. 22.

How closely was Jezebel's error related to that of the Nicolaitans in nearby Pergamum (cf. 2:15)? One answer is that it was the same. Thyatira was only about forty miles away, so Jezebel could have been a leader in the Nicolaitan movement (Caird). Two aspects of the error, eating meat sacrificed to idols and committing fornication, were certainly the same (cf. 2:14-15, 20). First John was written at about this time in Asia, and it tells of a separatist group that based its teachings on prophetic inspiration (1 John 2:19; 4:1-3) (Caird). Inasmuch as the Nicolaitans had a wide geographical representation (cf. 2:6), this could have been a branch of the same sect.

As convincing as this is, it fails to account for the dominance of the trade guilds in the Thyatiran culture, a condition that did not exist elsewhere. This in itself argues that the two heresies cannot be precisely identified. It seems most likely that the Nicolaitans, Balaam (cf. 2:14), and Jezebel had similar characteristics, but with differences that distinguished them as separate parties.[39] The particular thrust of Jezebel's teaching was probably, "Since an idol has no real existence (cf. 1 Cor. 8:4), you need not hesitate to go along with the simple requirements of the trade guild and participate in a common meal dedicated to some idol" (Mounce).

The situation was worse in Thyatira than in Pergamum, because here the heresy was not only propagated in the church, but it was also widely known to be so in churches in other cities (cf. 2:23) and was an error of long standing as indicated by the "children" of Jezebel (τὰ τέκνα, *ta tekna*, 2:23). These heretics prided themselves in their enlightened liberalism (τὰ βαθέα, *ta bathea*, "the deep things," 2:24), with the prophetic claim and powerful influence of the leader giving to it a significance it did not have in the other cities (Moffatt; Beckwith). Realizing the trade guild dominance of the economic life of the city, the Christian convert faced the questionable decision of com-

---

37. Vine, *Dictionary*, p. 280.
38. The possessive adjective ἐμούς supplies special emphasis to the expression (Lenski, *Revelation*, p. 116).
39. Hailey, *Revelation*, p. 137. Because the word order of πορνεῦσαι καὶ φαγεῖν is reversed from 2:14, the primary focus of Jezebel's system was probably sexual immorality (Charles, *Revelation*, 1:71).

promising his stand at least enough to participate in a common meal dedicated to a pagan deity (Mounce). For such a person it was a relief to discover on the authority of the Spirit (cf. *prophētin*, "prophetess," 2:20) that Christians need not separate themselves from such practices, least of all in matters related to business. They need not fear pagan immorality and sacrificial practices, because men and women in whom the Spirit dwells know that the flesh cannot defile the spirit.[40] With such teaching as this, Jezebel had gained and was gaining a considerable following.

2:21 Christ proceeds to describe His past dealings with this woman in order to show the seriousness of her negative influence on the church: καὶ ἔδωκα αὐτῇ χρόνον ἵνα μετανοήσῃ (*kai edōka autē chronon hina metanoēsē*, "and I gave her time that she might repent"). Her error must have had a long history. Otherwise, He could not state this about her.[41] Just how long He had waited after giving her a warning is not divulged, but it was long enough for her to have chosen the option of repentance (Charles). The time period stipulated began with a specific warning delivered at some particular point in the past. The aorist tense of *edōka* indicates this.[42] How the warning was transmitted to her is a matter of speculation. It probably came from John himself, either directly or indirectly, because of his position of authority among the churches of Asia. It seems to have been his role to rebuke such errant leaders in the churches (cf. 3 John 10) (Sweet). The warning could have come through some other agency, but John's awareness of the time and nature of the earlier warning furnishes further indication that he most probably was the agent.

Up to the point of writing, Jezebel had chosen not to amend her life by turning from her misguiding practices to God, however: καὶ οὐ θέλει μετανοῆσαι ἐκ τῆς πορνείας αὐτῆς (*kai ou thelei metanoēsai ek tēs porneias autēs*, "and she does not desire to repent of her fornication"). The durative force of the present tense of *thelei* conveys the sense, "she *still* does not wish to repent." She has no disposition to change at this point.[43] She will continue her present course of action (Swete; Beckwith). The statement is blunt and final (cf. Matt. 23:37).[44]

---

40. G. R. Beasley-Murray, *The Book of Revelation*, NCB (Grand Rapids: Eerdmans, 1978), p. 91.
41. Swete, *Apocalypse*, p. 43; Moses Stuart, *A Commentary on the Apocalypse* (Edinburgh: Maclachlan, Stewart, 1947), p. 482.
42. Robertson, *Word Pictures*, 6:309.
43. The preposition ἐκ following a form of μετανοέω is the usual construction in this book when the verb requires a noun to complete its meaning (cf. 2:22; 9:20, 21; 16:11). The construction is limited to this book. Acts 8:22 uses the preposition ἀπό in a similar situation. The infinitive μετανοῆσαι carries the ingressive force of the aorist tense (Alford, *Greek Testament*, 4:574; Charles, *Revelation*, 1:71; Robertson, *Word Pictures*, 6:309).
44. Robertson, *Word Pictures*, 6:309.

Her refusal to repent pertains specifically to her fornication. *Porneias* can be understood in a figurative sense to refer to corrupt doctrines she taught and religious infidelity she generated.[45] It was for attempting to seduce Israel from the worship of the true God to that of Baal that the OT Jezebel had been accused of harlotry (2 Kings 9:22) (Caird). Religious infidelity is often spoken of in the OT under the figure of harlotry (e.g., Jer. 3:6; Ezek. 23:19; Hos. 9:1). Similarly, participation in the guild feast involved professing Christians in the worship of other gods (Mounce). Yet the literal sense of the same noun in v. 20 argues strongly for a literal sense here. The same sin is referred to by the verb μοιχεύω (*moicheuō*, "I commit adultery"), which must refer to literal sexual sins. The orgies that followed the feasts dedicated to pagan gods were well-known happenings. Later in this book, the literal sin is mentioned alongside idolatry three times (cf. 9:21; 21:8; 22:15).[46] In addition, the OT Jezebel does appear to have been guilty of literal fornication as well as spiritual fornication (cf. 2 Kings 9:22, 30; Jer. 4:30; Nah. 3:4) (Alford). The cult of Baal that she championed was quite licentious in its practice, and she apparently was involved in its sinful excesses (Beasley-Murray). She may be more famous for her promotion of idolatry, but she must have been guilty of practicing and promoting sexual immorality also. The Thyatiran Jezebel was adamant in her refusal to turn away from the same.

2:22 The ἰδού focuses special attention upon the consequences of her refusal to repent as something unexpected and terrible (Alford): ἰδοὺ βάλλω αὐτὴν εἰς κλίνην (*idou ballō autēn eis klinēn*, "behold, I am casting her into a bed"). *Ballō* is the ordinary word for someone who is cast into a bed of sickness (cf. Matt. 8:6, 14; 9:2; Mark 7:30) (Alford; Lee). The more searching question connected with it is what kind of judgment it specifies. This depends on the meaning assigned to *klinēn* ("bed"). It can hardly be the usual *triclinium* on which participants reclined while eating meals at the guild feasts, though such is perhaps a source of the figure (Swete; Ramsay). It must be something of a devastating nature because of the θλῖψιν μεγάλην (*thlipsin megalēn*, "great tribulation") that parallels it later in the verse. Because the gospels recounting Christ's teachings had often used *ballō eis* to describe the casting of people into the place of eternal torment (cf. Matt. 3:10; 5:29; 7:19; 13:42, 50; 18:8, 9; Mark 9:45, 47; Luke 3:9; John 15:6) and because of later usage of the combination in this book (cf. Rev. 20:3, 10, 14, 15), it is possible that *klinēn* refers to hell.[47] The use of

---

45. Alford, *Greek Testament*, 4:574; Stuart, *Apocalypse*, p. 482; Mounce, *Revelation*, p. 104.
46. F. J. A. Hort, *The Apocalypse of St. John* (London: Macmillan, 1908), p. 30.
47. Lange, *Revelation*, p. 122.

bed to refer to future pestilence and death and even eternal perdition supports this possibility (cf. Isa. 14:11) (Alford). This seems to carry the symbolism a bit too far in this passage, however (Lenski).

The figure may be intended to contrast a sickbed with a bed of adultery (Beckwith). The bed was a common way of referring to illness in Scripture (cf. Ex. 21:18; Ps. 41:3; 1 Cor. 11:27-29) (Alford; Ladd; Mounce), and *klinēn* with *ballō* serves this purpose in Matt. 9:2 and Mark 7:30. It is perhaps a Hebrew idiom (Beckwith). Adultery is mentioned in the next clause, making the bed a powerful figure for sickness as a natural contrast to such sinful activity. She is punished in the same place where she sinned.[48] A possible allusion to Ps. 41:3 and the sentence construction of this verse, an example of Hebrew parallelism, further argue for understanding this as a bed of illness (Swete; Charles). This interpretation has its merits, but it also has a serious problem. In the context of these messages it is much too mild in relation to the seriousness of her sins to say merely that this woman is going to get sick (Lenski). Sickness is one of God's ways of dealing with erring believers, and it is highly doubtful that Jezebel had genuine faith in Christ.

Proposed as a stronger punishment is the symbolism of death. *Klinēn* is said to represent a funeral bier, with the observation that sickness as a punishment for sin at times reached the extent of death (cf. 1 Cor. 11:29-30) (Moffatt). The OT at times uses the bed in connection with death (cf. 2 Kings 1:4) (Lee). Κλίνη (*klinē*, "bed") in some contexts is known to have referred to a funeral bier, because a bed was laid in such a casket (Hort). The weakness of this explanation relates to the rarity with which such a meaning attaches to the noun and to the reference to death in 2:23. This would assign the same meaning as the threat, "I will kill with death," that the Lord is about to deliver. Such repetition is unlikely.

A final proposal is that *klinēn* is figurative language for the period of eschatological tribulation that comes in conjunction with Christ's second advent. If θλῖψιν μεγάλην (*thlipsin megalēn*, "great tribulation") with which the noun stands in parallel has such an eschatological connotation, this meaning is probable, because the woman and her following would then have the same destiny (Lenski). As noted above, the bed sometimes is emblematic of pestilence and death and even of eternal perdition. If eschatological tribulation eventually leads to perdition, arguments favoring the figurative meaning of hell are applicable here also. Further evidence for the eschatological nature of the warning stems from similar conclusions reached in con-

---

48. Richard Chenevix Trench, *Commentary on the Epistles to the Seven Churches in Asia* (London: Parker, Son, and Bourn, 1861), p. 141.

nection with the church in Ephesus (cf. 2:5) and particularly in connection with the one in Pergamum (cf. 2:16). Furthermore, the word
of encouragement to the faithful at Thyatira is based on the note of
the Lord's eschatological coming (cf. 2:25), making it probable that
the word of warning to the unfaithful is looking to the same future
coming. The probable accuracy of this interpretation will become
more evident in conjunction with the discussion of the parallel *thlipsin megalēn* later in v. 22. The severity of future pain, to be described
in detail later in the Apocalypse, furnishes a more forceful warning to
Jezebel and her "children" than does the threat of mere sickness.

The punishment of unrepentant Jezebel is shared by her unrepentant followers: καὶ τοὺς μοιχεύοντας μετ' αὐτῆς εἰς θλῖψιν μεγάλην (*kai
tous moicheuontas met' autēs eis thlipsin megalēn*, "and those who
commit adultery with her into great tribulation"). It is clear that
"those who commit adultery with her" are her followers, but it is not
so clear whether the adultery is to be understood literally or spiritually. If it is the latter, *moicheuontas* is a broad term to include both
literal fornication and eating things sacrificed to idols (cf. 2:20) (Alford; Lee). This aligns with its frequent usage in the LXX to describe
rebellious and idolatrous Israel (cf. Jer. 3:8; 5:7; Ezek. 16:17, 18, 22,
32; Hos. 2:4) (Alford; Swete). Yet in the context of this message which
thus far has been limited to literal sexual immorality, some indication of a switch to the figurative would be necessary if spiritual adultery were the meaning (Beckwith). The primary reference must be to
literal adultery as a comparison with Lev. 20:10 shows. This is probably an allusion to this OT passage that deals with literal adultery,
because the penalty there is θανάτῳ θανατούσθωσαν (*thanatō
thanatousthōsan*, "they shall be put to death with death"), which is
reminiscent of ἀποκτενῶ ἐν θανάτῳ (*apoktenō en thanatō*, "I will kill
with pestilence") in 2:23 (Alford; Lee). If it be objected that a church
commended as this one has been in 2:19 would not have tolerated the
promotion of sexual immorality (Caird), it needs to be remembered
also that the church was not so healthy in other respects and so may
have permitted some strange practices.

The articular present participle *tous moicheuontas* indicates a
group of people who were continually engaged in this activity with
Jezebel.[49] *Met' autēs* does not mean they shared in the act with her
personally, but that they participated by tolerating and encouraging
her or even followed her example by involving themselves in adultery
also.[50] Whereas the threatened punishment for Jezebel is to be cast

---

49. Robertson, *Word Pictures*, 6:310.
50. Alford, *Greek Testament*, 4:575; G. H. Lang, *The Revelation of Jesus Christ*
    (London: Oliphants, 1945), p. 122. When direct sharing in the act of adul-
    tery is in view, the verb μοιχεύω governs a direct object in the accusative
    case. See Jer. 3:9, LXX; Matt. 5:28.

eis klinēn ("into a bed"), the threatened punishment for these is that of Christ's casting them *eis thlipsin megalēn* ("into great tribulation"). Their fate may be different from hers (cf. 2:23) (Alford), but the Hebrew parallelism of the construction favors a similar or identical fate. Of course, θλῖψις (*thlipsis*, "tribulation") can be a general word referring to a severe judgment of suffering (Beckwith; Moffatt), but a number of significant considerations make a reference to the eschatological tribulation more probable. "Great" (*megalēn*) suggests that this must be the tribulation of the last days (Sweet). This same expression is used in Rev. 7:14 to refer to the period preceding the return of the Lord in power and great glory.[51] The absence of the article in the present verse is explained by this being the first mention of the period in the book (Smith). The article is used in 7:14 because of a previous mention of it. Jesus used the identical expression in an eschatological setting when referring to this future period in His Olivet discourse (Matt. 24:21). Since the encouragement to the faithful in 2:25 refers to His second advent, the case for a technical eschatological meaning of *thlipsin megalēn* is still stronger. In consideration that the main body of the Apocalypse (Revelation 4-19) includes a detailed description of this future period, it is exegetically sound to conclude that the threat to the followers of Jezebel is that of being thrust into this period of unparalleled misery.

As with Ephesus (cf. 2:5) and Pergamum (cf. 2:16), however, a way of escape remains available: ἐὰν μὴ *μετανοήσωσιν ἐκ τῶν ἔργων *αὐτῆς (*ean mē metanoēsōsin ek tōn ergōn autēs*, "if they do not repent of her works"). This is the way of repentance. The works from which they must turn away to be freed from the punishment are works that have sprung from Jezebel's influence (Beckwith). Even though in some cases committed by others, they are still her works.[52] She is the one who led them astray (Mounce). They too are guilty of the sin of adultery, though not necessarily with Jezebel in person. Her influence encouraged them to exercise the freedom to live licentiously, so these are "Jezebelian" works that they do.

2:23 An additional pronouncement against Jezebel's followers comes at the beginning of v. 23: καὶ τὰ τέκνα αὐτῆς ἀποκτενῶ ἐν θανάτῳ (*kai ta tekna autēs apoktenō en thanatō*, "and I will kill her children with pestilence"). One opinion is that these were the actual children of Jezebel, probably born through her adulterous activities (Beckwith). In the OT, death was the fate of children born to Ahab (2 Kings 10:7), and a comparison with Ahab's wife underlies much of this

---

51. J. B. Smith, *A Revelation of Jesus Christ* (Scottdale, Pa.: Herald, 1961), p. 77. Θλῖψις μεγάλη occurring at Acts 7:11 is clearly without eschatological connotation because it is part of an account of Israel's history.
52. Robertson, *Word Pictures*, 6:310.

message (cf. v. 20). According to Jewish and pagan belief, a parent's sin was visited upon his family (cf. Dan. 6:24) (Moffatt). This is the kind of judgment seen in the smiting of the child of David and Bathsheba also (cp. v. 23 with 2 Sam. 12:14) (Beckwith). One important difference exists here, however. The children smitten in 2 Kings 10 were Abab's children, not Jezebel's. The OT figure is therefore not a factor here (Alford; Beckwith).

The suggestion that these children were a future generation of Jezebel's followers who remained after the first generation had been judged (Lenski) has little merit. The message to this church is to the people alive at the time of writing. Her children must be her spiritual progeny who have wholeheartedly endorsed her sinful practices.[53] How then do they differ from "those who commit adultery with her" (v. 22)? Possibly her children are more ardent in their support of her, and receive a more severe punishment (Alford; Hort; Lee; Moffatt; Charles; Ladd; Sweet). Yet it is doubtful that their punishment is more severe than that of Jezebel herself. This may be another way of stating the same punishment already stipulated twice in v. 22, that of being cast into the "great tribulation" (cf. 6:7-8). Quite conceivably, this could be the same group described in two different ways, as participating in her sins (v. 22) and as embracing her teachings and ways (v. 23) (Beasley-Murray). "Children" is a customary way of referring to one's spiritual progeny. These people had embraced the antinomian doctrines of their spiritual mother and are properly referred to as her spiritual offspring. No distinction between these and her associates in v. 22 is intended (Mounce).

The threat to Jezebel's children is that they were to be killed with pestilence. This must be killing in a physical sense, because the whole expression is almost duplicated in Ezek. 33:27, LXX, where physical death through pestilence is in view.[54] *Thanatō* most probably means pestilence rather than its more common meaning of death. This is so not only because of the Ezekiel parallel (Charles), but also because of having this meaning elsewhere in the Apocalypse (cf. Rev. 6:8; 18:8; cf. 2 Sam. 24:13, LXX) (Lee; Moffatt; Bullinger). Though θάνατος (*thanatos*) is used to translate מוּת (*mût*, "die") and מָוֶת (*māwet*, "death") most often in the LXX, it almost always (35 times) is used to translate דֶּבֶר (*deber*, "pestilence"; Hort). This is a threat that could very well be implemented as part of the fourth seal judgment during the future period of tribulation (cf. Rev. 6:7-8).

---

53. Ibid.
54. In part, Ezek. 33:27, LXX, reads, θανάτω ἀποκτενῶ. A suggested parallel with Lev. 20:10, LXX, מוֹת־יוּמַת is interesting (Alford, *Greek Testament*, 4:575), but as a Hebrew reduplication, there would be neither force nor grammar for this expression (Hort, *Apocalypse*, p. 31).

Christ's dealings with the children of Jezebel will become a matter of public knowledge among the seven churches who on the basis of this knowledge will learn of His omniscience and righteous judgment: καὶ γνώσονται πᾶσαι αἱ ἐκκλησίαι ὅτι ἐγώ εἰμι ὁ ἐραυνῶν νεφροὺς καὶ καρδίας, καὶ δώσω ὑμῖν ἑκάστῳ κατὰ τὰ ἔργα ὑμῶν (*kai gnōsontai pasai hai ekklēsiai hoti egō eimi ho eraunōn nephrous kai kardias, kai dōsō hymin hekastō kata ta erga hymōn*, "and all the churches will know that I am the one who searches the reins and hearts, and I will give to each one of you according to your works"). Some have understood "all the churches" to mean all the churches everywhere to the end of time (Alford). The broader scope is seen as necessary to lift the whole of this threatening and its accompanying encouragements beyond proconsular Asia and to furnish a glimpse of the ecumenical character of these messages. The problem with this idea is that Jezebel would hardly have been known outside proconsular Asia because of limited communications with other parts of the Roman Empire (Ladd). The immediate reference is to these seven churches, but in the broader purpose of the book the seven represent the church universal of all times.

Gnōsontai indicates knowledge gained by observation and/or experience.[55] The OT passages of which this is an echo confirm that this is knowledge acquired by this means (cf. Ex. 7:5; 16:12; 29:46) (Charles). It will become well known in the future day of the Lamb's wrath that Jesus is aware of both outward conduct and inward thoughts and motives, and will judge righteously on the basis of such knowledge.[56] Some kind of special emphasis belongs to *egō eimi* ("I am"), either used absolutely to function as a title for Christ or to identify Him more emphatically with the participial predicate nominative, *ho eraunōn nephrous kai kardias* ("the one who searches the reins and hearts"), than would have been the case with *eimi* ("I am") alone. In the former case, it would be a self-declaration of deity (cf. John 8:24, 28, 58), and in the latter, an introduction of a Messianic or divine title.[57] The latter function is more obvious because the absolute use would result in an emphasis on deity (*egō eimi*) and omniscience (*ho eraunōn nephrous kai kardias*). At the beginning of this message He has already asserted His deity (ὁ υἱὸς τοῦ θεοῦ [*ho huios*

---

55. Γινώσκω is a synonym of οἶδα, which speaks of knowledge gained by reflection, a mental process based on intuition or information (cf. Rev. 2:9, 13, 19; 3:1, 8, 15).
56. Lange, *Revelation*, p. 123; Lenski, *Revelation*, p. 118. Γνώσονται is an ingressive future middle pointing to a particular point of time, "they shall come to know" (Robertson, *Word Pictures*, 6:310).
57. See discussion of ἐγώ εἰμι at Rev. 1:17.

tou theou, "the Son of God"]), and another statement of the same is unnecessary.[58]

"The one who searches the reins and hearts," an allusion to Jer. 17:10 (cf. also Ps. 7:9; Prov. 24:12; Jer. 11:20; 20:12), is a designation for one who has an intimate knowledge of man that pierces below superficial appearances. Just as in the Jeremiah passage, the point of this self-designation is that divine acquaintance with man's real, secret life forms the basis for an unerring and impartial judgment. Christ has demonstrated such omniscience in His appraisal of and strong words against Jezebel and her children. They cannot hide their evil from Him (Beckwith). The exercise of this divine attribute is spoken of in terms of a search[59] of *nephrous kai kardias.* The former noun refers literally to the "kidneys," but metaphorically to the inner parts of man's incorporeal being, particularly his will and affections (Swete; Lenski). The latter noun, when used alongside *nephrous,* focuses particularly on man's thoughts (Hort; Swete). Christ plumbs the depths of man's being, and on the basis of what He finds He will judge.

His future judgment is the second part of the twofold knowledge that all the other churches will glean from His dealings with Jezebel. *Dōsō hymin hekastō kata ta erga hymōn* ("I will give to each one of you according to your works") is a frequently stated basis for future judgment (e.g., Ps. 62:12; Prov. 24:12; Jer. 17:10; Rom. 2:6; 2 Tim. 4:14; Rev. 20:12-13). This, the Lord's own principle of judgment (cf. Matt. 7:16-20; 16:27), is stated four other times in this book (Rev. 18:6; 20:12, 13; 22:12) (Lee; Smith). The word used to indicate divine action in a general sense, *dōsō,* is used in v. 26 of this message to indicate God's gracious gift to the victors (cf. 2:7, 10, 17, 28; 3:21) (Lenski). *Hymin* ("you") is plural because the Lord speaks to the whole church composed of individuals and not just to the messenger representing the church (Swete; Morris). In itself it is personal, but the individualizing *hekastō* ("each one") makes the expression even more so (Lenski).

---

58. If the absolute use of ἐγώ εἰμι as a title for Christ were to be accepted, an interesting parallel to Rev. 2:18 exists: a statement of His deity (ὁ υἱὸς τοῦ θεοῦ, 2:18, and ἐγώ εἰμι, 2:23), a statement of His omniscience (ὁ ἔχων τοὺς ὀφθαλμοὺς αὐτοῦ ὡς φλόγα πυρός, 2:18, and ὁ ἐραυνῶν νεφροὺς καὶ καρδίας, 2:23), and an indication of His coming judgment (οἱ πόδες αὐτοῦ ὅμοιοι χαλκολιβάνῳ, 2:18, and δώσω ὑμῖν ἑκάστῳ κατὰ τὰ ἔργα ὑμῶν, 2:23). Even if the first of the three parallels fails to hold, however, the appropriateness of the self-designations in 2:18 to the message to follow is still obvious.

59. In Rom. 8:27, God searches the hearts (ὁ ἐραυνῶν τὰς καρδίας), and in 1 Cor. 2:10, the Holy Spirit searches all things (πάντα ἐραυνᾷ).

The principle of return to every single individual in proportion to works he has accomplished is the lesson to be gleaned by the churches through Christ's dealing with Jezebel and her children. These works (*erga*) are, to be sure, the real acts and verities of the inward man discerned by the piercing eye of God (cf. Matt. 15:19) (Alford; Hailey), but the nature of the word *erga* and the point of this statement demand that they be more than this. For other churches to learn the lesson of divine repayment for deeds performed, the deeds must be accomplishments with an outward appearance of such nature as to present public evidence (Lenski). These outward acts reflect a person's inner motives (cf. 1 Cor. 4:5) and are inseparable from them, but *erga* itself refers to the outworking of such motives as the basis for divine judgment.

2:24 Continuing His appraisal of the state of the church, Christ turns His attention to a brighter side of the church's constituency: ὑμῖν δὲ λέγω τοῖς λοιποῖς τοῖς ἐν Θυατίροις, ὅσοι οὐκ ἔχουσιν τὴν διδα-χὴν ταύτην, οἵτινες οὐκ ἔγνωσαν τὰ βαθέα τοῦ Σατανᾶ, ὡς λέγουσιν (*hymin de legō tois loipois tois en Thyatirois, hosoi ouk echousin tēn didachēn tautēn, hoitines ouk egnōsan ta bathea tou Satana, hōs legousin*, "but I say to the rest who are in Thyatira, as many as do not have this teaching, who have not known the deep things of Satan, as they say"). The adversative *de* ("but") marks a shift from pronouncing judgment upon the ungodly in the church to words of encouragement for the godly remnant among them. For the first time in these messages, a group within a local church is singled out as bearing a continuing true testimony for the Lord (Walvoord).

The second person pronoun *hymin* ("you") names the addressees of Christ's word of comfort, a designation that is further defined by the adjective *loipois* ("the rest").[60] This marks the faithful as those who had not been deceived by the cunning of Jezebel (cf. 1 Kings 19:18). The adjective does not necessitate that the remnant be in a minority.[61] Possibly they were a majority in the church in light of the Lord's praise for the church in 2:19. The group thus named is distin-

---

60. The plural pronoun ὑμῖν is another deviation from the more common singular pronoun addressing the messenger representing each church. Plural pronouns are also found in 2:10, 13, 23. Plural verbs that point to the people of the churches as opposed to their representative messenger occur in 2:10, 24, 25 (Smith, *Revelation*, p. 78). These occasional plurals confirm that words addressed to the messengers are intended ultimately for the people they represent.
61. In 1 Thess. 4:13, οἱ λοιποί refers to the pagan world which certainly was not a minority. In Rev. 9:20, οἱ λοιποί encompasses two-thirds of the whole earth (cf. also Rev. 19:21).

guished in two ways: they do not have the erroneous doctrine of Jezebel, and they have not known the deep things of Satan.[62]

"As many as do not have this teaching" is the first way of clarifying the identity of "the rest."[63] The shade of meaning assigned to *echousin* ("they have") deserves elaboration. Its occurrence here in proximity to its synonym κρατήσατε (*kratēsate*, "hold fast") in the next verse raises a familiar question regarding an intended distinction in meaning between the two. A similar issue has already been discussed in conjunction with the use of the verbs earlier (cf. 1:16; 2:1).[64] It was the conclusion before and probably should be again that *krateō* is a stronger verb than *echō*. To equate them here could imply that the remnant in Thyatira did not hold Jezebel's heresy firmly, but did hold it loosely. Jesus would not have condoned holding it at all. Obviously, the sense is that they were completely free from any contact with her false teaching.[65] They did not hold it at all, a suitable sense for *echousin* in comparison with *kratēsate*.[66] Whether Nicolaitan or not, Jezebel advocated a system of doctrine akin to that other heretical sect, and a remnant in Thyatira had wisely distanced themselves from it.

The second description of the faithful in Thyatira notes that they are the ones "who have not known the deep things of Satan, as they say." They compose a class of people[67] who have not experienced[68] the alleged deeper knowledge attained by those attached to the false system. Tradition reveals that a number of pagan religions and heretical sects boasted of their knowledge of "the deep things." The

---

62. Swete, *Apocalypse*, p. 45; Moffatt, "Revelation," 5:59; Lange, *Revelation*, p. 123.
63. The relative pronoun ὅσοι is quantitative (Lenski, p. 119). Its antecedent is τοῖς λοιποῖς. It includes all who (i.e., "as many as" = "all who") are designated as "the rest" (Robertson, *Word Pictures*, 6:310).
64. See discussion at 2:1.
65. Alford, *Greek Testament*, 4:576. Alford sees in the continuing action of the present tense of ἔχουσιν a further evidence of their complete separation from Jezebel's doctrine.
66. A distinction in meaning finds further confirmation in the side-by-side comparison of ἔχετε and κρατήσατε in 2:25, where a difference in emphasis is even more conspicuous.
67. The relative pronoun οἵτινες is generic, referring to a class of people: "which very ones." They were this kind of people. This pronoun is qualitative by background, but in Koine Greek it was gradually losing its qualitative force. Though John most frequently uses ὅστις as practically equivalent to ὅς (cf. Rev. 1:12; 9:8; 12:13; 17:12; 19:2), a few times (cf. Rev. 1:7; 9:4; 20:4) he uses it in its classical sense, "as much as" or "as many as" (Alford, *Greek Testament*, 4:576; Charles, *Revelation*, 1:73; Robertson, *Word Pictures*, 6:410).
68. Οὐκ ἔγνωσαν has the force of "not knowing by experience." See the discussion of γνώσονται at 2:23.

Ophites who worshiped the serpent and later Gnostic sects such as the Cainites, Carpocratians, and Naasenes are among them. They used the very language about Satan (or the serpent) as Paul had in reference to God (cf. 1 Cor. 2:10).[69] *Ta bathea* ("the deep things") is a substantive that designates matters that are hidden and beyond man's scrutiny.[70] It amounts to a claim of esoteric knowledge, perhaps even a superior morality, a higher law (Hort). If man is to know them, he must have supernatural help.

If this claim to know the deep things is accepted as characteristic of those who had been deluded, a question of how the expression is used remains. Is *ta bathea tou Satana* ("the deep things of Satan") phraseology taken over en toto from Jezebel's followers or the Nicolaitans (Beckwith), or did they use it as an expression of reproach against "unenlightened" Christians?[71] As stated above, some early sects are known to have used the total expression as a slogan (Alford; Charles; Moffatt). Such formed an exact counterpart to "the deep things of God" (1 Cor. 2:10) (Lee). It is next to impossible, however, to conceive of the total expression coming from professing Christians. "As they say" (*hōs legousin*) requires that "of Satan" come from the same lips as "the depths." They did not boast about "the depths," to which Christ added "of Satan." A Christian would hardly have bragged about his involvement in Satan worship.

It is more convincing to conclude that this was their way of claiming they could indulge in idol feasts, including their immorality, without sinning. From their perspective, they looked with scorn on their "weaker" fellow Christians.[72] The presence of this kind of professing Christians in Asia Minor is known from other contemporary sources. The false claim of sinlessness made by opponents of the apostle and the connection of the sinful ones making such a claim are noted in one of John's writings to Christians in this same area: "If we say that we have not sinned, we make Him a liar and His word is not in us. . . . In this are manifest the children of God and the children of the devil: everyone who does not practice righteousness is not from God, and he who does not love his brother" (1 John 1:10; 3:10). The proneness of heretics to ridicule the piety of other Christians is an established habit among them.[73]

It is possible that the words should rather be taken ironically on behalf of the author or faithful Christians. The thrust would be,

---

69. Robertson, *Word Pictures*, 6:311.
70. Joseph Henry Thayer, *A Greek-English Lexicon of the New Testament* (New York: American Book, 1889), p. 93.
71. Robertson, *Word Pictures*, 6:311.
72. Ibid.
73. Ibid.

"Whereas they claim to know the 'deep things of God,' in reality it is the 'deep things of Satan' that they know." The words thus become a sarcastic reversal of their main slogan.[74] By designating the Gnostic-like doctrine as "the depths of Satan," "the rest who are in Thyatira" would be showing their deep abhorrence of it (Lee). This meaning would also align with Jesus' labels for institutions in other cities, "the synagogue of Satan" in Smyrna (2:9) and "the throne of Satan" in Pergamum (2:13) (Lee; Beckwith). Furthermore, this would correspond with Jezebel's claim to be a prophetess (2:20), whereby she professed to introduce her followers to "the deep things of God" (1 Cor. 2:10; cf. Rom. 11:33; Eph. 3:18) (Ladd). As appealing as this reasoning is, the explanation falters in the words "as they say" (*hōs legousin*). To refer the "they" to "the rest who are in Thyatira" (Lee) ignores the necessity of assigning *legousin* a different subject from that of *egnōsan* ("know"). If both verbs had the same subject, an impossible sense would result: "the godly remnant has not known the depths of Satan as the godly remnant claims." To attribute the addition of "of Satan" to the Lord is also inadmissible, because if the claim of knowing deep things applies to part of the expression, it must apply to all. The situation in 2:9 is different. There an indication of Christ's assignment of satanic orientation is clear. This verse has no such indication (Beckwith).

It is better to view this as an actual claim of an element in the Thyatiran church, that a Christian should fully know "the deep things of Satan" in the sense that he ventures into Satan's strongholds to demonstrate the powerlessness of the enemy over him, or else to learn the real nature of sin in this firsthand way (Beckwith; Morris). They were probably part of the fanatical group in the province of Asia that held that a Christian could not sin (cf. 1 John 1:10; 3:9). They were similar to the group in Corinth who shared in idolatrous feasts and prided themselves in their knowledge and strength in proving the harmlessness of such participation. They even went to the extreme of claiming their actions would help the weaker brethren overcome their unfounded scruples and be built up in knowledge and strength.[75] On this ground Jezebel encouraged her followers to participate as fully as possible in the pagan society (Caird). A gnostically influenced Christian could well boast about knowing the deep things of Satan, because his "knowledge" told him that such things were

---

74. Hanns Lilje, *The Last Book of the Bible*, trans. Olive Wyon (Philadelphia: Muhlenberg, 1957), p. 86.
75. Beckwith, *Apocalypse*, p. 469. Οἰκοδομηθήσεται in 1 Cor. 8:10 is an ironical repetition of the argument of the strong. Paul turns its sense from "build up" to attach to it the connotation of "tear down."

unreal and harmless (cf. 1 Cor. 8:1-4) or because he was so sure of his sinlessness (cf. 1 John 1:8-9; 3:9) that he felt himself to be immune, i.e., beyond good and evil (Moffatt; Sweet). The heretics rejoiced in their freedom in the Spirit to explore the sphere of Satan's rule (Beasley-Murray). They proudly claimed to have done so.[76]

For those who have maintained purity from the defilement of Jezebel and her doctrine, the Lord has a promise: οὐ βάλλω ἐφ᾽ ὑμᾶς ἄλλο βάρος (*ou ballō eph' hymas allo baros,* "I do not cast on you another burden"). "Another burden" has at times been identified as the apostolic decree of Acts 15:19-21, 28-29 because *baros* ("burden") is also used in Acts 15:28.[77] Another tie-in lies in the coverage of the decree. Both that decree and the message to Thyatira forbid fornication and eating meat sacrificed to idols (Alford; Moffatt). With this identification of *baros,* the adjective *allo* ("another") points to the other two parts of the apostolic decree, abstaining from blood and things strangled, which are not specifically prohibited here (Charles). Yet similarities to the earlier Jerusalem decree could be accidental (Hort; Beckwith; Mounce). The fact is, the faithful in Thyatira were not perplexed because of a restriction of their Christian freedom by the earlier conciliar action. This was probably the last thing in their minds (Beckwith). Furthermore, this explanation leaves *allo* quite isolated. Something additional is needed to indicate a reference to the decree or to topics so remote as v. 20 (Beckwith).

A further suggestion has been that "another burden" refers to additional suffering. The use of ὑπομονήν (*hypomonēn,* "endurance"; 2:19) reflects persecution the faithful had already faced. Yet it is doubtful that the Lord could promise them that their suffering has now ended when He is about to challenge them to hold fast until He comes (2:25). Another possible meaning derives an implication from the previous exhortation for the followers of Jezebel to repent. If the

---

76. The parenthetical ὡς λέγουσιν is construed with what precedes rather than with what follows. If one takes it with what follows, it has two possible senses. The first is that the Lord promises no further burdens just as the false teachers had promised (Hort, *Apocalypse,* p. 31). The second is that the following promise of no further burden alludes to the conciliar decree of Acts 15:28, and the "they" refers to the apostolic teachers who composed that decree (Walvoord, *Revelation,* p. 76). The first possible sense is excluded by the observation that Jesus' actions are independent of what others have said. He is not guided by what the heretics have done. The second possible sense is eliminated because the apostles are nowhere in this context. To assume a reference to them is only a remote possibility. Besides, Jesus would not be under their authority. It is preferable to connect the parenthetical clause more closely with the preceding.

77. Robertson, *Word Pictures,* 6:311.

guilty are challenged to repent, by implication those who had not yet yielded to the temptations should continue faithful. This and no other burden will come to them. The problem with this understanding is that it leaves *allo* isolated (Beckwith). "Another" requires something more than an implication in its indication of something additional.

The best explanation is that the "burden" upon the faithful is that of resisting the pressure of Jezebel and her group. Choosing to abstain from her evil practices doubtless resulted in ridicule. Christ promises to place upon them no burden other than continuing to stand against her. Jezebel and her followers must bear the wrath of Christ, but all the faithful must endure is the social pressure resulting from their stand against fornication and eating meat sacrificed to idols. If this meaning is correct, *baros* carries the sense of something "weighty" or "important," which is legitimate for the word (cf. Matt. 23:23; 2 Cor. 10:10; 1 Thess. 2:6). In light of the pressure upon the faithful, it is a "weighty admonition" that the Lord is about to deliver in v. 25, "Hold fast what you have until I come." Grammatical usage permits a merging of the two statements to result in the following sense: "I put upon you no other weighty admonition than this: Hold fast what you have."[78] In this case the *allo* refers to the command at the beginning of the next verse. Their anxiety is thereby relieved. He casts (*ballō*) Jezebel and her children into conditions of unparalleled suffering (vv. 22-23), but He does not cast (*ou ballō*) upon the faithful anything worse than to keep doing what they already are doing.

2:25 The burden of resisting Jezebel in obedience to Christ's admonition becomes specific in v. 25: πλὴν ὃ ἔχετε κρατήσατε ἄχρις οὗ ἂν ἥξω (*plēn ho echete kratēsate achris hou an hēxō*, "other than [this], hold fast what you have until I come"). After *ouk allo* ("not another") *plēn* is often a preposition followed by an ablative (e.g., Gen. 39:6, 9 [LXX]; Mark 12:32). Because it is followed here by an independent clause, some have assumed that it begins a new sentence (Swete). As explained in connection with the discussion of *allo baros* in the previous verse, however, the best course here is to allow it to have its exceptive force. It introduces the one exception to the Lord's promise of no further burden.

Κρατέω (*Krateō*, "I hold fast") is a common metaphor to describe strict adherence to a tradition or teaching either in a good sense (cf. 2 Thess. 2:15; Rev. 2:13; 3:11) or in a bad sense (cf. Mark 7:3, 8; Rev. 2:14, 15).[79] Its several usages in these messages make it a sort of

---

78. Beckwith, *Apocalypse*, p. 470; Mounce, *Revelation*, p. 105. In comparisons, the usual construction after ἄλλος with a negative is the genitive case, or ἤ, or else πλήν with the genitive. Sometimes it may be followed by πλήν and an independent clause. In this instance πλήν means "other than" or "except."

79. William R. Newell, *The Book of Revelation* (Chicago: Moody, 1935), p. 60.

motto for several of the churches.[80] The other occurrences of the verb in these messages are present tenses, a factor that arouses curiosity about why the speaker chooses the aorist imperative *kratēsate*. One suggestion takes this as an ingressive aorist, "start holding fast," i.e., "once for all, take a firm hold upon what you have been taught" (Hort). This sense might imply that the readers did not have a firm hold already, however. A better way is to see the connotation of a constative aorist, "hold on as a single decisive effort."[81] The aorist imperative replaces the present imperative's emphasis on continuance with its focus on urgency. It is more vivid in setting forth the renewed and determined grasp of every intervening moment of the space prescribed (Alford).

The relative clause *ho echete* ("what you have") is the valued possession the faithful are told to cling to.[82] It is their Christian integrity (Beckwith). At least it includes their works for which they are so highly commended in v. 19 and their separation from the defilement of Jezebel noted in v. 24 (Swete). The length of the period during which the perseverance is required is set by the indefinite temporal clause *achris hou an hēxō* ("until I come"). *Hēxō* is used in place of ἔρχομαι (*erchomai*, "I am coming") to refer to Christ's second advent here and twice in the message to Sardis (cf. 3:3).[83] The nearness of His coming is held up as an incentive to stand true in the face of pressure to compromise right standards of behavior.

2:26 *Promise to the overcomer.* The order of the promise to the overcomer and the command to hear is reversed in this and the three remaining messages as compared with the first three. In this message alone the promise to the overcomer is connected with the preceding by the conjunction καί (*kai,* "and"). The reason for this is that the promise is closer in thought to the body of the message in this case (Alford; Hort; Walvoord). Here also the overcomer is more specifically defined by an adjoining participle and its phrase: ὁ νικῶν καὶ ὁ τηρῶν ἄχρι τέλους τὰ ἔργα μου (*ho nikōn kai ho tērōn achri telous ta erga mou,* "the one who overcomes and keeps My works until the end").

In the discussion of 2:7 the conclusion was that *ho nikōn* ("the one who overcomes") is not a member of a special class of Christians distinguished by their spirituality and power in contrast to other

---

80. Robertson, *Word Pictures,* 6:319.
81. Swete, *Apocalypse,* p. 46; Robertson, *Word Pictures,* 6:311. Lenski's suggestion of an effective aorist is unsatisfactory because it could imply that their holding fast would culminate at Christ's return.
82. Note the weaker word ἔχω, "have" or "hold," side-by-side with the verb κρατέω, which has the more intense meaning of "hold fast."
83. The two usages of ἥξω in 3:3 are future indicative and are identical in form with the verb here, but the same form can also be aorist subjunctive. The latter is more probable here because ἄχρις (ἄχρι) in Revelation usually introduces a clause with a subjunctive verb (cf. 7:3; 15:8; 20:3, 5).

genuine Christians who are not overcomers. The designation is rather a description of what is normal and what is expected of true followers of the Lord. Hence, the promise to follow is for all genuine believers in Thyatira who stand representatively for all Christians. *Kai ho tērōn* ("and keeps") is the same individual as designated by *ho nikōn*, not someone different.[84] The overcomer also obeys the word of the Lord by maintaining the practice of good works. Τηρέω (*Tēreō*, "I keep") is frequent in the gospel of John (twelve times), the epistle of First John (six times), and Revelation (nine times). Usually its object is τὸν λόγον (*ton logon*, "the word") or τὰς ἐντολάς (*tas entolas*, "the command-ments"). For it to be followed by *ta erga* ("the works") here offers the same idea in concrete form, the works being performed in com-pliance with God's commands (Swete; Beckwith). Works in these mes-sages are regularly presented as a test of character (Swete). "*My* works" are an obvious contrast to "*her* works" in v. 22. The works that belong to Christ are holy, but those of Jezebel were anything but holy.[85] *Achri telous* represents the same termination as is indicated by *achris hou an hēxō* in v. 25.[86] The "end" of the struggle to maintain an obedient life will coincide with the return of Christ to deliver the overcomer.

The substance of the promise to the overcomer in Thyatira, the only overcomer to receive a double promise,[87] alludes to Ps. 2:8-9, a promise to the Messiah of victory over His enemies. The first line of the promise guarantees that he will share the Messiah's victory over His enemies: δώσω αὐτῷ ἐξουσίαν ἐπὶ τῶν ἐθνῶν (*dōsō autō exousian epi tōn ethnōn*, "I will give to him authority over the nations"[88]).

---

84. The καὶ between the two participles may easily be another of the frequent ascensive uses of the conjunction: "he who overcomes, even he who keeps." The occurrence of the article with each participle has the effect of making the two participles equal. Its repetition with the second serves to emphasize the two conditions of success: "The victor is he who keeps Christ's works; he who keeps Christ's works is the victor" (Swete, *Apoc-alypse*, p. 46; Charles, *Revelation*, 1:74). The nominative case of the par-ticiples affords another example of the nominative absolute (cf. 3:12, 21), the person so designated being picked up by a dative αὐτῷ in the next clause (Robertson, *Word Pictures*, 6:311). More normal constructions are those found in 2:7, 17 and 6:4; 21:6 (Charles, *Revelation*, 1:74). The nomi-native absolute is common in John's other writings (cf. John 6:39; 7:38; 1 John 2:24, 27) (Lee, "Revelation," 4:529).
85. Alford, *Greek Testament*, 4:577; Moffatt, "Revelation," 5:60. Μου is a geni-tive of possession. The works are Christ's possession in the sense that they appropriately represent His attribute of holiness.
86. Robertson, *Word Pictures*, 6:312.
87. Note the two promises, the first included in δώσω (v. 26) and ποιμανεῖ (v. 27) and the second in δώσω (v. 28) (Charles, *Revelation*, 1:77).
88. Ἐθνῶν is best rendered "nations," not "Gentiles." The latter translation would exclude the people of Israel, a limitation that is unjustified in light of the universal sweep of the Messiah's dominion.

Exousian here takes the sense of the "authority" or "power" of ruling or governing.[89] That the Messiah's followers will share in His eschatological rule is a familiar prophetic theme (cf. 1:6; 12:5; 19:15).[90] This promise is fierce, including such ideas as destroying with a rod of iron and the shattering of a clay jar (2:27). Its violent nature is in keeping with the general tone of the message. A strong threat to the truth such as the teaching of Jezebel required a strong promise to bolster those who successfully stood against her (Swete; Beckwith). This promise is the first definitive reference in Revelation to the coming millennial kingdom, which Jesus is to establish when He returns to earth (Moffatt).

2:27 The next verse continues the promise based on Ps. 2:8-9: καὶ ποιμανεῖ αὐτοὺς ἐν ῥάβδῳ σιδηρᾷ, ὡς τὰ σκεύη τὰ κεραμικὰ συντρίβεται (*kai poimanei autous en rhabdō sidērą, hōs ta skeuē ta keramika syntribetai*, "And he will destroy them with a rod of iron, as vessels of a potter are dashed to pieces"). The overcomer will join Christ in destroying the nations who oppose Him. *Poimanei* has at times been rendered by the English verbs "shepherd" or "rule" in light of its literal meaning of "tend as a shepherd" (cf. 7:17; Matt. 2:6) and in light of its usage in reference to the functioning of church leaders (cf. Acts 20:28; 1 Pet. 5:2) (Lee; Walvoord). Yet neither of these meanings is strong enough to match the severity of destruction depicted in the shattering of clay containers to which the action is compared. The dashing to pieces of the vessels of the potter indicates in "ferocious detail" a rule of destruction (Moffatt). The function must compare with the meaning of *syntribetai* in the next line (Ladd). The same verb refers to actual destruction in 19:15 where it parallels πατάξῃ (*pataxē*, "he may strike") (Charles). In the LXX ποιμαίνω (*poimainō*, "I destroy") translates the Hebrew word meaning "break in pieces," a meaning that more accurately portrays the violence necessitated by this context.[91]

---

89. The author appears to distinguish carefully between ἐξουσίαν with and without the article. In the fourth gospel he never uses an article with the noun. In Revelation, the articular use occurs in contexts where full authority is implied (cf. 9:19; 13:4, 12; 16:9; 17:13). On the other hand, the anarthrous construction is chosen when authority is limited (cf. 2:26; 6:8; 9:3; 13:2, 5, 7; 14:18; 17:12; 18:1; 20:6). Three apparent exceptions to the former generalization come in 9:10; 11:6; 22:14 (Charles, *Revelation*, 1:75).

90. Beckwith, *Apocalypse*, p. 470; Robertson, *Word Pictures*, 6:312.

91. Alford, *Greek Testament*, 4:578. In noting John's habit of elsewhere translating the Hebrew text independently, Charles explains how the producers of the LXX erred and how John avoided the same error. It appears that the LXX translators understood תרעם from רעה and vocalized it תִּרְעֵם, resulting in the rendering ποιμανεῖς. They should have taken רעע as the root and vocalized it תְּרֹעֵם. John does not appear to have followed the LXX in his rendering of the Hebrew, however. Independently, he rendered

The objects of this destruction are designated by *autous*, which refers back to the "nations" of v. 26.[92] *En rhabdǭ sidērǡ* ("With a rod of iron") is also from Psalm 2. One opinion has it that this is a shepherd's oaken club, capped with iron and capable of inflicting severe punishment (Swete). Whatever its construction, it symbolizes a royal scepter of some kind, with which a rigorous rule is achieved.[93] The Messiah will shatter the power of all His enemies, allowing the overcomers to share this dominance with Him, a feature of His conquest that is developed further in 17:14 and 19:14 (Beckwith).

A comparison,[94] also from Psalm 2, shows how utterly devastating the conquest of the Messiah and His followers will be: *hōs ta skeuē ta keramika syntribetai* ("as vessels of a potter are dashed to pieces"). Vessels of a potter are made of clay that has been dried and cooked until quite brittle. Such material when struck with a sharp blow shatters into hundreds of pieces, a graphic picture of the collapse of the Messiah's enemies at their future confrontation with Him. Τρίβω (*Tribō*) has the basic meaning of "broken into many small pieces," "shattered," or "crushed." Addition of the σύν (*syn*, "with") prefix paints a picture of masses of fragments collapsing into a heap together (Alford). The future victory of the Messiah and those with Him will be complete.

The closing words of v. 27 elaborate on the source of the Messiah's power: ὡς κἀγὼ εἴληφα παρὰ τοῦ πατρός μου (*hōs kagō eilēpha para tou patros mou*, "as I also received from My Father"). It comes from His Father (cf. Ps. 2:7-8). He will bestow the power on others in the same way as He has received and still possesses[95] it.

2:28 The second promise to the Thyatiran overcomer comes in v. 28: καὶ δώσω αὐτῷ τὸν ἀστέρα τὸν πρωϊνόν (*kai dōsō autǭ ton astera ton prōinon*, "and I will give him the morning star"). In Rev. 22:16 Christ is "the bright morning star," but who or what is "the morning star"

---

the Hebrew correctly in adopting a secondary meaning of ποιμαίνω, "devastate" or "destroy" (cf. the LXX renderings of this verb in Ps. 80:14; Jer. 6:3; 2:16; 22:22; Mic. 5:5) (Charles, *Revelation*, 1:75-76).

92. The pronoun αὐτούς is masculine and its antecedent, ἐθνῶν, is neuter. As occasionally happens, the agreement between the two is *ad sensum* rather than strictly grammatical (Lenski, *Revelation*, p. 122).

93. Robertson, *Word Pictures*, 6:312.

94. It is possible to construe ὡς τὰ σκεύη τὰ κεραμικὰ συντρίβεται as a separate independent clause analogous with the construction of Ps. 2:9 on which the passage depends, but the grammatical flow of the present context is more coherent if it is taken as a subordinate clause clarifying the degree of devastation indicated by ποιμανεῖ (Beckwith, *Apocalypse*, p. 471).

95. Choice of the perfect tense of εἴληφα shows that He continues in possession of the power (Robertson, *Word Pictures*, 6:312).

promised here? Three proposals that cannot be taken too seriously are the resurrection of the Christian (Lee), fallen Lucifer (Alford), and the king of Babylon (Alford). Proponents of the resurrection of Christ cite Rev. 20:6 as giving the essence of the promise to the overcomer, but resurrection is not specifically in view in the present verse. Isaiah 14:12 is the chief support for the identification of fallen Lucifer, the picture of Lucifer being put under the feet of the saints, but an allusion to Lucifer is farfetched in this context. The king of Babylon also looks to Isa. 14:12 for support, because he is the one who pictures Lucifer there, but such a reference is even more farfetched than Lucifer. A fourth explanation is that the morning star refers to Venus, which from Babylonian times was a symbol for sovereignty (Beasley-Murray). In Roman times this star was more specifically a symbol for victory and sovereignty (Beasley-Murray). This is an interesting concept in that the second promise to the overcomer would become a reinforcement of the first already given in vv. 26-27 (Beasley-Murray). The proposal loses its plausibility, however, in light of the strong disdain for heathen idolatry expressed earlier in the message. Christ would hardly draw His symbolism from heathen thought.

Another identification for "the morning star" is Christ Himself, because He is "the bright morning star" later in the book.[96] Christ in His own Person will be the gift to the overcomer at the time of His second advent (Swete). On the surface, this seems obvious, but further reflection rules out this possibility. The very terms of the sentence itself make a separation between Christ and the gift of "the morning star" He bestows (Alford). It would be a strange way for Him to refer to Himself (Morris). A preferable understanding of the morning star is the promise that in the messianic kingdom, the righteous will shine as stars. Because the star of the morning was thought to be the brightest, the glory that will follow conquest over the Messiah's enemies (v. 27) is indirectly in view (Beckwith). Staunch adherence to the truth is similarly rewarded in Dan. 12:3 where the future privileges of the faithful are likened to the stars (cf. Esdr. 7:97; Enoch 104:2) (Moffatt; Beckwith). This conclusion also resembles the promise of Matt. 13:43 that "the righteous will shine as the sun in the kingdom of their Father" (Alford). The star appears as a symbol of royalty in Matt. 2:2, a factor that also enforces the idea of future rule (Lee).

This second promise to the Thyatiran overcomer, then, reinforces the first. It presents in symbolic form the role of the overcomer as ruling with the Messiah following the putting down of His enemies at His second advent (Smith).

---

96. Lee, 4:530; Robertson, *Word Pictures*, 6:312.

2:29 *Command to hear.* The call to give special attention, ὁ ἔχων οὖς ἀκουσάτω τί τὸ πνεῦμα λέγει ταῖς ἐκκλησίαις (*ho echōn ous akousatō ti to pneuma legei tais ekklēsiais,* "The one who has an ear, let him hear what the Spirit says to the churches"), is the same as that issued to the three earlier churches (2:7, 11, 17). Beginning with this message and continuing with the last three, it is at the end after the promise to the overcomer, instead of before the overcomer promise that ends the first three messages. No significant rationale for this change in sequence has been advanced (Lenski). The point is that the Thyatiran church, like the other six churches, must pay special heed to the analysis of Christ through the Holy Spirit regarding itself and those of the other churches also.

Additional Notes

2:19 The amount of emphasis residing in the three occurrences of σου in 2:19 deserves further explanation. The first is a vernacular possessive genitive that is itself unemphatic, but that in some way places greater emphasis upon its context.[97] The last two occurrences *are* emphatic, however. Two observations confirm this. The twofold repetition of the pronoun (second and third occurrences) shows that emphasis is intended: "the love and the faith, even the service and the endurance *that you show* and the works *that you do.*" Also the writer could not very well have written καί σου, because the unemphatic σου after an unemphatic word is not a probability.[98] Two uses of σου in Rev. 10:9 illustrate the same principles as this verse reflects (Charles). Another σου at the beginning of v. 20 brings to four the number of occurrences in just over one verse, another feature pointing to an intended emphasis on the last two in v. 19.

2:20 A substantial group of ancient sources has the pronoun σου after γυναῖκα, yielding the meaning "your wife." If this reading is correct, Jezebel was the wife of the messenger to the church. In its favor, the reading is the more difficult. Hardly any reason can be imagined that a scribe would have inserted it later (Alford). On the other hand, if ἄγγελος was taken to refer to an angelic being, its omission by a later scribe is quite natural (Alford). The external witnesses supporting inclusion of the pronoun, while substantial, are not nearly as impressive as those supporting the omission (Lee). Furthermore, it is doubtful that a messenger whose leadership in his own home had allowed his wife to degenerate to this point would have been chosen to represent the church in ministering to John on Pat-

---

97. Edwin A. Abbott, *Johannine Grammar* (London: Adam and Charles Black, 1906), p. 601.
98. Ibid., p. 606.

mos. Standards for church leadership covering this situation were already in place (cf. 1 Tim. 3:4, 12) and make the meaning this reading would convey next to impossible.

2:22 A few MSS read a future indicative μετανοήσουσιν rather than the aorist subjunctive, making this a simple condition, one assumed to be factual.[99] The weight of MS evidence for the aorist subjunctive is stronger, however. This construction is a more probable condition, usually future.

Another significant reading as an alternative for αὐτῆς is αὐτῶν, "their" works. The witnesses favoring the feminine singular are much more impressive, however. Jezebel was clearly responsible for the inferior quality of the deeds of her followers.[100]

---

99. Robertson, *Word Pictures*, 6:310.
100. Ibid.

7

Church of Complacency

E. THE MESSAGE TO SARDIS (3:1-6)

By the time the bearers of the Apocalypse reached the fifth city on their itinerary, their number would have dropped from seven to three. The three would have traveled thirty-three miles south from Thyatira to reach Sardis, which was perched on an elevated plateau 1,500 feet above the valley below and located at the western end of the Great King's highway from Susa.[1] To the Christian congregation of this strategically situated city came the following message from the glorified Lord.

Translation

[1]And to the messenger of the church which is in Sardis, write:

"These things says the one who has the seven spirits of God and the seven stars. I know your works, that you have a name that you live, and [yet] you are dead. [2]Prove yourself to be watchful, and establish the remaining things that are about to die, for I have not found your works fulfilled before My God. [3]Remember therefore how you have received and heard, and keep [strengthening what remains], and repent. If therefore you do not watch, I will come as a thief, and you will in no way know what hour I will come upon you. [4]But you have a

---

1. G. V. Caird, *A Commentary on the Revelation of St. John the Divine*, HNTC (New York: Harper & Row, 1966), p. 47.

few names in Sardis that have not defiled their garments, and they will walk with Me in white, because they are worthy. ⁵The one who overcomes thus will be clothed in white garments, and I will in no way wipe his name from the book of life, and I will confess his name before My Father and before His angels. ⁶The one who has an ear, let him hear what the Spirit says to the churches."

Exegesis and Exposition

3:1 *The address.* The address follows the same wording as the previous four with a new city inserted: καὶ τῷ ἀγγέλῳ τῆς ἐν Σάρδεσιν ἐκκλησίας γράψον (*kai tō angelō tēs en Sardesin ekklēsias grapson*, "and to the messenger of the church which is in Sardis, write"). Sardis was situated geographically on one of a series of alluvial hills that formed a transition from the lower elevation of the Hermus plain to the high elevation of Mount Tmolus. Each of these hills was shaped into the form of a small elongated plateau with steep sides. They terminated in the north in a sharp point and on the south in a neck of land that connected them to Mount Tmolus. Such a location made Sardis an almost impregnable natural fortress militarily. The small neck of land to the south provided the only access to the city, but even this was a steep, tedious, and winding climb, and so the city was easily defendable. The other sides of the city were smooth rock walls that were almost perpendicular, dropping down to the plain 1,500 feet below. This provided an ideal stronghold. At the same time, it limited the growth possibilities of the city.[2]

The city appears to have begun when the Lydian kingdom began in about 1200 B.C. Sardis apparently was called Hyde during the early days of the kingdom while serving as its capital. As the civilization and the kingdom grew larger and more complex, the elevated plateau on which the city stood was too small to serve as a capital, so a lower city was built on the western and northern sides of the original city and probably on the eastern side also. The old city served as an acropolis. Because of the great difference in altitude, the new city was in sharp contrast to the old. Since it was a double city, its name was pluralized, Σάρδεις (*Sardeis*), like that of Athens (Ἀθῆναι [*Athēnai*]) and some other cities (Ramsay).

Being the capital of Lydia, Sardis had a history of frequent wars. Whoever controlled Sardis controlled Lydia. In this role Sardis was pre-eminent in the eyes of the more Hellenistic cities of Asia to the west as the Oriental enemy in whose hands their fate rested. Most of them engaged Sardis in warfare and lost. It was a great, wealthy,

---

2. W. M. Ramsay, *The Letters to the Seven Churches of Asia* (New York: A. C. Armstrong, 1904), pp. 354-56.

impregnable city over which victory was practically impossible. In the ongoing rivalry between Asia and Europe it represented Asia, and the Greek colonies toward the coast to the west represented Europe. Sardis was an enemy of those Ionian cities. After learning from them it eventually conquered them and earned the acknowledged status of "Sardis the First Metropolis of Asia and of Lydia, and of Hellenism," a designation inscribed on their coins. The Hellenism that developed in Sardis was distinctive. To some degree it modified Asia, but in other ways this Greek spirit was itself modified. This Hellenism was not a racial type, but a kind of aspiration and aims. It reflected itself in a consciousness of individualism and in social and political structures (Ramsay).

By the middle of the sixth century B.C., the city attained such a high level of respect that when its downfall came at the hands of a little-known enemy the Greek cities received the news of it with disbelief. Despite an alleged warning against self-satisfaction by the Greek god whom he consulted, Croesus the king of Lydia initiated an attack against Cyrus king of Persia, but was soundly defeated. Returning to Sardis to recoup and rebuild his army for another attack, he was pursued quickly by Cyrus who laid siege against Sardis. Croesus felt utterly secure in his impregnable situation atop the acropolis and foresaw an easy victory over the Persians who were cornered among the perpendicular rocks in the lower city, an easy prey for the assembling Lydian army to crush. After retiring one evening while the drama was unfolding, he awakened to discover that the Persians had gained control of the acropolis by scaling one-by-one the steep walls (549 B.C.). So secure did the Sardians feel that they left this means of access completely unguarded, permitting the climbers to ascend unobserved. It is said that even a child could have defended the city from this kind of attack, but not so much as one observer had been appointed to watch the side that was believed to be inaccessible.[3]

History repeated itself more than three and a half centuries later when Antiochus the Great conquered Sardis by utilizing the services of a sure-footed mountain climber from Crete (195 B.C.). His army entered the city by another route while the defenders in careless confidence were content to guard the one known approach, the isthmus of land connected to Mount Tmolus on the south (Ramsay; Ford).

In A.D. 17 a severe earthquake did great damage to the city. Tiberius, the Roman emperor, was very generous in his donations and help extended to the city in its rebuilding efforts. In appreciation

---

3. Ibid., pp. 358-62; J. Massyngberde Ford, *Revelation*, vol. 38 of AB (Garden City, N.Y.: Doubleday, 1975), p. 412.

Sardis minted a special coin in honor of Tiberius and Rome, bearing his image and the inscription "Caesarean Sardis." This continued for quite some time even after the death of the imperial benefactor. The city also erected a temple in his honor and in honor of Empress Livia. She was portrayed as the mother goddess and he as her god-son (Ramsay).

By the time the Romans controlled Sardis, its greatness lay in the past. The acropolis ceased functioning as an important part of the living city and was viewed merely as a historical relic. Without the acropolis, Sardis's location had nothing to commend itself, and it was no longer inhabited. The chief town in the district became Salikli, about five miles to the east in a more convenient situation for travelers and trade at the foot of Mount Tmolus.[4] When the Turks later swarmed through the Hermus Valley, the acropolis was restored as a fortress and remained so until Islam completely exterminated Christianity in this valley during the Middle Ages (Ramsay). The modern city of Sart occupies the site of ancient Sardis.

In the prime of the Lydian Empire, its kings were quite wealthy. Their riches accumulated through trade, agriculture, and the commerce of the East. The accuracy of a legend about gold being discovered in the area is debated.[5] The early wealth of Sardis and the discovery of coinage made of a gold-silver alloy give considerable credibility to the report (Hemer). During the Roman period a semblance of the earlier wealth returned because of trade introduced through the city's proximity to a junction of the Roman system of roads in the area.[6] The main industry of this period was the production of woolen goods. It is said to be the first city to perfect the art of dyeing wool.[7] Jewelry found in the local cemeteries by archaeologists indicates that some of the city's vast wealth may have been derived from this source.[8]

Archaeological explorations that began in 1958 have disclosed

4. Ramsay, *Seven Churches*, p. 367. Hemer differs from Ramsay's portrayal of Sardis as a city in decay. He agrees that the time of its royal and military splendor had vanished, but emphasizes that it retained a high degree of commercial prosperity for a long time (Colin J. Hemer, *The Letters to the Seven Churches of Asia in Their Local Setting*, JSNTSup 11 [Sheffield: U. of Sheffield, 1986], p. 134). This is a well-taken corrective to balance the picture given by Ramsay.
5. Ramsay, *Seven Churches*, p. 357, denies its accuracy.
6. Henry Barclay Swete, *The Apocalypse of St. John* (London: Macmillan, 1906), p. 47.
7. R. H. Charles, *The Revelation of St. John*, 2 vols., ICC (New York: Scribner's, 1920), 1:78.
8. John F. Walvoord, *The Revelation of Jesus Christ* (Chicago: Moody, 1966), p. 78; Robert H. Mounce, *The Book of Revelation*, NICNT (Grand Rapids: Eerdmans, 1977), p. 109.

the presence of an important Jewish synagogue in Sardis as early as the first half of the third century A.D. It cannot be insisted that a synagogue existed there at the end of the first century A.D., because the one discovered was constructed more than a century later. It does, however, suggest that a large community of Jews lived there. Other evidence indicates that the presence of such a community extended back to an earlier date than that of the writing of the Apocalypse and that it may have been a center of the Jewish Diaspora.⁹ This is confirmed by what Josephus says regarding the existence of a wealthy and influential Jewish community in this city.¹⁰

Some evidence reflects the prominence of the imperial cult in Sardis. Several inscriptions indicate this, including one with an excerpt "the city of the Sardians, twice temple-warden, [honored?] the Imperator Caesar Aurelius Antoninus Verus Augustus."¹¹ It competed with other cities of Asia for the privilege of erecting a temple for emperor worship.¹² After the earthquake of A.D. 17, such a temple was erected. The dominant religion of the city, however, appears to be that of the general Anatolian religious forms: a worship of the forces of nature, which were viewed as subject to death but also as having the power of self-reproduction. There are abundant data to enforce the conclusion of a consuming preoccupation with the problems of death and immortality among these people. No unifying feature for all these that would be distinctive to Sardis has yet been discerned, however. The patron deity of the city was Cybele, a well-known goddess of the Anatolian variety, who elsewhere was known as Artemis (Ramsay; Hemer). Beginning in the fourth century B.C., the city had a temple dedicated to Artemis (Walvoord). Remains of this temple are visible on the site of the old city.

Pagan religions throughout the area attributed healing power to their deities, but in Sardis special emphasis focused on the power to restore life to the dead. This special power was connected with a hot springs about two miles from the city. These springs were viewed as visible manifestations of the power of the god of the underworld, which was prominent in the local religious legend (Ramsay).

The founding of the Christian church in Sardis is not mentioned in the NT. Perhaps it was founded in the early fifties A.D. through representatives of the apostle Paul during his three-year stay in

---

9. Ford, *Revelation*, pp. 410-12; Hemer, *Seven Churches*, pp. 136-37.
10. Josephus *Antiquities* 14.10.24; 16.6.4, 6; Ford, *Revelation*, p. 412.
11. Ford, *Revelation*, pp. 410-11.
12. Isbon T. Beckwith, *The Apocalypse of John* (New York: Macmillan, 1919), p. 472. Only nine years after its great earthquake, Sardis was one of eleven cities that bid for the honor of being the site of an imperial temple (Hemer, *Seven Churches*, p. 134).

Ephesus, a city fifty miles to the southwest. What is known from this message is that the church had passed its prime and, like the city in which it was located, its splendor was in the past (Charles). Unlike the church in Laodicea, these Christians did not boast about their riches. They simply grew careless and indifferent to spiritual things and gradually declined over the years.[13] Their church was perhaps the worst of the seven that are described in these chapters (Charles). It was not troubled by persecution from outsiders (Beckwith). Nothing is said about pressure from pagan religions, though doubtless there must have been some. Nor is anything said about opposition from the Jewish community, apostolic frauds, the Nicolaitans, and other sources that were problematic in other cities. Perhaps the city's long history of riotous living made it hard for Christians to resist the temptation to opt for an easier life. The church appears to have been well-thought-of by many, but unlike Jesus, these could not distinguish between the peace of well-being and the peace of death (Caird).

It is to the professing Christian community in such a situation that this fifth message is addressed.

Attributes of the speaker. To the Sardians Jesus introduces Himself as ὁ ἔχων τὰ ἑπτὰ πνεύματα τοῦ θεοῦ καὶ τοὺς ἑπτὰ ἀστέρας (*ho echōn ta hepta pneumata tou theou kai tous hepta asteras,* "the one who has the seven spirits of God and the seven stars"). The identity of "the seven spirits of God" has been discussed in connection with 1:4 above. There the conclusion was that the title is a reference to the Holy Spirit against a background of Zech. 4:1-10. That Christ holds the seven spirits is reminiscent of the doctrine of the procession of the Spirit from Christ (cf. John 15:26; Rom. 8:9). The identification of the seven eyes of Zech. 4:10 with the seven spirits in Rev. 5:6 symbolizes the Spirit's omniscience. His further identification with the seven lamps of Zech. 4:2 (cf. Rev. 4:5) is a picture of the testimony He bears. The author of this message is one who is represented among the churches by the third Person of the Trinity, who knows all and whose purpose is to testify through the seven lampstands established in these seven cities.

Christ also pictures Himself as holding the seven stars. As pointed out in the earlier discussion of 1:16 and 2:1, where the description or its equivalent is also used, this title speaks of Christ with special reference to His control over the churches. Here He reverts to *echōn* used earlier in 1:16 in place of the stronger κρατῶν (*kratōn,* "holding fast") that was used in 2:1. However, the word is still a symbol for authority and control. His constant control is not limited to the mes-

---

13. R. C. H. Lenski, *The Interpretation of St. John's Revelation* (Columbus, Ohio: Lutheran Book Concern, 1935), p. 136.

sengers, represented in the stars, but extends through them to the whole church. He wants to ensure that the lampstand in each community is shining brightly as it should. Sardis represents a situation where the church was surely not emitting spiritual light as it should have been.

A question about this self-designation of Christ pertains to its general nature. In each of the other messages, He describes Himself in terms that are relevant to the local situation, but nothing about this self-designation seems any more applicable to the Sardian situation than it does to the other cities. One suggestion is that the general nature of the description is designed to create special alarm resulting in repentance.[14] It introduces a message of rebuke and solemn denunciation, a tone reflected even in the promise of 3:5. The Lord of the church comes, armed with all the powers of the Spirit, searching the depths of hypocrisy, judging the worthlessness of works not done in faith (Alford). This message is certainly graver than any given thus far.[15] The negative character of this message may easily be granted, but does this in itself explain why the speaker would introduce Himself in terms unrelated to the specific situation He is addressing?

In a sense this message is not too different from the one to Ephesus. To both churches He introduces Himself as one who holds (or holds fast) the seven stars, both churches are said to have fallen from a former position (though the decline at Ephesus was of a much smaller degree) (cf. 2:5; 3:3), both are invited to remember and repent (2:5; 3:3), and the overcomers in both receive promises of "life" (2:7; 3:5) (Hemer). A better, though not altogether satisfying, explanation is to see in Christ's self-description of this fifth message a reference to the adequacy of the *life-giving* Spirit to resolve the problem of the deadness of the Sardian church.[16] Christ, the life-giver (cf. Rev. 1:18), imparts life through the Spirit (cf. Rom. 8:2).[17] In accord with the Holy Spirit's procession from the Son (cf. John 15:26),[18] it is Christ's part to bestow or withhold the powers of the life-giving Spirit on which the life of the church depends (cf. Acts 2:33; Eph. 4:7-8)

---

14. Henry Alford, *The Greek Testament*, 4 vols. (London: Longmans, Green, 1903), 4:579.
15. G. R. Beasley-Murray, *The Book of Revelation*, NCB (Grand Rapids: Eerdmans, 1978), p. 95.
16. James Moffatt, "The Revelation of St. John the Divine," in *The Expositor's Greek Testament*, ed. W. Robertson Nicoll (Grand Rapids: Eerdmans, n.d.), 5:364.
17. George E. Ladd, *A Commentary on the Revelation of John* (Grand Rapids: Eerdmans, 1972), p. 55; Alan F. Johnson, "Revelation," in *EBC*, ed. Frank E. Gaebelein (Grand Rapids: Zondervan, 1981), 12:448.
18. William Lee, "The Revelation of St. John," in *The Holy Bible*, ed. F. C. Cook (London: John Murray, 1881), 4:536.

(Swete). His power is sufficient to meet every need, even to the point of restoring life to those about to die (Hemer). This view cannot account for why no specific reference to life is found in the introduction, but its concept of the implication of such is supported by the position of contemporary Judaism that the two chief works of the Spirit were the inspiration of prophecy and the quickening of the dead (Beasley-Murray).

Knowledge about the people. Through the use of οἶδα (*oida*, "I know"), the Lord once again indicates His absolute clearness of mental vision that photographs all the facts of life as they pass by:[19] οἶδά σου τὰ ἔργα (*oida sou ta erga*, "I know your works"). "Your works" could be the past deeds of the church, which gave them the reputation of being alive, but they are more likely their present ones which, according to v. 2, are woefully inadequate.[20]

The character of their works becomes apparent in the remainder of v. 1: ὅτι ὄνομα ἔχεις ὅτι ζῇς, καὶ νεκρὸς εἶ (*hoti onoma echeis hoti zēs, kai nekros ei*, "that you have a name that you live, and [yet] you are dead"). The initial conjunction *hoti* ("that") introduces an object clause that inferentially states the substance of *sou ta erga* ("your works") (Alford). *Onoma* ("Name") usually refers to a proper name, but it has other well-established uses.[21] Commonly in Hellenistic Greek, it signified all that a name implies, such as rank, authority, fame, reputation, or character.[22] The suggestion that this refers to the proper name of a local church leader, "Zosimus" or "Zotikos," is to be rejected here as being much too fanciful and far-fetched (Alford; Lee). It must rather refer to the reputation of either the church in Sardis corporately (Lenski) or its members individually. At this early date the corporate reputation seems a bit unlikely, so it refers to the gener-

---

19. Swete, *Apocalypse*, p. 24. Οἶδα is also used in 2:2 (see discussion of the term at that point), 9, 13, 19; 3:8, 15.

20. Johnson, "Revelation," 12:448. Ἔργα is also used in 2:2 (see discussion of the term at that point), 5, 6, 19, 22, 23; 3:2, 8, 15. The position of σου is another instance of the vernacular genitive used rather frequently in this book (cf. 2:9, 19 [see discussion found in Additional Notes at this point]; 10:9; 18:4, 5; 21:3) (Charles, *Revelation*, 1:78).

21. Ὄνομα is used four times in this brief message (vv. 1, 4, 5 [twice]). Each time its meaning must be scrutinized because at least three different connotations are intended. In v. 4 it means "individual." The uses in v. 5 may combine the thoughts of "reputation" (v. 1) and "individual" (Hemer, *Seven Churches*, p. 143).

22. Richard Chenevix Trench, *Commentary on the Epistles to the Seven Churches in Asia*, 6th ed. (1897; reprint, Minneapolis: Klock & Klock, 1978), p. 165; Hermann Cremer, *Biblico-Theological Lexicon of New Testament Greek*, trans. William Urwick (Edinburgh: T. & T. Clark, 1895), p. 454; G. Abbott-Smith, *A Manual Greek Lexicon of the New Testament* (Edinburgh: T. & T. Clark, 1937), p. 319.

al reputation of individual Christians in the church (Trench). The use of *name* was a common way to refer to someone who was nominally a Christian, the word often contrasting semblance with reality.[23] In Hebrew thought name denoted inner reality or self-disclosure, but with the Greeks it spoke of an external or superficial estimate.[24]

As *erga* is defined by the first *hoti* clause of v. 1, *onoma* finds its explanation in the second *hoti* ("that") clause. The "name" or reputation of this church is to the effect that they live, i.e., they have spiritual life. *Zēs* ("you live") is from the verb ζάω (*zaō*, "I live"), which needs to be distinguished from the word-group of βίος (*bios*, "life"). The former refers to inner life, the latter to external.[25] In John's writings *zaō* is life that belongs primarily and essentially to God and Christ (cf. 1:18).[26] This is the word's connotation here. The recipients of the message had a semblance of possessing eternal life.

Herein lies the deception, however. "And [yet] you are[27] dead" reflects the superficiality of their Christianity. The so-called adversative use of the conjunction *kai* ("and") introduces this last clause of the verse. It more vividly portrays the contrast between what they were and what they pretended to be than would have been the case if the contrast had been made rhetorically complete by the use of an adversative conjunction such as ἀλλά (*alla*, "but") (Alford).

Nekros ("dead") refers to spiritual death. Physical death might be entertained as an option. A famous cemetery was only seven miles away from the city. Because Sardis was old and ineffective, its congregation was possibly made up of elderly people whose number was dwindling. It may have reached the point that it was unable to make new converts or even to maintain the present level of activity. This was not the case, however. The Sardian church was outwardly active, conveying the impression of liveliness. So *nekros* refers to an inward spiritual condition (Caird). Like the city, the church was existing in the past, so to speak. Its fame and the ministry of its members for Christ in the past were the basis for its present reputation. They had made peace with the surrounding society and fit in comfortably with their culture. The offense of the cross in that community had ceased

---

23. Alford, *Greek Testament*, 4:579; Beckwith, *Apocalypse*, p. 473; A. T. Robertson, *Word Pictures in the New Testament*, 6 vols. (Nashville: Broadman, 1933), 6:313.
24. J. P. M. Sweet, *Revelation* (Philadelphia: Westminster, Pelican, 1979), p. 99.
25. Richard Chenevix Trench, *Synonyms of the New Testament* (reprint; Grand Rapids: Eerdmans, 1953), p. 91.
26. Cremer, *Lexicon*, p. 273.
27. Εἶ is the present indicative of εἰμί, a tense indicating a state of being in present time. While maintaining a name, they had lapsed into a state that was incongruent with it (Swete, *Apocalypse*, p. 48).

to exist. A state of spiritual death pervaded the church (Johnson). They were void of real vitality and genuine fruitfulness. They had sunk into a deep sleep which, if not interrupted, would issue in death (cf. Matt. 8:22; Luke 15:24; Rom. 6:13; 2 Tim. 3:5; Jas. 2:17) (Alford; Swete). In this church and in the one at Laodicea no foes of the churches are mentioned, either inside or outside. Yet they are characterized as "dead" and "lukewarm." The deadness and lukewarmness must have been self-imposed (Lee). Yet conditions had not yet reached the point of no return in this church. Otherwise, Jesus could not have added the words ἃ ἔμελλον ἀποθανεῖν (ha emellon apothanein, "things which are about to die") in the next verse. There is yet enough hope to allow for an appeal to arouse themselves to living activity (v. 2) (Beckwith).

Some are of the opinion that Sardis pictures the deadness of Protestantism in the post-Reformation church.[28] Undoubtedly kinship exists between Sardis and any church that reflects a similar state of spiritual lifelessness, but it is completely unjustifiable to find in these words a prophetic significance pointing to a specific period of church history in John's future.[29] Principles of interpretation dictated by a grammatical and historical approach to the text require the primary application of these words to a church then-existent at the specified location in the Roman province of Asia. Sardis had sunk into a deep sleep and was near death (Alford).

3:2 *State of the church.* The divine prescription for curing the church's spiritual malady was watchfulness: γίνου γρηγορῶν, καὶ στήρισον τὰ λοιπὰ ἃ ἔμελλον ἀποθανεῖν (ginou grēgorōn, kai stērison ta loipa ha emellon apothanein, "prove yourself to be watchful, and establish the remaining things that are about to die"). *Ginou* possibly conveys the idea of "*be* watchful," but this meaning more likely would have been conveyed by a form of εἰμί (eimi, "I am").[30] The sense of "*become* watchful" with the connotation of "*prove yourself to be* watchful" is preferable.[31] Compliance with such a command is by its nature an ongoing process.[32] In paraphrase the sense might be given as "wake up and keep on watching."[33] The call to be constantly alert was

---

28. Walter Scott, *Exposition of the Revelation of Jesus Christ* (Swengel, Pa.: Bible Truth Depot, n.d.), pp. 92-93.
29. There is no exegetical ground for seeing a prophetic significance in any of the seven messages in Revelation 2-3. See separate Excursus on the Chronological Interpretation of Revelation 2-3 at the end of this volume.
30. Robertson, *Word Pictures*, 6:313.
31. F. J. A. Hort, *The Apocalypse of St. John* (London: Macmillan, 1908), p. 32; Hemer, *Seven Churches*, p. 143.
32. Note the focus on linear action by the present tense of γίνου.
33. Alford, *Greek Testament*, 4:580. The continuing nature of the action of a present periphrastic construction such as γίνου γρηγορῶν is difficult to

an invitation to a radical reversal of the Sardian believers' current attitude. Their complacency had lured them into surrendering their identification with Christ and His cause in favor of allowing their lives to blend more completely with their non-Christian surroundings (Johnson). Two notable incidents in the city's past history served as vivid reminders of the results of a lack of vigilance (Charles; Walvoord; Ladd; Hemer). Both in the fall of the city to the Persians (549 B.C.) and in its later conquest by Antiochus the Great (195 B.C.), local tragedies could have been averted through even a minimal amount of watchfulness, but there was none. The same was about to happen to the Christian community at the hands of its spiritual enemy. A quick return to vigilance was needed.

Jesus also commands the Sardian Christians to establish the worthwhile elements that remained from healthier days of their Christian experience. *Ta loipa* ("the remaining things") carries the force of "that which survives," a rather unusual meaning that is paralleled in Rev. 8:13; 9:20; 11:13 (Hemer). Being neuter gender, it obviously includes "those few remaining graces, which in your spiritual deadly slumber are not yet quite extinct" (Alford). The neuter can also include individuals viewed as living realities too, however.[34] The pressing need was for a reconstruction of both persons and principles on a solid foundation (Charles). That Jesus would issue such a command as is found in the urgent[35] *stērison* ("establish") shows that "you are dead" of v. 1 does not have an absolute sense.[36] Starting with wholesome spiritual principles and individuals that yet remained in the congregation, the church was to erect once again the impressive spiritual fortress that had once stood in this pagan city.

The remaining values were still declining as Jesus issued this command. In *ha emellon apothanein* He notes the Christians' imminent death. The tenses of the verbs picture them as having been on the verge of dying in the past and continuing up to the present moment with the imminent possibility of losing the last spark of life.[37] To respond positively to this command would be to avoid this ap-

---

capture in simple translation. A descriptive paraphrase such as this captures more of the elements of the meaning of the Greek text.

34. Robertson, *Word Pictures*, 6:314.

35. The verb στήρισον is an aorist imperative whose normal force denotes urgency: "Establish the remaining things, do it now!"

36. Trench, *Seven Churches*, p. 209.

37. Lenski, *Revelation*, p. 128. The imperfect ἔμελλον is epistolary, from the standpoint of the recipients of the message looking back to the time of John's vision, i.e., the time of the Lord's inquiry into the church's spiritual state (Swete, *Apocalypse*, p. 49; Lee, "Revelation," 4:537). The aorist ἀποθανεῖν is punctiliar, looking at the precise moment of death.

proaching death. A glimmer of hope is extended to this faltering church.

Clarification of the reason for the warning comes in the remainder of v. 2: οὐ γὰρ εὕρηκά σου *τὰ ἔργα πεπληρωμένα ἐνώπιον τοῦ θεοῦ μου (ou gar heurēka sou ta erga peplērōmena enōpion tou theou mou, "for I have not found your works fulfilled before My God"). Jesus' investigation[38] had yielded the conclusion that the general character and condition of the church were lacking (Beckwith). Peplērōmena ("fulfilled") could convey the notion that there remained an incompleteness in the full number of their deeds,[39] but the harsh tone of the message demands that it refer to the quality rather than the quantity of the works.[40] Though they were sufficient to give them a name before men, they were sadly deficient before God. Works that please God must proceed from a motivation of living faith, such a faith as was obviously missing in this church (Alford; Mounce). This is not the picture of a church in Sardis that was on its way and had not yet arrived. Unfortunately, it was stagnant and going nowhere. "Before My[41] God" is a reminder that God's evaluation is quite different from man's. Man looks on the outward appearance, but God on the heart (cf. 1 Sam 16:7).

3:3 Two occurrences of οὖν (oun, "therefore") mark out two parts of v. 3. The former introduces a gracious call to take advantage of the solution to the believers' problem of stagnancy (Lenski): μνημόνευε οὖν πῶς εἴληφας καὶ ἤκουσας, καὶ τήρει, καὶ μετανόησον (mnēmoneue oun pōs eilēphas kai ēkousas, kai tērei, kai metanoēson, "remember therefore how you have received and heard, and keep [strengthening what remains], and repent"). This portion of v. 3 prescribes the reme-

---

38. Εὕρηκά conveys the idea that the findings have been weighed and that the conclusion from the earlier process remains the same as it was initially. The perfect tense also allows that the search had not yet ended (Swete, *Apocalypse*, p. 50).

39. E. W. Hengstenberg, *The Revelation of St. John*, 2 vols. (New York: Carter and Brothers, 1852), 1:170; Caird, *Revelation*, p. 48; Johnson, "Revelation," 12:448.

40. J. B. Smith, *A Revelation of Jesus Christ* (Scottdale, Pa.: Herald, 1961), p. 83; Johnson, "Revelation," 12:448.

41. Seven other times in these messages Christ uses "My" to allude to His relationship with His Father and God (E. W. Bullinger, *The Apocalypse* or *"The Day of the Lord"* [London: Eyre and Spottiswoode, n.d.], p. 193). Cf. 2:27; 3:5, 12 [four times], 21. This recalls that He is Son of Man as well as Son of God (cf. 2:18) (Swete, *Apocalypse*, p. 50). "My God" from the lips of Christ occurs only here, four times in 3:12, and as a part of His cry of separation from the Father during His crucifixion (Matt. 27:46; Mark 15:34), and in anticipation of His ascension (John 20:17). "My Father" comes from His lips more than thirty-five times in the NT outside this book, mostly in the gospels of Matthew (13 times) and John (19 times).

dy for dying conditions in the church, continuing the command of v. 2 to reconstruct the impressive spiritual fortress that once stood in the city (note the verb *stērison*, v. 2).[42] Reconstruction can be accomplished in three steps: remember, keep, and repent.

Mnēmoneue ("remember") is not a bid to the readers to recall something from the past, but a command to keep in the forefront of their attention their rich spiritual heritage of the past as a motivating force in their restoration.[43] The basis for renewal is to bear constantly[44] in mind the manner in which they had received and heard the gospel. As elsewhere with other NT writers, the salutary effect of reflection upon one's first experience of salvation is recognized (cf. Gal. 5:7; Col. 2:6; Heb. 3:14; 10:32) (Smith). The Greek perfect and aorist tenses are used in the two verbs *eilēphas* ("you have received") and *ēkousas* ("you heard"), indicating that the hearing of the gospel was a momentary act and that results from the reception still abide. The deposit of doctrine that the church received was permanent (Alford; Swete; Charles; Mounce).

Tērei ("keep") states the second recommended step for restoration. This command, like the one to remember, is a present imperative to emphasize the need to "keep on keeping."[45] With no stated object, the reader must supply one from the context. One suggestion has been to supply "the gospel," the body of truth just alluded to in connection with the receiving and hearing, but this would require the earlier *pōs* to mean "what," a possibility that must be ruled out. The best object to supply comes from v. 2 in connection with the command to establish (or strengthen) the remaining things. Here is a call to devote

---

42. As often is the case in the gospel of John and the Apocalypse, οὖν resumes and coordinates what follows with the preceding (cf. Rev. 1:19; 2:5, 16; 3:19) (Swete, *Apocalypse*, p. 50; Lee, "Revelation," 4:537; Robertson, *Word Pictures*, 6:314). The second occurrence of the conjunction in v. 3 is also to be identified as the "resumptive" or "continuative" use of the conjunction. Because the latter term continues γίνου γρηγορῶν (v. 2) as the former one resumes the στήρισον of the previous verse in a chiastic arrangement, the flow of vv. 2-3 may be captured by "in strengthening the remaining things, remember how you have received . . . ; if you do not become watchful as I have just advised you to do, I will come as a thief."

43. Robertson, *Word Pictures*, 6:314; Leon Morris, *The Revelation of St. John*, TNTC (Grand Rapids: Eerdmans, 1969), p. 76.

44. Μνημόνευε is a present imperative, carrying an emphasis on continuous action.

45. Alford, *Greek Testament*, 4:580; Morris, *Revelation*, p. 76. Τηρέω is a characteristically Johannine word, being used eighteen times in his writings (e.g., John 2:8; 14:15; 1 John 2:3; cf. Rev. 1:3) (Harald Riesenfeld, "τηρέω, τήρησις, etc.," in *TDNT*, ed. Gerhard Kittel and Gerhard Friedrich, trans. and ed. Geoffrey W. Bromiley [Grand Rapids: Eerdmans, 1972], 8:142; Lee, 4:537). It signifies earnest attention (Sweet, *Revelation*, p. 99).

earnest attention to rebuilding on what was left from the earlier days of fruitfulness: "keep on giving earnest attention to the need to strengthen the leftover vitality." The dependence of the initial *oun* of v. 3 upon the verb *stērison* of v. 2, as noted above, lends support to this understanding.

Metanoēson ("repent") gives the third step on the road to spiritual recovery for this church. In contrast to the first two commands, which require a continued mental perspective, this one calls for a quick and decisive change of thought and behavior.[46] The Sardians needed to remember continually how they had received and heard the gospel, to give continued earnest attention to the need to strengthen the remnants of spiritual vitality, and to repent at that very moment in confession of and in turning away from their spiritual lethargy. Like the Ephesian church (2:5), they were to recall their former outlook and achievements, and do an immediate about-face in order to return to that condition. In the NT μετανοέω (*metanoeō*, "I repent") and its cognates take on the meaning of a regret over wrongdoing in the past, which regret results in a change of lifestyle for the better. It contrasts with another verb, μεταμέλομαι (*metamelomai*, "I regret"), which refers to a remorseful desire to undo things already done but has no implication of a change of heart as does *metanoeō*.[47]

The second οὖν (*oun*, "therefore") of v. 3 resumes the γίνου γρηγορῶν (*ginou grēgorōn*, "prove yourself to be watchful") of v. 2 (Swete): ἐὰν οὖν μὴ γρηγορήσῃς, ἥξω ὡς κλέπτης, καὶ οὐ μὴ γνῷς ποίαν ὥραν ἥξω ἐπὶ σέ (*ean oun mē grēgorēsēs, hēxō hōs kleptēs, kai ou mē gnōs poian hōran hēxō epi se*, "if therefore you do not watch, I will come as a thief, and you will in no way know what hour I will come upon you"). The earlier *oun* ("therefore") of the verse introduced a remedy for the dying condition of the church, but this one poses a threat that is predicated on an assumption that the remedy will not be accepted (Lenski). That a severe warning should follow so closely the prescription for a spiritual cure is somewhat surprising. Apparently Jesus did not anticipate that the church would accept His terms of restoration. Their present evil state was almost hopeless, as indicated in vv. 1 and 2, so it was highly improbable that they would turn back at this point (Alford).

---

46. Alford, *Greek Testament*, 4:380; Robertson, *Word Pictures*, 6:314; Morris, *Revelation*, p. 314. Μετανόησον is an aorist imperative rather than a present imperative.
47. Trench, *Synonyms*, p. 255; W. F. Arndt and F. Gingrich, *A Greek-English Lexicon of the New Testament and Other Early Christian Literature*, 2d ed. (Cambridge: U. Press, 1979), p. 512.

Grēgorēsēs ("you watch") alludes to their needed response in the same terms as in v. 2, but with a shift in emphasis to the initial act of recovery. The action of the aorist verb is well portrayed in "if you do not *wake up*."[48] They were still spiritually dead (cf. v. 1), not yet having awakened from their lethargy (Alford).

Failure to wake up exposed them to a possible surprise coming of the Lord. His coming[49] as a thief to Sardis has been the object of the same two interpretations as His coming to Ephesus (2:5). Some have made it a special coming in judgment upon this church at Sardis.[50] Acknowledging that the formula of coming as a thief usually applies to the suddenness of Christ's second coming, they see the formula applied here to a partial and special advent for judgment of a single church (Alford; Lee; Beasley-Murray). Another supporting observation cites Rev. 3:20 as another case where parousia language is used in reference to the present experience of Christians (Beasley-Murray). What this explanation fails to provide, however, is a reason the consequences of the coming are not stated. In other alleged cases of Christ's coming for special judgment (cf. 2:5, 16, 22-23), consequences are explicitly stated, but here no penal result is given. Apparently it is understood to be Christ's punishment of disloyalty at His second advent.

On the other side, support for a reference to Christ's second advent is convincing. The close connection between the coming of the Lord and present watchfulness indicates that the sin at Sardis included a failure to watch for the Lord's return.[51] The simile of coming as a thief is elsewhere used exclusively to refer to Christ's second advent (cf. Matt. 24:43; Luke 12:39; 1 Thess. 5:2; 2 Pet. 3:10; Rev. 16:15).[52] It was understood this way by four other NT writers: Matthew, Luke, Paul and Peter (Beasley-Murray). As in Paul's instruction to those at Thessalonica, this is a coming of the day of the Lord as a thief comes on those who are unprepared for His coming (Bullinger). The urgent call for repentance in these messages is based on the prospect of an imminent end.[53] This is the language that Jesus Him-

---

48. Robertson, *Word Pictures*, 6:314. The aorist is ingressive.
49. The same verb, ἥκω, is used here as occurs in 2:25 to refer to Christ's coming. Though the form ἥξω is used in 3:3 (twice) as it is in 2:25, here it is future indicative rather than aorist subjunctive. The spelling is the same, but sentence structure differs in the two verses.
50. Alford, *Greek Testament*, 4:581; Lenski, *Revelation*, p. 131; Frederick A. Tatford, *Prophecy's Last Word* (London: Pickering and Inglis, 1947), p. 61.
51. Trench, *Seven Churches*, pp. 170-71; Charles, *Revelation*, 1:81; Robert Govett, *The Apocalypse Expounded by Scripture* (London: Charles J. Thynne, 1920), p. 67.
52. Beckwith, *Apocalypse*, p. 474; Robertson, *Word Pictures*, 6:314.
53. J. Behm, "νοέω, νοῦς, etc.," in *TDNT*, 4:1004.

self used earlier when telling the twelve to watch for His return (Charles). John shared with the rest of the early church a belief in the imminent advent of Christ (Caird). A possible negative outcome of this advent is used here as an incentive for Christians in Sardis to wake up and stay alert, a motivaton used elsewhere.

As indicated earlier in connection with Ephesus (2:5), Pergamum (2:16), and Thyatira (2:22), some object to an eschatological coming of Christ here because such could not be conditioned upon nonrepentance in one city (Caird; Ladd; Morris; Mounce). The objection poses a difficult obstacle, but not an impossible one. In the ultimate sense, the timing of Christ's return is sovereignly determined by the Father (cf. Acts 1:7). From a human perspective, however, NT revelation shows that the coming will coincide with several other developments. It will coincide with the national repentance of Israel, as Peter declares in Acts 3:19-21. Both the return of Christ and Israel's repentance will follow upon the completion of the Body of Christ, according to Rom. 11:25-26. If Israel and the church will reach a certain spiritual level at the point when Christ returns, why not the rest of the world, known biblically as "Gentiles" (cf. 1 Cor. 10:32)? One mark of the degeneracy of the Gentile world is certainly the worsening moral condition of the professing Christian church as it comes under the influence of its surrounding culture. In the sovereign purpose of God, these three human indicators, the repentance of Israel, the fullness of the Body of Christ, and the bottoming out of Gentile morality, will occur simultaneously, and Christ will return. A threat of an eschatological coming of Christ to punish sleeping Sardis fits well into this broader picture.

To come as a thief is a proverbial expression for unexpectedness.[54] The figurative lesson of unexpectedness is reinforced by an explicit statement to this effect at the end of v. 3: *kai ou mē gnōs poian hōran hēxō epi se* ("and you will in no way know what hour I will come upon you"). In no uncertain terms, the Lord declares the church's ignorance of the timing of His return.[55] No one will be able to pinpoint the hour of His return, and so everyone will be caught by surprise. Of all people, citizens of this city could appreciate what it was

---

54. Morris, *Revelation*, p. 76. The choice of κλέπτης instead of λῃστής is appropriate. The former word depicts a thief who does his work with stealth, fraud, and secrecy, and the latter one is a robber who acts violently and in the open (Trench, *Synonyms*, p. 160; Marvin R. Vincent, *Word Studies in the New Testament* [New York: Scribner's, 1906], 2:591).
55. Alford, *Greek Testament*, 4:567; Robertson, *Word Pictures*, 6:314. The double negative οὐ μὴ with the aorist subjunctive γνῷς expresses an emphatic negation about the future more strongly than any other Greek construction.

to be completely surprised by the arrival of an opponent. The city had been captured twice in its history, once in 549 B.C. by Cyrus of Persia and again in 195 B.C. by Antiochus the Great, while its inhabitants were indifferently resting in its supposed impregnability. Would Christians there allow the same to happen to them at the hands of one whom they had made their spiritual opponent?

Jesus here repeats teaching that John had heard Him give many years before, lessons recorded in Matt. 24:42-43 and Luke 12:39. The difference here is the obvious application to a specific case where the watchfulness He had earlier commanded had been completely disregarded. Both this verse and Rev. 16:15 are based on this synoptic gospel tradition (Hemer). There are a remarkable number of allusions to the teachings of Christ in the gospels in this brief message to Sardis.

3:4 In recording the Lord's message to this church, John uses the strong adversative ἀλλὰ (*alla*, "but") to contrast the general character of the church with those few members who had not soiled their garments:[56] ἀλλὰ ἔχεις ὀλίγα ὀνόματα ἐν Σάρδεσιν ἃ οὐκ ἐμόλυναν τὰ ἱμάτια αὐτῶν (*alla echeis oliga onomata en Sardesin ha ouk emolynan ta himatia autōn*, "But you have a few names in Sardis that have not defiled their garments"). The church had a reputation for being alive (v. 1), but only a few of its number lived up to that reputation. The majority of members were a contradiction to what they as a church supposedly were.[57]

Onomata ("names") takes the sense it has in Acts 1:15 and Rev. 11:13, that of "persons," a meaning common in Koine usage.[58] The frequent use of this noun is one of the unusual characteristics of this message (cf. also 3:1, 5 [twice]). In each verse, however, it carries a different sense. These faithful people had not soiled their garments. *Emolynan* means "smear," "befoul," or "pollute," not "color" or "stain," which is the meaning of μιαίνω (*miainō*).[59] *Himatia* is the general word for garment, in contrast with a number of other words

---

56. Swete, *Apocalypse*, p. 50; Merrill C. Tenney, *Interpreting Revelation* (Grand Rapids: Eerdmans, 1957), p. 64.

57. Swete, *Apocalypse*, p. 50; Hengstenberg, *Revelation*, 1:172; Scott, *Revelation*, p. 96.

58. Lee, "Revelation," 4:537; G. Adolf Deissmann, *Bible Studies*, trans. by Alexander Grieve, 2d ed. (Edinburgh: T. & T. Clark, 1909), pp. 196-97; Robertson, *Word Pictures*, 6:315. The suggestion that ὀνόματα is synonymous with "reputation" (Hengstenberg, *Revelation*, 1:172) does not have much merit. Though the same noun in v. 1 smacks of empty profession, such a connotation is not present in this verse (Alford, *Greek Testament*, 4:581).

59. Trench, *Seven Churches*, p. 173; Robertson, *Word Pictures*, 6:315; Lenski, *Revelation*, p. 131.

sometimes translated the same way but referring to more specific kinds of garments.[60] Quite possibly this is an indirect reference to the local trade of woolen goods and dyed stuffs in Sardis (Moffatt). In the custom of pagan worship of the surrounding area, soiled clothes disqualified the worshiper and dishonored the god he tried to worship (Charles). This perhaps led to the figurative language chosen by the Lord here.

A number of suggestions about what it means to defile one's garments have been forthcoming. Among the less persuasive ones are the following, along with the reasons for rejecting them. (1) One idea is that the expression refers to the soiling of the conscience, but this view is too specific and no reference to the conscience is found in the context (Alford). (2) Another says it means the remnant had not soiled its robes of baptismal purity, but again, this confuses the picture because no reference to baptism is found in the context (Alford). (3) A further suggestion is that the words commend the remnant for abstaining from contact with the dead body of the rest of the church, but the statement of the verse contradicts this: the remnant had remained in the church and had not separated (Alford). (4) It refers to abstaining from moral impurity, particularly sexual immorality because this is the meaning of the verb in Rev. 14:4 (Moffatt). This view restricts unnecessarily the way in which the defilement can be contracted, however.

A suggestion that has a little more support is the one that connects the statement with Jude 23, where the soiling of the garment is traced to the flesh. The metaphor in Jude 23 is different from the present one, however (Hort). A more persuasive view holds that this is the figure of not having soiled their robes of righteousness put on by faith. This is the meaning of white garments in Rev. 19:8, and coincides with the idea of unsoiled robes washed white in the blood of the Lamb in 7:14 (Alford). It also fits with the broader phraseology of Scripture that speaks of the garments of salvation (Ps. 132:16; Isa. 61:10), being clothed with righteousness (Job 29:14; Ps. 132:9; Isa. 59:17; Eph. 6:14; Rev. 19:11, 14), and a robe of righteousness (Isa. 61:10) (Smith). Nevertheless, though righteousness by faith is unquestionably in the background, it is strange to speak of it as refraining from soiling one's garments.

Even closer to the truth is the proposal that freedom from defilement refers to keeping one's self from indulging in the pagan impurities at Sardis. Concession to heathen impurities had led to compromise and spiritual deadness (Mounce). Others had accommodated to the prevailing standards of a pagan city, but these believers had

---

60. Trench, *Synonyms*, p. 184; Arndt and Gingrich, *Lexicon*, pp. 376-77.

not. Soiling connotes a mingling of pagan practices with a Christian profession, thereby defiling the purity of one's alleged relationship with Christ (Johnson). These had not soiled their clothes, spiritually speaking, thereby not disqualifying themselves from the worship of the true God (Moffatt). The thing that spoils this view is the absence of any reference in this message to concessions made to heathen impurities. Such are found in other messages, but none in this one.

The best solution to what it means to keep one's garments unsoiled, therefore, is a general one. The language refers to those who have not soiled the purity of their Christian lives by falling into sin (Alford; Beckwith). This aligns with references to soiling in Rev. 7:14 and 22:14, both of which suggest contamination in general (Moffatt; Beckwith). Because the source of the potential contamination is nowhere indicated, it is best to adopt the broadest explanation and note that any sin into which Christians may fall can contaminate. The refreshing thing about this remnant in Sardis is that members had not fallen into sinful practices and so had remained pure in contrast to most of their fellow churchmen.

To this group that has avoided falling into sin Christ promises a future reward:[61] καὶ περιπατήσουσιν μετ' ἐμοῦ ἐν λευκοῖς (*kai peripatēsousin met' emou en leukois*, "and they will walk with Me in white"). The reward continues to picture ethical standards as a garment. Because of their refusal to defile their garments while under great cultural pressure to do so, Christ will replace their humanly preserved, clean garments with those that are white by divine standards. Because of the earlier contrast between soiled garments of sinful church members and unsoiled garments of faithful Christians, it seems evident that the whiteness of these new garments stands for holiness and purity (Beasley-Murray). Such garments are reserved for such as Christ Himself (Matt. 17:2; Mark 9:3; Luke 9:29), unfallen angels (Matt. 28:3; Mark 16:5; Rev. 15:6), the two men at Christ's ascension (Acts 1:10), and the glorified church (Rev. 19:8, 14) (Smith). White symbolizes purity in 7:9, 13 also.[62] Anticipation of wearing such apparel and enjoying the personal companionship of Christ provides ample incentive for continued faithfulness for the few in Sardis who were standing against the tide of apathy that had gripped the majority in the church.

---

61. This is the first eschatological promise to any of the churches that is not part of an overcomer statement (Charles, *Revelation*, 1:81). It expresses intimate fellowship with the Lord as His companions in the Messianic kingdom (Beckwith, *Apocalypse*, p. 475). The language of walking with God recalls the ethical walk of Enoch whose life pleased God (cf. Gen. 5:22) (Hort, *Apocalypse*, p. 33; Swete, *Apocalypse*, p. 51).

62. Robertson, *Word Pictures*, 6:315.

Other suggestions of what it means to walk in white are worthy of mention. A reference to white baptismal robes (Swete) is a bit far-fetched and unsupported in the context. A reference to Christ's glory at the transfiguration (Matt. 17:2) (Hort) is at best a secondary idea. A reference to spiritual bodies awaiting the faithful in heaven is a little more intriguing. In the Apocalypse spiritual bodies are referred to this way several times (6:11; 7:9, 13-14; 19:8).[63] This parallels the teaching of 2 Cor. 5:1, 4, where human bodies are viewed as garments to be taken off and spiritual bodies to be put on (cf. Matt. 13:43; 1 Cor. 15:43, 49, 54; Phil. 3:21) (Charles). Such garments are twice assumed at the resurrection (cf. Rev. 6:11; 7:9) (Lee). The formidable obstacle faced by this view is Rev. 19:8*b*, which identifies the white garments as the righteous deeds of the saints (Beasley-Murray).

The view that says walking with Christ in white refers to justification or the imputed righteousness of the saints is also worth attention (Morris). This figure is derived from an allusion to the itinerant ministry of Jesus in Galilee (cf. John 6:66). To walk with Christ is to enjoy the benefit of His justification (Mounce). The picture suggests associations with festivity (Eccles. 9:8), victory (2 Macc. 11:8), justification (Rev. 7:9 ff.; 19:8, 14), and the heavenly state or glorification (Dan. 7:9; Matt. 17:2), which all meet here. However, justification that is consummated in glorification dominates the context (Swete). One cannot question that those who walk in white are none other than the justified ones (Mounce), but there is nothing to show that this is the primary focus of the image of walking in white.

The suggestion that this figure would have recalled the pure white togas worn by Roman citizens at times in great triumph is tempting.[64] Such would have been of great encouragement in a city whose history was dominated by defeat and unfulfilled promise. Paul draws upon such imagery in Col. 2:15 and 2 Cor. 2:14-16 (Hemer). The problem is that the inhabitants of this city were so far removed from the city of Rome that they had probably never witnessed a victory celebration. Though they may have heard about it, the chance that this would come to their minds in a context such as this is remote.

So it is wisest to return to the primary notion of practical purity that will be imparted to the redeemed in their association with Christ, first in heaven and then on earth when He establishes His kingdom here. The worthiness of the faithful is given as a further reason for this promise: ὅτι ἄξιοί[65] εἰσιν (*hoti axioi eisin*, "because

---

63. Ibid.
64. Ramsay, *Seven Churches*, pp. 386-88; Hemer, *Seven Churches*, p. 147.
65. The gender of ἄξιοι is masculine in agreement with the sense of ὀνόματα, which is grammatically neuter. Because the noun refers to persons, it is natural for an adjective modifying it to be placed in the masculine gender (Alford, *Greek Testament*, 4:581).

they are worthy"). This worthiness does not derive ultimately from their own merit, however. The rest of the Apocalypse is against this (cf. 5:9-10) (Alford; Lenski). A relative worthiness of the saints, such as is in view here, is mentioned in a number of NT passages outside the Apocalypse (cf. Luke 20:35; Eph. 4:1; Phil. 1:27; Col. 1:10; 1 Thess. 2:12; 2 Thess. 1:5). Such must be the sense here (Swete). Elsewhere in the Apocalypse ἄξιος (*axios,* "worthy") is used in a good sense only when referring to God (4:11) and Christ (5:9). It is used in a bad sense in 16:6.[66]

3:5 *Promise to the overcomer.* According to this message to Sardis, the overcomer has a threefold blessing to anticipate. The first of these is being clothed in white garments: ὁ νικῶν *οὕτως περιβαλεῖται ἐν ἱματίοις λευκοῖς (ho nikōn houtōs peribaleitai en himatiois leukois,* "the one who overcomes thus will be clothed in white garments"). Coming on the heels of a similar eschatological promise that is not addressed to the overcomer (3:4), this promise adds insight to an understanding of what overcoming means. Overcoming is the same as not falling prey to the failure referred to earlier in the message, because walking with Christ in white is the hope offered to those who had not defiled their garments (3:4) as had the majority in the church (3:1-2).[67] The correspondence between the promise of v. 4 and the first promise of v. 5 unmistakably shows the overcomer to be in the class of the faithful remnant in the church (Alford). Of course, others in the church could join this faithful remnant through repentance (cf. 3:3), thereby becoming overcomers. Their failure to do so, however, would leave them in the category of nonovercomers who could expect the penalty assigned in 3:3.

The symbolic significance of being clothed, presumably by Christ,[68] in white garments has been variously explained. The suggestions here are even more numerous than for the "white" symbol in 3:4, including purity,[69] glory (cf. Rev. 3:18; 6:11; 7:9, 13-14; 19:14) (Johnson), victory (Alford), purity and victory (Caird), light,[70] sanctity (Hort), righteousness (Walvoord), and the color of heaven that includes purity, perfection, and glory (Swete; Lee). As shown already in the discussion of the color in 3:4, purity is the best connotation to

---

66. Robertson, *Word Pictures,* 6:315.
67. Moffatt, "Revelation," 5:364. Another instance that demonstrates the connection of overcoming with remaining faithful is the promise of 2:10 (Beckwith, *Apocalypse,* p. 475).
68. The verb is middle voice: "have himself clothed." Here and in Rev. 4:4 this verb is followed by ἐν and the locative of the item of clothing, but usually in this book the item is expressed by the accusative, whether the verb be middle or passive (cf. 7:9, 13; 10:1; 11:3; 12:1; 17:4; 18:16; 19:8, 13) (Swete, *Apocalypse,* p. 51; Robertson, *Word Pictures,* 6:315).
69. Robertson, *Word Pictures,* 6:315.
70. Trench, *Seven Churches,* pp. 172, 176.

attach to the white garments. This is the meaning of white robes in 7:9, 13 and elsewhere, and provides the best understanding of the promise here too (cf. Matt. 28:3).[71]

Being clothed "in white garments" has suggested to some a picture of the resurrected spiritual bodies of the saints, largely on the basis of a parallel with 2 Cor. 5:1, 4, where human bodies are viewed as garments to be taken off.[72] This view encounters difficulty in Rev. 19:8b, however. There the bright linen is equated with the righteous deeds of the saints (Beasley-Murray). Hence, it is better, as shown in earlier discussion of the white garments, to see them as symbolic of the eternal state of purity (Swete). The source of the image is doubtless Zech. 3:1-10 where the filthy garments of Joshua the high priest are replaced with clean ones. Overcomers are linked to the priesthood and priestly functions through this promise (cf. Ex. 28:39, 42; Ezek. 44:17, 18) (Alford; Lee; Moffatt). The thought pertains to their acceptability to God and the divine recognition of their office and ministry as priests of God (Walvoord).

The second promise to the Sardian overcomer advances the thought of the priestly purity of the overcomer: καὶ οὐ μὴ ἐξαλείψω τὸ ὄνομα αὐτοῦ ἐκ τῆς βίβλου τῆς ζωῆς (*kai ou mē exaleipsō to onoma autou ek tēs biblou tēs zōēs*, "and I will in no way wipe his name from the book of life"). Ἐξαλείφω (*Exaleiphō*, "I wipe out") speaks of the erasure of a name from a written page. The same verb in Acts 3:19 describes the blotting out of sins. In the LXX, it is used for the concept of "blotting names out from under heaven" in connection with an act of judgment (cf. Deut. 9:14; 25:19; 29:19). The same verb is also used in Ps. 68:29 (LXX; Ps. 69:28 in the English text) to speak of blotting out from the book of life the names of God's enemies. In the present verse it is a promise of deliverance rather than judgment through having one's name remain in the book of life.

The implications of not having one's name blotted out of the book of life have occasioned widespread discussion. One school of thought focuses on the analogous threat implied by the promise, the threat of having one's name removed from the book by the loss of salvation.[73] Revelation 20:12 shows that the absence of a person's name from the book means exclusion from the kingdom (Lee; Moffatt). Those whose loyalty to Christ wanes have no claim on eternal life (Johnson). The exalted Lord has power to strike names from the pages because He

---

71. Robertson, *Word Pictures*, 6:315.
72. Lee, "Revelation," 4:538; Charles, *Revelation*, 1:82; Moffatt, "Revelation," 5:364-65; Robertson, *Word Pictures*, 6:315.
73. John Peter Lange, *The Revelation of John*, Lange's Commentary, ed. E. R. Craven (Grand Rapids: Zondervan, 1968), p. 127.

wrote the book of life (cf. 13:8; 21:27) (Beasley-Murray). The next part of the verse about confessing the overcomer's name before the Father and His angels, a clear reminiscence of Christ's earlier words recorded in the synoptic gospels (cf. Matt. 10:32; Mark 8:38; Luke 9:26: 12:8), appears to support the possibility of losing one's salvation. In the face of this evidence, however, to assume that remaining in the book of life rests upon continuing loyalty to Christ ignores the fact that before all human faith or striving lie the divine choice and the divine initiative.[74] The worthiness of the faithful mentioned in 3:4 is based on divine grace (cf. 7:14) (Scott). It is incomprehensible that it could be lost through human unfaithfulness. Couple with these considerations the fact that Ps. 69:28 has the names of the wicked in the book of life, and the basis for an assumption that this refers to a loss of one's salvation is eliminated.

Another understanding is to take the "blotting out" as an example of litotes, a figure of speech in which an affirmative is expressed by the negative of a contrary statement. Coming by way of a denial of the opposite, this is an understatement to express emphatically the assurance that the overcomer's name will be retained in the book of life.[75] The purpose of the promise is to provide certainty and assurance to those who are "worthy" (cf. v. 4), not to indicate anything about the fate of those who do not overcome.[76] The message purposes to end on a note of hope and encouragement (Morris). The overcomer will be vindicated in the judgment. His name will not be removed from the roll of the kingdom, and he will enjoy eternal life (Beckwith; Beasley-Murray). The emphasis of this viewpoint is certainly valid in the context of the message to Sardis, but it fails to deal with one important factor: the promise to the overcomer is an empty one unless the possibility exists that such a blotting out could occur. What incentive is furnished by being promised deliverance from something that could not happen? Furthermore, the psalmist prays for the blotting out of the names from the book of life (Ps. 69:28), and in so doing

---

74. Caird, *Revelation*, p. 49; Beasley-Murray, *Revelation*, p. 98. Caird disputes this point by arguing that predestination to John was conditional, i.e., one cannot earn a place in the book of life, but he can forfeit that place. He sees the decrees of God as not being irreversible. The acceptance or the rejection of man may change them (Caird, *Revelation*, pp. 49-50). Such rationalization makes man the final court of appeal, however, and undervalues the sovereignty of God.
75. Swete, *Apocalypse*, p. 51; Alford, *Greek Testament*, 4:582; Morris, *Revelation*, p. 77; Lenski, *Revelation*, p. 134.
76. Lee, "Revelation," 4:538; Charles Caldwell Ryrie, *Revelation*, Everyman's Bible Commentary (Chicago: Moody, 1968), p. 28; Walvoord, *Revelation*, p. 82; Ladd, *Revelation*, p. 58; Homer Hailey, *Revelation, an Introduction and Commentary* (Grand Rapids: Baker, 1979), p. 147.

indicates that such is a distinct possibility. The "not blotting" referred to in this verse must be more than a figure of speech.

Another approach to this book-of-life issue is to identify the book with civic registers of living citizens that were kept in Sardis and other cities. When a person died, the name of that person was erased from the register (Moffatt; Hemer). This interpretation at times distinguishes the book of life in 3:5 from the books that are mentioned in 13:8 and 21:27, saying that the present book can have names removed from it because it includes those who merely profess Christ as well as those whose relationship to Him is genuine (Scott). Support for this assumption is cited in 3:1 where "a name that you live" indicates empty profession. Those whose names have been inscribed in this book, whether by outward admission to the church in baptism or by becoming living members of Christ by faith, if they endure to the end as His soldiers and servants and obtain the victory, will not have their names erased as will those who are mere professed members (Alford). This view fails to take several significant points into consideration. Ὄνομα (*Onoma*, "name") in 3:1 is used in quite a different sense from what it bears in 3:5. It has no bearing on this issue. This explanation fails to indicate why a person with an empty profession had his or her name written in the book of life in the first place. Civic registers contained only the names of the *living* (Swete). Perhaps the greatest shortcoming of this solution is its dissociation of the book of life here with the same object mentioned in 13:8 and 21:27. There is no ground for this.

A fourth possible solution remains for the problem posed by the nonerasure from the book of life. It is generally conceded that the concept behind the book of life has OT roots traceable all the way back to Ex. 32:32-33 (Hemer). One proposal is to distinguish the OT book of life from the NT one by theorizing that removal in the OT meant loss of physical life, and in the NT, loss of spiritual life (Sweet). This distinction is arbitrary, however. Consistency demands that both refer to relegation to spiritual death.

In both the Exodus passage and in Ps. 69:28, blotting out (ἐξαλείφω [*exaleiphō*, "I wipe away"] is the verb in both) from God's book (of life) is explicitly entertained as a possibility. No valid reason exists to deny the possibility here also. The rest of the OT allusions to having one's name recorded in heaven or in the book (of life) have connotations of blessing to people because their names remain written there (cf. Isa. 4:3; Dan. 12:1; Mal. 3:16). New Testament references to the same outside the Apocalypse also connote blessing to the ones whose names are written there (cf. Luke 10:20; Phil. 4:3), but in the Apocalypse sometimes the note is positive (cf. 21:27) and sometimes it is not (cf. 13:8; 17:8; 20:12, 15). In the latter case, the absence of one's name from the book denotes separation from God and eventually everlasting punishment resulting from His judgment.

So the possibility of having one's name erased from the book is real and needs to be accounted for in connection with the promise to the overcomer in Rev. 3:5 (Caird). Because it is the wicked whose names are blotted from the book in Ex. 32:33 and Ps. 69:28, a relevant question is, When or how did their names come to be written in the book of life in the first place? Revelation 13:8 lends itself to two possible interpretations. Either the book was written from the foundation of the world, or the Lamb was slain from the foundation of the world.[77] If the former is the meaning, the time of the writing is explicitly placed before the foundation of the world. If the latter interpretation of 13:8 is correct, the time is still, by implication, the same because it is "the book of life *of the Lamb*" (cf. Rev. 21:27). The slain Lamb (cf. Rev. 5:6) is the one to whom the book relates, and its existence can presumably be traced to the time (in God's eternal plan) of His slaying, i.e., before the foundation of the world (Caird). If this is when the writing happened, there remains the question of how the names, even of the wicked, were written in the book. The most obvious answer lies in the universal impact of the Lamb's slaying. In Rev. 5:9-10 the Lamb's worthiness is tied to His death and the consequent redemption provided thereby. Heavenly creatures acclaim the Lamb's worthiness in 5:11-12, and they are joined by all creation and its tribute to the Father and the Lamb in 5:13-14. Because it was by His sacrificial death that Christ won the right to break the seals of the seven-sealed scroll, disclose its contents, and put them into effect upon the whole world (cf. 5:5-6), it is evident that His death affected the whole world (Caird). If the book of life contains the names of all those for whom Christ died (Caird), Christ must in some sense have died for all men because at the beginning the names of all men were in the book. In the words of Johannine theology outside the Apocalypse, He died for "the world," no one excluded (cf. John 1:29; 3:16; 4:42; 1 John 2:2; 4:14).

This provision of eternal life for everyone is only potential, however. It becomes actual only when appropriated by each person. If a person experiences physical death, never having trusted Christ for forgiveness, his name is erased from the book of life. It is only those who receive Christ by faith that have their place in the book confirmed (Walvoord). Some in the Sardian church had professed a relationship to Christ (cf. 3:1) but had not demonstrated that their faith was genuine through an enduring loyalty to Christ. These were candi-

---

77. A choice between these two possibilities will be deferred until a discussion of Rev. 13:8.

dates for removal from the book. Not so with the overcomers, however. Through their faithfulness they had shown their relationship to Christ to be real, so the appearance of their names in the book of life was not only potential, it was also actual. Such names, Christ promises in 3:5, will never be wiped from the book.[78]

The third part of the threefold promise to the Sardian overcomer is in the concluding words of v. 5: καὶ ὁμολογήσω τὸ ὄνομα αὐτοῦ ἐνώπιον τοῦ πατρός μου καὶ ἐνώπιον τῶν ἀγγέλων αὐτοῦ (*kai homologēsō to onoma autou enōpion tou patros mou kai enōpion tōn angelōn autou*, "and I will confess his name before My Father and before His angels"). This is the second clear echo in this fifth message of the teachings of Jesus as recorded in the synoptic gospels (cf. Matt. 10:32; Luke 12:8-9) (Beckwith; Charles; Caird). The other conspicuous echo is the likening of Christ's coming to a thief (Rev. 3:3 with Matt. 24:42; Luke 12:39). Additional echoes from Jesus' earlier ministry include the command to watch (Rev. 3:3 with Matt. 24:42; 25:13; 26:41) and the blotting of a name from the book of life (Rev. 3:5 with Luke 10:20).[79] This message contains more of such references than any of the other six.

Coming immediately after the promise of not erasing the overcomer's name from the book of life, this promise implies that on that future day of reckoning the judge will acknowledge the names written in the book as those who belong to Him (Alford). All others will be excluded from the new Jerusalem (cf. Matt. 7:3; 25:12; Mark 8:38; Luke 9:26; Rev. 20:15; 21:27). Apparently most of the church in Sardis had been ashamed of the name of Christ in situations of pressure created by their culture and had failed to confess Him. A few, like the church in nearby Philadelphia (cf. 3:8), had not denied His name (cf. 3:4). Though the text does not divulge it, the problem in Sardis may have been the same as in Philadelphia, i.e., pressure to participate in a form of Jewish worship that denied Jesus' "name." This would agree with archaeological evidence that a large Jewish community existed here (Hemer). This cannot be asserted dogmatically, however.

---

78. Rev. 17:8 poses an apparent problem for this interpretation when it notes that the names of the "earth-dwellers" have not been written (οὐ γέγραπται) in the book of life from the foundation of the world. The problem may be resolved by distinguishing the two possible emphases of the perfect tense of γέγραπται, that of a completed process and that of continuing results following the completed process. It is not the completed process of writing before the foundation of the world that is being negated by οὐ. It is rather the continuing results: "whose names *do not remain written* in the book of life from the foundation of the world." They were there at one time, but they did not stay there. More details of this discussion will be found at the comments on 17:8.

79. Trench, *Seven Churches*, p. 169.

The point of the promise is that some were victors and could expect Christ to "say the same thing"[80] about them in the presence of the Father and His angels as they had said about Him while among their contemporaries on earth. He will affirm their worthiness and the legitimacy of their claim to the bliss of the future kingdom.

3:6 *Call to hear.* This fifth message closes with the familiar invitation: ὁ ἔχων οὖς ἀκουσάτω τί τὸ πνεῦμα λέγει ταῖς ἐκκλησίαις (*ho echōn ous akousatō ti to pneuma legei tais ekklēsiais*, "The one who has an ear, let him hear what the Spirit says to the churches"). In Revelation this is Jesus' repeated method of issuing an individualized call for the hearer to respond (cf. 2:7, 11, 17, 29; 3:13, 22; cf. also 1:3). In the gospels He uses the phrase seven times, the only variation being the pluralization of the "ears" (cf. Matt. 11:15; 13:9, 43; Mark 4:9, 23; Luke 8:8; 14:35).[81] Jesus is the only one in Scripture to use this invitation, and He reserves it for occasions when He is speaking of the need for significant changes to be made (Bullinger).

As in each of the seven messages, Christ is the speaker, but it is the Spirit (*to pneuma*) of Christ in the prophet, who is the mouthpiece of Christ, whose voice goes to the churches. The plural *ekklēsiais* is a reminder that although each message was specifically directed to one church, each church was also to profit from the instruction given to the others.

Additional Notes

3:2 Some early MSS support the omission of τὰ before ἔργα, resulting in the sense "any works of yours." This reading is preferred by some because it is the more difficult reading in light of the presence of the article with ἔργα in the other messages (cf. 2:2, 19; 3:8, 15) (Hort; Moffatt; Hemer). The reading that includes the article also has respectable MS support and is preferred by others who view the omission as an impossible reading (Charles; Beckwith; Mounce). They say it would make "your works" cover any and every Christian activity, thus contradicting the favorable word about the church in v. 4. The reasoning in support of the article's inclusion is stronger.

3:3 Two possible senses of πῶς have been proposed, a subjective one ("how") expressing the manner of their reception (Lee, "Revelation," 4:537), and an objective one ("what") introducing the content of what they had previously received (Mounce, *Revelation*, p. 111;

---

80. Ὁμολογήσω is the future form of ὁμολογέω, which is built from two words: ὁμός, which means "one and the same," and λέγω, which means "I say." Primarily it means to say the same thing as another, to admit the truth of an accusation or to affirm the truthfulness of an assertion (Vincent, *Word Studies*, p. 523).

81. Robertson, *Word Pictures*, 6:565; Morris, *Revelation*, p. 62.

Johnson, "Revelation," p. 449). The fact that they had initially received objective data, i.e., the apostolic tradition of the gospel (cf.
2:25) (Beasley-Murray, *Revelation*, p. 96; Johnson, "Revelation," 12:
449), and the need of an object for the next verb τήρει, something
received that they could keep (Beckwith, *Apocalypse*, p. 474; Mounce,
Revelation, p. 111), present the objective sense of the conjunction in a
positive light. Yet this meaning is not adequate to focus on the *quality*
of their fine beginning as a church. The normal force of πῶς is to
convey manner. Content would have been more clearly shown by
using ὅτι. The meaning "how" convincingly draws attention to the
heartiness, zeal, and love with which the church had received the
truth at first (Trench, *Seven Churches*, p. 169). Because there was no
heresy in this church, the church had not lost *what* it had received,
but the *how*, i.e., the manner in which she had once received it (Lee,
"Revelation," p. 537; Hemer, *Seven Churches*, p. 145).

Some authorities opt for an aoristic rather than a perfect sense of
εἴληφας, pointing out that the parallel with ἤκουσας requires this
(Lenski, *Revelation*, p. 130) and that other occurrences of the perfect
tense of this verb in the Apocalypse are aoristic in meaning (cf. 5:7;
8:5; 11:17) (Hort, *Apocalypse*, p. 33; Beckwith, *Apocalypse*, p. 474;
Moffatt, "Revelation," 5:364). Their reasons are unconvincing, however, as the other occurrences in Revelation are debatable just as this
one is and the "parallel" with ἤκουσας is actually a contrast insofar as
the tenses go. The best sense is that the aorist points to the time when
they heard the gospel (cf. 1 Thess. 1:5, 6; 2:13) and the perfect con-
cedes that they still possess this gift of God (Charles, *Revelation*, 1:80;
cf. Swete, *Apocalypse*, p. 50; Mounce, *Revelation*, p. 111). The sequence
of the two verbs that places receiving before hearing is surprising.
Obviously the hearing preceded the receiving. The effect of this arrangement is to focus more attention on εἴληφας: "remember how you
have received on the basis of what you heard."

The choice of an accusative case for ποίαν ὥραν is unusual for two
reasons: (1) A locative case (dative inflectional ending) normally
names a point in time, the accusative being reserved to expressing
duration of or limitation in time (Mounce, *Revelation*, p. 112). (2) The
source of this statement is Christ's earlier teaching as recorded in
Matt. 24:42-43 and Luke 12:39. In both cases Christ used a locative,
ποίᾳ ἡμέρᾳ. The explanation lies in a changing connotation of the
accusative case. Along the way it lost its usual significance of measure and duration and came to be used for other functions. This
happened in classical Greek as well as in Koine (Alford, *Greek Testament*, 4:581; Robertson, *Word Pictures*, 6:314; *A Grammar of the Greek
New Testament in the Light of Historical Research* [Nashville: Broad-

man, 1934], p. 470; Beckwith, *Apocalypse*, p. 474). Here it denotes a point in time as it does also in John 4:52 and Acts 20:16.

3:5 Some textual sources read the demonstrative pronoun οὗτος rather than the adverb οὕτως. In support of the pronoun it is sometimes argued that John would have used ὁμοίως ("likewise") or ὡσαύτως ("in like manner") rather than οὕτως to express similarity (Beckwith; Johnson). It is also noted that οὕτως creates certain syntactical problems when used with the articular participle as here (Beckwith), and that οὕτως could have arisen because of the usual confusion between ο and ω, and then have been retained as not being altogether without meaning (Alford). In response to these arguments, ὁμοίως or ὡσαύτως may have indicated a distinction between the overcomer and the unsullied of v. 4, which the writer did not intend (Beckwith). Besides this, οὕτως may have been viewed as superfluous and arbitrarily changed to οὗτος by a well-meaning copyist (Bruce M. Metzger, *A Textual Commentary on the Greek New Testament* [New York: United Bible Societies, 1971], p. 736). Because the MS evidence favoring the adverb is much stronger, it is the preferred reading (ibid.). Here is another of John's pleonastic uses of οὕτως (Lee). See the discussion of the adverb at 2:15.

8

Church of Promised Deliverance

F. THE MESSAGE TO PHILADELPHIA (3:7-13)

As the team from Jesus and John to the seven cities reached Philadelphia, their number had probably dwindled to two, the messengers to Philadelphia and Laodicea. Jesus' words to this church are as positive as those to any of the churches, possibly more so.

Translation

7And to the messenger of the church which is in Philadelphia, write:
  "These things says the holy one, the true one,
  who has the key of David,
  who opens and no one shuts,
  and shuts and no one opens;
8I know your works—behold, I have given an opened door before you, which no one can shut—that you have little power, and [yet] you kept My word, and did not deny My name. 9Behold, I am giving [some] of the synagogue of Satan, the ones who say that they themselves are Jews, and they are not but they lie—behold, I will make them come and bow down before your feet, and know that I have loved you. 10Because you have kept the word of My endurance, I will also keep you from the hour of trial that is about to come upon the whole inhabited earth, to try those who dwell upon the earth. 11I will come soon; hold fast what you have, that no one take your crown. 12The one who overcomes, I will make him a pillar in the temple of My God,

and he will not possibly go outside any longer, and I will write upon him the name of My God and the name of the city of My God, the new Jerusalem, which descends from heaven from My God, and My new name. ¹³The one who has an ear, let him hear what the Spirit says to the churches."

Exegesis and Exposition

3:7 *The address.* The familiar address this time incorporates a word that is used six times outside Revelation in the NT, Φιλαδελφεία (*Philadelpheia*, "Philadelphia") (Rom. 12:10; 1 Thess. 4:9; Heb. 13:1; 1 Pet. 1:22; 2 Pet. 1:7 [twice]; cf. Rev. 1:11). In all six it is a positive Christian virtue of "brotherly love," but here it is a place name: καὶ τῷ ἀγγέλῳ τῆς ἐν Φιλαδελφείᾳ ἐκκλησίας γράψον (*kai tō angelō tēs en Philadelpheią ekklēsias grapson*, "and to the messenger of the church which is in Philadelphia, write"). The city's name was chosen in recognition of the loyalty of Attalus II to his brother Eumenes II.[1]

The city of Philadelphia, now the site of the modern town of Alasehir, was located in Lydia about twenty-five miles southeast of Sardis. It lay in the valley of the Cogamis River, which was a tributary of the Hermus. At some point after 189 B.C., it had been founded by a Pergamenian king, either Eumenes II or his brother Attalus II, who correctly thought this to be an excellent site for a city. The long Cogamis Valley extends southeast from the Hermus Valley and connects into the side of the central plateau. It affords the best path for ascending from the Hermus Valley, about 500 feet above sea level, to the main plateau about 1,500 feet higher. Though the climb was steep, this was the path along which trade and communication from the harbor at Smyrna and from Lydia and the northwest regions were maintained with Phrygia and the east. It rivaled the road east from Ephesus in importance as a trade route. It also served as the imperial postal road during the first century A.D. Communications from Rome moved to Troas, whence they continued overland to Pergamum, Sardis, and then to Philadelphia and on to the east. Philadelphia was thus a stage on the main line of Imperial communication. In later Byzantine times, it became the greatest trade route of the whole country.[2]

Though not constructed primarily as a military fortress, the location was well suited for this. It stood on a broad hill that sloped up

---

1. W. M. Ramsay, *The Letters to the Seven Churches of Asia* (New York: A. C. Armstrong, 1904), p. 191.
2. Ibid., pp. 191-92; Colin J. Hemer, *The Letters to the Seven Churches of Asia in Their Local Setting*, JSNTSup 11 (Sheffield: U. of Sheffield, 1986), pp. 153-55.

from the valley toward Mount Tmolus on the south and east, but it did not merge with the rest of the mountains, being separated from them. Its other side was the plateau proper. With suitable fortifications on its lower slopes, it could be defended with relative ease (Ramsay).

The primary purpose for the city's establishment was consolidating, regulating, and educating the central regions that were subject to the Pergamenian kings. These rulers wanted Philadelphia to be a hub of Graeco-Asiatic civilization so as to spread the Greek language and manners in the eastern parts of Lydia and in Phrygia. It thus had a missionary function from the outset as an apostle of Hellenism in an Oriental land. It was successful in this effort to foster a unity of spirit, customs, and loyalty within the area, as evidenced by the vanishing of the Lydian language by A.D. 19 and the dominance of the Greek language as the only one spoken (Ramsay).

The city's geophysical location was not quite so fortuitous, however. It lay on the edge of the Katakekaumene, also spelled Catacecaumene (derived from κατακαύω [*katakauō*, "I burn down"]), a Lydian district where volcanoes at the time were quite active and where earthquakes were frequent. Even though the volcanic ash made the soil in the area unusually fertile, the volcanoes themselves posed a constant threat to the well-being of the area. In A.D. 17 an earthquake, unparalleled in the annals of history up to that time, destroyed twelve cities in the Lydian Valley, including Sardis and Philadelphia. It was this earthquake that brought Philadelphia to the attention of ancient writers. Three years later, the Greek writer Strabo tells of a lingering fear of the repeat of such a catastrophe that plagued the city subsequently, with aftershocks serving as reminders of the continuing danger. Though Sardis suffered more serious initial damage, Philadelphia was apparently nearer the epicenter of the quake and suffered substantial damage for a period of time long after the initial shocks. Some of the city's residents even chose to live outside the city in huts erected a distance away rather than return to rebuild their houses in the city. Probably the fears of the inhabitants were further kindled by later shocks in the area, notably the one that destroyed nearby Laodicea in A.D. 60. The city probably had not fully recovered from its disaster by the time the Apocalypse was written (Ramsay; Hemer).

The Roman emperor Tiberius provided substantial help in rebuilding the city after its major calamity. In return, Philadelphia joined the other cities that received help in erecting a monument in Rome as visible evidence of their gratitude. Another response was to establish a cult of Germanicus, named after the adopted son and heir of Tiberius. Germanicus was in Asia at the time, probably dis-

271

tributing the relief bounty for the ruined cities. Another response to the emperor's kindness was the adoption of a new city name, Neo-kaisareia ("new Caesar"; also spelled Neocaesarea), the new Caesar being either Tiberius, successor of Augustus, or Germanicus, successor of Tiberius. Though helped substantially, the economy and prosperity of Philadelphia were severely hampered for a long time as a result of the earthquake. The new name disappeared after twenty-five or thirty years, but Philadelphia was the only one of the cities to substitute a new name for its original name voluntarily.[3]

Later, during the reign of Vespasian (A.D. 70-79), it took another imperial title, Flavia. Two names for the city remained in use throughout the second and third centuries (Ramsay). Imperial actions also affected Philadelphia in the nineties, but this time adversely. Because of the earthquake, which drove them from the city proper, and because of the fertility of the soil, many of the people had turned to farming as a means of livelihood, specifically to the cultivating of vineyards. Apparently because of a famine, in A.D. 92 Domitian issued an edict that at least half the vineyards in the provinces be cut down and no new ones planted. This action was designed to increase production of corn which the Empire needed badly. This crisis affected Philadelphia more critically than any other, because no city of Asia depended on the fruit of the vine more than it. Dionysius, god of wine, was the principal deity. Corn was also produced, but not enough to support the area in years of a bad harvest. The people needed wine production to fall back on when times were bad. This series of events doubtless brought local disillusionment with the Roman emperor throughout this last decade of the first century A.D. (Hemer).

Few details are known about the religious inclinations of Philadelphia. The religion practiced there, judging from the coinage that has been recovered, was apparently of a Graeco-Asiatic nature. The roots appear to have been thoroughly Anatolian, but on the surface the Greek influence upon the area emerges (Ramsay). Archaeology has yielded no evidence of a Jewish synagogue in the city, but the message itself indicates there must have been one (cf. Rev. 3:9). It is difficult to explain how a city so economically bereft could have attracted a significant Jewish community in the Diaspora. Perhaps a partial explanation for their presence in the vicinity lies in Philadelphia's proximity to Sardis, where economic enticements were far more appealing (Hemer).

Attributes of the speaker. The character in which Christ desires the Philadelphians to conceive of Him is described by four self-

---

3. Ramsay, *Seven Churches*, pp. 397-98; Hemer, *Seven Churches*, p. 157. Sardis called itself "Caesareia" for a brief period following the earthquake, but this was only for a very short time.

designations, the first two of which are attributes of Christ: Τάδε λέγει ὁ ἅγιος, ὁ ἀληθινός, ὁ ἔχων τὴν κλεῖν Δαυίδ, ὁ ἀνοίγων καὶ οὐδεὶς κλείσει, καὶ κλείων καὶ οὐδεὶς ἀνοίγει (Tade legei ho hagios, ho alēthinos, ho echōn tēn klein Dauid, ho anoigōn kai oudeis kleisei, kai kleiōn kai oudeis anoigei, "These things says the holy one, the true one, who has the key of David, who opens and no one shuts, and shuts and no one opens").

Ho hagios ("the holy one") is a title that sometimes names the Father in this book (cf. Rev. 4:8; 6:10), but throughout the NT it is a common title for the Messiah (cf. Mark 1:24; Luke 1:35; 4:34; John 6:69; Acts 4:27, 30; 1 John 2:20). The OT reader would immediately see this connection also (cf. Ps. 16:10; Hab. 3:3; Isa. 40:25). Hagios characterizes Jesus, not so much as the sinless one, but as one especially set apart, belonging exclusively to God.[4] Though opposed and rejected by the synagogue of Satan (cf. 3:9), Christ remains characteristically holy. Hence, His words are also holy, carrying with them a mandate for obedience.

Ho alēthinos ("the true one") emphasizes Christ's genuineness. He is the real as opposed to the unreal. A cognate word, ἀληθής (alēthēs, "true"), speaks of what is true as fact, the opposite of spurious or imperfect.[5] This term has to do with reality, however. When confronted by Christ, we are confronted by no shadowy outline of the truth, but with the truth itself.[6] Occurring rather commonly in the Apocalypse, alēthinos is usually coupled with another adjective as it is with hagios here. In 3:14; 19:11; 21:5; and 22:6 πιστός (pistos, "faithful") is its complement, and in 15:3; 16:7; and 19:2 it is with δίκαιος (dikaios, "righteous").[7] This adjective is quite common in Johannine writings, occurring ten times in Revelation (3:7, 14; 6:10; 15:3; 16:7; 19:2, 9, 11; 21:5; 22:6) and twelve times in John's other writings. It has only five occurrences in the rest of the NT.[8]

Attempts to refine the interpretation even further disclose two

---

4. Isbon T. Beckwith, The Apocalypse of John (New York: Macmillan, 1919), p. 478.
5. G. Abbott-Smith, A Manual Greek Lexicon of the New Testament (Edinburgh: T. & T. Clark, 1937), p. 20. Inasmuch as Revelation never uses ἀληθής, some suggest that too clear-cut a distinction between the two adjectives not be drawn. This allows ἀληθινός to include several nuances in this book that might be relegated to ἀληθής under other circumstances (Colin Brown, "Truth," in NIDNTT, 3:893).
6. William Barclay, The Revelation of John, 2 vols. (Philadelphia: Westminster, 1960), 1:127.
7. James Moffatt, "The Revelation of St. John the Divine," in The Expositor's Greek Testament, ed. W. Robertson Nicoll (Grand Rapids: Eerdmans, n.d.), 5:366.
8. William Lee, "The Revelation of St. John," in The Holy Bible, ed. F. C. Cook (London: John Murray, 1881), 4:539; Beckwith, Apocalypse, p. 479.

possible nuances. One perspective presents the focus of the true as contrasted with the subordinately true, with all imperfect and partial realizations of the ideal,[9] and the other sees the true as contrasted with the absolutely false.[10] The former view sees an antithesis between the perfect and the imperfect, the ideal fully realized and the ideal only partially realized. Whatever Christ assumes by way of names, titles, or offices, it is realized to the *fullest* extent. This approach allows more for the word's basic connotation of "genuine" in comparison with *alēthēs* that means true, as noted above.[11] It also fits the context better when it depicts "the *real* Messiah" (Alford; Beckwith). It is more in accord with the wider usage of the word in all of Johannine literature to take this meaning (cf. John 1:9; 4:37; 7:28; 8:16; 1 John 5:20) (Swete; Beckwith). There is serious question whether a clear distinction between *alēthinos* and *alēthēs* can always be maintained, however (cf. John 7:28) (Alford). It is also objected that the meaning of "genuine" is limited to only Greek contexts, the present passage not fitting that description. In a Hebrew context such as this, *alēthinos* has more the meaning that God "keeps faith forever" (i.e., one who can be trusted to keep His promises) (cf. Ex. 34:6; Isa. 67:15).[12] These two objections raise a considerable question about this view.

The second perspective regarding *alēthinos* views it as contrasting the true with the absolutely false. The chief support for this understanding lies in the concept's contrast with the enemies of the church, who are called liars (cf. 3:9).[13] However, this reasoning fails to provide an adequate explanation of the word's use in Rev. 6:9 where the "genuine" connotation is required. This objection, along with the second objection to the first view, probably points to a more refined sense in which the first view should be endorsed as correct. Christ is true to His word and can be trusted to keep His promises.

---

9. Richard Chenevix Trench, *Commentary on the Epistles to the Seven Churches in Asia* (London: Parker, Son, and Bourn, 1861), p. 183; Henry Barclay Swete, *The Apocalypse of St. John* (London: Macmillan, 1906), p. 53; Lee, "Revelation," 4:539.
10. Henry Alford, *The Greek Testament*, 4 vols. (London: Longmans, Green, 1903), 4:583; F. J. A. Hort, *The Apocalypse of St. John* (London: Macmillan, 1908), p. 34; R. H. Charles, *The Revelation of St. John*, 2 vols., ICC (New York: Scribner's, 1920), 1:85-86; Beckwith, *Apocalypse*, p. 478.
11. Swete, *Apocalypse*, p. 53; Moffatt, "Revelation," 5:366; A. T. Robertson, *Word Pictures in the New Testament*, 6 vols. (Nashville: Broadman, 1933), 6:316.
12. Charles, *Revelation*, 1:86; George E. Ladd, *A Commentary on the Revelation of John* (Grand Rapids: Eerdmans, 1972), p. 58.
13. Alford, *Greek Testament*, 4:583; Robertson, *Word Pictures*, 6:318; Homer Hailey, *Revelation, an Introduction and Commentary* (Grand Rapids: Baker, 1979), p. 149.

His reliability derives from His being the *genuine* Messiah who can be relied upon. This explanation amounts to a slight revision of the first perspective but fits the situation of the Philadelphians quite well. Their persecution was so severe that their only hope of relief lay in the fulfilled promises of the *real* Messiah.

The third attribute of Christ in this sixth message notices His possession of the key of David. Eliakim, in a typical sense, held this key to the house of David, that is, he had authority over the royal treasury (cf. Isa. 22:22). As the root and offspring of David (cf. Rev. 5:5; 22:16), Christ in the fulfilled sense controls the entrance to David's house, which ultimately refers to the Messianic kingdom. His Davidic lineage and authority were alluded to in Rev. 1:5*a*. The claims of the Jewish element in Philadelphia were apparently to the contrary. These opponents could not accept that complete authority to admit or exclude from the city of David, the new Jerusalem, was His. The Jews, whose hostility is prominent in 3:9 of this message, denied that Jesus was the Messiah and claimed that they alone, not Jesus' followers, had access to the kingdom of David. The opening words of this message emphasize that the opposite is true. He is the genuine Messiah, and in the coming reign of glory His power to open the door to His own and close it to the self-styled "children of the kingdom" is established (Beckwith). With an authority like what He has over Hades (cf. Rev. 1:18), heaven and earth (Matt. 28:18), and His own house (cf. Heb. 3:6), He has regal dominion over the house of David.[14] The strong Jewish emphasis in Jesus' self-description makes this "the most distinctly eschatological of the seven epistles" (Beckwith).

The fourth part of Christ's self-description to this church is clearly derived from Isa. 22:22: *ho anoigōn kai oudeis kleisei, kai kleiōn kai oudeis anoigei* ("who opens and no one shuts, and shuts and no one opens").[15] Like Eliakim, except in a final sense, Jesus alone has the power to admit into or exclude from His kingdom. The extent to which He has shared this power with His church will be analyzed in the discussion of 3:8 below.

3:8 *Knowledge about the people.* Christ's intimate knowledge of the

---

14. Charles, *Revelation,* 1:86; Moses Stuart, *A Commentary on the Apocalypse* (Edinburgh: Maclachlan, Stewart, 1947), p. 490.
15. John is obviously not quoting the LXX in this allusion. It is also quite distinct from the MT. What appears in the Hebrew text as direct statements and finite verbs, in John's rendering becomes a series of dependent clauses, introduced by participles that are subsequently resolved into finite verbs. This is a Hebrew idiom used often by John. He deals with the text from Isaiah quite independently (Charles, *Revelation,* 1:86; Robertson, *Word Pictures,* 6:319).

situation in Philadelphia adds omniscience to His holiness, truthfulness, and omnipotence, cited in v. 7: Οἶδά σου τὰ ἔργα (*Oida sou ta erga*, "I know your works"). The works of this church are not defined immediately as they are with the other churches, their description being reserved until after a word of encouragement that the Lord injects at an unusually early point.

A minor debate has arisen regarding the proper punctuation of v. 8 in relation to the ἰδού (*idou*, "behold") clause. One opinion is that it should be set off from the rest of the sentence as a parenthesis, and the other wants to understand it as parallel with two other *idou* clauses in v. 9. The latter option sees the three clauses as telling what the Lord has given (v. 8a), what opposition He gives (v. 9a), and the victory He will give (v. 9b). The difficulty with this proposal is that it leaves the opening words of v. 8, "I know your works," dangling with nothing to complete them. The solution that takes the clause parenthetically is preferable (Alford; Hort; Charles; Beckwith), because it allows for taking *hoti* ("that") (v. 8) in a suitable sense to introduce a clause explaining the works mentioned immediately before the *idou* clause. Such an explanation follows the pattern of the rest of the messages in these chapters (Beckwith). The parenthetical nature of the clause is confirmed by noting the awkwardness of weaving the words beginning with the interjection "behold" and ending with "shut" into the flow of a larger sentence.[16]

Because of the extremity of this church's situation Jesus takes the unusual step of prematurely injecting this word of encouragement to the members, even before He finishes His acknowledgment of their works. Perhaps as He thought of the sterling quality of their works, the thought of deserved support merited this unique step. He speaks of giving or setting before the church an opened door: ἰδοὺ δέδωκα ἐνώπιόν σου θύραν ἠνεῳγμένην, ἣν οὐδεὶς δύναται κλεῖσαι αὐτήν (*idou dedōka enōpion sou thyran ēneǫgmenēn, hēn oudeis dynatai kleisai autēn*, "behold, I have given an opened door before you, which no one can shut").

Though some have theorized that *dedōka* is used Hebraistically to mean "set" (Charles; Beckwith), the better judgment is to take it with its usual force of "give," denoting something that is promised as a gift (Beckwith). The force is, "I have given, and it remains given."[17] The precise meaning of *thyran ēneǫgmenēn* ("opened door") has been a matter of dispute. A small minority explain it in the light of John

---

16. Alan F. Johnson, "Revelation," in *EBC*, ed. Frank E. Gaebelein (Grand Rapids: Zondervan, 1981), 12:452.
17. Ibid. The perfect tense conveys this combination of completion and continuing results.

10:1-9 where Christ is the door of the sheep and hence the door of salvation.[18] The sense is that Christ makes access to God sure, despite the trials and temptations of this life (cf. 3:8-10). Yet it is a strange thing for Christ to say of Himself, "Behold, I have set before you a door opened," so as to imply that He Himself was the door (Charles). The context of this statement is quite removed from that of John 10, so this proposal cannot be taken too seriously.

A second proposal, that the opened door speaks of expanded missionary opportunities, is widely held.[19] It rests heavily on the use of the open door terminology elsewhere in the NT in connection with unusual evangelistic and ministry opportunities (cf. 1 Cor. 16:9; 2 Cor. 2:12; Col. 4:3)[20] and on the strategic location of Philadelphia as a mission city. As indicated above in the discussion of the address of the message, Philadelphia was founded for the specific purpose of disseminating the Graeco-Asiatic culture and language in the eastern part of Lydia and in Phrygia.[21] Contextual support for this meaning may be cited in the very next verse. It consists of the promise of the conversion of their opponents, conversion being the goal of missionary outreach (Alford). As enticing as this explanation is, it faces serious objections. For one thing, a challenge to greater outreach would be a strange reason for Christ to interrupt His acknowledgment of the church's works with a parenthetical statement. It is much easier to see this as a promise brought forward in the message to encourage a persecuted people. Besides, the other two *idou* clauses in this message (3:9*a* and 3:9*b*) are words of encouragement, not challenges to greater service. In addition, such a statement about the church's future missionary work would hardly be structured grammatically as a parenthesis sandwiched between two parts of a sentence commending the church for its faithfulness (Beckwith; Johnson). Rejection of this missions connotation is further confirmed by consideration of the broad context of chapters 2-3 and the Apocalypse as a whole. Though symbolically they are pictured as "lampstands," which implies a witness to the world, the responsibility for spreading the gospel is not one of the activities urged upon these churches (Beckwith).

Overwhelming evidence points to a third explanation of the

---

18. Moffatt, "Revelation," 5:366; J. P. M. Sweet, *Revelation* (Philadelphia: Westminster, Pelican, 1979), p. 103.
19. Swete, *Apocalypse*, p. 53; Alford, *Greek Testament*, 4:584; Lee, "Revelation," 4:539; Ramsay, *Seven Churches*, pp. 404, 406; Charles, *Revelation*, 1:87; Robertson, *Word Pictures*, 6:317; John F. Walvoord, *The Revelation of Jesus Christ* (Chicago: Moody, 1966), p. 85.
20. Robertson, *Word Pictures*, 6:317.
21. Ramsay, *Seven Churches*, pp. 391-92; Walvoord, *Revelation*, p. 85; Johnson, "Revelation," 12:451.

"opened door" as the correct one. It speaks of a sure entrance into the messianic kingdom, promised to this church as a reward for their faithfulness. No one, not even those of "the synagogue of Satan," can shut them out. Jewish opponents would seek to deny Gentiles, such as Christians in this city, entrance into the messianic kingdom (Beckwith). This meaning is clear from the immediate context of the message.[22] The use of David's name just before recalls the Messiah's prerogative of admitting to or turning away from David's future kingdom (Rev. 5:5; 22:16; cf. Luke 1:32) (Johnson). David is always the type of the supreme ruler of the theocracy (cf. Jer. 30:9; Ezek. 34:23; 37:24; Hos. 3:5) (Lee). Furthermore, *ēneǭgmenēn* ("opened") is a form of ἀνοίγω (*anoigō*, "I open"), which is used twice at the end of v. 7 in describing Jesus' administration of His messianic office. If He who controls the opening and closing of access to the Davidic kingdom speaks of an opened door in the same breath as describing messianic prerogative, the inevitable conclusion is to see a reference to admission to that kingdom (Johnson). It is natural to refer to this final reward for fidelity immediately after "I know your works," because these works amounted to the church's faithful stand for Christ (Beckwith). The words *hēn oudeis dynatai kleisai autēn*[23] ("which no one can shut," 3:8) recall the words *oudeis kleisei* ("no one will shut") from v. 7 and come into play in connection with v. 9. This promise amounts to a promise of deliverance from their Jewish adversaries, a deliverance that will come at Christ's second advent (cf. 3:11).[24] Added affirmation of this solution comes in noting that it makes this *idou* clause a promise, thus paralleling the two *idou* clauses of v. 9. It also matches the distinctly eschatological tone of this message to Philadelphia.[25]

Jesus resumes His acknowledgment of the church's works following this inserted promise of access to the messianic kingdom: ὅτι

---

22. Ladd, *Revelation*, p. 59; Johnson, "Revelation," 12:452; Robert H. Mounce, *The Book of Revelation*, NICNT (Grand Rapids: Eerdmans, 1977), p. 117.
23. The combination ἥν . . . αὐτήν is an example of the pleonastic vernacular and Hebrew repetition of the personal pronoun αὐτήν after the relative pronoun ἥν (cf. also Rev. 7:2; 20:8). This construction seems to emphasize that someone was trying to shut the door, but was not able to interfere with the Lord who still keeps the door open (Lee, "Revelation," 4:540; Moffatt, "Revelation," 5:366; R. C. H. Lenski, *The Interpretation of St. John's Revelation* [Columbus, Ohio: Lutheran Book Concern, 1935], p. 140).
24. E. W. Bullinger, *The Apocalypse* or *"The Day of the Lord"* (London: Eyre and Spottiswoode, n.d.), p. 201.
25. Beckwith, *Apocalypse*, p. 480. One opinion is that the second and third solutions to the problem of the "opened door" are not mutually exclusive. The proposal acknowledges the correctness of the third view, but wants to give it an immediate application as a stimulus to evangelism (Hemer, *Seven Churches*, p. 162). The argumentation for this is weak, however.

μικρὰν ἔχεις δύναμιν, καὶ[26] ἐτήρησάς μου τὸν λόγον, καὶ οὐκ ἠρνήσω τὸ ὄνομά μου (*hoti mikran echeis dynamin, kai etērēsas mou ton logon, kai ouk ērnēsō to onoma mou,* "that[27] you have little power, and [yet] you kept My word, and did not deny My name"). Jesus makes three observations about their works. The first is *mikran echeis dynamin* ("you have little power"). Some argue that this alludes to the meager number of believers in the church and consequently the limited influence they exercised (Hort; Beckwith). Support for this theory comes from observing that the members of the church probably came from the lower classes (cf. 1 Cor. 1:26-27) in contrast with the wealth of their Jewish adversaries.[28] It is also observed that the church is not blamed for its lack of equipment, a factor beyond its control, but is praised for making good use of the slight resources at its disposal (Moffatt). Others are of the opinion that the church's "little power" refers to the small spiritual vitality of the believers in the church, noting that the expression obviously falls short of a full commendation (Walvoord). Although neither view has particularly strong support, the latter meets with formidable objections. This could hardly imply a limited spiritual vitality because it is part of the good qualities that constitute the commended works (Lee). It is further disproved by the commendations that are issued to the church in the remaining verses of the message.[29] "Little power" must refer to the church's limited influence because of its numerical smallness.

Contrasting with the church's little power is its obedience to Christ's word in a particular situation when members had been called upon to deny His name. *Etērēsas* ("you kept") and *ouk ērnēsō* ("you did not deny") are aorist tense verbs that, in contrast to the present tense *echeis* ("you have") just before, point to a specific historical trial faced by these people, a trial through which they passed victoriously. The Lord commends them for this. Apparently the Jews had on some occasion attempted to force them to disregard Christ's teachings and deny Him (cf. John 8:31ff.; Rev. 2:9; 3:9), but the people

---

26. The καὶ takes on an adversative force, "and yet," as it does frequently in the gospel of John (Charles, *Revelation*, 1:87).
27. The suggestion that ὅτι in this case is causal (i.e., "because") (Alford, *Greek Testament*, 4:584) cannot be taken seriously. This would leave the "works" undefined. The Lord's grounds for praising the church would be unstated in the message (Moffatt, "Revelation," 5:366). The meaning "that" is more satisfactory as a conjunction to introduce an elaboration of the "works" earlier in the verse. This is the force of ὅτι in parallel situations in other messages (cf. 2:2; 3:1, 15) (Lee, "Revelation," 4:539; Swete, *Apocalypse*, p. 54]).
28. Alford, *Greek Testament*, 4:584; Robertson, *Word Pictures*, 6:317.
29. Beckwith, *Apocalypse*, p. 481; J. B. Smith, *A Revelation of Jesus Christ* (Scottdale, Pa.: Herald, 1961), p. 87.

had survived the crisis without faltering, even though they were few in number.[30] The word He had given them, they did keep,[31] and refrained from a denial of Him in the face of their persecutors' threats.

3:9 *State of the church.* The second *idou* of this message calls special attention to a promise of God's working in the lives of the church's enemies, and thus introduces a second promise of Christ to the church: ἰδοὺ διδῶ ἐκ τῆς συναγωγῆς τοῦ Σατανᾶ, τῶν λεγόντων ἑαυτοὺς Ἰουδαίους εἶναι, καὶ οὐκ εἰσὶν ἀλλὰ ψεύδονται (*idou didō ek tēs synagōgēs tou Satana, tōn legontōn heautous Ioudaious einai, kai ouk eisin alla pseudontai,* "Behold, I am giving [some][32] of the synagogue of Satan, the ones who say that they themselves are Jews, and they are not but they lie"). The thought behind the statement is not formally completed until the third *idou* clause later in the verse because the object of *didō* ("I am giving") is not given in full, but the implicit idea is, "I am giving some of the synagogue as your converts" (Beckwith).

Didō ("I am giving") is an appropriate word choice because the predicted homage of these opponents will come as a gift from Christ. The sense may be more evident if the verb is taken Hebraically, "I am making (i.e., I will make) some of the synagogue." Such a Hebraism is used frequently in the LXX and is also found in Acts 2:27; 10:40; and 14:3. This idiomatic understanding is supported by the combination *idou didō*, which itself is a pure Hebraism with a future sense (cf. הִנְנִי נֹתֵן [*hinĕnî nōtēn*, "behold, I am giving"]) (Charles; Beckwith).

"The synagogue of Satan" was apparently composed of professing Jews, worshiping in the synagogue and claiming to be the true Israel (cf. John 8:31ff.). Satan is named as the leader of such a synagogue because of the persecuting habits of this group (cf. 2:9) (Moffatt). The claim[33] of these people that "they themselves were Jews" is understood by some as an indication that the ancestral title Jew has now been appropriated for the Christian church and that this racial succession has passed to Christianity (Moffatt). Nowhere does the verse

---

30. Lee, "Revelation," 4:540; Beckwith, *Apocalypse,* p. 481; Robertson, *Word Pictures,* 6:317.
31. The former μου is unemphatic, a vernacular possessive. Because of this, it throws emphasis on the rest of the clause, ἐτήρησας and τὸν λόγον (Charles, *Revelation,* 1:87).
32. In ἐκ τῆς συναγωγῆς there is an ellipsis of τινὰς as there is with the preposition ἐκ in 2:10. This idiomatic usage conveys the sense of "certain ones out of" or "some of the synagogue" (Trench, *Seven Churches,* p. 188; Marvin R. Vincent, *Word Studies in the New Testament* [New York: Scribner's, 1906], 2:593; Beckwith, *Apocalypse,* p. 188).
33. Τῶν λεγόντων is in apposition with the unexpressed τινὰς of the preceding ἐκ τῆς συναγωγῆς phrase. Its genitive ending is explained by attraction to the case of τῆς συναγωγῆς.

say this, however. It simply denies that because of its spiritual state, this particular group of Abraham's descendants was deserving of such recognition (cf. Rom. 2:28-29) (Ladd). According to John, a true Jew is one who has been forgiven through recognizing Jesus as his Messiah. A false Jew is one who rejects not only Jesus, but also those who believe in Jesus (cf. 2:9) (Johnson).

The author of these messages notes emphatically the falsity of the pseudo-Jewish claim with the words *kai ouk eisin alla pseudontai* ("and they are not but they lie"). The earlier part, "and they are not," constitutes a sufficient denial of their claim, but the issue is forcefully closed with the addition of "but they lie." In typically Johannine style (cf. John 8:44; 1 John 1:10; 2:4) an additional contrast is drawn between these false professors and the one who identifies Himself as "the true one" (v. 7).[34]

The third promise introduced by *idou* comes at the end of v. 9: ἰδοὺ ποιήσω αὐτοὺς ἵνα ἥξουσιν καὶ προσκυνήσουσιν ἐνώπιον τῶν ποδῶν σου, καὶ γνῶσιν ὅτι ἐγὼ ἠγάπησά σε (*idou poiēsō autous hina hēxousin kai proskynēsousin enōpion tōn podōn sou, kai gnōsin hoti egō ēgapēsa se*, "behold, I will make them come and bow down before your feet, and know that I have loved you"). This promise resumes the second promise and formally completes it, but in a slightly different form. The *idou poiēsō autous* ("behold, I will make them") restates the *idou didō ek tēs synagōgēs tou Satana* ("behold, I am giving [some] of the synagogue of Satan") and reveals that these false Jews will eventually be made to come and do homage before the feet of the Philadelphian church.

Christ purposes to cause these false Jews to do homage before Gentile Christians, the exact opposite of what the OT predicted about Israel in her kingdom. The allusion is to Isa. 60:14, on the basis of which the homage the Jews expected from the Gentiles will be rendered by them (the Jews) to the Christians (cf. also Isa. 45:14; 49:23; Ezek. 36:23; 37:28; Zech. 8:20-23) (Charles). The nature of the fulfillment of Christ's purpose has been identified either as the exaltation of the Philadelphian church, without implying salvation of those who are forced to come and worship (Charles; Johnson), or as a reference to an eschatological salvation of the Jews (Trench; Hort; Beckwith; Ladd).

In favor of the former option, Phil. 2:10-11 has been cited. As in this Pauline passage, some will bow remorsefully before Christ and some joyfully (Johnson). The reversed roles of Jews and Gentiles in the allusion to Isa. 60:14 is said to put Israel in the fold of those making acknowledgment and the church in the role of recipient of

---

34. Robertson, *Word Pictures*, 6:318.

that acknowledgment (Mounce). The Jews had rejected their Messiah and had forfeited their right to be called Jews.[35] This is the language of eschatological judgment rather than an anticipation of blessing. It simply says that the Jews will acknowledge their mistake in denying Christians a place in the kingdom.[36] The understanding that views the exaltation of the Philadelphian church but does not see the conversion of the professing Jews is rather convincing.

Yet so is the other perspective. In his picture of the heavenly city later in this book, John draws upon the same OT passages that talk about the salvation of the Jews (cf. Isa. 45:14; 60:14; Ezek. 36:23; 37:27-28) (Caird). Gentile kings are said to enter the heavenly city that is the outgrowth of the kingdom of David (Rev. 21:23-26; cf. 20:4-6) (Caird). This is a time of the future repentance of national Israel. The eschatological conversion of Israel as a reference is also supported by the verses that follow immediately. In 3:10-11 the focus is on the future and the return of Christ when this repentance will occur (Ladd). In light of the general nature of the application of all seven of these messages, the prophecy must look forward to the time when the whole church enters the messianic kingdom (Beckwith). The people of Israel will have an entirely different attitude toward the church as Christ's bride because they will by then have turned to Christ themselves. Another support for this interpretation is the use of *proskynēsousin* ("worship") (v. 9). Worship denotes abject submission and homage before the glory of the church and can hardly be practiced by anyone who has not become Christ's follower (Moffatt). The people of ethnic Israel who will have become Christians will willingly render such homage to members of the Body of Christ.

Though both views have impressive support, the second seems stronger. It is the future repentance of Israel resulting in respectful treatment of the church that is in view in this third promise to the Philadelphian church. The Lord does reverse the application of Isa. 60:14 and similar OT passages to make them apply to a predominantly Gentile church rather than Israel as the recipients of homage. Of course, as His self-description that opens this message recalls, Israel too will repent and be blessed after the establishment of the kingdom, in *direct* fulfillment of these same prophecies.

The last part of Christ's purposed compulsion of these false Jews will bring them to know of His love for this faithful group of Christians. Emphasis falls upon *egō* ("I") and *se* ("you") in His words

---

35. G. V. Caird, *A Commentary on the Revelation of St. John the Divine*, HNTC (New York: Harper & Row, 1966), p. 52.
36. Swete, *Apocalypse*, p. 55; G. R. Beasley-Murray, *The Book of Revelation*, NCB (Grand Rapids: Eerdmans, 1978), p. 101; Hailey, *Revelation*, p. 152.

egō ēgapēsa se ("I have loved you") (v. 9).[37] Jesus, the true Messiah of Israel, has loved the ones persecuted by the false Jews (Bullinger; Beckwith). An awareness of this loving relationship will characterize a convinced Jew at the time of the end as he looks back upon this period of persecution. The false Jews scoffed at the claim of the Philadelphian Christians that they were objects of the true God's love, but that will change when Israel repents.

3:10 Jesus' commendation of and promises to the people of this church have not ended. He next names their endurance as the ground for a further promise of deliverance from the predicted period of future suffering on the earth: ὅτι ἐτήρησας τὸν λόγον τῆς ὑπομονῆς μου, κἀγώ σε τηρήσω ἐκ τῆς ὥρας τοῦ πειρασμοῦ τῆς μελλούσης ἔρχεσθαι ἐπὶ τῆς οἰκουμένης ὅλης πειράσαι τοὺς κατοικοῦντας ἐπὶ τῆς γῆς (*hoti etērēsas ton logon tēs hypomonēs mou, kagō se tērēsō ek tēs hōras tou peirasmou tēs mellousēs erchesthai epi tēs oikoumenēs holēs peirasai tous katoikountas epi tēs gēs,* "because you have kept the word of My endurance, I will also keep you from the hour of trial that is about to come upon the whole inhabited earth, to try those who dwell upon the earth"). This commendation resembles the *etērēsas mou ton logon* of 3:8, but is more specific. Now it is especially the word of Christ's endurance (*ton logon tēs hypomonēs mou*) that they have kept.[38] With *mou* understood as a subjective genitive, this may be the endurance that Christ requires or the endurance that He Himself displayed (Beckwith). The genitives following ὑπομονή (*hypomonē*, "endurance") in Rev. 13:10 and 14:12 support the latter meaning, as do the references to Christ's own endurance in 2 Thess. 3:5 and Heb. 12:3.[39] The preferable understanding is that of His endurance through which He exemplified the quality to be emulated by His followers. This quality figures prominently into the theme of Revelation (cf. 1:9; 2:2, 3).

In response to the church's keeping of His standards, Christ promises to keep it from the hour of trial.[40] *Tērēsō* ("I will keep") is a form

---

37. These words are perhaps an allusion to Isa. 43:3-4 (Hemer, *Seven Churches,* p. 164).
38. The genitive τῆς ὑπομονῆς is objective: "the word *about* my endurance."
39. Hemer, *Seven Churches,* p. 165. Mueller proposes a result relationship for the genitive in τῆς ὑπομονῆς μου, yielding the meaning, "You have kept the word with the result of perseverance in Me." He refers it to the concept of abiding in Christ found elsewhere in Johannine literature (Theodore Mueller, "'The Word of My Patience' in Revelation 3:10," *Concordia Theological Quarterly* 46 [April-June 1982]: 34). This meaning, however, assigns to ὑπομονή a meaning that is unwarranted in the immediate context and the NT as a whole.
40. The conjunction-pronoun κἀγώ expresses reciprocity: "I on my side" (Alford, 4: 585). Τηρήσω (future tense) corresponds to ἐτήρησας (aorist tense): "because you did keep . . . I will keep" (Beckwith, *Apocalypse,* p. 483). The repetition of the same verb emphasizes reciprocal action, though shades

of τηρέω (*tēreō,* "I keep, preserve"). This is a verb that at times emphasizes watchful care. Such seems most appropriate here. A meaning such as "protect" or "preserve" is called for to counter the trials that will compose "the hour of trial." The promise to the church is some mode of complete preservation and protection during this crisis hour.[41]

The precise import of this fourth promise to Philadelphia hinges on a proper understanding of the full expression *kagō se tērēsō ek tēs hōras tou peirasmou* ("I will keep you from the hour of trial"). Understanding "the hour of trial" to be the future period of trouble just before Christ's personal return to earth, as will be clarified below, do these words promise preservation while present during the period or preservation by means of removal from the scene of the suffering?[42]

A frequently used support for the former of these two possibilities comes from John 17:15 where the combination τηρέω εκ (*tēreō ek,* "I keep from") also occurs.[43] In that passage it is argued that Christ does not ask for believers to be kept from the presence of the evil one. Rather He asks that they be enabled to stand successfully *in his presence,* i.e., to be kept safe from the power of Satan as he assailed them (Moffatt; Beckwith). In response, those who advocate removal from the scene rather than preservation through the midst point out three differences between the present verse and John 17:15: (1) In John 17:15 the preservation is from evil, but in Rev. 3:10 it is from a period of time during which judgment will fall on the world (Smith;

---

of meaning assigned to the two occurrences differ. Ἐτήρησας is a keeping by way of obedience, but τηρήσω is a keeping by way of protection and watchful care. A similar play on the tenses of this verb is found in John 17:6, 11, 12 (Robertson, *Word Pictures,* 6:318).

41. Jeffrey L. Townsend, "The Rapture in Revelation 3:10," *BSac* 137 (1980): 253.

42. Other views regarding the timing and nature of the deliverance from "the hour of trial" include the partial rapture view, which teaches that various groups will be taken from the scene of the trials at different times throughout the period, and the midtribulation rapture view, which has much in common with the view of removal of all believers from the scene of the trouble cited above. It differs from the mainstream pretribulation rapture only in its definition of "the hour of trial," which it limits to the last three-and-one-half years before Christ's personal return to earth (Gleason L. Archer, "The Case for the Mid-Seventieth-Week Rapture," in *The Rapture: Pre-, Mid-, or Post-Tribulational,* essays by Reiter, Feinberg, Archer, and Moo [Grand Rapids: Zondervan, 1984], pp. 118-19). Neither of these views is as well supported as the two discussed more fully in the text above.

43. The full text of John 17:15 is οὐκ ἐρωτῶ ἵνα ἄρῃς αὐτοὺς ἐκ τοῦ κόσμου ἀλλ' ἵνα τηρήσῃς αὐτοὺς ἐκ τοῦ πονηροῦ. Removal from the scene of Satan's activity is the very thing Christ does not request, according to the first half of the verse.

Johnson). (2) In John 17:15 the disciples were already in the midst of evil, but in Rev. 3:10 the plagues of the tribulation period are still future (Smith). (3) In John 17:15b the spiritual realm of the evil one (i.e., spiritual death) is in view, not the moral sphere of the evil one (i.e., the world system), so Rev. 3:10 *does* refer to preservation in a position outside the realm of "the hour of trial."[44] In an attempt to neutralize the first of these three differences, some have noted that "the hour of trial" is essentially equivalent to "trial," the emphasis being upon the experience within the time, not the period as such.[45] This is not convincing, however, because ὥρα (*hōra*, "hour") is a temporal term, attempts to water it down notwithstanding. It cannot be construed otherwise.[46]

Another evidence for the view of preservation through the midst of "the hour of trial" has been the preposition *ek* ("from"). Insistence upon the word's local meaning of "out from within" and the consequent notion of deliverance out from within is the focal point of this argument.[47] This preposition lays all the emphasis on emergence, that is the final victorious outcome of the keeping.[48] The combination *tēreō ek* ("I keep from") connotes protection issuing in emission, it is argued.[49] This meaning allegedly finds support in the similar passage, Rev. 7:14: οἱ ἐρχόμενοι ἐκ τῆς θλίψεως τῆς μεγάλης (*hoi erchomenoi ek tēs thlipseōs tēs megalēs*, "those who are coming out of the great tribulation"). Yet this line of reasoning is quickly erased by noting that in 7:14 the local use of the preposition is required by its use with *erchomenoi* ("coming"), a verb of motion. The verb in 3:10, *tēreō* ("I will keep"), provides no such requirement.[50] It could just as well mean preservation after removal *from* the period. "Issuing in emergence from" is too much to read into the preposition *ek*. It could just as well signify protection "by being kept from within." Evidently

---

44. Townsend, "Rapture," p. 259. Winfrey and Edgar furnish additional considerations showing the inapplicability of John 17:15 to support the posttribulational position (David G. Winfrey, "The Great Tribulation: Kept 'Out of' or 'Through'?" *GTJ* 3, no. 1 [Spring 1982]: 5-10; Thomas R. Edgar, "Robert H. Gundry and Revelation 3:10," *GTJ* 3, no. 1 [Spring 1982]: 37-39).
45. Beasley-Murray, *Revelation*, p. 101; Robert H. Gundry, *The Church and the Tribulation* (Grand Rapids: Zondervan, 1973), pp. 59-60; Johnson, "Revelation," 12:455.
46. Edgar, "Gundry and Revelation 3:10," pp. 39-42; Paul D. Feinberg, "The Case for the Pretribulation Rapture Position," in *The Rapture: Pre-, Mid-, or Post-Tribulational*, pp. 69-70.
47. Gundry, *Church and Tribulation*, p. 55.
48. Ibid., p. 57.
49. Ibid., p. 59.
50. Alford, *Greek Testament*, 4:585; Edgar, "Gundry and Revelation 3:10," pp. 22-29.

its combination with *tēreō* modifies its primary meaning of motion out from within to its secondary meaning of outside position.⁵¹

The conclusion that the meaning is deliverance for members of the Philadelphian church while they remain present during "the hour of trial" is beset by serious weaknesses. One of them is the obvious fact that saints present during the Tribulation period will not be exempt from harm. Many of them will suffer martyrdom (e.g., 6:9-11; 7:9-14) and will not be preserved (Smith; Johnson). The usual response to this is that believers are kept from the outpouring of divine judgments on a rebellious world, but not from the fierce persecution imposed on them by the beast (Ladd). Further, martyrdom holds no terror for the saint because physical death has no eternal significance (Ladd). The reward for the church's devotion, manifested already in the face of Jewish malice (cf. 3:8-9), will be fresh power to be loyal on a higher level, i.e., against a storm of Roman persecution (Moffatt). In other words, because the church was faithful to Christ in time of trial, He in turn would be faithful to it in the time of its *great* trial.⁵² This response is not satisfactory, however, because it would imply that Christ had not been faithful to them up to that point. Preservation normally means protection from death. What good does it do to be preserved from the physical consequences of divine wrath and still fall prey to a martyr's death? The source of the bodily harm is inconsequential when incentive to persevere is in view. A promise of preservation is meaningless if the saints face the same fate as sinners during the Tribulation.

Another weakness in the approach which sees this as a promise of preservation while remaining present during "the hour of trial" surfaces in the observation that this meaning would have been more obvious with the use of either the preposition ἐν (*en*, "in") or διά (*dia*, "through") with the genitive case.⁵³ *En* would have shown clearly that they would be preserved "in" the midst of "the hour of trial," and *dia* would have indicated their preservation "through" the midst of "the hour of trial." Yet neither of these was used. The answer that each of these falls short of *ek* in placing all the emphasis on emergence and a final victorious outcome⁵⁴ is unconvincing. Nothing indicates that the emergence will be "final," i.e., at the end of the period, rather than at the outset of the Tribulation.

The view that the promise consists of removal from the earth

---

51. Townsend, "Rapture," pp. 257-58.
52. Schuyler Brown, "The Hour of Trial, Rev. 3:10," *JBL* 85 (1966): 308-14.
53. Henry Clarence Thiessen, *Will the Church Pass Through the Tribulation?* (New York: Loizeaux, 1941), p. 24.
54. Gundry, *Tribulation*, p. 57.

prior to "the hour of trial" is well supported. Perhaps the most convincing of all is how well it fits the immediate context of the message to Philadelphia. It assures the faithful in Philadelphia who had already undergone their fiery test that they would be spared the stress and storm that were to come on others after the arrival of "the hour of trial" (Beckwith). Not only would they be spared the effects of the wrath of the Lamb (cf. 6:16-17), which would fall on the earth's rebellious, but also an intensified persecution at the hands of Satan's representatives, which is destined for believers during this period. This would encourage them in their present suffering to persevere a little longer, whereas the other option of preservation while remaining during the Tribulation would furnish no encouragement at all. The latter would be tantamount to a threat rather than a promise, a threat that for remaining faithful, they would experience worse persecution than they had already. Such is completely inappropriate at this point in the message where a promise to motivate the recipients is required. Rather, they were encouraged to bear their present suffering and continue their faithfulness and endurance, because of the promised deliverance from the time of trouble that would overtake the world, but would not overtake them (Walvoord).

The view that provides for removal from the scene is satisfying also because it allows for an adequate meaning of "*the hour* of trial," a period of time during which the trial exists. If the promise pertained to the trial itself, the deliverance conceivably could be only partial, but the promise is strengthened considerably by referring to the period itself (Walvoord). Illustrations of the use of "hour" where emphasis falls on the experience within the time, not the period itself (Matt. 26:45; Mark 14:35, 41; John 2:4; 7:30; 8:20; 12:23, 27; 13:1; 17:1),[55] are not relevant nor are they persuasive even if they were relevant. This promise of being kept from the hour falls into an entirely different category of meaning from the other passages.

Another consideration favoring removal before "the hour of trial" comes from John 12:27.[56] In part, this verse has the wording σῶσον με ἐκ τῆς ὥρας ταύτης (*sōson me ek tēs hōras tautēs,* "save Me from this hour"). Of particular interest is the occurrence of the verb *sōson,* a word akin to *tēreō* in referring to deliverance, combined with the phrase *ek tēs hōras,* the same phrase as in Rev. 3:10. In this other

---

55. Ibid., pp. 59-60; cf. Douglas J. Moo, "The Case for the Posttribulation Rapture Position," in *The Rapture: Pre-, Mid-, or Post-Tribulational,* p. 96.
56. Gundry uses John 12:27 in an entirely different way in arguing for ignoring "the hour" in the expression "the hour of trial," as noted above. The present discussion gives full consideration to seeing ὥρα as a period of time.

Johannine passage Christ prayed to be saved from the hour of His crucifixion, meaning obviously that, humanly speaking, He wanted to be delivered from the awful agony of that experience. In other words, He wanted to be spared the necessity of living through the time period when it took place. It was not that He prayed for strength to go through it without giving in or feeling its effects. This is a prayer for complete exemption from the hour of crucifixion. This meaning, transferred to Rev. 3:10, shows it to be a promise of complete exemption from "the hour of trial." In essence, the promise is, "I will protect you [at a place] away from the period of misery on earth." The contention that Jesus in John 12:27 had already entered into His hour of trial[57] cannot be sustained. The hour referred to was the hour of His impending crucifixion, which was yet future (cf. John 7:30).[58] So the comparable construction and terminology from another Johannine book lend weight to the view of removal from the scene of tribulation.

Aside from the detailed supports cited, the most natural understanding of the expression "kept from the hour" is not to be preserved through it, but to be kept safe in a place away from where it occurs.[59] The participle τῆς μελλούσης (*tēs mellousēs*, "which is about to") modifies *hōras* ("hour") rather than πειρασμοῦ (*peirasmou*, "trial"), showing that it is the hour, not the trial, that is prominent in the statement. It is exemption from the period of time that is promised. By implication, this deliverance will coincide with Christ's return mentioned in the very next verse: "I will come soon" (3:11). Believers on earth will meet the Lord in the air and thus escape the hour of trial (Smith). One cannot make good sense out of Rev. 3:10 otherwise. The statement does not refer directly to the rapture. What it guarantees is protection away from the scene of the "hour of trial" while that hour is in progress. This effect of placing the faithful in Philadelphia (and hence, the faithful in all the churches; cf. 3:13) in a position of safety presupposes that they will have been removed to another location (i.e., heaven) at the period's beginning.

Identification of *tēs hōras*[60] *tou peirasmou*[61] ("the hour of trial") is

---

57. A. T. Robertson, *A Grammar of the Greek New Testament in the Light of Historical Research* (Nashville: Broadman, 1934), p. 598; Gundry, *Tribulation*, p. 56.
58. Smith, *Revelation*, pp. 331-33; John A. Sproule, *In Defense of Pretribulationism* (Winona Lake, Ind.: BMH, 1980), p. 28; Townsend, "Rapture," p. 256.
59. Charles Caldwell Ryrie, *Revelation*, Everyman's Bible Commentary (Chicago: Moody, 1968), p. 30; Johnson, "Revelation," 12:455.
60. In this instance the noun ὥρας does not mean a literal sixty-minute hour, but has a more general meaning of "period" as it does frequently in the Apocalypse (cf. 3:3; 8:7; 9:15; 11:13; 14:7; 17:12; 18:10, 17, 19).
61. The English "trial" is the rendering chosen for πειρασμοῦ because through this time of misery some of the faithless may come to repentance. Yet the

not difficult. This is no mere general or personal stress that came upon the Christian community at Philadelphia.[62] In the first place it is directed against *tēs oikoumenēs holēs* ("the whole inhabited earth"), not just Philadelphia, and secondly, it is designed to try *tous katoikountas epi tēs gēs* ("those who dwell upon the earth"). This is a company of people constantly in view throughout the Apocalypse as objects of God's wrath because of their rebellion against Him.[63] Rather than a local and immediate application this expression anticipates a much more significant period that will impact the whole world just prior to Christ's personal return to earth. In the words of another, it is the imminent period of "broken days which in eschatological schemes was to herald the Messiah's return" (Moffatt). It is the time known to the Jews as the "Messianic woes," foretold in the visions beginning at Revelation 4 as coming upon the world. It is to be a time of distress on the world before the coming of Christ, one known as the Day of the Lord, the Tribulation, or the Great Tribulation (cf. Dan. 12:1; Joel 2:31; Mark 13:14; 2 Thess. 2:1-12; Rev. 7:14; 14:7). This accounts for Christ's words "I will come soon" in Rev. 3:11, immediately following. The trials of this period are designed to test the wicked, either to lead them to repentance or to punish them for failing to repent (cf. 9:20; 11:13; 16:11) (Alford; Beckwith; Johnson).

The widened scope of this promise meant that the Philadelphian Christians would triumph over the contempt and intrigues of their immediate Jewish foes, but also over the wider pagan opponents (Moffatt). Because this period of tribulation will immediately precede the coming of the Lord to earth in power and great glory (cf. Matt. 24:29, 30), and because the generation to whom John wrote these words has long since passed away, Philadelphia's representation of not just the other six churches of Asia but also of the church universal throughout the present age is evident (Smith).

The timing of "the hour of trial's" arrival is reflected by *tēs*

---

prevailing sense behind the word is affliction and calamity because it is directed primarily against "those who dwell upon the earth," i.e., those in rebellion against God. The definite article shows that this period was well known by the recipients of the Apocalypse (Alford, *Greek Testament,* 4:586).

62. Robertson, *Grammar,* p. 598; J. Barton Payne, *The Imminent Appearing of Christ* (Grand Rapids: Eerdmans, 1962), pp. 78-79.

63. Ladd, *Revelation,* p. 62; Johnson, "Revelation," 12:454. The phrase τοὺς κατοικοῦντας ἐπὶ τῆς γῆς is apparently from Hos. 4:1 where the LXX contains the phrase τοὺς κατοικοῦντας τὴν γῆν. There as here, the group is the object of God's judgment because of unfaithfulness. There it is limited to Israel, but in Revelation it includes all peoples. The phrase is used ten other times in Revelation and always in a bad sense. These are men given up to evil and hatred of God's saints (cf. 6:10; 8:13; 11:10 [twice]; 13:8, 12, 14 [twice]; 17:2, 8; Hort, *Apocalypse,* p. 35).

mellousēs erchesthai ("which is about to come"). The words describe "the hour" and show that it should be closely related to ἃ δεῖ γενέσθαι ἐν τάχει (*ha dei genesthai en tachei*, "things that must happen soon") and correspondingly also to ἔρχομαι ταχύ (*erchomai tachy*, "I will come soon"). "The hour of trial" was thought to be near by the early church, an impression that was justified in light of the participle *mellousēs* ("about to"). It was a period conceived of as about to happen at any moment. It was nearing daily and was something that could not be deferred much longer.[64]

3:11 *The Lord's coming.* The imminence of "the hour of trial" and the promise of the church's protection away from the scene of this hour accounts for the rather abrupt ἔρχομαι ταχύ (*erchomai tachy*, "I will come soon") at the beginning of v. 11. Christ promises to return soon to initiate "the hour of trial" on earth, but more relevant to those in the Philadelphian church, to deliver them from their difficult circumstances. The placement of this fifth promise at this point is clear implication that deliverance of the faithful will occur in conjunction with His coming. It holds open the possibility that His coming will happen before this generation passes, but does not guarantee it. This heightens the expectancy of Christ's coming soon, a possibility that is stressed further by the presence of *tachy* ("soon").[65] This kind of anticipation supplies motivation for the church to persevere (Swete).

Erchomai tachy ("I will come soon") is one of many recurrences of the book's keynote (cf. 1:7). Comparable expressions are found in 2:5 (where *tachy* ["soon"] is implied), 16; 22:7, 12, 20. A similar expression, ἥξω ὡς κλέπτης (*hēxō hōs kleptēs*, "I will come as a thief"), occurs in 3:3 and 16:5. These are sometimes warnings to the unfaithful to bring them to repentance (cf. 2:5, 16; 3:3; 16:5) and sometimes promises to the faithful to provide encouragement (cf. 3:11; 22:7, 12, 20). To Philadelphia it is, of course, for encouragement and comfort. This can hardly be His return to earth described in Rev. 19:11-21, because this phase of His coming will be preceded by all the events described in chapters 6-18. A return to earth could not be characterized as "soon" by any stretch of the imagination. It is rather an imminent event that will come suddenly and unexpectedly (Walvoord). Only this nearness of the Lord's coming to reward the faithful provides an effective motive to be tenacious (Alford; Moffatt).

His near return leaves only one course of action open to the faithful: κράτει ὃ ἔχεις (*kratei ho echeis*, "hold fast what you have"). Though

---

64. Swete, *Apocalypse*, p. 55; Walter Scott, *Exposition of the Revelation of Jesus Christ* (Swengel, Pa.: Bible Truth Depot, n.d.), p. 105.
65. Charles, *Revelation*, 1:90; Frederick A. Tatford, *Prophecy's Last Word* (London: Pickering and Inglis, 1947), p. 68.

no conjunction is used,[66] this clause is inferential, based on *erchomai tachy*. "Hold fast what you have" is sort of a motto for each church (cf. 2:25).[67] The degree of progress already achieved by the church (cf. 2:6, τοῦτο ἔχεις [*touto echeis*, "this you have"]) was a rich treasure (cf. 3:8, 10) and was to be clung to tenaciously in resistance against those who were trying to take it away (Alford). The promise of being kept from "the hour of trial" in v. 10 carries with it the responsibility of continued effort (*kratei*, "hold fast"), and the motive for doing so derives from the short interval remaining until Christ returns (*erchomai tachy*, "I will come soon").[68]

The enjoined tenacity has the goal of protection against the Philadelphians' having their crown stolen: ἵνα μηδεὶς λάβῃ τὸν στέφανόν σου (*hina mēdeis labē ton stephanon sou*, "that no one take your crown"). The robber would not steal the crown for himself, but simply to deprive the faithful of the benefit.[69] The benefit is called *ton stephanon sou* ("your crown"). The Smyrnan church was promised the same reward, except there the crown was equated to "life" (cf. Rev. 2:10). Perhaps here the more general meaning of victory attached to *stephanon* should remain undefined. The city was known for its games and festivals, so the word was not strange to the people. However, probably more to the point was the precariousness of life in a place so liable to ruin from natural disaster and economic change (Hemer). The believers' own steadfastness was an assurance that these catastrophes of the natural realm could not befall them in the spiritual realm. They were safe from all enemies.

3:12 *Promise to the overcomer.* The promise to the Philadelphian overcomer draws heavily upon the picture of the eternal state in Revelation 21-22: ὁ νικῶν[70] ποιήσω αὐτὸν στῦλον ἐν τῷ ναῷ τοῦ θεοῦ μου, καὶ ἔξω οὐ μὴ ἐξέλθῃ ἔτι, καὶ γράψω ἐπ᾽ αὐτὸν τὸ ὄνομα τοῦ θεοῦ μου καὶ τὸ ὄνομα τῆς πόλεως τοῦ θεοῦ μου, τῆς καινῆς Ἰερουσαλήμ, ἡ καταβαίνουσα ἐκ τοῦ οὐρανοῦ ἀπὸ τοῦ θεοῦ μου, καὶ τὸ ὄνομά μου τὸ

---

66. Both ἔρχομαι ταχύ and κράτει ὃ ἔχεις are emphatic because their connection with what precedes is only implied. Such instances of asyndeton serve to make the statements more penetrating.
67. Robertson, *Word Pictures*, 6:319.
68. Swete, *Apocalypse*, p. 56. The present imperative of κράτει brings out the continuing nature of command: "keep on holding fast." Ταχύ, of course, points out the brevity of the anticipated wait till Christ's return.
69. Alford, *Greek Testament*, 4:586. The rider on the red horse in Rev. 6:4 is similar to this thief. He takes peace from the earth, not so that he himself can enjoy it, but for the express purpose that earth's inhabitants can no longer enjoy it.
70. Ὁ νικῶν is a nominative absolute, a construction found in the promise to the overcomer in 2:26 and 3:21 also. It is resumed by two occurrences of αὐτὸν later in the sentence.

καινόν (*ho nikōn poiēsō auton stylon en tōͅnaōͅͅtou theou mou, kai exō ou mē exelthē ͤti, kai grapsō ep' auton to onoma tou theou mou kai to onoma tēs poleōs tou theou mou, tēs kainēs Ierousalēm, hē katabainousa ek tou ouranou apo tou theou mou, kai to onoma mou to kainon,* "The one who overcomes, I will make him a pillar in the temple of My God, and he will not possibly go outside any longer, and I will write upon him the name of My God and the name of the city of My God, the new Jerusalem, which descends from heaven from My God, and My new name"). This promise is the sixth one given to this church. This overcomer is none other than the one who keeps on holding fast (cf. v. 11). The message purposes to assure Christians of an eternally enduring place in the messianic kingdom and an open recognition of them as the people of God and of the Messiah (Beckwith). Hence, the promise to the overcomer must pertain to the ones just instructed to hold fast. The promise tells of the reward for their perseverance: a stable relationship to God and an absolute assurance (trebly verified) of eternal life (Moffatt).

The stable relationship to God is guaranteed by *poiēsō auton stylon en tōͅ naōͅ tou theou mou, kai exō ou mē exelthē eti* ("I will make him a pillar in the temple of My God, and he will not possibly go outside any longer"). The language is clearly metaphorical, as is evident from *stylon* ("pillar"). Because the person is likened to a pillar, *naōͅ* ("temple") must be metaphorical also (Charles). Hence, this promise is not inconsistent with the later statement that there is no temple in the heavenly Jerusalem (Rev. 21:22). The Jerusalem that comes down from heaven is all temple, and Christ's victorious ones are its living stones and pillars.[71] The Philadelphian Christians will be permanent, like a pillar in the Temple, and will stand when all else has fallen. They are assured of continuance in God's presence throughout all eternity (Walvoord). Christ once again refers to the Father as His God: *tou theou mou* ("my God"). In fact, He does so four times in this verse in order to emphasize this relationship (cf. also 3:2).[72]

The security of the overcomer is further elaborated upon by *kai exō ou mē exelthē eti*[73] ("and he will not possibly go outside any long-

---

71. Alford, *Greek Testament,* 4:586. Despite the explicit reference to the Temple, Wilkinson proposes the pillar promise to contain kingship and coronation allusions drawn from the history of Israel and the nations around them (Richard H. Wilkinson, "The ΣΤΥΛΟΣ of Revelation 3:12 and Ancient Coronation Rites," *JBL* 107, no. 3 [Sept 1988]: 498-99). The acknowledged unfamiliarity of the recipients with the customs involved (ibid., p. 500) is a serious deficiency for this theory.
72. The Father is called the God of Christ by NT writers in Heb. 1:9 and 1 Pet. 1:3. See note at Rev. 3:2 for other places where Christ calls the Father His God.
73. Possibly, a contrast with Philadelphia's sufferings from the great earthquake of A.D. 17 is in the background of this statement because many of

er"). The underscored[74] promise notices the fixity of character that will have been achieved and the oneness of the overcomer with God, making separation an impossibility. He will be the exact opposite of those who are refused entrance into the city (Swete; Charles; Walvoord).

The other part of the promise to the overcomer is an absolute assurance of eternal life. This is indicated by his reception of a threefold name: *grapsō ep' auton*[75] *to onoma tou theou mou kai to onoma tēs poleōs tou theou mou, tēs kainēs Ierousalēm, hē katabainousa ek tou ouranou apo tou theou mou, kai to onoma mou to kainon* ("I will write upon him the name of My God and the name of the city of My God, the new Jerusalem, which descends from heaven from My God, and My new name"). The threefold occurrence of *onoma* ("name") is impressive and amounts to a threefold assurance of his identity with God. To have "the name of My God" was equivalent to belonging to God, being endowed with divine power (Moffatt). This sets the overcomer in utter contrast with the assumptions of his present Jewish persecutors (Beckwith).

To have "the name of the city of My God" meant the right of citizenship in the new Jerusalem (Charles). This is "the new Jerusalem" that descends from God after the white throne judgment and the creation of the new heavens and the new earth (cf. 21:10 ff.). Like the holy city of 21:2, 10, this one is described as descending[76] out of heaven, "from My God" as Christ describes it. It is the successor to the old Jerusalem with which John was familiar (Swete). Citizenship in this city is yet another mark of assurance for the overcomer.

Christ's "new name" symbolizes the full revelation of His character promised to the overcomer at Christ's second advent. Currently, man is incapable of grasping the full theological significance of the incarnation, but that will change. When He comes, the victors will

---

the city's inhabitants lived outside the city after the destruction of their homes (Hemer, *Seven Churches*, p. 166).

74. The construction οὐ μὴ ἐξέλθῃ, a double negative followed by the aorist subjunctive, expresses emphatic negation.

75. It is sometimes suggested that the antecedent of αὐτὸν be understood as στῦλον, because inscriptions on pillars were a common feature of Oriental architecture. The nearer and preferable antecedent, however, is the unexpressed subject of ἐξέλθῃ, the overcomer. The victor receives the name on his forehead as in 14:1 and 22:4 (cf. Ex. 28:36-38) (Charles, *Revelation*, 1:92; Mounce, *Revelation*, p. 121; Hemer, *Seven Churches*, p. 166).

76. The case of ἡ καταβαίνουσα is nominative, contrary to what is normal. The participle is in apposition with Ἰερουσαλήμ (indeclinable) whose case is genitive in its agreement with πόλεως. The unusual construction is an instance of "irregular apposition" (Lee, "Revelation," 4:542). See the similar phenomenon in 1:5; 2:13, 20.

not only appreciate fully who Christ is, but they will bear His new name with Him (Charles; Mounce). Herein is further assurance.

3:13 *Command to hear.* What the Spirit through Christ has said to Philadelphia is an invitation to anyone in any of the churches to hear and heed: ὁ ἔχων οὖς ἀκουσάτω τί τὸ πνεῦμα λέγει ταῖς ἐκκλησίαις (*ho echōn ous akousatō ti to pneuma legei tais ekklēsiais,* "The one who has an ear, let him hear what the Spirit says to the churches").

Additional Notes

3:9 The combination ποιήσω . . . ἵνα introduces the purpose of Christ's compelling action. Ἵνα introduces a purpose clause with two future indicative verbs (ἥξουσιν and προσκυνήσουσιν) and one aorist subjunctive one (γνῶσιν). The combination of future indicative and aorist subjunctive in the same ἵνα clause is also found in 22:14. The future tenses following ἵνα are unusual, but constitute a construction characteristic of John's writings (cf. John 15:8; 17:2), especially in Revelation (cf. Rev. 6:4, 11; 8:3; 9:4, 5, 20; 13:12; 14:13; 22:14).[77]

An inversion of the logical sequence, known as *hysteron-proteron,* occurs here as it does frequently in the book. The writer tends to look first at the result, then at the steps leading to it. Here the "come and worship" is the result of "know." Only after knowing that Christ has loved this church will the opponents come and bow down before their feet (cf. also 3:17; 5:2, 5; 10:4, 9; 12:10; 19:13).[78]

---

77. Lee, "Revelation," 4:460, 540; Swete, *Apocalypse,* p. 65.
78. Beckwith, *Apocalypse,* pp. 243-44.

9
Church of Lukewarmness

G. THE MESSAGE TO LAODICEA (3:14-22)

The last of the seven messengers was left to carry out, probably alone, his mission, which must have been quite traumatic. His was the task of transmitting the most solemn message and sharpest rebuke given to any of the seven churches, to a prestigious congregation in a well-to-do community.[1] Here is a church that the Lord reprimands sternly for its lukewarmness. No commendation of any kind appears. The only encouragement in the message is the possibility it extends for repentance and overcoming.

Translation

14And to the messenger of the church that is in Laodicea, write:
"These things says the Amen, the faithful and true witness, the beginning of the creation of God. 15I know your works, that you are neither cold nor hot. I wish that you were cold or hot. 16Thus, because you are lukewarm and neither hot nor cold, I am about to spew you out of My mouth. 17Because you say, 'I am rich and have become rich and have need of nothing,' and [yet] you do not know that you are wretched and miserable and poor and blind and naked, 18I counsel you to buy from Me gold refined by fire that you may become rich,

---

1. E. W. Bullinger, *The Apocalypse* or *"The Day of the Lord"* (London: Eyre and Spottiswoode, n.d.), p. 204.

and white garments that you may be clothed and the shame of your nakedness may not be exposed, and eyesalve to anoint your eyes that you may see. [19]As many as I love, I reprove and chasten; be zealous, therefore, and repent. [20]Behold, I am standing at the door and knocking; if any hears My voice and opens the door, I will enter to him and will eat supper with him, and he with Me. [21]The one who overcomes, I will grant that he sit down with Me in My throne, as I also overcame and sat down with My Father in His throne. [22]The one who has an ear, let him hear what the Spirit says to the churches."

Exegesis and Exposition

3:14 *The address.* The message to Laodicea is addressed in the normal manner: Καὶ τῷ ἀγγέλῳ τῆς ἐν Λαοδικείᾳ ἐκκλησίας γράψον (*Kai tō angelō tēs en Laodikeiā ekklēsias grapson*, "And to the messenger of the church that is in Laodicea, write"). The name Laodicea is derived from combining λαός (*laos*, "people") with δικάω (*dikaō*, "I rule"). It conveys the sense "the rule of the people," i.e., a democracy.[2] Paul knew of this church during his first Roman imprisonment (A.D. 60-62), though he had not yet visited here personally (cf. Col. 2:1). He had written the people a letter, however, which perhaps can be identified with his NT epistle named Ephesians (cf. Col. 4:16).[3]

Laodicea was the most easterly and the southernmost of the seven churches addressed in the Apocalypse, though it was only slightly farther south than Ephesus. Ephesus was almost due west of Laodicea. It lay about 40 miles southeast of Philadelphia and was the natural terminal destination for those responsible for circulating this book. It was in the Lycus Valley at a critical juncture on a major highway. It was the highway that began at Ephesus in the west, ascended the Maeander Valley and continued eastward to enter the Gate of Phrygia. Beyond this gate was a much broader valley where Lydia, Phrygia, and Caria came together, a valley entered by the Maeander flow-

---

2. William R. Newell, *The Book of Revelation* (Chicago: Moody, 1935), p. 75.
3. Henry Barclay Swete, *The Apocalypse of St. John* (London: Macmillan, 1906), p. 59; Isbon T. Beckwith, *The Apocalypse of John* (New York: Macmillan, 1919), pp. 486-88; R. C. H. Lenski, *The Interpretation of St. John's Revelation* (Columbus, Ohio: Lutheran Book Concern, 1935), p. 151; G. V. Caird, *A Commentary on the Revelation of St. John the Divine*, HNTC (New York: Harper & Row, 1966), p. 56. If, as many NT students conclude, the words ἐν Ἐφέσῳ were missing from the autograph of Ephesians, it was probably a circular letter to all the churches in the Roman province of Asia, including Laodicea. Since the bearer of Ephesians and Colossians was Tychicus (Eph. 6:21-22; Col. 4:7-8), the reference in Col. 4:16 to "the [epistle] from Laodicea" could easily be what we know as Ephesians (Colin J. Hemer, *The Letters to the Seven Churches of Asia in Their Local Setting*, JSNTSup 11; Sheffield: U. of Sheffield, 1986], p. 181).

ing from the north. From the point where the Maeander joins its tributary, the Lycus River, the road follows the Lycus Valley eastward as the Maeander turns to the north at about this point and becomes too rugged for travel. The Lycus Valley is on two levels with Laodicea occupying the lower level and, not far away, Colosse the upper one about ten miles to the east. A third member of this tri-city combination was Hierapolis lying six miles due north of Laodicea, between the Lycus and the Maeander. The Lycus Valley was one of the most frequent routes of travel from the interior to the west because of the ease with which one could travel the road. Laodicea was situated as a guardian of this road, near the spot where the Lycus Valley opened into the Maeander Valley.[4] It also was the place where the road from Pergamum and Sardis on the north crossed the east-west route, on its way to the south coast (Hemer).

Though nearly impregnable because of the arrangement of the surrounding mountains, Laodicea was vulnerable because it was almost completely dependent on others for its water. This weakness hindered the city from taking military advantage of what was otherwise an ideal situation. The aqueducts that brought water into the city were underground, but an attacking enemy could easily learn of their existence and sever them, denying the city its needed water. These aqueducts had been unnecessary during the days of the city's early settlement. Water from the local stream was sufficient, but as the population increased, it became necessary to import water from outside sources (Ramsay; Hemer).

Little is known of the history of the founding of Laodicea. The probable founder was Antiochus II (261-246 B.C.), who named it for his wife Laodice whom he divorced in 253 B.C. With its Seleucid origin, it probably resembled Thyatira in constitution and law, but here again, records are too scarce to be dogmatic (Ramsay). Since the city was intended to strengthen the Seleucid hold on the land, its original population would have been chosen from among those loyal to the king. Most were probably Syrians, but a segment of the inhabitants may have been Jewish. Allowance must also be made for some Macedonian colonists. Later, after Phrygia was given to Eumenes by the Romans (189 B.C.), the loyalty of the city to the west was strengthened by importing new citizens loyal to the Pergamenians. Thus Laodicea and other cities of the Lycus Valley came to have very mixed populations (Ramsay; Hemer).

The city served as the judicial seat of the district of which it was a part. Its location at an important travel intersection also made it a

---

4. W. M. Ramsay, *The Letters to the Seven Churches of Asia* (New York: A. C. Armstrong, 1904), pp. 413-14; Hemer, *Seven Churches*, p. 178.

great commercial and financial center, a potential it realized after Rome took control of the area and brought peace to the land. It was an important manufacturing center, as well. The major product was a widely sought after soft wool that was glossy black in color. The wool was woven into garments for local use and export trade. It was in competition with its neighbors in Colosse and Hierapolis, where wool was also manufactured, but apparently was the economic victor because of the peculiar black and soft qualities of its own wool.[5]

The seat of a famous school of medicine was also located in Laodicea, though the temple of "the god of the valley," Men Karou, alongside which the school grew up, was about thirteen miles to the west. The Laodicean physicians followed the teachings of Hierophilos (350-250 B.C.), who advocated that compound diseases required compound medicines for treatment. They developed an unusual system of heterogeneous mixtures. A well-known medicine developed by the physicians of this school was applied to the eyes to cure eye diseases (Ramsay; Hemer). Commerce, manufacturing, and medicine combined to make Laodicea a wealthy city. Many of its citizens also were quite wealthy. The prosperity of the city was illustrated following a great earthquake of A.D. 60, which destroyed the city and other cities around it. As was its habit, the Roman government offered substantial aid in rebuilding the devastation. Yet Laodicea was not among those cities who received help. Whether the government refused to offer it because of their great wealth, or Laodicea refused it because they did not need it, is debated. Whatever the case, the reason was wealth. Even nearby Hierapolis, a prosperous city in its own right, received imperial aid for rebuilding. Laodicea not only received none, but its citizens even contributed heavily in helping rebuild some of the other cities.[6]

Laodicea occupied a strategic location as one of only two entrances into Phrygia from the west, the other entrance point being Philadelphia. As discussed earlier, Philadelphia fulfilled its duty of Hellenizing the portion of the region to which it had access, but Laodicea was a miserable failure in this regard. The portion surrounding Laodicea still spoke its native tongue, not Greek. No plausible explanation for the difference between the "evangelistic" success of the two cities has been advanced, but it interestingly parallels the spiritual success of the churches in the two as reflected in these last two messages of Revelation 2-3 (Ramsay).

---

5. Hemer, *Seven Churches*, pp. 181, 199-201; Ramsay, *Seven Churches*, p. 416.
6. Richard Chenevix Trench, *Commentary on the Epistles to the Seven Churches in Asia* (London: Parker, Son, and Bourn, 1861), p. 252; Beckwith, *Apocalypse*, pp. 486-87; Hemer, *Seven Churches*, pp. 192-96.

Inscriptions discovered in Laodicea furnish no evidence of the Jewish population in the city, though other records reflect a significant size and influence of the Jewish community there. Antiochus III reportedly settled 2,000 Jewish families in Lydia and Phrygia, according to Josephus. Laodicea, founded as a Seleucid city and on the borders of the two territories, was a natural center for the immigration. In 62 B.C. the Roman governor of Asia refused to allow Asian Jews to send their contributions to Jerusalem. Instead he seized the money. The amount seized in the district of Apameia of Phrygia, the district in which Laodicea was most prominent, indicates a population of 7,500 adult Jewish freemen (discounting women and children). A reference in the Talmud suggests that the Jews of Laodicea were the apex of ease and laxity. Jews in nearby Hierapolis are known to have been organized into trade guilds. Lessons about Laodicean Jews may be learned by analogy from this neighboring situation (Ramsay; Hemer).

The temple of the Phrygian god Men Karou was the center of society and administration as well as of religion for the valley where Laodicea was located. A market was there, protected by the sacred name, for trading with people from a distance. The medical school connected with the temple, as described above, was also there. When Hellenism found its home in the valley, the people continued to worship the god considered supreme in the district but imparted to him something of their own character and identified him with their own god Zeus. The Laodicean god was sometimes called Aseis, perhaps a Semitic word meaning "powerful." If the Semitic influence was present, it would indicate that the body of settlers from Syria brought in at the city's founding had imparted an element of their own character to the god also (Ramsay).

The introduction of Christianity into the Lycus Valley can be sketched from NT sources. The Holy Spirit prohibited Paul from entering Asia in A.D. 50 (Acts 16:6), forcing him to traverse only the northern borders of the province. He reached Ephesus via an overland route in A.D. 52, probably following the upland road through Tralla to the Cayster Valley (Acts 19:1). While he ministered in Ephesus, Epaphras evangelized the Lycus Valley, primarily Laodicea (Col. 1:6-7). By the time Paul wrote Colossians (A.D. 61), he had not personally visited Laodicea or Colosse (Col. 2:1). His intended visit to Colosse (Philem. 22) did not come until his release from Roman imprisonment (A.D. 62 or 63). Paul's "letter from Laodicea" (Col. 4:16) (our Ephesians) and his letter to Colosse were unusual, since Paul had not personally been in the Lycus Valley to found the churches. The suggestion that Archippus (Col. 4:17), a son of Philemon (Philem. 1:2), was responsible for the church in Laodicea is plausible. Churches in the three cities—Hierapolis, Laodicea, and Colosse—were closely related because of geographical proximity to each other, with the first two overshadowing the last because of their size and economic importance. Colosse had declined in importance through the decades of the first century A.D. (Hemer).

Attributes of the speaker. Christ's self-description to the church in Laodicea is threefold: Τάδε λέγει ὁ Ἀμήν, ὁ μάρτυς ὁ πιστὸς καὶ ἀληθινός, ἡ ἀρχὴ τῆς κτίσεως τοῦ θεοῦ (*Tade legei ho Amēn, ho martys ho pistos kai alēthinos, hē archē tēs ktiseōs tou theou,* "These things says the Amen, the faithful and true witness, the beginning of the creation of God"). The first title, *ho Amēn* ("the Amen"), is used only here as a personal name for Christ. Usually functioning as an adverb, the word has an article preceding it. This makes it a substantive and uses it to represent a quality par excellence.[7] It thus becomes a descriptive title for the Lord,[8] and pictures Him as the one in whom verity is personified (Beckwith). The Greek word, a transliteration of the Hebrew אָמֵן (*'āmēn,* "be firm"), means "verity" and implies certainty. The Hebrew source word signifies what is "fixed," "true," or "unchangeable."[9] A form of *'āmēn* is translated "truth" in the twofold occurrence of "God of truth" in Isa. 65:16. The concept in the use of *ho Amēn* is credibility, the certainty that all this person says will be accomplished.[10] Since the principal indictment against the Laodicean church is lukewarmness, Christ's attributes of sincerity and truth come to the forefront as He deals with those whose alleged devotion to Him is only superficial and not substantial.[11]

The second part of Christ's self-designation in this seventh message is *ho martys ho pistos kai alēthinos* ("the faithful and true witness"). This expression is an emphatic one intended to make *ho Amēn* more specific.[12] *Martys* ("witness") is sometimes used in a legal sense, sometimes in a historical sense, and sometimes in an ethical sense. In

---

7. Nigel Turner, *Syntax,* vol. 3 of *A Grammar of New Testament Greek* (Edinburgh: T. & T. Clark, 1963), pp. 113-14.
8. Walter Scott, *Exposition of the Revelation of Jesus Christ* (Swengel, Pa.: Bible Truth Depot, n.d.), p. 109.
9. Scott, *Revelation,* p. 109. See also the discussion of אָמֵן used as an adverb at 1:6.
10. Swete, *Apocalypse,* p. 59; F. J. A. Hort, *The Apocalypse of St. John* (London: Macmillan, 1908), p. 36; Henry Alford, *The Greek Testament,* 4 vols. (London: Longmans, Green, 1903), 4:588; James Moffatt, "The Revelation of St. John the Divine," in *The Expositor's Greek Testament,* ed. W. Robertson Nicoll (Grand Rapids: Eerdmans, n.d.), 5:370; Beckwith, *Apocalypse,* p. 488; Lenski, *Revelation,* p. 152; John F. Walvoord, *The Revelation of Jesus Christ* (Chicago: Moody, 1966), p. 90; Caird, *Revelation,* p. 57.
11. Albert Barnes, *The Book of Revelation* (New York: Harper, 1851), p. 1569.
12. Lenski, *Revelation,* p. 152. The "long attributive" construction gives the words more emphasis.

the last sense it came to be used of those who died because of their testimony for Christ (cf. 2:13). The present use is a narrow application of the historical sense. The thought of Jesus as a witness is a favorite one in John's writings (e.g., John 3:11, 32, 33), but it does not occur elsewhere in the NT.[13]

Several suggestions about the precise connotation of *martys* in this verse have emerged. One approach contends that its primary reference is to the witness borne by Christ during His earthly life.[14] This view notes its agreement with Paul's reference to Christ's witness before Pontius Pilate (cf. 1 Tim. 6:13) and both Jesus' (John 5:31; 8:14) and John's (John 19:35; 21:24) descriptions of Christ's earthly witness in John's gospel.[15] More impressive, however, is the obvious fact that this witness of Christ is quite remote from and therefore relatively irrelevant to the present situation.

Another idea relates the word to the witness borne in the Apocalypse.[16] Substantiation of this comes in noting that it concurs with the meaning of "the faithful witness" in 1:5[17] and that Christ's witnessing activity is a theme elsewhere in the Apocalypse (cf. 19:9, 11; 21:5; 22:6) (Beckwith). This meaning should be included, but it does not allow a wide enough scope for the word.

Still another way to explain the word is to limit its primary force to just this seventh message (Alford). Certainly it is because He is the faithful and true witness that His counsel and rebuke are to be taken seriously and His promises believed (Moffatt). This meaning is appropriate because Christ's trustworthiness stands in direct contrast to the unfaithfulness of the Laodicean church.[18] As in the other six messages, this explanation provides in the introductory self-designation an accented focus upon certain features of the message to follow (Alford). This view is persuasive, but is not broad enough to allow for references to Christ's faithful witness elsewhere in the book (cf. 1:5; 19:9, 11; 21:5; 22:6).

---

13. Trench, *Seven Churches*, p. 254; Swete, *Apocalypse*, p. 59; Lenski, *Revelation*, p. 152. The word μάρτυς occurs only here and in 1:5 in the NT as a reference to Christ. Its cognates express the same idea of testimony, however, and reflect John's concept of Christ in this regard.
14. Trench, *Seven Churches*, p. 254; R. H. Charles, *The Revelation of St. John*, 2 vols., ICC (New York: Scribner's, 1920), 1:14.
15. J. B. Smith, *A Revelation of Jesus Christ* (Scottdale, Pa.: Herald, 1961), p. 92.
16. Archibald Thomas Robertson, *Word Pictures in the New Testament*, 6 vols. (Nashville: Broadman, 1933), 6:286; Newell, *Revelation*, p. 75.
17. Robertson, *Word Pictures*, 6:286.
18. G. R. Beasley-Murray, *The Book of Revelation*, NCB (Grand Rapids: Eerdmans, 1978), p. 104; Robert H. Mounce, *The Book of Revelation*, NICNT (Grand Rapids: Eerdmans, 1977), p. 124.

The best way to take *martys* in 3:14 is to make it comprehensive in covering Christ's reliability as a witness to every divine revelation (Charles). This meaning agrees closely with that assigned in 1:5, and is especially well supported by the observation that a faithful witness can be trusted never to misrepresent His message by exaggeration or suppression, with His veracity extending not only to His character but also to the content of His message (Moffatt). This meaning is broad enough to provide for an allusion to the OT source of the total expression (Ps. 89:37 [38]; cf. Rev. 1:5) as well as agreeing with the focus of the book as a whole and the need expressed in the message to Laodicea. Christ is the epitome of veracity.

Pistos ("faithful") is an adjective expressing Christ's entire trust-worthiness as a witness (Trench; Beckwith). In the NT it describes one who is either trusting (cf. John 20:27; Acts 16:1) or trustworthy (cf. 1 Thess. 5:21; 2 Tim. 2:22; 1 John 1:9). It can be applied to man in either sense, each context being the determining factor, but it can be applied to God only in the latter sense as it is here. This title given to Christ stands in conspicuous contrast to the Laodicean church, which was neither faithful nor true.[19] *Alēthinos* supplies the dimension of "true" or "genuine" to Christ's witness. The picture of Christ is not merely that of His truthfulness, but goes beyond to portray the ex-emplification of the perfect ideal of a witness in whom all the highest conditions of a witness are met, one whose testimony never falls short of the truth (Trench; Swete; Moffatt; Beckwith; Lenski).

The third title adopted by Christ in this Laodicean message is *hē archē tēs ktiseōs tou theou* ("the beginning of the creation of God"). Among professing Christians whose devotion to Christ is lax or even nonexistent, one reaction of self-justification is to downgrade the Person of Christ by rationalizing that He is not so exceptional. Christ's choice of this title hints that such may have been happening. Such a Christological error is known to have existed some thirty-five years earlier in the neighboring church at Colosse (cf. Col. 1:15-20). Possibly the false teaching caused the lukewarmness, but it seems more probable that lukewarmness caused those of the Laodicean church to seek doctrinal grounds for their lack of loyalty to Christ. Whichever the case, doctrinal defection and moral laxity generally go hand-in-hand.

Heretical groups through the centuries of the Christian era, such as the Arians who denied the deity of Christ, have assigned a passive meaning to *archē*, "one begun." This advocates that Christ was the first created being and therefore not God.[20] The obvious fallacy in

---

19. Trench, *Seven Churches*, p. 254; Alford, *Greek Testament*, 4:362; Joseph Henry Thayer, *A Greek-English Lexicon of the New Testament* (New York: American Book, 1889), p. 512; Walvoord, *Revelation*, p. 90.
20. Swete, *Apocalypse*, p. 59; Robertson, *Word Pictures*, 6:320; Beckwith, *Apocalypse*, pp. 488-89.

this interpretation is conspicuous upon consideration of the closer context and the context of the book as a whole.[21] How could a created being command the degree of faithfulness outlined in the message to Laodicea, and how could He make such far-reaching promises as are extended to the repentant one and the overcomer? Such a low Christology is at variance with Rev. 1:18 and 2:8 where Christ is eternal, with 5:13 where He with the Father is distinguished from every created thing as an object of worship, with 19:10 where worship of a creature is forbidden, and with 22:13 where His name τὸ Ἄλφα καὶ τὸ Ὦ (*to Alpha kai to Ō*, "the Alpha and the Omega") necessitates His being the source of creation, not the result of it. This error is also out of accord with other Johannine writings which place so much emphasis on the deity of Christ (e.g., John 1:3; 5:18; 10:30) (Swete).

The view that takes *archē* in the active sense to mean "beginner," "originator," or "initiator" is clearly preferable. This is the meaning supported by Christ's use of the word in Rev. 22:13. At the end of the Apocalypse, it parallels not only *to Alpha* ("the Alpha") but also ὁ πρῶτος (*ho prōtos*, "the first"). To be "first," He must have also been the creator (Lee). This too is the meaning that corresponds with Paul's response to the doctrinal error that had arisen earlier in nearby Colosse and perhaps already existed in Laodicea because of the close communications that existed between churches in the two cities.[22] Paul had commanded that the letter to Colosse be read in Laodicea (Col. 4:16). Quite possibly, the Laodicean church had copied Colossians and treasured it as they treasured other Scripture. It could well be that John in his use of *hē archē tēs ktiseōs tou theou* was appealing to their close familiarity with Colossians. The similarities between the message to Laodicea and Paul's two epistles to churches in the Lycus Valley are striking (cp. Rev. 3:21 with Col. 3:1 and Eph. 2:6; Rev. 3:17-19 with Col. 1:27; 2:8, 18, 23 and with 2:2, 3).[23] Paul uses very similar terminology in Col. 1:15 where he calls Christ "the first begotten of all creation" and in Col. 1:18 where he calls Him "the beginning (ἀρχή [*archē*])." (Apparently both Col. 1:18 and Rev. 3:14 rest upon the use of *archē* in Prov. 8:22.) At that point in Colossians, he was developing Christ's uniqueness as creator and counteracting an error regarding the Person of Christ that reduced Him to the level of a hierarchy of mediating powers (Hemer). This is probably the point of *hē archē tēs ktiseōs tou theou* in Rev. 3:14 (Trench; Hort; Swete; Alford;

---

21. Alford, *Greek Testament*, 4:588; William Lee, "The Revelation of St. John," in *The Holy Bible*, ed. F. C. Cook (London: John Murray, 1881), 4:543; Beckwith, *Apocalypse*, p. 488.
22. Beckwith, *Apocalpyse*, p. 489; Robertson, *Word Pictures*, 6:321; Mounce, *Revelation*, p. 124.
23. Charles, *Revelation*, 1:94-95; Leon Morris, *The Revelation of St. John*, TNTC (Grand Rapids: Eerdmans, 1969), p. 82.

Moffatt; Beckwith; Lenski; Caird; Walvoord). Christ is unique and therefore pre-eminent. He has supreme authority and power to execute His word, including the warnings and promises in the message to follow (Beasley-Murray).

The words *tēs ktiseōs tou theou* ("the creation of God") require a sense that is inclusive of all creation. The meaning is the same as that of πάντα (*panta*, "all things") in John 1:3 and of τὰ πάντα (*ta panta*, "all things") in Col. 1:16. His creatorship of the whole universe also anticipates His creation of the new heaven and the new earth following His thousand-year reign on earth.[24]

The solemnity of the titles adopted by the Lord for His message to Laodicea prepares the way for the searching and severe criticism that follows (Swete).

3:15 *Knowledge about the people.* Christ gets straight to the point in stating His knowledge about this church: Οἶδά σου τὰ ἔργα, ὅτι οὔτε ψυχρὸς εἶ οὔτε ζεστός (*Oida sou ta erga, hoti oute psychros ei oute zestos*, "I know your works, that you are neither cold nor hot"). As in the previous messages, the Lord follows His self-description with *oida* ("I know"), a word depicting intimate knowledge that is complete and infallible (Swete; Lenski). When used of human knowledge, this word designates something known by observation; but referring to divine knowledge, it points to a comprehension that is absolute because it is based on omniscience.[25] The objects of His knowledge are *sou*[26] *ta erga* ("your works") as in four of the six earlier messages (Rev. 2:2, 19; 3:1, 8). In each case the works are more than the deeds done. They are a reflection of life and conduct in general, including outward and inward spiritual activities (Alford). They are evidence of the inward spiritual condition the Lord alone sees and knows directly (Beckwith; Lenski). It is by means of these that men prove what they actually are.[27]

Continuing the structure of two of the foregoing messages that have "I know your works" (Rev. 3:1, 8), this message employs a *hoti* ("that") clause to define what the works are. The characteristics may be good or bad. The good generally precedes the bad if there is any good to be commended, showing that the Lord is more disposed to look for the good than He is the bad. In Laodicea, however, no commendation is in order, so the message launches immediately into a rebuke that is the most scathing of any of the seven.[28]

---

24. Hermann Cremer, *Biblico-Theological Lexicon of New Testament Greek*, trans. William Urwick (Edinburgh: T. & T. Clark, 1895), p. 381.
25. Scott, *Revelation*, p. 111; W. E. Vine, *An Expository Dictionary of New Testament Words* (Old Tappan, N.J.: Revell, 1966), p. 298.
26. See additional note at 2:19 regarding this vernacular possessive genitive.
27. Cremer, *Lexicon*, pp. 256-57.
28. Barnes, *Revelation*, pp. 1551-52; Walvoord, *Revelation*, p. 91.

The Lord's evaluation of this church focuses on its mediocre demeanor in regard to spiritual things: *oute psychros ei oute zestos* ("you are neither cold nor hot"). These people had avoided the extremes of outright spiritual destitution, but they had also avoided unrestrained spiritual fervor. *Zestos* ("hot") is the easier of the two words to define. It is derived from ζέω (*zeō*, "I boil"), which in its participial form is usually translated "fervent" (cf. Acts 18:25; Rom. 12:11). Hot describes a person characterized by a healthy spiritual fervor. The picture is of one who has been heated to a boiling point by some outside source and has maintained that state (Alford; Charles; Beckwith; Lenski). The temperament of this church left much to be desired by way of devotion to Christ.

At the other pole, unanimity does not exist regarding the picture of *psychros* ("cold"). One opinion assigns no meaning to it, either positive or negative. The main reason for this is to avoid having Christ wish anyone to be spiritually destitute (cf. v. 15*b*).[29] This view conceives of *psychros-zestos* as a unit and of those who are not "cold-hot" as being indifferent to the responsibility of following Christ without distraction.[30] Combined, the two terms are another way of saying "lukewarm" (Beckwith; Johnson). Separated, the two words have no spiritual connotation. The water supply of Laodicea lies in the background of this explanation, which has no reference to spiritual fervor. The hot waters of Hierapolis had medicinal value, and the cool, pure water of Colosse provided refreshment. In contrast to these, the waters of Laodicea were halfway between in temperature and served no useful purpose, according to this opinion. This approach argues that Jesus rebukes the church for its lack of works, not its spiritual temperature, so no figurative significance is assigned to either of the three terms.[31]

Yet serious obstacles face this explanation. The cold-hot combination can hardly be intended as another way of saying lukewarm because in the very next breath Christ expresses His desire that the readers be one or the other (v. 15*b*). The combining of the two is not the answer. Further, ineffectiveness in service is a strange way for Christ to evaluate this church. The other messages define works in terms of inner qualities of the Christian life. Would He censure the

---

29. Mounce, *Revelation*, p. 126; Alan F. Johnson, "Revelation," in *EBC*, ed. Frank E. Gaebelein (Grand Rapids: Zondervan, 1981), 12:457.

30. Swete, *Apocalypse*, p. 60; Barnes, *Revelation*, p. 1569; Beckwith, *Apocalypse*, p. 489.

31. M. J. S. Rudwick and E. M. B. Green, "The Laodicean Lukewarmness," *ET* 69 (1957-58): 176-78; Peter Wood, "Local Knowledge in the Letters of the Apocalypse," *ET* 73 (1961-62): 263-64; Mounce, *Revelation*, pp. 125-26; J. P. M. Sweet, *Revelation* (Philadelphia: Westminster, Pelican, 1979), p. 107; Hemer, *Seven Churches*, pp. 187-91.

Laodiceans on the basis of external accomplishments? Probably not. How then is the objection that Christ would not want a church to be cold to be answered? The best suggestion is that spiritual coldness, even to the point of open hostility, is preferable to lukewarmness and repulsive indifference because it at least suggests that religion is something to be in earnest about. From an ethical standpoint, a frank repudiation is at least more promising than a half-and-half attachment (Alford; Moffatt; Caird). To prefer outright rejection over a halfway response is startling, to say the least, but to profess Christianity while remaining untouched by its fire is a disaster. There is more hope for the openly antagonistic than for the coolly indifferent.[32] The state of coldness is more conducive to a person's coming to Christ than the state of lukewarmness, as illustrated in the conversion of Saul of Tarsus (Walvoord; Beasley-Murray).

To suggest that the metaphors of hot and cold referring to spiritual temperature were unknown in early Christian times (Johnson) is erroneous. In two places the NT refers to those hot or fervent (ζέοντες [*zeontes*, "boiling"]) in spirit because of their spiritual ardor for the Lord (cf. Acts 18:25; Rom. 12:11). Such a metaphorical connotation is not only upheld at an early date; it is also required by the context of this message. Some reference to this people's inner inclination is a necessity. The opposite metaphorical force was common for *psychros*. It referred to spiritual indifference in other literature of the day, and in His Olivet discourse Jesus used a cognate word ψύχω (*psychō*, "I grow cold") to describe spiritual declension (BAGD).

It remains to assign the metaphorical *psychros* a more explicit meaning. One suggestion has been that it describes a backslidden Christian, based on the assumption that there would be no unbelievers in the church of Laodicea (Scott). This seems unlikely, however, because lukewarm better describes such a backslider. Another explanation identifies this person as an unbeliever who has never heard the gospel (Trench). This would allow lukewarm to speak of those who have heard the gospel, but have not responded in more than a superficial way. It would also agree with the Lord's words about a person who had never heard as being better off than the scribes and Pharisees (cf. Luke 7:36-50; John 9:41). The problem with this view is that it does not provide an adequate contrast with *zestos*. Coldness presupposes some contact with the gospel and a resulting negative response to it, not a complete unawareness of it.

The correct solution is to see a picture of an unbeliever who has rejected the gospel openly and aggressively (Alford; Lenski). This is the simplest and most straightforward meaning of the metaphorical

---

32. Morris, *Revelation*, p. 82; Homer Hailey, *Revelation, an Introduction and Commentary* (Grand Rapids: Baker, 1979), p. 158.

psychros and furnishes the most appropriate antithesis to the state of spiritual fervor denoted by *zestos* (Alford). So despicable did Christ find lukewarmness that He preferred to deal with an obstinate opponent of the gospel, recognizing the greater possibility of finding fertile soil for the message here than with a lukewarm, professing Christian. *Anything* is better than lukewarmness.

State of the church. Such is the perspective of the Lord on lukewarmness as He opens His discussion of the condition of this church: ὄφελον ψυχρὸς ἦς ἢ ζεστός (*ophelon psychros ēs ē zestos*, "I wish that you were cold or hot"). *Ophelon ēs*[33] expresses His frustrated longing that the readers be anything but lukewarm. This is a wish that is tainted with regret.[34] It is an expression of a holy impatience over the half-and-half position of this people in regard to spiritual issues (Trench). He would prefer either of the alternatives to what He finds to be their actual state.

3:16 That state is depicted graphically in the opening clause of v. 16: οὕτως, ὅτι χλιαρὸς εἶ καὶ οὔτε ζεστὸς οὔτε ψυχρός (*houtōs, hoti chliaros ei kai oute zestos oute psychros*, "thus, because you are lukewarm and neither hot nor cold"). The key term describing their state is *chliaros* ("lukewarm"). It appears only here in biblical Greek (Charles). Traditionally, the image behind this metaphor is related to the water supply in Laodicea. The city appears to have had difficulty in this regard. Some recent studies have proposed that the problem was impurities in the water that caused vomiting (Hemer), but this contradicts the plain testimony of the text. The problem was the temperature of the water. Neighboring Hierapolis had hot, spring water, valuable for its medicinal effects. In its journey to Laodicea it lost some of its heat and consequently medicinal value by the time it arrived either overland or by aqueduct in Laodicea.[35] Nearby Colosse had cool, life-giving water that was refreshing as a beverage (Hemer). The water in Laodicea was somewhere between these two in temperature. Such tepid water was sickening to drink on either a hot or a cold day.[36] The metaphorical meaning of this divine estimate of the church portrays most vividly the revulsion Laodicea provoked in Christ.

---

33. Ὄφελον is an aorist participle of ὀφείλω with which an original ἐστίν is understood (BDF, par. 67.2). Followed by an imperfect or aorist indicative, it expresses an unattainable wish, implying, "this is unfortunately not so" (BDF, par. 359.1). The present combination with the imperfect ἦς expresses a wish about the present (Robertson, 6:321). This is what the Lord wishes for them now as opposed to "what might have been."
34. Trench, *Seven Churches*, p. 258; Robertson, *Word Pictures*, 6:321; Lenski, *Revelation*, p. 155.
35. Swete, *Apocalypse*, p. 59.
36. Newell, *Revelation*, p. 76.

The obvious question is, What was the spiritual status of this people? Clearly their problem was not spiritual immaturity. Jesus would not express dissatisfaction of a young Christian passing though a justifiable stage of Christian growth. It is not sufficient to analyze them simply as spiritually complacent.[37] Nor can they be seen simply as those who have shown some interest in the things of God, but have fallen short of the true testimony of Christ.[38] Neither of these goes far enough in explaining the terrible plight of the ones addressed. Lukewarm is a description of church people who have professed Christ hypocritically but do not have in their hearts the reality of what they pretend to be in their actions.[39] Such hypocrisy offers the only possible reason Christ would prefer coldness to luke-warmness. In fact, the spirit of vv. 15-16 resembles His denunciation of the religious authorities of His day because of their hypocrisy, in contrast with His hopeful expectations with regard to harlots and tax-gatherers. A person who professes to be a Christian, but secretly has not believed in Christ, thinks that such a profession is enough to get him by. Nothing can be done with a nominal Christian who can-not recognize that he needs repentance and that Jesus is really out-side His life (Moffatt). The five adjectives that describe this church in v. 17 make it quite evident that, corporately speaking, they did not have a relationship with Christ as Savior.[40] This probably cannot be pressed to mean that there were *no* genuine Christians there. It sim-ply means they were so few in number and insignificant in influence that the Lord did not find it necessary to acknowledge their presence as He did in a similar situation with the church of Sardis (cf. 3:4). By and large, the church had come under the dominance of pretending Christians.

Christ's response to the Laodicean lukewarmness coincides with their disgusting spiritual state[41] and corresponds to threats made

---

37. Contra Swete, *Apocalypse*, p. 60; Lenski, *Revelation*, p. 154.
38. Contra Trench, *Seven Churches*, p. 260; William Kelly, *The Revelation* (London: Thomas Weston, 1904), p. 83. Assuming Hemer's theory about an aqueduct furnishing the city's water supply, Porter theorizes that the Laodiceans had acted unwisely in going to the expense of building an aqueduct that would bring them unusable water and sees their problem of spiritual deception mirrored in this (Stanley E. Porter, "Why the Laodiceans Received Lukewarm Water [Revelation 3:15-18]," *TynBul* 38 [1987]: 148-49).
39. Barnes, *Revelation*, p. 1570; Walvoord, *Revelation*, p. 92.
40. Johnson, "Revelation," 12:458. The adjectives are "wretched and miser-able and poor and blind and naked."
41. Οὕτως picks up the thought of οὔτε ψυχρὸς εἶ οὔτε ζεστός from v. 15 and shows correspondence between the seriousness of the church's condition and Christ's drastic response. For the sake of emphasis, the spiritual lapse causing His response is repeated, with slightly different wording, in the

against other churches with similar problems (cf. 2:5, 16, 22; 3:3) (Lee): μέλλω σε ἐμέσαι ἐκ τοῦ στόματός μου (*mellō se emesai*[42] *ek tou stomatos mou*, "I am about to spew you out of My mouth"). His warning to Laodicea continues the metaphor of the area's sickening water supply: if they continue foisting this spiritual sham upon Him, He has no choice but to respond by spewing them out of His mouth, as any person who has stomach sickness would.

Mellō ("I am about to") is informative in at least two regards. First, its use instead of another verb such as θέλω (*thelō*, "I wish") shows that there is yet opportunity for the Laodiceans to repent (cf. 3:18-20), thereby averting the coming wrath of God. The longsuffering of God is still at work and the judgment of God still pending (Trench; Alford; Moffatt; Beckwith; Lenski). Second, *mellō* indicates the imminence of the wrath to come on this church. This spewing out is not an immediate and special judgment. It is rather a warning of coming eschatological wrath (Charles). The language is intended to awaken the readers to the impending danger (Trench; Beckwith; Lenski). Here the threat of imminent peril parallels the promise of deliverance from imminent peril given the previous church (cf. τῆς μελλούσης [*tēs mellousēs*, "which is about to"], 3:10) (Scott).

Christ's disgust with tepid Christianity is reflected in "spew you out of My mouth." This is a most contemptuous expression, one He does not use elsewhere.[43] The Laodiceans were in a precarious predicament as a result of their own moral choice. They had cause for great alarm.

3:17 Some authorities by putting a comma at the end of v. 16 and a period after v. 17 make v. 17 an explanation of the threat issued in v. 16 (Trench). They note that it makes good sense to view the self-claim to riches as an adequate reason for the threat (Lee; Hailey). It makes better sense, however, to put a period after v. 16 and a comma at the end of v. 17, making v. 17 a basis for the counsel that is offered in v. 18 (Alford). A continuation of the terminology of riches, poverty, blindness, and nakedness from v. 17 to v. 18 makes this more natural. Such an arrangement also parallels the structure of 3:10 a few verses earlier (cf. also Rev. 18:7, 8) (Alford; Lee). This latter punctuation makes

---

ὅτι clause of v. 16 (cf. Rom. 1:15 for another illustration of οὕτως used in this manner) (Beckwith, *Apocalypse*, p. 489).

42. The basic meaning of ἐμέσαι is simply "to vomit." By His choice of this word the Lord expresses the utmost abhorrence by a denunciation that is unparalleled in the other six messages (Charles, *Revelation*, 1:96). An OT usage that is somewhat comparable to this metaphor is Lev. 18:25, 28; 20:22 where the land is said to "spew out" (Hebrew קָיא) its inhabitants in judgment.

43. Swete, *Apocalypse*, p. 60; Kelly, *Revelation*, p. 84; Smith, *Revelation*, p. 122.

vv. 17-18 an elaboration of what constitutes lukewarmness. The words of v. 17 are the boastful, self-appraisal of the Laodiceans. Their lukewarmness lay in their nonrecognition of their own need (Scott).

Their claim of riches receives special notice: ὅτι λέγεις ὅτι Πλούσιός εἰμι καὶ πεπλούτηκα καὶ *οὐδεν[44] χρείαν ἔχω (*hoti[45] legeis hoti Plousios eimi kai peploutēka kai ouden chreian echō,* "Because you say, 'I am rich and have become rich and have need of nothing'"). Their self-appraisal is at odds with their true condition (Scott). The possibility of this church's becoming blinded to spiritual things by its material wealth exists (Bullinger; Ramsay), because Laodicea was a wealthy city and complacency and self-satisfaction are often fostered by material comforts (Moffatt). The city's ability to handle its own damage after the earthquake of A.D. 60, independently of Rome, could contribute to the church's self-satisfaction. But other factors, such as an inefficiency (cf. Col. 4:17) and the absence of persecution or other special difficulties, could and probably did contribute more to the church's languid state (Moffatt). The citizenry of Laodicea in general was noted for its wealth. That does not demand that the constituency of the church was also well-to-do. This may or may not have been the case (Beckwith). It is difficult to conceive of a Christian congregation boasting about material riches (Johnson). Part of the church's problem may have been its inability to distinguish between material and spiritual prosperity.[46] The spirit of the surrounding culture may have crept in and paralyzed the spiritual life of the members (Johnson).

Even with the concession that the worldly wealth may have been a prominent factor, it still remains that the church's opinion of its spiritual status was baseless fiction (Alford). A primary reference to spiritual riches is obligatory because spiritual riches are the counterpart in v. 18. Only such a meaning corresponds to the "you do not know . . ." declaration that closes v. 17. A Gnostic spirit that pervaded the area was characterized by spiritual pride based on knowledge allegedly possessed by its adherents. The Laodicean church had not been immune to this influence. *Plousios eimi* ("I am rich") plainly states its claim to spiritual riches.

---

44. Οὐδέν is an adverbial accusative of reference: "I have need *with reference to nothing* (Swete, *Apocalypse,* p. 61; Charles, *Revelation,* 1:96). Its position first in the clause puts great emphasis upon it.
45. This first occurrence of ὅτι in v. 16 is causal. The second one in the verse, immediately after λέγεις, is recitative and functions similarly to quotation marks, introducing a direct quotation (Robertson, *Word Pictures,* 6:321). The third time in the verse, just after οἶδας, is the objective use, introducing a noun clause which gives the substance of what the Laodiceans did not know.
46. George E. Ladd, *A Commentary on the Revelation of John* (Grand Rapids: Eerdmans, 1972), p. 66.

The combination *plousios eimi kai peploutēka* ("I am rich and have become rich") is an example of the literary device called *hysteron-proteron* that John uses repeatedly in this book (cf. 3:9; 5:2, 5; 10:4, 9; 12:10; 19:13). It is an inversion of natural sequence. The perfect tense *peploutēka* carries the force of "I have got rich." As a result, the expression means, "my wealth is due to my own exertions" (Swete; Alford; Beckwith). Logically, the obtaining of wealth precedes the attainment of a rich status.

The elaboration *kai ouden chreian echō* ("and have need of nothing") further reflects the church's contented complacency. Whatever the people's condition, they were happy with it and regarded it highly. The Lord's subsequent picture of reality points to a false self-sufficiency based on wrong attitudes and a wrong interpretation of the facts (Swete; Moffatt; Walvoord).

The real condition of Laodicean Christianity stands in marked contrast to the supposition of the residents: καὶ οὐκ οἶδας ὅτι σὺ εἶ ὁ ταλαίπωρος καὶ ἐλεεινὸς καὶ πτωχὸς καὶ τυφλὸς καὶ γυμνός (*kai ouk oidas hoti sy ei ho talaipōros kai eleeinos kai ptōchos kai typhlos kai gymnos*, "and [yet][47] you do not know that you are wretched and miserable and poor and blind and naked"). From Jesus' perspective, their alleged spiritual prosperity was actually spiritual poverty. Only by remedying their ignorance of this could they hope to reverse the situation. They had imposed this dilemma upon themselves, and only by their own intelligent and volitional repositioning could they resolve the problem.

The Lord points His finger forcefully toward the messenger representing this church through His use of emphatic *sy* ("you"): "It is you, the boastful one, who is wretched . . ." (Swete; Alford; Moffatt; Lenski). As throughout these messages, the individual messenger is not singled out as the guilty party. He symbolizes the condition of the whole church.[48] Here was a church, rich in pride but poor in grace

---

47. The contrast indicated by the context is grounds for understanding καὶ as adversative in this instance.
48. The article in ὁ ταλαίπωρος is generic, referring to the assembly and not one individual (Kelly, *Revelation*, p. 86; Beckwith, *Apocalypse*, p. 490). It serves to unify all five adjectives that follow under one heading and provide a stinging portrayal of the church's ebbing spiritual state. The proposal that the article governs only the first two adjectives with the last three serving as elaborations of the first two finds some support in the subjective nature of the first two versus the objective conditions indicated by the last three and in the fact that only the last three are taken up in the counsel of v. 18 (Trench, *Seven Churches*. p. 266; Alford, *Greek Testament*, 4:590; Lee, "Revelation," 4:544; Charles, *Revelation*, 1:96-97). Yet the symmetry of the coordinate relationship of the words and the rhetorical force of the five versus the two in unifying the sharp emphasis

and ignorant of the poverty.[49] Its deplorable condition earns a multiple description: *ho talaipōros kai eleeinos kai ptōchos kai typhlos kai gymnos* ("wretched and miserable and poor and blind and naked"). *Talaipōros* ("wretched") is found only once elsewhere in the NT, in Rom. 7:24 where Paul cries, "O wretched man that I am." There Paul was well aware of his condition, but not so with the Laodiceans (Trench; Moffatt; Lenski; Walvoord). *Eleeinos* ("miserable") occurs in the NT only here and in 1 Cor. 15:19 where it describes the pitiable condition of one who doubts the doctrine of bodily resurrection. It pictures one worthy of extreme pity because he is in peril of eternal death if he should remain in his present state (Trench; Moffatt; Lenski; Walvoord). *Ptōchos* ("poor"), an adjective, is derived from πτώσσω (*ptōssō*), which names the action of one who crouches and cowers as a beggar. The idea is that of beggarliness or destitution that results from begging.[50] Of the five adjectives, this one is the most specific antonym of the Laodiceans' self-concept, that of being rich. *Typhlos* ("blind") was often used of mental blindness (e.g., Matt. 23:17). Written to a city famous for producing eye medications, its reference here is to an inability to see spiritual values (Trench; Beckwith; Walvoord). To be spiritually "naked" (*gymnos*) was especially shameful in a city famous for its woolen garments. Salvation is sometimes represented as a garment in the NT (cf. Matt. 22:11, 12; Rev. 6:11; 7:9, 13, 14).[51] A significant number of these church people were without it. This metaphor ends Christ's description of actual conditions in Laodicea (Beckwith).

3:18 To a people with such desperate needs Jesus extends His offer of help: συμβουλεύω σοι ἀγοράσαι παρ' ἐμοῦ χρυσίον πεπυρωμένον ἐκ πυρὸς ἵνα πλουτήσῃς (*symbouleuō soi agorasai par' emou chrysion pepyrōmenon ek pyros hina ploutēsēs*, "I counsel you to buy from Me gold refined by fire that you may become rich"). *Symbouleuō* in the active voice is only here and in John 18:14 in the NT. It means "I advise" or "I counsel." It is an invitation that leads and draws rather than demands (Trench; Swete; Lenski). Yet this is more than just a friendly invitation (Lenski). This word and the ones following express deep irony. Here is a church that needs nothing and yet needs counsel

---

upon σὺ is a more impressive syntactical arrangement (Swete, *Apocalypse*, p. 60; Beckwith, *Apocalypse*, p. 490; Robertson, *Word Pictures*, 6:322; Lenski, *Revelation*, p. 156; Mounce, *Revelation*, p. 126). It is probably the intended sense.

49. Robertson, *Word Pictures*, 6:322.
50. Thayer, *Lexicon*, p. 557; G. Abbott-Smith, *A Manual Greek Lexicon of the New Testament* (Edinburgh: T. & T. Clark, 1950), p. 393; Lenski, *Revelation*, p. 156.
51. Barnes, *Revelation*, p. 1571.

on the vital points of self-preservation (Alford). The solicitation to buy something that cannot be purchased with money further reflects the caustic tone of the Lord's words. The pronouns *soi . . . emou* are specific and emphatic: *"you* buy from *Me."*[52] "Your feeling of self-sufficiency is groundless. You are completely dependent on Me." The word *agorasai* ("to buy") is full of sarcasm. The substance of the counsel is to buy. The Lord asks those who live in a city noted for its riches to buy what they cannot afford (cf. Isa. 55:1). This is language that materialistic people can understand (Trench; Alford; Moffatt; Lenski).

The counsel is to buy three items, the first of them being *chrysion pepyrōmenon ek*[53] *pyros* ("gold refined by fire"). This is pure gold, all dross having been removed through the refining process. The picture of obtaining purity through a refining process is frequent in Scripture (cf. Ps. 66:10; Zech. 13:9; 1 Pet. 1:7; 4:12). Whether or not the purification comes through trials as it does elsewhere depends upon what symbolism is entailed in the *chrysion* ("gold"). Various suggestions have included gold's standing for divine righteousness,[54] religion,[55] grace,[56] a new and disciplined spirit (Charles), faith with its accompanying works (Trench; Swete), and all spiritual wealth as contrasted with the imaginary wealth in which the Laodiceans prided themselves (Alford). It is better to see white garments rather than gold as a symbol for divine righteousness. Religion in itself is not a thing of value in the Apocalypse, so it can be ruled out too. Grace is the divine source of benefits, not a character quality that this context requires. A new and disciplined spirit is a suitable opposite to the spiritually destitute state described in v. 17 (Charles). Such a spirit is none other than a new heart manifesting itself in righteous character (Charles). Yet this explanation is too narrow to distinguish the symbol of gold from those of white garments and eyesalve yet to come in v. 18. The same problem exists with the explanation that takes gold as a symbol for all spiritual wealth. The best identification is to inter-

---

52. Trench, *Seven Churches*, p. 267; Alford, *Greek Testament*, 4:590; Moffatt, "Revelation," 5:372; Robertson, *Word Pictures*, 6:322.
53. The preposition ἐκ has at times been taken in its basic meaning "out of" to indicate a picture of metal fresh from the smelting furnace. This adds the suggestions of brightness and newness to the basic idea of purity (Alford, *Greek Testament*, 4:590). Another notion is that it expresses the source of the gold (Swete, *Apocalypse*, p. 62). Both of these ideas read too much into the simple preposition, however. It is commonly used with a passive verb as here to express means by which, and should be assigned this simple force.
54. Kelly, *Revelation*, p. 86; Scott, *Revelation*, p. 114.
55. Barnes, *Revelation*, p. 1571.
56. Newell, *Revelation*, p. 77.

pret gold as a picture of high quality faith, a faith capable of withstanding trials and one that results in works. This symbolism was apparently common among early Christians (cf. Luke 12:21; 1 Tim. 6:18; James 1:3; 2:5; 1 Pet. 1:7; cf. Prov. 17:3; Zech. 13:9). It should be remembered, however, that associated with this purified faith that the Lord offers is a new heart. The new heart is also implied in the two symbols yet to come.

Each recommended purchase in v. 18 has its own purpose, that of refined gold being expressed by *hina ploutēsēs*[57] ("that you may become rich"). This purpose, as the other two also, corresponds to one of the three self-delusions of the Laodiceans expressed by the last three adjectives of v. 17. Such spiritual riches are the direct solution to abject spiritual poverty (cf. *ptōchos*, v. 17).

The counselor recommends, in the second place, the purchase of ἱμάτια λευκὰ (*himatia leuka*, "white[58] garments"): καὶ ἱμάτια λευκὰ ἵνα περιβάλῃ καὶ μὴ φανερωθῇ ἡ αἰσχύνη τῆς γυμνότητός σου (*kai himatia leuka hina peribalē kai mē phanerōthē hē aischynē tēs gymnotētos sou*, "and white garments that you may be clothed and the shame of your nakedness may not be exposed"). The significance of the white garments has been taken as either graces of the Christian life (Charles), white as simply the color of heavenly garments with no special significance,[59] the righteousness of Christ imputed (Lenski), or the righteous deeds of the saints.[60] To understand graces of the Christian life is too general to distinguish this from the other metaphors of v. 18. To find no special symbolic significance in the white garments is open to the same criticism. Support for imputed righteousness as the meaning lies in the frequent use of nakedness as a symbol for judgment (Beasley-Murray). Yet in this book righteousness is more than imputed. In Revelation righteousness is preeminently practical. The probable meaning of the putting on of these garments is the reception of an inner inclination toward righteous deeds, as referred to in Rev. 19:8 (Alford). This is practically synonymous with receiving a new heart and, of course, implies imputed righteousness as a basis.

The purpose of this second purchase is positive, the acquisition of clothing (*peribalē*), and negative, the avoidance of the shame of nakedness (*mē phanerōthē hē aischynē tēs gymnotētos sou*). This meets the need indicated by the *gymnos* of v. 17. The fulfillments of the positive

---

57. The aorist subjunctive πλουτήσῃς is ingressive in force, focusing particularly upon the initial acquisition of spiritual wealth (Alford, *Greek Testament*, 4:590; Robertson, *Word Pictures*, 6:322).
58. The contrast between white garments and those made of the glossy black wool manufactured in the city could hardly have been missed by the initial readers (Hemer, *Seven Churches*, p. 199).
59. Barnes, *Revelation*, p. 1566.
60. Kelly, *Revelation*, p. 86; Scott, *Revelation*, p. 114; Newell, *Revelation*, p. 78.

and negative sides of the remedy are not concurrent, however. The putting on of the garments Christ supplies comes at the moment of personal faith in Him, but the avoidance of shame will come at the time of His second advent. This is the shame of one who has professed Christ, but has not truly put on Christ (Trench). Shame and nakedness are frequently equated in Scripture (2 Sam. 10:4; Isa. 20:4; Ezek. 16:37; Hos. 2:3, 9; Nah. 3:5).[61] Also, nakedness is a standing symbol for adverse judgment (cf. Ezek. 16:35-43; Nah. 3:1-7; 2 Cor. 5:2-3; Heb. 4:13) (Beasley-Murray; Sweet). Not until the return of Christ for judgment will hidden issues of the heart become public. If the Laodiceans fail to repent, they will be utterly disgraced when Christ returns (Moffatt). *Phanerōthē* ("be exposed") is regularly used in the NT for divine manifestations or revelations of things hidden from men now or at the last day, especially the latter (e.g., 1 Cor. 4:5; 2 Cor. 5:11; Eph. 5:13; 1 John 3:2).[62] Reference to the revelation of man's inner condition at Christ's return is confirmed by usage of the same "clothing-nakedness" terminology in the parenthetical blessing pronounced in Rev. 16:15. This promise, given in connection with the next-to-the-last bowl judgment, comes in conjunction with Christ's prediction that He would come as a thief (cf. 3:3). The imminence of His coming is a consideration placed before this church in 3:20, as will be shown in the discussion below.

The third recommended purchase deals with improvement of eyesight: καὶ κολλούριον ἐγχρῖσαι τοὺς ὀφθαλμούς σου ἵνα βλέπῃς (*kai kollourion enchrisai tous ophthalmous sou hina blepēs*, "and eyesalve to anoint your eyes that you may see"). *Kollourion* ("eyesalve") is derived from κολλύρα (*kollyra*), which is a course bread, cylindrical in shape. This elongated lump was impregnated with medicines and used as a bandage for sore or weak eyes. The local reference of this word was to the Phrygian powder used at the medical school at Laodicea.[63] *Enchrisai* ("to anoint"), used only here in the NT, is the normal technical word for anointing the eyes. By common agreement, the anointing of the eyes is a spiritual anointing (as with χρῖσμα [*chrisma*, "anointing"], 1 John 2:20, 27; cf. John 9:6).[64]

The spiritual meaning behind the figure requires clarification.

---

61. Trench, *Seven Churches*, pp. 271-72. A subjective genitive yields good sense for τῆς γυμνότητος, "shame caused by nakedness," but·a genitive of apposition, "shame which is nakedness," is probably more accurate in light of Rev. 16:15 where shame and nakedness are equated.
62. Trench, *Seven Churches*, p. 271; Alford, *Greek Testament*, 4:591; Thayer, *Lexicon*, p. 649; Abbott-Smith, *Lexicon*, p. 465.
63. Barnes, *Revelation*, p. 1571; Charles, *Revelation*, 1:98; Robertson, *Word Pictures*, 6:322; Lenski, *Revelation*, p. 160.
64. Trench, *Seven Churches*, p. 272; Alford, *Greek Testament*, 4: 591; Barnes, *Revelation*, p. 1571.

The proposal that the eyesalve pictures the spiritual gift given by Christ to the believer, consisting of a new heart that enables him to fellowship with Christ (Charles) is too inexact to differentiate the eyesalve from the gold and the white garments. Another proposed meaning referring it to the Word of God (Lenski) or the gospel[65] misses the intention of these figures to refer to inner spiritual qualities rather than external data such as the Word or the gospel. A combination of two other proposals furnishes the best analysis. The eyesalve pictures the illuminating grace (Swete) or anointing[66] of the Holy Spirit (cf. 1 John 2:20, 27) along with the convicting ministry of the Spirit (cf. John 16:8-11) (Swete). The reproof of the Spirit that removes self-deception and bestows spiritual vision (Swete) should not be excluded, but the anointing or teaching ministry of the Spirit that provides illumination following conversion (Alford) is the more prominent.[67] As the cure for spiritual blindness, this is the best parallel to the eye medicine for which this city was famous.

The purpose of the final recommended purchase was the cure of spiritual blindness: *hina blepēs* ("that you may see"). This purpose corrects the spiritual problem represented by *typhlos* in v. 17. The tense of *blepēs* is present, a contrast with the tenses of *ploutēsēs* and *peribalē*, which are aorist. The comparison of these actions suggests that the two aorist verbs are instantaneous, coming at the point of conversion to Christ, and the present verb continues on throughout the Christian life. In other words, initial faith in Christ comes at the same time as the impartation of a new inclination toward righteousness. Spiritual discernment characterizes the Christian life from that point on.

Pedagogically, Christ's counsel to this church must have been quite effective. As shown in the discussion of this city at the beginning of the message, its everyday life was marked by its importance as a financial center, a manufacturing center for woolen garments, and a medical school famous for its eye medications. Spiritually speaking, however, the church was seriously lacking in three corresponding areas: genuine faith (i.e., gold), a disposition toward righteousness (i.e., white garments), and a discernment of spiritual matters (i.e., eyesalve). The church adherents' spiritual destitution is viewed in three aspects, all three of which could be resolved by a single act, by their acceptance of the gift of salvation from Christ.[68]

---

65. Barnes, *Revelation*, p. 1571.
66. Kelly, *Revelation*, p. 86; Newell, *Revelation*, p. 78.
67. The present tense of βλέπης and its focus on continuance of sight justifies this distinction. See additional comment below.
68. Charles, *Revelation*, 1:98-99; Beckwith, *Apocalypse*, pp. 490-91; Lenski, *Revelation*, p. 157; BDF, pp. 85-86.

3:19 A minority opinion is that 3:19-22 should be taken as an epilogue to all seven messages (Ramsay). This builds upon the absence of a conjunction to introduce v. 19 and the alleged need to have a single epilogue to conclude the literary composition of the seven messages (Ramsay). Also it is considered inappropriate to have Christ expressing love to a church that is so destitute (cf. 3:19) in the same way He did to the spiritually prosperous church at Philadelphia (cf. 3:9) (Ramsay). The theory of a single epilogue for all seven messages seeks further support in the absence of any direct reference to Laodicea after v. 18 (Ramsay) and in the way the promise to the overcomer in 3:21 overshadows those in the other messages (Alford).

A major problem with this view is that it leaves the seventh message without its own promise to the overcomer, without its own command to hear, and without its own exhortation. This is an unwarranted breach of the symmetry of this message in comparison to the others (Moffatt; Mounce). In regard to the love expressed to the undeserving Laodiceans, one can think of nothing more touching than Christ's reaching out to rescue the lukewarm readers in a manner comparable to the way He had encouraged the faithful (Hemer). The promise to the overcomer in Laodicea does not exceed the other promises. All seven words to the overcomer picture the future bliss of the new heaven and the new earth. Besides this, each promise has a wider application than just the individual church to which it is addressed (Lee). The argument of no direct reference to the Laodicean situation in vv. 19-22 has been debated. It seems that there was a local tradition about the coming of the Romans and exploiting the city after capture and about a later dynasty of kings from this city. This could be intended as a sharp contrast to Christ's suggestion of voluntary hospitality (3:20) and a close analogy to His invitation to sit with Him on His throne (3:21).[69]

It is more persuasive to understand vv. 19-22 as an integral part of the seventh message, allowing it the same structure as the other six (Swete). The tone of the message changes abruptly from spewing out in v. 16 to love in v. 19, the absence of a conjunction adding to the abruptness:[70] ἐγὼ ὅσους ἐὰν φιλῶ ἐλέγχω καὶ παιδεύω (*egō hosous ean philō elenchō kai paideuō*, "as many as I love, I reprove and chasten"). This free rendering of Prov. 3:12 (cf. Heb. 12:6) has at times been taken to speak of a different group from the one addressed in v. 16. It understands the words thus: "I have finished the description of My dealings with counterfeit Christians; now I turn My attention to the

---

69. Hemer, *Seven Churches*, pp. 202-7.
70. Ἐγώ is very emphatic both because of its initial position in the sentence and because it adds to the subject already stated in the verb φιλῶ.

faithful remnant there at Laodicea and dwell upon My dealings with
them." The abruptness of the statement plus the absence of a commendation of this church are taken to imply He now turns His attention to loyal followers (Smith). The hopelessly obdurate and impeni-
tent are outside Christ and are not objects of His love. The discipline
here applies to those who are born again, but who have become indis-
tinguishable from the lukewarm pretenders around them (Walvoord).

The case for identifying the addressees of v. 19 as the same group
as addressed above is stronger, however.[71] The censure already given
in vv. 15-18 does not mean hostility. It is rather an evidence of affection (Moffatt). The use of reproof and discipline to express love resides
in the source text of this allusion (cf. Prov. 3:11-12). The μέλλω (*mellō*,
"I am about to") of v. 16 has already served notice that the opportunity for repentance is open. The οὖν (*oun*, "therefore) that follows in
v. 19 shows that this relationship of love is not yet reciprocal and
should be sought through zeal and repentance. Most convincing is the
fact that Rev. 16:15 pronounces blessing upon those who respond out
of a state similar to that described in 3:18. The existence of a faithful
remnant in Laodicea should not be denied, but if referred to in this
message, members of the remnant would have been singled out more
clearly than by terminology such as in v. 19 (cf. 3:4).

Lukewarmness is not necessarily terminal. "As many as" (*hosous
ean*[72]) shows that Laodicea was treated no differently from the other
churches. Any and all whom Christ loves receive rebuke and discipline, no matter where they live. The choice of φιλέω (*phileō*, "I love)
over ἀγαπάω (*agapaō*, "I love") (cf. 3:9) is a bit puzzling. To understand the two words as identical in meaning (cf. John 5:20; 16:27;
20:2) (Alford; Johnson) fails to account for the proximity of the two in
the present context (cf. 3:9). Some distinction must be intended in
such a situation. Contextually, it is clear that the love for Philadelphia
sustains and safeguards those who are loyal and that for Laodicea
inflicts painful wounds upon the unworthy, to regain their loyalty
(Moffatt). *Phileō* is a love of personal affection that is quite consistent
with the severity of discipline associated with God's love.[73] It is more
human and more emotional than *agapaō* (Swete; Sweet) and it has

---

71. Charles, *Revelation*, 1:99; Beckwith, *Apocalypse*, p. 491; Robertson, *Word
    Pictures*, 6:323; Lenski, *Revelation*, p. 160.
72. Ὅσους ἐάν is an indefinite plural of the quantitative relative pronoun
    (Robertson, *Word Pictures*, 6:323). Perhaps "whomever" captures the
    thought in English as well as anything (H. E. Dana and Julius R. Mantey,
    A Manual Grammar of the Greek New Testament [New York: Macmillan,
    1927], pp. 259-60).
73. Lee, "Revelation," 4:545; William Barclay, *The Revelation of John*, 2d ed., 2
    vols. (Philadelphia: Westminster, 1960), 1:183; Mounce, *Revelation*, p. 128.

less depth (Walvoord). The word is probably chosen here to show that in spite of the church's poor attitude toward Him, He still has tender and affectionate feelings toward it (Hailey). The surprising choice of this emotional word comes as a touching and unexpected manifestation of love toward those who deserve it least among the seven churches (Charles). No special relationship of paternity can be read into the choice of this word, though such does exist in Prov. 3:12 and Heb. 12:6. Here is a case where Christ extends special treatment to a church in spite of its lukewarm condition.

The love of Christ toward these unexpected objects is what motivates Him to "reprove" (*elenchō*) and "chasten" (*paideuō*) them. *Elenchō* refers to a verbal rebuke designed to bring a person to acknowledge his fault. It attempts to correct by word as compared with *paideuō*, which accomplishes the same goal by act. The latter word has the basic connotation of "instruct" or "educate" and developed a meaning of "chasten" when the education process was expedited with correction. Here, it is the severe discipline of love.[74] Hopefully, the goal can be achieved by verbal rebuke only, but if this fails, chastening must follow. This is Christ's constant[75] method of dealing with person after person who falls into this category of need.

The course of action urged for the needy church comes at the end of v. 19: ζήλευε οὖν καὶ μετανόησον (*zēleue oun kai metanoēson*, "be zealous, therefore, and repent"). *Oun* shows the response recommended here to be the logical course in light of the Lord's loving reproof and chastening. *Zēleue* ("be zealous") denotes the new habit[76] to be embraced. A continuing zeal is commanded in place of lukewarm indifference that had characterized the people heretofore. By derivation the verb relates to *zestos* ("hot") in 3:15, 16, a connection that clarifies the fervency that Christ wants to become the spirit of this church. *Metanoēson* ("repent") points to the decisive change of purpose that the Lord commands (cf. 2:5, 16; 3:3).[77]

The relationship between the two actions commanded requires elaboration. One opinion is that the habit of zeal precedes the crisis decision of repentance as a description of how repentance is to be

---

74. Trench, *Seven Churches*, p. 277; Swete, *Apocalypse*, p. 63; Alford, *Greek Testament*, 4:591; Moffatt, "Revelation," 5:372; Vine, *Dictionary*, p. 183; Lenski, *Revelation*, p. 161.
75. Ἐλέγχω and παιδεύω with their present tenses match the indefinite ὅσους ἐάν (Lenski, *Revelation*, p. 160).
76. Ζήλευε, a present imperative, denotes the adoption of a continuing practice (Swete, *Apocalypse*, p. 63; Alford, *Greek Testament*, 4:591; Charles, *Revelation*, 1:100; Beckwith, *Apocalypse*, p. 491).
77. Moffatt, "Revelation," 5:372; Robertson, *Word Pictures*, 6:323; Lenski, *Revelation*, p. 161. The tense of the imperative μετανόησον is aorist, indicating a single turning point in the life of the repentant one.

carried out: "be zealous in your repenting."[78] Repentance is impossible for those who lack passion, is the reasoning (Sweet). Development of a burning zeal of love prior to repentance is an impossibility, however. The change of purpose must precede the zeal (Alford). Another way to approach the dilemma is to see zeal as a means of achieving repentance or "a right mind" (Swete; Charles). But zeal can hardly proceed from proper motives unless it follows repentance. The best answer is to understand another example of *hysteron proteron* (cf. 3:17). The act of repentance is necessary in order to effect the requisite pattern of zeal.[79] A decisive and effective change of purpose must come first (Alford). By arriving at a better mind, the church would no longer be tepid but fervent in spirit (Swete).

It remains to clarify the substance of this course of action. Does it consist of telling the bulk of the church to repent and become a part of the faithful remnant just referred to in *egō hosous ean philō* ("as many as I love")? Our earlier discussion of this clause precludes this meaning. The words are rather a command to the church as a whole to respond to the strong reproof already delivered so as to avoid the chastening of the Lord that will come imminently if it does not. The sense is, "Let My strong criticisms of you open your eyes at once to the need of repentance and also to the fact that it is really love on My part that prompts Me to reprove and chastise you. A realization of My loving concern, as well as your own desperate condition, should bring a resolute change of purpose and kindle within you a warm fervor of devotion that will dispense with lukewarmness."[80]

3:20 The note of deep affection expressed in v. 19 continues as the Lord says, ἰδοὺ ἔστηκα ἐπὶ τὴν θύραν καὶ κρούω (*idou hestēka epi tēn thyran kai krouō*, "Behold, I am standing at the door and knocking"). As in the message to Philadelphia (cf. 3:8,9), *idou* ("behold") focuses special attention on a promise of future blessing.[81] *Hestēka* ("I am standing"), fully expressed, means "I have taken My position and am standing."[82] It reflects a mental stance deliberately taken. *Krouō* ("am knocking"), on the other hand, speaks of an action that is continually going on.[83] Here is a picture of immediacy, in a sense, a

---

78. Barnes, *Revelation*, p. 1571.
79. Alford, *Greek Testament*, 4:591; John R. W. Stott, *What Christ Thinks of the Church* (Grand Rapids: Eerdmans, 1958), p. 123.
80. Cf. Moffatt, "Revelation," 5:372.
81. Moffatt calls this the "eschatological" ἰδού that is used frequently in the Apocalypse (cf. 1:7; 16:15; 21:3; 22:7, 12) ("Revelation," 5:373).
82. Bullinger, *Apocalypse*, p. 208. Ἕστηκα is a perfect tense of ἵστημι. The perfect of this verb in the NT is always intensive, emphasizing the continuing results of a completed process.
83. J. A. Seiss, *The Apocalypse*, 3 vols. (New York: Charles C. Cook, 1909), 1:167; Newell, *Revelation*, p. 79; Lenski, *Revelation*, p. 162; Merrill C.

greater closeness than in any of the previous messages.[84] The picture comes from Song of Sol. 5:2 where the bridegroom knocks and seeks to be admitted by the bride (Swete). Christ presents Himself as right on the verge of entering and so furnishes incentive for the church to heed the commands of v. 19 (Beckwith).

The spiritual connotation of *thyran* ("door") has been a matter for debate. A major group sees it as the door of the human heart, either that of an unbeliever (Trench), that of a believer,[85] or that of any person, regardless of spiritual condition.[86] In the case of the non-Christian, Christ would be offering the gospel of salvation from sins. In that of the believer, He would offer the opportunity of returning to fellowship. In the last case, He would simply say, "I'm here, no matter what the need is." An appropriateness is to some degree detectable in all three suggestions, but the fact is that the popular idea of Christ knocking at the door of men's hearts, though containing a great truth (cf. Luke 19:10), is not taught here (Beckwith).

The more probable identification is the eschatological door through which Christ will enter at His second advent. This picture stresses the urgency for people to seek a right relationship with Christ. A convincing proof of this view is that this figure was widely used among early Christians as a way of portraying the Lord's return (cf. Matt. 24:33; Mark 13:29; Luke 12:36; James 5:9).[87] It also parallels the command-incentive sequence in other messages, i.e., a reference to Christ's coming following the command for repentance (cf. 2:5, 16; 3:3) (Sweet). The source of the language of v. 20, Song of Sol. 5:1 ff., is also alluded to in Luke 12:35-38 where it is given a comparable eschatological sense (Moffatt). Jewish interpreters handled this OT passage in a similar way, using an allegorical sense to look forward to the coming of their Messiah (Sweet).

An objection to the foregoing explanation is that in other NT passages where the "door" figure is eschatological (cf. Matt. 24:33; Mark 13:29; Luke 12:36; James 5:9), Christ is seen as a judge or a rewarder of the faithful rather than a preacher of repentance as He is here (Charles). This observation ignores the strong judgmental language of 3:16, however, and cannot be taken seriously. In the seven messages, Christ fulfills the dual role of rewarder of the faithful and judge of the unrepentant. The alleged incompatibility of this view

---

Tenney, *Interpreting Revelation* (Grand Rapids: Eerdmans, 1957), p. 67; Walvoord, *Revelation*, p. 98.

84. Robert Govett, *The Apocalypse Expounded by Scripture* (London: Charles J. Thynne, 1920), p. 96.

85. Kelly, *Revelation*, p. 87; Beckwith, *Apocalypse*, p. 491.

86. Barnes, *Revelation*, p. 1571.

87. Robertson, *Word Pictures*, 6:323.

with the immediate context (Johnson) can also be dismissed as a serious obstacle to this view. The repentance commanded in v. 19 is obviously picked up in one's willingness to open the door in v. 20.

One implication of this eschatological view is how it appears to condition Christ's second advent on a positive human response to His invitation, rather than upon the sovereign choice of God (cf. Acts 1:6-7). This implication is similar to earlier portions of these messages that appeared to condition that advent on a negative response to His command to repent (e.g., 3:3). The problem is more apparent than real. As will be reflected more fully in discussion of the remainder of v. 20 below, the promised entrance of Christ and His consequent fellowship with the faithful one are realized in two phases: a preliminary phase that happens simultaneously with initial saving faith and the ultimate phase at the time of His second advent. A realization of the preliminary phase is assurance of participation in the ultimate phase. Saving faith assures a person of participation in the supper with Christ, which is viewed as imminent, but whose timing is not affected by when that saving faith occurs. The true Christian has, in a sense, *already* begun fellowship with Christ, but in another sense, his ultimate fellowship with Him has *not yet* begun.

A failure to recognize this dual nature of fellowship has prompted some to limit the time of the promise's application to the point of conversion (Trench; Alford; Charles; Beasley-Murray). It is seen as more of an evangelistic plea than as an admonition to prepare for the Lord's coming (Walvoord; Johnson). The evidence is quite convincing that the time of the promise's fulfillment is Christ's return, but this does not exclude a secondary reference to conversion, which is a prerequisite to participation in the blessings of that return. The eschatological tone of the promise is overwhelming: the "eschatological" *idou* ("behold") (cf. 3:8, 9) which introduces v. 20, the reference to the eschatological supper later in v. 20,[88] the broader context of the message (cf. 3:16, 18, 21), the analogy of five of the other six messages (excluding the one to Smyrna), the broader context of Revelation (cf. 16:15), and the connotation that first-century Christians put on the picture of Christ knocking at the door (cf. Matt. 24:33; Mark 13:29; Luke 12:36; James 5:9) (Moffatt; Beckwith; Mounce).

With allowance for a legitimate secondary application to a foretaste of ultimate fellowship with Christ, the primary reference of Christ's standing at the door and knocking must be to His eschatological coming that is pictured as imminent throughout these messages. Because of His longsuffering (cf. 1 Pet. 3:20; 2 Pet. 3:9), He keeps on

---

88. See discussion of δειπνήσω below in v. 20.

knocking, but at some point, unknown to human beings, that knocking will come to an end and He will enter earth's scene once again, both to deliver His faithful followers and to punish the rebellious. The promise of v. 20 predicts the fate of the former group, and the warning of v. 16 foresees that of the latter.

Christ proceeds to express the condition of blessing: ἐάν τις ἀκούσῃ τῆς φωνῆς μου καὶ ἀνοίξῃ τὴν θύραν (*ean tis akousē tēs phōnēs mou kai anoixē tēn thyran,* "if any hears My voice and opens the door"). The custom of the time was to speak and identify oneself when knocking at someone's door (cf. Acts 12:13-14),[89] so the opening of the door was in response to both the knock and the voice. The above discussion identifies this response with the repentance commanded in v. 19.[90] This is the climactic decision of a lost person in turning to Christ for salvation.[91] It is not a plea for the straying Christian to return to fellowship with Christ,[92] nor is it a general invitation to Christians and non-Christians alike.[93] The probable existence of a faithful remnant in Laodicea as in the other cities, though they are not mentioned, has already been noted. They do not need to open the door again. They have already done so, and Christ will enter at His second advent. This is an opportunity for those who have not yet experienced conversion to Christ to do so and thereby make ready for His return.

In return for this positive response Christ offers, εἰσελεύσομαι πρὸς αὐτὸν καὶ δειπνήσω μετ' αὐτοῦ καὶ αὐτὸς μετ' ἐμοῦ (*eiseleusomai pros auton kai deipnēsō met' autou kai autos met' emou,* "I will enter to him and will eat supper with him"). In light of conclusions already reached, this act of entrance is Christ's second advent as referred to by ἔρχομαι (*erchomai,* "I will come") in 3:11 and by ἥξω (*hēxō,* "I will come") in 2:25 and 3:3.[94] Such an identification also agrees with the eschatological nature of the supper referred to in *deipnēsō* ("will eat supper"), though opinion about the supper has not been unanimous. One different idea has been that the mention of supper could hardly have failed to remind the readers of the last supper in the upper room with Christ and the subsequent occasions when that meal was re-enacted in the ordinance of the Lord's Supper (Caird). A reference to this ordinance, sometimes called the Eucharist, is not supported in this strongly eschatological context. Though the Supper is a preview of the Lord's return (cf. Matt. 26:29), the language of this verse points

---

89. Trench, *Seven Churches,* p. 289; Barnes, *Revelation,* p. 1572.
90. Both ἀκούσῃ and ἀνοίξῃ are aorist tenses and constitute a natural expansion of the aorist imperative μετανόησον of 3:19.
91. Trench, *Seven Churches,* p. 279; Lenski, *Revelation,* p. 162.
92. Contra Swete, *Apocalypse,* p. 64; Bullinger, *Apocalypse,* p. 209.
93. Contra Robertson, *Word Pictures,* 6:323.
94. Moffatt, "Revelation," 5:373. Cf. also ἔρχομαι (Rev. 2:5, 16).

to a coming of the Lord that is much more personal and intimate than experienced in the corporate worship of the church (Swete; Beckwith; Caird). Other attempts at identifying this supper experience have usually referred it to present fellowship with Christ enjoyed by believers (Beasley-Murray; Mounce). These, however, fail to appreciate that Christ's present supping with believers is only a foretaste of the future. As part of the bride of Christ, believers will participate in the marriage supper of the Lamb (cf. Rev. 19:9) and in this manner celebrate in His future kingdom (cf. Luke 22:16, 29, 30) (Smith). The language of this promise makes it impossible to rule out a primary reference to the future messianic kingdom (Beasley-Murray; Mounce).

The "supper" picture of fellowship in the messianic kingdom was widespread in the early church (cf. Matt. 26:29; Mark 14:25; Luke 22:30) (Beckwith). So interpreted, this promise follows the pattern of Luke 12:25-38 (particularly v. 37) where a meal of fellowship follows the entrance of the master.[95] Future bliss was regularly conceived of as a feast (cf. Enoch 62:14) (Moffatt). Eating with the Messiah and ruling with Him (cf. Rev. 3:21) are regularly brought together (Swete; Beckwith). The contextual tie of this figure in the Apocalypse is with 19:9 and the invitation to the wedding feast there (Bullinger). That is the prophetic fruition of the promise made in Rev. 3:20.

Supper, the last meal of the day, was according to custom the usual occasion of hospitality in biblical times. Participation in such a meal was among the Orientals proof of confidence and affection (Swete; Charles). To be assured of such a meal opportunity with the Lord was a pledge of enjoying the closest possible association with Him. This is emphasized in the words *met' autou kai autos met' emou* ("with him and he with Me"). John's writings characteristically emphasize this sort of reciprocity (cf. John 6:56; 10:38; 14:20; 15:4, 5; 17:21, 26) (Alford; Beckwith; Lenski). The mutual exchange of camaraderie pictured in the present verse depicts ultimate closeness with Christ in the future.

3:21 *Promise to the overcomer.* The promise to the overcomer continues the same future incentive offered the lukewarm in Laodicea: ὁ νικῶν δώσω αὐτῷ καθίσαι μετ' ἐμοῦ ἐν τῷ θρόνῳ μου, ὡς κἀγὼ ἐνίκησα καὶ ἐκάθισα μετὰ τοῦ πατρός μου ἐν τῷ θρόνῳ αὐτοῦ (*ho nikōn*[96] *dōsō*

---

95. Moffatt, "Revelation," 5:373; R. J. Bauckham, "Synoptic Parousia Parables and the Apocalypse," *NTS* 23 (1977): 173.
96. Ὁ νικῶν is another instance of a nominative absolute, separated grammatically from the rest of the sentence for the sake of emphasis (cf. 2:26; 3:12). It is resumed by the dative αὐτῷ in the main clause of the sentence. The present tense of the participle reminds the readers that the overcomer will persevere (i.e., "keep on overcoming") (Moffatt, "Revelation,"

autǭ kathisai met' emou en tǭ thronǭ mou, hōs kagō enikēsa kai ekathisa meta tou patros mou en tǭ thronǭ autou, "the one who overcomes, I will grant that he sit down with Me in My throne, as I also overcame and sat down with My Father in His throne"). The genuine Christian, the one who overcomes by faith and is victorious over the world (cf. 1 John 5:4-5) (Walvoord), will join Christ not only in the great eschatological supper, but also will sit with Him on His throne to participate in ruling the world.

The promise, *dōsō autǭ kathisai met' emou en tǭ thronǭ mou* ("I will grant that he sit down with Me in My throne"), is an extension of the promise that Christ made to the Twelve while on earth that they would not only eat and drink with Him in His kingdom, but also sit upon twelve thrones, judging the twelve tribes of Israel (cf. Matt. 19:28; Luke 22:29-30). Paul expanded the promise to include all Christians as rulers and the broadened domain of the world, not just Israel (cf. 1 Cor. 6:2). The implementation of this promise is a central focus as the message of the Apocalypse progresses, culminating with Christ's reign in the millennial kingdom (cf. 5:10; 11:15; 20:4).[97]

The relationship of Christ's throne to the Father's in this verse has been understood in two ways. One way is to identify the two as one and the same throne (Alford; Moffatt). The other is to distinguish them, one in heaven belonging to the Father and the other on earth belonging to Christ as the son of David (Bullinger; Walvoord). The one throne approach is based largely on Rev. 22:1 where the same throne is said to belong to the Father and to the Lamb. The oneness of the Father and the Son and the future participation of believers in the glory of the Father and the Son (cf. John 17:22, 24) are also cited as supporting a single throne (Alford; Lee). In spite of this information, the fact remains that v. 21 distinguishes between two thrones and to merge them into one is to ignore the obvious.

The distinction between Christ's throne and the Father's is not merely rhetorical. It provides for different aspects of God's future program (cf. 1 Cor. 15:24-28) by recognizing the final earthly consummation of Christ's kingdom at His return (Johnson). His throne is the one to which He is heir as David's son (cf. Ps. 122:5; Ezek. 43:7; Luke 1:32) (Bullinger). He will occupy it when He comes in His glory (Luke 1:32; cf. Dan. 7:13-14; Matt. 25:31; Acts 2:30; Heb. 2:5-8; Rev. 20:4). Christ's occupancy of the throne of David is a major emphasis of Revelation from its very beginning to the very end (cf. 1:5, 7; 22:16). It

---

5:373; Beckwith, *Apocalypse*, p. 470; Robertson, *Word Pictures*, 6:324; Lenski, *Revelation*, pp. 90-94).

97. Swete, *Apocalypse*, p. 64; Alford, *Greek Testament*, 4:592; Charles, *Revelation*, 1:102; Robertson, *Word Pictures*, 6:624; Lenski, *Revelation*, p. 165.

is this throne upon the earth on which the overcomer is promised a place.

The pattern followed in sharing His throne with overcomers is that of the Father in sharing His throne with Christ: *hōs kagō enikēsa kai ekathisa meta tou patros mou en tō thronō autou* ("as I also overcame and sat down with My Father in His throne"). A comparison of Christ's relations with believers with the Father's relations with Him is characteristically Johannine (cf. John 15:9, 10; 17:21, 22; 20:21) (Moffatt). *Enikēsa* ("I overcame") looks back to the historical event[98] of Christ's death (Rev. 5:5, 9; cf. John 16:33) and *ekathisa* ("sat down") refers to His ascension following resurrection.[99] Unlike the overcomer to whom the promise is given, Christ's overcoming was through His sacrificial death. By means of this victory, He took His seat at the Father's right hand in heaven (cf. Ps. 110:1; Matt. 22:44; Acts 2:34; Eph. 1:20; Heb. 1:3; 8:1; 10:12; 12:2). The Father and His throne in heaven, which Christ now occupies with Him, will shortly become a focal point of the descriptions of the Apocalypse (cf. 4:2).

3:22 *Call to hear.* The Laodicean message closes with the familiar summons to a perceptive reception of what has been written: ὁ ἔχων οὖς ἀκουσάτω τί τὸ πνεῦμα λέγει ταῖς ἐκκλησίαις (*ho echōn ous akousatō ti to pneuma legei tais ekklēsiais*, "The one who has an ear, let him hear what the Spirit says to the churches"). As in the other messages, this was a comprehensive warning to each church to hear and apply what has been written not only to itself, but also to the other six. The message to Laodicea had particular relevance to the church in that city, but the sevenfold repetition of this command to hear shows the likelihood that some of the lessons were also needed in the other six churches.

Additional Notes

3:17 Some MSS read οὐδένος instead of οὐδὲν, according to the pattern of using a genitive with χρείαν ἔχω in 21:23. External evidence in support of the accusative here is strong enough to conclude that it is correct. John uses either the genitive or accusative in this situation. In 22:5, a similar textual variant occurs (Charles).

---

98. The verbs ἐνίκησα and ἐκάθισα are aorist tenses, allowing them each to refer to a single historical fact.
99. Trench, *Seven Churches*, p. 286; Swete, *Apocalypse*, p. 64; Alford, *Greek Testament*, 4:592; Robertson, *Word Pictures*, 6:324; Lenski, *Revelation*, pp. 164-65.

RETROSPECTIVE OVERVIEW OF THE SEVEN MESSAGES

Collectively, the seven messages form an indispensable part of the Apocalypse. In them are the practical lessons to be applied in light of coming events in God's prophetic program.

They also serve to unify the other parts of the book. Christ's self-descriptions, for the most part, draw from the introductory words and vision of Revelation 1: 2:1 draws from 1:13, 16; 2:8 draws from 1:17-18; 2:12 draws from 1:16; 2:18 draws from 1:14; 3:1 draws from 1:4, 16; 3:7 draws from 1:5*a*; 3:14 draws from 1:5*a*. They build upon Christ's initial appearance to John on Patmos and utilize characteristics of His Person depicted there to address areas of need in each church.

The warnings of the seven messages also reflect their unifying effect. They consistently point forward to the dreaded happenings to be foretold in chapters 4-19: 2:5 points to undesirable conditions after Christ's coming to initiate wrath; 2:16 points to His punitive coming described in Rev. 19:11-15; 2:22-23 points to the Great Tribulation, called by the same name in 7:14; 3:3 points to His coming to initiate the wrathful day of the Lord (cf. 6:17); 3:10 anticipates the hour of trial that is about to come on the whole world; 3:16 points to the threat of being spewed from His mouth into this period. The horrors of this coming period were designed to bring the disobedient in the churches to repentance. This course of action furnished their only hope of escaping the unparalleled suffering of those who will be alive during this time.

The promises of the seven messages also serve notice of the book's unity. They provide for escape from the miseries of Revelation 4-19 and for enjoyment of the privileges of the saints after Christ's triumphant return in Rev. 19:11-21: 2:7 looks forward to 22:2, 14; 2:10 looks forward to 22:2, 14; 2:11 looks forward to 20:14; 21:8; 2:17 looks forward to 19:9; 2:26-28 looks forward to 19:14-15; 3:4 looks forward to 19:8, 14; 3:5 looks forward to 20:12,15; 21:27; 3:8 looks forward to 22:16; 3:9 looks forward to 21:23-26; 3:10 looks forward to preservation from the period of Revelation 4-19; 3:11 looks forward to 21:2, 10; 3:20 looks forward to 19:9; 3:21 looks forward to 20:4. Incentives for faithfulness to Christ are abundant. The churches are encouraged to look beyond the present difficulties of the Christian life to derive courage to persevere.

These seven messages cannot be read apart from the rest of the Apocalypse, nor does the rest of the book mean anything without these seven. Chapters 2-3 explain why the rest of the book was written. The overall purpose is distinctly practical (cf. 1:3).

PART 3
The Publication of the Prophecy:
Its Future Expectation (4:1–22:5)

Part 3

The Fulfillment of the Prophecy
as Future Expectation (24:1–27:5)

10
The One Sitting on the Throne

After writing in chapter 1 of his past impressions resulting from his vision of the glorified Christ and in chapters 2 and 3 of present conditions in the churches through the seven messages of Christ to the churches, John now turns in chapter 4 to future anticipations stemming from the series of apocalyptic visions that he receives. This begins the principal prophetic portion of the Apocalypse.

A. THE OPENING OF THE SEVEN-SEALED SCROLL (4:1–8:1)

The prophecy pictures the divine manifestations of wrath under the figure of a scroll that is held in its roll form by seven seals that are broken one at a time as the separate stages are unveiled. The first scene pictures the throne room where the scroll will eventually appear.

1. THE SOURCE OF THE SCROLL (4:1–5:14)

In John's first apocalyptic vision, the seven-sealed scroll arises in a heavenly setting that is dominated by a throne, more specifically by the one sitting on that throne. Chapter 4 focuses on God the Creator who delivers the seven-sealed scroll, and chapter 5 on God (i.e., Christ) the Redeemer, the only one found worthy to take it and open the seals.[1]

---

1. Walter Scott, *Exposition of the Revelation of Jesus Christ* (Swengel, Pa.: Bible Truth Depot, n.d.), p. 119.

a. The One Sitting on the Throne (4:1-11)

Chapter 4 describes John's transition to a state that enabled him to view the heavenly scene. It also details the appearance of the person sitting on the throne and his surroundings. This information is pertinent as an introduction to the series of descriptions beginning in chapter 6, because it discloses the place where and the Person from whom the visitations originate.

Translation

¹**After these things I looked, and behold, a door opened in heaven, and the first sound that I heard [was] as [that] of a trumpet, speaking with me, saying, "Come up here, and I will show you things that must happen after these things." ²Immediately I came to be in the spirit; and behold, a throne stood in heaven, and upon the throne [was] one sitting, ³and the one sitting was similar in appearance to a jasper stone and a sardius, and a rainbow [was] around the throne similar in appearance to an emerald. ⁴And around the throne [I saw] twenty-four thrones, and upon the thrones [I saw] twenty-four elders sitting, clothed in white garments, and upon their heads [I saw] golden crowns. ⁵And from the throne were proceeding [flashes of] lightning and voices and [peals of] thunder; and seven torches of fire [were] burning before the throne, which are the seven spirits of God, ⁶and before the throne [there was something] like a sea of glass similar to crystal.**

"And in the middle of the throne and around the throne [were] four living beings, full of eyes in front and in back; ⁷and the first living being [was] similar to a lion, and the second living being [was] similar to an ox, and the third living being had the face as [that] of a man, and the fourth living being [was] similar to an eagle flying. ⁸And the four living beings, each one of them had six wings apiece, around and within full of eyes; and they do not have rest day and night, saying,

> **"Holy, holy, holy,**
> **Lord God, the Almighty,**
>   **who was and who is and who is coming."**

⁹**And whenever the living beings give glory and honor and thanks to the one who is sitting upon the throne, to the one who lives forever and ever, ¹⁰the twenty-four elders fall before the one sitting upon the throne and worship the one who lives forever and ever, and they cast their crowns before the throne, saying,**

> ¹¹**"You are worthy, our Lord and God,**
>   **to receive the glory and the honor and the power,**
> **because You created all things,**
>   **and because of Your will they were and were created."**

Exegesis and Exposition

At this point in the Apocalypse, John begins recording what is the heart of the book. The prophet has been prepared to receive it through his vision of Christ in chapter 1. In chapters 2 and 3 the Christian people of the seven churches of the province of Asia have received their instructions regarding moral preparation that is the intended practical effect of the prophecy. It now remains to proceed with the prophecy itself, in other words with ἃ δεῖ γενέσθαι ἐν τάχει (*ha dei genesthai en tachei,* "the things that must happen soon") (1:1).

4:1 *Invitation to heaven.* The former occurrence of the phrase μετὰ ταῦτα (*meta tauta,* "after these things") in v. 1 denotes the sequence in John's receipt of the revelation. It marks the beginning of a new[2] vision as it does a number of times in the book (7:9; 15:5; 18:1; 19:1; cf. μετὰ τοῦτο [*meta touto,* "after this"], 7:1). In this case, it introduces a new section of the book as the scene now changes from a picture of the glorified Christ walking among the churches on earth to that of the Father in the court of heaven.[3] Some uses of *meta tauta* in Revelation denote the sequence of fulfillment of events prophesied within a vision (cf. 1:19; 4:1 [second occurrence]; 9:12; 20:3), but this is not the primary force of the phrase here. This use marks a change in scene from Christ in authority over the churches and their messengers to a vision of the court of heaven.[4] It is true that the sequence of visions given to John may coincide with the sequence of events they predict (Scott), but whenever *meta tauta* is followed by εἶδον (*eidon,* "I looked," "I saw"), John's primary reference is to the beginning of a new vision.[5]

Some have argued that 4:1 is simply a transition from one part of the first vision to another.[6] Support for this comes from the observations that nowhere else in the book does *meta tauta* indicate a break in John's ecstatic state[7] and that *meta* means "immediately after" in

---

2. The first vision of the book extends from Rev. 1:10 to 3:22.
3. Henry Barclay Swete, *The Apocalypse of St. John* (London: Macmillan, 1906), p. 66; R. H. Charles, *The Revelation of St. John,* 2 vols., ICC (New York: Scribner's, 1920), 1:106; John Phillips, *Exploring Revelation* (Chicago: Moody, 1974), p. 97; John F. Walvoord, *The Revelation of Jesus Christ* (Chicago: Moody, 1966), p. 87.
4. Swete, *Apocalypse,* p. 66; James Moffatt, "The Revelation of St. John the Divine," in *The Expositor's Greek Testament,* ed. W. Robertson Nicoll (Grand Rapids: Eerdmans, n.d.), 5:375.
5. J. B. Smith, *A Revelation of Jesus Christ* (Scottdale, Pa.: Herald, 1961), p. 101.
6. Isbon T. Beckwith, *The Apocalypse of John* (New York: Macmillan, 1919), p. 494; William E. Biederwolf, *The Millennium Bible* (Grand Rapids: Baker, 1967), pp. 552-53; Richard J. Bauckham, "The Role of the Spirit in the Apocalypse," *EvQ* 52, no. 2 (April-June 1980): 68-69.
7. Henry Alford, *The Greek Testament,* 4 vols. (London: Longmans, Green, 1903), 4:593.

contrast to εἶτα (*eita*, "next"), which allows for an intervening period before the next item in the sequence.[8] The other extreme is to say that the first vision ended after 3:22, and a considerable period of time transpired before the beginning of the vision of 4:1.[9] This is generally associated with the rationale that John needed time to write down what he had just seen and heard.[10] The proper perspective is most probably to allow for a break in John's ecstatic state after 3:22 (see discussion of ἐγενόμην ἐν πνεύματι [*egenomēn en pneumati*, "I came to be in the spirit"] in 4:2 below), but to hold that a new vision began immediately thereafter. The implication of *meta* in meaning "immediately after" seems to require this. John had ample time to write down what he had seen and heard after the completion of the last of the visions contained in the book.

Immediately after Christ's completion of the messages to the seven churches, the majestic figure that first dominated John's attention (cf. 1:12-18) faces him no more, and he moves into a new phase of his revelatory experience: εἶδον, καὶ ἰδοὺ θύρα ἠνεῳγμένη ἐν τῷ οὐρανῷ (*eidon, kai idou thyra ēneǭgmenē en tǭ ouranǭ*, "I looked, and behold, a door opened in heaven"). *Eidon* ("I looked") does not mean that John turned in order to see as he did in the first vision (cf. 1:12), but simply that he came to recognize an object that was before him in prophetic vision. This action should not be equated with sight with the physical eye. Rather, it is sight with the eye of ecstatic vision as throughout the Apocalypse.[11]

The particle *idou* ("behold") calls special attention to the door that John sees. In this book it always indicates a special divine intervention.[12] This is not just another door, but is like a door set in the sky, permitting entrance to the heavenly regions (Beckwith). It should not be equated with the doors in 3:8 and 3:20. Nor is its opening the same as the opening of all heaven in John 1:51; Acts 7:56; or Rev. 19:11.[13] It actually stands in contrast to the usual apocalyptic and ecstatic symbol of "heaven opened" (cf. also Matt. 3:16; Acts 7:56;

---

8. James Glasgow, *The Apocalypse* (Edinburgh: T. & T. Clark, 1872), pp. 140-41.
9. E. W. Bullinger, *The Apocalypse* or *"The Day of the Lord"* (London: Eyre and Spottiswoode, n.d.), pp. 215-16; Moffatt, "Revelation," 5:376.
10. William Lee, "The Revelation of St. John," in *The Holy Bible*, ed. F. C. Cook (London: John Murray, 1881), 4:551.
11. Alford, *Greek Testament*, 4:593; W. Boyd Carpenter, *Revelation*, A New Testament Commentary for English Readers, ed. C. J. Ellicott (New York: Harper & Row, 1966), 3:551.
12. David E. Aune, *Prophecy in Early Christianity and the Ancient Mediterranean World* (Grand Rapids: Eerdmans, 1983), p. 279.
13. Swete, *Apocalypse*, p. 66; George E. Ladd, *A Commentary on the Revelation of John* (Grand Rapids: Eerdmans, 1972), p. 71.

10:11; 11:5) (Moffatt; Beckwith). This is a special door opened to admit John to heaven (cf. 1 Enoch 15:14; Test. Levi 5:1) (Bullinger). John may have seen inside while standing at the opened door, but it is more likely that he was taken up through the door into heaven (Alford). The participle *ēneǭgmenē* ("opened") indicates that the door had been previously opened and left that way for John's arrival.[14] He did not witness the actual opening of the door (Alford).

The door's location is fixed by the words *en tǭ ouranǭ* ("in heaven"). Chapter 4 and the chapters following indicate this to be the dwelling-place of God (cf. Rev. 3:12).[15] This is where Christ ascended following His resurrection (cf. Acts 1:10-11; 3:21; 7:55-56; Rom. 10:6; Col. 3:1; 1 Thess. 4:16).[16] Οὐρανός (*ouranos*, "heaven") sometimes refers to the "sky," but as the revelation to John continues, it will be seen as a place of conflict (cf. 12:7) and one that will eventually see destruction (cf. 21:1) (Mounce). John appears unaffected by the popular view of Judaism regarding a plurality of heavens (cf. 2 Cor. 12:2) (Charles). Of fifty-two uses of the word in the Apocalypse, only once is it plural and this perhaps under the influence of an OT passage being alluded to (Rev. 12:12; cf. Isa. 44:23) (Mounce). John spends most of his time in heaven through the remainder of the Apocalypse. The site of his vision does seem to return to earth at 10:1, but is back in heaven for 11:15-19. Chapter 12 appears to be located on earth, but for 14:18-20 he is back in heaven.

As he contemplated the door opened in heaven, John received specific instructions: καὶ ἡ φωνὴ ἡ πρώτη ἣν ἤκουσα ὡς σάλπιγγος λαλούσης μετ' ἐμοῦ λέγων, Ἀνάβα ὧδε, καὶ δείξω σοι ἃ δεῖ γενέσθαι μετὰ ταῦτα (*kai hē phōnē hē prōtē hēn ēkousa hōs salpingos lalousēs met' emou legōn, Anaba hōde, kai deixō soi ha dei genesthai meta tauta*, "and the first sound which I heard [was] as [that] of a trumpet, speaking with me, saying, 'Come up here, and I will show you things that must happen after these things'"). Most identify this voice with that of the glorified Christ in 1:10,[17] though some object that Christ cannot be

---

14. Swete, *Apocalypse*, p. 66; Robert H. Mounce, *The Book of Revelation*, NICNT (Grand Rapids: Eerdmans, 1977), p. 133. The perfect tense of the participle shows this. This is the first of five significant openings in the Apocalypse. In 11:19 and 15:5, it is the temple in heaven that is opened. In 19:11, heaven itself is opened, and in 21:12, "the books" are opened at the judgment of the white throne.
15. Leon Morris, *The Revelation of St. John*, TNTC (Grand Rapids: Eerdmans, 1969), p. 85.
16. John Peter Lange, *The Revelation of John*, Lange's Commentary, ed. E. R. Craven (Grand Rapids: Zondervan, 1968), 10:150.
17. William Milligan, *The Book of Revelation*, vol. 25 of The Expositor's Bible (New York: George H. Doran, 1889), p. 67; Beckwith, *Apocalypse*, p. 495; Morris, *Revelation*, p. 85.

the agent to show John a vision and at the same time be a part of the vision (cf. 5:6) (Beckwith). Objectors to referring the voice to Christ also contend that the voice of 1:10 is distinguished from that of Christ in 1:15 (Alford; Lee). The latter objection was shown to be unfounded in the earlier discussion of 1:15. The former one is met by noting that Christ does not actually appear here. Only His voice is heard. He does not become the active agent in "showing" until 6:1, after His appearance as the Lamb in 5:6 (Beckwith). The words *hē prōtē* ("the first") point clearly back to the voice that spoke first (cf. 1:10), and the *deixō* ("I will show") repeats the δεῖξαι (*deixai*, "to show") of 1:1 as part of the commission given to Christ (Beckwith). There can be little doubt that it is the voice of Christ summoning John upward.

Loudness marks the sound of the voice John heard here as it did in 1:10. Its comparison to a trumpet in the words *hōs salpingos*[18] ("as [that] of a trumpet") is almost identical with the comparison at 1:10. This sounds a note of authority with which the voice summoned John. Here the participle *lalousēs*[19] ("speaking") replaces λεγούσης (*legousēs*, "saying") of 1:11 in describing the voice. It was speaking with John and saying[20] the following words: *Anaba hōde* ("Come up here"). This summons, somewhat similar to the one given Moses at Mount Sinai (cf. Exod. 19:20, 24-25), has at times been understood as more than a summons to John. Because the rapture of the church comes at a time just prior to the events about to be related, some have taken it as a summons to the church into heaven at that future moment when Christ returns for her (Walvoord). This interpretation is supported by noting the similarity between this summons and the one the church anticipates at the rapture and by the absence of any reference to the church between Rev. 4:1 and 22:16.[21] It is acknowledged even by

---

18. For a discussion of the construction of a genitive following ὡς, see the additional note at 1:10.

19. Λαλούσης modifies ἦν, but is attracted to the genitive case of σάλπιγγος in much the same way as is λεγούσης in 1:10-11 (Beckwith, *Apocalypse*, p. 495). See the discussion at that point.

20. Λέγουσα, the feminine participle to modify the feminine ἡ φωνή, is to be expected rather than the masculine λέγων. The masculine follows natural gender, that of Χριστός, rather than strict grammatical agreement, however (Beckwith, *Apocalypse*, p. 495). This is one of the "severe" solecisms that Turner finds in the Apocalypse where λέγων and λέγοντες appear to be indeclinable (cf. also 5:12; 11:1, 15; 14:7; 19:6) (Nigel Turner, *Syntax*, vol. 3 of *A Grammar of New Testament Greek* [Edinburgh: T. & T. Clark, 1963], pp. 314-15). Also, an accusative case to agree with ἦν would have been expected, but here as elsewhere in the book, the writer is characterized by his rather free use of the nominative, particularly with participles (cf. 1:5; 2:20; 3:12; 14:14) (A. T. Robertson, *Word Pictures in the New Testament*, 6 vols. [Nashville: Broadman, 1933], 6:136).

21. Walvoord, *Revelation*, p. 103; Alan F. Johnson, "Revelation," in *EBC*, ed. Frank E. Gaebelein (Grand Rapids: Zondervan, 1981), 12:461.

some supporters of this view, however, that there is no authority for connecting John's summons with the rapture of the church (Walvoord). In fact, the two events are quite dissimilar in that John's body remained on Patmos throughout his experience, whereas at the rapture of the church the bodies of the saints will be transferred to heaven. Another basic difference is that John's summons is a command to receive revelation, but that of the church is one that accomplishes final salvation for the redeemed ones of the Body of Christ. Ἀναβαίνειν εἰς τὸν οὐρανόν (*Anabainein eis ton ouranon*, "to ascend into heaven") is one of the ways of describing a penetration into the heavenly mysteries (cf. Rom. 10:6; 2 Cor. 12:1-2) (Moffatt). This summons is best understood as an invitation for John to assume a new vantage point for the sake of the revelation he was about to receive (Ladd; Mounce).

The promise of *deixō soi* ("I will show you") is in execution of the plan of God the Father in granting to Christ the responsibility of transmitting the ἀποκάλυψις (*apokalypsis*, "revelation") to the churches (cf. *deixai* ["to show"], 1:1). His action, which fulfills this promise, begins in Rev. 6:1 where the Lamb initiates the process of breaking the seals of the seven-sealed scroll (Beckwith).

The caption for the promised revelation, *ha dei genesthai meta tauta* ("things that must happen after these things"), is familiar because of its earlier disclosure in Rev. 1:1, 19. *Ha dei genesthai* ("things that must happen") is retained from Rev. 1:1 as a fundamental prophetic expression originating in Daniel's prophecy.[22] *Genesthai meta tauta* ("happen after these things") recalls the last part of the three-fold outline of the book in Rev. 1:19, the first two parts being John's vision of the glorified Christ (1:9-16) and an evaluation of the present condition of the churches (chapters 2-3). The time has arrived to deal with what God has destined for the future (Charles). The events to be predicted are not just probable. They are fixed and certain because they are the outworking of God's will (cf. *dei*, "must") (Morris). Underlying every prophecy is the reality of God's hand in history. These predictions are not designed to satisfy human curiosity about the future, but to remind mankind of who is in control (Scott).

The latter occurrence of *meta tauta* ("after these things") in 4:1 differs from the former one in its function. It places the fulfillment of matters about to be prophesied subsequent to the conditions described in chapters 2-3, and does not pertain to the sequence in which John received his visions.[23] The prophecies will describe what will happen after the period of the churches has run its course.

---

22. See discussion of the expression at 1:1.
23. Smith, *Revelation*, pp. 101-2. The Westcott-Hort Greek text punctuated

4:2 *The heavenly throne.* Very quickly after the summons and promise of additional revelation, John entered another ecstatic state: εὐθέως ἐγενόμην ἐν πνεύματι (*eutheōs egenomēn en pneumati*, "immediately I came to be in the spirit"). The adverb *eutheōs* ("immediately") without a conjunction to connect the clause with v. 1, intensely describes John's instantaneous translation into a prophetic view of the heavenly sphere.[24] As already concluded in the discussion of 1:10, "in the spirit" is descriptive of the prophetic trance into which the prophet's spirit entered (Charles). This miraculous ecstatic state wrought by the Spirit of God was, to all intents and purposes, a complete translation from Patmos to heaven. All of the prophet's senses were operative: his ears heard, his eyes saw, and his emotions were as real as though his body was literally in heaven instead of remaining on Patmos.[25]

Because this was John's condition throughout the first vision of 1:10–3:22, the relationship of this experience with the previous one needs clarification. Several possibilities exist. It may be that the additional challenge to come up to heaven and enter a distant open door required a stronger spiritual endowment than previously when he simply remained on Patmos to receive the vision (Alford). This fresh outpouring of the Spirit may enable him to view a new and more sublime vision (cf. Ezek. 11:1, 5) (Lee). This explanation is not convincing, however. The text contains no indication that a force of the Spirit mightier than before came upon the seer (Beckwith). The alleged parallel to Ezek. 11:1, 5 is not relevant, because the two verses speak of two separate functions of the Spirit. Here Rev. 1:10 and 4:2 are the same function (Charles). The same objections hold in nullifying the suggestion that 4:2 depicts a higher degree of inspiration.[26]

Another suggestion is that *egenomēn en pneumati* ("I came to be in the spirit") merely marks a continuation of the same state in which John already found himself, and serves only as a reminder of this fact.[27] In other words, the expression implies no more than what is already expressed in μετὰ ταῦτα εἶδον (*meta tauta eidon*, "after these

---

the end of v. 1 and the beginning of v. 2 so as to connect μετὰ ταῦτα with the beginning of v. 2 rather than with the end of v. 1. Evidence from Rev. 1:10, 19 and from Daniel 2:28, 29, 45 points strongly to the correctness of putting no punctuation after γενέσθαι and putting a period after ταῦτα (Swete, *Apocalypse*, p. 67; Beckwith, *Apocalypse*, p. 495).

24. Lange, *Revelation*, p. 150.
25. J. A. Seiss, *The Apocalypse*, 3 vols. (New York: Charles C. Cook, 1909), 1:99.
26. Contra Swete, *Apocalypse*, p. 67.
27. Charles, *Revelation*, 1:110; Beckwith, *Apocalypse*, p. 596; Mounce, *Revelation*, p. 133. Robertson suggests viewing ἐγενόμην as an effective aorist in 4:2 in comparison with its use as an ingressive aorist in 1:10 (*Word Pictures*, 6:326).

things I saw") (4:1) (Charles). This explanation, however, does in-justice to the tense and meaning of *egenomēn* ("I came to be") and disregards the force of the adverb *eutheōs* ("immediately"). A change of some sort transpired here, one that is marked by suddenness.

It is best to conclude that John had returned to his normal senses after the first vision ended in 3:22 and now returns to the same state in which he had been so as to receive a second vision (Charles; Ladd). This is the most natural understanding of the language (Beckwith; Mounce). It is the repetition of the expression from 1:10 that implies an intermittent state when the trance left him (Morris). Apparently the first vision (1:10–3:22) ended, and immediately after, this new summons with its consequent ecstatic renewal came.

Another use of ἰδοὺ (*idou*, "behold") marks a new special divine intervention at the beginning of John's new vision: καὶ ἰδοὺ θρόνος ἔκειτο ἐν τῷ οὐρανῷ (*kai idou thronos ekeito en tō ouranō*, "and behold, a throne stood in heaven"). *Thronos* ("throne") originally might have been used for an oracular seat, a teacher's chair, a judge's bench, or even a favorable combination of planetary positions. It later came to be reserved for kings and gods.[28] Here it is the central point of a huge room of indescribable beauty with God Himself the central figure (Beckwith). In the OT Temple God's throne was a prominent part (cf. Ps. 9:4). The OT also at times pictures heaven itself as God's throne (cf. Isa. 66:1) and sometimes sees Him enthroned in heaven (cf. 1 Kings 22:19; Pss. 11:4; 47:8; Isa. 6:1; Ezek. 1:26; Dan. 7:9). This last picture is the symbolism required in this verse, though the picture of the throne room also merges with that of a heavenly temple (Rev. 16:17; cf. Ps. 18:6; Mic. 1:2; Hab. 2:20) (Swete; Charles). The temple and the throne are interrelated throughout the book (cf. 7:15; 11:19). The heavenly throne was probably a part of the heavenly temple as seen by the presence of the golden altar of incense and the ark of the covenant therein also (cf. 8:3; 11:19) (Charles).

The throne of God is extremely prominent throughout John's prophecy, being explicitly mentioned in every chapter except chapters 2, 9, 10, 15, 17, and 18. In Revelation 15 heaven is seen as a temple without an explicit reference to the throne. *Thronos* is used thirteen times in the eleven verses of chapter 4 (cf. 4:2 [twice], 3, 4 [three times], 5 [twice], 6 [twice], 9, 10 [twice]), eleven of the occur-rences referring to the throne of God and the other two to the thrones upon which the twenty-four elders sat (cf. 4:4). It is used thirty-seven times in the whole book. The major focus of chapter 4 upon the throne is its symbolism of God's sovereignty exercised in judgment.

---

28. J. Massyngberde Ford, *Revelation*, vol. 38 of AB (Garden City, N.Y.: Dou-bleday, 1975), p. 70.

From this point of origination proceeds the outworking of God's wrath described in the body of the Apocalypse (cf. 6:10, 16-17; 14:7; 15:1; 16:5, 19; 18:20; 19:2, 11). Though evil reigns for a time on earth, God will ultimately prevail.[29]

John did not see the throne being put into position.[30] According to the connotation of the verb *ekeito* ("stood"), he merely observed it standing in its place.[31] The fact that John has now in his prophetic apprehension "arrived" in heaven where he saw the throne is shown by the words *en tǭ ouranǭ* ("in heaven").

"And upon the throne [was] one sitting" (καὶ ἐπὶ τὸν θρόνον κα-θήμενος, *kai epi ton thronon kathēmenos*) brings the climax of John's initial look at the heavenly throne room. This person is undoubtedly God the Father, because He is distinguished from the Lamb in 5:5, 7; 6:16; 7:10 and from the Spirit in 4:5 (cf. 19:4) (Alford; Bullinger; Charles). Suggestions as to why John did not name Him more directly have included a reluctance to mention the divine name for the same reason it is avoided in later Hebrew literature[32] and the impossibility of expressing in a word the awesomeness of this Person (Alford). The best explanation is that he probably did not intend an anthropomorphic representation. Portraying the glory of God was the objective, not a detailed description of the Father's appearance.[33]

The combination *kathēmenos* ("sitting") and the preposition *epi* ("upon") frequently designates God throughout the book. The sitting posture denotes the activity of reigning, not resting or a cessation of priestly functioning as in Heb. 1:3; 10:12; 12:2. Efforts to explain the variety of cases employed after the preposition have not produced conclusive results.[34] The consensus is that the reason for the pattern

---

29. Thomas F. Glasson, *The Revelation of John,* CBC (Cambridge: U. Press, 1965), p. 39.
30. Biederwolf, *Millennium Bible,* p. 553.
31. Swete, *Apocalypse,* p. 67; Fritz Rienecker, *A Linguistic Key to the Greek New Testament,* trans. and ed. Cleon L. Rogers, Jr. (Grand Rapids: Zondervan, 1980), p. 822. Κεῖμαι functions as a passive of τίθημι, so ἔκειτο is equivalent in meaning to ἐτέθη (cf. John 2:6; 19:29; 21:9) (Swete, *Apocalypse,* p. 67; Rienecker, *Linguistic Key,* p. 822).
32. Beckwith, *Apocalypse,* p. 496. Yet elsewhere John does specifically name Him as God: 7:10, 15; 12:5; 19:4.
33. Alford, *Greek Testament,* 4:594; Walvoord, *Revelation,* p. 105. Aune compares the one sitting upon the throne to the Roman emperor whose major role was one of administering justice and who administered his responsibility in a passive manner (David E. Aune, "The Influence of Roman Imperial Court Ceremonial on the Apocalypse of John," in *Papers of the Chicago Society of Biblical Research* 28 [1983]: 8-9). This is part of his case for understanding John to model the ceremonial of the heavenly throne room after the ceremonial of the imperial court (ibid., pp. 5-6). Elements of his comparison are interesting, but not persuasive.
34. Charles concludes that the participle in the nominative and accusative as a general rule is followed by ἐπί and the accusative, the participle in the

of variations is not yet known. God is simply pictured throughout the book as "the one who sits upon the throne" (Bullinger).

4:3 John proceeds with his description of this central person of his vision: καὶ ὁ καθήμενος[35] ὅμοιος ὁράσει λίθῳ ἰάσπιδι καὶ σαρδίῳ (*kai ho kathēmenos homoios horasei lithǭ iaspidi kai sardiǭ* ("and the one sitting was similar in appearance to a jasper stone and a sardius"). He resembled a jasper stone and a sardius. Before the task of defining the two stones and their colors, it is necessary to reach some conclusion about how much to press the details of the description in a quest for John's meaning. In other words, How is the expression *homoios horasei*[36] ("similar in appearance") to be understood? On one side are those who see no need to analyze the symbolism of the scene in detail. The objective is only the general impression created by the archetypical imagery, an impression of transcendent glory (Beckwith; Mounce; Johnson). This approach usually compares various OT attempts to give visible pictures of the glory of God. In Ezek. 1:26-28, God and His throne are like the brilliance of glowing metal, of fire and brightness all around. In Ex. 24:10, God appears standing on a pavement of sapphire. In Dan. 7:9, His raiment was as white as snow and His throne as fiery flames, and many thousands were standing before Him. In 1 Kings 22:19, He is seen on His throne with all the host of heaven standing around Him. In Isa. 6:1, He sits on His throne, lofty and exalted, with the train of His robe filling the Temple.[37] These represent a variety of ways of describing the glory of God (Ladd).

This attitude in approaching the text encounters the danger of overlooking important lessons. Details of Scripture are always significant. There must be a reason for the use of these symbols instead of others. Granted that the precise symbolic import of some of the stones in the vision may be difficult to comprehend, other parts of the vision are relatively clear in their symbolic import. For example,

---

genitive by ἐπί and the genitive, and the participle in the dative (or locative) by ἐπί and the dative (or locative) (*Revelation*, 1:12-13). Alford proposes that the first mention in a context is always accusative to suggest *motion toward* and that no apparent rationale prevails regarding the usage of the genitive and the dative (*Greek Testament*, 4:594). The accusative following the preposition is found in 4:2, 4; 6:2, 4, 5; 14:14; 17:3; 19:11; 20:4, 11. The genitive after ἐπί is used in 4:10; 5:1, 7; 6:16; 14:15, 16; 17:1; 19:18, 19, 21. The comparable uses of the dative are in 4:9; 5:13; 7:10, 15; 19:4; 21:5.

35. In v. 3 the participle καθήμενος is articular rather than anarthrous as in v. 2. The function of the article with it in v. 3 is to denote another reference to the same person previously referred to in the context.

36. Ὁράσει is a use of the instrumental case with a word expressing likeness (ὅμοιος) (A. T. Robertson, *A Grammar of the Greek New Testament in the Light of Historical Research* [Nashville: Broadman, 1934], p. 530). This usage draws upon the associative idea of that case.

37. Beckwith, *Apocalypse*, pp. 496-97; Robertson, *Word Pictures*, 6:326.

the rainbow later in v. 3 paints the picture of divine judgment, including the hope of deliverance therefrom for those who benefit from the covenant symbolized thereby (Bullinger). Without the rest of the Bible, the conclusion might be to consider the details relatively meaningless, but in light of Scriptures that form such a vital background for John and his readers, one can hardly conclude other than that the details have deep significance (Walvoord). This is further confirmed by a recollection of the symbolic (cf. ἐσήμανεν [esēmanen, "he signified") nature of the manner in which the revelation was communicated to John.

Modern ignorance of ancient terminology makes precise identification of the stones quite tentative (Morris). Probably the equation of *iaspidi* ("jasper stone") to the modern jasper which is dull and opaque (Alford) is wrong because the modern stone is hardly considered costly as the text implies.[38] Unlikelihood exists in regarding it as green jade or quartz (Lee) too, because this duplicates the color of the emerald at the end of the verse. To view it as a species of red stone has support from Isa. 54:12,[39] but this would create an overlap with the parallel term *sardiǭ* ("sardius"), which on all hands is acknowledged to be fiery red (Alford). The key to probable identification of this stone is Rev. 21:11 where it represents a watery crystalline brightness (Alford; Morris). The modern jasper is opaque, but the ancient stone must have been translucent rock crystal, possibly a diamond.[40]

There is basic agreement regarding the sardius. It was a fiery, deep red stone, most likely a carnelian. In antiquity, it was most often the one used for engraved gems (Swete; Charles). It is the stone for which the city of Sardis was named (Swete).

Based on the identifications of the stones above, one is justified in assigning a symbolic connotation to them. Suggested symbolisms have included judgment by water and judgment by fire, the goodness of God in nature and His severity in judgment, deity and humanity, and the holiness of God and the justice of God (Alford). The last seems most probable because the same mixture of white light (i.e., the diamond) with fire (i.e., the carnelian) pervades the OT and apocalyptic visions of divine majesty (cf. Ezek. 1:4; 8:2; Dan. 7:9; cf. Rev. 1:14; 10:1) (Alford). The picture is that of His anger because of His holy nature reacting in response to the prevailing sinfulness of mankind, resulting in the judgment He is about to send upon the earth (Smith).

---

38. Beckwith, *Apocalypse*, p. 597; Robertson, *Word Pictures*, 6:326.
39. Robertson, *Word Pictures*, 6:326.
40. Charles, *Revelation*, 1:114; G. R. Beasley-Murray, *The Book of Revelation*, NCB (Grand Rapids: Eerdmans, 1978), p. 113; Mounce, *Revelation*, p. 134.

The impression of coming judgment because of the infinite disparity between God's holiness and man's sinfulness is tempered by the next part of the statement: καὶ *ἶρις κυκλόθεν τοῦ θρόνου ὅμοιος ὁράσει σμαραγδίνῳ (*kai iris kyklothen tou thronou homoios horasei smaragdinō*, "and a rainbow [was] around the throne similar in appearance to an emerald"). Throughout the LXX τόξον (*toxon*) (cf. especially Gen. 9:8-17) is used to indicate a bow (cf. Rev. 6:2). ᾽Ιρις (*Iris*, "rainbow") is used in Ex. 30:24 to mean "cassia" and in Rev. 10:1 to mean "rainbow." It is not used elsewhere in the Greek Bible. The exact shape of the *iris* ("rainbow") has been discussed. Both semicircular and circular shapes have been proposed (Beckwith). The parallel in Ezek. 1:28 suggests a semicircle, but the adverbial preposition *kyklothen*[41] ("around") that accompanies the noun here argues more strongly for a complete circle, a sort of halo (cf. 10:1) (Beckwith). Another preposition such as ὑπεράνω (*hyperanō*, "above") or ἐπί (*epi*, "over") would be more probable if an arc of a circle had been the shape. The circular shape is probably the reason for the choice of *iris* rather than *toxon* (Swete).

The notion that *iris* ("rainbow") is not to be singled out for detailed analysis but is only a part of the larger picture (Mounce) robs this figure of its important contribution to the context. John's use of the OT is never just decorative. Other allusions in this chapter to Genesis and Exodus show clearly that this rainbow is a reminiscence of the covenant that God made with Noah (cp. 4:1 with Gen. 15:1; 4:1 with Ex. 19:20, 24; 4:5 with Ex. 19:16; 4:8 with Ex. 3:14; 4:11 with Gen. 1:1).[42] It is much more satisfactory to acknowledge that it is a reminder that God's mercy is as great as His majesty, i.e., that there will be no triumph of God's sovereignty at the expense of His mercy.[43] The disasters portrayed in the following pages cannot be interpreted as meaning that God has forgotten His promise to Noah. This symbol is in contrast to the note of terror struck in v. 5*a*, as well as counterbalancing the hint of coming wrath in v. 3*a* (Moffatt; Beasley-Murray).

The rainbow is distinguishable from other rainbows, however. It has a green color "similar in appearance to an emerald" (*homoios horasei smaragdinō*). A fairly good consensus exists that σμαράγδινος (*smaragdinos*) refers to what is called an emerald in modern times.

---

41. The preposition κυκλόθεν is a cognate of the noun κύκλος which means "ring" or "circle" (G. Abbott-Smith, *A Manual Greek Lexicon of the New Testament* [Edinburgh: T. & T. Clark, 1950], p. 260).

42. J. P. M. Sweet, *Revelation* (Philadelphia: Westminster, Pelican, 1979), p. 118.

43. G. V. Caird, *A Commentary on the Revelation of St. John the Divine*, HNTC (New York: Harper & Row, 1966), p. 63.

This poses a slight problem with the interpretation of *iris* as a rainbow, because a rainbow has seven colors.[44] Perhaps the best answer that can be posed at this point is that the rainbow possessed a number of shades of green similar to a rainbow. The symbolism of the stone seems to lie in its green color, which represents the grace and mercy of God.[45] This is a fitting reinforcement to the allusion to mercy provided by the rainbow, whose appearance is compared to the emerald.

4:4 Besides the circular rainbow, twenty-four thrones were also positioned around the throne: καὶ κυκλόθεν τοῦ θρόνου θρόνους εἴκοσι τέσσαρες (*kai kyklothen tou thronou thronous eikosi tessares*, "and around the throne [I saw] twenty-four thrones"). The text does not specify whether the additional thrones were smaller, lower, or both, but they were surely subordinate to the throne around which they were arranged. Possibly some connection should be made with the thrones spoken of in Col. 1:16, where thrones are part of a listing of an angelic hierarchy that also includes dominions (κυριότητες [*kyriotētes*]), principalities (ἀρχαί [*archai*]), and powers (ἐξουσίαι [*exousiai*]) (Beckwith). How close the relationship is depends upon how the occupants of the thrones are identified.

These occupants number the same as the thrones, twenty-four: καὶ ἐπὶ τοὺς θρόνους εἴκοσι τέσσαρας πρεσβυτέρους καθημένους περιβεβλημένους ἐν ἱματίοις λευκοῖς, καὶ ἐπὶ τὰς κεφαλὰς αὐτῶν στεφάνους χρυσοῦς (*kai epi tous thronous eikosi tessaras presbyterous kathēmenous peribeblēmenous en himatiois leukois, kai epi tas kephalas autōn stephanous chrysous*, "and upon the thrones [I saw] twenty-four elders sitting, clothed in white garments, and upon their heads [I saw] golden crowns"). They are called *presbyterous* ("elders") and are the first group of created beings to come to John's attention in this heavenly setting. From ancient times, πρεσβύτερος (*presbyteros*, "elder") denoted an official position (Bullinger), but specific identification of this prominent group has been difficult. Attempts to identify the elders have fallen into two broad categories, one saying that they are men and the other that they are angels. Each category has three variations, the former one saying that the men are either representatives of Israel, representatives of the church, or representatives of both. The latter category sees the angels as representatives either of

---

44. Lee, "Revelation," 4:533. Because of this difficulty, Beasley-Murray proposes that σμαραγδίνῳ is a colorless rock crystal through which light would become a rainbow of prismatic colors (*Revelation*, p. 113).
45. Swete, *Apocalypse*. p. 68; Alford, *Greek Testament*, 4:596; Bullinger, *Apocalypse*, p. 217; Homer Hailey, *Revelation, an Introduction and Commentary* (Grand Rapids: Baker, 1979), p. 168.

the OT priestly orders or of the faithful of all ages, or as a special class or college of angels.

Understanding the elders as representing men finds its strongest support in the observation that πρεσβύτεροι (*presbyteroi*, "elders") is more easily applied to men than it is to angels (cf. Heb. 11:2).[46] The strength of this is somewhat minimized, however, by the observation that the LXX reading of Isa. 24:23 refers to a heavenly assembly, presumably angels, whose members are heavenly beings called τῶν πρεσβυτέρων (*tōn presbyterōn*, "the elders") (Beckwith). The grouping of elders with angelic beings throughout Revelation adds credence to the possibility of the term's referring to angels (e.g., 7:11; 19:1-4) (Ladd). There is some validity to distinguishing between πρεσβυτής (*presbytēs*), which means "old man," and πρεσβύτερος (*presbyteros*), which means "elder" (Bullinger). The former word is limited to human beings, but the latter can serve as an official title without regard to which order of created being one belongs.

A further support cited for referring *presbyterous* to human beings is that white clothing in Revelation is generally the clothing of saints (cf. 3:5, 18) (Smith; Sweet; Johnson). Granting this to be a possible general practice in Revelation does not demand that it be an exclusive practice, because it is an argument from silence. Nothing in the text requires this guideline. The practice of the NT more widely indicates that no such restriction was observed by the other writers, even by John himself in his gospel (John 20:12; cf. Matt. 28:3; Mark 16:5; Acts 1:10) (Johnson). It is hardly persuasive to identify *presbyterous* as men on this basis.

Another evidence cited to prove that the elders are men is that crowns of gold are usually associated with redeemed men, not angels (Sweet; Johnson). Sometimes only the church is seen as represented, because only the church will have achieved victory by this time in the tribulation. Neither Israel nor angels will have yet been rewarded (Walvoord). These are again arguments from implication, not explicit statements of Scripture, however. Nothing in Scripture prohibits angels from wearing this crown. Certainly golden crowns do not denote redemption in Rev. 9:7, and probably not in Rev. 14:14. Since nothing in the context of chapter 4 speaks directly of redemption, another connotation is probable. Crowns of gold could denote the royal dignity of those associated with the throne of God (cf. 1 Kings 22:19; Ps. 89:7) (Johnson).

It is true that the description of the elders includes items that are promised to the overcomers in the churches: white garments (Rev.

---

46. F. W. Grant, *The Revelation of Jesus Christ* (New York: Loizeaux, n.d.), p. 33; Ford, *Revelation*, p. 71.

3:5), crowns (Rev. 3:11), and thrones (Rev. 3:21). It is also true that elders were sometimes a representative group, whether it be those in local churches (cf. Acts 14:23; 15:6; 20:17; 21:18) or the twenty-four who represented the thousands of priests in Israel (cf. 1 Chron. 24:7-19).[47] This does not dictate, however, that this was always true. There is no compelling evidence here that they represent a larger body (Bullinger). Nowhere in the context is it suggested. Furthermore, throughout the book, they are distinguished from the saints (cf. 7:13-14; 14:3; 19:4-8) (Ladd; Johnson). Identifying them as men because of the thrones they occupy fails to recognize an important distinction: they are seated on their thrones already, but men will not be so positioned until some point in the future (Rev. 20:4; cf. 1 Cor. 6:2).[48]

Another argument in favor of the human identification of the elders comes from the number twenty-four.[49] It is said to symbolize the combined number of the twelve patriarchs of Israel and the twelve apostles (Alford). This view notes that the elders were representatives of the people of Israel in the OT (Ex. 4:29; 12:21; 19:7; 24:1; cf. Heb. 11:2) and of the churches in the NT (Acts 14:23; 20:17; 21:18) (Lee). The description of the new Jerusalem in Rev. 21:12-14 is taken as verification of this, because both groups are a part of the heavenly city. The analogy of Christ's earlier statement about the twelve apostles sitting on twelve thrones judging the twelve tribes of Israel is also taken as proof (cf. Matt. 19:28; Luke 22:30). The dual reference to the song of Moses and the song of the Lamb in Rev. 15:3 also provides some support for this view (Alford; Lee). As promising as this reasoning is, it cannot override the distinctions between the saints and the elders already cited. It also introduces a concept that is foreign to the norm of primitive Christianity, the idea the church could be com-

---

47. Lee, "Revelation," 4:554; Smith, *Revelation*, p. 106; Walvoord, *Revelation*, p. 106; L. W. Hurtado, "Revelation 4-5 in the Light of Jewish Apocalyptic Analogies," *JSNT* 25 (1985):113.
48. Swete, *Apocalypse*, p. 69; Charles, *Revelation*, 1:128-30; Morris, *Revelation*, p. 88. Biederwolf responds that the thrones may be viewed in an idealized manner. Their actual existence is yet future, but they are already potentially realized (*Millennium Bible*, p. 556). Yet it is doubtful that the tension between the "already" and the "not yet" of the Christian life is applicable at this point, in light of the apparent chronological unfolding of the Apocalypse (i.e., Rev. 20:4 comes subsequent to Rev. 5:4).
49. Ford suggests that the number twenty-four relates to a list of ruling fathers in Israel such as is enumerated in Sirach 44-49: Enoch, Noah, Abraham, Isaac, Jacob, Moses, Aaron, Phinehas, Joshua, Samuel, Nathan, David, Solomon, Hezekiah, Josiah, Jeremiah, Ezekiel, Zerubbabel, Jeshua, Nehemiah, Joseph, Shem, Seth, and Adam. On this basis, she concludes that the twenty-four elders represent Israel (*Revelation*, p. 80). The correspondence in the number of names is interesting but probably nothing more than coincidental.

posed of a fusion or combination of peoples of the Old and New Covenants such as this view would require (Moffatt; Beckwith). The church is not a composite of two groups, but one people. Rev. 21:12-14 does not represent a true coordination of Jewish and Christian churches. This would have required twenty-four gates or twenty-four foundations (Charles).

The second group of interpretations understand the twenty-four elders to be angelic beings. As a group, these encounter the immediate objection that angels cannot sing about their own redemption the way these elders do in Rev. 5:9-10 (Seiss). This objection is based, however, on an acceptance of an incorrect textual variant that includes the first person pronoun "us" in the song about redemption.[50] Furthermore, the four living beings, whom no one attempts to identify with redeemed humanity, also join in singing that song. Some go even further in objecting to the elders being angels by observing that angels in the Bible never sing. This objection is questionable, however. The Bible never says that angels cannot sing. The angelic host that appeared to the shepherds at Christ's birth seems to demonstrate otherwise (Luke 2:13-14). It is certain that angels have a great interest in salvation (cf. 1 Pet. 1:12). It is probably not beyond their capability to sing about it.

To see the twenty-four angels as representative of the faithful of all ages, because believers share the throne of their Lord and reign with Him (Rev. 1:6; 3:21; 20:4, 6; 22:5; cf. 2 Tim. 2:12), wearing crowns as they do so (Rev. 3:11), is an inviting possibility. This is the kingly privilege of the faithful (Charles). Yet the fact remains that in the context it is nowhere hinted that the elders are symbols of a larger group. There is no compulsion that they stand for something else (Bullinger).

Taking the twenty-four angelic beings to be representative of the OT priestly orders furnishes an explanation for the number twenty-four (cf. 1 Chron. 23:3-4; 24:4; 25:9-31). The elders function in a quasipriestly fashion in offering the prayers of the saints (cf. Rev. 5:8) in the heavenly archetype of the earthly Temple with its accessories (cf. Heb. 8:5) (Bullinger; Charles; Beasley-Murray; Mounce). The nature of their priestly function is in doubt, however. Rather than priestly, theirs is the responsibility of leading in worship for all creation (Beckwith). Their attire of golden crowns and white robes and their functions are royal rather than judicial or sacerdotal (Swete; Moffatt). This obstacle for the priestly representation view is added to

---

50. Bullinger, *Apocalypse*, pp. 219-20; Mounce, *Revelation*, p. 135. See the additional note at 5:9 for further details about the textual problem there.

the broader objection of having no contextual indication that the elders represent anyone.

The remaining explanation appears to be the correct one, that the twenty-four elders are a special class or college of angels, beings of high authority that belong to the court of God in heaven.[51] In this book they are always grouped with angels rather than men, but are distinguished from other angelic subgroups (cf. 7:9-11; 19:1-4) (Ladd). That they are such a class of angels is well borne out when one of the elders performs the same function of offering bowls of incense that is later performed by an angel (cf. 5:8; 8:3). In addition, in 7:13 the phrase "one of the elders" indicates that the elders were separate created beings rather than corporately representing a larger group. He is separate and different both from the great multitude and from John (cf. also 5:5) (Bullinger). In 7:14, this elder acts as an agent of revelation in much the same manner as angels function in the book (cf. 1:1; 17:3; 22:6). Such duties belong only to angels (cf. Dan. 9:21-27) (Charles). This particular group of angels primarily assists in execution of the divine rule of the universe. Very probably they are part of the assembly of heavenly beings that are regularly pictured as present with God in heaven (cf. 1 Kings 22:19; Ps. 89:7; Isa. 24:23) (Ladd).

The twenty-four elders, for several reasons, appear to be subordinate to the four living beings introduced in 5:6. For one thing, they respond to the signal of the four to fall down and worship in 4:9-10 (Charles). Again, whenever the two orders come together in the Apocalypse, the living beings are always listed first (cf. 4:9-10; 5:6, 8, 14; 14:3) (Charles). There are three apparent exceptions to this sequence: here (4:4, 6) where the living beings are placed last to prepare for their song in 4:8, which introduces the sequence of 4:9-11; and in 7:9-11 and 19:1-4 where the sequence is determined by distance from the throne, the outer echelons being given first (Charles). In 7:9-11, the most distant group, the redeemed multitude, comes first, followed by angels, elders, and living beings, the living beings being closest of all. The situation in 19:1-4 is similar with the redeemed multitude being omitted.

As noted above, white apparel is generally characteristic of angelic beings (cf. Matt. 28:3; Mark 16:5; John 20:12; Acts 1:10). The twenty-four elders are no exception: *peribeblēmenous en himatiois leukois* ("clothed in white garments"). When they received the garments is not disclosed. The point is that they are now so clothed.

A further feature of the twenty-four was their headpieces: *kai epi*

---

51. Bullinger, *Apocalypse,* p. 219; Lange, *Revelation,* p. 152; Moffatt, "Revelation," 5:378; Beckwith, *Apocalypse,* pp. 498-99; Phillips, *Revelation,* p. 103.

tas kephalas autōn stephanous chrysous ("and upon their heads [I saw] golden crowns"). As noted above, the golden crowns suggest royalty. "Crowns" (*Stephanous*) had a variety of uses in the ancient world. They were used in heathen religious worship and as a means of facilitating the reception of oracles from heathen gods. They were part of the dress at feasts, being considered as having some kind of magical protective power. In politics, they were a mark of dignity, and in battle, a means of protection and victory. They were used to crown the winner in athletic competition as a bestowal of honor to him and to the god to whom the festival or events were dedicated. In the victor's hometown at a final celebration, he would offer the wreath or crown to his own deity. Crowns were worn at weddings and funerals as well.[52] They were manufactured by weaving a garland of oak, ivy, parsley, myrtle or olive wood, or an imitation of these in gold as in the present case. The other kind of crown in the Apocalypse is the δι-άδημα (*diadēma*, "crown"). It is more directly representative of kingly authority than στέφανος (*stephanos*), but the latter can be emblematic of royalty. Such is the case with the golden crowns of the elders.

4:5 *Activities around the throne.* Beginning at v. 5, several active aspects of the heavenly scene that greeted John are noted, including flashes of lightning, voices and peals of thunder (v. 5*a*), the burning of torches (v. 5*b*), the worshipful songs of four living beings (vv. 6-8),[53] and the twenty-four elders (vv. 9-11). This series of actions is initiated by the words καὶ ἐκ τοῦ θρόνου ἐκπορεύονται ἀστραπαὶ καὶ φωναὶ καὶ βρονταί (*kai ek tou thronou ekporeuontai astrapai kai phōnai kai brontai*, "and from the throne were proceeding [flashes of] lightning and voices and [peals of] thunder"). The origin of these phenomena was *ek tou thronou* ("from the throne"). This is a reverent way of saying that the one who sits upon the throne is responsible for them. They were proceeding from Him.[54] They are graphically[55] pictured as emanating from His Person. Here is another reminiscence of the circumstances at the giving of the law on Mount Sinai (cf. Ex. 19:16) (Swete).

---

52. Walter Grundmann, "στέφανος, στεφανόω," in *TDNT*, 10 vols., ed. Gerhard Friedrich, trans. and ed. Geoffrey W. Bromiley (Grand Rapids: Eerdmans, 1976), 7 (1971):631.
53. No action accompanies the description of the sea of glass in v. 6*a*.
54. Morris, *Revelation*, p. 88. John is somewhat reluctant to describe in detail the one who sits upon the throne. This is another indication of that reluctance.
55. The conspicuous change in tense from the aorist ἐγενόμην in 4:2 to the present ἐκπορεύονται in 4:5 is a stylistic device to increase vividness. Ἐκπορεύονται is a historical present, graphically representing the action as currently in process. This is the kind of description as might be rendered by an eyewitness of the events (Carpenter, *Revelation*, p. 552; Robertson, *Word Pictures*, 6:327-28).

Astrapai kai phōnai kai brontai ("[flashes of] lightning and voices and [peals of] thunder") are important in Revelation in tying the manifestations of God's displeasure in the remainder of the book to His throne. They are found in conjunction with the seventh seal (Rev. 8:5), the seventh trumpet (Rev. 11:19), and the seventh bowl of wrath (Rev. 16:18) (Mounce). In each instance, they are in the setting of this heavenly temple where the throne stands (Mounce). In the OT, such phenomena are common manifestations of the glory of God (e.g., Ex. 9:23, 28; 1 Sam. 7:10; 12:17-18) and a display of His omnipotence (cf. Ps. 29:3), particularly as exercised in judgment against a sinful world (cf. Ezek. 1:4, 13, 24).[56] The most direct allusion of these "judgment" phenomena is to the occasion of the giving of the law to Moses where occurrences of φωναὶ καὶ ἀστραπαί (*phōnai kai astrapai*, "voices and [flashes of] lightning") are recorded (Ex. 19:16 [LXX]; cf. 1 Sam. 2:10; Job 37:2-12; Ps. 18:13-15) (Swete; Ladd; Beasley-Murray; Ford). The Hebrews made no great distinction between the *phōnai* ("voices") and the *brontai* ("[peals of] thunder"). Their close relation can be seen in Ps. 77:18 (76:19, LXX) and Job 37:4 (Charles), though the "voices" may refer to the "roar and furious noise of a tempest" that usually accompany lightnings and thunders (Beckwith). These visible and audible displays are another reminder that the throne, which is centerpiece of this heavenly scene is, first and foremost, a throne of wrath.

A second activity seen in heaven is the burning of seven torches: καὶ ἑπτα λαμπάδες πυρὸς καιόμεναι ἐνώπιον τοῦ θρόνου, ἅ εἰσιν τὰ ἑπτὰ πνεύματα τοῦ θεοῦ (*kai hepta lampades pyros kaiomenai enōpion tou thronou, ha eisin ta hepta pneumata tou theou*, "and seven torches of fire [were][57] burning before the throne, which are the seven spirits of God"). The *lampades* ("torches") should be distinguished from the λυχνίαι (*lychniai*, "lampstands") of 1:12, 20. They were used outdoors rather than indoors. They were better suited for open air because of less likelihood that they would be extinguished by gusts of wind (cf. John 18:3) (Lenski). This feature, coupled with the use of *kaiomenai* ("burning") elsewhere in the Apocalypse (cf. 8:8, 10; 19:20; 21:8), indicates that the torches emitted "a blazing and fierce" light rather than

---

56. Lange, *Revelation*, p. 152; R. C. H. Lenski, *The Interpretation of St. John's Revelation* (Columbus, Ohio: Lutheran Book Concern, 1935), p. 176; Biederwolf, *Millennium Bible*, p. 557; Ladd, *Revelation*, p. 76.
57. As elsewhere in this book (cf. 4:6b, 7), ἦσαν must be supplied to make the thought complete. The resulting periphrastic imperfect, [ἦσαν] καιόμεναι, provides a picture of a steady and continuous burning before the throne. This distinguishes these torches from those in Ezekiel's vision. The latter flashed here and there (Swete, *Apocalypse*, p. 70; Beckwith, *Apocalypse*, p. 499; Morris, *Revelation*, p. 89).

a calm and soft one.[58] Fire in this book symbolizes judgment, and these torches are no exception. Here is the divine preparedness for the battle against wickedness (cf. Judg. 7:16, 20; Nah. 2:3-4) (Seiss). The close proximity of these torches "before the throne" (*enōpion tou thronou*) harmonizes with the continuing emphasis of the chapter upon God's wrath against sinful humanity.

The text removes all doubt concerning the specific representation of the torches. The words *ha eisin ta hepta pneumata tou theou* ("which are the seven spirits of God") equate them with a Person already introduced in Rev. 1:4, the Holy Spirit.[59] There He was seen as part of the source of divine grace and peace with which the prophet greeted the seven churches. Here His role as consumer of the ungodly is more prominent.[60] A further correlation to His presence in this scene may also be His part in creation and preservation of the natural world, which comes into focus at the end of the chapter (4:11; cf. Gen. 1:2; 2:7; Ps. 104:29-30) (Ladd). A picture of a heavenly court poised to launch its massive program to purify God's creation is enhanced by this additional feature.

4:6 Another part of the scene that catches John's attention is, like the seven torches, in close proximity to the throne.[61] This was something like a sea of glass: καὶ ἐνώπιον τοῦ θρόνου ὡς θάλασσα ὑαλίνη ὁμοία κρυστάλλῳ (*kai enōpion tou thronou hōs thalassa hyalinē homoia krystallǭ*, "before the throne [there was something] like a sea of glass similar to crystal"). Words could hardly describe it, because he had seen nothing exactly like it on earth. All he could do was draw a comparison to describe in a limited way what he saw in the vision (Alford; Charles). It reminded him of a sea made out of glass.

The OT and some apocryphal sources mention the concept of a watery expanse between earth and heaven and various earthly representations of it which may bear some relationship to this sea (Gen. 1:7; Ex. 24:10-11; 1 Kings 7:23; Ps. 104:3; Ezek. 1:22, 26; cf. 2 Enoch 3:3; T. Levi 2:7). The inexplicit nature of John's description at this point poses a special challenge in explaining the significance of this feature.

---

58. Milligan, *Revelation*, p. 68.
59. See especially Zech. 4:2, 6 for the origin of the seven torches. It appears that there is also some allusion to Ezek. 1:13 where the torches move among the cherubim as the Spirit of God moves among the churches (Beasley-Murray, *Revelation*, p. 115). For a detailed discussion of how this symbolism for the Holy Spirit came to be used, see the Exegesis and Exposition at 1:4.
60. Alford, *Greek Testament*, 4:597; Biederwolf, *Millennium Bible*, p. 557.
61. The preposition ἐνώπιον emphasizes nearness to the throne (Morris, *Revelation*, p. 89).

One suggestion takes the sea as representing the blood of Christ.[62] It sees an analogy with the waters of the Red Sea, which point forward to the redemption sung about in Rev. 5:9-10 (Sweet). This view has practically nothing tangible as its basis, however. Another approach sees in the sea a picture of the providence of God (Lenski). Again, however, little by way of substantive evidence supports this.

Two other views assume that the sea has negative connotations. One interprets it to stand for everything that is recalcitrant to the will of God (Caird). The starting point of this reasoning is the Babylonian creation myth, alleged to lie behind the biblical account of creation as well as the imagery of this chapter (Caird). The perspective of the Apocalypse is taken to be that the sea belongs to the old order (cf. Rev. 21:1), which stands for everything opposed to God's will. It is the reservoir of evil from which arises the evil monster (cf. Rev. 13:1) and through which the redeemed must pass in a new Exodus (cf. Rev. 15:2-3) (Caird). The theory of an origin of the imagery from a pagan source is quite tenuous, however. Even if it was true it is doubtful that John would have been aware of this negative symbolism.

The other negatively oriented theory about the sea is a bit narrower, limiting its symbolism to a reservoir of evil from which the monster of evil arises in Rev. 13:1 (Caird). Along with the support cited for the previous view, it adds another consideration from Mesopotamian mythology, that God at creation defeated the dragon of the sea and imposed order on chaos. The chaos might return, such as at the time of the Flood. Such a connection between great bodies of water and chaos are reflected in the emphasis of Christian baptism in saving from such chaos (cf. 1 Pet. 3:20-21) (Sweet). An adequate rebuttal of this view is to note that later references to the watery sea in this book do not necessarily set the tone for interpreting the sea of glass in heaven (Morris). The sea of glass may be an intentional reversal of this negative sea imagery (cf. Exod. 24:10; Ezek. 1:22, 26) (Johnson).

Each of the four remaining views has an element of validity, but none seems to be comprehensive enough. First, it is certainly a visual phenomenon that adds to the awesome splendor of the throne room scene (Mounce). In this regard, it resembles the theophany of Ex. 24:10 where under the feet of God was "as it were a paved work of sapphire stone" (Beckwith). In the OT concept God's throne apparently stood on the waters above the firmament (Gen. 1:7; Ps. 104:3; cf. 2 Enoch 3:3) (Charles; Mounce). But awesome splendor does not go far enough in explaining this sea. Second, and more specifically, the sea enhances God's separateness from His creatures by suggesting the

62. William Hendriksen, *More Than Conquerors* (Grand Rapids: Baker, 1944), p. 105.

vast distance that separated John from the throne of God (Swete; Mounce). A comparison with Ex. 24:10; Job 37:18; and Ezek. 1:22 suggests a reference in these words to the clear ether in which the throne of God is supported. Such a space in front of the throne symbolically insulates God from John and everyone else. It is a picture of majestic repose and ethereal purity (Alford). In the words of another, the sea is "a symbol of God's separateness . . . and a threat against those who dishonor His creation and persecute His servants."[63] Though containing an element of truth, this view of an emphasis on separation is unsubstantiated in this context.

A third view contributes more to the growing picture of the sea of glass, the view that it stands for the sanctifying power of the Word of God (Walvoord). This draws upon the relationship of this part of the scene to the lavers in the Tabernacle (Ex. 30:18-21; cf. 1 Kings 7:38-39) and the molten sea in Solomon's Temple (1 Kings 7:23-37). Both were for priestly purification (Scott; Caird). This approach to the sea of glass, similar to crystal, highlights the clearness and beauty of a scene of holiness typified by both the glass and the crystal (Scott). Certain emphases of this view are misleading, however. It is erroneous to introduce references to the part played by the Word of God into this picture of cleansing. Nothing supports it contextually. The same is true of some who see a picture of the ordinance of baptism in the inferential reference to water. This has no support.

An affirmation of the idea of purity comes from a fourth view, which sees the purity, calmness, and majesty of God's rule symbolized.[64] The picture of purity is confirmed in Rev. 15:2 where this same sea of glass is mixed with the fire of purity (Alford). The concept of calmness adds too much, however. It is pressing the figure too far to contrast this with the turbulence of the sea upon which the harlot sits in Rev. 17:1, 15[65] and the troubled sea picturing the confusion of nations in Dan. 7:2-3 (cf. Rev. 13:1) (Lee).

In summary, "[something] like a sea of glass similar to crystal" pictures the splendor and majesty of God on His throne that set Him apart from all His creation, a separation stemming from His purity and absolute holiness, which He shares with no one else. The term *krystallō* ("crystal") enhances the emphasis on God's purity. It comes from κρύος (*kryos*, "ice, frost") and is used only here and in Rev. 22:1

---

63. Martin Kiddle, *The Revelation of St. John*, MNTC (London: Hodder and Stoughton, 1940), p. 89.
64. Charles, *Revelation*, 1:118; Lenski, *Revelation*, p. 178; Robert A. Jamieson, A. R. Fausset, and David Brown, *A Commentary Critical, Experimental and Practical on the Old and New Testaments*, 6 vols. (Grand Rapids: Eerdmans, 1945), 6:673.
65. Contra Alford, *Greek Testament*, 4:598.

in the NT. Its cognate κρυσταλλίζω (*krystallizō*, "be crystal-clear") is found in Rev. 21:11. In the LXX renderings of Job 38:29 and Ps. 147:17 *krystallọ* means "ice," but in Ezek. 1:22 "crystal" is its preferred rendering. The comparison of glass to crystal in Rev. 4:6 is striking, because glass manufactured in these ancient times was usually semi-opaque. Here it is "crystal-clear" and therefore takes on extremely high value as is implied in Ezek. 1:22 (Swete).

A third activity in this heavenly scene revolves around four living beings, now introduced for the first time, who receive major attention in vv. 6b-8: Καὶ ἐν μέσῳ τοῦ θρόνου καὶ κύκλῳ τοῦ θρόνου τέσσαρα ζῷα γέμοντα ὀφθαλμῶν ἔμπροσθεν καὶ ὄπισθεν; καὶ τὸ ζῷον τὸ πρῶτον ὅμοιον λέοντι, καὶ τὸ δεύτερον ζῷον ὅμοιον μόσχῳ, καὶ τὸ τρίτον ζῷον ἔχων *τὸ πρόσωπον ὡς ἀνθρώπου, καὶ τὸ τέταρτον ζῷον ὅμοιον ἀετῷ πετομένῳ. Καὶ τὰ τέσσαρα ζῷα, ἓν καθ' ἓν αὐτῶν ἔχων ἀνὰ πτέρυγας ἕξ, κυκλόθεν καὶ ἔσωθεν γέμουσιν ὀφθαλμῶν; καὶ ἀνάπαυσιν οὐκ ἔχουσιν ἡμέρας καὶ νυκτὸς λέγοντες, Ἅγιος ἅγιος ἅγιος κύριος ὁ θεὸς ὁ παντοκράτωρ, ὁ ἦν καὶ ὁ ὢν καὶ ὁ ἐρχόμενος (*Kai en mesọ tou thronou kai kyklọ tou thronou tessara zọa gemonta ophthalmōn emprosthen kai opisthen; kai to zọon to prōton homoion leonti, kai to deuteron zọon homoion moschọ, kai to triton zọon echōn to prosōpon hōs anthrōpou, kai to tetarton zọon homoion aetọ petomenọ. Kai ta tessara zọa, hen kath' hen autōn echōn ana pterygas hex, kyklothen kai esōthen gemousin ophthalmōn; kai anapausin ouk echousin hēmeras kai nyktos legontes, Hagios hagios hagios, kyrios ho theos ho pantokratōr, ho ēn kai ho ōn kai ho erchomenos*, "And in the middle of the throne and around the throne [were] four living beings, full of eyes in front and in back; and the first living being [was] similar to a lion, and the second living being [was] similar to an ox, and the third living being had the face as [that] of a man, and the fourth living being [was] similar to an eagle flying. And the four living beings, each one of them had six wings apiece, were full of eyes around and within; and they do not have rest day and night, saying, 'Holy, holy, holy, Lord God, the Almighty, who was and who is and who is coming'").

The location of the four living beings is fixed by the words *en mesọ tou thronou kai kyklọ tou thronou* ("in the middle of the throne and around the throne"). *Mesọ* ("middle") probably means that the four were in the immediate vicinity of the throne and encircling it, one on either side, one behind and one in front. The *kyklọ* ("around") furnishes the picture of the circle, with one always seen before the throne and the others on either side and behind.[66] They form an inner

---

66. Rienecker, *Linguistic Key*, p. 823; Mounce, *Revelation*, p. 137. Their position is thus distinguished from that of the living beings in Ezekiel who seem to be supporting the throne (cf. Ezek. 1:22, 26) (Charles, *Revelation*, 1:118).

circle closest to the throne as they offer worship to the one sitting on the throne (cf. Rev. 5:8; 19:4) (Charles). Whether they are still or in motion around the throne is not disclosed, but a rapid circular movement is suggested by a similar picture in Ezek. 1:12 (Swete; Beckwith).

Zōa ("living beings") is a noun related to the verb ζάω (zaō), which means "to live." It is not derived from the verb meaning "I create" (κτίζω, ktizō), so it should not be rendered "living creatures."[67] Nor are they "beasts" (cf. θήριον [thērion], Rev. 13:1; 17:3) and to be labeled as "living beasts" as in the KJV (Bullinger). Their description shows them to resemble the seraphim of Isaiah (Isa. 6:2) and the cherubim of Ezekiel (Ezek. 1:4-14; 10:1). Their likeness to Ezekiel's חַיּוֹת (ḥayyôt, "living beings") who are identified with the cherubim is closer (cf. Ezek. 9:3; 10:2 ff., 20 ff.) (Bullinger; Swete).

Identification of the four living beings has been a major subject of discussion. One of the earliest proposals equated them with the four NT gospels, but the equation has been reached by different means.[68] The church Father Irenaeus said the human face of the third beast represented Matthew, the eagle of the fourth the gospel of Mark, the ox of the second Luke, and the lion of the first being John. Victorinus said the man pictured Matthew, the lion Mark, the ox Luke, and the eagle John. Augustine identified the lion with Matthew, the man with Mark, the ox with Luke, and the eagle with John. Athanasius referred the man to Matthew, the calf (i.e., ox) to Mark, the lion to Luke, and the eagle to John. Seemingly, almost every combination has been suggested. In modern times, it has been noted that Matthew, which presents Jesus as King, is aptly represented by the Lion of the tribe of Judah, that Mark, which presents Jesus as the Servant of the Lord, is fittingly pictured by the ox, that Luke, which emphasizes Jesus' humanity, is well represented by the human-like third being, and that John, which features the deity of Christ, is connected with the eagle (Walvoord). The unanimity of the early church regarding acceptance of some combination of such symbolism is remarkable. Yet early interpretation must be evaluated and, if farfetched, be rejected. The suggestion of having animals standing for NT books is certainly imposing (Bullinger). Another reason for the inappropriateness of connecting a book with one of the living beings is that the inner significance of the characters does not completely match in any case, no matter which combination is chosen (Alford). The arbitrary character

---

67. Lenski, *Revelation*, p. 179. The word, partly Anglicized, forms a component of English words such as zoology, zoological, zoophyte, zootomy, and zoonymy.
68. Charles, *Revelation*, 1:124; William Barclay, *The Revelation of John*, 2 vols., 2d ed. (Philadelphia: Westminster, 1960), 1:198-204.

of assigned representations is verified by the variety of suggested identifications (Lee). Further, it is pointless to have four gospels guarding the tree of life (cf. Gen. 3:24), as beings similar to these do, or occupying prominent places in the temple in heaven (Bullinger).

Another suggestion regarding the four living beings has been that they symbolize the attributes of God, the lion for courage, boldness, and victorious sacrifice, the ox for patience, the human figure for sympathy, and the eagle for soaring aspiration, contemplation, and striving after ideal. They present in material form what would otherwise be invisible to the natural eye.[69] This view is interesting, but it has little support except rationale that lacks substantive biblical orientation. Besides, it has been well observed that it is wrong to identify the four so closely with God, because they never receive worship. They rather are pictured as worshipers (Bullinger). The attributes of God could hardly assume that role.

Another approach to the symbolism of the four is to equate them to the four points of the zodiac because they correspond closely to these signs of the ox, the lion, the scorpion, and the aquarius.[70] Ezekiel (whose living beings these resemble), because he lived in Babylon, would have seen the large, winged, ox-like and lion-like figures with human heads that stood at entrances to temples in that country. These are thought to have been modeled after stellar constellations (Beasley-Murray). These four constellations stood in the four quarters and were thought to be connected with the winds from the four directions also (Charles). As interesting as these phenomena are, John probably knew nothing of Babylonian mythology, so the suggestion is only a remote possibility (Mounce). Furthermore, the living beings have no astrological significance insofar as the rest of the Apocalypse is concerned (Caird).

An additional idea is that the four picture the standards of four tribes of Israel—Judah, Reuben, Ephraim, and Dan (cf. Num. 2:2, 10, 18, 25)—thereby representing Israel (Scott; Walvoord). This is hardly the case, however. In Rev. 5:13, the whole created world is distinctly contrasted with the four living beings. These are a traditional order of heavenly beings, none of whom personifies the people of God or the created universe. Otherwise, John would have stipulated so in an explanatory phrase such as he uses from time to time (cf. Rev. 1:20; 4:5; 5:6) (Beckwith). Other views, that they represent the four princi-

---

69. Biederwolf, *Millennium Bible*, p. 560; Walvoord, *Revelation*, pp. 110-11.
70. Charles, *Revelation*, 1:118-23; Beasley-Murray, *Revelation*, p. 117. Moffatt lists the four signs of the zodiac as the bull, the archer, the lion, and the eagle ("Revelation," 5:380).

pal apostles or that they represent redeemed glorified men,[71] falter for this last reason also (Beckwith).

It appears that several observations about the four living beings are valid. First, they are an exalted order of angelic beings, as indicated by their special proximity to the throne of God.[72] Though they are distinguished from angels in such places as 5:8, 11 and 7:11 (Bullinger; Lee), the distinction can be explained by their exalted state among their fellow angels.

Second, they have something to do with the judicial authority of the throne (Scott). The present scene and its emphasis upon God's judicial dealings with the creation provide part of the hint. Added to this is the suggestion that the number four speaks of universality as in "the four winds." It is the recognized signature of creation, especially as it is the witness and manifestation of God (Lee; Caird). The four likenesses represent each part of the animal creation (Scott; Morris). Their participation in the administration of divine justice is evident later in the book (e.g., Rev. 6:1, 3, 5, 7).

Third, their representation of animate creation is also apparent. The relation of these four to creation is reflected in the song in Rev. 4:9-11 and 15:7 (Alford; Bullinger; Moffatt). The related living beings in Ezekiel symbolize worldwide power, which upholds and pervades while it transcends creation. The same idea is present here (Swete). Their distinction from creation in 5:13 has already been noted, but it is possible for them as angelic beings to be reminders of the divine immanence in nature and still maintain their distinction from the created world (Mounce).

Fourth, the analogy of these angelic beings to the seraphim of Isa. 6:1-3 and the cherubim of Ezek. 10:2, 14, 20 is apparent. They are a high order of angels, perhaps the highest, comparable to the beings described in these OT sources (Ladd). They are four in number as in Ezekiel (Ezek. 1:5). They are full of eyes as are the cherubim in Ezek. 10:12. Individually, they have the faces of the lion, the ox, a man, and the eagle as in Ezekiel (Ezek. 1:10). Each has six wings as do the seraphim of Isaiah (Isa. 6:2). Their ascription of praise to God (Rev. 5:8) is the same as that of the seraphim in Isaiah (Isa. 6:3) (Alford; Beckwith). Their name *zǭa* ("living beings") is derived directly from Ezek. 1:5, the name being used interchangeably with "cherubim" in Ezekiel (cf. Ezek. 9:3; 10:2, 20) (Swete; Bullinger; Beckwith). Certain differences between the living beings in Revelation and the OT

---

71. Seiss, *Apocalypse*, 1:106-7; Lehman Strauss, *The Book of Revelation* (Neptune, N.J.: Loizeaux, n.d.), p. 135.
72. Beckwith, *Apocalypse*, p. 501; Biederwolf, *Millennium Bible*, p. 558.

cherubim and seraphim are obvious,[73] but remarkable similarities between them necessitate assigning the four in Revelation to a comparable angelic order as the ones in the OT.

A merging of these four aspects results in the following identification of the four living beings of the Apocalypse: they are of an exalted angelic order engaged in worship, who bear a special relationship to those angelic beings described in Ezekiel and Isaiah and whose special function in the context of the Apocalypse is the administering of divine justice in the realm of animate creation.

The first characteristic of the four living beings is furnished in the words *gemonta ophthalmōn emprosthen kai opisthen* ("full of eyes in front and in back"). This is similar to Ezekiel's living beings who have eyes in "their whole body, and their backs, and their hands, and their wings" (Ezek. 10:12), but Ezekiel first ascribes the eyes to their wheels instead of to the beings themselves (Ezek. 1:18). The thorough endowment of eyesight capabilities of the four beings here is emphasized through statements of the completeness (*gemonta,*[74] "full") of their coverage and the dual positions of the eyes (*emprosthen kai opisthen,* "in front and in back"). Both emphasize the alertness and comprehensive knowledge of these beings (Mounce). Nothing relevant to their sphere of responsibility happens without their knowledge because of their "unsleeping watchfulness" (Scott). This is not to attribute to them omniscience such as belongs to God alone, but rather to state that God has created them with such penetrative intel-

---

73. Differences between the four living beings of the Apocalypse and the OT cherubim and seraphim include the following: in Ezekiel, each has four faces (Ezek. 1:6, 10), whereas in Revelation, the four faces are distributed among the four, one face apiece. In Ezekiel, the cherubim have only four wings instead of the six found in Revelation. In Ezekiel, the cherubim are winged supporters of God's throne, carrying Him as He moves throughout the world, but in Revelation, the beings attend the throne room of God's glory, leading in adoration directed toward Him and the Lamb. In Ezekiel, it is the wheels that are full of eyes (Ezek. 1:18), though Ezekiel 10:12 appears to assign the same to the beings, but in Revelation, the beings themselves are full of eyes (Alford, *Greek Testament*, 4:599; Beckwith, *Apocalypse*, pp. 500-1). The Ezekiel beings have wheels (Ezek. 1, 10), but those of the Apocalypse have none. The throne was above the beings in Ezekiel, but here they surround it (Scott, *Revelation*, p. 127). Though closely akin to the cherubim of Ezekiel, these four living beings are not the same because of several essential differences (Charles, *Revelation*, 1:119).

74. The participle γέμοντα represents the verb γέμω and appears relatively infrequently in biblical Greek, only eight times in the LXX, and four times in the NT outside Revelation (cf. Matt. 23:25, 27; Luke 11:39; Rom. 3:14). In the Apocalypse, however, it is relatively frequent, appearing seven times (cf. Rev. 4:6, 8; 5:8; 15:7; 17:3, 4; 21:9) (Swete, *Apocalypse*, p. 71).

ligence that they are immediately aware of happenings pertaining to their judicial responsibility.

4:7 John next notes the distinct characteristics of each of the four living beings. In contrast to Ezekiel's living beings, each one of whom had four facial appearances, each of these four has only one likeness. Though John says in reference to the third being only that the similarity applies to the face, it is most probable that all four likenesses relate only to facial features.[75] Ezekiel's beings resemble human beings in form more generally (cf. Ezek. 1:5). Analogy would imply that the same is true here.

Since the four living beings of Revelation have already been identified as an exalted angelic order with a special relationship to animate creation, it only remains to specify what in animate creation is stressed by each. The first is *homoion*[76] *leonti* ("similar to a lion"). Among the wild animals the lion is viewed as "king of the jungle" and, in general, represents what is the most noble; so this first being should be understood in this sense.[77] The likeness of the second being is given in *homoion moschǭ* ("similar to an ox"). The ox pictures that part of animate creation that is strongest. The Greek word in general usage sometimes refers to a calf in distinction from the grown bullock, but the LXX regularly uses it to refer to an ox, regardless of age (cf. Ex. 21:36; Lev. 22:23; cf. also Gen. 12:16; Exod. 29:10) (Alford). Regarding the third of the living beings, his appearance is described by *echōn*[78] *to prosōpon hōs anthrōpou* ("having the face as [that] of a man"). The human face is emblematic of intelligence and reason. This being points to that part of animate creation that is the wisest, the human race.[79] The fourth living being is *homoion aetǭ petomenǭ* ("sim-

---

75. Beckwith, *Apocalypse*, p. 502; Robertson, *Word Pictures*, 6:329.
76. This verse has three occurrences of ὅμοιον to describe the living beings through comparison with animals. See the additional note on Rev. 1:15 for comments regarding ὅμοιος followed by a dative substantive.
77. Swete, *Apocalypse*, p. 71; Bullinger, *Apocalypse*, p. 224; Norman B. Harrison, *The End* (Minneapolis: Harrison Service, 1948), p. 76; Ford, *Revelation*, p. 75; Rienecker, *Linguistic Key*, p. 822.
78. The participle ἔχων is masculine. Because it modifies the neuter ζῷον, a neuter participle would be expected. This is another example of natural agreement rather than grammatical agreement. The participle is conformed to the gender of the being specified, as is true with λέγων in Rev. 4:1 (Alford, *Greek Testament*, 4:599). The living beings are invested with intelligence and thus conceived of in a generic masculine sense (Swete, *Apocalypse*, p. 72). This participle functions as a finite verb in its clause (James Hope Moulton, *A Grammar of New Testament Greek*, vol. 1, *Prolegomena*, 3d ed. [Edinburgh: T. & T. Clark, 1908], pp. 222-24; Robertson, *Historical Research*, pp, 1132-35).
79. Swete, *Apocalypse*, p. 71; Ford, *Revelation*, p. 75; Rienecker, *Linguistic Key*, p. 822.

ilar to an eagle flying"). He is symbolic of what is swiftest in animate creation.[80] Together, then, the four living beings picture all animal life from the perspectives of greatest nobility, strength, wisdom, and speed.

4:8 Further features of the living beings are added by the words *ta tessara zōa, hen kath ' hen autōn echōn*[81] *ana pterygas hex, kyklothen kai esōthen gemousin ophthalmōn* ("the four living beings, each one of them having six wings apiece, were full of eyes around and within"). The six wings possessed by each[82] of the four recalls the seraphim of Isaiah's vision (cf. Isa. 6:2). Because specific symbolism for the wings is not stated here, some have supposed that the wings depict swiftness and unlimited mobility in responding to God's commands (cf. Ps. 18:10; Ezek. 10:16) (Swete; Mounce; Johnson). The close relationship of this part of their appearance with the seraphim of Isaiah suggests explaining the wings' purpose in that light. In Isa. 6:2, two wings covered the face, denoting awe, because the seraphim dared not look at God; two covered the feet, denoting humility, because they stand in His presence; and with two they would fly, denoting obedience, because they are ready to carry out His commands (Lee).

After the parenthetical note about the wings, John continues his observation about the four living beings: "the four living beings . . . were full[83] of eyes around and within."[84] This is a partial reiteration of v. 6 which described the four as being "full of eyes in front and in back." There the assigned significance of the eyes was alertness and comprehensive knowledge. This also implies a constant vigilance over God's creation (Swete; Ford).

---

80. Swete, *Apocalypse*, p. 71; Harrison, *End*, p. 76; Bullinger, *Apocalypse*, p. 224; Ford, *Revelation*, p. 75; Rienecker, *Linguistic Key*, p. 822.
81. The masculine ἔχων modifies the neuter ἐν according to natural agreement rather than strict grammatical agreement, as noted in connection with the same participle in Rev. 4:7. This participle, like the comparable one in 4:7, functions as a finite verb in its clause.
82. The distributive force of the statement is emphatic, being accomplished through two grammatical devices. The first is the idiom ἐν καθ' ἐν αὐτῶν (literally, "one by one of them") utilizing the distributive sense of εἷς, a practice that was common in later Greek (Robertson, *Historical Research*, p. 675). The other is through the distributive sense of the preposition ἀνά which carries the sense of "each" (Turner, *Grammar*, pp. 265-66).
83. The verb γέμουσιν is plural even though the subject τὰ τέσσαρα ζῷα is neuter plural, which generally governs a singular verb. The existing construction has the effect of individualizing each one of the living beings (Robertson, *Word Pictures*, 6:329).
84. Another possibility is to understand the participle ἔχων with a copula as elsewhere in the Apocalypse, giving it the force of a finite verb. The subject τὰ τέσσαρα ζῷα would have two predicates, ἔχων and γέμουσιν, resulting in the sense, "the four living beings, each one of them, had six wings apiece [and] were full of eyes around and within." The parenthetical arrangement is preferable, however (Moffatt, "Revelation," 5:380).

A slight difficulty is encountered in explaining how *kyklothen kai esōthen* ("around and within") conveys the idea of thorough coverage of the beings with eyes. "Around" and "within" are not precisely contrasting terms, so a bit of confusion results in trying to picture the placement of the eyes on the beings. A few scribes in ancient times sensed this difficulty and reflected their confusion by altering the text with the addition of ἔξωθεν καὶ (*exōthen kai*, "outside and") before *esōthen* ("within"). The reading is correct as it stands, however, and the picture must be constructed on this basis. One response to it rejects all efforts at such a reconstruction by renouncing all efforts to reproduce details. The justification for this is the book's alleged purpose to stir the imagination, not to represent a precise picture (Mounce). This rationale is reinforced by the assertion that the combination *kyklothen kai esōthen* is a meaningless phrase (Charles). Both awkwardness and meaninglessness as reasons for rejecting a pictorial representation are inadequate, however. If John saw it, it must be conceptually reproducible. What the expression means is that the living beings had eyes all around their bodies and on the undersides of their wings, as suggested of the cherubim in Ezek. 10:12.[85] Being so full of eyes positioned in this manner, they are able to move their wings without ever disrupting their vision.[86] *Kyklothen* ("around") is almost equivalent to ἔμπροσθεν καὶ ὄπισθεν (*emprosthen kai opisthen*, "in front and in back") in 4:6, and *esōthen* ("within") is a new detail added at this point.

The particular activity of the living beings is described in the words *kai anapausin ouk echousin hēmeras kai nyktos legontes,*[87] *Hagios hagios hagios, kyrios ho theos ho pantokratōr, ho ēn kai ho ōn kai ho erchomenos* ("and they do not have rest by day and by night, saying, 'Holy, holy, holy, Lord God, the Almighty, who was and who is and who is coming'"). They offer incessant praise before the throne of God. Such unending tribute is characteristic of descriptions of heaven in other apocalyptic works (cf. 1 Enoch 39:12; 2 Enoch 19:6; 21:1; T. Levi 3:8) (Beckwith). Their continuous praise must be understood in light of their other functions, however. It is not to be interpreted as meaning they have no other duties and functions. For example, in Rev. 6:1, 3, 5, 7 they are responsible for summoning the riders to advance in portrayal of future wrath against rebellious mankind. This does not violate the statement about ceaseless praise, because

---

85. Beckwith, *Apocalypse*, p. 502; Biederwolf, *Millennium Bible*, p. 560.
86. Carpenter, *Revelation*, p. 553.
87. Once again, a participle agrees with the sense of its antecedent rather than its grammatical gender. Λέγοντες is masculine plural, modifying the neuter plural τὰ τέσσαρα ζῷα which is the unexpressed subject of ἔχουσιν earlier in the clause. See the note on ἔχων earlier in v. 8.

"they do not have rest" is qualified by the words "by day and by night."[88] The manner of expression in Greek indicates that it is a *kind* of time expressed rather than the extent of time.[89] It is analogous with Paul's statements to the Thessalonians regarding his own labors to support himself "by night and by day" (1 Thess. 2:9; 2 Thess. 3:8). This does not mean that he worked around the clock at earning money, excluding even ministry opportunities, but that he did night labor and day labor to provide funds to live on. So it is with the four living beings. They have no rest from their occupation with offering tribute to God. This is their consuming practice whenever they are not otherwise engaged in carrying out God's will. Whenever they do this, their offering of praise becomes the invitation for the twenty-four elders to do the same (cf. 4:9-11).

The song of the four living beings focuses on three aspects of God's essential nature: His holiness, His omnipotence, and His eternality (Charles). Psalms 93, 97, and 99 are psalms that connect the holiness of God with His reign over the world. This is a fitting theme to which to return in light of the arrival, prophetically speaking, of that eschatological period when His reign will come to fruition (Bullinger). Holy is a fitting description of God in comparison to His creation. The threefold ascription of holiness to Him, *Hagios hagios hagios* ("holy, holy, holy"), sometimes referred to as the *Trisagion*, repeats Isa. 6:3 (cf. 1 Enoch 39:12) and attests to the primary place of praise in the presence of God (Charles). The formula may refer to the three Persons of the Holy Trinity,[90] but it is difficult to press the point. More than likely, the repetition is for the sake of emphasis.[91] God's distance from an unholy creation is thereby highlighted (Beckwith).

A second aspect of God's essential nature comes to the fore in His title *kyrios ho theos ho pantokratōr* ("Lord God the Almighty").[92] This

---

88. Alford proposes that ἡμέρας καὶ νυκτός be connected with the participle λέγοντες that follows, partly because καὶ joins the two nouns rather than ἤ and partly because of a judgment of the ear (*Greek Testament*, 4:599). It is better grammatically to understand the expression with what precedes, because it is quite rare for such an adverbial qualifier to precede a participle that it modifies.

89. Lenski calls this a genitive of time within (*Revelation*, p. 185). Dana and Mantey's terminology would term it an adverbial genitive of time (H. E. Dana and Julius R. Mantey, *A Manual Grammar of the Greek New Testament* [New York: Macmillan, 1927], p. 77). Expression of the extent of time of their praise would have been in the accusative case. This more likely would have indicated that their tribute was never interrupted.

90. Harrison, *End*, p. 79.

91. BDF, par. 493(1).

92. The LXX rendering of Isa. 6:3 is ἅγιος ἅγιος ἅγιος κύριος σαβαώθ. John has substituted ὁ παντοκράτωρ for σαβαώθ, following the pattern of the LXX translation of צבאות in all the OT prophets except Isaiah. He has also

is a title by which the Father is known in Rev. 1:8. It is a title especially applied to Him as the series of wrathful acts against a rebellious world moves to its climax (cf. Rev. 11:17; 15:3; 16:7, 14; 19:6, 15; 21:22). The one seated upon the throne is the omnipotent one. He is in the unique position to administer justice in a creation that has chosen to disregard His standards of righteousness. The living beings acknowledge Him as the sole possessor of this prerogative.

They sing also about His eternality: *ho ēn kai ho ōn kai ho erchomenos* ("who was and who is and who is coming"). This title of the Father was first encountered in Rev. 1:4 (cf. Rev. 1:8; 11:17), but a shift in emphasis occurs here with the switch in position between *ho ēn* ("who was") and *ho ōn* ("who is"). Earlier uses of the title have emphasized His present existence by giving *ho ōn* the first position, but here *ho ēn* is first, giving His past existence more attention (Bullinger). Very possibly the change in sequence is traceable to the emphasis of the present chapter on the creative activity of God (cf. 4:11) (Moffatt). The close relation of the four living beings to creation adds to this likelihood. Perhaps their voicing of *ho erchomenos* ("who is coming") is somewhat akin to the eager longing of creation for its own redemption as expressed in Rom. 8:19-22 and as ultimately fulfilled in Rev. 20:11; 21:1 (Swete).

A complete absence from this song of any direct reference to salvation has caused some surprise. The reason is that redemption has not yet entered the picture, and will not do so until the next scene of this vision in chapter 5. All praise to God thus far centers in His creative endeavors.[93] The song is quite in keeping with the progress of the revelation to John up to this point. This continual song from the four living beings underscores the central role of the one sitting upon the throne in the present setting. As the absolutely holy one, He is thoroughly entitled and has ample might to initiate stringent measures against His own creation in order to return it to its original holy state.

4:9 The fourth activity around the throne is described in vv. 9-11. It is the song of the twenty-four elders. Before recording the song itself, John explains what occasions the singing: καὶ ὅταν δώσουσιν τὰ ζῷα δόξαν καὶ τιμὴν καὶ εὐχαριστίαν τῷ καθημένῳ ἐπὶ *τῷ θρόνῳ τῷ ζῶντι εἰς τοὺς αἰῶνας τῶν αἰώνων (kai hotan dōsousin ta zǭa doxan kai timēn kai eucharistian tǭ kathēmenǭ epi tǭ thronǭ tǭ zōnti eis tous aiōnas tōn aiōnōn*, "and whenever the living beings give glory and honor and

---

substituted a frequently used phrase from the MT of Ezekiel, אדני יהוה (κύριος ὁ θεὸς), for Isaiah's κύριος (cf. Ezek. 6:3, 11; 7:2, 5; 8:1, etc.) (Charles, *Revelation*, 1:127).
93. Milligan, *Revelation*, p. 74.

thanks to the one who is sitting upon the throne, to the one who lives forever and ever"). The elders await the signal of the four living beings before proceeding with their tribute to the one seated upon the throne. They engage in such vocal worship only when the four do, according to the introductory clause of v. 9. For those who explain the song of the four in 4:8 differently from the above explanation, this has posed a problem of inconsistency. When they take the praise of v. 8 as continuous and unbroken, they cannot harmonize this with the intermittent nature of the elders' song as indicated in vv. 9-10.[94] One way around the difficulty is to avoid "strict logic" or "pedantic literalness" in literature of this type.[95] Yet such an escape amounts to a flight from rationality. John must have intended some coherent relationship between the worship of the two groups.

Removal of the alleged inconsistency lies in the explanation of 5:8 already furnished. The praise of that verse is not actually continuous or unbroken, but it comes on specific occasions as recorded elsewhere in 11:16-17 and 19:4 (Moffatt; Beasley-Murray). Whenever appropriate and whenever permitted by freedom from other responsibilities, the praise is forthcoming. The construction of the temporal clause in v. 9 clarifies the periodic nature of the prayers. It is an indefinite temporal clause that conveys the idea of repetition: "whenever the living beings give glory and honor and thanks."[96] Every time one group sings, so does the other.

It is interesting that the song of v. 8 is considered as giving[97] "glory and honor and thanks" (*doxan kai timēn kai eucharistian*). The three words are not used in v. 8, but they describe the song. The first two words point to the perfections of God, holiness, omnipotence, and eternality, as emphasized in the previous song, whereas the last one expresses gratitude for His gift of creation (Swete). This is the praise that God is worthy to receive from His creatures (cf. Ps. 29:2; 1 Enoch 61:10-11) (Charles).

The one sitting upon the throne is further identified by the words *tō zōnti eis tous aiōnas tōn aiōnōn* ("to the one who lives forever and ever"). The expression is used again in v. 10 and in Rev. 10:6; 15:7. Its apparent source is the LXX rendering of Dan. 4:34 [Theodotion], τῷ ζῶντι εἰς τοὺς αἰῶνας (*tō zōnti eis tous aiōnas*, "to the one who lives forever"), and Dan. 12:7, τὸν ζῶντα εἰς τὸν αἰῶνα (*ton zōnta eis ton aiōna*, "the one who lives forever") (cf. Dan. 6:26; Deut. 32:40), with

---

94. Barclay, *Revelation*, 1:206; Charles, *Revelation*, 1:125.
95. Barclay, *Revelation*, 1:206; Morris, *Revelation*, pp. 91-92.
96. Robertson, *Word Pictures*, 6:330; Swete, *Apocalypse*, p. 73; Charles, *Revelation*, 1:127; Beckwith, *Apocalypse*, p. 503.
97. Δώσουσιν should not be understood in the sense of imparting to God qualities that He does not already possess. These are characteristics that inhere in Him (Beckwith, *Apocalypse*, p. 503).

the addition of *tōn aiōnōn* ("and ever") to strengthen the expression. This is another way of describing God's eternality, comparable to the last part of the four beings' song, *ho ēn kai ho ōn kai ho erchomenos* ("who was and who is and who is coming") (Charles). The same quality is attributed to Christ in Rev. 1:18.

4:10 The threefold response of the twenty-four elders comes in v. 10: πεσοῦνται οἱ εἴκοσι τέσσαρες πρεσβύτεροι ἐνώπιον τοῦ καθημένου ἐπὶ τοῦ θρόνου καὶ προσκυνήσουσιν τῷ ζῶντι εἰς τοὺς αἰῶνας τῶν αἰώνων, καὶ βαλοῦσιν τοὺς στεφάνους αὐτῶν ἐνώπιον τοῦ θρόνου⁹⁸ λέγοντες (*pesountai hoi eikosi tessares presbyteroi enōpion tou kathēmenou epi tou thronou kai proskynēsousin tō zōnti eis tous aiōnas tōn aiōnōn, kai balousin tous stephanous autōn enōpion tou thronou legontes,* "the twenty-four elders fall before the one sitting upon the throne and worship the one who lives for ever and ever, and they cast their crowns before the throne, saying"). Though a part of creation themselves, the twenty-four view creation as outside themselves in this song in order to ascribe praise to Him who called them as well as the rest of creation into being (Alford).

Whether the response of the elders to the living beings is because of their submission in rank or because of expediency cannot be stated with absolute certainty,⁹⁹ but at least some element of the former seems probable in light of the living beings' greater proximity to the throne. This is the first of six times in the Apocalypse when the elders prostrate themselves (*pesountai*, "fall") before either God or the Lamb (cf. also 5:8, 14; 7:11; 11:16; 19:4). Three times they are joined by the four living beings (cf. 5:8; 7:11; 19:4) and once by all the angels (cf. 7:11). Here they alone fall before God who sits upon the throne. Their prone posture is for the sake of worshiping the eternal one (*tō zōnti eis tous aiōnas tōn aiōnōn*, "the one who lives for ever and ever"), the same title as the one worshiped by the four living beings in v. 9. *Proskynēsousin* ("worship") here governs a dative expression as its object, as is generally the case in Revelation when it carries the meaning of "worship" rather than "do homage to."¹⁰⁰ Their own beauty and excellencies mean nothing to the twenty-four elders. They give no indication of self-infatuation. Rather, out of reverence and because of a spirit of deep humility they direct their adoration to the eternal God, the creator of all and the sovereign over all.¹⁰¹ Their third act, preparatory to bursting forth in song, is to cast their crowns before the throne (*balousin tous stephanous autōn enōpion tou thronou*). Ev-

---

98. For the variation in cases when θρόνος is the object of ἐπί, see note at 4:2.
99. Carpenter, *Revelation*, pp. 553-54.
100. See Additional Notes for a discussion of various constructions with προσκυνέω.
101. Morris, *Revelation*, p. 92; Biederwolf, *Millennium Bible*, p. 560.

erything revolves around the throne and Him who sits upon it; this is the center of attention in this heavenly scene. One suggestion is that the crowns connote a victory of the elders, won through God's grace (Swete), but our earlier discussion (cf. 4:4) shows the crowns to be emblematic of royalty. Such marks of high dignity they voluntarily surrender by casting them before the throne so that greater honor may accrue to God.

4:11 Their song differs from that sung by the four living beings in v. 8. Apparently a great variety of songs resound around the throne (Morris). The song of the elders resembles John's summary of the four beings' song in v. 9, because both attribute glory and honor to God. The song of the elders, however, is more focused on the wonders of God's creation as evidence of His glory and power.[102] It begins with a declaration of His worthiness: ἄξιος εἶ, ὁ κύριος καὶ ὁ θεὸς ἡμῶν, λαβεῖν τὴν δόξαν καὶ τὴν τιμὴν καὶ τὴν δύναμιν (*axios ei, ho kyrios kai ho theos hēmōn, labein tēn doxan kai tēn timēn kai tēn dynamin,* "You are worthy, our Lord and God, to receive the glory and the honor and the power").

Like the song of the four living beings in v. 8, this song gives praise to God also, but in contrast to the earlier song, the elders' song addresses God directly.[103] *Axios* ("worthy") was used in the political language of the day on such occasions as when the emperor marched in triumphal procession. In the ultimate sense, however, to attribute worthiness to anyone less than the one upon the throne is blasphemous (Mounce). The elders' use of the first person plural pronoun *hēmōn* ("our") in addressing God has been taken by some as a sign that they represent redeemed humanity, but this is hardly the case inasmuch as humanity is only part of what Christ redeemed (Alford). Besides, use of the first person plural pronoun is not proof that one has experienced redemption. Christ Himself uses the first person possessive in this book to refer to "*My* God" (cf. 3:12). The one sitting on the throne is the Lord and God of unfallen angelic beings just as He is of redeemed humanity. It must be reiterated that creation, not redemption, is the subject of the present song.

This is a tribute to God's worthiness "to receive glory and honor and power" (*labein*[104] *tēn*[105] *doxan kai tēn timēn kai tēn dynamin).* The

---

102. Milligan, *Revelation,* pp. 74-75.
103. Mounce, *Revelation,* p. 140. Note the second person singular εἶ and the second person singular pronouns σύ and σου.
104. As with δώσουσιν in 4:9, λαβεῖν does not designate an imparting of qualities to God, but is in recognition and proclamation of His true character (Beckwith, *Apocalypse,* p. 73). It almost carries the connotation that He "reserves to Himself" power and honor and glory.
105. The use of the article with each member of this series may have a demonstrative force, pointing back to the previous reference to the items

first two terms of this tribute coincide with the first two in John's description of the living beings' song (5:9), but the third term, *tēn dynamin* ("power"), replaces the εὐχαριστίαν (*eucharistian*, "thanks") of the earlier song. The reason for the change is the particular focus of the elders in this song upon God's creative power (Alford). Doxologies throughout the book are composed of elements dictated by their respective contexts. As the song of the living beings in 4:8 has for its theme the holiness, omnipotence, and everlastingness of God, aspects of His essential nature, so the one in the present verse revolves about the theme of God's glory as reflected in His works, especially His work of creation (Charles).

This particular reason for the declaration of God's worthiness comes in the last half of the song: ὅτι σὺ ἔκτισας τὰ πάντα, καὶ διὰ τὸ θέλημά σου ἦσαν καὶ ἐκτίσθησαν (*hoti sy ektisas ta panta, kai dia to thelēma sou ēsan kai ektisthēsan*, "because You created all things, and because of Your will they were and were created"). Such an acknowledgment of God's creative work recalls Pss. 33:6-9; 102:25; 136:5-9 (Beckwith; Walvoord). In adding to the song of the four living beings, the term *ektisas* ("You created") focuses upon a frequent Hebrew theme, God's mighty display of power in creation, as a basis for praise (Beckwith). Though redemption does not become a reason for praise until chapter 5 (cf. 5:8-9), this song prepares the way for the climactic announcement that the long-awaited redemption of creation is on the brink of fulfillment (Bullinger).

It has been proposed that the phrase *dia to thelēma sou* ("because of Your will") is directed against the false notion of some apocalyptic writings that the world was created for man or, more specifically, for Israel or the righteous in Israel (Charles; Beasley-Murray). The notion is certainly false, but the antithetical idea that God created for His own pleasure (cf. KJV) misses the thrust of the context too (Alford). The phrase focuses upon the operating cause of the creation of the universe.[106] This context and the Apocalypse as a whole emphasize God's power as the creator. He and He alone is the one and only cause of creation (Moffatt). It is insufficient to object that this reason for God's worthiness is already expressed in the *hoti* ("because") clause as a whole and that this would add nothing new. To emphasize its importance, God's creative activity is purposely restated in this *dia* phrase and again restated in the remaining words *ēsan kai ektisthēsan*

(i.e., two of the three) in 5:9: "the same glory and the same honor," as just mentioned. In this doxology and in the one of 5:13, the article is used with each quality, giving each one an individual emphasis, but in 5:12, one article covers the entire list, viewing them as a single entity (Robertson, *Historical Research*, p. 758).

106. John R. W. Stott, *What Christ Thinks of the Church* (Grand Rapids: Eerdmans, 1958), p. 167.

("they were and were created"). The song accumulates emphasis on God's creative work through a threefold statement that He did it.

The combination *ēsan kai ektisthēsan* has occasioned various explanations. One takes the former verb to express the existence of creation in the will of God before its actual existence and the latter verb to refer to the actual creation (Swete; Charles). In other words, *ēsan* looks back to the eternal past and *ektisthēsan* pictures the genesis of nature (Swete). This view furnishes a possible explanation of the imperfect tense of *ēsan*, but it introduces into the context a completely foreign element, the thought of the *potential* existence of creation (Beckwith). The imperfect tense could just as well view the state of creation immediately after the initial creative act.

Another approach to this combination of verbs has been to understand the second as explanatory of the first.[107] Existence, first thought of as an accomplished fact, is made more specific by the latter verb (Beckwith). This proposal is modeled after the creation account in Genesis where the general description of man's creation in Genesis 1 is followed by a more detailed account in Genesis 2 (Charles; Beckwith; Ladd). The debilitating deficiency of this view is the difference between the two verbs. They convey two significantly distinct thoughts, and construing the latter as elaboration of the former is impossible.

A third explanation for the two-verb combination is the figure of *hysteron proteron*, because of the non-chronological arrangement of the two: certainly the κτίσις (*ktisis*, "creation") must exist before one can say *ēsan*. The latter verb is proposed to be the act of creation, and the former one the process of creation (Moffatt). Though *hysteron proteron* is a common literary device of this author (cf. Rev. 3:9, 17) (Beckwith), it is unnecessary to resort to it because of the reverse chronological sequence of the two verbs.

The writer may be thinking logically rather than chronologically. The simplest and most satisfactory explanation is that the two verbs speak of the simple fact of the creation's existence (*ēsan*) and then of the fact of the beginning of its existence (*ektisthēsan*) (Alford; Ladd). All created things (*ta panta*) existed in contrast to their prior nonexistence, and God gave them that existence by a specific act of His own power.

With the song of the twenty-four elders this initial scene in the throne room closes. John's invitation to heaven (4:1), the heavenly throne (4:2-4), and activities around the throne (4:5-11) made a deep impression on the seer as they do upon any who seriously ponder

---

107. This is the epexetical use of καὶ that is so common in the style of the Apocalypse (Beckwith, *Apocalypse*, p. 504).

their implications. Here is the headquarters of the holy, omnipotent, and eternal God who requires His standards to be met by His creation. If they are not, His wrath must inflict penalties upon the rebellious who are among the works of His hand.

Additional Notes

4:1 An apparent similarity exists between the structure in the Apocalypse and that of the fourth gospel. In John 1:1-18 the prologue suggests the scope of the book, in 1:19–2:11 is revealed the Redeemer to be described in the book, and the conflict of Jesus' ministry begins in John 5. John 2:12–4:54 does not speak so much of victory in the struggle itself as it does about the victory that prepares us for the struggle and provides hope before the struggle begins. So it is in the Apocalypse that after revealing the scope of the book and the historical background, John first relates those truths that give assurance of God's ultimate victory through the struggles about to be related. God is on His throne and in control of the world's destiny. For His redeemed ones, victory is secure.[108]

4:3 A few MSS read ἱερεῖς rather than ἶρις. The mistake apparently arose through an error in hearing by a scribe writing from dictation, because the two words had similar pronunciations. The slight MS support for this variant and the difficulty created by the reading of "*priests* around the throne" indicate that the alternative cannot be taken seriously. The presence of priests in the throne room is nowhere else indicated in Rev. 4:1–22:5.

4:4 The sudden changes from the nominative cases of θρόνος (4:2), ὁ καθήμενος (4:3), and ἶρις (4:3) to the accusative cases of θρόνους (4:4), πρεσβυτέρους (4:4), and στεφάνους (4:4) could be traced to John's "liberal" grammatical practices (Alford), but more probably they are attributable to a change of perspective within his own mind from that of ἰδού in 4:2-3 to that of εἶδον in 4:4 (Swete; Beckwith). As a demonstrative particle, the former word is followed by nominatives, and the latter word, as a finite verb, governs the accusatives. Very possibly, the close connection between the two in 4:1 (εἶδον, καὶ ἰδού) indicates an association so close between the two words in the author's mind that the use of one evokes the idea of the other. Certainly this kind of change is an insufficient reason for concluding that v. 4 is a later addition by the author, as is sometimes held. John's frequent habit of incorporating such stylistic changes is a strong warning against such a conclusion (Charles).

4:7 Several variants appear as alternatives to the words τὸ πρόσωπον ὡς ἀνθρώπου. A difficulty that has given rise to these variations

108. Milligan, *Revelation*, p. 65.

is the stand-alone genitive ἀνθρώπου. Because no substantive is present for it to qualify, more significant proposals in ancient textual sources have included changing it to a nominative ἄνθρωπος, removing the ὡς that precedes it, and adding ὅμοιον just before it. These are obvious attempts to alleviate the strain of an unusual construction. A textual change is not necessary, however. Simply to understand that the genitive itself implies a pronominal substantive, is sufficient: "[that] of a man."

4:9 Instead of the dative τῷ θρόνῳ some MSS read a genitive τοῦ θρόνου. Efforts thus far to distinguish the nuances of meaning with various cases after the preposition ἐπί have proved fruitless. See the note at 4:2 in this regard. Fluctuations in MS sources between the dative and genitive, as here, are especially noticeable (e.g., Rev. 5:13; 6:16; 7:15). The dative is preferred here because of support from stronger MS sources and because of dissimilarity with the genitive in the very next verse. Later scribes would tend to eliminate such conspicuous differences.

The use of future indicatives (δώσουσιν, πεσοῦνται, προσκυνήσουσιν, βαλοῦσιν) in 4:9-10 is rather unusual and has been the subject of some debate. Turner traces them to Semitic influence, saying they are literal renderings of the Hebrew imperfect.[109] This Hebrew tense can denote future time in some instances, but here the action is past. His view lacks any supporting evidence, however. Another explanation has it that these are usual uses of the future tense with the idea that a present act continues into the future (Beckwith). This seems absurd, however. This would mean that the elders are continually falling and throwing their crowns (πεσοῦνται, and βαλοῦσιν 4:10). Besides this, in 4:4 they are seated on thrones and not in a "falling" posture. The best understanding takes the verbs as frequentative futures. The aspect of time is de-emphasized, and eternal repetition implied.[110] This is certainly the meaning furnished by the context (Moffatt). Ὅταν with the future indicative conveys the notion of repetition rather than unbroken continuance, which the more usual subjunctive would have implied.[111] The frequentative force also follows the pattern of the Hebrew imperfect of which this usage may be a reflection (Lee; Beckwith).

4:10 In Rev. 7:11; 11:16 19:4, 10; 22:9, προσκυνέω with the dative speaks of worshiping God, but in Rev. 13:4, the worship of the dragon. In 19:10, it is likewise with the dative as John attempts to worship the

---

109. Turner, *Grammar*, p. 86.
110. Alford, *Greek Testament*, 4:601; Beckwith, *Apocalypse*, p. 503; Biederwolf, *Millennium Bible*, p. 560.
111. Alford, *Greek Testament*, 4:601; Robertson, *Word Pictures*, 6:330.

angel. The verb's use with an accusative object, on the other hand, means "do homage to," directed toward the beast (or his image) as in Rev. 13:12; 14:9, 11; 20:4. Apparent exceptions to this distinction made by the author are Rev. 13:4, 15; 16:2; 19:20, where the verb has the beast as its dative object. Yet each of these passages has a variant reading that offers the possibility of the accusative (Charles). In classical Greek, προσκυνέω with the accusative was used consistently to denote worship, but in the LXX it is used over a hundred times with the dative to represent worship of the true God, the accusative being used only in exceptional cases.[112] The synoptic gospels, in contrast with the LXX, use the verb with the accusative to denote the worship due to God or His Son. John's gospel uses it with both the dative and the accusative, but when with the latter, it is qualified so as to point specifically to worship of the Father rather than pagan gods.[113] In the Apocalypse, John appears to follow the LXX pattern more closely. The dative emphasizes the idea of "prostrating oneself *to* a person, idol, or God," and the accusative means "adore" without this emphasis.[114] Charles contends that the case usage in the gospel of John is the direct opposite of what it is in the Apocalypse (Charles), but this is an invalid assertion, based on a failure to discern carefully the nuances of meaning in John 4:21-24 where the verb is followed by the dative twice and the accusative four times.

Peterson has noted a distinction between worship in heaven and worship on earth in the Apocalypse.[115] His point is well taken that worship on earth contrasts with that in heaven as represented in the doxologies and acclamations of the book. It consists of obeying the commands and admonitions of the book and living in a godly way.[116]

112. Edwin A. Abbott, *Johannine Vocabulary* (London: Adam and Charles Black, 1905), pp. 134-35.
113. Ibid., pp. 139-42.
114. Edwin A. Abbott, *Johannine Grammar* (London: Adam and Charles Black, 1906), p. 78.
115. David Peterson, "Worship in the Revelation to John," *Reformed Theological Review* 47, no. 3 (September-December 1988): 70-75.
116. Ibid., p. 73.

11
The Seven-Sealed Scroll of the Lamb

Having been given the setting of the heavenly throne room, the prophet now views a second scene in this same setting. The centerpiece of this new scene is a remarkable scroll and a single individual who is qualified to take it from the hand of the one on the throne.

b. The Seven-Sealed Scroll of the Lamb (5:1-14)

Translation

¹And I saw on the right hand of the one sitting upon the throne a scroll written [upon], inside and on the back, sealed with seven seals. ²And I saw a strong angel proclaiming in a loud voice, "Who is worthy to open the scroll, even to break its seals?" ³And no one in heaven or on earth or under the earth was able to open the scroll or to look at it. ⁴And I began crying loudly because no one was found worthy to open the scroll or to look at it. ⁵And one of the elders said to me, "Stop crying; behold, the lion who is of the tribe of Judah, the root of David, has overcome that He may open the scroll and its seven seals."

⁶And I saw in the middle of the throne and of the four living beings and in the middle of the elders a Lamb standing as one slain, having seven horns and seven eyes which are the seven spirits of God sent into all the earth. ⁷And He came and took [it] from the right hand of the one sitting upon the throne. ⁸And when He took the scroll, the four living beings and the twenty-four elders fell before the Lamb, each one having a harp and golden bowls full of incense, which is the prayers of the saints. ⁹And they sang a new song, saying,

"You are worthy to take the scroll
and to open its seals,
because You were slain and have redeemed for God
    with Your blood
[some] from every tribe and tongue and people and nation,
¹⁰and You made them a kingdom and priests to our God,
    and they shall reign on the earth."

¹¹And I looked, and I heard the voice of many angels around the throne and of the living beings and of the elders, and their number was ten thousands of ten thousands and thousands of thousands, ¹²saying with a loud voice,

"Worthy is the Lamb who was slain to receive
the power and riches and wisdom and strength
and honor and glory and blessing."

¹³And every creature that is in heaven and on the earth and under the earth and on the sea, and all things in them, I heard saying,

"To the one sitting upon the throne and to the Lamb
[be] the blessing and the honor and the glory and the
might forever and ever."

¹⁴And the four living beings kept saying, "Amen"; and the elders fell and worshiped.

Exegesis and Exposition

5:1 *The seven-sealed scroll in the Father's possession.* Four new scenes (5:1; 5:2-5; 5:6-10; 5:11-14) of the vision currently in progress are introduced by καὶ εἶδον[1] (*kai eidon*, "and I saw") in chapter 5 (cf. vv. 1, 2, 6, 11). The throne room described in chapter 4 functions as the setting of these scenes, the first of which introduces a scroll whose contents comprise essentially the remainder of the Apocalypse: Καὶ εἶδον ἐπὶ τὴν δεξιὰν τοῦ καθημένου ἐπὶ τοῦ θρόνου βιβλίον γεγραμμένον *ἔσωθεν καὶ ὄπισθεν, κατεσφραγισμένον σφραγῖσιν ἑπτά (Kai eidon epi tēn dexian tou kathēmenou epi tou thronou biblion gegrammenon esōthen kai opisthen, katesphragismenon sphragisin hepta,* "And I saw on the right hand of the one sitting upon the throne a scroll written [upon], inside and on the back, sealed with seven seals").

The scroll lies *on (epi)* the open palm of the one sitting upon the

---

1. The normal function of καὶ εἶδον in Revelation is to introduce similar or closely related events within the same vision. Μετὰ ταῦτα εἶδον, on the other hand, introduces a separate and distinct vision (cf. 4:1). Thus the general scene is the same in chapter 5 as in chapter 4. The only difference is that a particular incident is now seen for the first time, being introduced by καὶ εἶδον (Henry Alford, *The Greek Testament,* 4 vols. [London: Longmans, Green, 1903], 4:603; William Lee, "The Revelation of St. John," in *The Holy Bible,* ed. F. C. Cook [London: John Murray, 1881], 4:563).

throne.² Several have taken the words to indicate that it was held *in* His hand, arguing that an object in the form of a roll could rest upon an open hand only by an act of balancing.³ This explanation is severely weakened, however, by noting that the sense of *in* would have required the preposition ἐν (*en*, "in") as John uses it in Rev. 10:2, 8 (cf. Ezek. 2:9), rather than *epi*.⁴ The hand could be cupped to retain a round object without balancing, yet still be open. The natural meaning of *epi* followed by the accusative case is "on" or "upon" (Swete; Alford). The position of the scroll in God's possession indicates its divine source, the supreme authority of the revelation contained in it, and the assurance of adequate power to translate its contents into action.⁵

A *biblion* ("scroll") was made by processing either papyrus or skins from different kinds of animals.⁶ Possible OT parallels to this scroll are Isa. 29:11-12; Jer. 36:10-25; Ezek. 2:9-10; Dan. 12:4. A few have proposed that this was a book, consisting of separate leaves fastened together in a codex like a modern book.⁷ This is based on the assumption that only a flat book could rest on an open hand (Moffatt) and on the use of ἀνοῖξαι (*anoixai*, "to open") later in the chapter (Charles; Beckwith). A scroll is unrolled, but a book is opened, is the reasoning.⁸ The possibility of a scroll's resting on an open hand has already been shown, however. The question of the use of *anoixai* for unrolling a scroll is answered simply by referring to Isa. 37:14, LXX,

---

2. Henry Barclay Swete, *The Apocalypse of St. John* (London: Macmillan, 1906), p. 75; R. H. Charles, *The Revelation of St. John*, 2 vols., ICC (New York: Scribner's, 1920), 1:136.
3. James Moffatt, "The Revelation of St. John the Divine," in *The Expositor's Greek Testament*, ed. W. Robertson Nicoll (Grand Rapids: Eerdmans, n.d.), 5:383; Isbon T. Beckwith, *The Apocalypse of John* (New York: Macmillan, 1919), p. 507; R. C. H. Lenski, *The Interpretation of St. John's Revelation* (Columbus, Ohio: Lutheran Book Concern, 1935), p. 192.
4. Beckwith, *Apocalypse*, p. 507; A. T. Robertson, *Word Pictures in the New Testament*, 6 vols. (Nashville: Broadman, 1933), 6:332.
5. J. B. Smith, *A Revelation of Jesus Christ* (Scottdale, Pa.: Herald, 1961), p. 111.
6. J. Massyngberde Ford, *Revelation*, vol. 38 of AB (Garden City, N.Y.: Doubleday, 1975), p. 84. The ending -ιον usually indicates the diminutive form of a noun, in this case "a little scroll," but in ordinary usage the diminutive force of this word had vanished, leaving it as the practical equivalent of βίβλος. When a diminutive sense was desired, another word was used, one such as βιβλαρίδιον (cf. Rev. 10:2).
7. Theodor Zahn, *Introduction to the New Testament*, 3 vols., trans. John Moore Trout et al. (Grand Rapids: Kregel, 1953), 3:405-6; Charles, *Revelation*, 1:137; Moffatt, "Revelation," 5:382-83.
8. Charles, *Revelation*, 1:136-37; Beckwith, *Apocalypse*, p. 507. According to this approach, a roll-form would have required another verb such as ἀνειλεῖν (cf. Ezek. 2:10, LXX), ἀνελίσσειν (cf. Rev. 6:14), or ἀναπτύσσειν (cf. Luke 4:17) rather than ἀνοῖξαι.

where the verb is used in such a situation.[9] In the Apocalypse, this verb is particularly fitting because of the seals that must be broken or opened to divulge the scroll's contents (cf. 5:9) (Beckwith). Two reasons are particularly persuasive in concluding that *biblion* here is in a roll-form. One is the appropriateness of the adverbial expression *esōthen kai opisthen* ("inside and on the back") to a scroll as opposed to a book. "Inside" means inside the scroll before unrolling, and "on the back" refers to the back side of the scroll after it is unrolled.[10] The other reason is that papyrus codices did not originate until the second century A.D. or perhaps the late first century at the earliest.[11] John's work under the primitive conditions of Patmos could therefore hardly have been in a book format.[12] It must have been in the form of a scroll, such as is found in Ezek. 2:9 and 3:1.[13]

Another issue of far-reaching exegetical import pertaining to *biblion* relates to its contents. A number of proposals have appeared. First, it represents the book of the New Covenant because the promised kingdom to be instituted in Rev. 20:1 ff. is in fulfillment of that covenant (cf. Jer. 31:31-34).[14] This is unlikely, however, because the new covenant of Jeremiah is one of mercy, and the setting of this scroll is dominantly one of judgment.[15] A second proposal has been

---

9. Charles, *Revelation*, 1:137. In Luke 4:17, an impressive accumulation of MSS attests the reading ἀνοίξας rather than ἀναπτύξας to describe Jesus' opening of the Isaiah scroll in the synagogue at Nazareth. Most recently, however, the textual preference of some authorities has been for the latter reading, even though it enjoys what is probably weaker external support.
10. Robertson, *Word Pictures*, 6:332.
11. Bruce M. Metzger, *The Text of the New Testament*, 2d ed. (New York: Oxford, 1968), p. 6.
12. Alan F. Johnson, "Revelation," in *EBC*, ed. Frank E. Gaebelein (Grand Rapids: Zondervan, 1981), 12:465.
13. Swete, *Apocalypse*, p. 75; Alford, *Greek Testament*, 4:603; Friedrich Düsterdieck, *Critical and Exegetical Handbook to the Revelation of John*, Meyer's Commentary, trans. and ed. Henry E. Jacobs (New York: Funk & Wagnalls, 1887), pp. 205-6; Beckwith, *Apocalypse*, p. 505; John Peter Lange, *The Revelation of John*, vol. 10 of Lange's Commentary, ed. E. R. Craven (Grand Rapids: Zondervan, 1968), p. 115; Walter Scott, *Exposition of the Revelation of Jesus Christ* (Swengel, Pa.: Bible Truth Depot, n.d.), p. 131; Robertson, *Word Pictures*, 6:332; George E. Ladd, *A Commentary on the Revelation of John* (Grand Rapids: Eerdmans, 1972), p. 79; G. V. Caird, *A Commentary on the Revelation of St. John the Divine*, HNTC (New York: Harper & Row, 1966), p. 70; G. R. Beasley-Murray, *The Book of Revelation*, NCB (Grand Rapids: Eerdmans, 1978), p. 120; Ford, *Revelation*, p. 84; Robert H. Mounce, *The Book of Revelation*, NICNT (Grand Rapids: Eerdmans, 1977), p. 143.
14. Robert Govett, *The Apocalypse Expounded by Scripture* (London: Charles J. Thynne, 1920), p. 118.
15. E. W. Bullinger, *The Apocalypse* or *"The Day of the Lord"* (London: Eyre and Spottiswoode, n.d.), p. 232.

that the scroll is a testament or will assuring that the inheritance is reserved by God for the saints.[16] Several reasons support the plausibility of this interpretation. In that day a Roman will had to be sealed seven times to make it authentic, reminiscent of the seven seals on this scroll (Moffatt; Beckwith). Also, Rev. 11:15 announces the inheritance of Christ and the saints who will reign with Him (cf. Rev. 5:9) (Johnson). This explains the tone of tumultuous joy that prevails in Revelation 5, i.e., an enthronement that initiates the new era of salvation (Beasley-Murray). The problem with this "inheritance" theory is that the Apocalypse nowhere else supports it. The only reference to an inheritance is in Rev. 21:7 and is quite incidental (Moffatt). The seals and trumpets do not deal with the inheritance of the saints, but with the plagues of judgment to be heaped upon rebellious humanity (Ladd). This view fails, too, in its disagreement with the emphasis on overflowing judgment found in the context of Ezekiel, which appears to give rise to the scroll symbolism (Beasley-Murray).

A third view is that the scroll represents the Lamb's book of life so prominent elsewhere in Revelation (cf. 3:5; 13:8; 17:8; 20:12, 15; 21:27) (Mounce). The fullness of the scroll (i.e., "written [upon], inside and on the back") could point to the seemingly limitless number of names recorded therein (cf. Rev. 7:9) (Ladd). If this were the meaning, however, John's purpose in recording the book's contents would be to divulge the identity of the redeemed, a purpose that is suggested nowhere in the Apocalypse (Caird). As the seals of this book are broken, only tribulation is divulged (Beckwith). The process of breaking the seals is meaningless unless it relates to the remainder of the Apocalypse (Caird).

A fourth explanation for *biblion* holds that it represents God's redemptive plan foreshadowed in the OT and completed in the NT (Swete; Caird; Ford). This view fits the character of the Apocalypse as a sustained meditation on the OT in light of the Christian gospel (Caird). It also provides for the prominence of the death of Christ in chapter 5 (cf. vv. 6, 9), but it is particularly good in showing how God's redemptive plan, foreshadowed in the OT, asserts His sovereignty over a sinful world and so achieves the purpose of creation (Caird). Yet the shortcomings of this view are even more persuasive. The opening of the seals does not relate to the past, i.e., the redemptive work of Christ's death, as this view holds, but to things yet future at the time of writing (Alford). Nor does the view account for the

---

16. Zahn, *Introduction*, 3:395-96; Moffatt, "Revelation," p. 383; J. A. Seiss, *The Apocalypse*, 3 vols. (New York: Charles C. Cook, 1909), 1:272; Beasley-Murray, *Revelation*, pp. 120-23.

obvious relation of the scroll to the wrathful contents of the Apocalypse itself (Beckwith). In other words, it is inconsistent with the process described, beginning in chapter 6 (Swete). Nevertheless, the view commendably notes an element that must not be missed, that somehow the scroll pertains to the accomplishment of God's original purpose for His creation.

A fifth analysis of the scroll is that it represents Christ's title-deed or contract-deed to the world.[17] Favorable evidence for this explanation shows that it has much to offer in the formulation of a satisfactory solution. This kind of contract was known all over the Middle East in ancient times and was used by the Romans from the time of Nero on. The full contract would be written on the inner pages and sealed with seven seals. Then the content of the contract would be described briefly on the outside. All kinds of transactions were consummated this way, including marriage-contracts, rental and lease agreements, release of slaves, contract-bills, and bonds.[18] Support comes also from Hebrew practices. The Hebrew document most closely resembling this scroll was a title-deed that was folded and signed, requiring at least three witnesses. A portion of text would be written, folded over and sealed, with a different witness signing at each fold. A larger number of witnesses meant that more importance was assigned to the document. Such a document was used to prolong the proceedings when writing a bill of divorce. It was also used in Jeremiah 32 in the recovery of a lost estate (Bullinger). The similarity of *biblion* to the title-deed of Jer. 32:10-14 makes it tempting to identify it as a title-deed to all creation, which was forfeited through the entrance of sin in Genesis 3 and reclaimed by Christ through His redeeming death (Johnson). This fits the emphasis on creation in the song of Rev. 4:11 and the note of great joy that prevails in Revelation 5 (Beasley-Murray). This explanation approximates the true interpretation, but it still lacks one important element: it fails to account for the contents of the book as reflected in the seal-breaking process beginning in Revelation 6 (Swete). An accurate analysis must account for the contents of the book as reflected in the Apocalypse itself (Beckwith).

A sixth interpretation of the contents of *biblion* is the correct one. It contains the counsels of God as revealed in the visions beginning at chapter 6. Viewed from God's perspective, these are the judgments

---

17. H. A. Ironside, *Lectures on the Book of Revelation* (New York: Loizeaux, n.d.), p. 88.
18. Ford, *Revelation*, p. 92; Beasley-Murray, *Revelation*, pp. 120-23. Apparently wills or testaments were not done in this format because their contents were always kept secret.

that will fall upon the earth during a relatively brief period, eventually at their conclusion issuing in the coming of the promised Messiah and His kingdom. It is a "history" of the future that gives the successive steps leading to the inauguration of the world-kingdom of Christ.[19] That an actual reading from the scrolls is nowhere recorded in the Apocalypse (Alford; Lee) is no serious problem to this view. The contents are enacted, not read. This is so obvious that elaboration is almost superfluous. Later discussions will show that the seventh seal contains the seven trumpet judgments (cf. Rev. 8:6–11:15) and that the seventh trumpet contains the seven bowls of wrath (Revelation 16-19) (Johnson), so here in this scroll is a comprehensive account of the future wrath of the Lamb (cf. 6:17). The horrors of the seal visions alone are sufficient to earn the title "the scroll of doom" (Moffatt). The relation of the scroll to the vision of chapter 4 makes clear the plan of Revelation: the eternal and almighty God of Revelation 4 presents in this seven-sealed scroll the decrees of His will regarding the consummation of His kingdom (Beckwith). Subsequently, when the Lamb breaks the seals, it is not merely a disclosure of the scroll's contents, but an activation of those contents (Caird).

This appraisal of the scroll concurs with the nature of Ezekiel's scroll containing "words of lament and mourning and woe" (Johnson). Daniel heard similar data from the angel (cf. Dan. 10:21), but was not permitted to give detailed circumstances of the latter days (Dan. 12:1-4, 9; cf. also Dan. 8:26) (Bullinger; Moffatt). The hiddenness of the destiny of the world and the events of the last days spoken of in the OT (cf. Isa. 29:11; Dan. 8:26) is now about to end. Just as promised to John in Rev. 4:1, the seals will be broken and everything about the future revealed (cf. Rev. 1:19; 22:10) (Swete; Charles; Beckwith). The enactment of these events in the heavenly throne room supplies a pattern to be followed in the future fulfillment of God's will when the very same events transpire in the reality of world history (Beckwith; Mounce). The purging effect of God's wrath will touch the entire sphere of God's creation (4:11; cf. Rom. 8:18-25). The effects of sin will disappear, and earth will be restored to its rightful owner. The consequences of this scroll's contents are immeasurable and eternal.

The first of two descriptions of the scroll is furnished in *gegrammenon esōthen kai opisthen* ("written [upon], inside and on the back"). *Gegrammenon* ("written") was often used to describe ancient docu-

19. Swete, *Apocalypse*, p. 74; Alford, *Greek Testament*, 4:603; Bullinger, *Apocalypse*, p. 231; Beckwith, *Apocalypse*, p. 505; Scott, *Revelation*, p. 131; Lenski, *Revelation*, p. 194; William E. Biederwolf, *The Millennium Bible* (Grand Rapids: Baker, 1967), p. 561; Scott, *Revelation*, p. 131; Ladd, *Revelation*, p. 81.

ments whose authority continued in force.[20] Punctuating the verse so as to join *esōthen kai opisthen* ("written [upon], inside and on the back") to it agrees with a comparable connection of words in Ezek. 2:10.[21] Writing on a scroll was usually limited to one side of the writing material, the inner side of the roll, but sometimes extended to the outer side or back of the material. The latter is the case here and in Ezekiel's parallel. The "spill-over" onto the back symbolizes the fullness of the contents.[22] The decrees of God contained herein are extensive and comprehensive.[23] They constitute the whole counsel of God regarding the future of the world. No further revelation may be anticipated (cf. Rev. 22:18) (Scott).

The second descriptive word about the scroll is the expression *katesphragismenon sphragisin hepta* ("sealed with seven seals"). *Katesphragismenon* ("sealed") is stronger than the simple verb for sealing, its intensification of meaning emphasizing the security of the sealing.[24] This enhances the secrecy of the scroll's contents and is an appropriate emphasis in connection with a document that none but the Lamb is worthy to open.[25] The seal on a scroll kept it closed. It symbolizes an event still hidden in mystery, but divinely decreed. Such imagery is borrowed from Isa. 29:11-12 (Lee). Such a seal was an impression usually made on clay, wax, or some other soft material that restricted an unauthorized person from access to the contents.[26] Use of seven such seals stresses the profundity of the mysteries contained inside.[27]

---

20. Gottlob Schrenk, "γράφω, γραφή, κ. τ. λ.," in *TDNT*, 10 vols., ed. Gerhard Kittel and Gerhard Friedrich, trans. and ed. Geoffrey W. Bromiley (Grand Rapids: Eerdmans, 1976), 1 (1964):748-49; Fritz Rienecker, *A Linguistic Key to the Greek New Testament*, trans. and ed. Cleon L. Rogers, Jr. (Grand Rapids: Zondervan, 1980), p. 824.

21. Zahn proposes that a comma be placed after ἔσωθεν and that ὄπισθεν be connected with κατεσφραγισμένον to harmonize with his explanation of βιβλίον as a book rather than a scroll. To him, "on the back" would be a seal on the edge opposite the viewer (Zahn, *Introduction*, 3:405-6). This is grammatically possible but not probable, because ὄπισθεν as an adverbial modifier in Revelation and elsewhere in the NT always qualifies the verb preceding it, never the one following it (Johnson, "Revelation," 12:466).

22. Charles, *Revelation*, 1:138; Beckwith, *Apocalypse*, p. 506; John F. Walvoord, *The Revelation of Jesus Christ* (Chicago: Moody, 1966), p. 113.

23. Mounce, *Revelation*, p. 143; Rienecker, *Linguistic Key*, p. 824.

24. The κατά prefix on κατεσφραγισμένον has a perfective force. Isa. 29:11 and Dan. 8:26 emphasize a secure sealing of information about the future in a different way.

25. Swete, *Apocalypse*, p. 75; Beckwith, *Apocalypse*, p. 506; Biederwolf, *Millennium Bible*, p. 561.

26. Gottfried Fitzer, "σφραγίς, σφραγίζω," *TDNT*, 7 (1971):939-40; Ford, *Revelation*, p. 84; Rienecker, *Linguistic Key*, p. 824.

27. Charles, *Revelation*, 1:138. Roman law required a will to be sealed seven

The manner in which the seals were affixed remains a question. The common way of sealing a scroll was to place its seal or seals on the outer edge so that they all had to be broken before any of the scroll's content could be read (Moffatt; Beckwith). Further, someone has observed that this is the only way John could have seen all seven (Johnson). Yet, is it? The seals could have been clearly visible at one end (i.e., longitudinal edge) of the scroll, though spaced at intervals throughout the inner part of the roll (Alford). Though contrary to known customs of the day, this is the only explanation that harmonizes with the progressive nature of the revelation associated with the breaking of the seals, one by one (Walvoord; Mounce). As each seal is broken and the next section of the scroll unrolled to permit viewing, the clear implication of the text is that the dramatization that follows represents that portion of the scroll. The beginning of the scroll's enactment does not await the opening of all seven seals fastened along the single outer extremity of the papyrus roll.[28] It is granted that nothing is read verbatim from the scroll, but with the severing of each successive seal, part of the scroll's contents is revealed in prophetic symbolism.[29] Picturing the seals at one end of the scroll is most probable.

5:2 *Credentials necessary to open the scroll.* The second scene of chapter 5 (5:2-5) revolves about finding someone with the necessary credentials to break the seals on the scroll. At first, no one qualified can be found, causing the prophet deep grief. Then comes good news of the discovery of such a person, bringing an end to John's weeping. The issue of worthiness is first raised by a strong angel: καὶ εἶδον ἄγγελον ἰσχυρὸν κηρύσσοντα ἐν φωνῇ μεγάλῃ, Τίς ἄξιος ἀνοῖξαι τὸ βιβλίον καὶ λῦσαι τὰς σφραγῖδας αὐτοῦ (*kai eidon angelon ischyron kēryssonta en phōnē megalē Tis axios anoixai to biblion kai lysai tas sphragidas autou,* "And I saw a strong angel proclaiming in a loud voice, 'Who is worthy to open the scroll, even to break its seals?' ").

Efforts to identify this strong angel have pointed to Gabriel and Michael. He is perceived as the angel Gabriel, because elsewhere in Scripture Gabriel functions as a messenger of God (cf. Dan. 8:16; 9:21; Luke 1:19, 26) and Gabriel was the one who ordered Daniel to close and seal the book (Smith). His identity as Michael rests upon

---

times, as illustrated by the wills of Roman emperors Augustus and Vespasian and their successors (Ethelbert Stauffer, *Christ and the Caesars* [Philadelphia: Westminster, 1955], pp. 182-83; Emmett Russell, "A Roman Law Parallel to Rev. V," *BSac* 115 [July 1958]: 258-64). As noticed above, however, it is doubtful that Roman custom furnishes the best explanation of this scroll.

28. Leon Morris, *The Revelation of St. John*, TNTC (Grand Rapids: Eerdmans, 1969), p. 94; Ford, *Revelation*, p. 92.

29. Charles, *Revelation*, 1:137; Beckwith, *Apocalypse*, pp. 507, 515.

Michael's rank as an archangel and because of his special interest in the events of the last days (cf. Dan. 12:1-3; Jude 9) (Scott). The obstacle to accepting either of these identifications is that neither here nor in two other mentions of a "strong angel" in Revelation is a name assigned. If this angel were known by name elsewhere in Scripture, his name probably would have been given. Because it is not, he is best left unnamed and identified only as a mighty angel who performs God's will (Beckwith). *Ischyron* ("strong") denotes active power rather than a reserve of secret strength (Swete). Such an angel actively exerts his might in fulfillment of God's purposes.

His strength displays itself here in proclaiming his God-given message in a loud voice. That he proclaims (*kēryssonta*) rather than says adds emphasis to his question. That he does so in a loud voice (*phōnē megalē*) is a demonstration of his strength.[30] The combination of his strength and loud voice results in a proclamation that can reach remotest extremities of the universe (Beckwith). A loud voice (or loud voices) is rather common in the Apocalypse (cf. 1:10; 5:12; 6:10; 7:2, 10; 8:13; 10:3; 11:12, 15; 12:10; 14:7, 9, 15, 18; 16:1, 17; 19:1, 17; 21:3). The utterances of these loud voices are always articulate, with one possible exception (cf. 10:3), and deserve special attention.[31]

The strong angel asks an intriguing question about finding a worthy person to break the seals of the scroll. The adjective *axios* ("worthy") originally meant "of proper weight," but its meaning developed to cover qualities other than weight. It is a synonym of ἱκανος (*hikanos*, "sufficient," "competent," or "fit"). Both words refer to quality of being, person, power, or attainment.[32] The shade of difference between them is that worthiness (ἀξιώτης [*axiōtēs*]) is the inner ethical presupposition of the ability (ἱκανώτης [*hikanōtēs*]) to open this seven-sealed scroll. The worthiness required for this is so great that no created being can even contemplate it, much less attain it (Bullinger).

Only by anticipating the remainder of chapter 5 can the nature of this worthiness be assessed. One suggestion is that it is based on the rank or office of the Lamb who meets the criteria (Beckwith). His Messianic authority as the scion of David is certainly part of the picture, according to 5:5 (Moffatt), but this explanation alone ignores

---

30. Robertson, *Word Pictures*, 6:333; Smith, *Revelation*, p. 112; Walvoord, *Revelation*, pp. 113-14.
31. Charles, *Revelation*, 1:139, 261.
32. Alford, *Greek Testament*, 4:606; Charles, *Revelation*, 1:139; Beckwith, *Apocalypse*, p. 508; Lenski, *Revelation*, p. 194. A comparison of ἱκανός in Matt. 3:11 with its parallel ἄξιος in John 1:27 shows the close relationship between the two words. Another interesting comparison is τίς ἄξιος here with τίς ἱκανός in 2 Cor. 2:16.

the worthiness on moral grounds of which *axios* speaks. To explain the worthiness as designating the Lamb's inner moral competency has merit (Charles). This fits the meaning of *axios* (cf. John 1:27) (Swete; Lee; Charles) and agrees with 5:9 where the Lamb's worthiness relates to His act of total self-sacrifice (Mounce). Yet this explanation alone fails to account for explicit references to moral competency in the context of chapter 5. The best resolution is to refer the worthiness to both Christ's office and His moral competency.[33] In 5:9 the explicit statement is that His worthiness is based on His redemptive death, and in 5:5 it is strongly implied that His worthiness is tied to His Messianic office. The two aspects of His Person cannot be separated.

The sequence of actions in *anoixai to biblion kai lysai tas sphragidas autou* ("to open the scroll, even to break its seals") is unusual because one would normally break the seals of a scroll before opening it. Several have rendered the *kai* by "and" rather than "even" and cited this as another example of *hysteron proteron*.[34] The reason for the reversed order is, according to this view, that the content of the scroll is of first importance and the breaking of the seals is only an incidental step in discovering those contents (Mounce). This misses the point of the figure of speech called *hysteron proteron*, however. When the opening of the scroll is placed first because it is the first necessity, the "last-first" terminology does not apply (Swete). Because of this last observation, some contend that this is only an apparent *hysteron proteron* (Swete). This too falls somewhat short of the mark, however, because the opening of the scroll and the breaking of the seals are so nearly identical as demonstrated in Rev. 5:5. The best solution is to understand *kai* as epexegetical, meaning "even," and the breaking of the seals as a closer specification of what is involved in opening the scroll (Lenski). In 5:5, a comparable construction with an epexegetical *kai* occurs: "to open the scroll, even its seven seals." These words show that the opening and the breaking are essentially the same actions.

Another inquiry regarding *anoixai* ("to open") explores what the precise import of the opening is. That it denotes the interpretation of the OT by the coming and teaching of Christ can be dismissed, because the scroll cannot be identified with the OT (Swete). That it denotes the allegorical interpretation of Scripture can likewise be eliminated, because nothing in the immediate context or the rest of the book offers any ground for this (Swete). A third suggestion is a bit

---

33. Robertson, *Word Pictures,* 6:333; Lenski, *Revelation,* p. 194.
34. Charles, *Revelation,* 1:139; Beckwith, *Apocalypse,* p. 508; Robertson, *Word Pictures,* 6:333.

more plausible, that the opening signifies an enlargement, development, and continuation of the book of Daniel, describing from God's side the judgments necessary to fulfill all He has foretold (Bullinger). A fourth suggestion is related to the third, but is broader: the opening is the revelation of divine counsels and judgments (Charles). Both the third and fourth suggestions falter in one important respect, however. If only revelation were included in the opening of the scroll, others worthy of the task could have been found. The OT prophets, for example, revealed the future (cf. Amos 3:7), but they were unable to implement their predictions in history (Beckwith). So *anoixai* must include not only the telling of the prophecies contained in the scroll, but also the ability to make them come true (Beckwith; Lenski). As the Lamb breaks the seals, one by one beginning in chapter 6, therefore, His execution of the events foretold in each section of the scroll is entailed also.

5:3 A search of the universe fails to disclose anyone able to open the scroll or look at it: καὶ οὐδεὶς ἐδύνατο ἐν τῷ οὐρανῷ οὐδὲ ἐπὶ τῆς γῆς οὐδὲ ὑποκάτω τῆς γῆς ἀνοῖξαι τὸ βιβλίον οὔτε βλέπειν αὐτό (*kai oudeis edynato en tọ ouranọ oude epi tēs gēs oude hypokatō tēs gēs anoixai to biblion oute blepein auto*, "and no one in heaven or on earth or under the earth was able to open the scroll or to look at it"). *Edynato* ("was able") speaks of the same ability as *axios* of the previous verse. It brings out the connection in the author's mind between "worthiness" and "ability" or "competence." Its tense (imperfect) shows that all creation's inability and unworthiness to open the scroll was a chronic and ongoing condition. *Oudeis edynato* ("no one was able") describes the unaltered and complete impotence of created beings to perform the function. The possibility is reduced to a vanishing point after a search produces no one in region after region (Morris).

The threefold division of creation expressed in *en tọ ouranọ oude epi tēs gēs oude hypokatō tēs gēs* ("in heaven or on earth or under the earth") follows the OT pattern found in Ex. 20:4, 11 and Ps. 146:6 (cf. Phil. 2:10). A similar pattern is used in the Babylonian division of the world into heaven, earth, and water. Here the comprehensive expression is an emphatic designation of the whole universe (Charles; Beckwith). A quasi-ascensive scale is implied in the three parts. As each region declines the challenge of producing someone able to open the scroll, eventually the possibilities are exhausted (Swete). Identification of the third member, "under the earth," has at times made it the place of departed human spirits,[35] but to do justice to the comprehensiveness of the total expression, all created beings must be

---

35. Düsterdieck, *Revelation*, p. 207; Lange, *Revelation*, p. 158; Lenski, *Revelation*, pp. 194, 212.

included. Thus the underworld is best identified here as the place of departed spirits, including demons (Moffatt).

Since no one can open the scroll, no one can examine its contents. *Blepein auto* ("to look at it") does not mean that no one is able to look at the exterior cover of the scroll, as would be the case if *oute* ("or") introduced a climax.[36] The expression means rather that because of an inability to break the seals, no one could read the scroll's contents.[37]

5:4 John was deeply grieved to the point of tears over the lack of a qualified being: καὶ *ἔκλαιον πολὺ ὅτι οὐδεὶς ἄξιος εὑρέθη ἀνοῖξαι τὸ βιβλίον οὔτε βλέπειν αὐτό (kai eklaion poly hoti oudeis axios heurethē anoixai to biblion oute blepein auto*, "And I began crying loudly because no one was found worthy to open the scroll or to look at it"). One opinion is that John started to cry, but something happened to stop him before he started.[38] The qualifying adverb *poly* ("loudly") indicates that he did actually begin sobbing. Κλαίω (*Klaiō*, "I cry") is used a number of times in the NT to describe professional mourning (e.g., Matt. 2:18; Mark 5:38, 39; Luke 7:13, 32; 8:52). In fact, the weeping of Jesus contrasts sharply with those in mourning over the death of Lazarus when John uses δακρύω (*dakryō*, "I weep") rather than *klaiō* to describe his crying (cf. John 11:33, 35) (Ford). While in this instance it would be a mistake to imply that John's response to the situation was anything less than heartfelt, it is still quite probable that his was a loud wail, as the word usually denoted. The addition of "loudly" indicates an even louder outcry.[39] This weeping was unrestrained emotion by one who was in an ecstatic state (Swete).

An inquiry into the specific reasons for John's emotional outburst is revealing. A first response might be that he wept over the moral incapability of all created beings.[40] This explanation is too superficial, however. The sequence of revelatory experience through which John had just come demands a more profound reason. After all, he had long before known about the depravity of man and the sin-cursed world. A second possibility is that he wept because he feared that the hoped-for revelation, promised in Rev. 4:1, would now be withheld.

---

36. Alford, *Greek Testament*, 4:606. The climactic sense of the phrase οὔτε βλέπειν αὐτό would be, "nor even so much as to look upon the book."
37. Düsterdieck, *Revelation*, p. 207; Beckwith, *Apocalypse*, p. 508.
38. Düsterdieck, *Revelation*, p. 207; Beckwith, *Apocalypse*, p. 508. Ἔκλαιον, an imperfect tense, is understood as inchoative, a usage that can in some instances indicate an action begun but not completed.
39. Only one other time in the NT is κλαίω qualified in this manner by an adverb, in the description of Peter's weeping following his denials. There the adverb is πικρῶς (Matt. 26:75) (Smith, *Revelation*, p. 112).
40. Swete, *Apocalypse*, p. 77; cf. also Bullinger, *Apocalypse*, p. 236; Charles, *Revelation*, 1:189; Lenski, *Revelation*, p. 195.

Such revelation depended on the opening of the scroll.[41] Though closer to the truth, this view is deficient in depicting John in the wrong light. In his condition, he was certainly not one who wept in disappointment because his curiosity was apparently going to be left unsatisfied. The most plausible reason for his sobbing is his fear that the events contained in the revelatory scroll would remain unfulfilled, thus thwarting the purposes of God (Caird). As already shown in the discussion of v. 2 above, opening the scroll included the power to implement the things revealed therein, so the disappointment is over more than just a withholding of revelation. John was not weeping for his own sake, but over the apparent indefinite postponement of God's final and decisive action (Mounce). He did not want to see God's vindication of His people as a part of the OT Messianic hope deferred for an undetermined period (Caird). So he broke out in tears.

5:5 At this point, a member of the angelic order of elders intervened to relieve his distress: καὶ εἷς ἐκ[42] τῶν πρεσβυτέρων λέγει[43] μοι, Μὴ κλαῖε (*kai heis ek tōn presbyterōn legei moi, Mē klaie,* "and one of the elders said to me, 'Stop crying'"). No symbolic meaning in such intervention is to be sought. The elder merely functions as a mediator, as angels of other orders do on occasion (cf. Rev. 17:1; 21:9) (Swete; Beckwith). An elder steps forward to inform or guide the seer regarding another matter in Rev. 7:13.

His directive at this point is *mē klaie* ("stop crying"). The angelic messenger sees beyond John's limited human perspective that such sorrow is inappropriate and instructs him to cease wailing.[44] Essentially the same directive came from Jesus' lips twice, once on the occasion of raising the widow's son at Nain (Luke 7:13), and again when He was about to raise Jairus's daughter from the dead (Luke 8:52). Weeping was not fitting on those occasions because of what Jesus was about to do—raise people from death. It was unfitting for

---

41. Swete, *Apocalypse,* p. 77; Charles, *Revelation,* 1:139; Moffatt, "Revelation," 5:383; Beckwith, *Apocalypse,* p. 508; Homer Hailey, *Revelation, an Introduction and Commentary* (Grand Rapids: Baker, 1979), p. 175.
42. The construction εἷς ἐκ occurs twelve times in the gospel of John and eight times in this book, replacing a partitive-genitive construction. It is found only ten times in the rest of the NT (Charles, *Revelation,* 1:139; Robertson, *Word Pictures,* 6:333). This is a substantial support for the apostolic authorship of the Apocalypse.
43. The tense of λέγει is present. It is a historic use of the tense, carrying an aoristic force. When used among a number of aorist and imperfect tenses, it adds great vividness to the narrative (Lenski, *Revelation,* p. 196).
44. Prohibitions with μή and the present imperative normally call for the cessation of action already in progress (Lenski, *Revelation,* p. 196). Only when contextual factors dictate can the construction indicate another sense such as forbidding to undertake a habitual course of action.

John because of what Jesus was about to do—open the seven-sealed scroll: ἰδοὺ ἐνίκησεν ὁ λέων ὁ ἐκ τῆς φυλῆς ᾽Ιούδα, ἡ ῥίζα Δαυίδ, ἀνοῖξαι τὸ βιβλίον καὶ τὰς ἑπτὰ σφραγῖδας αὐτοῦ (*idou enikēsen ho leōn ho ek tēs phylēs Iouda, hē rhiza Dauid, anoixai to biblion kai tas hepta sphragidas autou,* "behold, the lion who is of the tribe of Judah, the root of David, has overcome that He may open the scroll and its seven seals"). For this reason, the elder forbids John to weep any longer.

He prefaces his great announcement with *idou* ("behold"), a common practice throughout the Apocalypse (Lenski). Victory is emphasized in his spirited explanation to John.[45] Immediately following *idou, enikēsen* ("has overcome") quickly brings attention to this as an occasion for joy rather than sorrow. The verb in this context deserves the strong force of "overcome" or "conquer," though in some contexts it may carry a lesser import of "prevail" (Alford). This is the word's meaning throughout the book when God's people are the victors (e.g., 2:7, 11; 12:12; 15:2) (Beckwith). This fits the picture of Israel's conquering Messiah who as a lion will defeat the enemies of God (Johnson). The meaning takes its cue from the great historical fact of Christ's victory at the cross, referred to already in Rev. 3:21.[46] God's purposes will not be thwarted through a permanently closed scroll as John feared, said the elder, so the prophet can stop sobbing.

The descriptive titles identifying the victorious Christ are quite meaningful. *Ho leōn ho ek tēs phylēs Iouda* ("The lion who is of the tribe of Judah") comes from Gen. 49:9 where Judah is so described. It aptly pictures kingly might and boldness (cf. Prov. 28:1). Here that tribe's noblest son is fitly called its lion (Swete; Beckwith; Lenski). Here is one whose strength, majesty, courage, and menace as well as His intellectual excellence resemble qualities of the "king of the jungle" (Ford).

A second title used to refer to Christ is *hē rhiza Dauid* ("the root of David"). Here *rhiza* ("root") refers to what springs from and therefore represents a root. It is a metaphorical term for "offspring."[47] John's fondness for this title accounts for his use of it again in 22:16.[48] The full title *hē rhiza Dauid* derives from Isa. 11:1, 10 (cf. also Jer. 23:5;

---

45. The position of the verb at the very beginning of its clause produces this emphasis (Walvoord, *Revelation*, p. 114; Mounce, *Revelation*, p. 144).
46. Swete, *Apocalypse*, p. 77; Moffatt, "Revelation," 5:384. The tense of the verb is aorist, stating the great historical fact of the once-for-all conquest of Christ over the power of darkness. On this basis, He is empowered to open the book (Charles, *Revelation*, 1:140; Lenski, *Revelation*, p. 196; Morris, *Revelation*, p. 92).
47. Alford, *Greek Testament*, 4:606-7; Lange, *Revelation*, p. 157.
48. In Rev. 22:16, the καί before τὸ γένος is apparently epexegetic as an explanation of ῥίζα (Smith, *Revelation*, pp. 112-13).

33:15) and describes Christ's headship in the final Davidic kingdom (cf. Rom. 15:12) (Beckwith; Lenski; Mounce). His Davidic descent was frequently acknowledged among early Christians (Moffatt). Both "the lion of the tribe of Judah" and "the root of David" are familiar OT Messianic titles, but they are linked together only here in the NT (Johnson).

An interpretive issue related to *hē rhiza Dauid* is whether it has in view Christ's human nature or His divine nature. A reference to His divine nature would come from seeing Christ as the divine root that brought forth David.[49] In the present context, however, attention is upon the origin of Jesus, not of David. It is by virtue of Jesus' membership in David's family that He is called the greatest of the tribe of Judah and a branch from the root of David.[50] In this chapter, Christ achieves victory and exaltation through suffering. This focuses attention on His humanity (Alford). The combination of *rhiza* with ῥάβδος (*rhabdos*, "scepter") in the LXX rendering of Isa. 11:1 (cf. Isa. 11:10; Ezek. 19:11, 12, 14) has Messianic connotations stemming from His Davidic lineage.[51]

The purpose of Jesus' victory is expressed by *anoixai* ("that He may open"). This is a shade different from calling the opening a *result* of His victorious redemptive work,[52] because at the time of winning the victory the result was only anticipated. It is also better to see the opening as a purpose of rather than what constitutes the victory,[53] because the significance of the opening of the seals is far-reaching, including also the implementation of what is revealed. The opening of the scroll is best seen as the object or purpose of Jesus' conquest. The reason He won the victory was to enable Him to open this scroll of destiny and its seals and implement God's purposes throughout the final stages of human history (Charles).

5:6 *Transfer of the scroll to the Lamb.* The third scene of chapter 5 (5:6-10) introduces the main character of the heavenly drama. He takes the scroll from the one sitting upon the throne, and angelic beings in the immediate vicinity respond in a moving tribute to Him. Verse 6 describes His position and appearance: καὶ εἶδον ἐν μέσῳ τοῦ θρόνου καὶ τῶν τεσσάρων ζῴων καὶ ἐν μέσῳ τῶν πρεσβυτέρων ἀρνίον

---

49. Alford, *Greek Testament*, 4:607; Biederwolf, *Millennium Bible*, p. 562.
50. Robertson, *Word Pictures*, 6:333-34.
51. Moffatt, "Revelation," 5:384. Δαυίδ, though indeclinable, clearly functions as a genitive case here. The issue that correlates to the divine-human problem in the expression is whether the genitive is objective, i.e., the root that produced David (divine nature), or subjective, i.e., the root that David produced (human nature). The latter option is correct.
52. See Beckwith, *Apocalypse*, p. 508.
53. Lee calls such an "infinitive epexegetic" ("Revelation," 4:565).

ἑστηκὸς ὡς ἐσφαγμένον, ἔχων κέρατα ἑπτὰ καὶ ὀφθαλμοὺς ἑπτά (*kai eidon en mesǭ tou thronou kai tōn tessarōn zǭōn kai en mesǭ tōn presbyterōn arnion hestēkos hōs esphagmenon, echōn kerata hepta kai ophthalmous hepta*, "And I saw in the middle of the throne and of the four living beings and in the middle of the elders a Lamb standing as one slain, having seven horns and seven eyes").

A correct understanding of the Lamb's position depends upon the connotation of the two *en mesǭ* ("in the middle") phrases. One explanation has dismissed the details of the description as unimportant, saying that it is wrong to attribute to the apocalyptist a precise diagram. The resultant idea proposed is "in the very midst of the group formed around the throne by the other beings" (Swete; Charles; Beckwith). In ignoring the individual aspects of the description, however, this approach does an injustice to the word picture that John paints. A second explanation is similar in saying that the two phrases are not spatial, but that they relate the Lamb to the throne as the symbol of power, to the four living beings as the agents of infinite providence, and to the elders. As the person in the middle, He directs this power and its two classes of agents (Lenski). To ignore the spatial connotations of the description, however, is to render the words meaningless.

A third way to take the phrases yields the sense "between the throne and the four living creatures (on the one side) and the elders (on the other)." In this case, the Lamb would stand somewhere between the inner concentric circle of the living creatures and the outer concentric circle of the twenty-four elders (Swete; Charles). Placing Him some distance from the throne could explain His need to come (ἦλθεν [*ēlthen*]) (v. 7) in order to receive the scroll from the one sitting upon the throne.[54] This sense would agree with the Semitic idiom as illustrated in Lev. 27:12, 14 of the LXX (Alford). This kind of Hebraism is widely illustrated in the Greek OT (e.g., Gen. 1:4, 7, 18; 2:7; 3:15; 9:16, 17) (Swete; Charles; Caird). Yet this view poses a serious problem of inconsistency with Rev. 3:21, which says that Jesus sat down with the Father on His heavenly throne.

A fourth view sees the Lamb standing in the center of all the angelic creatures, both living beings and elders, who surround the throne (Mounce). This is the force of the same phrase in Rev. 4:6 (Mounce). It also agrees with the general place of the Lamb throughout the book. He is the centerpiece of all (Swete). Furthermore, it concurs with Rev. 7:17, which thus locates the Lamb (cf. also Rev. 3:21) (Caird; Ladd). This view takes the two *en mesǭ* phrases in parallel with each other, which emphasizes that the Lamb stood in the center of all the beings named (Charles). This view admittedly cannot

---

54. Robertson, *Word Pictures*, 6:334.

answer why it was necessary for the Lamb to come in order to take the scroll (v. 7) (Charles; Caird; Beasley-Murray). Yet the suggestion that places Him on the outer periphery temporarily, before approaching the throne, runs counter to Rev. 3:21 (cf. Acts 7:56; Heb. 10:12). Hence, the "coming" of v. 7 must depict merely His movement from beside the Father to a position where He could receive the scroll.

After fixing the position of the leading character, John supplies details of His appearance. He calls Him a lamb (*arnion*). *Arnion* will be used frequently in the remainder of the Apocalypse, becoming almost a semi-technical term to describe the crucified Messiah.[55] Elsewhere in the NT it occurs only at John 21:15, but the LXX uses it four times. In formation, the word is a diminutive of ἀρήν (*arēn*, "lamb"), but the diminutive aspect should not be pressed to mean "little lamb" any more than the diminutive of θηρίον (*thērion*, "beast") to which *arnion* is opposed later in the book should be pressed to mean "little beast." The concept behind *arnion* comes from Isa. 53:7, though the LXX uses ἀμνός (*amnos*, "lamb") in that passage. The gospel of John follows the LXX in the use of *amnos* (cf. John 1:29, 36). The choice of the diminutive *arnion* here probably is designed to enhance the contrast between a lamb and a lion, both of which are descriptive of aspects of Christ's Person (cf. 5:5). He combines the meekness and gentleness of a lamb with the majesty of a lion as well as with the horns of power yet to be named in v. 6 (Alford; Swete; Moffatt; Beckwith).

Yet this contrast in characteristics is not universally accepted. Because *arnion* depicts the glorified Christ, enthroned with God, and destined to be victorious over all opposing forces, both human and divine (cf. 6:16; 17:14), some prefer the translation "ram" for the word.[56] Such a rendering gives prominence to His wrath (6:16) and His warfare and triumph (17:14). It also harmonizes with His horns of power mentioned later in v. 6 and explains the similarity of this passage to Dan. 8:3.[57] The plausibility of this alternative is in question, however. Elsewhere in Jewish Greek usage, the term only means "lamb" or "little lamb" (Charles; Moffatt; Beckwith). It is Christ's death as a sacrificial lamb with its redemptive results that qualifies

---

55. Charles, *Revelation*, 1:141; Moffatt, "Revelation," 5:385; Beckwith, *Apocalypse*, p. 509. Ἀρνίον occurs 29 times in 11 chapters (cf. chaps. 5, 6, 7, 12, 13, 14, 15, 17, 19, 21, 22). All uses refer to Christ except 13:11 where a likeness of one of the two beasts of Revelation 13 to a lamb is expressed.
56. Joachim Jeremias, "ἀρνίον," *TDNT*, 1 (1964):340-41; Ford, *Revelation*, p. 86.
57. Moffatt, "Revelation," 5:384; Ford, *Revelation*, p. 86. Moffatt proposes a possible astral origin of a ram in the Persian zodiac.

Him to open the scroll (cf. Rev. 5:9) (Beckwith). Provision for this aspect of His Person is necessary in the current description.

The next part confirms this conclusion: *hestēkos hōs esphagmenon* ("standing as one slain"). A slain ram would signify a collapsed power. This is out of place in the Apocalypse. A slain lamb is perfectly appropriate to the intended paradox. On one hand, the elder has described this Person as the lion of the tribe of Judah (5:5), depicting supreme power. On the other, His appearance is that of "a lamb standing as having been slain," which speaks of supreme self-sacrifice (Swete). These figures draw attention to the unique characteristics combined in the life of Christ. His supreme self-sacrifice leads to His supreme power, so there is no contradiction between the two (Charles).

The participle *hestēkos* ("standing") portrays the Lamb as standing in its natural living position. He is not dead. Even though slain, He is erect and alive in this heavenly scene. To be sure, the marks of His death are visible, but because of His resurrection, they are not debilitating.[58] The other participle *esphagmenon* ("one slain") depicts Christ's present state resulting from death. The present and eternal reality remains as a consequence of His historical crucifixion.[59] Special attention to Christ's death is not just incidental. Subsequent discussion will show it to be *the* accomplishment that enables Him to take and open the seven-sealed scroll (cf. Rev. 5:9). The question whether *esphagmenon* presents Christ as a martyr killed by violent means or as a passover lamb that bears the marks of slaughter has been asked. Favoring the former is the usual use of σφάζω (*sphazō*, "I slaughter") (Ford). Yet the word's usage in secular Greek certainly included a sacrificial connotation. The sacrificial note is predominant in its use in the LXX (Sweet). The use of *arnion* ("lamb") in v. 6 lends itself to the emphasis as does the reference to redemption in 5:9. In a book so filled with Exodus-style terminology as Revelation, a reference to the passover lamb is to be expected. This conclusion is confirmed by the attention to the passover lamb in the gospel of John also (cf. John 1:29; 19:14, 31-36) (Beasley-Murray). The objection that

---

58. Alford, *Greek Testament*, 4:607; Swete, *Apocalypse*, p. 78; Beckwith, *Apocalypse*, p. 510. The participle is perfect tense. In the NT the perfect tense of ἵστημι is always intensive, emphasizing the continuing results of a past act.
59. Lenski, *Revelation*, p. 200; J. P. M. Sweet, *Revelation* (Philadelphia: Westminster, Pelican, 1979), p. 128. The participle is an intensive use of the perfect tense and thus points out the continuing character of the Lamb. It resembles Paul's use of ἐσταυρωμένον in 1 Cor. 2:2: the nature in which Paul presented Christ in his preaching was that of "one crucified."

the verb nowhere in the NT outside Revelation refers to Christ's sacrificial death can be answered by noting the presence of its cognate noun as a part of the sacrificial terminology in the LXX rendering of Isa. 53:7 (Swete). The further objection that a slain sacrificial lamb would have a throat wound, rather than those in the hands and on the side as Christ's were (Lee; Moffatt; Scott), presses the details of the similarity excessively. The general point is that the death wounds on the body still remain.

A further feature of this character's appearance comes in the phrase *echōn*[60] *kerata hepta kai ophthalmous hepta* ("having seven horns and seven eyes"). In the OT the horn is a symbol of strength or power. As a Hebrew metaphor, it occurs in Num. 23:22 and Deut 33:17 (cf. also 1 Sam. 2:1; 2 Sam. 22:3; 1 Kings 22:11; Pss. 75:4; 132:17; Dan. 7:20-21; 8:5). In the later books of the OT it symbolizes dynastic force or kingly dignity and is thus used in the Apocalypse several times (cf. Rev. 12:3; 13:1; 17:3, 12).[61] The horns are seven in number, indicating the fullness of Christ's power, because seven is the perfect number. The Lamb with seven horns is, then, an all-powerful warrior and king.[62]

The Lamb's seven eyes have been construed as indicating that the Lord is about to remove iniquity from the land of Israel, based on the context of Zech. 3:9 and 4:10 (Bullinger). This presses the meaning of the OT source of the words too far, however. The interpretation of the symbol that takes the eyes as representing sight, intelligence, and wisdom in their fullness, in other words, omniscience, is preferable.[63] This brings out more clearly the Zecharian emphasis upon the eyes of the Lord that range to and fro throughout the earth.[64] Nothing escapes the notice of the Lamb. Not only is He omnipotent, as indicated by His seven horns, He is also omniscient.

---

60. The participle ἔχων is masculine in order to agree with the natural gender of the person named by the noun ἀρνίον. Grammatical agreement would have called for a neuter participle to agree with the neuter ἀρνίον, but because the person symbolized by the noun is a male, the masculine participle is chosen.

61. Swete, *Apocalypse*, p. 78; Düsterdieck, *Revelation*, p. 211; Bullinger, *Apocalypse*, p. 138; Charles, *Revelation*, 1:141; Beckwith, *Apocalypse*, pp. 509-10; Lenski, *Revelation*, p. 200; Caird, *Revelation*, p. 75; Mounce, *Revelation*, p. 146.

62. Swete, *Apocalypse*, pp. 78-79; Charles, *Revelation*, 1:141; William Kelly, *The Revelation* (London: Thomas Weston, 1904), p. 90; Ladd, *Revelation*, p. 87.

63. Swete, *Apocalypse*, pp. 78-79; Charles, *Revelation*, 1:141; Moffatt, "Revelation," 5:384; Scott, *Revelation*, p. 135; Beckwith, *Revelation*, p. 510; Robertson, *Word Pictures*, 6:334-35; Lenski, *Revelation*, p. 200; Smith, *Revelation*, p. 113; Caird, *Revelation*, p. 75.

64. Robertson, *Word Pictures*, 6:335.

His means for implementing His omniscience is further explained in the relative clause that closes v. 6: οἵ εἰσιν τὰ *ἑπτὰ πνεύματα τοῦ θεοῦ ἀπεσταλμένοι εἰς πᾶσαν τὴν γῆν (*hoi eisin ta hepta pneumata tou theou apestalmenoi eis pasan tēn gēn,* "which are the seven spirits of God sent into all the earth"). This symbolic representation of the Holy Spirit[65] arises from the relationship of the third Person of the Trinity to the second Person. The Holy Spirit proceeds from the Son just as He does from the Father (cf. John 15:26). He is Christ's agent for keeping in touch with the affairs of the world, as the participial phrase *apestalmenoi eis pasan tēn gēn* ("sent into all the earth") suggests.

᾽Αποστέλλω (*Apostellō,* "I send"), a keyword in the gospel of John (e.g., John 20:21, 22) (Sweet), means to send as an official representative (Charles). Because *apestalmenoi* ("sent") agrees in gender with *ophthalmous* ("eyes"), it is sometimes taken to mean that the eyes have been sent out into all the earth.[66] Zech. 4:10, the OT source of this picture, favors this (Charles). Yet the present context supports so strongly the sending forth of the seven spirits as agents of divine providence that it is better to take the words in a slightly different sense from that in Zechariah (Charles). So the participial agreement with its antecedent is according to sense rather than strictly grammatical.[67] The Holy Spirit is Christ's agent for assimilating what is going on throughout the whole world, and this relationship is represented symbolically in the imposing picture of the Lamb in the throne room.

5:7 After describing the Lamb's position and appearance, John records the transfer of the scroll from the Father to the Lamb: καὶ ἦλθεν καὶ εἴληφεν ἐκ τῆς δεξιᾶς τοῦ καθημένου ἐπὶ τοῦ θρόνου (*kai ēlthen kai eilēphen ek tēs dexias tou kathēmenou epi tou thronou,* "and He came and took [it] from the right hand of the one sitting upon the throne"). *Ēlthen kai eilēphen* ("he came and took") is another example of a Semiticism that abounds in the Greek translation of the OT (e.g., ἔρχεται . . . καὶ εἶπεν [*erchetai . . . kai eipen,* "he came . . . and said"], 1 Sam. [Kings] 20:1).[68] Though *ēlthen* ("he came") may describe the Lamb's actual advance toward the throne, the decision reached regarding His position in 5:6 renders such unnecessary. He is already

---

65. See discussion at Rev. 1:4.
66. Robertson, *Word Pictures,* 6:335.
67. Beckwith, *Apocalypse,* p. 510. Πνεύματα is neuter and ἀπεσταλμένοι is masculine. Beckwith's suggestion of having two antecedents, both "eyes" and "spirits" (ibid., pp. 510-11), is syntactically unacceptable.
68. Gustaf Dalman, *The Words of Jesus* (Minneapolis: Klock & Klock, 1981), p. 21; Charles, *Revelation,* 1:cxlviii, 143. Cf. Rev. 8:3; 17:1; 21:9 for other examples of this same Hebraism.

seated beside the Father on the throne. It is only necessary that He position Himself to accept the scroll from the Father. Such a presentation is all that is signified by *ēlthen*.

The transaction depicted in this exchange is reminiscent of Dan. 7:9-14, which describes from a slightly different perspective the ultimate triumph of Christ (Bullinger; Walvoord). By permitting the Lamb to take the scroll, the one sitting upon the throne authorizes Him in a symbolic way to execute His plan for the redemption of the world. The Lamb and only the Lamb is qualified to do this because of His victorious death on the cross and the redemption secured thereby (Johnson). In other words, the exchange of the scroll from the Father to the Lamb fulfills Rev. 1:1, "the revelation . . . which God gave Him to show" (Beckwith).

A question has come about how a lamb, an animal which has no hands, could take something from the open hand of the one on the throne. One answer resorts to the principle that scriptural symbols are not always capable of visual or artistic representation (Lee; Mounce). A preferable explanation is to postulate that at this point the Lamb may have resumed human form. He must do so at some point to enable Him to open the seals of the seven-sealed scroll (cf. 6:1, 3, 5, 7, 9, 12; 8:1) and eventually appear personally as the rider on a white horse (cf. 19:11). Possibly this transformation occurred here, though the text does not mention it, enabling Him to take the scroll from the Father.

His acceptance of the book is expressed by *eilēphen* ("took"), a perfect tense of the Greek verb λαμβάνω (*lambanō*, "I take"). Two schools of thought exist regarding the significance of this perfect tense. One says it is an intensive perfect and emphasizes the permanent results of the Lamb's receipt of the scroll. He receives the book as an abiding possession (cf. Rev. 3:3).[69] The other sees a genuinely aoristic or historical perfect. In other words, though the tense is perfect, it has the force of an aorist and simply notes the occurrence of an act without any special implications of the action (Charles; Beckwith; Lenski). The former understanding does better justice to the climactic nature of the scene, though the latter position has much to say in its favor. Beckwith notes that the aoristic use of the perfect tense of this verb is common (Beckwith, *Apocalypse*, p. 511). Others observe this same characteristic in the Pauline epistles and subapostolic literature (Rom. 5:2; 2 Cor. 1:9; 2:13; 7:5; cf. Mark 5:15) (Swete, *Apocalypse*, p. 79; Moulton, *Grammar*, 1:145; Charles, *Revelation*, 1:144;

---

69. Swete, *Apocalypse*, p. 79; A. T. Robertson, *A Grammar of the Greek New Testament in the Light of Historical Research* (Nashville: Broadman, 1934), p. 897.

BDF, par. 343). A recent study has proposed that the perfect tense for the Greek aorist is accounted for by the same Semitic influence that is evident elsewhere in the Apocalypse (Steven Thompson, *The Apocalypse and Semitic Syntax* [Cambridge: Cambridge U., 1985], p. 44). On the other hand, most traditional evidence for taking the perfect in an aoristic sense comes from writings outside the Apocalypse. Such does not necessarily apply to the style of this book. As already discussed at Rev. 3:3, a good case can be made for distinguishing the perfect from the aorist sense. This is especially true here where the very next verse uses an aorist of the same verb (cf. ἔλαβεν, 5:8). The special contribution of the perfect here comes by taking it as a dramatic use of the tense. This offers a more vivid picture (cf. also 7:13, 14; 8:5; 11:17; 19:3) (Lee, "Revelation," 4:567; Robertson, *Word Pictures*, 6:335). What occurs here is a dramatic description of a transaction that affects the future course of the world including all mankind. It must be construed in as vivid and realistic a way as possible. Attributing the full force to the perfect tense of *eilēphen* best accomplishes this objective.

5:8 This momentous transfer of the scroll evokes an overwhelming response from the special orders of angelic creation in heaven: καὶ ὅτε ἔλαβεν[70] τὸ βιβλίον, τὰ τέσσαρα ζῷα καὶ οἱ εἴκοσι τέσσαρες πρεσβύτεροι ἔπεσαν ἐνώπιον τοῦ ἀρνίου, ἔχοντες ἕκαστος κιθάραν καὶ φιάλας χρυσᾶς γεμούσας θυμιαμάτων, αἵ εἰσιν αἱ προσευχαὶ τῶν ἁγίων (*kai hote elaben to biblion ta tessara zǭa kai hoi eikosi tessares presbyteroi epesan enōpion tou arniou, echontes hekastos kitharan kai phialas chrysas gemousas thymiamatōn, hai eisin hai proseuchai tōn hagiōn*, "and when He took the scroll, the four living beings and the twenty-four elders fell before the Lamb, each one having a harp and golden bowls full of incense, which is the prayers of the saints").

This verse begins a demonstration caused by the thrill of satisfaction over Christ's worthiness to receive the scroll and open its seals (Moffatt). When the Lamb took the book, the four living beings and the twenty-four elders fell[71] before Him in worship (Swete). His taking of the scroll marks the initiation of proceedings to convert its contents into reality and eventually usher in the promised kingdom,

---

70. The aorist ἔλαβεν resumes the tense of ordinary narration (Swete, *Apocalypse*, p. 79).
71. The falling down (ἔπεσαν) of these angelic beings depicts the awful solemnity of the occasion (Smith, *Revelation*, p. 114). In 4:10, the 24 elders fall before the one sitting upon the throne and worship the one who lives forever and ever. In 5:14, only the elders fall in worship. In 7:11, all the angels fall before the throne on their faces and worship God. In 11:16, the 24 fall upon their faces before God and worship Him. In 19:4, the 24 and the four living beings fall and worship God who sits upon the throne.

the determined opposition of all foes notwithstanding. This is more than sufficient to evoke overflowing praise from this heavenly company (Lenski).

A further expression expands upon the way the twenty-four elders express their worship: *echontes hekastos kitharan kai phialas chrysas gemousas thymiamatōn* ("each one having a harp and golden bowls full of incense"). These words apply to the elders alone, though it is possible grammatically that the masculine participle *echontes* ("having") incorporates the neuter *zōa* ("living beings") also. The fact is that the details of the following description are not appropriate to the living beings. To see them as possessing harps and bowls is unnatural, and to attribute to them priestly functions ignores the priestly function that is distinctive to the elders (Swete; Charles; Lenski).

The musical instrument of the elders, *kitharan* ("a harp"), is the traditional one associated with psalmody in the OT. It, like the lyre, is associated with joy and gladness (cf. 1 Chron. 25:1, 6; 2 Chron. 29:25; Pss. 71:22; 92:3; 149:3) (Swete; Bullinger). It also is regularly connected with prophecy (cf. 1 Sam. 10:5; 1 Chron. 25:3; Ps. 49:4). More than any other musical instrument, the harp is employed in Scripture in direct praise and worship of God (Scott). Later in the Apocalypse, it is used to describe celestial music in 14:2 and 15:2 (Swete; Ladd).

The other vehicles of worship employed by the elders are "golden bowls" (*phialas chrysas*). Φιάλη (*Phialē*, "bowl") ordinarily depicted a small slender bottle with a narrow neck, but the article referred to here was used for offering incense and must have been a container with a large open mouth. The English words *bowl* and *saucer* better represent the present idea.[72] Golden bowls were the kinds of receptacles that belonged to the OT altar (cf. Zech. 14:20). The LXX uses *phialē* frequently to name vessels found in the Tabernacle and the Temple (e.g., Ex. 27:3; Num. 4:14; 2 Chron. 4:21 [22]) (Bullinger).

The bowls were full of incense (*gemousas thymiamatōn*). The use of incense in this setting resorts to anthropomorphism to describe the worship of heaven. The reference is to the Hebrew ritual where efficacy of an offering as acceptable comes only when it was accompanied by incense. This symbolized the sweet odor of prayer rising to God (Beckwith). Here it is a symbol of the prayers of the saints, as in Ps. 141:2 and Luke 1:10 (Swete; Charles). In OT worship the offering of incense was the prerogative of the priest (cf. Num. 16:6, 7) (Ford).

One proposal has *hai eisin hai proseuchai tōn hagiōn* ("which is

---

72. Lange, *Revelation*, p. 159; Henry George Liddell and Robert Scott, *A Greek-English Lexicon*, 9th ed. (Oxford: Clarendon, 1940), p. 1930.

the prayers of the saints") as a gloss that was not a part of the text of 5:8 originally. It is said to interfere with the purely heavenly nature of the present scene by inserting prematurely an element that is earthly (cf. 5:13).[73] It is argued that this scene is one of praise, not of prayer, and that prayer for a speedy accomplishment of God's will regarding the kingdom is out of place (Beckwith). For such reasons, the claim is that this relative clause is imported from 8:3 (Charles; Beckwith).

This proposed gloss misses the tendency of John to take earthly realities into account when dealing with heavenly scenes (Sweet). Besides this, it is yet to be established that these are the prayers of saints on earth rather than in heaven. Subsequent discussion of v. 8 will show the latter to be quite a viable option. Because of the extreme subjectivity of the arguments favoring a gloss and because no manuscript evidence supports the omission of these words, it is far better to understand them not as a later addition, but as originally penned by the author at the time of writing (Lenski).

This relative clause serves to identify the symbolism of *thymiamatōn* ("incense"). Though in gender the relative pronoun *hai* ("which") agrees with *phialas* ("bowls"), it has *thymiamatōn* as its antecedent. This is the natural sense dictated by the context. The feminine gender of the pronoun *hai* is explained by its attraction to the gender of the feminine predicate nominative of the relative clause *hai proseuchai* ("the prayers"). Prayers of saints are elsewhere symbolized this way (cf. Ps. 141:2) (Swete; Charles). The fragrant smoke of incense ascending from a worshiper or an altar was cited widely in ancient times as a natural picture of prayer ascending from earth to heaven (Moffatt). The elders' possession of bowls of incense recalls the view of Judaism that angels were carriers of the prayers of men.[74] Rev. 8:3 resorts to this function of angels in connection with human prayer also (Beckwith).

It has been suggested, without specific support, that only the general prayers of the saints are in view here (Swete). The grounds are better for seeing them as specific prayers of saints from this future time of trial—prayers that seek the sending forth of judgment and the inauguration of Christ's kingdom (cf. Luke 18:7-8).[75] The connection of similar prayers with the vindication of martyrs of this future time in 8:3-5 argues for such specificity. A reference to the

---

73. Beckwith, *Apocalypse*, p. 512. Moffatt parallels this to another gloss found in 19:8b, τὸ γὰρ βύσσινον τὰ δικαιώματα τῶν ἁγίων ἐστίν ("Revelation," 5:385).

74. Rienecker, *Linguistic Key*, p. 825.

75. Beckwith, *Apocalypse*, p. 512; William R. Newell, *The Book of Revelation* (Chicago: Moody, 1935), pp. 97, 99. See the Excursus on the Imprecatory Prayers of the Apocalypse at the end of this volume.

coming reign of the saints in 5:10 lends support from the immediate context (Johnson). In 6:10, the martyrs petition God for His judgment on their murderers. This adds to the case for restricting these prayers to specific goals of vindication (Johnson).

Who then are the saints (*tōn hagiōn*), the holy ones whom God has separated to Himself through Christ, the Spirit, and the gospel, the ones who offer these prayers? Are these the saints down through the ages, as some contend (Swete; Charles; Ladd)? This certainly is the sense of *tōn hagiōn* throughout the NT (e.g., 2 Cor. 1:1; Phil. 1:1) and, some would say, throughout Revelation too (cf. Rev. 8:3, 4; 11:18; 13:7, 9, 10; 14:12; 16:6; 17:6; 18:20, 24; 19:8; 20:9; 22:21) (Beckwith; Ladd; Johnson). This would seem to be especially true in Rev. 11:18; 16:6; 18:20, 24 where the designation is associated with the prophets and the apostles (Ladd). The problem with this broad definition of saints is that the saints from all ages are now in heaven, and praise rather than prayer for a specific need is what concerns them (Scott). With saints in heaven who will have been a part of this future period of trouble on earth, as these saints appear to be (cf. 6:9-11), the case is different. Having been martyred by the enemies of God, they have special cause to pray for vindication while the period progresses. The Apocalypse describes a witnessing company of saints on earth during the apocalyptic outpouring of wrath (cf. 12:17; 13:7-10) who will be objects of the beast's persecution. These will be the ones who cry out to God for vindication after their martyrdom (Scott). The symbol of their prayers in this scene, preparatory to the opening of the seven seals, furnishes a hint as to the part these prayers will play once the period symbolized by the seals begins.

5:9 The song prompted by the transfer of the scroll to the Lamb is full and enlightening: καὶ ᾄδουσιν ᾠδὴν καινὴν λέγοντες, Ἄξιος εἶ λαβεῖν τὸ βιβλίον καὶ ἀνοῖξαι τὰς σφραγῖδας αὐτοῦ (*kai ạdousin ọdēn kainēn legontes, Axios ei labein to biblion kai anoixai tas sphragidas autou*, "and they sang a new song, saying, 'You are worthy to take the scroll and to open its seals'"). The first part of the song declares the worthiness of the Lamb to acquire the scroll and divulge and implement its contents.

Before amplifying the song itself, however, one must identify those who sing. The plural subject of the verb *ạdousin* ("they sang"[76])

---

76. The tense of ᾄδουσιν is present, but is best rendered by an English past tense because this is a historical use of the present tense necessitated by the verb's parallelism with the aorist ἔπεσαν (5:8) (Moffatt, "Revelation," 5:386; Lenski, *Revelation*, p. 205). Another explanation of the present tense as expressing the continual nature of the singing, the ongoing task of the elders (Alford, *Greek Testament*, 4:609; Charles, *Revelation*, 1:146), is unconvincing. The historical present lends vividness to the narrative. For

could be the twenty-four elders only, or it could include both the four living beings and the twenty-four elders. Limiting it to the elders only has in its favor the limitation of the *echontes* ("having") phrase of v. 8 to the elders alone (Mounce). Since the living beings have no harps, it is observed, they have nothing for musical accompaniment as the elders do (Charles). This limitation, however, overlooks the possibly parenthetical nature of the *echontes* phrase at the end of v. 8 (Mounce) and the already-demonstrated capability of the four living beings (cf. 4:8). The most natural sense accepts *ạdousin* as having the same subject as the verb of the first half of the compound sentence, *epesan* ("they fell") (5:8). This indicates that there were twenty-eight singers, four living beings and twenty-four elders. The number increases to include all creation by the end of the chapter (cf. 5:13) (Johnson).

The "new song" (*ọdēn kainēn*) sung by this heavenly chorus was originally a song of praise inspired by gratitude for new mercies. A song thus named is mentioned six times in the Psalms (Pss. 33:3; 40:3; 96:1; 98:1; 144:9; 149:1), but in the "new song" of Isa. 42:10, the words have fuller content, corresponding to the deeper sense of "new things" in Isa. 42:9. That deeper sense is that however great the glories of things in the past, those will be dim in comparison to the splendor of things to come. The new song of v. 9 belongs to this new cycle (Charles). This is a song composed especially for a great occasion, one celebrating the redemption of the saints (Swete). Earlier songs in Revelation 4 have celebrated God as the creator (Ladd). Now the divine cause has entered a new stage, calling for a new celebration (cf. Rev. 14:3) (Beckwith). *Kainēn* ("new") in the Apocalypse signals something regarding the quality of a thing, not new in reference to time (Charles). The temporal connotation would have been conveyed by νέος (*neos*, "new"). This is the description of a song that is new in nature, different from the usual, impressive, better than the old, and superior in value.[77]

The first word of the song, *axios* ("worthy"), captures the theme of the whole song, the worthiness of the Lamb to receive the scroll and open its seals (cf. 5:4-5).[78] It is significant that here Christ is addressed as worthy in the same manner as the Father was in 4:11 (*axios ei*, "You are worthy") (cf. also 5:12) (Sweet). He who takes the

---

an example of this use of the present tense in the close context, see λέγει in 5:5 and the comments there.

77. Johannes Behm, "καινός, καινότης, κ. τ. λ.," in *TDNT*, 3 (1966):447.
78. The infinitive λαβεῖν is used as a modifier of the adjective ἄξιος, telling the aspect of worthiness that is in view (H. E. Dana and Julius R. Mantey, *A Manual Grammar of the Greek New Testament* [New York: Macmillan, 1927], p. 219; Rienecker, *Linguistic Key*, p. 825).

scroll and puts its contents into effect exercises the divine function of judgment and sovereignty. He too is God (Beasley-Murray).

The reason for the Lamb's declared worthiness is expressed in a twofold manner. The first part is the remainder of v. 9: ὅτι ἐσφάγης καὶ ἠγόρασας τῷ θεῷ *ἐν τῷ αἵματί σου ἐκ πάσης φυλῆς καὶ γλώσσης καὶ λαοῦ καὶ ἔθνους (hoti esphagēs kai ēgorasas tō theō en tō haimati sou ek pasēs phylēs kai glōssēs kai laou kai ethnous, "'because You were slain and have redeemed for God with Your blood [some] from every tribe and tongue and people and nation'")*. This deals with the payment of the price of redemption and justifies the ascription of worthiness just given (Bullinger; Lenski). The aorist indicatives *esphagēs* ("You were slain") and *ēgorasas* ("You have redeemed") look back to the once-for-all action of the work at Calvary (Charles; Lenski; Morris). The former verb also describes the death of Christ in vv. 6 and 12 of this chapter as well as in Rev. 13:8. In Rev. 6:9 and 18:24, it refers to the death of Christian martyrs (Swete; Charles). The latter verb relates that through His death Christ has purchased the faithful for God by the shedding of His blood. Paul and Peter also look at salvation as a matter of purchase (cf. 1 Cor. 6:20; 7:23; Gal. 3:13; 1 Pet. 1:18-19; 2 Pet. 2:1). Since the background of the term is the purchasing of slaves in a market place, the term may look back to the Christian's release from the bondage of sin to allow the redeemed to become ἅγιοι (*hagioi*, "saints") (Swete; Charles; Ladd; Hailey). This meaning finds additional support in noting that the passover lamb was sacrificed to provide for the forgiveness of Israel's sins, suggesting the same function of the Lamb in this chapter (Beasley-Murray). This is also the sense usually given to redemption by Paul and Peter.[79]

Yet the question is whether the broader context of Revelation limits this redemption to that from sin alone or expands the redemption to include also the eschatological aspects detailed later in the book. The latter appears to be the case. This is a redemption from *all* hostile power (Charles). The songs of redemption in 14:2-3 and 15:2-4 pertain to redemption from the forces of the beast (Sweet). Furthermore, the immediate context speaks of an emancipation that results in the creation of a new people of God to rule upon the earth (cf. 5:10) (Beasley-Murray).

The Person for whose benefit the purchase was made is none other than God Himself, as *tō theō* ("for God") indicates.[80] Those purchased are destined for His service. As in 1:5, *en tō haimati sou* ("with

---

79. Robertson, *Word Pictures*, 6:336.
80. Swete, *Apocalypse*, p. 81. The dative τῷ θεῷ is a dative of advantage.

Your blood") shows the means whereby the redemption was accomplished. The cost of the purchase was the blood of the Lamb.[81]

The redeemed ones come from every part of the human race. *Ek pasēs phylēs kai glōssēs kai laou kai ethnous* ("[some] from every tribe and tongue and people and nation") indicates that the number includes some from every conceivable background (Lenski). Yet the expression is not all-inclusive. It does not attribute the same universal scope to the redemptive power of Christ's death as 1 John 2:2 does (Swete; Charles). The expression is partitive, i.e., only part of the total number actually enjoy the benefits of that death. The benefits of Christ's redemptive work must be appropriated by placing faith in Him.

The four terms *pasēs phylēs kai glōssēs kai laou kai ethnous* occur five times in Revelation (cf. 7:9; 11:9; 13:7; 14:6),[82] but never in the same order as here. The origin of the expression is the prophecy of Daniel (cf. Dan. 3:4, 7, 29; 5:19; 6:25; 7:14) (Charles). The enumeration includes representatives of every nationality, without distinction of race, geographical location, or political persuasion (Swete). A suggestion that the list be limited to redeemed Jews only or redeemed Gentiles only (Ford) misses the breadth intended. This is the totality of humanity among which the Jews have been scattered (Smith). In perceiving the universal thrust of the words, some have refrained from seeking distinctive meanings for the individual terms (Alford; Mounce). This too is a mistake because the individual reference of each word must be allowed for. Behind *phylēs* ("tribe") is the idea of the same descent. It is a group belonging to the same clan and united by family lineage (Lenski; Hailey). People speaking the same language are intended in *glōssēs* ("tongue") (cf. Acts 2:4, 6, 8, 11) (Lenski; Hailey). *Laou* ("people") unites a people of the same race or stock (Hailey) or possibly of the same interests (Lenski). The group indicated by *ethnous* ("nation") is one bound together by political unity (Lenski) or perhaps, more broadly, by habits, customs, and peculiarities.[83] People of every lineage, language, race, and political orientation are represented in this broad company of the beneficiaries of Christ's redemption.

---

81. Ibid.; Robertson, *Historical Research*, p. 589; Charles, *Revelation*, 1:147; Lenski, *Revelation*, p. 206.
82. Similar combinations of four terms are found in 10:11 and 17:15, with βασιλεῦσιν substituted for φυλῆς in 10:11 and ὄχλοι substituted for the same word in 17:15.
83. Hermann Cremer, *Biblico-Theological Lexicon of New Testament Greek*, trans. William Urwick (Edinburgh: T. & T. Clark, 1895), p. 227.

5:10 The second part of the twofold reason for the ascription of worthiness to the Lamb comes in a sketch of the benefits accruing to the redeemed: καὶ ἐποίησας αὐτοὺς τῷ θεῷ ἡμῶν βασιλείαν καὶ ἱερεῖς, καὶ *βασιλεύσουσιν ἐπὶ τῆς γῆς (*kai epoiēsas autous tọ theọ hēmōn basileian kai hiereis, kai basileusousin epi tēs gēs,* "and You made them a kingdom and priests to our God, and they shall reign on the earth").

A further result of the Lamb's sacrifice is the establishment[84] of the redeemed as a kingdom and priests: *kai epoiēsas autous tọ theọ hēmōn basileian kai hiereis* ("and You made them a kingdom and priests to our God"). The threefold occurrence of this theme in Revelation (cf. also Rev. 1:6; 20:6) indicates that talk about such a spiritual heritage was common parlance among Christians of John's day (Swete). As God's possession,[85] the redeemed will not merely be God's people over whom He reigns, but will also share God's rule in the coming millennial kingdom (cf. 1 Cor. 4:8; 6:3) (Charles; Ladd). This kingdom is the goal toward which the program of God is moving as emphasized by *basileusousin* ("they shall reign") later in v. 10 (cf. Rev. 20:4). The idea of priesthood found in *hiereis* ("priests") means full and immediate access into God's presence for the purpose of praise and worship (Ladd). It also includes the thought of priestly service to God (Mounce). Though believers are currently viewed as a royal priesthood (1 Pet. 2:5, 9; cf. Ex. 19:6), this is only preliminary to the fullness of the way they will function alongside Christ in the millennial kingdom.[86]

Kai basileusousin epi tēs gēs ("and they shall reign on the earth") explains more fully the earlier *basileian* ("kingdom"). The fact that believers will serve as reigning powers means that they will be the equivalent of kings (Charles; Beckwith). Spelled out more particularly in 20:4 regarding the millennial kingdom and in 22:5 regarding the eternal state, they will join with Christ in His continual reign following His second advent to the earth. This all stems from the epoch-determining redemptive work of the Lamb.

5:11 *Universal tribute to the worthy Lamb.* A fourth occurrence of καὶ εἶδον (*kai eidon,* "and I looked") signals another subsection of this vision of the throne room in Revelation 4-5. This one begins with a sweeping expression that includes all levels of heavenly angelic beings: καὶ ἤκουσα φωνὴν ἀγγέλων πολλῶν κύκλῳ τοῦ θρόνου καὶ τῶν

---

84. The aorist ἐποίησας connotes finished result. As commonly the case in the heavenly songs of this book, it is proleptic, anticipating the culmination of the process being carried out at the time the song is sung (Swete, *Apocalypse,* p. 81; Beckwith, *Apocalypse,* pp. 512-13).
85. Τῷ θεῷ (5:10) has a possessive sense: "belonging to God" as His peculiar people (Beckwith, *Apocalypse,* p. 513).
86. Newell, *Revelation,* p. 13.

ζῴων καὶ τῶν πρεσβυτέρων (*kai ēkousa phōnēn angelōn pollōn kyklǭ tou thronou kai tōn zǭōn kai tōn presbyterōn*, "and I heard the voice of many angels around the throne and of the living beings and of the elders"). Along with his sight of this angelic host, John heard the sound they were making (*kai ēkousa phōnēn*, "and I heard the voice"). For the first time a more general company of angels designated by *angelōn pollōn* ("many angels") joins the heavenly chorus heretofore composed of only the living beings and the elders (cf. 4:8, 10-11; 5:8-9). According to *kyklǭ tou thronou* ("around the throne"), they surround the previously described throne on which the Father and the Lamb sat, an inner circle of the four living beings, and a larger circle of the twenty-four elders.[87]

The number of this combined company defies calculation: καὶ ἦν ὁ ἀριθμὸς αὐτῶν μυριάδες μυριάδων καὶ χιλιάδες χιλιάδων (*kai ēn ho arithmos autōn myriades myriadōn kai chiliades chiliadōn*, "their number was ten thousands of ten thousands and thousands of thousands"). Clearly the purpose of this parenthetical[88] expression is not to be numerically explicit, but to stipulate the extremely high number of heavenly beings joining this attribution of worthiness to the Lamb.[89] The expression is an echo of Daniel's description of the attendants of the Ancient of Days in one of his prophecies (Dan. 7:10; cf. also Ps. 68:17-18) (Sweet).

The sequence that places the larger number, *myriades myriadōn* ("ten thousands of ten thousands"), before the smaller one, *chiliades chiliadōn* ("thousands of thousands"), is puzzling, so much so that one has suggested that it is a later addition to the text (Charles). The omission of the latter number from the Latin Vulgate and a quotation of one little-known church Father are offered in support. Yet aside from these two relatively unimpressive ancient witnesses, the words appear in every manuscript containing this section. Another suggestion has it that the reversal of sequence is without significance (Mounce), but this explanation does not account for the data of the text. It can only be hypothesized that this is a mild *hysteron proteron*.[90] The word order is deliberate and the resultant anticlimax brings even more emphasis to the expression. When ten thousand is multiplied by itself, even this does not match the number of angels involved. The leftover still comes to a figure amounting to a thousand

---

87. Lenski, *Revelation*, p. 209; Biederwolf, *Millennium Bible*, p. 565.
88. The participle λέγοντες (5:12), though nominative, resumes ἀγγέλων πολλῶν . . . καὶ τῶν ζῴων καὶ τῶν πρεσβυτέρων from the first part of v. 11, making the last half of v. 11 parenthetical (Lee, "Revelation," 4:569).
89. Arndt and Gingrich, *Lexicon*, p. 531.
90. Robertson, *Word Pictures*, 6:336.

multiplied by itself. This is an apocalyptic symbol for countless thousands of angels who lift their voices in this great doxology.[91]

5:12 The song they sing comes in v. 12: λέγοντες[92] φωνῇ μεγάλῃ, Ἄξιόν[93] ἐστιν τὸ ἀρνίον τὸ ἐσφαγμένον λαβεῖν τὴν δύναμιν καὶ πλοῦτον καὶ σοφίαν καὶ ἰσχὺν καὶ τιμήν καὶ δόξαν καὶ εὐλογίαν (*legontes phōnē megalē, Axion estin to arnion to esphagmenon labein tēn dynamin kai plouton kai sophian kai ischyn kai timēn kai doxan kai eulogian*, "saying with a loud voice, 'Worthy is the Lamb who was slain to receive the power and riches and wisdom and strength and honor and glory and blessing'"). *Legontes* ("saying") is used in 4:8, 10 and in 5:13 as well as here to introduce utterances of angels. All four appear to be songs, though only one has an explicit indication as *ǎdousin* ("they sang") to prove it. Because of this, the other three could be chants rather than songs (Mounce), but a comparison of 5:12 with 5:9-10 leads to the inevitable conclusion that both are songs. In 5:9 *legontes* is an amplification of *ǎdousin*, which is a clear reference to singing (Mounce). From this comparison it is concluded that *legontes* can include songs as well as speeches. This angelic host cannot be denied the ability to sing.

They do sing, and they do so with a loud voice (*phōnē megalē*) comparable to the one in which the strong angel issued his proclamation earlier in the chapter (cf. 5:2). Though they stand outside personal involvement in Christ's redemption, they are far from being disinterested spectators (cf. Eph. 3:10; 1 Pet. 1:12). They recognize the splendor of His sacrificial act and its infinite merit by offering a fuller doxology than the one to God the creator in 4:11 (Swete).

This doxology of the angels is phrased in the third person rather than in the second (cf. 4:11; 5:9): *axion estin* ("worthy is"). It is thus addressed to all those who sustain a relationship to the Lamb that they may register agreement with the thrust of the doxology (Lenski). The analogy of other doxologies shows the meaning not to be that God has given Christ the seven capacities and powers in the following list, but it is rather that Christ is worthy to receive adoration for these things that He already possesses (Beckwith).

The slain Lamb is not only worthy to take the seven-sealed scroll

---

91. Lenski, *Revelation*, p. 210; Rienecker, *Linguistic Key*, p. 825.
92. Λέγοντες is nominative even though its antecedents in v. 11*a* are genitive. After the parenthesis of v. 11*b*, it is as though John resumed his thought with words such as "and the angels lifted up their voice, saying" (Lee, "Revelation," 4:569).
93. The gender of the adjective ἄξιος is neuter because of grammatical agreement with the neuter noun ἀρνίον, though some MSS have a masculine ἄξιος (Robertson, *Word Pictures*, 6:337). Support for the masculine reading is negligible, however.

and open its seals (cf. 5:4-5, 7), but according to this heavenly ascription He is also worthy to receive recognition for a complex[94] of qualities composed of seven parts: *dynamin* ("power"), *plouton* ("riches"), *sophian* ("wisdom"), *ischyn* ("strength"), *timēn* ("honor"), *doxan* ("glory"), and *eulogian* ("blessing"). The repetition of *kai* ("and") between each member of the series gives a kind of solemn dignity to each word even though the group is viewed as a single complex expression.[95] It requires each of the seven features of the Lamb's worthiness to be reflected upon separately (Bullinger).

Dynamin brings out the sense of omnipotent power (Lenski). It differs from χράτος (*kratos*, "strength") in its emphasis upon Christ's ability, while the other word depicts the presence and actual use of force.[96] This word occurs along with three others in this series, *plouton*, *ischyn*, and *doxa*, in the similar doxology of 1 Chron. 29:11-12 [LXX], the earliest known heptad of such titles of honor (Swete; Charles). *Plouton* includes not just spiritual wealth, but also unconditional wealth in all realms as befitting an all-sufficient God.[97] The term is especially appropriate for Christ in light of 2 Cor. 8:9 and Eph. 3:8 (Morris). His *sophian* designates the attribute of God that demonstrates itself in the conscious and purposeful creation and government of the world, appointing limits and goals in the execution of His will and the molding of destiny. It establishes the rule of righteousness on earth and is the moral power pervading and effecting the progress of world history.[98] To believers Christ becomes the wisdom of God (cf. 1 Cor. 1:24, 30) (Morris). Christ's *ischyn* is also divulged in earlier books of the NT (cf. Luke 11:22; Eph. 6:10; 2 Thess. 1:9) (Swete). Strength is His possession whether actively exerted or not (Lenski).

Timēn refers to the honor that is God's rightful possession.[99] Another NT writer says Christ's honor is due Him because of His sacrificial death (Heb. 2:9; cf. Phil. 2:11).[100] When associated with *doxa*, *timē* denotes a position of honor that is only one part of *doxa*. *Doxa* is

---

94. The lone article τήν at the beginning of the list governs the whole list and binds the qualities together into a single expression. Together the seven tell with completeness what the Lamb is worthy to receive (Charles, *Revelation*, 1:149; Beckwith, *Apocalypse*, p. 513).
95. Robertson, *Historical Research*, p. 427. Referred to as *polysyndeton*, this practice enhances rhetorical emphasis by producing the impression of extensiveness and abundance. It gives the impression of an exhaustive summary (BDF, par. 460 [3]).
96. Wilhelm Michaelis, "χράτος," in *TDNT*, 3 (1966):905-6.
97. Alford, *Greek Testament*, 4:610; Düsterdieck, *Revelation*, p. 215.
98. Cremer, *Lexicon*, p. 871.
99. Arndt and Gingrich, *Lexicon*, p. 825.
100. Morris, *Revelation*, p. 101.

the higher term, connoting "divine and heavenly radiance," the loftiness and majesty of God and even the being of God, the mode of His being.[101] In regard to Christ, *doxa* is elsewhere associated with Him in His incarnation (John 1:14; Heb. 2:9). *Eulogian* is "blessing" or "praise," that quality of Christ evoking man's thankful response for benefits received (cf. εὐχαριστίαν [*eucharistian*, "thanks"], 4:9). It is what makes Him worthy of the ascription of praise. It creates in the creature a willingness, unaccompanied by coercion, to return blessing for blessing conferred. A distinction between the actual offering of praise for blessings received and the acknowledgment of what He possesses in Himself, His intrinsic praiseworthiness, is clearer in the similar doxology of 1 Chron. 29:11-13 (Alford; Beckwith).

Two explanations have been offered for the word order of this doxology. One sees the seven attributes as composing two divisions, one of four and one of three, with the first four being objective, those qualities that the Lamb assumes, and the last three being subjective, human recognition of the Lamb (Charles; Lenski). The reasoning is that His victorious death has earned Him honor and glory and praise and brought Him the power to bestow incalculable riches on His people and to solve the mystery of the future (Moffatt). This arrangement agrees with the sequence of power-related words producing benefit elsewhere in the Apocalypse (11:17) and in the NT (Eph. 1:18-19; 2 Cor. 3:7-8; 4:4) (Moffatt). A serious deficiency in this suggested arrangement, however, is the governance of the entire series by one article, *tēn*. This offers strong reason to see all seven qualities as belonging intrinsically to Christ rather than assigning some of them to the expressions of a human response to Christ. Even the last item, *eulogian*, as the acknowledgement of what He possesses in Himself, is distinguishable, at least in thought, from what the creature returns to Him (Beckwith).

The other explanation for this doxology's peculiar word order accounts for it by noting the writer's desire to emphasize the contrast between *to arnion to esphagmenon*, which is expressive of weakness, and the first four terms in the list, which focus on power. By putting these items at the very beginning, the contrast is enhanced (Charles). This approach avoids segregating into categories a list that is unified by a single article at the beginning. It is also more sensitive to the double emphasis of the chapter on the contrast between the Lion and the Lamb, between power and meekness. The more usual sequence in doxologies addressed to God puts "honor," "glory," and "blessing" toward the beginning (Charles), but here the "power" terms are put forward to emphasize the power of the Lamb. Although it is true that

---

101. Gerhard Kittel, "δοκέω, δόξα, κ. τ. λ.," in *TDNT*, 2 (1965):237.

the Lamb is about to assume this power through opening the seals (cf. 11:17) (Charles), this doxology is offered in recognition of the power He already possesses (Bullinger; Charles; Beckwith).

5:13 With the conclusion of the angelic doxology, the company of singers now broadens to incorporate the whole creation: καὶ πᾶν κτίσμα ὃ ἐν τῷ οὐρανῷ καὶ ἐπὶ τῆς γῆς καὶ ὑποκάτω τῆς γῆς καὶ ἐπὶ τῆς θαλάσσης, καὶ τὰ ἐν αὐτοῖς πάντα, ἤκουσα λέγοντας[102] (*kai pan ktisma ho en tō ouranō kai epi tēs gēs kai hypokatō tēs gēs kai epi tēs thalassēs, kai ta en autois panta, ēkousa legontas,* "and every creature that is in heaven and on the earth and under the earth and on the sea, and all things in them, I heard saying"). This song by all creation climaxes the description of the throne room in chapters 4-5. Revelation 4 focused upon the one sitting upon the throne, and Rev. 5:1-12 on the Lamb. The song and description of 5:13-14 conjoin the glory of the one on the throne and that of the Lamb. The worship offered to both is united in one great closing doxology acclaimed by all created things throughout the entire universe.[103]

The threefold division of creation of Rev. 5:3 is now a fourfold one through the addition of the sea (*epi tēs thalassēs*). The gathering is no longer just representative; it is exhaustive, not one creature being omitted (Swete; Charles). *Ktisma* ("creation") in the NT is invariably a concrete term referring either to "a creature" or "a created thing."[104] In the present passage it clearly refers to intelligent animated creation (Alford). It is hardly possible, for example, that *pan ktisma ho en tō ouranō* ("every creature that is in heaven") could include the sun, moon, and stars or the birds of the sky (Charles). The creatures are intelligent beings who have an intellectual appreciation of God and the Lamb. Neither is it proper to limit *pan ktisma ho en tō ouranō* by excluding the living beings and elders involved in the song of 5:11-12 and in the pronouncing of "Amen" and worshiping in 5:14, though the possible antiphonal arrangement of 5:9-13 makes this appealing.[105] This would ignore the obviously intended climax by making the song nonuniversal. The chorus, being universal, must

---

102. The participle λέγοντας is masculine agreeing in sense with a personification of τὰ . . . πάντα, though some MSS have λέγοντα, which would be in grammatical agreement with τὰ . . . πάντα (Robertson, *Word Pictures*, 6:337). Its case is accusative because it functions as a modifier of an understood direct object of ἤκουσα. John hears the personified creatures when they say the words of the song (Lenski, *Revelation*, p. 212).

103. Charles, *Revelation*, 1:154. The order of Rev. 5:12-13 is the same as that of Ps. 103:20-22 where the worship of all creation follows that of angels (Moffatt, "Revelation," 5:387).

104. Swete, *Apocalypse*, p. 83; Düsterdieck, *Revelation*, p. 215; Lenski, *Revelation*, p. 211.

105. Contra Beckwith, *Apocalypse*, p. 514.

embrace all those previously mentioned (Alford). The resumptive phrase *kai ta en autois panta* ("and all things in them") lends weight to this conclusion that the living beings and elders are included among the singers (Charles).

The total expression is possibly an echo of Ps. 146:6, which speaks of God "who made heaven and earth, the sea, and all that is in them." The entirety of intelligent life in God's creation joins in, even fallen angels imprisoned "under the earth" (cf. 2 Pet. 2:4; Jude 6) and unredeemed humanity who must someday join in recognizing the preeminent qualities of God and the Lamb (cf. Phil. 2:9-11). As is the case with other heavenly songs of this book, this one is anticipatory of the great future day when no one will withhold from God His due.[106] The program of God as portrayed in the Apocalypse progresses toward this goal.

The climactic song is brief, but forceful: τῷ καθημένῳ ἐπὶ τοῦ θρόνου καὶ τῷ ἀρνίῳ ἡ εὐλογία καὶ ἡ τιμὴ καὶ ἡ δόξα καὶ τὸ κράτος εἰς τοὺς αἰῶνας τῶν αἰώνων (*tō kathēmenō epi tou thronou kai tō arniō hē eulogia kai hē timē kai hē doxa kai to kratos eis tous aiōnas tōn aiōnōn*, "'To the one sitting upon the throne and to the Lamb [be] the blessing and the honor and the glory and the might forever and ever'"). The conjunction of God and the Lamb as joint-objects of this doxology here and in Rev. 7:10 reflects the mature theological perspective of this book regarding the Person of Christ. The throne of both is one and the same, and worship offered to one is worship offered to the other (Charles). The doxology has four members, three of them being identical with the last three of the doxology of v. 12, though in a different order. The fourth member is *to kratos* ("might"), which is found in a doxology elsewhere only at Rev. 1:6. This word denotes active power in contrast to a reserve of secret strength expressed by *ischyn* ("strength") in the doxology of v. 12 which it replaces. This is also an appropriate term for God and Christ (cf. Eph. 1:19; 6:10) (Swete; Lenski).

Four articles, three occurrences of *hē* ("the") and one of *to* ("the"), individualize the four members of this doxology, in contrast to the grouping of the seven in the previous doxology under the governance of a single article (cf. 5:12). This causes each term to stand out by itself, as the same construction does in 4:11 (Swete; Lenski). The use of *kai* ("and") between each term serves further to heap up the ascriptions like a great tower of praise (Lenski). Endless blessing and honor and glory and strength belong to the one sitting upon the throne and to the Lamb. Their exaltation is not temporary. It endures infinitely

---

106. See comments about ἐποίησας (5:10) for another example of heavenly anticipation of what will be accomplished throughout creation.

as the concluding *eis tous aiōnas tōn aiōnōn* ("forever and ever") emphatically notes (Swete). With complete unanimity, the entire universe joins in the deserved acclamation.

5:14 Fittingly, the four living beings close the doxology of every creature with a solemn "Amen" of confirmation: καὶ τὰ τέσσαρα ζῷα ἔλεγον, Ἀμήν (*kai ta tessara zōa elegon, Amēn*, "and the four living beings kept saying, 'Amen'"). They pronounced the first doxology of 4:8 and now conclude the final one (Charles). They do not say it just once, but as the verb tense indicates, they keep repeating it over and over.[107] The suggestion that it was repeated after each attribute of the doxologies of 5:12-13 (Mounce) certainly adds drama to the scene, but it is only conjecture.

Amēn ("Amen") is used in more than one sense in the Apocalypse.[108] The idea that this is a "detached Amen" uttered by someone different from those voicing the doxology as in 1 Chron. 16:36 and Ps. 106:48 (Charles) perhaps misses the point that the four living beings were among those singing the doxology of v. 13. A better analysis is to classify it with the "Amens" where no change of speakers occurs, as in Rev. 1:6, 7 and frequently throughout the NT. After the vast company became silent, the four living beings voiced their complete agreement with what they along with the rest had just spoken.

The twenty-four elders terminate the whole series of praise-utterances with actions accompanied by no recorded words: καὶ οἱ πρεσβύτεροι ἔπεσαν καὶ προσεκύνησαν (*kai hoi presbyteroi epesan kai prosekynēsan*, "and the elders fell and worshiped"). This is a fresh act of homage by them. As they fell before the one sitting upon the throne in 4:10, so now they prostrate themselves in worship before Him and the Lamb. Symbolically they acknowledge their complete subjection to Them and seek to exalt Them in praise and adoration.

Additional Notes

5:1 The difficulty of conception involved in ἔσωθεν καὶ ὄπισθεν has occasioned several variations among textual sources. The only other reading with substantial support is ἔσωθεν καὶ ἔξωθεν. Besides enjoying the support of a weaker group of MSS, this latter alternative clearly arose when a scribe could not conceive of how a scroll could be written upon "inside and on the back." The precise opposite of "inside" is "outside," so he felt he was correcting someone's earlier error by changing "on the back" to "outside." "Inside and on the back" does lend itself to rational explanation, however, as the Exegesis and Exposition comments show.

---

107. Lenski, *Revelation*, p. 212. This is an iterative use of the imperfect tense.
108. See discussion of the word at Rev. 1:6.

5:4 A significant group of MSS and Fathers insert the personal pronoun ἐγώ as the subject of ἔκλαιον. What makes this reading appealing is its difficulty: in such a context as this, why would a scribe add something to make the prophet the center of attention? "And *I on my part* started to cry" takes attention away from the main figure who is about to be introduced in vv. 5-6. Here is a reading that is so difficult that it appears to be next to impossible. Because the group of sources that omits the pronoun is also respectable, the reading without ἐγώ is preferred.

5:6 A few early textual witnesses omit ἑπτά from this relative clause. Its inclusion is clearly the easier reading because of earlier references to the "seven spirits" in the Apocalypse (cf. 1:4; 3:1; 4:5), and it is difficult to explain how a scribe could omit it. Even though its omission is the harder reading, support for omission in the textual witnesses is much weaker than that of those including it. It is therefore better to conclude that ἑπτά was in the autograph.

5:9 A difficult textual issue with far-reaching implications stems from the inclusion of ἡμᾶς in the text of v. 9 either between θεῷ and ἐν, in place of τῷ θεῷ, or just before τῷ θεῷ. The position of the pronoun varies in different MSS, with stronger witnesses supporting the first and third sequences. If any one of the three readings including ἡμᾶς is correct, it would mean that those singing this song are among the redeemed. This would necessitate a reconsideration of the conclusions reached above regarding the identities of the four living beings and the twenty-four elders. Unquestionably MS support for inclusion of the pronoun is impressive, with two major uncial MSS placing it between θεῷ and ἐν. The single most reliable uncial in Revelation omits it from the text.

A number of internal factors militate against the inclusion of ἡμᾶς as part of the text of the autograph. A most obvious one is the impossibility of reconciling the first person plural with the third person plurals that are clearly the correct readings in the next verse (cf. αὐτούς and βασιλεύσουσιν in 5:10) (Beckwith). Such an abrupt switch from first person to third person renders the language of the song meaningless, so the reading must be judged as impossible. Another considerable obstacle to the inclusion of ἡμᾶς is that it would necessitate identifying the four living beings as redeemed ones. A number of commentators readily identify the twenty-four elders this way by virtue of their being the ones who sing this song. They fail to notice that the living beings are also among the singers. As observed in earlier discussion of the identity of the living beings, the case for their being among the redeemed is next to nonexistent. A third problem with including the pronoun is grammatical. Elsewhere in the Apocalypse, where John has an expression comparable to ἐκ πάσης φυλῆς καὶ γλώσσης καὶ λαοῦ καὶ ἔθνους in 5:9, he does not preface it with a pronoun as would be the case here with the inclusion (cf. 7:9; 11:9). This author uses ἐκ as a partitive genitive frequently (cf. 2:10; 3:9; 5:5, 9; 6:1; 7:9, 13; 9:13; 11:9; 13:3; 14:10; 15:7; 17:1, 2, 6 [twice], 11; 18:3; 20:12; 21:9) as is also common in other Johannine literature (e.g., John 1:41; 3:1; 6:8, 70, 71; 7:40, 50; 16:17; 2 John 4) and sometimes prefaces it with εἷς (cf. 5:5; 6:1; 7:13; 9:13; 13:3; 15:7; 17:1; 21:9; cf. also John 1:41; 6:8, 70, 71; 7:50), but never does he do so in the Apocalypse with a personal pronoun.[109] In cases where it stands alone, a pronoun such as τὶς is implied in the preposition ἐκ.

All in all, the reading that omits ἡμᾶς must be judged as correct. It is the one that as the original best accounts for how the others must have arisen.[110]

5:10 Two important uncial MSS and a few other ancient sources offer the present tense βασιλεύσουσιν as a possible reading instead of the future βασιλεύσουσιν. From one perspective, the present-tense reading has the advantage of being the harder reading, this because of the future tenses of βασιλεύω elsewhere in the book (cf. 20:6; 22:6) (Swete). A copyist with the Millennium of chapter 20 in mind would naturally change the puzzling present tense to a future, but no reason is apparent that he would change a future to a present (Sweet). From another perspective, because the song deals with what the redeemed have already been made (cf. ἐποίησας, 5:10), a present tense is the easier reading (Alford), though a futuristic use of the present tense would also harmonize with the future reign of the saints (cf. 20:4) (Johnson). Reference to a present reign, however, is highly improbable in this setting (Mounce), and the reasoning about how a scribe would react in light of Rev. 20:6 misses the point that that verse may talk about resurrected martyrs only. The present verse talks about all the redeemed (Caird). The case for the present tense is severely weakened by the fact that one of the two major MSS supporting it also has a present tense of the verb in 20:6, where it is clearly a mistake. This opens the possibility that the same scribe made the same mistake in 5:10.[111] Because this is a reign "upon the earth" (5:10) like that in 20:4, the future tense is the clear preference.

Another variant in this verse reads βασιλεύσομεν, the first person plural, rather than βασιλεύσουσιν, the third person plural. It rests upon such weak MS evidence, however, that it is not worthy of serious consideration.

---

109. Cf. Charles, *Revelation*, 1:cxxix.
110. Bruce M. Metzger, *A Textual Commentary on the Greek New Testament* (New York: United Bible Societies, 1971), p. 738.
111. Ibid.

12
The First Six Seals, "The Beginning of Birth Pains"

The source of the seven-sealed scroll is now fully described. The scene is set and the time has arrived to begin breaking the seals, one by one.

2. THE OPENING OF THE FIRST SEAL: PEACEFUL CONQUEST (6:1-2)

Translation

¹And I looked when the Lamb opened the first of the seals, and I heard one of the four living beings saying as the voice of thunder [speaks], "Come." ²And I looked, and behold, a white horse, and the one who sat upon it had a bow, and a crown was given to him, and he went forth conquering and that he might conquer.

Exegesis and Exposition

6:1 On the heels of the creationwide doxology that closes chapter 5, the action anticipated when the seven-sealed scroll first appeared, i.e., the opening of its seals (5:5), begins: καὶ εἶδον ὅτε ἤνοιξεν τὸ ἀρνίον μίαν ἐκ τῶν[1] ἑπτὰ σφραγίδων (*kai eidon hote ēnoixen to arnion*

---

1. Both occurrences of ἐκ τῶν in v. 1 are ablatives used with the preposition to denote a partitive sense, a usage quite common in the Apocalypse (A. T. Robertson, *Word Pictures in the New Testament*, 6 vols. [Nashville: Broadman, 1933], 6:339). This performs essentially the same function as the partitive genitive (Henry Barclay Swete, *The Apocalypse of St. John* [London: Macmillan, 1906], p. 85). For more details on this usage see the additional note on the textual issue in Rev. 5:9.

mian ek tōn hepta sphragidōn, "and I looked when the Lamb opened the first of the seals"). *Kai eidon* ("And I looked") marks this development as a new aspect of the vision already in progress throughout chapters 4 and 5. Yet from another perspective, the words mark the commencement of the revelation proper, the first five chapters having been introductory.[2] Revelation 1 was John's preparation to receive the information. Revelation 2-3 informed the seven churches of moral preparation necessary to avoid the horrors of "the hour of trial." Revelation 4-5 described the throne room from where the dreaded punishment was to proceed and the seven-sealed scroll in that room, which contained the divine purgings to come. Only now in chapter 6 does the revelation of those punishments begin, and along with the revelation a dramatization by way of an "advance showing" of the Lamb's implementation of those punishments against a rebellious world. After five chapters of rather elaborate preparation, "the things that must happen soon" (Rev. 1:1; 4:1) begin to unfold.

Eidon ("I looked") specifies the role of the prophet: he is to be an eyewitness of this dramatization of future events.[3] John's role is explicit only one other time in the opening of the seals, in 6:12 where the combination *kai eidon hote ēnoixen* ("and I looked when He opened") is repeated. The special attention resulting from this combination should be noted.[4] It comes here because this begins the whole seal opening process. In 6:12, it prefaces a description of the sixth seal and its far-reaching impact. As for introduction to the rest of the seals, *hote ēnoixen* ("when He opened") without *eidon* ("I looked") is used, except for the seventh seal, which substitutes *hotan* ("whenever") for *hote* ("when") (cf. 6:3, 5, 7, 9; 8:1).[5] No explicit attention is given in the other cases to John's personal observation of what transpires.

Each time, with the opening of a seal, nothing is read from the scroll (Lenski), but actions occur that unquestionably match the corresponding part of the scroll exposed through each consecutive seal.[6] The first four openings have features in common: each is preceded by an utterance from one of the four ζῷα (*zōa*, "living beings") and fol-

---

2. Swete, *Apocalypse*, p. 84; T. Randell, *Revelation*, The Pulpit Commentary, ed. H. D. Spence and Joseph S. Exell (Chicago: Wicox and Follett, n.d.), p. 182.
3. Walter Scott, *Exposition of the Revelation of Jesus Christ* (Swengel, Pa.: Bible Truth Depot, n.d.), p. 146.
4. R. C. H. Lenski, *The Interpretation of St. John's Revelation* (Columbus, Ohio: Lutheran Book Concern, 1935), p. 217.
5. Robertson, *Word Pictures*, 6:339.
6. Isbon T. Beckwith, *The Apocalypse of John* (New York: Macmillan, 1919), p. 515.

lowed by the appearance of a colored horse and his rider who has some sort of power over the earth. This puts the first four into a group that is in some ways distinct from the other three.[7]

The Lamb (*arnion*) is in the description of the throne room in Revelation 4-5. His function as the revealer commences as He opens the first seal (cf. 5:5-7) (Swete; Beckwith). He is the only one worthy to set in motion the events contained in the scroll.[8] He is the opener of each one of the seals, and in connection with the seventh one, He uses angels to blow the trumpets (8:2, 6) and pour out the bowls of wrath (15:1; 16:1) (Scott).

Mian ek tōn hepta sphragidōn could be rendered "one of the seven seals" or "the first of the seven seals." The cardinal *mian* can mean "first," though another word πρῶτος (*prōtos*) is the more common word used as an ordinal to convey this meaning (cf. Matt. 28:1).[9] The use of words that are distinctively ordinal numbers in listing the rest of the seals (6:3, 5, 7, 9, 12; 8:1) argues for the ordinal meaning here. By assigning the ordinal meaning, some have concluded that there is a special correspondence between the contents of each of the first four seals and the particular living being whose voice is heard.[10] This is plausible with the first being and his likeness to a lion whose strength may be symbolic of victory,[11] but the next three seals and living beings do not correspond.[12] The ordinal meaning "first" is correct, but no correspondence of each seal's content with the likeness of each living being is detectable.

This first seal and all those to follow should be understood in the same symbolic sense. To take any of them as a symbol of God's eternal protection of believers in Christ[13] is to be totally oblivious to the description of Rev. 5:2-7. Whereas σφραγίζω (*sphragizō*, "I seal") may signify the believer's security in some instances (cf. Eph. 1:13; 4:30), such a meaning is far removed from the context of the Apocalypse. Here the seals hold the scroll closed and indicate that its judgmental

---

7. Swete, *Apocalypse*, pp. 84-85; Alan F. Johnson, "Revelation," in *EBC*, ed. Frank E. Gaebelein (Grand Rapids: Zondervan, 1981), 12:472.
8. Robert H. Mounce, *The Book of Revelation*, NICNT (Grand Rapids: Eerdmans, 1977), p. 152.
9. Robertson, *Word Pictures*, 6:339.
10. J. Otis Yoder, cited in J. B. Smith, *A Revelation of Jesus Christ* (Scottdale, Pa.: Herald, 1961), p. 121.
11. William Lee, "The Revelation of St. John," in *The Holy Bible*, ed. F. C. Cook (London: John Murray, 1881), 4:571.
12. J. P. M. Sweet, *Revelation* (Philadelphia: Westminster, Pelican, 1979), p. 139.
13. Marvin Rosenthal, *The Pre-Wrath Rapture of the Church* (Nashville: Thomas Nelson, 1990), p. 145.

contents are a profound secret.[14] These seals denote protection from tampering and a hiding from unauthorized eyes (Lenski).

The future point at which the symbolic opening of the seals will take place has been the object of some discussion. One opinion has been that the events represented will occur before the period of trouble, often called "the Tribulation," just before Christ's return to earth.[15] A reason for this lies in the opinion that the seven seals are arranged at the outside edge of the scroll in such a manner that all must be broken before the scroll can be opened (Ladd). The equation of the seals with Matt. 24:6-14 is correct (Scott), but the placement of the events of the Matthew passage prior to the Tribulation is not. Further, as noted in earlier discussion of Rev. 5:1, the seals are not placed on the leading edge of the scroll. They are at the end of the scroll where they are visible at various points within the spiraled roll.

The opinion of the majority that places the events within the tribulation is much more convincing.[16] The happenings enumerated follow the pattern of Jesus' Olivet discourse (cf. Matthew 24-25; Mark 13; Luke 21), sometimes called the "Little Apocalypse," which He delivered on the Tuesday before His crucifixion. The similarities are so close that some venture to call that discourse the main source of the seal judgments (Charles; Beasley-Murray). Throughout apocalyptic literature, the sword, famine, pestilence, and earthquake recounted here as well as in the Olivet discourse, related to the last days (Beckwith). In Jewish and Babylonian literature, also, such an expectation of civil strife as these seals include was one of the precursors of the personal return of the Deliverer (Charles). In His teaching Jesus divided the time into two periods, the beginning of birth pangs (Matt. 24:8) and the Great Tribulation (Matt. 24:21). The former part closely parallels the first four seals in particular. So an important key in fixing the time period of the seals in this message was given by Christ some sixty-five years earlier when He taught about the future time of trial on earth.

Immediately after the opening of the seal, John heard one of the four living beings issue a summons: καὶ ἤκουσα ἑνὸς ἐκ τῶν τεσσάρων ζῴων λέγοντος ὡς *φωνὴ βροντῆς, *Ἔρχου (*kai ēkousa henos ek tōn*

---

14. R. H. Charles, *The Revelation of St. John*, 2 vols., ICC (New York: Scribner's, 1920), 1:137.
15. Scott, *Revelation*, p. 158; George E. Ladd, *A Commentary on the Revelation of John* (Grand Rapids: Eerdmans, 1972), p. 96.
16. Charles, *Revelation*, 1:64; E. W. Bullinger, *The Apocalypse* or *"The Day of the Lord"* (London: Eyre and Spottiswoode, n.d.), p. 255; Beckwith, *Apocalypse*, p. 515; Robertson, *Word Pictures*, 6:339; G. R. Beasley-Murray, *The Book of Revelation*, NCB (Grand Rapids: Eerdmans, 1978), pp. 129-30; Johnson, "Revelation," p. 472.

tessarōn zǭōn legontos hōs phōnē brontēs, Erchou, "and I heard one of the four living beings saying as the voice of thunder [speaks], 'Come'"). The place of the four living beings in the implementation of God's judgmental activity has been noted in earlier discussion (cf. 4:6). The comparison of the first being's voice also suggests a judgmental tone. *Hōs phōnē brontēs* ("as the voice of thunder [speaks]") betokens a coming storm (cf. Rev. 14:2; 19:6).[17] This is the only seal accompanied by such a voice of thunder. Βροντή (*Brontē*, "thunder") has only two occurrences in the NT outside the Apocalypse. Both are relevant to John, the author of Revelation. One is in Mark 3:17 where he and his brother James have the title "sons of thunder," apparently because of their inclination toward a stormy temperament. The other is in John's gospel and accompanies a heavenly response to Jesus' prayer (John 12:28-29). The latter is apparently indicative of a theophany, i.e., a manifestation of God. Thunder accompanied the theophany at Mt. Sinai at the giving of the Torah (Ex. 20:18).[18] A comparable manifestation is signaled by the thunderous voice of this living being.

Erchou ("Come") is a present imperative that states the summons. The strictly linear force of the present tense should not be pressed here.[19] "Keep on coming" would be inappropriate for this context. Ἔρχομαι (*Erchomai*, "I come") is a common word for making a public appearance, especially in reference to a divine epiphany. Here its association is with the manifestation of the wrath of God (Ford).

Three objects of the summons have been proposed: John,[20] Christ,[21] and the first horseman.[22] John as a possibility rests strongly on a textual variant that adds "and see" to the summons and upon the καὶ εἶδον (*kai eidon*, "and I looked") that begins v. 2. Besides resting on a weak textual foundation,[23] this interpretation does not say where John was to come. He was already in heaven (in the spirit, that is). Was he to cross the glassy sea and come to the throne itself? Probably

---

17. John F. Walvoord, *The Revelation of Jesus Christ* (Chicago: Moody, 1966), p. 124.
18. J. Massyngberde Ford, *Revelation*, vol. 38 of AB (Garden City, N.Y.: Doubleday, 1975), p. 97.
19. Robertson, *Word Pictures*, 6:339.
20. Albert Barnes, *The Book of Revelation* (New York: Harper, 1851), p. 137; Randell, p. 183; Walvoord, *Revelation*, p. 125.
21. Henry Alford, *The Greek Testament*, 4 vols. (London: Longmans, Green, 1903), 4:613; Swete, *Apocalypse*, p. 85.
22. Robertson, *Word Pictures*, 6:340; James Moffatt, "The Revelation of St. John the Divine," in *The Expositor's Greek Testament*, ed. W. Robertson Nicoll (Grand Rapids: Eerdmans, n.d.), 5:388; Mounce, *Revelation*, p. 152; Ladd, *Revelation*, p. 96.
23. See Additional Notes for a discussion of the evidence.

not (Alford). Such a meaning would have added an adverb such as ὧδε (hōde, "here"). Erchomai alone can hardly carry the sense of "draw near" (Alford).

The second view says Christ is the object because He is addressed by the same summons in 22:17, 20 (Alford; Swete). In Revelation the word always refers to Christ's coming, it is argued (Swete; Ford). This view is quite superficial, however, in its disregard of the immediate context. Most of its supporters base their conclusion on the erroneous assumption that the living beings represent nature and are calling for the redemption of creation through the coming of Christ (cf. Rom. 8:22-23). These present scenes are unrelated to that final renewal, however (Beckwith). The clear meaning is a summons to the first horseman. The response to the command of v. 1 is the immediate appearance of a white horse in v. 2. The same is true with the other three commands in vv. 4, 5, and 8. The context demands that all four of the summonses be addressed to the horsemen and their horses (Beckwith).

6:2 In response to the summons of the first living being, a white horse with its rider appears: καὶ εἶδον, καὶ ἰδοὺ ἵππος λευκός, καὶ ὁ καθήμενος ἐπ' αὐτὸν ἔχων τόξον (kai eidon, kai idou hippos leukos, kai ho kathēmenos ep' auton echōn toxon, "And I looked, and behold, a white horse, and the one who sat upon it had[24] a bow"). The familiar kai eidon ("and I looked") introduces another development in the action. At this stage it prompts a question about what John saw after seeing the first seal broken and hearing the first summons. Possibly it was the first of a series of pictures drawn on the newly opened scroll, but nothing in the text suggests some kind of graphic representation. Possibly it was writing on the scroll that John read or had read to him, but nothing is stated about his reading from the scroll[25] or hearing something read to him (Lee). The statement that he saw (kai eidon) only suggests a scenic representation or dramatic production in which a succession of horses was introduced, possibly accompanied by written statements in the scroll of the events referred to, though a reading of a written statement is never referred to.[26] Rather than reading from the scroll, the seer witnesses a prophetic event enacted in vision. This dramatic exhibition powerfully reinforces the prophecy given. If this connection between scroll and visual demonstration did not exist, the whole imagery of the scroll on the hand of

---

24. Ἔχων, though it is a present participle, functions as a finite verb here. The literal sense obtained by understanding a form of εἰμί with it to constitute a periphrastic tense-form is "was having," but it reads more smoothly as "had."

25. Robertson, *Word Pictures*, 6:339.

26. Barnes, *Revelation*, p. 137.

God (5:1) and the process of breaking the seals would have no significance. It would only confuse the ongoing revelation (Beckwith). As the Lamb breaks the seals, one by one, He reveals the contents and symbolism to John in a vivid and dramatic fashion.[27] The startling character of this new development in the vision is reflected in the addition of *kai idou* ("and behold") (cf. also 6:5, 8) (Walvoord).

The imagery of the four horses in 6:1-8 is similar to Zech. 1:7-11, and the afflictions resemble those predicted in Jer. 14:12; 24:10; 42:17. In Zechariah, special meanings of the colors of the horses are not as apparent as they are here in Revelation. In Zechariah, the horses are sent to patrol the earth, but in Revelation, their release brings great disaster to the earth (Mounce). As is often the case (cf. Job 39:19-25; Ps. 76:5-6; Prov. 21:31), horses are connected with war and conquest,[28] and horsemen are associated with an omen of the end (Moffatt).

In Zech. 6:2-3 the horses are red, black, white, and grizzled or "dappled" in color. Here the first horse is white.[29] A popular suggestion has been that white is a symbol for victory, as evidenced in the practices of both the Romans and Persians.[30] The horse with its rider is said to represent brilliant, unchecked, yet almost bloodless victory.[31] It must be granted that this first horse is associated with victory, as evident in the words νικῶν (*nikōn*, "conquering") and νικήσῃ (*nikēsē*, "he might conquer") later in v. 2, but the question is whether the horse's color is intended to convey a meaning that is otherwise present in the verse. This is improbable. A better proposal is that white carries the primary symbolism of righteousness and holiness.[32] This is certainly more consistent with usage of the color throughout the Apocalypse where it is constantly associated with Christ's righteousness or with His spiritual victory (cf. 1:14; 2:17; 3:4-5, 18; 4:4; 6:11; 7:9, 13-14; 14:14; 19:11, 14; 20:11) (Ladd; John-

---

27. Robertson, *Word Pictures*, 6:339.
28. Ibid.; Scott, *Revelation*, p. 147; Lenski, *Revelation*, p. 220.
29. Λευκός refers to almost anything that has the general color of white, so the first horse could be gray or white (Ford, *Revelation*, p. 97). In comparison with the colors of the other horses, however, pure white is intended here.
30. Swete, *Apocalypse*, pp. 85-86; Moffatt, "Revelation," 5:389; Beckwith, *Apocalypse*, p. 517; Robertson, *Word Pictures*, 6:340; Scott, *Revelation*, p. 147; Randell, *Revelation*, p. 183.
31. Scott, *Revelation*, p. 147; F. C. Jennings, *Studies in Revelation* (New York: Publication Office "Our Hope," n.d.), p. 201.
32. J. A. Seiss, *The Apocalypse*, 3 vols. (New York: Charles C. Cook, 1909), 1:314; William R. Newell, *The Book of Revelation* (Chicago: Moody, 1935), p. 102; Lenski, *Revelation*, p. 222; Robert Govett, *The Apocalypse Expounded by Scripture* (London: Charles J. Thynne, 1920), p. 87.

son). The obvious objection to this explanation is the possibility that the horse's rider represents the forces of evil, as will be shown below. If, however, his is only a feigned righteousness, a counterfeit of the true, the objection is overruled. The white horse, then, emerges as an emblem of righteousness, though there is no guarantee that the righteousness is more than apparent.

The identity of *ho kathēmenos ep' auton* ("the one who sat upon it") must also be established. Suggestions are plentiful. Those who interpret Revelation as referring exclusively to John's past have identified the horse's rider as the Roman emperor, basing their theories on bloody feuds, pestilences, martyrdoms, and other agitations under Roman emperors of the first century A.D. (Lenski; Moffatt). The paralleling of this seal and the others with events of John's recent past is quite arbitrary, however. Things of this kind happened many times before and many times since (Moffatt). A second way to take the rider is as representative of the Word of God, which is to judge the world (cf. John 12:48*b*) (Lenski). This view is farfetched and out of touch with the context, however. The interpretation that the rider is a personification of judgment, primarily conquest, to be sent upon the earth is a little better (Beckwith). This fits the imagery of Zech. 1:8 and 6:1-8 where horsemen and chariots are divine instruments of judgment on the enemies of God's people (Johnson) and where the rider is also a member of a closely knit group of four (Beckwith). The difficulty with this view is its generality. It does not specify which judgment or judgments are in view. The judgments of the other three riders are rather specific, so this one should be too.

A fourth approach to identifying the rider has him representing the victorious course of the gospel (Alford; Ladd). The advantage here is a resemblance to the Olivet discourse, whose similarity to the seals has already been noted, in predicting the advance of the gospel throughout the world (cf. Matt. 24:14; Mark 13:10) (Ladd; Johnson). It also provides a sense in which final and permanent victory is achieved (Alford). Yet this understanding comes up short in its failure to account for the early period of the gospel, which was not one of continuing triumph (*nikōn*, "conquering") (Moffatt). Nor does it account for the details of the first seal, such as the bow and the crown (Beasley-Murray). To connect this rider with such a positive force as the gospel is to forget that he along with the next three are part of ἀρχὴ ὠδίνων (*archē ōdinōn*, "the beginning of birth-pains") (Matt. 24:8; Mark 13:8) (Charles).

A fifth view identifies the rider with the Parthian invasion of the Roman Empire early in the Christian era (Moffatt). The victorious nature of the conquest, the well-known use of the bow as a weapon, and their fame as horsemen are among the elements often cited to support the Parthian reference.[33] The failure of the Parthian identification to correspond to the end-time nature of these four horsemen, however, negates this as the correct solution. Sixth, it has been proposed that the rider refers to warfare in general and the Parthians in a secondary way (Charles). This view does justice to the warlike symbolism of the bow and the horse, as well as providing a correspondence to the wars and rumors of wars in the parallel accounts of the Olivet discourse (Lee; Beckwith; Charles). It also allows for the striking similarity to the Parthian invaders. The problem with it is its failure to cope with the details of the text. Warfare in general is not specific enough to realize the specific nature of fulfillment required by this context. The same objection may be lodged against a seventh interpretation, which identifies the rider with triumphant militarism.[34] This is so general that it reveals nothing about the future.

An eighth understanding of the rider has identified him with the Jewish Messiah. This enjoys wide support, based on his similarity to the rider of Rev. 19:11-16 whose identity is unquestionable (Swete; Lee). It fits the imagery of the source visions of Zechariah 1:8; 6:1-8, where the horsemen and chariots are divine instruments of judgment on the enemies of God's people (Johnson). The color white is associated with Christ throughout the book, as already noted (Johnson). Only Christ can ride a horse that is white, the color of righteousness (Mounce). The triumph of Christ before the beginning of woes is promised in Mark 13:10 (Beckwith).

Nonetheless, as many pluses as this view has, its weaknesses are even more impressive. The major one is contextual: the Messiah cannot be put on the same plane as the three riders to follow. The four have an essential likeness to each other, clearly belonging together as part of *archē ōdinōn* ("the beginning of birth-pains") (Mark 13:8) (Moffatt; Charles). The Messiah is out of place in this company. In addition, the differences between this rider and the one in Rev. 19:11-16 are pronounced. The latter one is called "faithful and true," but the former one is not so characterized in that his goal is unjust conquest (Johnson). The rider in 19:11-16 is none other than the Lamb who opened the first seal, negating the possibility of His also being the rider revealed by that seal (Moffatt; Beckwith). In 19:11-16, the rider is present in triumph, followed by the host of heaven, but here the rider works in bodily absence, being only a symbol rather

---

33. Moffatt, "Revelation," 5:389; Beckwith, *Apocalypse*, p. 519; G. V. Caird, *A Commentary on the Revelation of St. John the Divine*, HNTC (New York: Harper & Row, 1966), p. 80.
34. Swete, *Apolypse*, p. 86; William Barclay, *The Revelation of John*, 2 vols., 2d ed. (Philadelphia: Westminster, 1960), 2:3.

than the embodiment of His victorious kingdom (Alford). This rider wears a victor's wreath and carries a bow, but the one in chapter 19 is crowned with many diadems and has a sharp sword issuing from His mouth (Mounce). Finally, it is out of keeping with the dramatic plan of the book for the triumph of Christ to transpire until a long series of judgments have run their course (Beckwith).

If the first rider is not the Messiah, then, he must be someone resembling the Messiah. He has been closely identified with the world ruler who is pictured as the first beast of Revelation 13.[35] He will come as a counterfeit Christ. The general accuracy of this explanation is verified through comparison with the parallel accounts of these end-times in Matt. 24:5; Mark 13:6; Luke 21:8 (cf. also Matt. 24:24) (Bullinger; Johnson). First in sequence among the signs spoken of earlier by Christ was the emergence of many "impostor" christs. It is futile to turn elsewhere for an understanding of this first rider. This conclusion agrees with the character of the other three riders also. All of them are associated with the great end-time impostor and his forces. The book is full of satanic imitations of Christ and His conquest, including the crowns of 12:1, 2 and the victories of 11:7 and 13:7 (Sweet; Ford). This rider is one of them.

Yet to identify him as the world ruler himself is not quite accurate. This rider, like the other three, is not an individual, but a personification of a growing movement or force that will be at work during this future period. Christ spoke of many impostors. These will join hands in a concerted effort to unseat Him from His throne. The beast out of the sea (cf. Rev. 13:1-8) will be a part of this movement and on his way to the top, but at the time represented by the first seal, he will not have risen to be the pre-eminent one of the movement. At the very beginning of the period, called "the beginning of birth-pains," he will be one of many impostors who constitute this antichristian force of which this first rider is an emblem.

The words *echōn toxon* ("had a bow") draw attention to the character of this rider (Charles). His bow furnishes the means of carrying out the tasks attributed to him. The bow traditionally has been associated with one who is a warrior. Frequently it is a symbol for victory (cf. Zech. 9:13-14) (Lenski; Ladd). This is certainly the case here, as the remainder of v. 2 indicates. The absence of any reference to arrows accompanying the bow has been taken as significant by some, but not by others. One approach says the bow presupposes the presence of arrows, and sees in it the symbol of lightning-like spir-

---

35. Walvoord, *Revelation*, p. 127; Jack MacArthur, *Expositional Commentary on Revelation* (Eugene, Ore.: Certain Sound, 1973), p. 137.

itual operations issuing from Christ Himself.[36] Aside from its wrong identification of the rider, this view is also excessively spiritualized in its interpretation. It is better to take the absence of arrows from the description as a symbol of bloodless victory. The bow indicates that war is threatened, but never actually occurs because victory is accomplished through peaceful means (Scott; Walvoord). Worldwide peace is the condition at the end of the first-seal period, because one of the results of the second seal is to take that peace away (cf. 6:4). Without arrows, the bow is not a deadly weapon as the sword under the second seal is. Wherever active warfare is described, specific mention is usually made of arrows also (cf. Num. 24:8; Ps. 45:5; Zech. 9:14) (Scott). Because death is not alluded to under this seal, this explanation of the bow without arrows is preferable.

The unfolding drama indicates a further detail about the first rider: καὶ ἐδόθη αὐτῷ στέφανος (*kai edothē autǭ stephanos*, "and a crown was given to him"). The idea that he forced someone to give him this crown[37] is unsubstantiated. It was given to him not as something he personally acquired or earned, but by permission of a higher authority to whom all beings are ultimately submissive.[38] In Revelation *edothē* ("was given") speaks of divine permission for evil powers to carry out their wicked mission (cf. 9:1, 3, 5; 13:5, 7, 14, 15) (Caird). All events in the apocalyptic section of the book are initiated from the throne described in chapter 4 (Bullinger), and must be understood in that light. Though indirect, all that transpires under the seals is in implementation of the "book of doom" through the agency of the Lamb introduced in chapter 5.

The intended symbolism of *stephanos* ("a crown") deserves clarification. One proposal is that of a conquest, the ultimate victory of good over evil (Charles; Ladd), but this requires an identification of Christ as the rider, which is unacceptable. A better way refers the word to imperial dignity awarded before a distinguished career of conquest (Scott). It has no allusion to ultimate outcome. This better fits the identity of the rider.

A final word about this rider establishes his success: καὶ ἐξῆλθεν νικῶν καὶ ἵνα νικήσῃ (*kai exēlthen nikōn kai hina nikēsǭ*, "and he went forth conquering and that he might conquer"). As noted above, his victories will come through peaceful means. Yet the nature of his victories is far different from those earlier in this book. Christians

---

36. John Peter Lange, *The Revelation of John*, vol. 10 of Lange's Commentary, ed. E. R. Craven (Grand Rapids: Zondervan, 1968), p. 171.

37. Jennings, *Revelation*, p. 201.

38. MacArthur, *Revelation*, p. 137.

overcome (νικάω [*nikaō*, "I conquer"], the same word as here) spiritual enemies through their faithfulness to Christ (Rev. 2:7, 11, 17, 26; 3:5, 12, 21; cf. 1 John 5:4, 5). Christ won a spiritual victory (*nikaō* again) through the redemption He accomplished at the cross (Rev. 3:21; 5:5, 9). The triumphs of the rider of the first seal are purely temporal. To equate his victory with that of Christ through His death and resurrection[39] fails to comprehend the moral character of these four riders. The former form of *nikaō, nikōn* ("conquering"), portrays the rider's career as one marked by a long series of victories.[40] The latter form, *nikēsē* ("that He might conquer"), points to an ultimate victory.[41] His victory is final only in a limited sense, however (Walvoord). It is complete in the sense that the counterfeit Christian forces of the future will attain worldwide domination, but that domination will be only temporary. The real King of kings will appear and put an end to it (cf. Rev. 19:11-16).

Additional Notes

6:1 A few MSS read the dative inflectional ending φωνῇ instead of the nominative φωνή. This would be an instrumental use of the dative case or an instrumental of manner (Swete). It would say the being speaks "as with the sound of thunder." Besides enjoying weak MS support, the dative reading would be the easier one for a copyist in light of other comparable usages in the book (cf. 5:12; 6:10). He would hardly change it to a nominative, but could likely have changed it from a nominative to a dative. The correct reading is the nominative. It is perhaps a pendent nominative: "as a voice of thunder [speaks]" (Alford).

Some MSS add the words καὶ ἴδε after ἔρχου here and also in vv. 3, 5, 7. The MS evidence is fairly evenly divided between the two possible readings, but the ἔρχου alone has much stronger support based on internal considerations. An accidental omission of the other two words four times is unlikely, and an addition of the last two words by a well-meaning copyist or copyists because of εἶδον at the beginning of v. 2 is quite plausible. Without realizing the other possible options as to the object of the summons, he may well have thought he was restoring a previous accidental omission that clarifies that

---

39. Lange, *Revelation*, p. 17.
40. Beckwith, *Revelation*, p. 519; Scott, *Revelation*, p. 147. Νικῶν is a present participle whose durative force denotes the continuous nature of the conquests.
41. Beckwith, *Revelation*, p. 519; Seiss, *Apocalypse*, p. 315; Robertson, *Word Pictures*, 6:340; Lenski, *Revelation*, p. 223. Νικήσῃ is an aorist subjunctive. The culminative aspect of the conquest is what is emphasized in this use of the tense.

object. The omission of the last two words is chosen as the correct reading.

3. THE OPENING OF THE SECOND SEAL: WARFARE AND BLOODSHED (6:3-4)

Translation

3And when He opened the second seal, I heard the second living being saying, "Come." 4And another fiery-red horse came forth, and to the one who sat upon him it was given to take peace from the earth, even that they might slay one another, and a great sword was given to him.

Exegesis and Exposition

6:3 The Lamb's opening of the second seal resulted in John's hearing of a summons from the second living being: καὶ ὅτε ἤνοιξεν τὴν σφραγῖδα τὴν δευτέραν, ἤκουσα τοῦ δευτέρου ζῴου λέγοντος, Ἔρχου (*kai hote ēnoixen tēn sphragida tēn deuteran, ēkousa tou deuterou zōou legontos, Erchou,* "And when He opened the second seal, I heard the second living being saying, 'Come' "). Little disagreement exists over the general nature of the second seal. It brings war, internal strife, and international and civil strife to the world (Swete; Charles; Beckwith; Walvoord). The specific point of its application is in question, however.

One perspective denies the seal any particular application in history (Beckwith; Lenski). It holds that many such "red horses" have been ridden down through the centuries.[42] This fails to account for the specific end-time nature of these seals, however. Another view restricts it to warfare against Christians by the Romans during the early Christian era.[43] It emphasizes the nearness of these events to John's time based on the imminence stated in Rev. 1:1 (Hailey). Among other flaws, this explanation suffers from the fatal one of overlooking the obvious fact that the seals are not directed against Christians, but against earth-dwellers who are in rebellion against God (cf. 3:10). Another way of explaining the seal differs only slightly. It takes it as referring to the presence of Roman legions and the peace they brought through warlike means (Ladd). Yet this ignores the purpose of the Roman prefects to preserve peace, not take it away (Bullinger). Also this interpretation is out of keeping with John's portrayal of Messianic judgments of the last days (Beasley-Murray).

The correct analysis of the second seal assigns it to some point

---

42. Robertson, *Word Pictures,* 6:341.
43. Homer Hailey, *Revelation, an Introduction and Commentary* (Grand Rapids: Baker, 1979), p. 190.

within the period called "the beginning of birth-pains" (cf. Matt. 24:8) (Charles; Beasley-Murray; Johnson). This phase constitutes the beginning of a broader period called "the tribulation" (2 Thess. 1:6), which will precede the personal return of the Messiah to earth to set up His reign. Such an assignment of the seal is fixed by Christ's parallel teaching in His Olivet discourse where He predicts wars and rumors of wars and nations antagonistic toward one another as part of the period that will signal His return (Matt. 24:6-7a; Mark 13:7-8a; Luke 21:9-10) (Bullinger; Walvoord). Because Jesus later in that discourse introduces the seventieth week of Daniel by referring to its midpoint (Matt. 24:15; Mark 13:14), probability is on the side of equating the Tribulation period with that seventieth week and "the beginning of birth-pains" with the first half of that week. Further confirmation of this application of the second seal comes from the sword carried by the rider. Eschatological tradition holds that the creator of this end-time strife will carry a sword (cf. Isa. 27:1; 41:2; 51:19; 65:12) (Charles). While the sword in prophetic literature is sometimes that of the Lord Himself, at other times it is a sword that He gives to His enemies that they may destroy one another. This latter sense applies here.

6:4 Subsequent elaborations regarding the second seal include a second horse with its rider: καὶ ἐξῆλθεν ἄλλος ἵππος πυρρός, καὶ τῷ καθημένῳ ἐπ' αὐτὸν ἐδόθη αὐτῷ λαβεῖν τὴν εἰρήνην *ἐκ τῆς γῆς (kai exēlthen allos hippos pyrros, kai tō̦ kathēmenō̦ ep' auton edothē autō̦ labein tēn eirēnēn ek tēs gēs, "and another fiery-red horse came forth, and to the one who sat upon him it was given to him to take the peace from the earth").

"Another" (allos) indicates that this rider is another of the same kind as the one to whom John called special attention under the first seal through his words kai eidon, kai idou ("and I looked, and behold") (6:2) (Scott). It not only shows a connection between the two, it also implies a separation in time.[44] As is obvious from the fact that peace and war cannot exist simultaneously, the events of the first two seals do not occur at the same time.

The horse's color, pyrros ("fiery red"), intimates the nature of afflictions under the second seal. It is a span of slaughter and bloodshed (cf. 2 Kings 3:22, 23) (Scott; Lenski; Mounce). The horse is "red as fire" (Ford). This is warfare in its most feared form.[45] Attempts to identify the rider on such a horse more specifically have produced a variety of unsatisfactory suggestions. To call him the devil (Lenksi) is unsupported and somewhat fanciful. To identify him with Nero

---

44. Oliver B. Green, *The Revelation* (Greenville: S.C.: Gospel Hour, 1967), p. 195.
45. Lange, *Revelation*, p. 164; Ladd, *Revelation*, p. 100.

makes this a scroll of history rather than prophecy. To call him anti-christ, as some would the first rider too,[46] is groundless. Besides the need to distinguish the two from each other, there is a difficulty in assigning the same identity to the third and fourth riders, as this might imply. To say this rider represents that which opposes the going forth of the Word of God under the first seal (Hailey) rests on a misunderstanding of the seals. All the seals have as their objects the earth-dwellers who stand in rebellion against God in this book (cf. Rev. 3:10). A fifth view, which depersonalizes the second rider and makes him representative of forces of war and bloodshed with their consequent horrors, is the best understanding.[47] This observes the parallelism between the seals and the Olivet discourse.

The words *edothē autō* ("it was given to him") recall that this rider is an agent appointed by God for a specific purpose (Scott). The purpose is stated and then clarified. The initial statement of it is that he is "to take the peace from the earth" (*labein tēn eirēnēn ek tēs gēs*). Whatever restraints have existed up to this point, his charge is to remove them. A consequent question relates to the time of this termination of peace. One idea has been that it coincides with a breaking of the covenant with Israel by the "prince who is to come" in Daniel 9:26-27.[48] This is identical with the abomination of desolation spoken of by Christ (Matt. 24:15; Mark 13:14). A better solution, however, places it during the first half of Daniel's seventieth week rather than at the midpoint. The analogy of the sequence in the Olivet discourse (Matt. 24:6-7*a;* Mark 13:7-8*a;* Luke 21:9-10) is a strong reason. Jesus called this development part of the beginning of birth pangs, so they belong with the preliminary part of the period (Bullinger).

Eirēnēn ("peace") refers to the normal state of affairs, which corresponds to the will of God. Sometimes it is restricted to man's inner being, but not here. It is the outward peace of the whole world that this rider removes.[49] *Tēn eirērēn* is more specifically a false peace, an imitation of the everlasting peace to come under the Messiah's rule.[50]

---

46. MacArthur, *Revelation*, p. 143.
47. Lange, *Revelation*, p. 165; Jennings, *Revelation*, p. 202.
48. Green, *Revelation*, pp. 197-98.
49. Werner Foerster, "εἰρήνη, εἰρηνεύω, κ. τ. λ.," in *TDNT*, 10 vols., ed. Gerhard Kittel and Gerhard Friedrich, trans. and ed. Geoffrey W. Bromiley (Grand Rapids: Eerdmans, 1976), 2 (1965):412.
50. Charles, *Revelation*, 1:166. The article τὴν refers to the previously existing peace created under the first seal, which is now disturbed by some force causing discord and bloodshed (Barnes, *Revelation*, p. 146). Alford's suggestion of making the article distributive, i.e., peace in its entirety, and not relating it back to the first seal (Alford, *Greek Testament*, 4:614) is based on a weak rationale regarding the function of the article. Alford is forced to such an explanation because of his erroneous assumption that the first four seals are simultaneous.

It has been created by forces associated with the first seal. This is another reminder of the sequential nature of the seals (Johnson). Events portrayed in each member of the series follow those represented in the previous one. They are not simultaneous.

The domain from which the peace is removed is specified in *ek tēs gēs* ("from the earth"). This is the earth in general, not some limited part of it such as Judea or the Roman Empire (Alford). The impact of these seals is worldwide. John's vantage point is heaven, but he sees the scenes being enacted before him as taking place on earth (except for the fifth seal, 6:9-11, which is specifically placed in heaven, of course). The description of the earthquake of 6:12-17 is a good example of this (Beckwith).

The clarification of this divine agent's purpose is in the words καὶ[51] ἵνα ἀλλήλους σφάξουσιν[52] (*kai hina allēlous sphaxousin*, "even that they might slay one another"). This is the positive side of warfare corresponding to the negative side just stated (Swete). A few want to give *sphaxousin* ("that they might slay") a sacrificial connotation because of the earlier use of the same verb for the sacrificial Lamb (Rev. 5:6).[53] The verb is used with the noun μάχαιρα (*machaira*, "sword") in the OT in connection with Abraham's offering of Isaac as a sacrifice (Gen. 22:6, 10 [LXX]) (Lee). Further, it is used to mean the slaying of martyrs because the verb comes again in such a connection under the fifth seal (Rev. 6:9) (Lee). Yet *machaira* is used freely in connections that are nonsacrificial (Rev. 13:10; cf. John 18:10). NT usage as a whole does not support the specialized limitation to sacrificial martyrdom (Mounce). Besides, it is questionable whether martyrs under the fifth seal are viewed as sacrificial victims. The altar mentioned there (6:9) may well be the golden altar of incense rather than the altar of burnt offering. In this case, no sacrifice would be involved. All in all, it is better to assign *sphaxousin* a broad connotation of the violent taking of life through warfare (Lenski). This will be a visitation resulting in great carnage.

A further identifying feature granted this rider by authority from heaven is noted in the words καὶ ἐδόθη αὐτῷ μάχαιρα μεγάλη (*kai edothē autō machaira megalē*, "and a great sword was given to him").

---

51. This is another of the many epexegetical uses of καὶ in this book. Because the ἵνα clause it introduces is not grammatically parallel to the λαβεῖν infinitival clause that precedes it, probability is on the side of taking this clause as a clarification of what has gone before rather than as an additional purpose.

52. The future indicative of σφάξουσιν, rather than the more common aorist subjunctive, imparts the result of the purpose with a special matter-of-fact emphasis: "that they may slay one another which they also shall" (Alford, *Greek Testament*, 4:614).

53. Lee, "Revelation," 4:573; Newell, *Revelation*, p. 103; Hailey, *Revelation*, p. 190.

Machaira sometimes referred to a short knife carried in a sheath at the girdle (cf. John 18:10), but at other times it named a long sword carried in battle by Roman soldiers and others. The latter is the meaning here.[54] Symbolically, it spoke of bloodshed, violent death (cf. Rom. 8:35), war (cf. Gen. 31:26), the power of authorities to punish criminals (cf. Rom. 13:4), and international strife (Swete; Charles; Ford). All of these pictures are appropriate except the next to the last. Punishment of criminals does not belong here.

How specific is the sword symbolism? Does it refer to all deadly instruments down to the present?[55] The thrust of Christ's use of it in Matt. 10:34 (cf. Luke 12:51) presents the sword as representing developments throughout this age (Alford). This fails to account for the peculiar application of the seals to the last days, however. So does the view that refers the sword to Rome in placing Rome side-by-side with the Parthians (Moffatt). The sword is better seen as a symbol for a specific period of dreadful bloodshed.[56] Because it has not yet occurred on the scale that it will someday, the relegation of it to "the beginning of birth-pains" in the future is necessary.

Additional Notes

6:4 The substitution of ἀπό or ἐπί for ἐκ in various witnesses does not have sufficiently strong MS evidence to merit serious consideration. Stylistic matters may have prompted the substitutions.[57] The reading containing ἐκ has much stronger support.

4. THE OPENING OF THE THIRD SEAL: WIDESPREAD FAMINE (6:5-6)

Translation

5And when He opened the third seal, I heard the third living being saying, "Come." And I looked, and behold a black horse, and the one who sat upon him had a balance in his hand. 6And I heard [something] like a voice in the middle of the four living beings saying, "A measure of wheat for a denarius, and three measures of barley for a denarius; and do not hurt the olive oil and the wine."

Exegesis and Exposition

6:5 The opening of the third seal followed by the summons of the third living being brings another startling new development.[58] It is a

---

54. Swete, *Apocalypse*, p. 86; Robertson, *Word Pictures*, 6:341; Mounce, *Revelation*, p. 154.
55. Lange, *Revelation*, p. 165.
56. W. Michaelis, "μάχαιρα," in *TDNT*, 4 (1967):526.
57. Bruce M. Metzger, *A Textual Commentary on the Greek New Testament* (New York: United Bible Societies, 1971), p. 740.
58. Special attention is called to what he saw through the words καὶ εἶδον, καὶ ἰδού as in 6:2.

sorrowful picture: καὶ ὅτε ἤνοιξεν τὴν σφραγῖδα τὴν τρίτην, ἤκουσα τοῦ τρίτου ζῴου λέγοντος, Ἔρχου. καὶ εἶδον, καὶ ἰδοὺ ἵππος μέλας, καὶ ὁ καθήμενος ἐπ᾽ αὐτὸν ἔχων ζυγὸν ἐν τῇ χειρὶ αὐτοῦ (kai hote ēnoixen tēn sphragida tēn tritēn, ēkousa tou tritou zǫou legontos, Erchou. kai eidon, kai idou hippos melas, kai ho kathēmenos ep᾽ auton echōn zygon en tē cheiri autou, "And when He opened the third seal, I heard the third living being saying, 'Come.' And I looked, and behold a black horse, and the one who sat upon him had[59] a balance in his hand"). The horse's color is black, suggesting a time of lamentation and mourning (Scott). The sorrowing results from a scarcity of food and anxiety created by this shortage (cf. Lam. 4:8-9). Provisions are so expensive that only the wealthy have enough.[60]

The black horse's rider has been identified in different ways. One way is to call him the antichrist,[61] but it is doubtful that any of the riders can be personalized. All are personifications of forces or movements. Another idea is to see the rider as industrialism, commercialism, international finance, and commerce (Lenski). This, however, ignores the obvious intent of the seal to signify famine. Prophets have predicted other famines and their predictions have been fulfilled (cf. 2 Kings 6:25; 7:1; Acts 11:28). Why should the obvious be ignored here by looking for something whose indirect effect is famine (Bullinger)? This rider should be identified as a personification of famine (Charles; Beckwith). Under the second seal, the world has experienced widespread war. Hunger is one of the aftermaths of war.[62] This answer also satisfies the sequence of Jesus' parallel prophecy in the Olivet discourse: famine follows international strife (Matt. 24:7b[63]) (Bullinger).

One way of portraying scarcity is the zygon ("balance"), which the rider holds in his hand. This is the word used to name a yoke worn by cattle, but here it refers to a bar with scales at both ends of it or else with a weight at one end and a pan suspended from the other.[64]

---

59. For an explanation of this translation of the participle ἔχων, see note on the comparable rendering at 6:2.
60. Moffatt, "Revelation," 5:390; Lange, *Revelation*, p. 165; Ladd, *Revelation*, p. 100; Walvoord, *Revelation*, p. 129; Mounce, *Revelation*, p. 152.
61. MacArthur, *Revelation*, p. 151.
62. Robertson, *Word Pictures*, 6:341.
63. Mark and Luke place earthquakes between international strife and famine in their accounts of the Olivet discourse (Mark 13:8b; Luke 21:11). Apparently Jesus' teaching was more extensive than what is recorded, leaving each writer free to choose a sequence. It would appear that earthquakes accompany the conditions of shortage, making the problem even worse.
64. Barnes, *Revelation*, p. 140; Charles, *Revelation*, 1:166; Lenski, *Revelation*, p. 226.

Careful weighing of food shows it to be in short supply.⁶⁵ Eating food by weight denotes conditions of famine (cf. Ezek. 4:16-17) (Beckwith).

6:6 John next hears a special announcement: καὶ ἤκουσα ὡς φωνὴν ἐν μέσῳ τῶν τεσσάρων ζῴων λέγουσαν, Χοῖνιξ σίτου δηναρίου, καὶ τρεῖς χοίνικες κριθῶν δηναρίου· καὶ τὸ ἔλαιον καὶ τὸν οἶνον μὴ ἀδικήσῃς (kai ēkousa hōs phōnēn en mesǭ tōn tessarōn zǭōn legousan, Choinix sitou dēnariou, kai treis choinikes krithōn dēnariou; kai to elaion kai ton oinon mē adikēsēs, "And I heard [something] like a voice in the middle of the four living beings saying, 'A measure of wheat for a denarius, and three measures of barley for a denarius; but⁶⁶ do not hurt the olive oil and the wine'"). This time the announcement does not come from the four living beings as the earlier three summonses have. There is a degree of uncertainty in his description: hōs phōnēn en mesǭ tōn tessarōn zǭōn legousan ("[something] like a voice in the middle of the four living beings saying") (Alford; Lee). Such vagueness characterizes this writer from time to time (cf. 8:1; 14:3; 19:1, 6). The voice comes from the heavenly presence, from the middle of the four living beings, but it is difficult to specify beyond this (Beckwith).

A number of proposals must be sifted. One is that the voice is nature's protest against famine, reflecting the interests of the four living beings who represent what is best in nature.⁶⁷ This misconstrues the statement as though en mesǭ ("in the middle") reads ex mesou ("from the middle") (Beckwith). It is not an utterance of these four beings. It is also misleading to identify the four closely with the natural world (Beckwith). Another way of handling the issue is to avoid identification of the voice by noting that it is not emphasized (Lenski). What is emphasized are the agents of providence represented in the announcement. This observation is valid, but does not exclude an investigation of the source of the voice. A third suggestion deserves the same response: the voice is mysterious and unidentified (Beckwith; Ford). But the mystery should not discourage inquiry. The general location from which the voice comes, the middle of the four living beings, is where the throne is (5:6), so most plausibly the speaker is either the Lamb or God. The Lamb is the initiator of the seal judgments, and it is reasonable that He announce the scarcity of staple foods (Smith; Mounce), but perhaps the case for assigning the announcement to the one sitting upon the throne is stronger. He is the ultimate source of all these judgments (Lee; Scott). In former times He sent famines (e.g., 2 Kings 8:1; Jer. 16:4; Hag. 1:11; 2:16-17) (Bul-

---

65. Lange, *Revelation*, p. 172; Mounce, *Revelation*, p. 155.
66. The context requires an adversative καὶ here because conditions of plenty that follow stand in direct contrast with the scarcity that has preceded.
67. Swete, *Apocalypse*, p. 87; Barclay, *Revelation*, 2:8.

linger). It is fitting that He announce this future famine. When taking into account that the unidentified voice under the fifth seal (cf. 6:11) is the voice of God, evidence for identifying Him as the speaker here is slightly stronger.

Choinix sitou ("a measure of wheat") is a quantity of wheat that equals slightly less than a quart (dry measure).[68] Wheat was the main food of the ancient world, a better grain worth more than barley (Ladd). This much wheat was only enough to sustain for one day a person of moderate appetite (Alford; Moffatt; Charles). Famine condition prices required a full day's pay to purchase this minimum ration. A denarius[69] was the average day's wages for a working man.[70] The minimum daily food requirement of barley was three measures because it was cheaper than the better food, wheat. These two foods were basic for the whole population.[71] By buying the cheaper commodity a laborer could obtain three measures and have enough for himself and his family, but each person received less nutritional value (Charles). The purchasing power of a denarius drops far below what is normal and results in widespread hunger.[72]

The famine will not be universal, however. Protection of an element of the population from it is reflected in the words *kai to elaion kai ton oinon mē adikēsēs* ("but do not hurt the olive oil and the wine"). *To elaion* ("olive oil") was used for lamps, healing, and anointing at feasts. Its symbolic connotation under this seal has been in question. One explanation sees olive oil as part of the staple food supply as were wheat, barley, and wine, whether in a time of shortage or prosperity (cf. Deut. 7:13; 11:14; 28:51; 2 Chron. 32:28; Neh. 5:11; Hos. 2:8, 22; Joel 2:19; Hag. 1:11), and the prohibition not to hurt the olive oil means a limitation to the scarcity. In other words, the third seal will entail poverty, but the famine will be only partial, not severe (cf.

---

68. G. Abbott-Smith *A Manual Greek Lexicon of the New Testament* (Edinburgh: T. & T. Clark, 1950), p. 482.
69. Δηναρίου is a genitive of price, one of the "looser genitives" that Robertson analyzes as being in reality an objective genitive (A. T. Robertson, *A Grammar of the Greek New Testament in the Light of Historical Research* [Nashville: Broadman, 1934], pp. 500-501).
70. Swete, *Apocalypse*, p. 88; Ladd, *Revelation*, p. 100; MacArthur, *Revelation*, p. 151.
71. Swete, *Apocalypse*, p. 88; Scott, *Revelation*, p. 150; Theodore H. Epp, *Practical Studies in Revelation*, 2 vols. (Lincoln, Neb.: Back to the Bible, 1969), 2:60.
72. Swete, *Apocalypse*, p. 88; Charles, *Revelation*, 1:167; Seiss, *Apocalypse*, 1:332; Govett, *Apocalypse*, p. 90; Scott, *Revelation*, p. 150. Estimates place the price of these commodities anywhere from eight to twelve times the usual cost (Bullinger, *Apocalypse*, pp. 257-58; Moffatt, "Revelation," 5:390; Beckwith, *Apocalypse*, p. 520; Mounce, *Revelation*, p. 155; Johnson, "Revelation," 4:474).

Ps. 104:14-15).[73] This line of thinking points out that the stipulated price of the wheat and barley also places a limitation on the rider. He could have charged two denarii rather than one, making the famine even more severe (Alford; Swete). Yet oil and wine were more in the category of luxuries than wheat and barley (Moffatt).

For this reason, the other analysis of the prohibition sees olive oil as particularly associated with the rich and concludes that the wealthy are unhurt by the famine. The lesson is a disparity between the poor and the rich. Comfort is denied the common worker, but the rich pass through the trial unscathed (Moffatt; Scott; Lenski). Some argue against this by noting the universal nature of the seal visitations (Beckwith) and by reasoning that the Lamb would not issue an order favoring the rich and aggravating the bad circumstances of the poor (Mounce). Yet the force of objections is mitigated by remembering that the rich will get their judgment under the sixth seal (Beasley-Murray). The problem with taking this as a reference to limited famine is that it underrates the severity of the seals. This famine will be serious enough to make it unique in history up to that time. The world has already seen many limited famines, but never one like this. The limitation proposal cannot explain the exorbitant price of grain (Beckwith). People could not live on olive oil and wine, so they must be seen as extras (Scott). The seal judgments will not limit human suffering. They will enhance it. So it is wrong to take a major feature such as this prohibition against hurting the oil and the wine and interpret it as a limitation on human hardship. It indicates rather the inequity that will prevail. The poor will have it extremely hard while the wealthy will experience no interruption to their luxurious lifestyle.

A question about the relation of this famine to the one under the next seal is in order. In view of the increasing intensity of hardship as the seals progress, it is proper to rate the fourth-seal famine as more severe (Mounce). This is verified in the widespread death under that seal. Yet the third-seal famine will still be the most severe ever to grip the world up to that time.

The symbolic meaning of *to elaion* applies also to *ton oinon* ("the wine"), but with the latter a clarification is needed. Wine is thought by some to refer to communion or to some element of Jewish liturgy. If this be so, the meaning would be that believers would be spared the misery of this famine (Ford). One of the Dead Sea Scrolls mentioning a feast of oil and wine is offered as support (Ford), as is the use of wine

---

73. Alford, *Greek Testament*, 4:616; Beckwith, *Apocalypse*, p. 521; Barclay, *Revelation*, 2:6.

in James 5:14.[74] A more likely reference, however, is to those during a time a famine who are not denied the practice of self-indulgence (Beasley-Murray). This can hardly be a promise of reprieve for believers.

Another suggested connotation of the wine ties it to an edict of Roman emperor Domitian in A.D. 92, prohibiting the planting of new vineyards and ordering the destruction of half the existing ones (Charles). This was done because of a lack of cereals and a superabundance of wine (Swete). The reaction of the populace was so strong that he had to withdraw the decree. This circumstance made the command "do not hurt the wine" particularly vivid in the minds of the readers (Moffatt; Beckwith). The problem with this connection is that Domitian's decree had nothing to do with a famine. It was issued to protect Italian vine growers (Beckwith). The edict may have been an occasion of, but not the cause for, this aspect of the third seal. The shortage of bread and the plentifulness of wine was an old Jewish expectation (Charles). The tendency to exaggerate the significance of contemporary events or events of the recent past to explain various parts of the Apocalypse is widespread. Such events may add color or hint at the nature of the ultimate fulfillment, but they cannot be taken as adequate interpretations. Final fulfillment awaits the period just prior to Christ's second coming. The predictions are not just intended to trigger something in the memories of the earliest readers.

The prohibition *mē adikēsēs* ("do not hurt"), addressed presumably to the third rider, is phrased so as to forbid even the beginning of damage to the wine.[75] Thereby the privileged lifestyle of the rich remains completely intact.

5. THE OPENING OF THE FOURTH SEAL: DEATH TO A FOURTH OF EARTH'S INHABITANTS (6:7-8)

Translation

7And when He opened the fourth seal, I heard the voice of the fourth living being saying, "Come." 8And I looked, and behold a pale green horse, and the one who sat upon him had the name "Death," and Hades was following with him; and authority over one-fourth of the earth was given to them, to kill with the sword and with famine and with pestilence and by the beasts of the earth.

---

74. Hanns Lilje, *The Last Book of the Bible* (Philadelphia: Muhlenberg, 1957), p. 126.
75. The aorist ἀδικήσῃς is ingressive: "do not begin to hurt" (Swete, *Apocalypse*, p. 88; Moulton, *Grammar*, 1:124-25; Robertson, *Word Pictures*, 6:342). This is generally the case with prohibitions using μή and the aorist subjunctive.

Exegesis and Exposition

6:7 A conspicuous increase in severity comes with the opening of the fourth seal: Καὶ ὅτε ἤνοιξεν τὴν σφραγῖδα τὴν τετάρτην, ἤκουσα φωνὴν τοῦ τετάρτου ζῴου λέγοντος, Ἔρχου (*Kai hote ēnoixen tēn sphragida tēn tetartēn, ēkousa phōnēn tou tetartou zōou legontos, Erchou,* "And when He opened the fourth seal, I heard the voice of the fourth living being saying, 'Come'").

The increased intensity raises the question of the time of this visitation. One placement locates it in the latter half of Daniel's seventieth week, following the rationale that the former part of the week is a time of relative tranquility and the fourth seal reflects awful conditions more characteristic of the latter three-and-one-half years (Walvoord). This perspective misreads Dan. 9:26-27, however. This OT prophecy indicates peaceful conditions between Israel and the Roman prince during the first half of the week, but does not rule out the devastation of this seal as occurring simultaneously with the continuing enforcement of a treaty between these two parties. It is the peaceful covenant that will be broken at the midpoint of the week. Conditions of widespread suffering and death could precede this.

The possibility of assigning the fourth seal to some period of past history must also be ruled out. Never has there been a time when the four afflictions of the fourth seal have operated simultaneously over a fourth of the earth.[76] The best proposal is to assign this seal to the same period as the first three seals, the time of "the beginning of birth-pains." Along with famine, *thanatō* ("pestilence") will also contribute its share of misery to this period (Lee). Jesus chose a different word, λοιμοί (*loimoi,* "pestilences"), to speak of the problem in His Olivet discourse (cf. Luke 21:11[77]), but both words describe sweeping plagues that will assail the world's population. It will be a time of awful misery.

6:8 In response to the fourth summons, John saw a fourth horse with its rider: Καὶ εἶδον, καὶ ἰδοὺ ἵππος χλωρός, καὶ ὁ καθήμενος

---

76. Bullinger, *Apocalypse,* p. 261. Attempts to overcome this objection to referring the seal to the past period of church history have caused some to propose that the first four seals occur simultaneously and that all four extend throughout the church's history (Alford, *Greek Testament,* 4:618; Lee, "Revelation," 4:576). In this way, examples of each variety of human tragedy can be cited. Even this, though, falls far short of the extensive scope of the forces and movements foreshadowed in the seals. It also overlooks significance of the consecutive opening of the seals which apparently signals the consecutive fulfillment of what is contained in each one.

77. Matthew and Mark did not include a reference to pestilence in their accounts of the Olivet discourse.

ἐπάνω αὐτοῦ ὄνομα αὐτῷ ὁ Θάνατος, καὶ ὁ ᾅδης ἠκολούθει μετ᾽ αὐτοῦ· καὶ ἐδόθη αὐτοῖς ἐξουσία ἐπὶ τὸ τέταρτον τῆς γῆς, ἀποκτεῖναι ἐν ῥομφαίᾳ καὶ ἐν λιμῷ καὶ ἐν θανάτῳ καὶ ὑπὸ τῶν θηρίων τῆς γῆς (Kai eidon, kai idou hippos chlōros, kai ho kathēmenos[78] epanō autou onoma autō ho Thanatos, kai ho hạdēs ēkolouthei met᾽ autou; kai edothē autois exousia epi to tetarton tēs gēs, apokteinai en rhomphaiạ kai en limō kai en thanatō kai hypo tōn thēriōn tēs gēs, "And I looked, and behold a pale green horse, and the one who sat upon him had[79] the name 'Death,' and Hades was following with him; and authority over one-fourth of the earth was given to them, to kill with the sword and with famine and with pestilence and by the beasts of the earth"). The word to describe the fourth horse's color, *chlōros* ("pale green"), is the color of grass and other vegetation in Mark 6:39 and Rev. 8:7; 9:4, but in the present connection, designates the yellowish green of decay, the pallor of death.[80] It is a pale ashen color that images a face bleached because of terror.[81] It recalls a corpse in the advanced state of corruption (Ford).

Speculation about the personification of this rider has varied. The suggestion that he represents the release of the devil and his deadly spiritual forces is based on an unjustified allegorization of the words (Lenski). He has been tied to the four instruments with which God threatened Jerusalem of old (cf. Ezek. 5:17; 14:21). The listing of troublous sources later in v. 8 is comparable to those of old (Beckwith), but this explanation fails to account for Hades as the rider's companion. Pestilence has been another identification of the rider. This is reasonable because his name *Thanatos* ("Death") is the same as the word translated "pestilence" (*thanatō*) later in the verse, and pestilence quite often follows famine (cf. Jer. 14:12; Ezek. 5:17; 14:21; Luke 21:11) (Johnson). Yet this rider's work includes more than pestilence (Beckwith). The presence of Hades with this rider shows

---

78. This nominative case of the participial substantive is cited by Alford as pendent (i.e., an independent nominative) (*Greek Testament*, 4:617). Yet this usage is not comparable to the independent nominatives in 3:12, 21 where no καί separates the nominative from the remainder of the sentence to follow. Because καί separates it from the following here, the substantive is best taken as the subject of an independent clause with an understood verb to be supplied.
79. Literally, the dative of possession could be rendered "a name to him, 'Death.'" The suggested rendering is necessary to convert this construction into an independent clause in English. The words ὄνομα αὐτῷ ὁ θάνατος are an anacoluthon in grammatical structure like that of John 3:1, meaning "His name was death" (Alford, *Greek Testament*, 4:617; Robertson, *Word Pictures*, 6:342).
80. Lange, *Revelation*, p. 274; Beckwith, *Apocalypse*, p. 523; Scott, *Revelation*, p. 152.
81. Swete, *Apocalypse*, p. 88; Barclay, *Revelation*, 2:9.

that his impact upon the population covers more (cf. Rev. 1:18; 20:13, 14; Isa. 28:15; Hos. 13:14) (Beckwith). It is therefore best to see this rider as a personification of death viewed comprehensively.[82] Only death can have Hades as its inseparable companion.

The variation of prepositions from *ep'* ("upon") in 6:2, 4, 5 to *epanō* ("upon") in this case has brought the suggestion that this rider was "above" his horse rather than on it.[83] Probably some distinction between the two prepositions is intended, but to have the rider hovering "above" his horse presses the difference too far. The difference between the two is much smaller, the latter word being prompted perhaps by the joint-appearance of Hades with Death as the rider in this case (Moffatt).

A case has been made for rendering the rider's name *Thanatos* as "Pestilence" because the same noun means that later in the verse and also in Rev. 18:8 (Charles; Moffatt), but this occurrence of the word requires the broader sense of "Death" as reflected in the above discussion (Beckwith; Scott). For an identification of *ho hạdēs* ("Hades"), an earlier discussion of the word at Rev. 1:18 should be compared. There the name had a local usage, but here Hades is personified. With an etymological meaning of "unseen," at times it refers to a condition into which all humans pass at the time of physical death (Scott). At other times, however, it is the intermediate place of only the ungodly, whereas believers go immediately into the presence of the Lord (Lenski). Together with *Thanatos*, it broadens the seal to comprehend the implications of death for both the material and immaterial parts of man.

Whether Hades is pictured as on foot, riding a separate horse, or riding the same horse depends on how *ho hạdēs ēkolouthei met' autou* ("Hades was following with him") is understood.[84] Obviously there is no fifth horse, so the symbolism of the four horsemen must be maintained (Beasley-Murray; Ford). If Hades is not mounted, he is on foot and apparently acts as death's hearse, standing ready to engulf and detain Death's victims (Alford; Scott; Beasley-Murray). Because the two are inseparable (cf. Rev. 1:18; 20:13, 14) (Swete; Mounce), Hades apparently is able to maintain the horse's pace so as to keep up with Death's movements.

Because they are granted power to do their work together (cf. *autois*, "to them"), they must remain together in the portrayal before

82. Swete, *Apocalypse*, p. 88; Lange, *Revelation*, p. 165; Beckwith, *Apocalypse*, p. 522; Lenski, *Revelation*, p. 224.
83. Alford, *Greek Testament*, 4:614; Randell, *Revelation*, p. 186.
84. The opinion that the phrase is an interpolation and was not in the autograph of Revelation (Charles, *Revelation*, 1:170-71) has no MS evidence to support it and cannot be accepted.

the seer's eyes. A suggestion that *autois* be referred to all the horses and riders under all four seals arises from the unity of the first four seals (Walvoord). *Kai edothē autois exousia epi to tetarton tēs gēs, apokteinai en rhomphaią kai en limọ̄ kai en thanatọ̄ kai hypo tōn thēriōn tēs gēs* ("And authority over one-fourth of the earth was given to them, to kill with the sword and with famine and with pestilence and by the beasts of the earth") has at times been taken as a separate sentence, a succinct summary statement of all four seals (Mounce). Yet it is awkward to cross the boundaries erected by the separate seals to justify such an inclusive antecedent for the pronoun. Besides this, it is difficult to see how the rider on the white horse could have killed through the use of wild beasts, if he killed at all (Mounce). The natural antecedents for *autois* under the existing framework are Death and Hades. In binding them together, the pronoun observes the constancy of their companionship.

The ravages of this fourth seal are staggering, but limited in comparison with what comes later (Beckwith; Ladd). If today's world population figure of five billion is used, *to tetarton tēs gēs*[85] ("one-fourth of the earth") means that Death and Hades have authority, which they apparently will exercise, to take the lives of one and a quarter billion people. The magnitude of this catastrophe can hardly be grasped because nothing comparable has happened throughout history (Swete). If limited to two continents, which it will probably not be (Beckwith; Lenski; Mounce), it will amount to the elimination of people from two of the world's most populous ones (Walvoord).

The suggestion that *apokteinai en rhomphaią kai en limọ̄ kai en thanatọ̄ kai hypo tōn thēriōn tēs gēs* ("to kill with the sword and with famine and with pestilence and by the beasts of the earth") serves no purpose and is a later addition to the text (Charles) has no evidence to support it. These are ravages associated with Ezekiel's warning to Jerusalem (cf. Ezek. 14:12-21), the same four being listed in Ezek. 14:21 (Alford). Three of the four—sword, famine, and pestilence—are associated with each other often in the OT (cf. 1 Chron. 21:12; Jer. 14:12; 21:7; 24:10; 44:13; Ezek. 5:12; 6:11, 12, etc.). It is in keeping with the habit of this writer to echo OT themes in his descriptions of God's future spoken judgments.

The first three items in the list are different means[86] that God will

---

85. Τῆς γῆς can at times depict only "the land" of Israel, but here it refers to the whole earth (Walvoord, *Revelation*, p. 130). It is an instance of the partitive genitive, this time without the preposition ἐκ (Robertson, *Word Pictures*, 6:343).

86. The first three words are introduced by the preposition ἐν with its instrumental meaning. This is appropriate when inanimate things are in view (Beckwith, *Apocalypse*, p. 523).

allow Death and Hades to use in removing human life: sword, famine, and pestilence.[87] The sword is a symbol of death by violent means, perhaps in warfare. Famine has already come on the scene under the third seal, but will worsen under the fourth so that sizable numbers of people will die from it. The inclusion of pestilence means that fatal diseases will be rampant and many will fall victim to them. The last item on the list points to actual agents[88] of destruction: wild beasts who roam the earth, looking for prey and taking advantage of all who are defenseless (cf. Num. 21:6; Deut. 32:24; Josh. 24:12; 2 Kings 2:24; 17:25; Isa. 30:6; Jer. 5:6; Ezek. 14:21; 33:27) (Bullinger).

After such terrifying developments, could matters get worse? How can the gloom of the fourth rider be exceeded? The remaining seals will tell. After all, these are only "the beginning of birth-pains."

Additional Notes

6:8 A few MSS, including some significant ones, omit αὐτοῦ, leaving ἐπάνω to function as an adverb: "and the one who sat above." Its omission is certainly the more difficult reading. It is easy to see how copyists might have added αὐτοῦ to make the meaning correspond to 6:2, 4, 5. Yet the strength of MS evidence supporting the inclusion is great enough to support that reading, with the conclusion that its absence in the other witnesses was accidental.[89]

6. THE OPENING OF THE FIFTH SEAL: PRAYERS FOR DIVINE VENGEANCE (6:9-11)

The fifth seal differs from the rest. It has no summons from a living being and no horse and rider like the first four. It is unlike the sixth seal with its vast upheavals and the seventh with its foreboding silence. Its inclusion of martyrdom is appropriate because such often accompanies political, economic, and social chaos as depicted under the first four seals (Ford). The reference to martyrdom fits well with the sequence of the companion prophecies of Christ in the Olivet discourse. He had taught earlier about the hardships awaiting His

---

87. Θανάτῳ is an example of metonymy whereby the effect is used in place of the cause that produces it (Bullinger, *Apocalypse*, p. 259). It depicts death brought about by the special cause of disease. This meaning for the word is fixed by its association with the other three judgments here and by a comparison with Ezek. 14:2 [LXX], where it is so translated (cf. also Jer. 14:12; 21:7) (Swete, *Apocalypse*, p. 89; Alford, *Greek Testament*, 4:617; Lee, "Revelation," 4:476; Beckwith, *Apocalypse*, p. 423; Scott, *Revelation*, p. 152; Lenski, *Revelation*, p. 231).
88. The preposition ὑπό rather than ἐν appropriately expresses the agency of animate creatures in inflicting death (Alford, *Greek Testament*, 4:617).
89. Metzger, *Textual Commentary*, pp. 740-41.

followers during the future "beginning of birth-pains" (cf. Matt. 24:9-10; Mark 13:9-13; Luke 21:12-17) (Charles).

Translation

⁹**And when He opened the fifth seal, I saw under the altar the souls of those slain because of the Word of God, even because of the testimony that they used to have, ¹⁰and they cried out with a loud voice, "How long, holy and true Master, will you not judge and avenge our blood from those who dwell upon the earth?" ¹¹And a white robe was given to each of them, and it was said to them that they should rest for a little time yet, until both their fellow slaves and their brothers who were about to be killed as also they themselves [had been] should have their number made complete.**

Exegesis and Exposition

6:9 A different kind of scene greeted John's eyes after the Lamb opened the fifth seal: καὶ ὅτε ἤνοιξεν τὴν πέμπτην σφραγῖδα, εἶδον ὑποκάτω τοῦ θυσιαστηρίου τὰς ψυχὰς τῶν ἐσφαγμένων διὰ τὸν λόγον τοῦ θεοῦ καὶ διὰ τὴν μαρτυρίαν ἣν εἶχον (*kai hote ēnoixen tēn pemptēn sphragida, eidon hypokatō tou thysiastēriou tas psychas tōn esphagmenōn dia ton logon tou theou kai dia tēn martyrian.hēn eichon,* "and when He opened the fifth seal, I saw under the altar the souls of those slain because of the Word of God, even because of the testimony that they used to have").

The significance of the difference is missed by those who explain the fifth seal's impact as producing martyrdom. They say it represents the difficulty of sharing one's faith, even to the point of having one's blood poured out by God's enemies as an offering to Him.[90] This is unacceptable because it ignores the basic fact that the seal judgments are God's wrath against the earth dwellers (cf. Rev. 3:10; 6:10), not against the redeemed. Martyrdom for Christ's sake can hardly be looked upon as a judgment from God. It is particularly out of keeping with the other judgments of this series. The nature of the fifth-seal judgment is gleaned from the cry of the martyrs in 6:10. Their prayers for God's vengeance against the earth dwellers are heard and certain vindication against their slayers is more fully assured.[91] God will surely avenge Himself against His enemies, but these prayers serve to confirm this. Prayers of the persecuted for judgment is a recognized influence in bringing about the end-time happenings (cf. Luke 18:7) (Beckwith). Earth's rebels have already had a taste of suffering under the first four seals, but the worst for them is yet to come, particularly under the seventh seal and the seven trumpet

---

90. Barclay, *Revelation*, 2:524; Rosenthal, *Pre-Wrath Rapture*, pp. 142-43.
91. MacArthur, *Revelation*, p. 105.

judgments. From a human standpoint, these prayers serve to make a dismal future ever more frightening because of the intercession of those especially precious in God's sight.

As expected, there is debate about the time of the fifth seal too. One suggestion places it in the past, associating it with martyrdoms under the first-century Roman emperors Nero and Domitian (Charles). At the time John wrote, these were the latest victims to be martyred for Christ (Moffatt). This can hardly be the answer, however. If these prayers are uttered in conjunction with other end-time happenings, these martyrs must be killed during that period, because their persecutors are still alive when they pray. Otherwise, their prayers would be meaningless. Another idea is to locate the martyrs throughout the Christian era (Lenski), but this falters on the same ground as the first. These martyrs must belong to the group to be slain during the time of trouble just before Christ returns. The parallelism with Christ's Olivet discourse necessitates this (Alford; Lee).

Because of the difference in nature between this seal and the first four, it has been supposed that it is not consecutive as the rest are (Alford). The particular "days" of this seal (or any other, for that matter) are never stipulated as they are in connection with the trumpet judgments to follow (cf. Rev. 10:7) (Alford). This reasoning is insufficient to demonstrate the point, however. The consecutive opening of the seals speaks of a consecutive fulfillment. Time yet remains before the end when this seal is opened (6:11), whereas under the seventh seal a point is reached when the climax is no longer delayed. So the offering of these prayers should be placed after the events represented in the first four seals and shortly before the events of the sixth seal. All six have as objects of judgment the rebellious earth dwellers.

Though not explicitly stated, the vision at this point reverts to the heavenly throne room. Dead people do not cry out on earth, and direct access to the holy and true master is possible only in heaven. Hence, *tou thysiastēriou* ("the altar") must be in heaven as it is everywhere else in this book (cf. Rev. 8:3, 5; 14:18) except in 11:1. What was a throne room in chapters 4-5 is now God's temple (cf. 11:19; 14:15, 17; 15:5, 8; Ps. 18:6; Mic. 1:2; Hab. 2:20). The combined conception of heaven as a kingly palace and as a temple occurs elsewhere in Scripture (Pss. 11:4; 29:9-10; Isa. 6:1) (Beckwith).

The nature of what is symbolized by *tou thysiastēriou* is important in tracing the continuity of the Apocalypse. One supposition is that it is the heavenly altar after which the altar of burnt offering was patterned.[92] Another sees it as the one after which the golden altar of

---

92. Swete, *Apocalypse,* p. 90; Lange, *Revelation,* p. 174; Scott, *Revelation,* p. 154.

incense was patterned (Beckwith). A third sees the altar as a blending of the two (Mounce). This last possibility can be dismissed in light of the radically different functions of the two altars. The purpose of interpretation is to clarify, not confuse, the issue of the altar's significance in the Apocalypse.

The altar-of-burnt-offering identification has merit because the blood of the sacrifices was poured at the bottom (cf. *hypokatō* ["under"]) of that altar (cf. Lev. 4:7).[93] Calling this an altar of sacrifice is also supported by the use of *esphagmenōn* ("slain"), a word frequently connected with animal sacrifices in the OT (Alford). The prominence of the altar of burnt offering led to its being referred to often as "the altar" as it is here (cf. *tou thysiastēriou*) (Lee). The concept of a martyr offering His blood as a sacrifice to God is paralleled elsewhere in the NT (cf. Phil. 2:17; 2 Tim. 4:6) (Beckwith).

The problems with identifying this as the altar of burnt offering are clearcut, however. If this were the altar of burnt offering, the souls of the martyrs would more likely be "on" rather than "under" the altar (Johnson). In the OT, it was the blood that was beneath the altar of burnt offering, but here it is the souls. The parallelism does not fit. Another weakness of the view is that it undercuts the uniqueness of the Lamb's sacrificial death (cf. 5:9). Since the once-for-all death of Christ, no more sacrifices are needed for redemption. Only the altar of incense is needed in heaven (Ladd; Morris). In the alleged parallels cited in Paul's writings (Phil. 2:17; 2 Tim. 4:6), no shedding of blood is involved because Paul uses σπένδω (*spendō*, "I pour out"), which refers to the drink offering (cf. Gen. 35:14; Num. 15:5-7) rather than the burnt offering. This carries no connotation of sacrificial death. Furthermore, it is not completely accurate to speak of the altar of burnt offering as the preeminent altar. The noun θυσιαστήριον (*thysiastērion*, "altar") is used without qualification to refer to the golden altar of incense several times in this book (cf. 8:3, 5; 14:17-18). The true assessment is that 6:9 is the only mention of an altar in Revelation with some apparent ties to the altar of burnt offering, except for the one in 11:1 that may well be an earthly rather than a heavenly altar.

An identification of this with the golden altar of incense is more probable. Throughout the book the heavenly altar is connected with the execution of judgment for which the saints are praying, and the prayers of the saints for judgment are symbolized by incense (cf. 5:8; 8:3, 4) (Beckwith). The contextual development of the Apocalypse is strong enough a consideration to require one altar and only one in

---

93. Robertson, *Word Pictures*, 6:343.

heaven. Otherwise, the continuity of the impact of the saints' prayers is lost.[94] In this work, heaven is often spoken of in terms of a sanctuary (11:19; 14:15, 17; 15:5, 8; cf. Heb. 9:24). The altar of incense was located adjacent to that sanctuary, but the altar of burnt offering was not. All factors considered, seeing this as the heavenly altar after which the golden altar of incense in the earthly Tabernacle and Temple was modeled is the wiser choice.

The term *tas psychas* ("the souls") refers to the total person as a rational being,[95] but whether or not it has implications regarding an intermediate body for the dead is debated. The fact that each one of these is given a στολὴ λευκή (*stolē leukē*, "white robe") may imply a body, because a robe cannot clothe what is immaterial (Bullinger; Walvoord). Yet this probably presses the symbolical scene too far. This vision is not designed to teach the condition of the saints between death and the coming of the Lord (Alford; Ladd). It is best to see *tas psychas* as referring to what once animated the bodies in contrast with the spirit (Lenksi). As is often the case with ψυχή (*psychē*, "soul"), the word refers to the "lives" or "persons" of the martyrs (Bullinger; Johnson). It was their lives that they had given up for Christ's sake. John saw only the souls, because their bodies had not yet been resurrected (cf. Rev. 20:4) (Lee).

Who were these martyrs? To generalize and say they represent all Christian martyrs of every age (Ladd) loses sight of the fact that their persecutors are still alive on earth at the time they pray. Much discussion has been devoted to saying they are the church in its suffering state (Swete). When it is noted that Stephen did not cry out for vengeance against his murderers (Acts 7:60) (Scott), it is adequate to respond that these martyrs are in heaven, not still upon the earth (Caird; Sweet). The spirit of the gospel is not to pray for vengeance (Lee; Bullinger), but these past martyrs are now beyond their mortal state and no longer subject to its limitations. Yet an assignment of these martyrs to the past does not account for the fact that the persecutors still live on earth as the prayers are uttered (Walvoord). The best rationale supports putting these martyrs in the prophetic seventieth week of Daniel (Walvoord), probably the first half of the week. This seal foretells miseries still to come by way of additional plagues that must happen soon, just before the personal return of Christ (Beckwith). The active role of the prayers of these martyrs and other saints in promoting the seventh seal, the seven trumpets, and the

---

94. Johnson, "Revelation," 12:475; see Excursus 2: The Imprecatory Prayers of the Apocalypse at the end of this volume.
95. MacArthur, *Revelation*, p. 165.

seven bowls should not be underestimated (e.g., 8:3-5). They bear a direct relationship to this future period of tribulation.[96]

The reason for the murder of these souls is expressed in *dia ton logon tou theou* ("because of the Word of God"). As with Rev. 1:2, 9, where the same expression occurs, a precise definition is desirable. Suggestions that it refers to the gospel given by God to men, including the truths of the resurrection and lordship of Christ (Ladd), that it is the confession of the one living and true God as contrasted with polytheism and Caesarism (Swete), that it is the Word of God and its claims upon the conscience of man (Scott), and that it is the divine revelation of Jesus in the gospel (Beckwith) all lack relevance to the context of Revelation. The proper way is to let the words that follow it furnish the definition. The Word of God here is none other than "the testimony received from Jesus" (Mounce). This takes the *kai* ("even") immediately after *theou* ("God") to have its ascensive force, as is often the case in this book.[97] This matches the nature of the construction in the two earlier passages (cf. Rev. 1:2, 9).

Because *martyrian* ("testimony") is not followed by a genitive as in 1:2, 9, it is sometimes taken in a different sense, that of a testimony the martyrs themselves have borne and suffered for (Swete). This interpretation fails to notice the implication of *eichon* ("they used to have"[98]), though. First and foremost, this is a testimony they held, not so much one they preached (cf. 12:17; 20:4; John 5:38; 14:21) (Beckwith; Mounce). This matches the conclusions reached in comparable uses of the noun earlier (cf. 1:2, 9) (Beckwith). This is "the testimony which they had received from the faithful witness and which they continued to hold" (Lee). The objection that this could hardly be limited to possessing the testimony and still be the cause of their martyrdom (Alford) is answered by viewing the testimony as a badge of allegiance to Christ, one that was visible to others. Their loyalty to Christ was conspicuous, and preaching it was only one way it showed (Smith). The ultimate cause of their martyrdom was their possession of this testimony.

6:10 Their plea to God is in the form of a question: καὶ ἔκραξαν φωνῇ μεγάλῃ λέγοντες, Ἕως πότε, ὁ δεσπότης ὁ ἅγιος καὶ ἀληθινός, οὐ κρίνεις καὶ ἐκδικεῖς τὸ αἷμα ἡμῶν ἐκ τῶν κατοικούντων ἐπὶ τῆς γῆς (*kai*

---

96. Govett, *Apocalypse*, p. 93; H. A. Ironside, *Lectures on the Book of Revelation* (New York: Loizeaux, n.d.), pp. 111-12; Epp, *Revelation*, p. 64; Charles Caldwell Ryrie, *Revelation*, Everyman's Bible Commentary (Chicago: Moody, 1968), p. 46.

97. Beckwith, *Apocalypse*, p. 526; Robertson, *Word Pictures*, 6:343.

98. The imperfect tense εἶχον conveys the constancy of their possession of the witness of Christ. Their clinging to His testimony was what produced their death (Robertson, *Word Pictures*, 6:343). Except for 1 Tim. 3:7, the combination of ἔχω with μαρτυρία serving as its object is found only in John's writings (cf. John 5:36; 1 John 5:10).

ekraxan phōnē megalē legontes, Heōs pote, ho despotēs ho hagios kai alēthinos, ou krineis kai ekdikeis to haima hēmōn ek tōn katoikountōn epi tēs gēs, "and they cried out with a loud voice, 'How long, holy and true Master, do you not judge and avenge our blood from those who dwell upon the earth?'").

Their prayer contrasts greatly to that of Stephen in Acts 7:60. It calls for vengeance rather than for the forgiveness Stephen sought for his oppressors. It is tempered by an acknowledgement that the martyrs' cause rests with one who is "holy and true" (Beckwith), but this prayer follows the pattern of the "imprecatory" psalms of the OT such as Ps. 74:9-10. The inspired psalmist could pray unselfishly as can these martyrs, but a prayer for pardon is more appropriate for a time of grace. When grace has exhausted its longsuffering, however, only judgment is left and prayers for righteous retribution are appropriate (Lenski). Such prayers come not just from a thirst for revenge. They are at least in part a protest against iniquity (Beckwith; Caird).

The manner of the petition is extraordinary. It is an outcry (*ekraxan*, "they cried out") and it comes in a loud voice (*phōnē megalē*). Κράζω (*Krazō*, "I cry out") describes the cry of Isaiah the prophet in Rom. 9:27 and the fervent prayer of the Spirit in the hearts of God's children in Gal. 4:6 (Ford). It is a strong word, emphasizing the urgent need of the hour in light of the coming kingdom (Beckwith). The verb tense shows this to be a single, definite appeal, not one that was continually urged.[99]

Heōs pote ("How long") is found frequently in the LXX (Charles). It is the well-known cry of suffering Israel (Scott). This perplexing question has been on the lips of the righteous almost since the beginning of the human race. It is the appeal of Abel's blood in Gen. 4:10 (Ford). Here the cry is addressed to *ho despotēs* ("master"), probably a title for God the Father (Swete; Lenski). The title carries the implication of divine might, majesty, power, and authority.[100] It is not the common word for "lord" in the NT, but recognizes more the absolute power of God. Only here is it applied to God.[101] The two qualities ascribed to God, *ho hagios kai alēthinos* ("holy and true"), are appropriate to His action in response to this prayer. He is holy in His apartness from evil and true in His faithfulness to His Word. He cannot tolerate iniquity. He must avenge.[102] The same two are applied to Christ in Rev. 3:7.

The carefully stated appeal avoids the mistake of telling God

99. Charles, *Revelation*, 1:174, 176. Ἔκραξαν is an aorist indicative.
100. Moffatt, "Revelation," 5:391; Lange, *Revelation*, p. 176.
101. Robertson, *Word Pictures*, 6:344; Alford, *Greek Testament*, 4:619; Ladd, *Revelation*, p. 105; Mounce, *Revelation*, p. 158.
102. Alford, *Greek Testament*, 4:619; Lange, *Revelation*, p. 176; Beckwith, *Apocalypse*, p. 526.

what He must do and when He must do it. It simply poses the question of how long He is refraining from judging the unrighteous and avenging the blood of the righteous who have been slain. The object of *krineis* ("judge") is not stated but is assumed to be the earth-dwellers named in the next clause. The blood of the righteous draws special attention, as did the blood of Abel. The petition is to carry out vengeance against those who have shed that blood,[103] *tōn katoikountōn epi tēs gēs* ("those who dwell upon the earth"). Throughout the Apocalypse, this expression is a semitechnical designation for mankind in their hostility to God (cf. 3:10; 8:13; 11:10; 13:8, 12; 17:2, 8) (Ladd; Mounce). They are the avowed opponents of the servants of God.[104] They are ungodly people who have no home but earth and want no home but earth (Lenski). It is not just the beast from the sea who will appear later to vent his wrath against the people of God. The whole race is in rebellion and is set on removing as many of God's servants as possible. Heard in this prayer are the voices of those who fall victim to them during the period called "the beginning of birth-pains."

6:11 God's immediate response to the martyrs' appeal is by way of symbolic act and spoken word: καὶ ἐδόθη αὐτοῖς ἑκάστῳ στολὴ λευκή, καὶ ἐρρέθη αὐτοῖς ἵνα ἀναπαύσονται ἔτι χρόνον μικρόν, ἕως *πληρωθῶσιν καὶ οἱ σύνδουλοι αὐτῶν καὶ οἱ ἀδελφοὶ αὐτῶν οἱ μέλλοντες ἀποκτέννεσθαι ὡς καὶ αὐτοί (*kai edothē autois hekastō stolē leukē, kai errethē autois hina anapausontai eti chronon mikron, heōs plērōthōsin kai hoi syndouloi autōn kai hoi adelphoi autōn hoi mellontes apoktennesthai hōs kai autoi, "and a white robe was given to each of them, and it was said to them that they should rest for a little time yet, until also their fellow slaves, even their brothers, who were about to be killed as also they themselves [had been], should have their number made complete"). The symbolic act is the granting to each one of a white robe (*stolē leukē*). *Stolē* was a robe of state, flowing to the feet. Here it is a reward of grace (cf. also Rev. 7:9, 14) (Lenski). It betokens the honor bestowed upon the faithful. Its color, *leukē* ("white"), pictures blessedness and the beauty of holiness. Here is the glory of the reward promised, similar to that promised the overcomers in the messages to the seven churches (e.g., Rev. 3:5) (Beckwith).

The issue of robes related to the existence of material bodies in heaven has been broached earlier. Jewish apocalyptic tradition consistently used white robes to represent the body of glory, i.e., the

---

103. Whenever ἐκδικεῖν is followed by ἐκ, the preposition introduces the persons from whom the vengeance is exacted (Charles, *Revelation*, 1:175).
104. Lange, *Revelation*, p. 176.

resurrection body. It is supposed that John was influenced by this (cf. 1 Enoch 62:16; 2 Enoch 22:8) (Caird; Mounce). Paul's teaching is sometimes cited as an analogy to this (cf. 1 Cor. 15:35ff.; 2 Cor. 5:1ff.; Phil. 3:21) (Caird). This reasoning overlooks the clear teaching that the resurrection body will not be received until Christ's return, however (cf. Rev. 20:4-5) (Beckwith; Ford). White robes are too common a figure to be interpreted so specifically without some further definition (cf. 3:18; 7:13-14; 22:14) (Mounce). Besides, if these robes represented intermediate bodies, the martyrs would have received them at death and would not have had to wait till some later time (Ladd). It must be concluded that these robes do nothing to advance the theological opinion about an intermediate body granted to the saints between death and bodily resurrection.

The spoken word to the martyrs, presumably from the Lord,[105] is rather difficult to analyze because of the two possible senses of *anapausontai* ("they should rest"). There is little question that it includes the thought of abstaining from their cry of vengeance and resting from their toil and pain. A case can be made for limiting the advice to this (Beckwith; Swete). The cognate noun ἀνάπαυσιν (*anapausin*, "rest") in Rev. 4:8 is limited to such a connotation. Yet this limitation determines that the word to them was an admonition to control their impatience, an unworthy trait to attribute to glorified beings in heaven. It is more in keeping with the scene to see the term as denoting not only an indication to stop the cry for vengeance, but also to rest in blessedness (Alford). It harmonizes better with their faultlessness to tell them to rest in the enjoyment of their heavenly benefits (Mounce). This is the meaning of the verb in Rev. 14:13.[106] Though *anapausontai* in itself does not express the idea of blessedness (Beckwith), the additional thought is inevitable in the context. An invitation to such rest is inseparable from the bliss of those already in glory with Christ.

The phrase *eti chronon mikron* ("for a little time yet") expresses the extent[107] of the proposed rest. The identical expression comes from the lips of Jesus twice, once in John 7:33 and once in John 12:35. The same words minus the *eti* ("yet") are used in Rev. 20:3 to tell of Satan's brief period of freedom after the Millennium. In the former case (John's gospel) the time is not more than about a year, and in the latter, just a matter of days. The proposal that it here points to the indefinite future, possibly hundreds of years from the persecution of

---

105. Ἐρρέθη is a passive voice that leaves the speaker unidentified (Lenski, *Revelation*, p. 238), but there can be little doubt that it is God who offers this word.

106. Alford, *Greek Testament*, 4:620; Robertson, *Word Pictures*, 6:344.

107. The accusative χρόνον μικρόν is an adverbial use of the accusative case to express extent of time (Robertson, *Word Pictures*, 6:344).

Christianity under the Roman emperor Trajan to the time of the Waldensians (A.D. 98-1209) or later,[108] is demeaning to the martyrs. Indefiniteness in such a situation is worse than no reply at all. Another idea is to equate the expression with the time of Satan's intensified wrath mentioned in Rev. 12:12 (Hailey). It makes sense that the two periods should coincide, because Satan in his wrath will take it out on those who will yet be martyred (Swete). His "little time" comes to an end when he is defeated and bound (cf. Rev. 20:1-3). The little time of the saints ends then too, for that is when they are raised to sit on thrones and reign for a thousand years (Hailey). The possibility of these two periods coinciding cannot be ruled out, but the verbal similarity between this verse and 12:12 is not striking. There the expression is ὀλίγον καιρόν (*oligon kairon*, "a brief season") compared to *chronon mikron* here. The verbal similarity to Rev. 10:6 is more convincing. There the angelic announcement is χρόνος οὐκέτι ἔσται (*chronos ouketi estai*, "there will be no more time [or delay]"). This is obviously the announcement of the end of the delay of which God informs the martyrs in 6:11 (Lee). As allowed above, this fifth-seal delay may coincide with the period of Satan's special wrath, but whether it does or not, it is important to note the advance in time between this seal and the special announcement in 10:6.

The remainder of v. 11 explains the need for the delay in God's final avenging of the martyrs' blood: *heōs plērōthōsin kai hoi syndouloi autōn kai hoi adelphoi autōn hoi mellontes apoktennesthai hōs kai autoi* ("until also their fellow slaves, even their brothers, who were about to be killed as also they themselves [had been], should have their number made complete"). Others were yet to give their lives for Christ. The number set in God's predetermined plan had not at this point been reached (Lenski). This roughly parallels concepts that Jesus taught in Matt. 23:29-32, particularly 23:32 (Beasley-Murray). The idea of a set number of elect ones, particularly those who are to die for their faith, is also found in extrabiblical tradition (cf. 1 Enoch 47:4; 2 Esdr. 2:41; 2 Apoc. Bar. 30:2) (Beckwith; Mounce). Πληρόω (*Plēroō*, "I complete") is used to speak of completing stipulated periods of time (cf. Luke 21:24; Acts 7:23, 30; 9:23; 24:27), but only here does it specify the reaching of a predetermined number of people. In fact, there is some theological objection to the notion that God has decreed a certain number of martyrs (Ladd). Yet these words lend themselves to that sense.

Kai hoi syndouloi autōn kai hoi adelphoi autōn may suggest two classes of people, "their fellow slaves and their brothers" (Lee). The first group is willing to be killed, but will not necessarily suffer mar-

---

108. Lange, *Revelation*, p. 176; Lee, "Revelation," 4:578.

tyrdom, and the second group includes the ones who will be killed (Swete; Smith; Hailey). Yet there is no ground for concluding that members of the former group will not experience death. They are in the same category as those already martyred (v. 9) and those yet to be martyred, according to the rest of the statement. There can be no full number reached unless all fall in the classification of those who give their lives. The participial clause *hoi mellontes apoktennesthai* ("who were about to be killed") modifies both groups and puts them into a single class. The redefinition offered in the second part is a sort of *hendiadys* (Bullinger). "Their fellow slaves" is made more specific by "even their brothers."[109]

The word to the souls under the altar gives them reassurance that God will eventually avenge their blood, but the time for the culmination of that vengeance has not yet arrived. One feature that must yet transpire beforehand is the increase of their number through additional martyrdoms. The earth dwellers under the dawning leadership of the beast from the sea will take an even greater toll of human lives before Christ finally intervenes through His personal arrival back on earth. Until then, the already martyred are told to rest and enjoy their state of blessedness already attained.

Additional Notes

6:11 Four possible readings are offered by various MS sources: the aorist passive subjunctive πληρωθῶσιν, the aorist active subjunctive πληρώσωσιν, the future passive indicative πληρώσονται, and the future active indicative πληρώσουσιν. MSS supporting both indicative readings are weak, so the last two options may be dismissed. The active subjunctive reading results in a sense such as "until their fellow servants complete [their course]" or "until they fulfill [their Christian calling]" (cf. Acts 13:25; 20:24; 2 Tim. 4:7) (Johnson). This is the harder of the two subjunctive readings because some direct object must be supplied, and πληροῦν is not used absolutely without an object anywhere else (Alford). It is so hard that it probably should be ruled impossible (Swete). The active subjunctive may have arisen through a copyist's error of sight or hearing. Because of the extreme difficulty of this reading and because of stronger MS testimony the aorist passive subjunctive is chosen. It too is somewhat difficult, but not impossible.

---

109. Beckwith, *Apocalypse*, p. 527. The first καί of the clause means "also," and the second one is epexegetic, as the word frequently is in this book. The idea of the two groups takes the two occurrences in combination to mean "both . . . and" (cf. Swete, *Apocalypse*, p. 92).

7. THE OPENING OF THE SIXTH SEAL: COSMIC AND TERRESTRIAL
DISTURBANCES (6:12-17)

Such judgments as occur under this seal are widely cited in apocalyptic descriptions of the end-time (Beckwith).

Translation

12And I looked when He opened the sixth seal, and a great earthquake occurred, and the sun became black as sackcloth of hair, and the whole moon became as blood, 13and the stars of heaven fell to the earth, as a fig tree casts its figs when shaken by a strong wind, 14and heaven was separated into parts as a scroll being rolled up, and every mountain and island were moved from their places. 15And the kings of the earth and the chief ones and the military commanders and the rich and the strong and every slave and free person hid themselves in the caves and in the rocks of the mountains. 16And they said to the mountains and rocks, "Fall on us and hide us from the face of the one sitting upon the throne and from the wrath of the Lamb, 17because the great day of their wrath has come, and who is able to stand?"

Exegesis and Exposition

6:12 After the opening of the sixth seal, John's attention is captured by sights that are nothing short of breathtaking: καὶ εἶδον ὅτε ἤνοιξεν τὴν σφραγῖδα τὴν ἕκτην, καὶ *σεισμὸς μέγας ἐγένετο (*kai eidon hote ēnoixen tēn sphragida tēn hektēn, kai seismos megas egeneto,* "and I looked when He opened the sixth seal, and a great earthquake occurred"). A great earthquake was the first thing to meet his eyes.

It is necessary, before examining the earthquake and other happenings in the series, to consider two questions about the series of events as a whole. The first is whether the descriptions should be understood symbolically or literally. Symbolic language is understood by a good number of commentators.[110] Among the reasons given is the established tradition of earlier prophetic pictures of the day of the Lord that can be traced through contemporary apocalyptic literature. Because of this tradition, which did not entertain the possibility of such literal happenings, no first-century readers would have taken these details literally (Mounce). Also, OT prophets are cited to prove the figurative nature of the language. Isaiah 2:12-19 is said to use the earthquake as a symbol for overthrowing human arrogance (Caird). The rolling up of the sky and the shaking of the stars picture the punishment of principalities and powers who stand be-

---

110. E.g., Ironside, *Revelation,* p. 114; Scott, *Revelation,* pp. 158, 160; Barclay, *Revelation,* 2:15; Caird, *Revelation,* p. 89.

hind the authority of human kings in Isa. 34:2-4 (Caird). Jesus applied Hos. 10:8 to the destruction of Jerusalem, not to an ultimate cosmic catastrophe (cf. Luke 23:28-31) (Caird). Yet this reasoning presupposes nonliteral meanings in the OT passages, which may not be valid. The most conspicuous deficiency of a symbolic explanation of the features of the sixth seal is that the things allegedly symbolized by the convulsion of the heavens (6:12-14), i.e., a convulsion of the nations, are described in literal terms (6:15-17) alongside the heavenly phenomena. The same distinction between a shaking of heavens and a convulsion among the people of earth is made in the OT counterpart to this description, Hag. 2:21-22 (Bullinger). The seal would hardly contain two descriptions of the same thing.

Perhaps the most convincing reason to take the events of this seal literally is Jesus' plain words in the companion Olivet discourse about coming earthquakes (Matt. 24:7; Mark 13:8; Luke 21:11).[111] His language could hardly have been figurative. Besides this, nothing short of an apparent awesome dissolution of the world would have such a devastating effect on the heart of mankind as this seal does (Mounce). Such physical upheavals as are noted here agree with the character of the period being described (Walvoord). The literal fulfillment of these words is necessary to do justice to OT prophecy, the Olivet discourse, and the truth of the dependence of the creation upon its Creator (Ladd).

Two precautionary words about the literalness of the sixth seal are in order. The suggestion of combining symbolic and literal (Mounce) is fraught with hermeneutical difficulty. It may be granted that the physical happenings result in political and social turmoil, but the first cause of all this is the cosmic and terrestrial disturbances. The other precaution is against stark literalness. The language is semipoetic or hyperbolic. The falling of the stars and the rolling up of heaven are only apparent (Ladd). If the moving of mountains and islands from their places (6:14) were universal and complete, there would be no hiding places left for men to seek (6:15-16). At the same time, the phenomena are so severe that they are unparalleled in human history. They are shattering enough to leave human beings with the full impression that the ultimate end has arrived, but they are not comprehensive enough to amount to a total destruction of creation's order. Human life continues after these disruptions.

The second preliminary question about the sixth seal delves into the time of its fulfillment. Does it come at the time of the end when Christ returns[112] or is it a forerunner of the last calamities (Beck-

---

111. Robertson, *Word Pictures*, 6:344-45.
112. Jennings, *Revelation*, pp. 212-14; Lenski, *Revelation*, p. 240.

with)? The strongest consideration for the former possibility is the parallelism between this seal and Matt. 24:29, which Jesus places "after the tribulation of those days" (Lee). It is the usual perspective of this approach that this is one of the three places in Revelation where John attains the brink of the last day (cf. 11:15-19; 16:17-21) (Lee; Beasley-Murray). The other two relate to the seventh trumpet and the seventh bowl. A crippling facet of this interpretation, however, lies in the fact that men still have opportunity to seek hiding places (6:16), an opportunity they will not have at the time Jesus returns (Hailey).

The preferable placement of this seal is some time in advance of the very end. In the plan of this book, this cannot be the absolute end because the seventh seal has not yet been opened. These events are not the immediate heralds of the end as similar ones are in the gospels. The end cannot come until the great persecution and martyrdom of the faithful has run its course (cf. Rev. 6:11) (Charles). Such physical upheavals as come under this seal apparently occur while the Tribulation is in progress and then are repeated on an even more devastating scale at the very end of the period (cf. Matt. 24:29).[113] Revelation 16:18 speaks of another earthquake at the very end (i.e., under the seventh bowl) that is unparalleled in human history. As severe as the sixth-seal earthquake is, no such statement accompanies its description. So the sixth-seal events are best understood as a preliminary foreshadowing of what Jesus places immediately after Daniel's seventieth week and immediately before His personal return (Bullinger).

The first part of this fear-evoking series is *seismos megas* ("a great earthquake"). Such a happening lies in a traditional eschatological scheme. This one is a forerunner of the final catastrophes yet to come (cf. Isa. 2:19; 29:6; Hag. 2:6, 7; Zech. 14:4, 5) (Beckwith). The English word *earthquake* is not quite adequate to describe this seal because the heavens are shaken along with the seas and the dry land. One suggested rendering is "convulsions" (Bullinger). These convulsions are precursors of the end, but do not announce immediate final judg-

---

113. Another viewpoint that denies the repetition of these cosmic disturbances suggests that they occur after the Great Tribulation (Matt. 24:29), but before the period of the outpouring of God's wrath consisting of the seventh seal, the seven trumpets and the seven bowls (Rosenthal, *Pre-Wrath Rapture*, pp. 141-42). This perspective rests upon a questionable distinction between the Great Tribulation and the period of God's wrath. It also stumbles at the fact that God's wrath has already begun at least as early as the sixth seal (cf. Rev. 6:17) and the fact that Christ placed His return to earth immediately after the termination of the Great Tribulation (Matt. 24:29-31), leaving no time for an alleged period of wrath after the Great Tribulation.

ment (Charles; Walvoord; Mounce). Their chronological placement is best accomplished through comparison with Jesus' Olivet discourse. In all the accounts of His listing of events during "the beginning of birth-pains," earthquakes come at the end or toward the end (Matt. 24:7; Mark 13:8; cf. Luke 21:11) and before the abomination of desolation at the midpoint of Daniel's seventieth week (Matt. 24:15; Mark 13:14). Neither Matthew's nor Mark's account of the discourse mentions the rest of the phenomena of this seal, but Luke's account of the discourse does allude to "fearful and great signs from heaven" in connection with the events of the other seals (Luke 21:11). The placement of these events just before the beginning of the last half of the prophetic week of Daniel is most likely.

The next four parts of the sixth-seal series pertain to heavenly occurrences: καὶ ὁ ἥλιος ἐγένετο μέλας ὡς σάκκος τρίχινος, καὶ ἡ σελήνη ὅλη ἐγένετο ὡς αἷμα, καὶ οἱ ἀστέρες τοῦ οὐρανοῦ ἔπεσαν εἰς τὴν γῆν, ὡς συκῆ βάλλει τοὺς ὀλύνθους αὐτῆς ὑπὸ ἀνέμου μεγάλου σειομένη, καὶ ὁ οὐρανὸς ἀπεχωρίσθη ὡς βιβλίον ἑλισσόμενον (*kai ho hēlios egeneto melas hōs sakkos trichinos, kai hē selēnē holē egeneto hōs haima, kai hoi asteres tou ouranou epesan eis tēn gēn, hōs sykē ballei tous olynthous autēs hypo anemou megalou seiomenē, kai ho ouranos apechōristhē hōs biblion elissomenon,* "and the sun became black as sackcloth of hair, and the whole moon became as blood, and the stars of heaven fell to the earth, as a fig tree casts its figs when shaken by a strong wind, and heaven was separated into parts as a scroll being rolled up").

In OT prophecy of an apocalyptic type, references to the darkening of the sun are common (cf. Isa. 13:10; Ezek. 32:7-8; Joel 2:10, 31; Amos 8:9; cf. Matt. 24:29; Mark 13:24-25; Luke 21:25) (Swete). The literal darkening of the sun will be a blackness comparable to *sakkos trichinos* ("sackcloth of hair"). This black garment was made of course cloth and worn as a visible expression of mourning and despair (cf. Isa. 50:3) (Beckwith; Lenski).

The reddening of the moon was another precursor of end-time judgment.[114] The reddish color expressed by *hōs haima* ("as blood") probably derives from the deep copper color of the moon during an eclipse when observed through atmospheric conditions (cf. Joel 2:31; Acts 2:20) (Swete; Beckwith). Because "the whole moon" (*hē selēnē holē*) is affected, this is a total eclipse that contributes to the panic of the world's population.

6:13 The third heavenly disturbance sees an unparalleled outbreak of meteors and comets (Seiss; Lenski). The noun *asteres*

---

114. Jennings, *Revelation*, p. 215.

("stars") can refer to larger heavenly bodies such as the sun, but its meaning is not limited to this. Its meaning is broad enough to include smaller objects that hurtle through space from time to time. In this case the stars are not the ultimate reference because they are still in place by the time of the fourth trumpet. The phenomenon is so large scale that it appears from man's perspective that the stars are falling, when in reality it is probably a very large meteor shower that invades the terrestrial atmosphere (Hailey). This is another aspect of "fearful and great signs from heaven" (Luke 21:11) that will strike terror in the hearts of men. The scope of the astral movement is so violent that it is likened to a fig tree that loses its unripe figs in a severe wind storm (*sykē ballei tous olynthous*[115] *autēs hypo anemou megalou seiomenē*). The sight will be awe-inspiring because these heavenly bodies will appear to be dropping like figs from a tree.

6:14 The fourth disturbance from above will affect the whole expanse of heaven as man sees it. Heaven will appear to split and roll back in two opposite directions: *kai ho ouranos apechōristhē hōs biblion elissomenon* ("and heaven was separated into parts as a scroll being rolled up"). The divided portions will shrivel, curl up like paper, and form a roll on either hand (cf. Isa. 34:4).[116] This is the human perception of the magnitude of the disturbance, but is not the ultimate passage of the heavens, which does not come until Rev. 20:11; 21:1 (cf. Ps. 102:25-26; Matt. 24:35; Mark 13:31; Luke 21:33; Heb. 1:10-12; 2 Pet. 3:10) (Beckwith). The impression of all these heavenly phenomena is that the universe is coming apart.

The account of the sixth seal returns to the earth at this point: καὶ πᾶν ὄρος καὶ νῆσος ἐκ τῶν τόπων αὐτῶν ἐκινήθησαν (*kai pan oros kai nēsos ek tōn topōn autōn ekinēthēsan*, "and every mountain and island were moved from their places"). The moving of the mountains with their islands is probably tied to the great earthquake in v. 12 and possibly to volcanic disturbances through which mountains and islands rise and disappear. This aspect of the upheaval has no precedent in OT prophecy or in apocalyptic writings (Charles; Beckwith). Because Jesus used the moving of a mountain in a figurative way to challenge His disciples' faith (Matt. 21:21; Mark 11:23; cf. 1 Cor. 13:2), some want to take this description to speak figuratively of the unsettling of established international powers (Swete; Charles; Scott). This is unconvincing, however, and would break the pattern already ob-

---

115. Ὀλύνθους refers to figs that grow under leaves during the winter, but seldom ripen. They become the untimely figs of spring and thus dry up and drop off during a dry wind (Swete, *Apocalypse*, p. 93; Lenski, *Revelation*, p. 241).

116. Swete, *Apocalypse*, p. 93; Mounce, *Revelation*, p. 162; Green, *Revelation*, p. 210.

served in the rest of the series. In other parts nonliteral elements are clearly indicated as similes (cf. *hōs*, "as," in vv. 12 [twice], 13, 14). No such indicator is present here (Smith). Such a geophysical change of the earth's surface occurs later on a much larger scale (cf. Rev. 16:20). A shifting in the earth's crust at this point is quite consistent with this.[117] John's language, however, must be hyperbolical here. The complete removal of every mountain would leave no hiding places for men to seek (6:16) (Beckwith). Many will be moved and even disappear, but complete abolition of all mountains will come at the seventh bowl judgment (cf. Rev. 16:20). At that point, no mountains will be found.

6:15 The resultant impact of the six-part upheaval upon humans will be nothing short of devastating: καὶ οἱ βασιλεῖς τῆς γῆς καὶ οἱ μεγιστᾶνες καὶ οἱ χιλίαρχοι καὶ οἱ πλούσιοι καὶ οἱ ἰσχυροὶ καὶ πᾶς δοῦλος καὶ ἐλεύθερος ἔκρυψαν ἑαυτοὺς εἰς τὰ σπήλαια καὶ εἰς τὰς πέτρας τῶν ὀρέων (*kai hoi basileis tēs gēs kai hoi megistanes kai hoi chiliarchoi kai hoi plousioi kai hoi ischyroi kai pas doulos kai eleutheros ekrypsan heautous eis ta spēlaia kai eis tas petras tōn oreōn*, "and the kings of the earth and the chief ones and the military commanders and the rich and the strong and every slave and free person hid themselves in the caves and in the rocks of the mountains"). Every category of humanity is covered by the sevenfold classification with special attention focused upon the upper classes in the first five items of the list.[118] *Hoi basileis tēs gēs* ("the kings of the earth") are the highest rulers, the heads of state of heathen nations (Swete; Charles; Lenski). *Hoi megistanes* ("the chief ones") are high-ranking officials of the kings' courts, civil officials in charge of implementing the executive functions of government (Beckwith; Lenski). *Hoi chiliarchoi* ("the military commanders") is the word for the Roman tribune (Moffatt). The name signifies that such an officer commanded a thousand men (Swete; Beckwith). At the command of such leaders armies advanced into battle (Mounce). Military might often determined the direction a nation would go. *Hoi plousioi* ("the rich") controlled the commerce of their various regions. The power of money in this world's society is undeniable. *Hoi ischyroi* ("the strong") are those who exercised great influence over significant numbers of people, whether through bodily strength, force of personality, or some other means (Lenski). These five classes are as impressive as any the human race has to offer.

The remaining people are covered by two more categories, considered as one group: *pas doulos kai eleutheros* ("every slave and free

---

117. Robertson, *Word Pictures*, 6:346.
118. Listings of humanity by category are characteristic of this author, with similar ones being found in Rev. 13:16 and 19:18.

person").[119] Together slaves and freemen made up the lower class of society without significant influence on other people but still frightened by the cosmic and terrestrial upheavals they had experienced.

All divisions of people responded in the same way. They "hid themselves in the caves and in the rocks of the mountains" (*ekrypsan heautous eis ta spēlaia kai eis tas petras*[120] *tōn oreōn*). They were seeking shelter from the collapse of the natural world. The uniqueness of what they saw told them that the routinization of nature to which they had become so accustomed was at an end and that the only alternative left was to hide. It was not rational to hide in the very mountains that were being shaken by earthquake (vv. 12, 14), but rationality was no longer an option. This was the only place they could think of.

6:16 Their impulse was: it is better to perish here than to remain and face the one sitting upon the throne and the wrath of the Lamb: καὶ λέγουσιν τοῖς ὄρεσιν καὶ ταῖς πέτραις, Πέσετε ἐφ' ἡμᾶς καὶ κρύψατε ἡμᾶς ἀπὸ προσώπου τοῦ καθημένου ἐπὶ τοῦ θρόνου καὶ ἀπὸ τῆς ὀργῆς τοῦ ἀρνίου (*kai legousin tois oresin kai tais petrais, Pesete eph' hēmas kai krypsate hēmas apo prosōpou tou kathēmenou epi tou thronou kai apo tēs orgēs tou arniou*, "and they said[121] to the mountains and rocks, 'Fall on us and hide us from the face of the one sitting upon the throne and from the wrath of the Lamb'"). The urgent[122] cry of people throughout the world is a call for those very mountains where they have gone into hiding to fall on them, a fate that is relatively better than having to face the awful agony of God's wrath. Three such cries are recorded earlier in Scripture, in Isa. 2:19 (cf. also Isa. 2:10, 21); Hos. 10:8; and Luke 23:30 (Hailey). The setting of each is a time of national calamity for Israel. All three are to some degree prophetic of the very time about which the sixth seal speaks. This is a graphic picture of terror and despair, probably the same general category of mourning spoken of already in Rev. 1:7 (Beckwith).

What sinners dread most is not death, but having to stand before a holy and righteous God. This is reflected in *krypsate hēmas apo prosōpou tou kathēmenou epi tou thronou* ("hide us from the face of

---

119. Πᾶς governs both δοῦλος and ἐλεύθερος, uniting them into one group covering the entire lower class (Lenski, *Revelation*, p. 242).

120. Πέτρας means "rocks," but it also designates "rocky masses" or "cliffs." Sometimes it even labeled a rocky chain of mountains (Lenski, *Revelations*, p. 242; Oscar Cullmann, "πέτρα," in *TDNT*, 6 [1969]:95).

121. Λέγουσιν is a vivid dramatic use of the present tense (Robertson, *Word Pictures*, 6:346; Leon Morris, *The Revelation of St. John*, TNTC [Grand Rapids: Eerdmans, 1969], p. 111). This is essentially the same as the historic present.

122. The aorist imperatives πέσετε and κρύψατε carry the note of urgency as is always true of the aorist imperative (Robertson, *Word Pictures*, 6:346).

the one sitting upon the throne") (Swete). More specifically, they dread "the wrath of the Lamb" (*tēs orgēs tou arniou*). Ὀργή (*Orgē*, "wrath") in most of its NT usages is a technical term for the eschatological visitation of God by way of temporal punishments against rebellious mankind (e.g., 1 Thess. 1:10; 5:9). Five other occurrences in Revelation (6:17; 11:18; 14:10; 16:19; 19:15) make this a rather frequent concept. The ten occurrences of the related word θυμός (*thymos*, "anger") (Rev. 12:12; 14:8, 10, 19; 15:1, 7; 16:1, 19; 18:3; 19:15) give an accurate impression of the nature of the seal, trumpet, and bowl visitations. Some question has been raised about the phrase "the wrath of the Lamb" because of the peaceful role of the Lamb elsewhere in the Apocalypse (Charles). It is an unusual expression inasmuch as the wrath of the incarnate Jesus became visible only when He twice cleansed the Temple. The word *orgē* is used only once in connection with His actions in the gospels (Mark 3:5) (Mounce). Yet His wrath is joined with God's wrath in the coming visitations (Beckwith). He is a Lamb, but He also has horns (Rev. 5:6) and He is lionlike (Rev. 5:5) as well as gentle. Paradoxically, the contrasting qualities merge in one person. This is the wrath of sacrificial love whose only option after rejection is to punish evil with utmost severity (Morris). That panic-stricken men would recognize the Lamb's role in inflicting their misery is remarkable.

6:17 The depth of their theological apprehension is even more remarkable in their grasp of the eschatological accountability that provokes this wrath: ὅτι ἦλθεν ἡ ἡμέρα ἡ μεγάλη τῆς ὀργῆς *αὐτῶν, καὶ τίς δύναται σταθῆναι; (*hoti ēlthen hē hēmera hē megalē tēs orgēs autōn, kai tis dynatai stathēnai?* "because the great day of their wrath has come, and who is able to stand?"). Mankind in his rebellion correctly[123] analyzes the cosmic and terrestrial disturbances as a part of the great end-time day of wrath from the one sitting on the throne and from the Lamb.

The verb *ēlthen* ("has come") is aorist indicative, referring to a previous arrival of the wrath, not something that is about to take place.[124] Men see the arrival of this day at least as early as the cosmic upheavals that characterize the sixth seal (6:12-14), but upon reflec-

---

123. Beckwith's proposal that this is the mistaken cry of men with which John would not agree (*Apocalypse*, p. 530) apparently rests upon a misunderstanding of the prolonged nature of the pouring out of God's wrath. Before being climaxed at its very end by Christ's personal return (Rev. 19:11-16), it will impose upon the world all sorts of temporal suffering because of man's rebellion against God.

124. Swete, *Apocalypse*, p. 95; Alford, *Greek Testament*, 4:622; J. Dwight Pentecost, *Things to Come: A Study in Biblical Eschatology* (Grand Rapids: Zondervan, 1958), p. 184.

tion they probably recognize it was already in effect with the death of one-fourth of the population (6:7-8), the worldwide famine (6:5-6), and the global warfare (6:3-4). The rapid sequence of all these events could not escape public notice, but the light of their true explanation does not dawn upon human consciousness until the severe phenomena of the sixth seal arrive.

The cumulative effect of the events produces the inevitable conclusion about the presence of *hē hēmera hē megalē tēs orgēs autōn* ("the great day of their wrath"). It is difficult to capture the Greek wording in English without a periphrasis such as "the day, that great day."[125] "The great day" is a title borrowed from the OT (Joel 2:11, 31; Zeph. 1:14; Mal. 4:5). Its mention is common in the NT also (e.g., Matt. 7:22; 1 Thess. 5:2; 2 Pet. 3:10). It is the central period into which all eschatological expectations converge (Beckwith). The primary passages from which John draws his images in the description of the sixth seal prove the reference of this phrase to be to the day of the Lord (Joel 2:11, 30-31; cf. Isa. 2:10-11, 19-21; 13:9-13; 34:4, 8; Ezek. 32:7-8; Hos. 10:8) (Beasley-Murray).

From the broad perspective of Scripture, the day of the Lord will be a time when God's wrath puts extended pressure on His enemies (Isa. 3:16-24; 13:9-11; Jer. 30:7; Ezek. 38-39; Amos 5:18, 19; Zeph. 1:14-18). By using terminology descriptive of the day of the Lord, Jesus identified part of that day with the Great Tribulation in particular and the whole of Daniel's seventieth week in general (cp. Matt. 24:21 with Jer. 30:7; Dan. 12:1; Joel 2:2). At the outset of the day of the Lord, human trials will be prolonged and comparable to a woman's labor before giving birth to a child (Isa. 13:8; 26:17-19; 66:7-9; Jer. 30:6-8; Mic. 4:9, 10; cf. Matt. 24:8; 1 Thess. 5:3).[126] This phase of growing human agony will be climaxed by the Messiah's personal return to earth to terminate the period of turmoil through direct judgment. Armageddon (Rev. 16:16; 19:11-21) and the series of Tribulation visitations that precede it are inseparable parts of the day of the Lord. God's eschatological wrath is a unit. This does not end the day of the Lord, however. Following Christ's personal intervention will come an extended time of blessing and prosperity for those who remain to populate the earth. As the OT makes quite clear, these times too are within the day of the Lord (e.g., Isa. 30:23-25; 35:1-10; Joel 3:18; Zech. 14:6-11). The day of the Lord, therefore, will include the seventieth week of Daniel's prophecy, the time of Christ's personal return, and His reign over the earth subsequent to that.[127]

---

125. Alford, *Greek Testament*, 4:622. The second article lifts the adjective from its mere epithetic function and makes it almost a title.
126. Pentecost, *Things to Come*, p. 230; Alva J. McClain, *The Greatness of the Kingdom* (Grand Rapids: Zondervan, 1959), pp. 186-91.
127. Cf. Kenneth L. Barker, "Zechariah," in *EBC*, 7:619-20; Robert L. Thomas,

Efforts to limit the day of the Lord to Armageddon only[128] do not account for all the data of Scripture. It has already been shown that the events of the sixth seal, which are so clearly placed within the day of the Lord in the OT, are not a collapse of the physical universe such as will accompany Christ's personal return (Smith; Caird). Unquestionably, "the day of the Lord" in Scripture includes terrors that immediately precede the personal return of Christ. The sixth seal can hardly be the arrival of Christ, because in the plan of this book the seventh seal has yet to be opened. The sixth seal cannot be anticipatory of the great day of wrath about to happen, because it would have the earthlings announcing the soon-arrival of something that will, as Scriptural teaching indicates, catch them by complete surprise (cf. 1 Thess. 5:2; 2 Pet. 3:10). This is not the actual end, but an anticipation of worse to come under the seventh seal (Swete). The happenings thus far are not introductory to or an accompaniment of the great day of the Lord. They are the beginning of the woes that compose that day and in themselves are prophetic of more dreadful calamities yet to come under the seventh seal (Beckwith). This opening phase of the day of the Lord should be identified closely with "the hour of trial" (3:10) and the period of the seals in its entirety. So with a general knowledge of what the Bible teaches about the future, the unsaved world correctly notes that "the great day of their wrath" is already in progress.

The final part of their words, *kai tis dynatai stathēnai?* ("and who is able to stand?"), raises the question of who will have the capacity to survive what the future holds. The question does not refer to standing before God to be judged.[129] It has to do with remaining on earth and maintaining an existence with the awareness that hardships will worsen as the intensity of God's wrath grows. The question is rhetorical and has the effect of an unequivocal assertion that no one will survive. The prophet Nahum asks the same question about that future day: "Who can stand before His indignation? Who can endure the burning of His anger? His wrath is poured out like fire, and the

---

"1 Thessalonians," in *EBC*, 11:281; Robert L. Thomas, "2 Thessalonians," in *EBC*, 11:314, 319-23.

128. Robert H. Gundry, *The Church and the Tribulation* (Grand Rapids: Zondervan, 1973), pp. 91-92. The generalization that sometimes the paralleling of events of the day of the Lord and passages in Revelation is more apparent than real (ibid., p. 91) does injustice to how close a connection John and his first-century readers must have made between the details of the Apocalypse and their OT source. A systematic analysis of the Apocalypse, such as the current investigation of the sixth seal, renders inescapable the conclusion that John thought and his readers understood the words about tribulation prior to Christ's return to be talking about the day of the Lord described in the OT.

129. Contra Moffatt, "Revelation," 5:394.

rocks are broken up by Him" (Nah. 1:6). The despair of mankind is complete. What an incentive for people in the seven churches to follow Christ faithfully and seek deliverance from this indescribably terrifying period (cf. Rev. 3:10-11).

Additional Notes

6:12 The inclusion of ἰδού before σεισμός by some witnesses is typical (cf. 6:2, 5, 8), but those that support it are weaker than those that exclude it from the text. It should not be read here. Other textual variations in this clause have even weaker support than the inclusion of ἰδού and should not be considered serious possibilities.[130]

6:17 An impressively strong group of MSS support the singular αὐτοῦ instead of the plural αὐτῶν. The plural is preferred, however, because with its ambiguity, it is the harder reading. A copyist more easily would have changed it to a singular to agree with the Lamb as the source of wrath in the previous verse. MS support for the plural is also quite substantial.[131]

Sproule raises the possibility, without endorsing it, that ἦλθεν is a dramatic aorist that would give no time indication for the beginning of the great day of wrath (John A. Sproule, *In Defense of Pre-Tribulationism* [Winona Lake, Ind.: BMH, 1980], pp. 54-55). The only time an aorist indicative speaks of something future or something about to happen, however, is if it is a dramatic aorist (H. E. Dana and Julius R. Mantey, *A Manual Grammar of the Greek New Testament* [New York: Macmillan, 1927], p. 198), a futuristic aorist (BDF, par. 333 [2]), or a proleptic aorist (Nigel Turner, *Syntax*, vol. 3 of *A Grammar of New Testament Greek* [Edinburgh: T. & T. Clark, 1963], p. 74). Some contextual feature must be present to indicate clearly these exceptional usages. No such feature exists in the context of the sixth seal, so these special uses are not options here. Rosenthal cites a use of the same verb form in Rev. 19:7 to demonstrate its futuristic connotation (*Pre-Wrath Rapture*, pp. 166-67), but this usage is in one of the heavenly songs that often in the Apocalypse utilize proleptic aorists (e.g., Rev. 11:15-19). His citation of ἦλθεν in Mark 14:41 is not relevant to the sixth seal, because the historical context of that passage clearly refers to Christ's coming crucifixion. The verb in Rev. 6:17 must be a constative aorist looking back in time to the point in the past when the great day of wrath arrived.

130. Metzger, *Textual Commentary*, p. 741.
131. Ibid., pp. 741-42.

13
The Slaves of God

The assertion that no one will survive the crescendo of God's wrath, as implied in the question of panic-stricken humanity (6:17), is corrected by two new visions injected after the conclusion of the sixth seal. The first pictures angelic actions of restraint and sealing.

8. THE SLAVES OF GOD (7:1-17)

a. Those on Earth: The 144,000 (7:1-8)

Translation

¹**After this I saw four angels standing at the four corners of the earth, holding firmly the four winds of the earth, that the wind should not blow upon the earth or upon the sea or against any tree. ²And I saw another angel ascending from the rising of the sun, having the seal of the living God, and he cried out with a loud voice to the four angels to whom it was granted that they should hurt the earth and the sea, ³saying, "Do not hurt the earth or the sea or the trees until we seal the slaves of our God upon their foreheads." ⁴And I heard the number of those sealed, one hundred forty-four thousand, those who were sealed from every tribe of the sons of Israel:**

⁵**from the tribe of Judah twelve thousand sealed,**
from the tribe of Reuben twelve thousand,
from the tribe of Gad twelve thousand,
⁶**from the tribe of Asher twelve thousand,**

from the tribe of Naphtali twelve thousand,
from the tribe of Manasseh twelve thousand,
⁷from the tribe of Simeon twelve thousand,
from the tribe of Levi twelve thousand,
from the tribe of Issachar twelve thousand,
⁸from the tribe of Zebulun twelve thousand,
from the tribe of Joseph twelve thousand,
from the tribe of Benjamin twelve thousand sealed.

Exposition and Exegesis

The two visions of chapter 7 separate the sixth and seventh seals.[1] The obvious purpose of this pair of visions is to contrast the preparedness of God's people to face the emergency with the panic of the world that is completely unprepared.[2] They answer the question, "Who shall be able to stand?" (6:17), and act as a stimulus for hope for the believing remnant during this future period. Though the world around is apparently falling apart, God's restraining and protecting hand is outstretched to undertake the cause of the faithful. They need not share the despair of the earth-dwellers.

Because the visions constitute a pause in the chronological progression represented by the opening of the seals, they have been called a parenthesis between the sixth and seventh seals,[3] but there is some objection to this because the visions are an integral part of the book's movement.[4] Regardless of terminology, the function of the visions is agreed upon. They reflect that the status of believers at this point in the series is radically different from that of the world's rebels.

7:1 Four angels move to center-stage as the new vision begins: μετὰ τοῦτο εἶδον τέσσαρας ἀγγέλους ἑστῶτας ἐπὶ τὰς τέσσαρας γωνίας τῆς γῆς, κρατοῦντας τοὺς τέσσαρας ἀνέμους τῆς γῆς, ἵνα μὴ πνέῃ ἄνεμος ἐπὶ τῆς γῆς μήτε ἐπὶ τῆς θαλάσσης μήτε ἐπὶ πᾶν δένδρον (*meta touto eidon tessaras angelous hestōtas epi tas tessaras gōnias tēs gēs, kratountas tous tessaras anemous tēs gēs, hina mē pneę anemos epi tēs gēs mēte epi tēs thalassēs mēte epi pan dendron*, "after this I saw four angels standing at the four corners of the earth, holding the four winds of the earth, that the wind should not blow upon the earth or upon the sea or against any tree"). That this is a new vision is shown by the phrase

---

1. Rev. 10:1–11:13 produces a similar break between the sixth and seventh trumpets.
2. Henry Barclay Swete, *The Apocalypse of St. John* (London: Macmillan, 1906), p. 95.
3. Robert H. Mounce, *The Book of Revelation*, NICNT (Grand Rapids: Eerdmans, 1977), p. 164.
4. R. C. H. Lenski, *The Interpretation of St. John's Revelation* (Columbus, Ohio: Lutheran Book Concern, 1935), p. 244.

meta touto ("after this") that introduces the scene. In the discussion of μετὰ ταῦτα (*meta tauta*, "after these things") at Rev. 4:1, it was observed how that expression followed by εῖδον introduces a new vision. *Meta touto* ("after this") does the same, with the singular *touto* ("this") rather than the plural *tauta* ("these things") viewing the events of the sixth seal as a single entity.

Because the placement of this vision's fulfillment depends to some degree on the time of the sealing mentioned in 7:3, it is advantageous to deal with that issue here. One opinion places it after the seventieth week of Daniel, viewing the setting of both visions of the chapter as the millennial earth.[5] The placement of both visions on earth, however, is highly questionable because of the presence of the four living beings and 24 elders in 7:11. These groups are in heaven. Another suggested time of the scene is at the beginning of the seventieth week.[6] The stillness before the four winds blow is taken as an indication that the time of tribulation has not yet begun (Bullinger). Because of an analogy with Zech. 6:5, the four winds are identified with the four horsemen met earlier, so the vision carries back in time prior to the first seal (Caird). This last observation is based on a mistranslation of Zech. 6:5, however. The verse says that the four chariots "are *going forth to* the four winds of heaven," not that they *are* the four winds (Mounce). As for the significance of the stillness, it is doubtful conjecture to use it as a basis for making this vision retroactive.

The natural meaning of the text places the sealing and the vision as a whole just after the sixth seal. Revelation 7 is an interlude between the sixth and seventh seals. This is proved by the change in tone from the subject matter of the sixth seal and by the delay until Rev. 8:1 in the opening of the seventh seal (Johnson). The description is provided to answer the question of 6:17 by way of showing that some will survive and even prosper spiritually under the blessing of God during earth's terrors.[7] At the sixth seal there has been chronological progression up to the midpoint of the seventieth week. As will be shown below, the sealing comes to protect those who serve

---

5. Walter Scott, *Exposition of the Revelation of Jesus Christ* (Swengel, Pa.: Bible Truth Depot, n.d.), p. 162.
6. E. W. Bullinger, *The Apocalypse* or *"The Day of the Lord"* (London: Eyre and Spottiswoode, n.d.), p. 279; G. V. Caird, *A Commentary on the Revelation of St. John the Divine*, HNTC (New York: Harper & Row, 1966), p. 94; Alan F. Johnson, "Revelation," in *EBC*, ed. Frank E. Gaebelein (Grand Rapids: Zondervan, 1981), 12:477.
7. James Moffatt, "The Revelation of St. John the Divine," in *The Expositor's Greek Testament*, ed. W. Robertson Nicoll (Grand Rapids: Eerdmans, n.d.), 5:394.

God from the effects of the trumpet judgments during the last half of the week. It is a valid question as to why the people of God do not have such protection from the wrath of God during the first half of the week. Perhaps the indirect nature of the wrath's early manifestation does not require it. The text is not explicit on this point. The evidence is sufficient for placing this sealing just before the midpoint of the seven-year Tribulation, at the end of the period called "the beginning of birth pains." Though the *meta touto* indicates a change of vision, this does not mean there is no relationship to the sixth seal.[8]

The agents in control of the four winds are *tessaras angelous* ("four angels"). These are somewhat comparable to the angel of fire in 14:18 and the angel of water in 16:5 (Swete). They are of a somewhat lower station than the living beings and the elders and have charge of the forces of nature. One in this class could be described as a στοιχεῖον (*stoicheion*, "spirit," "demon," or "genius").[9] The angels control the forces of nature and in Jewish tradition were viewed as a somewhat inferior angelic order.[10] Such a categorization is without biblical basis, however. All that can be stated with confidence about these is that they had the particular responsibility assigned to them in this text.[11]

The four are located *epi tas tessaras gōnias tēs gēs* ("at the four corners of the earth"). Though sometimes taken as reflecting the ancient cosmology of a square earth,[12] this is an accommodative term used to designate the four directions of the compass, the whole earth (cf. Isa. 11:12; Rev. 20:8).[13] The earth is not a flat square with four corners (Lenski). The language is figurative to indicate the worldwide nature of these angels' responsibility. These four points of the compass are points of origination from which the four winds proceed (cf. Jer. 49:36; Matt. 24:31).[14] The threefold repetition of the numeral *tessaras* ("four") is a means of marking the universality of this angelic action.[15] In light of this emphasis, *gēs* ("earth") should not be limited

---

8. Contra Isbon T. Beckwith, *The Apocalypse of John* (New York: Macmillan, 1919), p. 541.
9. R. H. Charles, *The Revelation of St. John*, 2 vols., ICC (New York: Scribner's, 1920), 1:203.
10. William Barclay, *The Revelation of John*, 2 vols., 2d ed. (Philadelphia: Westminster, 1960), 2:23.
11. Henry Alford, *The Greek Testament*, 4 vols. (London: Longmans, Green, 1903), 4:622.
12. J. Massyngberde Ford, *Revelation*, vol. 38 of AB (Garden City, N.Y.: Doubleday, 1975), p. 115.
13. Mounce, *Revelation*, p. 165; Homer Hailey, *Revelation, an Introduction and Commentary* (Grand Rapids: Baker, 1979), p. 201.
14. Swete, *Apocalypse*, p. 95; William Lee, "The Revelation of St. John," in *The Holy Bible*, ed. F. C. Cook (London: John Murray, 1881), 4:586.
15. Scott, *Revelation*, p. 163; J. B. Smith, *A Revelation of Jesus Christ* (Scottdale, Pa.: Herald, 1961), p. 128.

to the land of Palestine or to the Roman world of the time in any of its three uses in v. 1. It is the earth in its largest sense (Scott).

The realm of control of the four angels is shown in the words *kratountas tous tessaras anemous tēs gēs* ("holding the four winds of the earth"). Κρατέω (*Krateō*) means "hold fast," "hold firmly," or "detain." At each of four points of the compass one of the four winds is held prisoner by an angel who controls its movements. The mission of the four angels is to prevent outbreaks of elemental fury (Swete). The strength of the verb's meaning implies that the winds are struggling to get loose, but are being restrained.[16] The four winds picture God's destructive action against the earth in prophetic literature (cf. Jer. 49:36-38; Dan. 7:2; Hos. 13:15) (Mounce). The Jewish concept was that winds blowing from the four quarters, i.e., due north, south, east, and west, were favorable, but those blowing from angles or the four corners, i.e., east-northeast, west-northwest, etc., were harmful (cf. 1 Enoch 34:2-3; 76:1-14) (Charles). Revelation 7:1 speaks only of unfavorable winds, those that when unleashed will bring harm to the earth (7:2-3).

Whether or not to attach special symbolic significance to these winds has been debated. Seeing no special meaning is argued for by Mark 13:27 where Jesus uses the four winds merely to speak of universality (Lenski). The case here is different, though. They are agents of destruction, and the safeguarding of the elect in that earlier discourse by Jesus is not in view at this point in Revelation (Moffatt). One approach assigning special significance to the winds identifies them as the divine judgments under the first six seals (Lee), particularly the four horsemen of the first four seals (Caird). This connection, which makes 7:1-3 retrospective, rests largely on understanding Zech. 6:5 to say that the four horses are "the four winds of heaven," and thereby identifying the four horsemen with the four winds also.[17] As already indicated, this is probably a mistranslation of Zech. 6:5, however, so there is no identification of the horses with the winds (Mounce). A retrospective understanding of Rev. 7:1-3 ignores *meta touto* ("after this") in 7:1 and the chronological sequence that it represents.

It is wiser to see the winds as a picturesque apocalyptic way of referring to the plagues that are shortly to happen to mankind.[18] Because of the fluidity of apocalyptic language, the release of the winds is not mentioned later, being replaced by the seven angels with

---

16. Scott, *Revelation*, p. 164; Lenski, *Revelation*, p. 247. See the discussion of κρατέω at 2:1.

17. Caird, *Revelation*, p. 94; G. R. Beasley-Murray, *The Book of Revelation*, NCB (Grand Rapids: Eerdmans, 1978), p. 142.

18. George E. Ladd, *A Commentary on the Revelation of John* (Grand Rapids: Eerdmans, 1972), p. 111.

trumpets, at whose sounding the plagues fall upon the earth (Johnson). The first two trumpet judgments affect the same parts of creation as the winds, i.e., the earth, the trees, and the sea (cf. 8:6-9), so the angelic restraint here is in essence a delaying of the initiation of the trumpet series. Further confirmation of the connection between the four winds and the coming trumpet judgments comes in the sealing that must precede the release of the winds (cf. 7:2-4). As reflected in Rev. 9:4, this protects the servants of God from the effects of the trumpets as the sealing of Ezek. 9:4-8 protected the righteous remnant from the ministers of slaughter in Jerusalem. Such a mark set on certain people protects them from the harm inflicted on the rest (Beckwith). The regular use of winds to depict destructive forces from God coincides with this interpretation.

Some argumentation has sought to prove that Rev. 7:1-8 is from another source and was a later addition to the Apocalypse, because the section is so Jewish and so detached from the rest of the book (Charles; Moffatt; Mounce). A Christian writer, it is argued, would hardly have listed the twelve tribes separately as is done in vv. 5-8 in speaking of the church as the 144,000. This line of reasoning overlooks the relation between the winds and the trumpet judgments alluded to above, however. As a matter of fact, it does fit into the flow of the Apocalypse quite smoothly. The problem with the section's Jewishness is only apparent, resting on a misunderstanding of the identity of the 144,000. If national Israel instead of the church is in view, the difficulty dissolves. This issue will be addressed beginning at 7:4.

The angelic restraint exists *hina mē pneę̄ anemos epi tēs gēs mēte epi tēs thalassēs mēte epi pan dendron*[19] ("that the wind should not blow upon the earth or upon the sea or against any tree"). The nature of the construction and the verb tense could suggest the sense, "lest a wind keep on blowing."[20] This would indicate that the winds of de-

---

19. The preposition ἐπί occurs three times in this series. In the first two instances it governs the genitive case (i.e., τῆς γῆς and τῆς θαλάσσης) and in the last the accusative (i.e., πᾶν δένδρον). The reason for the difference is that the wind is conceived of as blowing *upon* the surface of the land and sea and *against* every tree (Swete, *Apocalypse*, p. 96; Beckwith, *Apocalypse*, p. 541).

20. A. T. Robertson, *Word Pictures in the New Testament*, 6 vols. (Nashville: Broadman, 1933), 6:348. The present subjunctive πνέῃ focuses on the durative aspect of verbal action. The relative rarity of the present subjunctive indicates that whenever it is used, its design is to indicate continuity, particularly in John's writings (Edwin A. Abbott, *Johannine Grammar* [London: Adam and Charles Black, 1906], pp. 369, 381; A. T. Robertson, *A Grammar of the Greek New Testament in the Light of Historical Research* [Nashville: Broadman, 1934], pp. 889-90).

struction had already begun to mount (Mounce). Yet they had not yet struck, as this verse indicates. The world was in every other way ready. Only the detail of the sealing of the 144,00 remained before the unleashing of these destructive winds.

It is doubtful that *tēs thalassēs* ("the sea") should be invested with the symbolic connotation of nations and people in anarchy (cf. Isa. 57:20; Dan. 7:2,3) or that *dendron* ("tree") should be taken as representative of the might and pride of the earth (cf. Ezek. 31:3-9; 14-18; Dan. 4:10, 22).[21] No symbolism is involved. The terms should be taken literally as they are in connection with the first two trumpet judgments (Lenski).

7:2 The next sight to greet John's eyes was a fifth angel: καὶ εἶδον ἄλλον ἄγγελον ἀναβαίνοντα ἀπὸ ἀνατολῆς ἡλίου (*kai eidon allon angelon anabainonta apo anatolēs hēliou*, "and I saw another angel ascending from the rising of the sun"). Various special identities that have been assigned to this angel have included Christ, the Holy Spirit, an archangel, a special messenger from Christ, and the prophet Elijah (Lee). These are all mistaken for two reasons. First, *allon* ("another") expresses numerical difference and indicates another of the same kind. This angel is of the same character as the first four (Hailey). Second, by use of the first person plural in this angel's address to the other four (σφραγίσωμεν [*sphragisōmen*, "we seal"] and ἡμῶν [*hēmōn*, "our"], 7:3), he identifies himself with them in a common task (Alford; Scott). He is best seen as another of the spirit beings who is distinguished because of the exalted mission committed to him.

John sees him "ascending from the rising of the sun" (*anabainonta apo anatolēs hēliou*). It is implied that he has been occupied with some earlier service on earth and now rises to the sky to deliver his message to the four angels (Swete). Whatever his earlier involvement, it appears to have been to the east of Patmos, in the direction of Palestine and the countries beyond it. The usual way of designating the sunrising in the LXX is ἀπὸ ἀνατολῶν (*apo anatolōn*, "from the risings"), though the singular *anatolēs* ("rising") is sometimes used (cf. Gen. 19:2; Num. 3:38). Nevertheless, *hēliou* ("of the sun") is sometimes expressed (Josh. 1:15; 13:5; Isa. 11:11, 14).[22]

Though it has been taken as merely a picturesque detail or an impossible question to answer (Charles; Mounce), in light of the im-

---

21. Contra Scott, *Revelation*, p. 164; Leon Morris, *The Revelation of St. John*, TNTC (Grand Rapids: Eerdmans, 1969), pp. 112-13; Ford, *Revelation*, p. 115.
22. Swete, *Apocalypse*, p. 96. Though raptured in his spirit to the heavenly throne-room (cf. 4:1-2), it appears that through the process of these heavenly revelations, John maintained the geographical perspective of where this visionary experience began.

portance of the east elsewhere in Scripture (e.g., Rev. 16:12) it appears relevant to ask why this angel came from the east. A promising suggestion is that the picture is that of divine salvation that also comes from the east (Swete; Alford; Charles). It is recalled that Paradise was set up in the east (Gen. 2:8) and the glory of God comes to the Temple from the east (Ezek. 43:2) (Beasley-Murray). This direction also was the area whence the magi came at Jesus' birth (Matt. 2:1), indicating the direction from which the Messiah was expected to come.[23] Jesus is called "dayspring" (ἀνατολή [anatolē]) (Luke 1:78) and "morning star" (Rev. 22:16), which signals the arrival of daylight through the rising of the sun in the east (Sweet). Israel, so prominent in the first part of this chapter, will experience salvation through the "sun-rising" of Christ.[24] This is the reason the east suggests a message of cheer and encouragement (Hailey), but the significance of the east is not limited to just cheer and encouragement. The east is the direction of Palestine and is appropriate because in this section the twelve tribes of Israel are the ones sealed (Swete), but this is only part of this direction's significance. God has chosen to reveal His salvation from this area of the world. It is, then, appropriate that the angel should come from there.

In his possession the fifth angel had an item that is the focus of attention: ἔχοντα σφραγῖδα θεοῦ ζῶντος (echonta sphragida theou zōntos, "having the seal of the living God"). A σφραγίς (sphragis, "seal") was usually a signet ring that an oriental monarch affixed to give validity to official documents or to mark his property (cf. Gen. 41:42; Esther 3:10; 8:2, 8; Dan. 6:17). It was used to authenticate and to protect (Swete; Mounce; Ladd). This text does not explicitly say what this seal is, but Rev. 14:1 suggests that it is the name of the Lamb and that of His Father (cf. Isa. 44:5) (Beckwith; Mounce). Χάραγμα (Charagma, "mark") is the word to describe the label placed on the followers of the beast in Rev. 13:6, 7. It carries the connotation of branding or tattooing such as was practiced by pagan religions. This is an appropriate association for that terminology. Sphragis on the other hand had a rich meaning in Christian usage, including that of ownership (2 Cor. 1:22), authentication (John 6:27), and protection leading to final salvation (Eph. 1:14; 4:30) (Sweet). The seven seals (sphragisin) of the scroll (cf. Rev. 5:1) currently in the progress of being opened are an exception to this favored sense, of course. The present seal is distinguished from them because it is distinctively the one that is theou zōntos ("of the living God").

---

23. Mounce, *Revelation*, p. 167; J. P. M. Sweet, *Revelation* (Philadelphia: Westminster, Pelican, 1979), p. 148.
24. F. C. Jennings, *Studies in Revelation* (New York: Publication Office "Our Hope," n.d.), p. 222.

"The living God" is a familiar expression in both the OT (e.g., Josh. 3:10; Ps. 42:2; Hos. 1:10) and the NT (twice in Matthew, once in Acts, seven times in the Pauline epistles, four times in Hebrews). Similar references to God occur in Rev. 4:9, 10; 10:6; 15:7, where εἰς τοὺς αἰῶνας τῶν αἰώνων (*eis tous aiōnas tōn aiōnōn*, "forever and ever") accentuates the unending nature of God's existence. In its various forms, this kind of reference to Him emphasizes the contrast between the one eternal God and innumerable transitory gods of the heathen (Swete; Bullinger; Charles). His uniqueness and eternality assure the accomplishment of His purpose for His people (cf. 10:6; 15:7) (Beckwith). The title adds solemnity and vitality to the seal it identifies (Alford).

The symbolism of this seal is a rather evident allusion to Ezek. 9:4 where a man provided with a writing kit is bidden to set a mark on the foreheads of the righteous (Swete). This is a protective measure for them in view of an impending massacre in Jerusalem (Beckwith). The parallel between that case and the present one is in the protection afforded by the seal from forthcoming judgment (Charles). The preserving effect of the seal is explicit in connection with the fifth trumpet judgment (Rev. 9:4), but is implied in the other trumpets also.

The fifth angel directs his instruction to the other four: καὶ ἔκραξεν φωνῇ μεγάλῃ τοῖς τέσσαρσιν ἀγγέλοις οἷς²⁵ ἐδόθη αὐτοῖς ἀδικῆσαι τὴν γῆν καὶ τὴν θάλασσαν (*kai ekraxen phōnē megalē tois tessarsin angelois hois edothē autois adikēsai tēn gēn kai tēn thalassan*, "and he cried out with a loud voice to the four angels to whom it was granted that they should hurt the earth and the sea"). As did the souls under the altar (6:10), "he cried out with a loud voice" (*ekraxen phōnē megalē*) (Swete). This loud cry reflects the urgency of his mission. His first concern is protection of God's slaves on earth. Before the four angels release the elements which will wreak havoc on parts of the natural world, these saints must receive their mark of exemption from the ill effects of God's visitations against the rest of mankind.

7:3 The message of the angel ascending from the east explicitly fixes the sequence of the sealing and the release of the four winds: λέγων, Μὴ ἀδικήσητε τὴν γῆν μήτε τὴν θάλασσαν μήτε τὰ δένδρα ἄχρι σφραγίσωμεν τοὺς δούλους τοῦ θεοῦ ἡμῶν ἐπὶ τῶν μετώπων αὐτῶν (*legōn, Mē adikēsēte tēn gēn mēte tēn thalassan mēte ta dendra achri sphragisōmen tous doulous tou theou hēmōn epi tōn metōpōn autōn*,

---

25. The combination of a relative pronoun οἷς pointing forward to a functioning personal pronoun αὐτοῖς in the relative clause is another of the frequent indications of Semitic influence on the language of the Apocalypse. See 3:8; 7:9; 13:8, 12; 20:8 for other illustrations of this construction (Charles, 1:87, 205).

"saying, 'Do not hurt the earth or the sea or the trees until we seal the slaves of our God upon their foreheads'"). The prohibition *mē adikēsēte* ("do not hurt") tells the four angels to continue their restraint of the four winds a little longer. They are not even to allow the damage to begin[26] until the sealing work is done. Ἀδικέω (*Adikeō*, "I hurt") often means "I do wrong" elsewhere in the NT (e.g., Matt. 20:13; Acts 7:26; Rev. 22:11), but here it alludes to acts of judgment against the cosmos.[27] The four angels had power to damage "the earth or the sea or the trees" (*tēn gēn mēte tēn thalassan mēte ta dendra*[28]) in that their function was to set free the four winds and thus cause ruin (Lee).

Their infliction of destruction must wait *achri sphragisōmen tous doulous tou theou hēmōn epi tōn metōpōn autōn* ("until we seal the slaves of our God upon their foreheads"). The angel from the east includes others who assist him in the sealing task (Beckwith). The first person plural of *sphragisōmen* ("we seal") perhaps refers to help from the angels holding the four winds as assistants in the task of sealing (Lee), in which case they would be agents of God's mercy as well as agents of His wrath. Whoever the agents of sealing are, their mission is executed on behalf of *tous doulous tou theou hēmōn* ("the slaves of our God"). A closer look at the purpose of the sealing and the identity of these slaves is necessary.

One approach to the sealing ties it to the sacrament of baptism through a reference to Ezek. 9:4-6 where "the mark" was the Hebrew letter ת (*t*) which in its old form was shaped like a cross. The sign of the cross recalls that water baptism has replaced the Old Covenant circumcision.[29] The connection between this seal and baptism is quite remote, however. The sacramental view could hardly be correct, because here the seal is in the hands of an angel or several of them (Swete; Beckwith; Beasley-Murray; Mounce).

The seal is rather a pledge of security, but the security has been differently defined. One definition says it protects from the demonic

---

26. As is most often the case with prohibitions expressed by μή and the aorist subjunctive, this is an ingressive use of the aorist: "do not begin to hurt" (Robertson, *Word Pictures*, 6:349).

27. Gottlob Shrenk, "ἀδικός, ἀδικία, κ. τ. λ.," in *TDNT*, ed. Gerhard Kittel and Gerhard Friedrich, trans. and ed. Geoffrey W. Bromiley (Grand Rapids: Eerdmans, 1976), 1 (1964):160-61.

28. The same three spheres of nature are in v. 1, but in v. 2 the trees are omitted from the list of areas impacted by the winds controlled by the four angels.

29. Lee, "Revelation," 4:587. Some early Christian writings saw in Paul's words on the sealing of the Spirit (2 Cor. 1:22; Eph. 1:13; 4:30) references to water baptism and identified that sealing with the one here (Hermas *Sim.* 9, 16:3-4).

influences during the reign of Antichrist, but not from physical harm, from plagues, from the Antichrist himself, or from spiritual apostasy.[30] The factor that most favors this view is the clear indication that the seal exempts its bearers from the demonic plague of locusts in Rev. 9:4,[31] assuming that that plague is demonic. In spite of this favorable element, this places an unwarranted restriction on the protection. The destructive forces set in motion in connection with the seventh seal and the seven trumpets are not limited to demonic agencies (Beckwith). Though this seal may not protect from harm inflicted by human agencies (cf. 13:7; 20:4), it must protect from all the divine plagues that come against only those allied against God (cf. 16:2) (Johnson).

Another way to view the sealing is as an immunity from death (Scott). The reasoning is that they are already God's bondservants, so the sealing cannot be for spiritual salvation. The later appearance of this same group with the Lamb on Mount Zion (14:1-5) means they will enjoy physical preservation until they meet Christ at His return to earth (Walvoord). These being the elect of Israel, they will be gathered by the Lord after the Tribulation (cf. Matt. 24:31), having been protected and preserved unscathed (Bullinger). Though this explanation has merit, it does not handle all the data adequately. For this author, martyrdom is the ultimate goal of Christian faith. The highest place in the future awaits the martyrs. He certainly would not exclude the 144,000 from that number. They are not secured from physical death as Rev. 13:15 so distinctly indicates.[32] If God allows the beast to dispose of the two witnesses (Rev. 11:7), He certainly will not isolate the 144,000 from terminal harm inflicted by this archenemy.[33]

Another possibility is that the sealing protects the saints from destruction as in Ezekiel's vision. Though they must suffer, many of them even to the point of martyrdom, they will finally be brought to safety in the eternal kingdom (Beckwith). The book's emphasis on the need for endurance (cf. 13:10; 14:12), the prophecy of coming martyrdoms (cf. 6:11), and similar forebodings of distress (cf. 3:10) show that the saints will not escape suffering during these end times (Beckwith). It is inevitable that some of the plagues, such as the ones under the first four trumpets, will have some adverse effect upon them. Notwithstanding these apparently accurate observations, this approach

---

30. Charles, *Revelation*, 1:205; R. H. Charles, *Studies in the Apocalypse* (Edinburgh: T. & T. Clark, 1913), pp. 124-25.
31. Charles, *Revelation*, 1:205.
32. Ibid., 1:195-96.
33. Jennings, *Revelation*, p. 224.

overlooks a basic fact: the source of the saints' suffering is not God, but the enemies of God. God's wrath is not to be directed against His own, but against His enemies. It is from these enemies that His slaves will receive all sorts of bad treatment. The sealing does not protect from them, but it does protect from Him.

The best analysis of the seal is that it protects against the disasters that the four winds will bring to the earth (Beckwith; Caird). The context of 7:1-3 is in preparation for the judgments of the seventh seal that includes the seven trumpets. Thus the sealing must relate to these judgments. The command "do not hurt" implies that after the sealing is finished, the judgments that are next in the divine program (i.e., Revelation 8) will come (Smith). For what imaginable reason could such a prohibition be uttered, unless those who are sealed are being designated for some purpose connected with the work of destruction of the four angels, and for what purpose could they be marked out except for that of exemption? This is an important lesson that carries over from the parallel situation in Ezek. 9:4-7 where the faithful are sealed as protection against the divine slaughtering of the inhabitants of Jerusalem (Johnson). The parallel device of the beast to mark his own as special associates in his cause (cf. Rev. 13:16; 14:9, 11; 16:2; 19:20) shows this sealing of God's own to be in the character of a special guarantee of an alliance with Him in the future developments on earth (Moffatt).

Apparent weaknesses in this definition of the seal include its inability to explain why the sealing did not come before the judgments of the first six seals, protecting God's servants from the harm inflicted under the fourth and sixth seals (cf. 6:8, 17).[34] It also cannot account for the apparent effect of some of the future plagues upon them (e.g., 8:6–9:17), though some of them are specifically limited to God's enemies (Revelation 9;16) (Beckwith). The only response to these alleged deficiencies is to assume God's protection of them throughout. Perhaps sealing was unnecessary to protect God's people during the first six seal judgments because of their lesser intensity, but with the more direct nature of His visitations under the trumpets, a decisive step of protection is in order. How God protects His own from such as the first four trumpets with their devastating effects on the world of nature is not disclosed. It can only be assumed that He will do so.

A few comments about the identity of "the slaves of our God" (*tous doulous tou theou hēmōn*) are in order, though a more definitive discussion of who they are is more appropriate in v. 4. The designation *doulous* (cf. Rev. 1:1; 2:20; 19:2, 5; 22:3, 6) links these people with angels in the service of God (cf. Rev. 19:10).[35] *Hēmōn* ("our"), being

---

34. Lee, "Revelation," p. 585; Charles, *Revelation*, 1:195.
35. Robertson, *Word Pictures*, 6:349.

used in an address by angels to angels, picks up the bond of a common service that unites angels with the human servants of God.[36] "Our God" comes from angelic lips in 7:12; 19:1, 5 and from human lips in 7:10; 12:10.[37] The question of whether or not these are Jewish Christians only may be raised because of the obviously wider scope of the meaning of δούλοις (*doulois*, "slaves") in Rev. 1:1. This earlier reference to Christians of all backgrounds is sometimes taken to dictate the same here (Lenski). The surrounding context of 7:4-8 makes this conclusion untenable, however. The upcoming list of the twelve tribes, which further identifies the slaves, differentiates these slaves from those in 1:1 and requires this narrower understanding.

The placement of the seal is *epi tōn metōpōn*[38] *autōn* ("upon their foreheads") (cf. Ezek. 9:4). It was not uncommon for a soldier or a guild member to receive such a mark as a religious devotee. The mark was a sign of consecration to deity (Ford). The forehead was chosen because it was the most conspicuous,[39] the most noble, and the part by which a person is usually identified (Lenski). It will be obvious to whom these slaves belong and whom they serve.

7:4 John's report in v. 4 assumes that the sealing of v. 3 has taken place between the verses: καὶ ἤκουσα τὸν ἀριθμὸν τῶν ἐσφραγισμένων, ἑκατὸν[40] τεσσαράκοντα τέσσαρες χιλιάδες, ἐσφραγισμένοι ἐκ πάσης φυλῆς υἱῶν Ἰσραήλ (*kai ēkousa ton arithmon tōn esphragismenōn, hekaton tessarakonta tessares chiliades, esphragismenoi ek pasēs phylēs huiōn Israēl*, "and I heard the number of those sealed, one hundred forty-four thousand, those who were sealed from every tribe of the sons of Israel"). John heard the number of the ones identified by the seal from an undisclosed source. Perhaps the fifth angel of 7:2-3 is the announcer (Lee).

Various efforts have sought to determine the significance of the number 144,000. An understanding of the number as symbolical divides it into three of its multiplicands, 12 × 12 × 1000. From the symbolism of the three it is concluded that the number indicates fixedness and fullest completeness.[41] Twelve, a number of the tribes,

---

36. Swete, *Apocalypse*, p. 97; Charles, *Revelation*, 1:206.
37. "My God" is the phraseology of Christ in Rev. 3:2, 12.
38. The writer uses the genitive of this noun after ἐπὶ whenever it is plural (9:4; 14:1; 22:4) and the accusative whenever it is singular (13:16; 17:5; 20:4) except in 14:9 where he has ἐπὶ τοῦ μετώπου (Charles, *Revelation*, 1:206). It is difficult to assign any special significance to this difference.
39. John Peter Lange, *The Revelation of John*, vol. 10 of Lange's Commentary, ed. E. R. Craven (Grand Rapids: Zondervan, 1968), p. 189.
40. Ἑκατὸν τεσσαράκοντα τέσσαρες χιλιάδες is a nominative absolute, agreeing in case with neither ἀριθμόν, which is accusative, nor ἐσφραγισμένων, which is genitive (Robertson, *Word Pictures*, 6:350).
41. Alford, *Greek Testament*, 4:624; Charles, *Revelation*, 1:206; Lenski, *Revelation*, p. 154.

is both squared and multiplied by a thousand. This is a twofold way of emphasizing completeness (Mounce). It thus affirms the full number of God's people to be brought through tribulation (Ladd). The symbolic approach points out the impossibility of taking the number literally. It is simply a vast number, less than a number indefinitely great (cf. 7:9), but greater than a large number designedly finite (e.g., 1,000, Rev. 20:2) (Lee). Other occurrences of the numerical components that are supposedly symbolic are also pointed out, 12 thousand in Rev. 21:16, 12 in Rev. 22:2, and 24, a multiple of 12, in Rev. 4:4. This is done to enhance the case for symbolism (Johnson). Though admittedly ingenious, the case for symbolism is exegetically weak. The principal reason for the view is a predisposition to make the 144,000 into a group representative of the church with which no possible numerical connection exists. No justification can be found for understanding the simple statement of fact in v. 4 as a figure of speech. It is a definite number in contrast with the indefinite number of 7:9. If it is taken symbolically, no number in the book can be taken literally. As God reserved 7,000 in the days of Ahab (1 Kings 19:18; Rom. 11:4), He will reserve 144,000 for Himself during the future Great Tribulation.[42]

One literal understanding of the number sees it as indicating the count of persons who will be brought safely through the Tribulation (Walvoord). As exhibited above, however, it is questionable that sealing guarantees complete physical preservation during this period. A better understanding of 144,000 takes it as a select group of martyrs during the Tribulation period.[43] Usually those who hold the view do so with the mistaken idea that the purpose of the sealing is for martyrdom rather than protection, however (Kiddle; Caird). They coincide with those yet to be martyred in 6:11 and with the picture of 144,000 martyrs presented in 14:1-5 (Mounce). Besides a misunderstanding of the purpose of the sealing, the problem with this view is that it leaves no room for a believer who will not face martyrdom in the last days (cf. 13:15) (Mounce). This is not the total number of believers of that last time, only a special group of them set aside for

42. Bullinger, *Apocalypse*, p. 282. Geyser is correct in observing that the predominant concern of the Apocalypse is "the restoration [on earth] of the twelve tribes of Israel, their restoration as a twelve-tribe kingdom, in a renewed and purified city of David, under the rule of the victorious 'Lion of the Tribe of Judah, the Root of David' (5. 5; 22. 16)" (Albert Geyser, "The Twelve Tribes in Revelation: Judean and Judeo Christian Apocalypticism," *NTS* 23, no. 3 [July 1982]: 389). He is wrong, however, in his theory that this belief characterized the Judean church only and was not shared by Gentile Christianity spearheaded by Paul (ibid., p. 390).
43. Martin Kiddle, *The Revelation of St. John*, MNTC (London: Hodder and Stoughton, 1940), pp. 135-36.

the purpose of witnessing to a rebellious world. Nothing is said here about the rest of the saved. It is only noted that these will have special protection from the wrath of God while they witness. After their witness is concluded, martyrdom may well be their fate, as subsequent discussion of Rev. 12:13 and 14:1-5 will reflect. Through the placement of this vision, it may be concluded that the period of their witness will coincide with the seventh seal and the seven trumpets, or the last half of Daniel's seventieth week. This group of almost 150,000 will carry God's message to the world during these difficult days.

For purposes of emphasizing that every tribe is included, *es-phragismenoi*[44] *ek pasēs phylēs huiōn Israēl* ("those who were sealed from every tribe of the sons of Israel") is added to supplement the numerical total. This, along with the naming of each individual tribe and the repeated number 12,000 in vv. 5-8, furnishes the strongest possible indicator that representation will come from every division of God's people (Beckwith).

A key issue remaining to be clarified is which people of God is indicated by this expression. The answer lies in determining the proper sense of *Israēl* ("Israel"). An exorbitant amount of discussion has sought to build a case that the term refers to spiritual Israel, which is the church (Ladd). Other places in this book and in the NT that are said to justify this identification include Matt. 19:28; Rom. 2:29; 4:11; 9:6-8; Gal. 3:29; 6:16; Phil. 3:3; James 1:1; 1 Pet. 1:1; 2:4, 9; Rev. 1:6; 2:9; 3:9; 18:4,[45] but they do not. It is not possible to examine each of these passages here, but a generalization that covers them all is that they come no closer to proving that the church is the new Israel than the passage currently under discussion. The same debate about the accuracy of this identification pertains in all the places cited, so no contribution is made by these other allegedly relevant texts to resolving the dilemma of the meaning of *Israēl* in Rev. 7:4. This same issue has been touched upon earlier in this work at Rev. 2:9 and 3:9.

---

44. An accusative singular rather than the nominative plural ἐσφραγισμένοι to agree with τὸν ἀριθμὸν might have been expected, but the nominative in such an appositional phrase is the custom of this writer (Beckwith, *Apocalypse*, p. 542). The plural number of the participle is explainable because τὸν ἀριθμόν is a collective noun and can have a plural sense. Thompson cites this as a participle used as a finite verb, a result of Aramaic influence on the Greek style (Steven Thompson, *The Apocalypse and Semitic Syntax* [Cambridge: Cambridge U., 1985], pp. 69). This appears to be an unnecessary assumption.

45. Swete, *Apocalypse*, p. 99; Lee, "Revelation," 4:588; Beckwith, *Apocalypse*, p. 535; Moffatt, "Revelation," 5:395; Robertson, *Word Pictures*, 6:350; Ladd, *Revelation*, pp. 115-16; Mounce, *Revelation*, p. 168; Johnson, "Revelation," 12:479-80.

Proponents of the position that the church is the new Israel also resort to theological rationale to prove their case. One example of such is the reasoning that a reference to the whole body of the church, including both Jew and Gentile, is most conformable to conceptions of the NT in general as well as to those of the Apocalyptist. It does least violence to the universalistic spirit of the book (Beckwith). It provides for greater unity between this group and the one spoken of in the last half of Revelation 7 (Johnson). A variation of this theological reasoning looks to Matt. 19:28 and concludes that Jesus' promise to the twelve apostles of sitting on twelve thrones judging the twelve tribes of Israel leads to the conclusion that the church is the new Israel (Mounce). Another deduces that the sealing must be coextensive with the peril and must embrace the entire Christian community, for God would not secure some of His servants and leave others unprotected.[46] Still another approach is that John evidently foresees the day when the human race will be divided under two allegiances, those having the seal of God and those having the mark of the beast. The 144,000 must include all living believers, therefore, and not just Jews (Beasley-Murray). Although under other circumstances these theological observations might be quite logical and convincing, in the present situation they fall far short of presenting a tight case for the point they seek to make.

No clear-cut example of the church being called "Israel" exists in the NT or in ancient church writings until A.D. 160.[47] Galatians 6:16, where "the Israel of God" can and probably does refer to some group other than the church as a whole, is no exception. This fact is crippling to any attempt to identify Israel as the church in Rev. 7:4. Such an attempt becomes even more ridiculous because it necessitates typological interpretation that divides the church into twelve tribes to coincide with the listing of Rev. 7:5-8, even with all the irregularities in that list.[48] This step is even more anomalous in light of the irregularities in the listing adopted in vv. 5-8. The approach is so misconceived that it does serious violence to the context (Beasley-Murray). It cannot be exegetically sustained.

The term *Israēl* must be referred to the physical descendants of Abraham, Isaac, and Jacob.[49] This is the natural understanding and the word's normal usage in the NT as well as the OT.[50] This accounts

---

46. Charles, *Revelation*, 1:200-1.
47. Peter Richardson, *Israel in the Apostolic Church* (Cambridge: Cambridge U., 1969), pp. 74-84, 206.
48. John F. Walvoord, *The Revelation of Jesus Christ* (Chicago: Moody, 1966), p. 143.
49. Jennings, *Revelation*, pp. 222-29.
50. J. A. Seiss, *The Apocalypse*, 3 vols. (New York: Charles C. Cook, 1909), 1:161; Walvoord, *Revelation*, p. 142.

for the detailed division of the people of God into twelve families answering individually to the twelve tribes of Israel in vv. 5-8, and is the explanation favored by the earliest Christian tradition.[51] A tie-in of the term to the church through the twelve apostles (cf. Matt. 19:28) is improbable because Rev. 21:12, 14 makes a clear distinction between the two groups of twelve. It is also in harmony with Paul's clear distinction between two groups of God's people, Israel and the church, as developed in Romans 9-11. In about eighteen lists of the sons of Jacob or Israel in the OT, different tribes are omitted at different times, but the number of them is always twelve. This is another indication that ethnic Israel is in view (Scott). This identification of the group best accounts for the distinction between them and the innumerable multitude in the next vision who come from all ethnic backgrounds (7:9).[52]

Numerous objections to this natural understanding of the name have been registered. It is proposed that the name *Israēl* could have undergone a change in meaning by the time this book was written (Johnson). The conflict between the Roman emperor and the church in the background of the Apocalypse necessitates that the 144,000 must be the church, says another (Moffatt). A further criticism says that particularist language must be metaphorical because the literal meaning of the term is obsolete and impossible in the Apocalypse (Moffatt). It is also concluded that God would not overlook the church in such a sealing process, saying that if there were two bodies of elect ones, both would have been sealed (Swete). A further claim is that seeing a reference to national Israel here seriously complicates the book of Revelation by introducing racial distinctions that no longer exist in the NT purview.[53] A reference to national Israel here is cited as pressing the logic of the book into an improbable sequence whereby only Jews are saved, but only Gentiles without the seal survive the great ordeal to enter God's presence (7:9-17) (Caird). Another objection to the literal understanding is the observation that it is impossible because ten of the twelve tribes lost their identity in the Assyrian captivity and the remaining two lost theirs when Jerusalem fell in A.D. 70 (Lenski; Mounce).

All of these objections are philosophically possible, but lack specific biblical data to confirm their logic. On the other hand, the fac-

---

51. Beckwith, *Apocalypse*, p. 535; Charles, *Revelation*, 1:193; Moffatt, "Revelation," 4:395.
52. Lee, "Revelation," 4:588; William Kelly, *Lectures on the Revelation* (London: G. Morrish, n.d.), p. 158; Walvoord, *Revelation*, p. 142.
53. Mounce, *Revelation*, p. 168. A point of discussion could be raised as to how giving a literal interpretation to Ἰσραήλ complicates one's understanding of the Apocalypse. The confusion arises from preconceived notions brought to the text, not from a literal interpretation.

tors favoring the literal meaning of *Israēl* are verifiable in Scripture through a literal understanding of the promises to ethnic Israel in the OT and NT. Israel has not and will not lose her distinctive national identity before God, regardless of human proposals to the contrary. Hence support for a literal understanding of the proper names in this paragraph is the outgrowth of interpreting the Bible in its natural sense. Any other interpretation has to struggle for supporting evidence.

Most of the opposition cited against the literal view is cleared up elsewhere in this exposition, but one argument deserves specific refutation, the one about the lost tribes of Israel. Though the identity of the tribe members is lost to mankind, it is still known to God who will be in charge of the sealing when it takes place (Walvoord), so this consideration is not prohibitive to the literal view.

It is, therefore, unquestionable that at this point in the progressive unveiling represented by the seven-sealed scroll the focus of attention falls upon God's earthly people about whom so much of God's plan for the world revolves. This is not the entirety of the faithful remnant of Israel,[54] but a group of them charged with a special responsibility of witnessing for Christ during the world's darkest hour, as will be reflected in later discussion (cf. 12:17; 14:1-5).

7:5-8 At this point comes a listing of the twelve components that make up the 144,000: ἐκ φυλῆς Ἰούδα δώδεκα χιλιάδες ἐσφραγισμένοι, ἐκ φυλῆς Ῥουβὴν δώδεκα χιλιάδες, ἐκ φυλῆς Γὰδ δώδεκα χιλιάδες, ἐκ φυλῆς Ἀσὴρ δώδεκα χιλιάδες, ἐκ φυλῆς Νεφθαλὶμ δώδεκα χιλιάδες, ἐκ φυλῆς Μανασσῆ δώδεκα χιλιάδες, ἐκ φυλῆς Συμεὼν δώδεκα χιλιάδες, ἐκ φυλῆς Λευὶ δώδεκα χιλιάδες, ἐκ φυλῆς Ἰσσαχὰρ δώδεκα χιλιάδες, ἐκ φυλῆς Ζαβουλὼν δώδεκα χιλιάδες, ἐκ φυλῆς Ἰωσὴφ δώδεκα χιλιάδες, ἐκ φυλῆς Βενιαμεὶν δώδεκα χιλιάδες ἐσφραγισμένοι (*ek phylēs Iouda dōdeka chiliades esphragismenoi, ek phylēs Rhoubēn dōdeka chiliades, ek phylēs Gad dōdeka chiliades, ek phylēs Asēr dōdeka chiliades, ek phylēs Nephthalim dōdeka chiliades, ek phylēs Manassē dōdeka chiliades, ek phylēs Symeōn dōdeka chiliades, ek phylēs Leui dōdeka chiliades, ek phylēs Issachar dōdeka chiliades, ek phylēs Zaboulōn dōdeka chiliades, ek phylēs Iōsēph dōdeka chiliades, ek phylēs Beniamein dōdeka chiliades esphragismenoi,* "from the tribe of Judah twelve thousand sealed, from the tribe of Reuben twelve thousand, from the tribe of Gad twelve thousand, from the tribe of Asher twelve thousand, from the tribe of Naphtali twelve thousand, from the tribe of Manasseh twelve thousand, from the tribe of Simeon twelve thousand, from the tribe

---

54. The repeated ἐκ in 7:5-8 expresses the partitive idea, showing that an elect group is chosen from the tribes (Johnson, "Revelation," 12:483).

of Levi twelve thousand, from the tribe of Issachar twelve thousand, from the tribe of Zebulun twelve thousand, from the tribe of Joseph twelve thousand, from the tribe of Benjamin twelve thousand sealed").

The repetition of the number 12 in the above list has evoked discussion about its significance. The suggestion that it is not literal but intensely symbolic, speaking of divine government in the earth executed through the tribes of Israel,[55] cannot be taken too seriously, because the number is surely literal sometimes. Why not here? In light of the conclusion reached about the identity of *Israēl*, 12 in the present connection must have a connection with Abraham's natural descendants, but beyond this it may also be a way of expressing the corporate identity of the elect people of God as reflected in the special effort to preserve the number at times (cf. Acts 1:25-26) (Lenski; Johnson).

The birth of Jacob's 12 sons is described in Gen. 29:32-35:18. Other lists of them are found in Gen. 35:22-26; 46:8-25; 49:3-27; Ex. 1:2-5; Num. 1:5-15; 2:3-31; 13:4-15; 26:4-51; 34:19-28; Deut. 27:12-13; 33:6-25; Josh. 13:7-22:34; Judg. 5:12-18; 1 Chron. 2:1–8:40; 12:24-37; 27:16-22; Ezek. 48:1-7, 23-28, 31-34. These are 19 arrangements of the names that differ from each other in one way or another, and the listing in Rev. 7:5-8 agrees with none of them (Beckwith). In the OT lists, sometimes the order of birth is followed (Gen. 29:32–35:18). At other times, it is the order of Jacob's blessing them (Gen. 49:3-27), the order of encampment (Num. 2:3-31), the order of the census before the invasion of Canaan (Num. 26:4-51),the order of blessing and cursing (Deut. 27:12-13), the order of Moses' blessing (Deut. 33:6-25), the order of "the princes" (Num. 1:5-15), the order of inheritance (Josh. 13:7–22:34), the order by the wives and concubines (1 Chron. 2:1–8:40), and the order of the gates of the city (Ezek. 48:31-34). The last list is closest to the order of the present list if it is rearranged according to direction into north, west, south, and east and if Judah's name is placed first (cf. Rev. 5:5). This list includes Levi and Joseph as John's list does (Lee).

The proposal that the unusual inclusion of Levi carries the lesson that all alike are now priests and have access to God can hardly be valid, because in some OT lists where territorial division is in view (1 Chron. 6:1-81), Levi is also included (Alford). Other peculiarities of this list have been the objects of special discussion. One is the reason for Judah's heading the list of the sons of Israel. It is totally unsatisfactory to use this and the missing names of some of the tribes to

---

55. Jennings, *Revelation*, p. 225.

argue that this is not physical, but spiritual Israel (Ladd). The discussion of *Israël* in 7:4 has shown this. It is also unsatisfactory to say there is no assignable reason in this case.[56] A listing that is random and without reason raises serious questions about why the list was included in the text. The conspicuous reason for Judah's first position lies in Christ's membership in that tribe, giving it priority.[57] This is supported by the title "the lion of the tribe of Judah" in Rev. 5:5 (cf. Heb. 7:13-14) (Lee; Johnson) and by comparison with OT lists where Judah comes first. In all such nongeographical or spatial listings in the OT, there is a connection with the Messianic expectation through Judah (Gen. 49:10; 1 Chron. 2:3–4:43; 5:2) (Johnson). The primacy of Judah, therefore, focuses more attention on the central role of the Lion-Lamb in the events of the seven-seal drama (e.g., 5:4-5; 6:16-17).

Another peculiarity of the list is the absence of the tribe of Dan. A number of explanations of this have been offered. The one that explains it as a textual corruption through which Dan was replaced by Manasseh is a remote possibility because of the sparsity of manuscript support (Beckwith; Mounce). Another, a favorite of pre-Christian Jewish tradition and the early church, was that the Antichrist was to arise from this tribe, and for this reason, it was not included.[58] Based in part on a rabbinic interpretation of Jer. 8:16, the early church saw this omission as an outgrowth of Dan's territory being one of the places where Jeroboam set up his idolatrous calf-worship (1 Kings 11:26; 12:28-30) (Caird). Another reason for this interpretation was Jacob's prophecy about Dan in Gen. 49:17, relating him to the serpent and what is diabolical.[59] As much attention as this view has drawn, it is too fanciful to be taken seriously.

A related explanation has it that the tribe of Dan had become extinct. It did not return from captivity and found no place in the reckoning of all Israel in 1 Chronicles 4-7 (Alford; Lee). The discontinuance of this tribe coincides with a haggadic interpretation of Gen. 49:17; Deut. 33:22; Jer. 8:15; 1 Chron. 27:22 as being the last mentions of them (Lee; Moffatt). Yet this distinction cannot be limited to Dan. Other tribes had likewise died out insofar as human observation could discern, and they are not omitted from the list.[60] Another way of explaining the absence of Dan is to postulate that no significance can be attached to it (Lenski). The practice of omitting names from

---

56. Contra Alford, *Greek Testament*, 4:625.
57. Charles, *Revelation*, 1:194; Mounce, *Revelation*, p. 169.
58. Alford, *Greek Testament*, 4:625; R. H. Charles, *The Apocrypha and Pseudepigrapha of the Old Testament*, 2 vols. (Oxford: Clarendon, 1913), 2:334; Beckwith, *Apocalypse*, p. 543.
59. Jennings, *Revelation*, p. 227.
60. Charles, *Revelation*, 1:208.

such lists was widespread, as with the absence of Simeon and Issachar from Deuteronomy 33, of Simeon and Judah from Judges 5, and of Gad and Asher from 1 Chronicles 27 (Beckwith; Lenski). Yet an omission from an apocalyptic list may very well be more significant than omissions from these earlier lists.

Another proposal to explain why Dan is omitted is that Dan left his inheritance and moved north to Laish and practiced idolatry (Hailey). This tribe was given an inheritance by lot just like the rest, but chose to move away and settle in the vicinity of Tyre and Sidon, thereby rejecting the word of the Lord. Being the only tribe that failed to conquer its territory (Judg. 1:34), it turned to idolatry as an alternative to obeying God (Judg. 18:14-31). Idolatry in particular was the blight upon Dan. Deuteronomy 29:18-21 requires the blotting out of the name of anyone who introduces idolatry into Israel (cf. also Deut. 29:24-26) (Bullinger). The Scripture gives regular notice of this tribe's offensiveness in this regard (Judg. 18:2, 30, 31; 1 Kings 11:26; 12:28-30) (Bullinger). The only narrative in the OT in which Dan played a part is the one related to the worship of idols in Judg. 18:1-31. Idolaters will be excluded from the new Jerusalem (Rev. 22:15) (Lee). Though Dan is included in the future distribution of the land (Ezekiel 48), it appears that this branch of the family will be excluded from the protective sealing prior to the trumpet judgments because of the blot upon Dan's history caused by idolatry (Bullinger; Smith). The other tribes were guilty of the same sin, but Dan was the leader in idolatrous practices.

The absence of Ephraim's name from the list of tribes creates another dilemma. Was it because Ephraim played a role in leading the northern tribes into idolatry or because he is really included in the name of his father Joseph? Ephraim like Dan was addicted to idolatry according to Judg. 17:1-13; 18:2, 30, 31; 1 Kings 12:25-29; Hos. 4:17, but probably it was the unsavory memory of Ephraim in other matters that caused its omission too. Ephraim was foremost in the defection from the house of David (2 Sam. 2:9; Isa. 7:9, 17) and was an ally of the enemies of Judah (Isa. 7:2, 5; cf. Hos. 5:3) (Lee). There were certain "untheocratic" recollections connected with this name that probably led to the substitution of Joseph's name (Smith). Such a substitution occurs elsewhere (Judg. 1:22, 35), being based on the fact that the tribe of Ephraim, like that of Manasseh, is closely associated with their father Joseph through whom they received their inheritance (Josh. 17:16-17). The inclusion of Joseph in the present list accomplishes the purpose of including Ephraim without the unpleasant connotation that the name carried.

Another peculiar characteristic of the breakdown of Rev. 7:5-8 is the inclusion of Manasseh and Joseph in the same list. This cannot be accounted for as an inadvertent slip.[61] No significant textual support exists to show this. Nor is it a matter of no special significance. It must be significant because the prophet included the list in his prophecy. It is also unacceptable to say that Manasseh was added to bring the number back to 12 after the exclusion of Dan.[62] Manasseh was the faithful son of Joseph. Because Joseph was given a double portion by Jacob in recognition of his favoritism toward Joseph (Gen. 37:3; Josh. 17:16-17), this is a fitting tribute to Manasseh's faithfulness.

Irregularities in this listing of the 12 tribes are undeniable. The preceding discussion seeks to explain some of them, but doubtless has not captured the full significance of these peculiarities. What can be said with certainty is that these are the ones protected from the effects of God's wrath through the future trumpet judgments.

b. Those in Heaven: The Innumerable Multitude (7:9-17)

The second picture injected as a contrast to the panic of earth's inhabitants under the sixth seal (cf. 6:17) has its setting in heaven. This group, like the 144,000, is unhurt by the effects of God's wrath, but for a different reason. They have at this point been removed from the earthly scene of the wrath and have no need of protective sealing. Someone might ask, "Are the 144,000 the only ones who have maintained their composure under the first six seals?" This vision responds to such a question negatively. A vast throng has turned to God during this period and have now passed into His immediate presence through death.

Translation

[9]After these things I looked, and behold, a great multitude, which no one could count, [some] from every nation and [all] tribes and peoples and tongues, [was] standing before the throne and before the Lamb, clothed in white robes, and palm branches were in their hands. [10]And they cried out with a loud voice, saying,

"Salvation to our God who sits upon the throne and to the Lamb."
[11]And all the angels were standing around the throne and the elders and the four living beings, and they fell before the throne upon their faces and worshiped God, [12]saying,

"Amen; blessing and glory and wisdom and thanksgiving and honor and power and strength to our God forever and ever; Amen."

---

61. Ibid.
62. Contra Mounce, *Revelation*, p. 170.

¹³And one of the elders answered, saying to me, "Who are these who are clothed in white robes and whence have they come?" ¹⁴And I said to him, "My lord, you know." And he said to me, "These are those who are coming out from the Great Tribulation, and they have washed their robes and made them white in the blood of the Lamb.
    ¹⁵Because of this they are before the throne of God,
    and they serve Him day and night in His temple,
    and the one who sits upon the throne will [be a]
      tabernacle over them.
    ¹⁶They will not hunger anymore or thirst anymore,
    nor will the sun fall upon them
    nor will any heat,
    ¹⁷because the Lamb who is at the midpoint in front
      of the throne will shepherd them,
    and lead them to springs of the water of life;
    and God will wipe away every tear from their eyes."

Exegesis and Exposition

The vision begun at this point offers a number of contrasts to the previous one. In 7:1-8, the number of people is definite, but here it is indefinite. In the earlier vision the group is from the 12 tribes of Israel, but in the latter one, from every nation. In the former case, the people are prepared for imminent peril, but in the latter, they are victorious and secure (Swete).

7:9 The method of introducing this vision indicates that it is new and distinct from the previous one: μετὰ ταῦτα εἶδον, καὶ ἰδοὺ ὄχλος πολύς (*meta tauta eidon, kai idou ochlos polys,* "after these things I looked, and behold, a great multitude"). Different theories have sought to account for how this vision fits the development of chapter 7. One sees this as a continuation of the vision of vv. 1-8 (Hailey), but this would necessitate identifying as one the two multitudes that are so clearly distinct. *Meta tauta eidon* ("After these things I looked") indicates a vision that is distinct from the preceding one (Alford; Ford). It is not a connective phrase advancing what John has just seen by way of a causal connection, i.e., the fruit of the ministry of the 144,000 being the Gentile multitude of the second vision.[63] Conditions depicted in the two visions appear to be simultaneous rather than consecutive. Those saved through the witness of the 144,000 are not yet saved because the time of their formal witness has not yet begun. This simultaneity also negates placement of the vision before rather than during the Great Tribulation.[64] The vision's placement in

---

63. Contra Lenski, *Revelation,* p. 255.
64. Contra Walvoord, *Revelation,* p. 145.

the book before the accounts of the last and greatest tribulation shows that this last phase has not yet arrived.[65] The connective expression *meta tauta eidon* simply shows that this is a new vision and that John received it immediately after the vision of 7:1-8.

Wide variety has characterized the opinions about the identity of *ochlos polys* ("a great multitude"). Making the multitude a symbolic representation of those who are finally victorious in salvation (Alford; Lenski; Hailey) presents a number of difficulties. It fails to note the connection of this crowd with the future Great Tribulation in 7:14,[66] and is not in keeping with the point reached in the breaking of the seals (Beckwith). To identify these with the elect of all ages is to ignore the definite terminology that limits them to a specific group of people (Walvoord).

Another identification of *ochlos polys* says they are "tribulation saints," those coming out of Daniel's seventieth week at its end. This takes the vision as proleptic, much the same as Rev. 14:1-5.[67] It anticipates the issue of final judgment and represents the servants of God as already delivered from the evil to come (Swete). Such a proleptic scene would place the people of the multitude on earth, however, but this vision has them still in heaven. The end has not yet been reached. The seventh seal has not yet been broken (Beckwith). A widely held view of *ochlos polys* makes them identical with the 144,000 sealed earlier in the chapter (Beckwith; Beasley-Murray; Johnson), but the two groups cannot be the same. The earlier one was numbered, but this one is innumerable.[68] One is exclusively Jews, the other is not.[69] One is facing the period of wrath, the other has been delivered from it (Beckwith; Scott). This multitude includes far more than the 144,000 of the earlier group (Mounce).

Another idea about *ochlos polys* is worthy of notice, that it is limited to martyrs who immediately receive their white robes at death.[70] Though they are not explicitly called martyrs, the fact that their deaths have come in connection with the Great Tribulation, a time of intense martyrdom, implies that they are (Ladd; Johnson). Their white robes connect them with the martyrs under the altar in 6:9-11 (Johnson). Scripture nowhere else speaks of a group clad in white robes except in these two places (Smith). All saints will eventually have white robes, but the nonmartyrs must wait until after the

---

65. Charles, *Revelation*, 1:202.
66. Ibid., 1:199; Johnson, "Revelation," 12:484.
67. Charles, *Revelation*, 1:202; Ladd, *Revelation*, p. 118.
68. Robert H. Gundry, *The Church and the Tribulation* (Grand Rapids: Zondervan, 1973), p. 81.
69. Ibid.
70. Charles, *Revelation*, 1:210.

final judgment.[71] Their purity symbolized by the whiteness of their robes is more pronounced than that of normal Christian forgiveness and holiness. The emphatic language of 7:14 indicates this. In the Apocalypse, the mystic union of the believer with Christ usually comes forward when martyrs and confessors are mentioned (cf. 14:13) (Moffatt). A theme of the whole book is the glorification of martyrdom.[72]

Yet it is not just the martyrs who have washed their robes in the blood of the Lamb. All Christians have (Beckwith; Morris). This author has a way of making clear his references to martyrs (cf. "slain for the Word of God," 6:9; "beheaded for the testimony of Jesus," 20:4) (Beckwith). The erroneous idea that martyrs washed their robes in their own blood rests on a misreading of the text. It is the blood of Christ, the same blood that is the ground of salvation for all. This is not to say that the multitude does not include the martyrs of 6:9-11 and perhaps others. It simply is not limited to them (Hailey).

The best solution is to identify this vast crowd as Gentile and Jewish believers who have died either natural or violent deaths during the period of the first six seals and come out from the Great Tribulation. The universality of terminology agrees with this as does the placement of the vision between the sixth and seventh seals (Beckwith). They are seen in heaven at a point simultaneous with the completion of the sealing of the 144,000 on earth.

The time frame represented by the vision has not escaped close scrutiny. Theories have said the multitude is seen before the seven-year Tribulation, during the seven-year Tribulation, after the seven-year Tribulation, during the Millennium, and in the eternal state. Placement before the Tribulation has little support and encounters the obstacle of being placed well after the seal judgments have begun, presumably at the Tribulation's beginning (Beckwith). Putting the scene after the Tribulation has the advantage of comparing this scene with others in the book, where the author reaches a certain crisis or turning point and inserts an anticipatory glimpse of the end of the Tribulation to encourage his readers (cf. 14:1-5).[73] In the anticipatory passages, however, there is usually a clear sign of the proleptic nature of the vision. Such is missing here.

The idea of a millennial setting for the scene has distinct advantages. The Feast of Tabernacles, which is reflected in this scene (cf. σκηνώσει [skēnōsei, "(be a) tabernacle"]), was a feast of rest (Deut. 16:13-15; Neh. 8:15) (Lee) and a type of the millennial age. The cry of

---

71. Ibid.
72. Ibid., 1:202.
73. Ibid.; Beckwith, *Apocalypse*, p. 540; Ladd, *Revelation*, p. 118.

"salvation" in 7:10 recalls the "Hosanna" (i.e., "save now") uttered during this same feast (Lee). The silence of the account regarding death and resurrection is another indication that this is a projection forward to the time of the Millennium.[74] The larger context of the vision points to a time when the complete number of the redeemed stand before God and the blessings of the eternal state are about to be realized (Mounce). The main problem with this view is that it cannot account for the placement of the vision as early as chapter 7, nor can it account for the heavenly location of the scene (Beckwith; Walvoord). The throne and the temple are given as the location (7:11, 15). The only throne and temple introduced thus far in the book are in heaven (cf. chaps. 4-5).

The eternal state view looks to the description of the bliss of the saints in this scene as its main support. Revelation 7:15-17 pictures the enjoyment of God's presence and protection from all adversity such as characterize the time of consummation (cf. Rev. 7:15 with 21:3; 22:3; and 7:17c with 21:4a).[75] These are conditions of coming eternal glory (Swete; Mounce). This positioning of the scene encounters two of the same difficulties as the millennial placement, the vision's early location in Revelation 7 and the heavenly location of the scene. If this were the eternal state, one would have expected to find conditions similar to the ones described in Revelation 21-22. For example, Rev. 21:22 says there is no temple in the eternal state, but there is here (7:15).

The best of the alternatives is to put this vision during the seven-year Tribulation period. The placement of this vision during the final series of God's judgments against the earth shows that the climax of those judgments has not yet come.[76] This multitude is seen serving God in heaven (cf. 7:15) before the arrival of the millennial kingdom.[77] Some aspects of the celestial city and eternal bliss have already arrived for them, but the dominant picture is that of a heavenly triumph. The Tribulation is partly past and partly future.[78] To a great extent, the vision's perspective depends on the time and aspect of the participle ἐρχόμενοι (erchomenoi, "are coming out"). The correct analysis of 7:14, as will be shown in the comments below, pictures the multitude as coming out of the Great Tribulation at the time that John views them (Johnson). According to the placement of this vision

---

74. Ford C. Ottman, *The Unfolding of the Ages* (Grand Rapids: Kregel, 1905), pp. 181-89.
75. Alford, *Greek Testament*, 4:626; Charles, *Revelation*, 1:201; Beckwith, *Apocalypse*, p. 539; Scott, *Revelation*, p. 175.
76. Charles, *Revelation*, 1:202.
77. Ibid., 1:201; Beasley-Murray, *Revelation*, p. 145.
78. Cf. Caird, *Revelation*, p. 103.

between the sixth and seventh seals, this would be a point just before the midpoint of Daniel's seventieth week.

The scene transpires in heaven, before the throne of God and of the Lamb becomes part of the new heavens and the new earth (cf. 22:3) (Ladd). The presence of the elders and the living beings (cf. 7:11) verifies that this is still the heavenly throne room introduced earlier in chapters 4-5 and not in an earthly setting.

Further data about this great multitude follows in v. 9: ὃν[79] ἀριθμῆσαι αὐτὸν οὐδεὶς ἐδύνατο, ἐκ παντὸς ἔθνους καὶ φυλῶν καὶ λαῶν καὶ γλωσσῶν, ἑστῶτες ἐνώπιον τοῦ θρόνου καὶ ἐνώπιον τοῦ ἀρνίου, περιβεβλημένους στολὰς λευκάς, καὶ φοίνικες ἐν ταῖς χερσὶν αὐτῶν (*hon arithmēsai auton oudeis edynato, ek pantos ethnous kai phylōn kai laōn kai glōssōn, hestōtes enōpion tou thronou kai enōpion tou arniou, peribeblēmenous stolas leukas, kai phoinikes en tais chersin autōn*, "which no one could count, [some] from every nation and [all] tribes and peoples and tongues, [was] standing[80] before the throne and before the Lamb, clothed in white robes, and palm branches were in their hands").

The clause *hon arithmēsai auton oudeis edynato* ("which no one could count") should not be taken to imply that someone tried to count the multitude. No such attempt was made, but if it had been, it would surely have failed.[81] The universality of the source of this multitude is stressed by the fourfold division *ek pantos ethnous kai phylōn kai laōn kai glōssōn* ("[some] from every nation and [all][82] tribes and peoples and tongues") (Mounce). A very similar expression has already been discussed at 5:9, and others will come at 11:9; 13:7; 14:6; 17:15. The universal source does not mean, however, that all people

---

79. The construction ὃν . . . αὐτόν is Semitic as in 3:8, the relative pronoun looking forward to the personal pronoun. As in 3:8 and 7:2, the two should be read as one (Robertson, *Word Pictures*, 6:350). Other instances of this Semitic-influenced construction are in Rev. 12:6; 13:8, 12; 17:9 (Thompson, *Apocalypse*, p. 112).

80. The participle ἑστῶτες functions as a finite verb as is often the case in this book (e.g., 4:8; 6:2). This quite possibly is a reflection of the Aramaic influence on the Greek of the Apocalypse (cf. Thompson, *Apocalypse*, pp. 67-69).

81. Alford, *Greek Testament*, 4:626. Ἐδύνατο, an imperfect tense, serves the same purpose as the classical ἂν δύναιτο in expressing this shade of thought.

82. After the singular ἔθνους, the other three terms in the series are plural. This is "a curious and irregular change" (Moffatt, "Revelation," 4:398). Because of it, the sense of the singular παντὸς probably carries over to the three plural terms, changing from "every" to "all" in the English translation. All four terms in the similar series at 11:9 and 17:15 are plural, but no form of the adjective πᾶς occurs in these. All four terms in the series at 5:9; 13:7; and 14:6 are singular with some form of πᾶς governing them.

are part of this vast multitude.[83] The partitive *ek* ("[some] from") means that only some from each grouping will be represented. A little later, others from these same groups will celebrate over the death of God's two witnesses (cf. 11:9-10).

In his vision, John sees the multitude "standing before the throne and before the Lamb" (*hestōtes*[84] *enōpion tou thronou kai enōpion tou arniou*). This is the same throne that has been the center of attention since chapter 4 (Scott). Such a position vividly portrays the multitude as both virtuous and victorious. Until now, only the living beings, elders, and other angels have appeared in the presence of God and the Lamb. They are still here (cf. 7:11) and are now joined in the presence chamber by this vast assembly of redeemed people (Swete). The writer's description is not explicit as to where the redeemed company stands in relation to the others, but it must be presumed that they occupy a position more remote from the throne than the angelic orders (Swete).

The apparel of the persons in the crowd tells more about their status: *peribeblēmenous*[85] *stolas*[86] *leukas* ("clothed in white robes"). In John's day, white robes were emblematic of rejoicing associated with victory (Beckwith). Here they indicate not only victory, but also the righteousness obtained through the death of Christ (cf. 7:14)

---

83. Representative universalism is the teaching of the Apocalypse here and throughout (David Peterson, "Worship in the Revelation to John," *Reformed Theological Review* 47, no. 3 [September-December 1988]: 73 [n]). Not all possess the faith that lies at the heart of the confession of 7:10. Many cling to their rebellion against God (e.g., Rev. 16:9, 11, 21).

84. The plural number of ἑστῶτες modifying the singular ὄχλος is explained on the basis of the latter word's being a collective noun. The crowd is thought of as resolved into the plurality of its countless constituents (Swete, *Apocalypse*, p. 100).

85. Two proposals of how to explain the accusative περιβεβλημένους modifying either the nominative ὄχλος or the nominative ἑστῶτες have emerged. Swete proposes that this along with other grammatical irregularities in this verse and the next is an indication that the writer is in sympathy with the rapture and abandon of the moment (*Apocalypse*, p. 100). Such a fluctuation between nominative and accusative is common in this book when preceded by εἶδον and ἰδού (Robertson, *Word Pictures*, 6:351; BDF, par. 160 [2]; Nigel Turner, *Syntax*, vol. 3 of *A Grammar of New Testament Greek* [Edinburgh: T. & T. Clark, 1963], p. 314). A more recent proposal has been to account for the accusative through Semitic influence on the Greek construction rather than calling it a solecism. The participle would then be an adverbial accusative in imitation of the comparable Hebrew construction (Thompson, *Apocalypse*, pp. 78-79). This suggestion is intriguing, but does not appear to rest upon as solid a foundation in the broad context of the book as the earlier one.

86. Στολὰς λευκάς is a predicate accusative retained with the passive verb of clothing περιβεβλημένους. Comparable constructions are found in 7:13; 10:1; 11:3; 12:1; 17:4; 18:16; 19:13 (Robertson, *Word Pictures*, 6:351).

(Mounce). The palms carried in their hands (*kai phoinikes en tais chersin autōn* ["and palm branches were in their hands"]) confirm the victory symbolism of the robes (Caird).

This further detail about the multitude furnishes a rich picture of their triumph. According to oriental thought, a palm was a perfect tree because it embodied everything a tree should have (Lenski). Palm branches were regarded as appropriate at any season of joy or triumph, such as the triumphal entry of Christ (John 12:13). They were prominent at the Feast of Tabernacles, being used to construct the shelters on the housetops required for that occasion. Another allusion to the σκηναί (*skēnai*, "tabernacles") used at this feast may be latent in σκηνώσει ἐπ᾽ αὐτούς (*skēnōsei ep᾽ autous*, "will [be a] tabernacle over them") later in this vision (7:15). The Greeks and Romans employed palm branches with the same symbolism.[87] This multitude is exuberant in celebration of its victory.

7:10 Their joyful song appropriately points to the one responsible for their success: καὶ κράζουσιν[88] φωνῇ μεγάλῃ λέγοντες, Ἡ σωτηρία τῷ θεῷ ἡμῶν τῷ καθημένῳ ἐπὶ τῷ θρόνῳ καὶ τῷ ἀρνίῳ (*kai krazousin phonē megalē legontes, Hē sōtēria tō theō hēmōn tō kathēmenō epi tō thronō kai tō arniō*, "And they cried out with a loud voice, saying, 'Salvation to our God who sits upon the throne and to the Lamb' "). The picture of the verb tense of *krazousin* ("they cry out") is that they "keep on crying out."[89] They never stop. Nor are their voices subdued. They do it *phonē megalē* ("with a loud voice").[90] The strong expression reflects the depth of gratitude of the crowd and a determination to give credit where credit is due, to God and the Lamb.

Hē sōteria ("Salvation") sounds the chief note of this song (cf. 12:10; 19:1) (Swete). This salvation is not their own achievement, but that of God and of the Lamb.[91] Two rather distinct connotations have been attached to the word. One takes it in a comprehensive sense of deliverance from sin with all its dire consequences (Lenski; Mounce). This sense best describes the use of the same word in 12:10 and 19:1 (Beckwith). In both of the other passages, the reference is to the accomplished salvation of the saints. A factor that causes hesitation in

---

87. Swete, *Apocalypse*, p. 100; Moffatt, "Revelation," 4:398; Beckwith, *Apocalypse*, p. 544.
88. As was true with the participle ἑστῶτες of the previous verse, the grammatically singular ὄχλος, being a collective noun, is viewed as plural by the plural verb κράζουσιν.
89. Alford, *Greek Testament*, 4:627. The tense is present.
90. For other examples of the combination κράζω φωνῇ μεγάλῃ, see 6:10; 7:2; 10:3; 19:17. Revelation 14:15; 18:2 vary from this combination only in minor ways.
91. Charles, *Revelation*, 1:211.

accepting this view is that John never uses σώζω (sōzō, "I save") to denote salvation from sin as other NT writers do (Caird). It is questionable as to whether he uses the noun sōtēria in this sense too.

The other suggested connotation for hē sōtēria is "victory." This multitude is celebrating its triumphant passage through persecution. Another look at 12:10 and 19:1 shows this meaning to be appropriate there too. In 12:10, it is victory over the dragon, and in 19:1, victory over Babylon and the persecutors of the saints. The word frequently carries the meaning of "victory" in classical Greek and in the LXX (Caird). Because these are people coming out from the Great Tribulation (7:14), triumph over persecutors is certainly a cause for celebration.[92] It is true that spiritual cleansing is pictured in this vision, such as would fit with the comprehensive sense of deliverance from sin (7:14), but the more restricted sense of the noun is in keeping with the context of this vision and of the book as a whole.[93]

A background of the Feast of Dedication has been proposed for this vision (Sweet). Palm branches were carried at this time of celebrating the Maccabean cleansing of the Temple from the desecration of Antiochus Epiphanes (2 Macc. 10:6-7; 1 Macc. 4:54-59; cf. 13:51). Palm branches carried at Jesus' triumphal entry perhaps were intended to evoke the spirit of this feast too, because shortly afterward Jesus proceeded to cleanse the Temple. This scene in heaven could be in celebration of the defeat of the kingdom of the beast and its desecration of the Temple (Sweet). A better case can be made, however, for the Feast of Tabernacles as the background. The Feast of Dedication was only secondary and derived some of its elements from the Feast of Tabernacles. The reference to God's being a tabernacle over His people in 7:15 is an important signal of this connection (Lee). This reference to salvation recalls the hosanna (i.e., "save now") uttered during the Feast of Tabernacles (2 Macc. 10:6-7). Another part of the feast was the prominence of water (cp. 7:17 with John 7:37-39) (Sweet). This multitude has now entered into its heavenly rest, another symbolic feature of the tabernacles celebration (cf. Deut. 16:13-15; Neh. 8:15) (Lee). Then, of course, there were the palm branches mentioned above. This annual time of joyfulness among the Jews furnishes a glimpse of the elation of this multitude now in heaven.

The words tō theō hēmōn tō kathēmenō epi tō thronō kai tō arniō ("to our God who sits upon the throne and to the Lamb") ascribe the

---

92. Swete, Apocalypse, p. 100; Robertson, Word Pictures, 6:351.
93. In light of this conclusion, the article ἡ with σωτηρία points out the particular deliverance this multitude has just experienced, not the salvation wrought by God from sin, death, and damnation (contra Lenski, Revelation, p. 258).

victory to God and to the Lamb. "Our God" shows that God belongs to the elect just as He does to the Lamb (cf. John 20:17; Rev. 3:12). Σωτήρ (Sōtēr, "Savior" or "Victor"), a title so freely attributed to the Roman emperor by the cities of Asia, belongs only to God and Christ in the ultimate sense (Swete). The multitude appropriately acknowledges this fact on this grand occasion of ongoing celebration.

7:11 The vibrant song of the multitude prompts the angelic host of heaven to renew its worship: καὶ πάντες οἱ ἄγγελοι εἰστήκεισαν κύκλῳ τοῦ θρόνου καὶ τῶν πρεσβυτέρων καὶ τῶν τεσσάρων ζῴων, καὶ ἔπεσαν ἐνώπιον τοῦ θρόνου ἐπὶ τὰ πρόσωπα αὐτῶν καὶ προσεκύνησαν τῷ θεῷ (kai pantes hoi angeloi heistēkeisan kyklō tou thronou kai tōn presbyterōn kai tōn tessarōn zōōn, kai epesan enōpion tou thronou epi ta prosōpa autōn kai prosekynēsan tō theō, "and all the angels were standing[94] around the throne and the elders and the four living beings, and they fell before the throne upon their faces and worshiped God"). These are presumably the same ones who endorsed the ascription of praise in 5:11-12 (Swete).

Though angels do not experience victory and salvation in the same sense as humans, they still rejoice over a repentant sinner (Luke 15:10) and have an intense desire to know more about the salvation that is available to men (1 Pet. 1:12) (Beckwith; Hailey). It is no surprise that they were standing around the throne at the critical point represented in this vision. As in 5:11, they form a circle around the throne outside the elders and the living beings. Though not explicitly stated, the situation probably requires that they be nearer the throne than the multitude.[95]

At this point the angels "fell before the throne upon their faces" (epesan enōpion tou thronou epi ta prosōpa autōn) much in the same manner as the twenty-four elders were known to do (cf. 4:10; 11:16). This posture is appropriate for those who worship God. The expression prosekynēsan tō theō ("they worshiped God") or a close equivalent shows worship to be a regular practice of heavenly angelic orders (cf. Rev. 4:10; 5:14; 11:16; 19:4). John is instructed to do the same toward the end of his revelatory experience (Rev. 19:10; 22:9).

7:12 The worship by the angels consists of an endorsement of the tribute of the multitude (7:10) and then a tribute of their own: λέγοντες, Ἀμήν· ἡ εὐλογία καὶ ἡ δόξα καὶ ἡ σοφία καὶ ἡ εὐχαριστία καὶ ἡ τιμὴ καὶ ἡ δύναμις καὶ ἡ ἰσχὺς τῷ θεῷ ἡμῶν εἰς τοὺς αἰῶνας τῶν αἰώνων· ἀμήν (legontes, Amēn; hē eulogia kai hē doxa kai he sophia kai hē eu-

---

94. Εἰστήκεισαν is a pluperfect form of ἵστημι. The pluperfect of this verb always conveys an imperfect sense (Alford, *Greek Testament*, 4:627; Lenski, *Revelation*, p. 258).

95. Swete, *Apocalypse*, p. 101; Charles, *Revelation*, 1:211.

charista kai hē timē kai hē dynamis kai hē ischys tǭ theǭ hēmōn eis tous aiōnas tōn aiōnōn; amēn, "saying, 'Amen; blessing and glory and wisdom and thanksgiving and honor and power and strength to our God forever and ever; amen'"). The first *Amēn* ("Amen") is their solemn confirmation of the tribute of the redeemed multitude to God because of the victory He has brought (cf. 1:6, 7; 5:14; 19:4).[96] Then follows their own tribute in the form of a sevenfold doxology similar to the one addressed to the Lamb by an innumerable multitude of angelic beings in 5:12.[97] The connection of their doxology with that of the large crowd of human beings shows that, though in itself it is quite general, it refers to the final victory of the redeemed (Beckwith).

Eulogia, literally "good speaking," means "blessing" or "praise." This is what is due to God on behalf of the liberated multitude. It finds a place in the doxologies of 5:12, 13 also (Swete). *Doxa* ("glory") is honor derived from earning a good reputation.[98] Here it is the radiance of the divine Person (Mounce), particularly because of His work of deliverance. The word occurs in doxologies at 1:6; 4:11; 5:12, 13; 19:1 also. *Sophia* is wisdom, the divine knowledge of God exhibited in His plan of salvation (Mounce). It is in another doxology at 5:12 (Swete). *Eucharistia* is made up of two parts, the first meaning "well" and the second "to give freely." It denotes gratitude.[99] The thanksgiving of the creature is inevitable in view of God's victorious accomplishments. The doxology of 4:9 also contains this word (Swete). *Timē* is "honor" or "esteem" in recognition of God's provision of salvation.[100] This term is in three other doxologies: 4:11; 5:12, 13. *Dynamis* ("power") is God's omnipotence, His ability to act effectively against all opposition (Lenski; Mounce). He has delivered this multitude from the most formidable forces earth has to offer. Its other doxological uses are at 4:11; 5:12; 19:1. *Ischys* ("strength") refers to a quality one possesses, whether he exerts it or not (Lenski). In this case, God has exhibited His strength in history in delivering this

---

96. Swete, *Apocalypse,* p. 101; Charles, *Revelation,* 1:212; Beckwith, *Apocalypse,* p. 544; Lenski, *Revelation,* p. 259; Hailey, *Revelation,* p. 208.
97. Unlike the doxology of 5:12, this one has the article with each member. This follows the pattern of the doxologies at 4:11 and 5:13. See the note at 4:11. The repetition of the article serves to give each item in the doxology an individual emphasis (Mounce, *Revelation,* p. 172). The seven items in this doxology do not coincide with the seven in 5:12, or with any of the previous doxologies (Swete, *Apocalypse,* p. 101). No particular significance to the order of the terms has been detected.
98. W. E. Vine, *An Expository Dictionary of New Testament Words* (Old Tappan, N.J.: Revell, 1966), p. 158.
99. G. Abbott-Smith, *A Manual Greek Lexicon of the New Testament* (Edinburgh: T. & T. Clark, 1950), p. 190.
100. Jennings, *Revelation,* p. 230.

throng from the clutches of the enemy. The word is in a doxology again at 5:12 (Swete).

In voicing their praise, the angels address the words *tǭ theǭ hēmōn* ("to our God"). Like the redeemed before them (7:10), they claim God as their own (Swete). As with the doxology of 5:13, this exaltation of God is not temporary. It continues *eis tous aiōnas tōn aiōnōn* ("forever and ever"). The final *amēn* ("amen") validates the truthfulness of their characterizations of God.

7:13 At this point commences an interview between one of the 24 elders and John, which serves to identify the innumerable multitude more explicitly: καὶ ἀπεκρίθη εἷς ἐκ τῶν πρεσβυτέρων λέγων μοι, Οὗτοι οἱ περιβεβλημένοι τὰς στολὰς τὰς λευκὰς τίνες εἰσὶν καὶ πόθεν ἦλθον; (*kai apekrithē heis ek tōn presbyterōn legōn moi, Houtoi hoi peribeblēmenoi tas stolas tas leukas tines eisin kai pothen ēlthon?* "and one of the elders answered, saying to me, 'Who are these who are clothed in white robes and whence have they come?'"). This exemplifies the dialogue format used from time to time to convey an explanation of a vision (cf. Jer. 1:11, 13; Amos 7:8; 8:2; Zech. 4:2, 5).[101] This tool shows that visions were not given for the purpose of spectacular displays, but to convey revelation, the details of which were not to be missed (Swete). This time, an elder intervenes as at 5:5 to interpret the vision by anticipating the question that John was getting ready to ask (cf. Josh. 9:8; Jonah 1:8).

Apekrithē ("he answered") is unusual in this situation because no question has been asked before the elder speaks. This is a frequent usage of the verb in the LXX and NT in imitation of a Hebrew idiom that introduces an utterance called forth by something, not just a question, that has preceded. Here it is a response to a fresh set of circumstances.[102] In addition the larger construction, *kai apekrithē . . . legōn* ("and he answered . . . saying"), is Semitic and is frequent in the gospel of John and the synoptic gospels (e.g., Matt. 25:45; Mark 15:9; Luke 3:16; John 1:26; 12:23). It occurs only here in the Apocalypse.[103]

With his question the elder immediately directs attention to the white-clad multitude.[104] Their garments, *tas stolas tas leukas*[105] ("in

---

101. Charles, *Revelation*, 1:212; Beckwith, *Apocalypse*, p. 544; Mounce, *Revelation*, p. 173.
102. Charles, *Revelation*, 1:212; Beckwith, *Apocalypse*, p. 544.
103. Charles, *Revelation*, 1:212; Robertson, *Word Pictures*, 6:352.
104. The expression οὗτοι οἱ κ. τ. λ. is a so-called prophetic predicate nominative that is put before its subject τίνες εἰσὶν to give it more emphasis (Robertson, *Word Pictures*, 6:352).
105. The articular construction τὰς στολὰς τὰς λευκάς is due to previous mention of στολὰς λευκάς in this context at 7:9.

white robes"), are the feature that attracts attention and serves as their main identifying mark (Swete). The elder never asks for John's estimate of the number. He inquires only as to their identity which indicates their character (*tines*, "who") and their origin (*pothen*, "whence") (Moffatt). The aorist tense of *ēlthon* ("have they come") does not exclude the possibility that some at this point are still exiting from the scene of what will be the Great Tribulation, thereby adding to the already huge number that John sees.[106]

7:14 John's response to the elder's interrogation portrays his bewilderment: καὶ εἴρηκα αὐτῷ, Κύριέ μου, σὺ οἶδας (*kai eirēka autō, Kyrie mou, sy oidas*, "and I said to him, 'My lord, you know'"). As with the perfect tense εἴληφεν (*eilēphen*, "took") in 5:7, the perfect *eirēka* ("I said") has been construed as both the quasi-aoristic use of the perfect and a regular use of the perfect (cf. also 8:5; 19:3).[107] Better judgment dictates a choice of the latter possibility. The usual force of the perfect, i.e., continuing results of a completed process, more vividly portrays how the whole scene was still fresh and vivid in John's mind as though it had just happened and the echo of his own voice yet remained (cf. κέκραγεν [*kekragen*, "he cried out"], John 1:15).[108]

John's address of the elder as *kyrie mou* ("my lord") may be a general way of showing respect either to an angel or a redeemed person or an address that was particularly suitable in light of the angelic status of the elder (Swete; Ladd). The latter option is more feasible because of the way the term is used in the LXX, particularly in addressing persons in OT apocalyptic writings (Dan. 10:16, 17; Zech. 1:9; 4:5, 13; cf. Gen. 19:2).[109] This address displays an especially deep reverence and respect such as John shows elsewhere in the book toward heavenly beings (19:10; 22:8, 9) (Alford; Moffatt; Mounce). It falls short of the worship reserved for God and the Lamb alone, however.

John's words *sy oidas* ("you know") are both a confession of ignorance and an appeal for information (Swete). In another setting, the identical words could be an expression of full confidence (cf. John 21:15, 16, 17), but not primarily so here.[110] The *sy* ("you") is emphatic, carrying the nuance, "It is you who know," in his conversation with the elder (Beckwith; Morris).

The question of why John did not recognize the great multitude is

---

106. A discussion of the *Aktionsart* of οἱ ἐρχόμενοι in 7:14 will show the plausibility of this (Charles, *Revelation*, 1:212).
107. Swete, *Apocalypse*, p. 102; James H. Moulton, *A Grammar of New Testament Greek*, vol. 1, *Prolegomena* (Edinburgh: T. & T. Clark, 1908), p. 145; Charles, *Revelation*, 1:212.
108. Robertson, *Word Pictures*, 6:352.
109. Swete, *Apocalypse*, p. 102; Charles, *Revelation*, 1:212.
110. Robertson, *Word Pictures*, 6:352.

interesting. It could have been the location of the scene. As one steeped in the OT, he might have expected such a scene of blessedness to be on earth rather than in heaven. It could have been the time period from which the participants were drawn, the future Tribulation. These in the vision had not yet lived on earth to permit John to meet them. It could have been the vast numbers that were perplexing to John. Jesus had taught that only few would be chosen (Matt. 7:13,14; 22:14). It may have been the variety of nationalities involved in the scene. Though by now John was well aware that God had opened the door of faith to the Gentiles, to have all racial backgrounds represented may have overwhelmed him. Probably all these factors contributed partially to John's response to the elder even though he had limited insight into an explanation of each. His response was simply a request for further enlightenment because he did not know fully how to answer the elder's question (Lenski).

The elder's response to John's dilemma is a full one, occupying the remainder of chapter 7. The first words are more specifically helpful in identifying the multitude: καὶ εἶπέν μοι, Οὗτοί εἰσιν οἱ ἐρχόμενοι ἐκ τῆς θλίψεως τῆς μεγάλης, καὶ ἔπλυναν τὰς στολὰς αὐτῶν καὶ ἐλεύκαναν αὐτὰς ἐν τῷ αἵματι τοῦ ἀρνίου (*kai eipen moi, Houtoi eisin hoi erchomenoi ek tēs thlipseōs tēs megalēs, kai eplynan tas stolas autōn kai eleukanan autas en tō haimati tou arniou,* "And he said to me, 'These are those who are coming out from the Great Tribulation, and they have washed their robes and made them white in the blood of the Lamb'").

The key identifying mark of the innumerable multitude lies in the words *hoi erchomenoi ek tēs thlipseōs tēs megalēs* ("those who are coming out from the Great Tribulation"). One approach to the participle *hoi erchomenoi* ("those who are coming") is to accentuate its function as a substantive. In this case, no essential time element or aspect of action is in view. "Such people as come" or "the comers" is its idea (Alford; Swete; Beckwith). The time of the exit must be determined from the context, which in this case shows them to have departed already at the time anticipated in the vision (cf. present participles in 15:2; 20:10) (Beckwith). This represents an explanation of the articular participle, which is quite valid grammatically. With such adjectival participles the *Aktionsart* of the Greek tense is often rendered unnoticeable, but sometimes contextual warrant exists for stressing the kind of action expressed by the Greek verb tense. Such an exception occurs here.

The usual force of the present tense is to portray continuous action. The Semitic-style construction of the statement favors allowing this sense here.[111] The switch to the finite verbs *eplynan* ("they

---

111. Charles, *Revelation*, 1:213.

washed") and *eleukanan* (they made . . . white") recalls the frequent
occurrence of a Hebrew participle or infinitive followed by finite
verbs (e.g., Jer. 23:32; Amos 5:7). The same Semitism has occurred
earlier in Revelation (1:5-6; 2:20).[112] The participle's parallelism with
the finite verbs serves to emphasize the durative force of its present
tense: "those who are in the process of coming." Because it is simply
part of the elder's question to stimulate John's curiosity, the aorist
ēlthon ("have they come") of 7:13 does not necessarily imply that their
number is complete and negate the idea that they are still arriving.
Nor do the two aorists *eplynan* and *eleukanan* negate the durative
notion of the participle (Beasley-Murray), because the cleansing of
the multitude occurred prior to their departure from earth. The present participle gives the impression that the persecution of the saints
will be a prolonged process that from John's standpoint was partly
past and partly future (cf. 6:9-11). But for the saints' standpoint it
gives the impression that entry into heaven follows immediately after
physical death (Caird). Resurrection of their bodies awaits the personal return of Christ to earth (cf. 20:4), however.

The saints' point of departure is the earth, the scene of "the Great
Tribulation" (*tēs thlipseōs tēs megalēs*). The same meaning attaches to
the expression here as was adopted at 2:22 in Christ's message to
Thyatira. This is a period of eschatological tribulation immediately
before Christ returns in power to establish His kingdom. It cannot be
simply general tribulation that began in John's time.[113] This is a
worldwide crisis among all nations that could hardly reflect the localized situation of John's time or shortly thereafter (Moffatt). It cannot be the destruction of Jerusalem of A.D. 70, the subject of Christ's
remarks on the Mount of Olives (cf. Matt. 24:1-3, 21, 29),[114] because
this was not the ultimate fulfillment of His prophecies there. Nor can
the reference be to all the tribulations throughout the age of the
church,[115] because the definite article *tēs* ("the"), the whole vision,
and its relation to the rest of the book eliminate the possibility of
such a general understanding.[116] This must relate to the future time
of punitive action anticipated in Rev. 3:10 as "an hour of trial" and
spoken of in Rev. 6:17 as "the great day" of the wrath of God and of the
Lamb (Johnson). Paul also anticipates such a period of God's punitive
action against the world (1 Thess. 5:3; 2 Thess. 1:6-10). Jesus coined
the expression "the great tribulation" (Matt. 24:21) and limited it to
the second half of Daniel's seventieth week (Matt. 24:15-22; Mark

---

112. Ibid., 1:202.
113. Contra Lange, p. 191; Hailey, p. 210.
114. Contra Hailey, *Revelation*, p. 209.
115. Contra Alford, *Greek Testament*, 4:628; Lenski, *Revelation*, p. 261.
116. Charles, *Revelation*, 1:199; Walvoord, *Revelation*, p. 145.

13:14-20; cf. Dan. 9:27).[117] It will be a period that will exceed all past and subsequent sorrows endured by the earth whose length will be 1,260 days (Rev. 11:3; 13:5) (Scott).

It is the superlatively great crisis of trial through which all rebels against God must pass just before Christ's second coming.[118] The servants of God will not suffer the direct effects of God's wrath. They will be untouched by it (Caird). The saints on earth will not be exempt from the ire of God's enemies during this period, however. During both the Great Tribulation and the three-and-one-half years of tribulation before it, they will bear the brunt of suffering caused by anti-God animosities. The intensity of persecution will be a marked increase over that experienced before this end-time arrives and will increase again when the seven-year period reaches its midpoint. Some will already have been martyred by the end of the sixth seal (cf. 6:9-11) and many more persecuted in other ways.

John witnesses the emergence of this multitude from such strife at a point just before the abuse of the saints is to become worse under the leadership of the beast out of the sea (cf. Rev. 13:7). He sees them coming "out from" (*ek*[119]) the Great Tribulation. They have already suffered to a degree, but will be spared the worse times of those saints who survive the first half of the week.

The final words of v. 14 tell how the constituency of the innumerable multitude gained its right to be a part of the victory celebration: *kai eplynan tas stolas autōn kai eleukanan autas en tō haimati tou arniou* ("and they have washed their robes and made them white in the

---

117. The correspondence of the first six seals of Revelation 6 with the earlier portions of Jesus' Olivet discourse makes a connection with His use of the expression even more compelling.

118. Charles, *Revelation*, 1:213; Lee, "Revelation," 4:592; Beckwith, *Apocalypse*, p. 545; Mounce, *Revelation*, p. 73.

119. The preposition ἐκ is flexible enough in its meaning to support a meaning of either coming "out of" the Great Tribulation while it is in progress or coming "out from" the Great Tribulation before it begins. Two related considerations decide for the latter alternative. One is the point at which the vision occurs, i.e., between the sixth and seventh seal. The seventh seal coincides with the last three-and-one-half years of Daniel's seventieth week. The other consideration is the specific way in which Christ limited "the great tribulation" to the last half of the seventieth week (Matt. 24:15, 21). Since that portion has not yet arrived in the progress of Revelation, the deliverance of this multitude must come before it begins. A third possible understanding that it is a departure after the Great Tribulation is completed (Marvin Rosenthal, *The Pre-Wrath Rapture of the Church* [Nashville: Thomas Nelson, 1990], p. 185) can be dismissed because it neglects the ongoing nature of the departure indicated by the present participle ἐρχόμενοι and rests on an unwarranted distinction between the Great Tribulation and the day of the God's wrath.

blood of the Lamb"). This descriptive picture has as its background Gen. 49:11 and Ex. 19:10, 14. Judah is said to have washed his garments in "the blood of grapes" in the former passage, and in the latter, the children of Israel wash theirs in readiness for the descent of the Lord upon Mount Sinai (Beasley-Murray; Mounce). Soiled garments illustrate sinfulness in Isa. 64:6 and Zech. 3:3. The representation of the removal of sin by the idea of cleansing and whiteness comes from Ps. 51:7 (LXX 50:9) and Isa. 1:18.[120]

In modern thought, making anything white by washing it in blood is paradoxical and even shocking, but it was not so with John and those with an OT background. To them such washing denoted spiritual purity. Not just any blood would accomplish the cleansing. The blood of martyrs shed for the Lamb's sake would not even do it. It had to be the blood of the Lamb's great sacrifice to produce the whiteness (Rev. 1:5; 5:9; cf. Rom. 3:25; 5:9; Eph. 1:7; Col. 1:20; Heb. 9:14; 1 Pet. 1:2, 19; 1 John 1:7) (Swete; Mounce). The aorist indicatives of *eplynan* ("they have washed") and *eleukanan* ("made . . . white") look back to the time when the cleansing occurred in the life of each member of the crowd, while they were still on earth. Through faith they appropriated the cleansing provision of the Lamb's sacrifice (cf. Acts 15:9) (Swete). The washing and the whitening are one, not two separate acts with the latter referring to a later process of sanctification (Alford). They are here by virtue of receiving God's forgiveness and Christ's imputed righteousness by faith. The Lamb's blood made it possible.[121]

7:15 The white robes (7:9, 13) and the cleansing they picture (7:14) are the basis for the position of this multitude before the throne: διὰ τοῦτό εἰσιν ἐνώπιον τοῦ θρόνου τοῦ θεοῦ (*dia touto eisin enōpion tou thronou tou theou*, "because of this they are before the throne of God"). *Dia touto* ("because of this") bases the multitude's heavenly presence on the washing-whitening process at the end of v. 14. The members' purity, derived from faith in the Lamb and His sacrificial work, has fitted them for the presence of God and given them grounds to stand before His throne (cf. 7:9) (Alford; Swete).

Standing before God's throne does not mean idleness for this throng. Members have an assigned function, which they fulfill willingly: καὶ λατρεύουσιν αὐτῷ ἡμέρας καὶ νυκτὸς ἐν τῷ ναῷ αὐτοῦ (*kai latreuousin autō hēmeras kai nyktos en tō naō autou*, "and they serve

---

120. Swete, *Apocalypse*, p. 103; Charles, *Revelation*, 1:214.
121. The preposition ἐν has its instrumental use here. This is proved by a comparison with διὰ τὸ αἷμα τοῦ ἀρνίου in Rev. 12:11, where διά expresses the means of the victory of the brothers (Charles, *Revelation*, 1:214).

Him day and night in His temple"). Priestly service indicated by the verb *latreuousin* ("they serve") is the continuous[122] occupation of the white-robed crowd. This is the word in Heb. 8:5 that describes the ritual service of OT worship under the law (Beckwith). Its use in the LXX is limited to a reference to service rendered to higher powers.[123] It and its cognate words speak of the service rendered to God by Israel (Acts 26:7; Rom. 9:4; Heb. 9:1, 6). This word is broader than its synonym λειτουργέω (*leitourgeō*, "I serve"), which in the OT was limited to priests and Levites. It covers more than the area of priestly ministry,[124] but its connection with *naọ* ("temple") in this verse shows that priestly service is in view here (cf. 1:6; 5:10; 20:6). Of course, this is not the service of external rites, but of spiritual worship. This is praise to and adoration of God such as has already been voiced in v. 10, the same service of worship as referred to in Rev. 22:3 (Mounce).

The unbrokenness of the multitude's worship is emphasized in *hēmeras kai nyktos*[125] ("day and night"). This is an idiomatic way of saying "unceasingly" or "without pause" (Mounce). It must be presumed that a distinction between day and night does not exist in heaven, because of the condition in the new Jerusalem that excludes night (Rev. 22:5). The figurative language recalls that here on earth changes of day and night affect mankind continually, but in heaven they will do so no longer (Lenski). The service of worship by the victorious crowd continues without interruption.

The location of the worship *en tọ naọ autou* ("in His temple") has created difficulty for some when compared with Rev. 21:22, which says there is no temple in the new Jerusalem that John saw descending from heaven. It does not appear to be a detail absent from the original vision that was added later.[126] No manuscript evidence supports this theory. Nor is it necessary to call it an error corrected by later revelation in Rev. 21:22.[127] The two passages need not be a description of the same scene. A theory that has a semblance of plausibility understands the temple here to be on earth during the Millennium (cf. Isa. 56:5-7; Ezek. 40-44) and the one in 21:22 to be after the

---

122. Λατρεύουσιν is a present tense. The present carries its usual durative force in this case.
123. Richard Chenevix Trench, *Synonyms of the New Testament* (1880; reprint, Grand Rapids: Eerdmans, 1958), p. 125.
124. Trench, *Synonyms*, pp. 126-27.
125. The expression ἡμέρας καὶ νυκτός is an adverbial genitive of time just as the same expression is in Rev. 4:8 (Robertson, *Word Pictures*, 6:353). The uninterrupted duration hereby indicated adds to the same connotation of the verb tense of λατρεύουσιν. See note at that point.
126. Contra Charles, *Revelation*, 1:215.
127. Contra Swete, *Apocalypse*, p. 104.

Millennium (Scott). The absence of any mention of the death and resurrection of those in the multitude is cited as proof that this is a projection forward to the time of the Millennium.[128] This is unconvincing, though, because 7:9-13 clearly places this scene in the throne room described in Revelation 4-5 (Alford; Ladd; Walvoord).

Another effort identifies both vv. 15-17 and Revelation 21-22 as descriptions of the final state of the saints. The worship setting of the former scene and the city imagery of the latter are said to justify the differing perspectives regarding the presence and absence of a temple (Johnson). Identification of the two scenes is made on the basis of identical wording at certain points (cp. 7:17c with 21:4a; 7:15 with 21:3 and 22:3),[129] and the difference in perspective is justified on the basis of the "fluidity" of apocalyptic language (Ladd). In one situation, it is the condition of the church before the new age that is reflected; in the other, it is after the initiation of the new order when they will serve God without a temple (Beasley-Murray). This kind of explanation evades what the text actually says, however. Besides the temple, there are distinct differences between the two scenes, as already pointed out.[130]

This is a picture of the whole of heaven as a sanctuary in which God's people are priests (Walvoord; Morris). This heavenly temple stands in the existing heaven (Rev. 11:19).[131] This is a view of the saints after death, not after the ultimate judgment. They are not yet in their final state of glory, but in the presence of God awaiting the culmination of His wrath against the earth (cf. Acts 7:59; Phil. 1:23) (Hailey). The harmonization of the sanctuary in 7:15 and the statement of 21:22 that there is no longer a sanctuary is that the present passage describes a heavenly scene just before the midpoint of the seven-year Tribulation, whereas the later one is descriptive of the eternal state. This time-frame is shown by the position of this passage in the immediate context of Revelation.

The elder's explanation of the multitude's identity next states three of God's future[132] provisions for those people. The first provision comes at the end of v. 15: καὶ ὁ καθήμενος ἐπὶ τοῦ θρόνου σκην-

---

128. Ottman, *Unfolding*, pp. 181-89.
129. Charles, *Revelation*, 1:201; Beckwith, *Apocalypse*, pp. 544-46.
130. See discussion of Rev. 7:9.
131. Charles, *Revelation*, 1:215.
132. At this point comes a transition from the present tense of λατρεύουσιν to the future tense of σκηνώσει and the subsequent verbs in the indicative mood. From speaking of what he currently beholds before him in vision, he turns to prophesying and foretelling the future of this multitude (Swete, *Apocalypse*, pp. 104-5; Charles, *Revelation*, 1:215; Beckwith, *Apocalypse*, p. 546).

ὡσει ἐπ᾽ αὐτούς (*kai ho kathēmenos epi tou thronou skēnōsei ep' autous*, "and the one who sits upon the throne will [be a] tabernacle over them"). Σκηνόω (*Skēnoō*, "I tabernacle"), a word used only in Johannine writings in the NT (John 1:14; Rev. 12:12; 13:6; 21:3), has the idea of tent-camping. It always speaks of God or heavenly beings. It reflects what in the OT was typified by the Shekinah, or the immediate presence of God, above the mercy seat (Ex. 40:34-38; 1 Kings 8:13), the Tabernacle in the wilderness (Lev. 26:11-12), and the cloud by day and the pillar of fire by night (Ex. 13:21-22) (Swete; Lenski). The verb behind Shekinah is שָׁכַן (*šākan*, "he dwells"). It has practically the same consonants as the Greek verb *skēnoō* (Sweet). The immediate presence of God to shelter and protect from all harm is what is promised here (cf. Isa. 4:5-6).[133] It corresponds to the OT promise that God will dwell in the midst of His people (Lev. 26:11-12; Ezek. 37:27; Zech. 2:10, 11; 8:3, 8; cf. Rev. 13:6; 21:3) (Moffatt).

7:16 Two more provisions for the heavenly multitude are given in v. 16. The first has to do with necessities for bodily nourishment: οὐ πεινάσουσιν ἔτι οὐδὲ διψήσουσιν ἔτι (*ou peinasousin eti oude dipsēsousin eti*, "they will not hunger anymore or thirst anymore"). This promise, along with several of the remaining ones in this chapter, is drawn from Isaiah's description of the exiles returning from Babylon (Isa. 49:10, LXX) (Swete). The wording is identical except for the addition of the two occurrences of *eti* ("anymore"). This promise was particularly attractive in an ancient land where both hunger and thirst were constant threats, but the deeper meaning of the satisfaction of spiritual hunger and the quenching of spiritual thirst is the force here (cf. John 4:14; 6:35; 7:37) (Mounce). The words are all the more meaningful to those who have just come from an experience of severe persecution (Beckwith). The point of the figurative language is that the tormenting conditions known on earth will have ended (Beasley-Murray). In another sense, of course, hunger and thirst will never know satiety. This is reflected in the access of the blessed to the "springs of the water of life" in v. 17. Paradoxically, the saved will always thirst for God, but that thirst will always be satisfied. What this part of v. 16 refers to, therefore, is the absence of unsatisfied desire.[134]

The other provision stated in v. 16 also alludes to Isa. 49:10: οὐδὲ

---

133. Charles, *Revelation*, 1:215; Mounce, *Revelation*, p. 175. Σκηνόω followed by μετά (Rev. 21:3) or ἐν (John 1:14) means "I dwell among," an indication of fellowship, but the same verb followed by ἐπί as it is here means "tabernacle over" as a covering of protection (Beckwith, *Apocalypse*, p. 545).

134. Charles, *Revelation*, 1:216; Morris, *Revelation*, pp. 118-19.

μὴ πέσῃ[135] ἐπ᾽ αὐτοὺς ὁ ἥλιος οὐδὲ πᾶν καῦμα (*oude mē pesę ep' autous ho hēlios oude pan kauma*, "nor will the sun fall upon them nor will any heat"). The wording of the Isaiah passage is οὐδὲ πατάξει αὐτοὺς καύσων οὐδὲ ὁ ἥλιος (*oude pataxei autous kausōn oude ho hēlios*, "nor will burning heat smite them nor will the sun"). The *kausōn* ("burning heat") was the burning wind from the desert, or the sirocco, a familiar phenomenon to Isaiah's readers in their local setting. It is changed to *pan kauma* ("any heat"), a scorching heat of any kind that does not have the local geographical connotations of the other term (Swete). The overpowering reality of the sun is familiar to practically everyone, regardless of where he lives.[136] Under the fourth bowl of God's wrath the heat of the sun will become more oppressive than ever before (καῦμα μέγα [*kauma mega*, "great heat"], 16:9). This multitude will not be subjected to this, of course.

7:17 How God can so provide for His people is explained in v. 17: ὅτι τὸ ἀρνίον τὸ ἀνὰ μέσον τοῦ θρόνου ποιμανεῖ αὐτούς, καὶ ὁδηγήσει αὐτοὺς ἐπὶ ζωῆς πηγὰς ὑδάτων· καὶ ἐξαλείψει ὁ θεὸς πᾶν δάκρυον ἐκ τῶν ὀφθαλμῶν αὐτῶν (*hoti to arnion to ana meson tou thronou poimanei autous, kai hodēgēsei autous epi zōēs pēgas hydatōn; kai exaleipsei ho theos pan dakryon ek tōn ophthalmōn autōn*, "because the Lamb who is at the midpoint in front of the throne will shepherd them, and lead them to springs of the water of life; and God will wipe away every tear from their eyes"). The *hoti* ("because") introduces the cause of which the provisions just listed are the effects. In short, the respective roles of the Lamb and God will bring the benefits promised.

The Lamb apparently occupies a slightly different position from the one in 5:6. There He was ἐν μέσῳ τοῦ θρόνου (*en mesǫ tou thronou*, "in the middle of the throne"), but here He is *ana meson tou thronou* ("at the midpoint in front of the throne"). *Ana meson* usually means "between or "among," but this meaning does not fit here (cf. Matt. 13:25) (Swete). He now stands in the foremost place before the middle of the throne (Beckwith). He is between the one sitting on the throne and the four living beings with the 24 elders who stand around it (Lee).

The Lamb's function as shepherd comes into view with *poimanei* ("he will shepherd"). The idea of Jesus as shepherd is well known in the rest of the NT (John 10:11, 14; Heb. 13:20; 1 Pet. 2:25; 5:2-4), but

---

135. The construction οὐδὲ μή followed by the aorist subjunctive πέσῃ is an example of the future of emphatic negation, emphasizing the utter impossibility of the sun's falling upon this crowd. It complements the future tenses of the six indicative verbs of 7:15*b*-17 in pointing to a fruition of the promises at some point yet to arrive.

136. Lange, *Revelation*, p. 192.

the idea of a lamb shepherding is an intriguing exchange of roles because of the boldness of the mixed metaphors. The shepherd figure is common in Johannine writings (John 10:1-30; 21:15-17). It probably builds on the OT picture of God as shepherd (Isa. 40:11; Ezek. 34:23) (Swete; Mounce). It is particularly relevant to Ps. 23:1-4, but the other three uses of ποιμαίνω (*poimainō*, "I shepherd") in Revelation (2:27; 12:5; 19:15) deal with His destroying (or ruling) the nations with a rod of iron and draw from Ps. 2:9 (Mounce). The synoptic gospels and the gospel of John view Christ's shepherding in relation to present life on earth (Matt. 2:6; John 10:1, 16), but the Apocalypse sees the saints as God's flock in heaven. In Isa. 53:6, 7 (cf. 1 Pet. 2:25), the wayward roving habits of sheep illustrate the proneness of God's people to wander, and the patient submissiveness of a lamb for sacrifice pictures the patience of the servant of the Lord. The characteristic of wandering is absent from the present passage, but the quality of the Lamb's patience is still prominent (Moffatt). He will patiently care for His sheep, guarding them from any further torments such as plagued their earthly sojourn.

In addition, He will "lead them to springs of the water of life" (*hodēgēsei autous epi zōēs pēgas hydatōn*). Besides protecting the sheep, the shepherd is responsible to provide for their refreshment. *Hodēgēsei* ("He will lead") continues the picture of shepherdly care as a means of showing the eternal blessedness awaiting those who belong to God (Lenski; Hailey). The same verb is used in the LXX to describe God's guidance of Israel (Ex. 15:13; Deut. 1:33) and of individual lives (Pss. 5:9; 85 [MT86]:11) and in the NT to describe the work of the Holy Spirit (John 16:13) and of Christ in the future order (here) (Swete). It is used in a literal sense of leading or escorting the blind in Matt. 15:14 and Luke 6:39, and is a combination of the common Greek noun ὁδός (*hodos*), which means "road," "path," or "way," and the verb ἡγέομαι (*hēgeomai*), which means "lead."[137] Along with *poimanei*, it adds local color for Christians of the province of Asia, particularly in the Lycus Valley around Laodicea where sheep and shepherds were common.

The destination of the flock under the shepherd's leadership is *epi zōēs pēgas hydatōn*[138] ("to springs of the water of life"). The word order

---

137. Abbott-Smith, *Lexicon*, pp. 309-10.
138. The plural nouns πηγὰς ὑδάτων (cf. Rev. 8:10; 14:7; 16:4) are somewhat unusual in comparison to similar expressions τῆς πηγῆς του ὕδατος τῆς ζωῆς in 21:6, ποταμὸν ὕδατος ζωῆς in 22:1, and ὕδωρ ζωῆς in 22:17. In these other comparable expressions, the nouns are singular when they occur. The plurals here probably come from the influence of the Hebrew text of Isa. 49:10 where the LXX rendering πηγῶν ὑδάτων reflects the plural and dual Hebrew nouns מַבּוּעֵי מָיִם (Swete, *Apocalypse*, pp. 105-6).

of the expression puts greatest emphasis on *zōēs* ("life").[139] God who is the fountain of life (Ps. 35:10 [MT36:9]) is the one to whom the Lamb will lead His sheep (Rev. 21:6; 22:1, 17; cf. John 4:12, 14; 7:38-39) (Swete). All that life means, the essence of life, will belong to the victorious company of the redeemed in eternal bliss (Lenski). At such a fountain as this the spiritual thirst of the saints (cf. 7:16) will be satisfied.

The other means of providing for the needs of God's people will be the role of God Himself in counteracting sorrow: *kai exaleipsei ho theos pan dakryon ek tōn ophthalmōn autōn* ("and God will wipe away every tear from their eyes"). Tears in the eyes denote the sorrow of God's people because of the pressures of life on earth. The OT source of this promise to remove any lingering effects of that sorrow is Isa. 25:8. The contrast between the recent struggles of this multitude and the exuberance for which they are destined is pictured as a sudden change from sorrow to delight. It enhances the magnitude of their eternal bliss.[140] The promise is restated in practically identical wording in Rev. 21:3.

The ultimate fulfillment of these seven promises (7:15*b*-17) will come in the eternal state described more fully in Revelation 21-22, but John's "snapshot" of the innumerable multitude catches them in heaven at a point just before the beginning of the last half of the seven years of Daniel's seventieth week.

---

139. A grammatical parallel to this expression is in 1 Pet. 3:21, σαρκὸς ἀπό-
θεσις ῥύπου, where the emphasis falls on σαρκός.
140. Charles, *Revelation*, 1:217.

Excursus 1: The Chronological Interpretation of Revelation 2-3

Widespread interest has been attached to the interpretation of the seven church messages of Revelation 2-3, and each approach is usually an outgrowth of the time period or periods to which these messages are assigned. Viewpoints varying from past to future application have been advanced, but the most prominent may be discussed under three headings: the prophetical, the historico-prophetical, and the historical.

THE PROPHETICAL INTERPRETATION

The prophetical interpretation looks upon these seven messages as being entirely future in their significance. There is absolutely no historical meaning in them; their import is intended for assemblies yet to be established on the earth. The assemblies are Jewish in their makeup and dare not be identified with the Body of Christ. The seven will occupy their places on the earth during the eschatological day of the Lord.[1]

Support mustered for this view includes the following arguments:

1. Verse 19 of chapter 1 testifies to the unity of the Apocalypse, not to its twofold or threefold division, and therefore chapters 2-3 relate

---

1. E. W. Bullinger, *The Apocalypse* or *"The Day of the Lord"* (London: Eyre and Spottiswoode, n.d.), p. 68.

to the future just as do the portions beginning with chapter 4.[2] One's acceptance of this proof must hinge on his understanding of Revelation 1:19, and there is no unanimity in regard to this verse. For example, many hold that the verse expresses a threefold division, not a single entity.[3] Still others see a twofold division. Consequently, the unity of the verse becomes of doubtful value in supporting the prophetic view.

2. It is the further argument of this viewpoint that the angels of Revelation 2-3 necessitate a connection with Israel rather than with the Christian church. With this the case, it is proposed, these churches must exist after the Gentile church is removed, i.e., in the future day of the Lord.[4] Here, once again, the answer lies in questioning the premise of the argument: Are angels *never* mentioned in relation to the church? The answer must be negative in the light of such passages as 1 Cor. 11:10.

Furthermore, it is possible to answer the angel argument by interpreting these seven angels to be human messengers. Contrary to Bullinger's assumption, this is possible without making angel a title for a church officer. They may be messengers in the common usage of the term without necessitating any implications regarding church composition, i.e., Jewish versus Christian.

3. Proof for the prophetic perspective is also sought in evidence that no churches existed in some of these cities at this early date. This is done particularly in relation to the church in Thyatira, the basis of the assumption being statements by Tertullian (A.D. 145-220) and by Epiphanius (about A.D. 367).[5] If no church existed at the time of the Apocalypse's composition, it stands to reason that one will exist in the future day, it is said.

It should be observed, however, that historical evidence to disprove the existence of this church is scanty. Tertullian does not agree with the truthfulness of this assertion, but merely cites the claims of certain sects.[6] Epiphanius too was answering unorthodox objections of the Alogi to the genuineness of the Apocalypse.[7] The absurdity of this position is readily seen when one recollects the evidence of the Apocalypse itself. Whatever author may be suggested (if not the apostle John, as we believe), "he would not have assumed as fact a thing

---

2. Charles H. Welch, *This Prophecy* (England: Leonard A. Canning, n.d.), pp. 59-61.
3. For discussion of this point, see my "John's Apocalyptic Outline," *BSac*, 123 (October-December 1966): 334-41.
4. Bullinger, *Apocalypse*, pp. 66-68.
5. Ibid., p. 70.
6. Ibid.
7. Ibid.

known to be erroneous."[8] How much more true this is with the inspired apostle as author.[9]

The conclusion must be, "The seven churches of Asia Minor were real churches. . . . They existed as actual historical entities in a province of Roman Asia in the closing decades of the first century."[10]

Evidence fails to support the prophetic view. Therefore the historicity of these churches must be admitted, as is normal in the case of such literature, and the messages to them cannot be assigned to the future day of the Lord in their interpretation.

THE HISTORICO-PROPHETICAL INTERPRETATION

The second viewpoint, the historico-prophetical, has had a remarkable popularity among expositors of the nineteenth century.[11] It was not, however, unknown to earlier interpreters.[12] This approach acknowledges the historical existence of the first-century churches addressed in the messages, but at the same time assigns a prophetic significance to them. This prophetic feature purportedly outlines the seven periods of church history from the time of composition to the coming of Christ for the church. Some advocates of this theory even

---

8. Isbon T. Beckwith, *The Apocalypse of John* (New York: Macmillan, 1919), p. 340; cf. William Henry Simcox, *The Revelation of St. John the Divine,* CGT (Cambridge: U. Press, 1893), p. 61.
9. Advocates of the prophetic view also argue on the basis of a difference in emphasis between these messages and the epistles of Paul. These are said to be grounded in a system of works whereas literature of the church rests on the system of grace (Bullinger, *Apocalypse,* pp. 63, 162-63). It is true that no classic passages on the doctrine of grace can be found in these letters, but this is far from saying that they do not rest on a grace principle. Works in the Christian life are in no way incompatible with grace, even in the writings of Paul (cf. Eph. 2:8-10). It is the concept of works done in compliance with Mosaic law that the apostle rules out, because they exclude the grace method of approaching God (cf. Rom. 3:21-22). On the other hand, however, good works are the necessary counterpart of faith and grace, and the emphasis upon such in these chapters is not per se an argument against relating them to the dispensation of grace.
10. Carl F. H. Henry, "Lessons from the Apocalypse," *Christianity Today* 9 (December 4, 1964): 16.
11. To name just a few, L. R. Conradi, *The Impelling Force of Prophetic Truth* (London: Thynne, 1935), pp. 30-31; John Peter Lange, *The Revelation of John,* vol. 10 of *Lange's Commentary,* ed. E. R. Craven (Grand Rapids: Zondervan, 1968), p. 139; Arno C. Gaebelein, *The Revelation* (New York: Publication Office "Our Hope," 1915), p. 33; J. B. Smith, *A Revelation of Jesus Christ* (Scottdale, Pa.: Herald, 1961), pp. 61-62.
12. Richard Chenevix Trench, *Commentary on the Epistles to the Seven Churches in Asia* (London: Parker, Son, and Bourn, 1861), pp. 301-3. Trench lists among others the Franciscan Abbot Joachin of Floris (died 1202), the Puritan Thomas Brightman (died 1607), Joseph Mede (died 1638), and Cocceius (died 1669).

go so far as to say that the prophetic interpretation overshadows the historical in importance.[13] This is not true of the majority, however.

The more prominent points of evidence favoring the historico-prophetic interpretation are as follows:

1. One reason advanced lies in the "difference and even opposed moral conditions" found in the various churches.[14] So varied are the descriptions of the different churches, these could not characterize the state of the church in general at that time or at any other time.

Such reasoning as this rests upon the presupposition that each description characterizes the whole body of professing Christians at a given moment.[15] This is nowhere stated, however. It is true that whatever is said to one church will have usefulness in connection with the others (i.e., "He who has an ear, let him hear what the Spirit says to the churches"), but this does not imply that the principal virtues or faults of one church are meant as the main characteristics of others. In other words, advice that has urgent application in Laodicea may represent one of the lesser needs in Philadelphia and elsewhere. There is, therefore, nothing in the messages to preclude their application to different local congregations existing simultaneously in the last decade of the first century, or for that matter, in any other period.

2. It is further argued that the contents of the seven messages hint at their prophetic significance.[16] By this is meant the language of the two chapters relating to the second advent, which implies that the latter churches (or last church) continue up to the time of Christ's second coming.

How far this line of reasoning can be pursued is questionable, however, especially when there are possible references to Christ's coming in two of the first three messages and a clear reference to His coming as early as the fourth message. In fact, one might easily conclude from the language utilized that Christ's coming was as near for the first church, Ephesus, as for the last, Laodicea.

There is also the idea that the progressive development of evil portrayed in these messages is indicative of their prophetic character.[17] Yet one cannot fully agree with this trend when he finds, for example, in Sardis one of the two worst spiritual states and in Philadelphia one of the two best spiritual states.[18] To describe accurately

13. Gaebelein, *Revelation*, p. 33.
14. William Kelly, *Lectures on the Revelation* (London: G. Morrish, n.d.), p. 24; cf. Smith, *Revelation*, p. 61; J. N. Darby, *Notes on the Apocalypse* (London: G. Morrish, n.d.), p. 11.
15. Kelly, *Lectures*, p. 24.
16. William Kelly, *The Revelation* (London: Thomas Weston, 1904), p. 75.
17. John F. Walvoord, *The Revelation of Jesus Christ* (Chicago: Moody, 1966), pp. 52-53.
18. Philip Schaff, *History of the Christian Church*, 8 vols. (Grand Rapids: Eerdmans, 1910), 1:451-52.

the growing failure in the church, Philadelphia should have been placed early in chapter 2, certainly before Sardis and not vice versa, if declining spiritual states were a mark of these two chapters.

3. Probably the most widely used piece of evidence in favor of the historico-prophetical approach is the theory of a correspondence between seven periods of church history and the seven messages. It is argued that the successive periods of church history, as they have unfolded, are in themselves a substantiation of this viewpoint because of the high degree of correlation between them and the spiritual conditions outlined in the seven messages. Lange comments: "Ephesus is manifestly a picture of the church toward the end of the apostolic time, whilst Laodicea pictures it as it shall be in the last time."[19] In commenting upon Lange's position, Craven, his American editor, adds, "The proof . . . that the Seven Churches are, in their order, representative of the predominant characteristics of the Church in the seven periods of her history is based entirely on observation of history."[20] In the terminology of Ironside, the key that fit the lock and opened up the explanation of the messages was the noticed similarity between them and the development of church history.[21] Many other expositors from a wide assortment of backgrounds have flocked to the opinion that a correspondence between church history and these seven messages exists.[22]

In spite of the abundance of impressive voices to speak in favor of the correlation of the passage with church history, there comes, however, the frequent question, "Does it really fit?" In speaking of the concept of successive church periods, Godet writes, "One may, doubtless, by taking up this latter stand-point, succeed in bringing out some ingeniously conceived points of harmony, but they always have a somewhat arbitrary character."[23] Is the application of these mes-

---

19. Lange, *Revelation*, p. 139.
20. Ibid., p. 141. Grant describes this most important principle as "the suitability of application itself" (F. W. Grant, *The Prophetic History of the Church* [New York: Loizeaux, 1902], p. 5). Scofield agrees with the importance of this point: "Most conclusively of all, these messages do present an exact fore-view of the spiritual history of the church, and in this precise order" (C. I. Scofield, ed. *Scofield Reference Bible* [New York: Oxford, 1917], pp. 1331-32).
21. H. A. Ironside, *Lectures on the Revelation* (New York: Loizeaux Brothers, n.d.), pp. 35-36.
22. From very early times the historico-prophetical treatment of the seven letters has come from the pens of writers of the continuous-historical persuasion in regard to the Apocalypse. Joseph Mede is one example of this variety. Cf. William Milligan, *Discussions on the Apocalypse* (London: Macmillan, 1893), p. 269. Therefore, the historico-prophetic approach cannot be limited to the futurist viewpoint of the book.
23. F. Godet, *Studies in the New Testament* (New York: Hodder and Stoughton, n.d.), pp. 303-4. Milligan agrees that the correspondence is artificial: "The

sages really arbitrary, as Godet suggests? This is the question that must be faced squarely before giving credence to the historico-prophetic conclusion.

There does appear to be evidence to support this arbitrary character. It can be discerned by examining a standard work on church history. Schaff, in speaking of the periods of church history, notes, "In regard to the number and length of periods there is, indeed, no unanimity."[24] He then goes on to observe that if any general agreement exists, it is in respect to a threefold division into ancient (A.D. 1-590), medieval (A.D. 590-1517) and modern (A.D. 1517-1880) periods. If a further breakdown is desired, Schaff proposes a division of each of the three into three subdivisions, resulting in nine, not seven periods of church history.[25]

The same diversity of opinion that exists among church historians is found in the writings of expositors of the historico-prophetic school. The limited scope of the present treatment forbids an exhaustive comparison of the differences, but a typical example will suffice to illustrate the point: The message to Sardis (Rev. 3:1-6) has been variously interpreted in its prophetic meaning. Craven makes this "the period blending with the spiritual declensions of the preceding [period], and extending through the dark ages to the Reformation."[26] Conradi, on the other hand, refers the Sardian message not to the pre-Reformation church, but to the church of the Reformation itself: "Surely Christ did not overlook this second greatest event in human history [i.e., the Reformation] when He gave the forecast to the seven churches, but pointed it out, as we shall see, very fittingly in the Sardis state."[27]

One can, apparently, make the words to Sardis fit either of the two epochs, depending on whether he emphasizes the good features regarding the church or the bad. The inevitable course in this case must be to apply the term "arbitrary" to such a method of interpretation. Can it be said honestly that this is the key which fits the lock and opens up the explanation of the messages, when in reality the key is so poorly defined? The shape of the key varies radically from one interpreter to the next, and so who is to say finally what "the key" is?[28]

---

history of the church cannot be portioned off into successive periods marked by characteristics to which those noted in the seven epistles correspond" (Milligan, *Apocalypse*, p. 269).

24. Schaff, *History*, 1:14.
25. Ibid., 1:14-19.
26. Lange, *Revelation*, p. 141.
27. Conradi, *Prophetic Truth*, p. 248.
28. A further objection to the historico-prophetic view is that it limits the scope of the seven messages to Western Christianity. Boyer responds to

The truthfulness of Trench's observation, thus, is well-attested: "There is no agreement among themselves on the part of the interpreters of the historico-prophetical school. Each one has his own solution of the enigma, his own distribution of the several epochs; or, if this is too much to affirm, there is at any rate nothing approaching to a general consensus among them."[29]

It would appear, then, that this historico-prophetical system is beset by difficulties and unsupported by any conclusive evidence.[30] A final alternative is yet available to the interpreter of Revelation 2-3, however.

THE HISTORICAL VIEW

The possibility still remaining is the purely historical view. This is the viewpoint that takes Christ's words as being strictly appropriate to the historical situations of seven first-century churches of Asia Minor. It does not deny that these seven represent spiritual states that characterize local churches of all locations and all times within the Christian era, but it does deny that a given spiritual state is more prevalent at one time than it is at another. In other words, the symbolic states are simultaneous rather than consecutive, in their coverage of the church age. The supports for the historical view may be summed up as follows:

1. The whole context of the Apocalypse necessitates this interpretation. It is foundational in understanding this book to recognize its emphasis upon the imminency of Christ's return, and the purely historical approach is the only one that allows for this meaning along with maintaining the historical existence of the seven churches.

The historico-prophetical view cannot make such a claim, because a consistent application of its interpretation would mean that

---

this by noting that the Greek word for *lampstands* shows the seven churches to be true churches, presumably limiting them to churches in the Western world. Because Western Christianity has been the major center for world evangelism, he finds this limitation of the prophecy justified (James L. Boyer, "Are the Seven Letters of Revelation 2-3 Prophetic?" *GTJ* 6, no. 2 [Fall 1985]: 272). In the scope of almost two thousand years of church history, his response is conspicuously fallacious. It is totally unrealistic to assume that the only true churches have belonged to Western Christianity.

29. Trench, *Seven Churches*, p. 248.
30. One further argument, the incredibility of not having predictions to cover the church age in Revelation, is worthy of brief notice (Scofield, ed., *Scofield Reference Bible*, p. 1331). This is unacceptable as evidence, however, because it denies God the prerogative of remaining silent when He chooses. Furthermore, there is found elsewhere ample revelation regarding the progress of the church in the present age (Walvoord, *Revelation*, p. 52).

Christ's coming is imminent for only one of the churches, the last. This would be the only one pictured prophetically for which Christ's coming was an any-moment expectation. On the contrary, however, there are definite references to His imminent return in the fourth and sixth messages, and possible references in the first, third, and fifth messages. If the historico-prophetical be the correct viewpoint, Christ would be guilty of deceiving those other churches, for His coming could not possibly take place within their periods of church history. Philadelphia, for example, was given a false hope of deliverance as an encouragement in persecution, because Christ's coming could not occur until the Laodicean period. The folly of accusing Christ of such moral conduct is apparent, and consequently the inability of the historico-prophetical approach in allowing for the doctrine of imminence throughout the church age must be admitted.[31]

It is revealing that Harrison uses the supposed prophetic character of these messages to disprove the imminency of Christ's return; he speaks of "a seven-fold historical development of the Church (Revelation 2 and 3), evidently requiring an extended period of time."[32] By this observation he argues against a Scriptural teaching of an any-moment return of Christ, for Christ spoke these words to a generation during whose existence He could not have come back. Harrison's case is not convincing, however. If one is forced to choose between the imminent return of Christ and the prophetic nature of the seven messages, there is no question that the decision of Scripture is in favor of Christ's imminent return.

The realization must be that Christ's return was just as much a possibility for the Ephesians as it was for the Laodiceans. This is possible when "the things that are" (Rev. 1:19) are represented by

---

31. F. C. Jennings, recognizing the problem of harmonizing the doctrine of imminence with the historico-prophetical scheme, seeks to reconcile the two by postulating a late discovery of the prophetic element. "The church at large has not discerned this interpretation of these letters until the last century. . . . If the Lord's people could say we are clearly only in one of the earlier conditions of the churches and others must yet intervene, it would destroy absolutely the sense of any immediate coming" (*The Seven Letters* [New York: Publication Office "Our Hope," 1909], pp. 64-65). Has this "discovery" been confined to the nineteenth century, however? Apparently not. See footnote 12 above for writers of a much earlier date who held this position. Boyer's defense against the "nonimminence" criticism of the historico-prophetic view follows similar lines: because the prophetic element in the seven messages was implicit rather than explicit, it could not have been understood before its fulfillment (Boyer, "Seven Letters," pp. 269-70). The existence of "implicit" prophecy in the Bible has not been demonstrated.

32. Norman B. Harrison, *The End* (Minneapolis: Harrison Service, 1948), p. 237.

seven simultaneous "church pictures" rather than seven successive ones. With this understanding of the words, the church age could have been very short, even terminating in the generation of John the apostle.

The characteristic of simultaneity is also an answer to two additional arguments utilized by the historico-prophetical school: (1) The words "the things that are" (*ha eisin*) in 1:19 are said to support this interpretation (William Kelly, *The Revelation*, p. 75). According to the threefold division of the verse and thus of the entire book, chapters 2-3 must encompass the whole scope of the church's earthly existence. To comprehend the condition of the Christian church from John's time to the events depicted at the beginning of chapter 4, it is necessary to posit seven consecutive stages of church history, moving in order from the first message to the last. (2) It is also held that the number seven is a number of revolution of time, indicating in these chapters a prophetic sampling of seven successive conditions of the whole visible church (Joseph Mede, *The Works of Joseph Mede* (London: J. L., 1650), pp. 296, 905; see also Kelly, *Revelation*, p. 75, and *Lectures*, pp. 24-25). Because seven is the number of totality, the entire age of the church must be encompassed in seven consecutive epochs. Yet neither argument necessitates succession as opposed to simultaneity. There is no valid objection to making each of the seven messages applicable to the entirety of the period; the concept of totality is equally applicable in this sense as in that of consecutive periods, as Godet writes: "The number *seven* indicates here, as it always does, a totality. But the idea of the book is that of a simultaneous, not that of a successive, totality, as those think who see in these seven churches the portraiture of the principal phases of the history of the church. . . . It is the starting-point of the Lord's progress which should be here indicated, this starting-point is the state of the church at the time of the vision, and not the unrolling of its future history, which is contained rather in the subsequent vision" (*Studies*, pp. 303-4). Because the historical view alone allows for such simultaneity and imminence, it is acceptable in view of the context of the Apocalypse.

2. A second reason for adopting the historical point of view lies in the absence of any word of Scripture to indicate an additional prophetic outlook in these two chapters. Walvoord agrees that no such statement is to be found when he says: "The prophetic interpretation of the messages to the seven churches . . . is a deduction from the content, not from the explicit statement of the passage."[33]

Admittedly to speak of this absence is an argument from silence,

---

33. Walvoord, *Revelation*, p. 52.

but coupled with the Scripture's usual unambiguity in such matters, it assumes increasing importance. Customarily, when the Bible makes a declaration regarding the future, there is no room for doubt about its character as prophecy.[34] But to those who "superinduce upon it [a literal sense] a prophetical," Trench poses the following searching questions: "What slightest hint or intimation does the Spirit of God give that we have here to do with the great successive acts and epochs of the kingdom of God in the course of its gradual evolution here upon earth? Where are the fingerposts pointing this way? What is there, for instance, of chronological succession? Does not every thing, on the contrary, mark simultaneity, and not succession?"[35]

There are no such pointers to lead the expositor to any conclusion other than the historical.

3. As a third factor to support the historical interpretation, attention is called to the kind of literature in Revelation 2-3. This is normal epistolary style, quite similar to the epistles of Paul and other NT writers. In these other writings, no serious thought is ever given to finding a typical prophetic meaning in a passage that manifestly deals with a historical situation in the city or cities addressed.[36] Instead the words are interpreted in light of the historical context. In other words, what did they mean to the first-century recipients of Asia Minor?

Such should be the case in the messages of the Apocalypse. Darby, himself an advocate of the historico-prophetical view, admits that these two chapters differ from the prophetic portions of the book.[37] Though not considering the difference sufficient to rule out the prophetic from the nonapocalyptic second and third chapters, Darby

---

34. Boyer responds to this criticism by noting that sometimes Biblical prophecy is implicit rather than explicit (Boyer, "Seven Churches," p. 269). The analogies used to prove his point are not relevant, however.
35. Trench, *Seven Churches*, pp. 307-8.
36. Kelly finds in Daniel 3-6 a case in which there is supposedly a mingling of the prophetic with the historical. He contends that the historical events recorded there have a deeper, more profound meaning than mere history. There is typical meaning in these happenings, and the types serve as prophetic hints to prepare the ground for the predictions beginning in Daniel 7 (*Lectures*, pp. xii-xiii). For one to find validity in this approach, he must first demonstrate satisfactorily that such literary principle exists in Daniel. Some would feel that such a treatment of a historical passage is highly allegorical and differs little from the method of the Alexandrian school. One is tempted to feel that the "technical minuteness of application" to which Kelly so strongly objects (ibid.) might be none other than the grammatico-historical method of interpretation. To rest one's case upon such precarious hermeneutics is highly inadvisable.
37. Darby, *Apocalypse*, p. 10.

significantly does note the difference in literary construction. Except for occasional references to future events such as the coming of the Lord or the hour of trial, the messages treat historical conditions and circumstances and do not partake of the apocalyptic character that dominates the book after the third chapter.

Understanding the normal method of interpreting epistolary literature to be historical, then, one concludes that there is this additional factor in favor of the historical viewpoint.

After all the evidence is tallied, one is inclined to accept the appraisal of Lee: "One cannot, however, overlook the historical character which is stamped on the Epistles throughout . . . and which distinctly points to a state of things actually before St. John's mind as existing in the several Churches. . . . That such teaching is applicable for reproof or for encouragement throughout all future time, is firmly to be maintained; but that definite periods of the Church are here predicted, or that these Epistles refer severally to successive aspects of the Divine Kingdom, may well be doubted."[38]

Such a conclusion is not at all inconsistent with the dispensational approach to the Scriptures. In fact, it harmonizes perfectly with the doctrine of Christ's imminent return throughout this age, which doctrine is so intimately associated with the pretribulational coming of Christ for His church.

Furthermore, the historical interpretation encourages a sound application of the grammatico-historical method of interpretation to the messages, such as might not be possible if the interpreter is diverted by his consideration of prophetic details. These two chapters are rich in truth for local congregations throughout this age, when understood in the light of their surroundings, and the student of God's Word would do well to make full and proper use of them in his ministry.

---

38. William Lee, "The Revelation of St. John," in *The Holy Bible*, ed. F. C. Cook (London: John Murray, 1881), 4:513-14.

Excursus 2: The Imprecatory Prayers of the Apocalypse

A rarely discussed, but very prominent, source of God's eschatological wrath is the prayers of the saints. These prayers loom large in the Apocalypse and in each case take on a vindictive tone. In order to understand these prayers adequately, four related themes must be clarified.

ALTAR(S)

Bearing upon the prayers of the saints in the Apocalypse is the matter of the heavenly altar or altars. The noun θυσιαστήριον (*thysiastērion,* "altar") occurs eight times in Revelation, and only once is an earthly altar in view (11:1). The remaining occurrences always connect either directly or indirectly with the saints' petitions in heaven.

Although there is no doubt that the earthly altar is the altar of burnt offering,[1] the case for the heavenly altar is not nearly so clear-cut. The heavenly sanctuary formed the pattern after which the earthly was constructed (Heb. 9:24), but it is debatable whether one or two altars should be visualized there.

It is quite certain that the golden altar of incense came before the

---

1. In Rev. 11:1 John is instructed to measure the sanctuary (ναός [*naos*]) first, and then there is the word about the altar. The altar of incense was related to the sanctuary, and therefore the altar referred to here is outside and could be only that of burnt offering.

mind of the apostle John in his ecstatic state. Otherwise there would be no explanation of the golden altar that is found twice (8:3; 9:13) because the altar of burnt offering, the other alternative, was overlaid with bronze, not gold (Ex. 38:1ff.).

Whether one can demonstrate the presence of the altar of burnt offering in heaven is another question, however. The only serious possibility of such is John's vision of the fifth seal judgment (6:9-11).[2] Several characteristics of this altar call to mind the altar of burnt offering:

1. The souls (ψυχὰς, *psychas*) of the martyrs are pictured under the altar, a feature resembling the pouring of blood (symbolic of life, [ψυχή, *psychē*], Lev. 17:11, LXX) at the base of the altar of burnt offering (Lev. 4:7).

2. The souls under the altar have been slain (τῶν ἐσφαγμένων, *tōn esphagmenōn*, 6:9). The same word is descriptive of the sacrificial Lamb in 5:6. The lamb as a type of Christ, the Lamb of God, was slain at the altar of burnt offering (Lev. 1:1-9). If this connection be correct, the life of the martyr is looked upon as a sacrifice. Parallel teachings from Paul are often cited to support the sacrificial nature of the martyr's death (Phil. 2:17; 2 Tim. 4:6). In neither passage, however, does Paul refer to the burnt offering. Rather he, by use of σπένδω (*spendō*, "I pour out"), makes reference to the drink-offering (Gen. 35:14; Num. 15:5-7), which does not necessarily carry the connotation of sacrificial death.

3. The use of *to thysiastērion* without added specification is always a reference to the altar of burnt offering, according to some authorities. Although this observation seems valid in nonapocalyptic literature and seems to hold true also in Rev. 11:1, it is highly questionable whether such is the case in general with apocalyptic writings. The unqualified noun in several passages of Revelation is obviously the golden altar of incense (8:3, 5; 14:18 with 8:3, 5 and 9:13).

Thus it can be seen that although the evidence is not overwhelming, there is some ground for finding the altar of burnt offering in 6:9-11. This has been the reason some commentators postulate two heavenly altars.[3]

---

2. One explanation finds in 8:3-5 both the altar of burnt offering and the altar of incense. According to this arrangement the angel goes first to the altar of burnt offering (8:3*a*), then to the altar of incense (8:3*b*), and finally back to the altar of burnt offering (8:5). Yet the strong emphasis upon incense throughout the passage and later references to the altar (9:13; 14:18; 16:7) seem to exclude the burnt offering from this passage. Cf. Isbon T. Beckwith, *The Apocalypse of John* (New York: Macmillan, 1919), pp. 552-53.

3. Henry Barclay Swete, *The Apocalypse of St. John* (London: Macmillan, 1906), pp. 90, 108.

There is still serious doubt, however, about the plurality of altars. In fact, the contextual development of the Apocalypse is strong enough to demand one altar and one altar only, and this is the same one that is constantly related to the prayers of the saints. At the same time, it is possible to explain the slight evidence in favor of the altar of burnt offering in another way[4] and therefore conclude that there is only one heavenly altar, the one resembling the golden altar of incense.

The mention of a heavenly altar in this book thus calls to mind the prayers of the saints because this is the particular function of the golden altar. The definiteness of the first mention of the altar in the Apocalypse (*tou thysiastēriou*, 6:9) presupposes a prior knowledge of this altar. Though the specific piece of furniture has not been mentioned in the earlier description of the heavenly throne room, it is assumed in connection with the incense (and prayers) in possession of the twenty-four elders (5:8). It is not uncommon in this book for heaven to be described by the terminology of a sanctuary (11:19; 14:15, 17; 15:5, 8; cf. Heb. 9:24). Hence the presence of the altar of incense is quite logical. The care of this altar is committed to one particular angel who, remaining unnamed, has authority to dispense the hot coals of the altar (8:3, 5; 14:18).

THE INCENSE

Also prominent in connection with the prayers of the saints is the incense itself. The concept of incense under the Old Covenant suggested divine acceptance, and the same acceptance is granted prayers when in association with incense. When acceptance is granted, the answer is also guaranteed. In other words, incense gives efficacy to the worship accompanying it, and the smoke cloud (cf. 8:4) symbolizes the divine acceptance (cf. Gen. 8:21; Deut. 33:10, ASV marg.; Ps. 141:2).

In the two places where incense is mentioned (5:8; 8:3-4), there are different relationships that it sustains to the prayers:

1. In 5:8 the prayers are themselves identical with the incense. There has been discussion regarding the antecedent of the relative pronoun αἵ (*hai*, "which") in this verse, and hinging upon this decision is the thing with which the prayers of the saints are equated. The feminine form would seem to require the bowls φιάλας (*phialas*, "bowls") as the antecedent.[5] Yet it appears more natural to under-

---

4. R. H. Charles, *The Revelation of St. John*, 2 vols., ICC (New York: Scribner's, 1920), 1:172-74, 226-30.
5. Henry Alford, *The Greek Testament*, 4 vols. (London: Longmans, Green, 1903), 4:709.

stand a reference to the θυμιαμάτων (*thymiamatōn*, "incense"), which stands just before the pronoun, in spite of the difference in gender. The well-known grammatical phenomenon of attraction, in this case the attraction of the relative to its predicate nominative προσευχαί (*proseuchai*, "prayers"), is adequate to explain the difference.[6] In such case, the incense symbolizes the prayers that are to become a vital factor in the sending forth of judgment upon the earth.

2. The imagery is slightly different in 8:3-4. Twice the incense is mentioned in connection with the prayers. Although different authorities interpret the two datives προσευχαὶς (*proseuchais*, "prayers") either as two instrumental cases to denote accompaniment or as two dative cases to denote benefit, a more proper course would appear to be understanding a dative of advantage in verse 3 and an instrumental of association in verse 4.[7] The incense is given on behalf of the prayers, to help them and make them acceptable (8:3), and it ascends before God along with the prayers themselves (8:4).

The association of the prayers with the incense, therefore, whatever form it may take, is a pledge of the success of the prayers.

THE PRAYERS THEMSELVES

It now remains to follow the progress of the prayers and answers through the Apocalypse. From the earliest moment of the unfolding drama of divine punishment, the prayers are seen. They appear in the introductory picture of the throne room of the heavenly temple and become conspicuous in response to the Lamb's procurement of the seven-sealed book or scroll (5:7-8). The scroll contains revelation of the very judgments that we later will learn are the objects of these prayers.

The next glimpse of the prayers comes as the Lamb opens the fifth seal of the scroll (6:9-11). Here it is not all the saints who pray; it is rather the martyrs. They are asking vengeance on their persecutors.

The character of this seal has often been a source of confusion. Seiss is typical of those who find the effect of this seal to be the slaughter of the faithful preachers of the gospel.[8] Such an opinion runs contrary to the purpose of the seals, however. The whole series is directed against the rebellious inhabitants of the earth (cf. 3:10a), not against the godly remnant. Such is certainly true of the first four and

---

6. Charles, *Revelation*, 1:145.
7. J. A. Seiss, *The Apocalypse*, 3 vols. (New York: Charles C. Cook, 1909), 2:26; A. T. Robertson, *Word Pictures in the New Testament* (Nashville: Broadman, 1933), 6:357.
8. Seiss, *Apocalypse*, 1:348.

sixth seals. It would be a strange reversal to have God direct the fifth seal judgment against His own people.

Consequently, one must consider another possibility, that the judgment lies not in the persecution, but in the prayers of the persecuted. Martyrdom will doubtless be an aspect of this phase of the Tribulation period, but not originating with God. The guilty parties are God's enemies, who in turn become the objects of the martyrs' petitions, once these saints have entered their heavenly rest. Their prayers for revenge upon their enemies are viewed as the fifth judgment against the earth-dwellers.

The consequences of these prayers far exceed the terrifying effects of the first four seals. The prayers at this stage of the period look forward to a future fulfillment, much worse for the enemies than anything thus far. This worsening progression is due at least in part to the sincere request for divine vengeance.

God's response to the petitioners notes the need for further delay until the answer may become actual. The expression ἔτι χρόνον μικρόν (*eti chronon mikron*, "yet a little time") (6:11) looks forward to a time when additional martyrs will have joined their number, and when together the two groups will make up the full complement of those who are to die in this manner (cf. 10:6).

The fulfillment of the prayers is begun in connection with their next mention (8:3-5). The scene around the same heavenly altar and the same atmosphere of vengeance as in chapter six show that this is a continuation of what was begun earlier. But now not just the martyrs are in prayer. "All the saints" (8:3; cf. 7:10-17) are making heavenly prayers on this occasion.

The description of the prayers in association with an appearance of the seven angels with trumpets shows beyond a shadow of a doubt that the trumpet judgments come in answer to the petitions. It is not without significance that the same altar is the source of both the prayers ascending to God and the fire that when cast toward the earth provokes the physical disturbances, marking the initiation of the trumpet judgments. This series in turn leads up to and includes final victory over God's enemies.[9]

The next reference does not mention the prayers themselves, but they are recognized by the altar that is the source of the sixth trumpet judgment (9:13). Here is a continuation of the answer that has begun

---

9. It is helpful in tracing the chronology of the Apocalypse to note the time lapse between the fifth seal and the beginning of the trumpet series. Such a sequence militates against recapitulation, i.e., that the trumpets retrace the same period covered by the seals. This is evidence to support the telescopic view, which allows the trumpets to come at a period after the first six seals.

at 8:3-5 in conjunction with the first trumpet. The added impact of the narrative here is to point out the increasing intensity of the prayers' consequences. The destruction of one-third of the world's population far outstrips the wrath manifested up to this point, thus signaling the near completion of God's answer to His petitioning saints.

Following the sixth trumpet, there comes an announcement of "no more delay" (10:6; cf. 6:11). The time of the seventh trumpet is that appointed in God's plan for the completion of His answer to His saints. What has come heretofore was part of the answer, but only a preliminary part. The consummation has now been reached.

What is contained in the next notice is centered in another mention of the one heavenly altar (14:18). Here is found a foreview of the great bloodshed of 19:11-21. The seer is given to see a proleptic picture of what will result from the seventh trumpet, i.e., the seven last plagues.[10] At the moment of this picture the number of martyrs is complete, allowing the fulfillment of the saints' prayers in a final sense.

Once again the altar is heard. This time it is in the midst of the climactic series of plagues (16:7). The cry vindicates God in His just dealings with rebellious humanity. His judgments are just because they come as divine vengeance for the shedding of the saints' blood.

The prayers have been fully answered from the perspective of the heavenly multitude in 19:1-2. Their blood has been fully avenged at the hand of the great harlot. The song once again is proleptic, anticipating the final victory of 19:11-21.

In this brief survey it becomes very impressive that whatever the other factors may be, to some extent God's future outpouring of wrath upon a rejecting world will come in answer to heavenly petitions offered by His saints.

THE MORALITY OF IMPRECATION

The ethical problem involved with imprecation has more frequently been discussed in studies of the Psalms,[11] yet a similar problem appears in the one-sided nature of the imprecatory prayers of the Apocalypse. It should be understood that *imprecatory* is not neces-

---

10. In the telescopic understanding of the seals, trumpets, and bowls, the seven trumpets are included in the seventh seal, and the seven bowls or seven last plagues are included in the seventh trumpet.
11. Cf. Chalmers Martin, "Imprecation in the Psalms," in *Classical Evangelical Essays in Old Testament Interpretation*, ed. Walter C. Kaiser, Jr. (Grand Rapids: Baker, 1972), pp. 113-32.

sarily synonymous with *wicked* or *immoral*. The correct sense includes the invoking of judgment, calamity, or curse.[12]

But even with the proper definition there is a pronounced absence of such utterances in portions of the NT relating to the church, the Body of Christ. In fact, the very opposite kind of expression seems to predominate: "I exhort therefore, first of all, that supplications, prayers, intercessions, thanksgiving, be made for all men" (1 Tim. 2:1). It is noteworthy that Paul did not write "*against* all men," but "*for* all men" (italics added). The closest approximation to imprecation in the NT epistles appears in 1 John 5:16: "There is a sin unto death: not concerning this do I say that he should make request." Even here, however, we do not find direct imprecation, but rather a withholding of intercession.

In other parts of the NT also the emphasis is upon praying for the well-being of others, even when they are the enemies of God's people: "Pray for them that persecute you" (Matt. 5:44).

The proper reconciliation of these two extremes lies in the presence of some special revelation that has been given to certain of the saints at times, a gift that is not in general characteristic of the present time.[13] This gift relates to an understanding of which persons are reprobate, a knowledge possessed only in divine perspective. In describing the divinely inspired writer of an imprecatory psalm, one has said: "There must have been such enlightened and enlarged views of God's justice . . . that the psalmist, wrought up to the highest sympathy with this fundamental attribute of Jehovah, anticipated the doom of the ungodly, and devoted them at once to destruction. . . . God through him, could doom, in direct terms, the guilty, or he could inspire him to pray for speedy judgments to fall upon them."[14] Because the Psalms were written from the divine viewpoint and because this viewpoint must always be correct, the morality of the imprecatory psalms is no longer a problem, as long as it is absolutely certain that it rests upon God's omniscience and righteousness, and not upon human impulse.

Such is the divine point of view that characterizes the saints who pray in the Apocalypse. They are, to be sure, not writers of inspired Scripture as the psalmist, but their condition of having moved on to their heavenly abode guarantees the absence of any selfish motives in their prayer life. They have now taken on conformity to the image of

---

12. Johannes G. Vos, "The Ethical Problem of the Imprecatory Psalms," *WTJ* 4 (1941): 123.
13. Ibid., pp. 136-37.
14. John J. Owens, "The Imprecatory Psalms," *BSac* 13 (July 1856): 556.

Christ, except for bodily resurrection, which is still future for them. It is, therefore, no problem for them to see matters as God does, and through prayer to hasten the satisfaction of His justice in the lives of the rebellious of the earth, those who will never repent.

God will honor these prayers because it is in perfect conformity with His will to avenge His elect (Luke 18:7-8). Such action on His part can even be characterized as good news by those in proper relation to Him (Rev. 10:7). It is good in that His justice is thereby completely satisfied. Even though it may be a source of misery to those who become victims of such vengeance, vengeance of this kind has been an integral part of God's dealings with the enemies of righteousness since the earliest history of man (Gen. 4:10) and will continue to be until the consummation of human history.

The grace of God, represented by the sacrificial Lamb in Revelation 5:6, must be tempered by the wrath of God, represented by the seven-sealed scroll and the prayers of the saints in Revelation 5:7-8. The longsuffering of God, which spares the world for the moment, will at some point in the future reach its limit, and then will begin the exercise of the imprecatory prayers of the saints.